Algebra 2

HOLT, RINEHART AND WINSTON

A Harcourt Classroom Education Company

Austin · New York · Orlando · Atlanta · San Francisco · Boston · Dallas · Toronto · London

Requests for permission to make copies of any part of the work should be mailed to the following address: Permissions Department, Holt, Rinehart and Winston, 1120 South Capital of Texas Highway, Austin, Texas 78746-6487.

Acknowledgments appear on pages 1093-1094, which are extensions of the copyright page.

Printed in the United States of America

ISBN: 0-03-052223-4

1 2 3 4 5 6 7 8 9   032   03 02 01 00 99

AUTHORS

James E. Schultz, *Senior Series Author*
Dr. Schultz has over 30 years of experience teaching at the high school and college levels and is the Robert L. Morton Professor of Mathematics Education at Ohio University. He helped to establish standards for mathematics instruction as a co-author of the NCTM *Curriculum and Evaluation Standards for School Mathematics* and *A Core Curriculum: Making Mathematics Count for Everyone.*

Wade Ellis, Jr., *Senior Author*
Professor Ellis has co-authored numerous books and articles on how to integrate technology realistically and meaningfully into the mathematics curriculum. He was a key contributor to the landmark study *Everybody Counts: A Report to the Nation on the Future of Mathematics Education.*

Kathleen A. Hollowell
Dr. Hollowell is an experienced high school mathematics and computer science teacher who currently serves as Director of the Mathematics & Science Education Resource Center, University of Delaware. Dr. Hollowell is particularly well versed in the special challenge of motivating students and making the classroom a more dynamic place to learn.

Paul A. Kennedy
A professor in the Department of Mathematics at Southwest Texas State University, Dr. Kennedy is a leader in mathematics education reform. His research focuses on developing algebraic thinking by using multiple representations and technology. He has been the author of numerous publications and he is often invited to speak and conduct workshops on the teaching of secondary mathematics.

CONTRIBUTING AUTHOR

Martin Engelbrecht
A mathemematics teacher at Culver Academies, Culver, Indiana, Mr. Engelbrecht also teaches statistics at Purdue University, North Central. An innovative teacher and writer, he integrates applied mathematics with technology to make mathematics accessible to all students.

TECHNOLOGY WRITER AND CONSULTANT

Betty Mayberry
Ms. Mayberry is the mathematics department chair at Gallatin High School, Gallatin, Tennessee. She has received the Presidential Award for Excellence in Teaching Mathematics and the Tandy Technology Scholar award. She is a Teachers Teaching with Technology instructor and a popular speaker for the effective use of technology in mathematics instruction.

Project Editors
Andrew Roberts, *Senior Editor*
June Turner, *Associate Editor*

Editorial Staff
Gary Standafer, *Associate Director*
Marty Sopher, *Managing Editor*
Vicki Payne, *Editor*
Laurie Baker, *Senior Copyeditor*
Cindy Foreman, *Copyeditor*

Book Design
Diane Motz, *Senior Art Director*
Lisa Woods, *Designer*
Ed Diaz, *Design Associate*

Image Services
Elaine Tate, *Art Buyer Supervisor*
Coco Weir, *Art Buyer*

Photo Research
Cindy Verheyden, *Photo Researcher*
Jerry Cheek, *Assistant Photo Researcher*

Photo Studio
Sam Dudgeon, *Senior Staff Photographer*
Victoria Smith, *Photography Specialist*

Editorial Permissions
Carrie Jones

Manufacturing
Jevara Jackson, *Manufacturing Coordinator*

Production
Gene Rumann, *Production Manager*
Rose Degollado, *Senior Production Coordinator*
Susan Mussey, *Senior Production Coordinator*

Cover Design
Pronk and Associates

Design Implementation
Pronk and Associates

Research and Curriculum
Mike Tracy, Joyce Herbert, Kathy McKee
Guadalupe Solis, Jennifer Swift

iv

Table of Contents

MATH CONNECTIONS

Coordinate Geometry 23, 27, 34 **Statistics** 38, 39, 60, 74
Geometry 31, 35, 47, 49, 75, 76, 79

APPLICATIONS

Science
Agriculture 19, 44
Anatomy 42, 79
Health 37, 43, 59, 68
Medicine 48
Meteorology 10, 19, 69
Physics 19, 32, 33, 35, 36
Temperature 46

Social Studies
Demographics 10, 40
Government 43, 60
Psychology 72

Language Arts
Communicate 7, 17,
   25, 33, 40, 48, 57, 67
Etymology 42, 69

Business and Economics
Business 10, 60, 75
Communications 12
Construction 19, 77
Consumer Economics 50, 75
Economics 10
Manufacturing 61, 66
Marketing 42
Real Estate 69
Sales Tax 7
Taxes 18, 40, 50, 54

Life Skills
Academics 28, 56, 58
Banking 50
Freight Charges 74
Fund-raising 59
Income 4, 5, 8, 9, 28, 33, 50, 51
Personal Finance 76

Sports and Leisure
Entertainment 68
Recreation 29, 30, 50, 51, 67, 69
Sports 39, 41, 69, 77
Travel 21, 22, 25, 27, 60

MATH CONNECTIONS

Geometry 99, 102, 104, 109
Statistics 91, 149

Transformations 126, 127, 130, 132

APPLICATIONS

Science
Chemistry 100, 121, 147
Engineering 100
Health 133
Medicine 97, 98
Meteorology 86
Physics 94, 98, 100, 141
Space Science 93, 101, 110, 117, 132
Temperature 116, 118

Social Studies
Current Events 92
Demographics 92, 116

Language Arts
Communicate 90, 98, 107, 114, 121, 128, 139
Etymology 90

Business and Economics
Business 90, 92, 116, 123
Manufacturing 116, 128, 129, 130
Real Estate 123
Taxes 88

Life Skills
Consumer Economics 106, 109, 114, 115, 117, 123, 126, 129, 131, 132, 146, 149
Income 107, 108, 124, 131
Transportation 107, 111

Sports and Leisure
Entertainment 102
Puzzles 123
Sports 146

Other
Genealogy 101

SYSTEMS OF LINEAR EQUATIONS & INEQUALITIES 154

MATH CONNECTIONS

Coordinate Geometry 169
Geometry 162, 177, 184, 192

Maximum/Minimum 188, 189, 190, 191, 192
Transformations 197, 200, 201

APPLICATIONS

Science
Agriculture 187, 188, 191, 193
Aviation 195, 201
Chemistry 156, 158, 163
Engineering 209
Health 182, 193, 201
Nutrition 170

Language Arts
Communicate 160, 168, 176, 182, 191, 199
Synonyms 186

Business and Economics
Broadcasting 206
Business 164, 165, 168, 170, 171, 185, 186, 193, 194
Economics 207
Fuel Economy 172, 174, 176
Investments 170
Landscaping 171
Manufacturing 184, 192, 206, 209
Small Business 161, 178, 194

Life Skills
Consumer Economics 163, 178
Fund-raising 177
Income 162, 170, 185, 209
Transportation 193

Sports and Leisure
Drama 179
Entertainment 185
Recreation 177
Sports 163, 170, 177, 198, 199, 200, 206

Other
Criminology 184

MATH CONNECTIONS

Coordinate Geometry 219, 221, 227, 230, 241
Geometry 249, 255

Probability 258
Transformations 220, 221, 222, 230, 265

APPLICATIONS

Science
Anatomy 267
Chemistry 250
Cryptography 234, 237, 239, 241
Networks 228, 229, 232, 233
Nutrition 227, 229, 230, 231

Social Studies
Geography 222

Language Arts
Communicate 220, 229, 239, 248, 256

Business and Economics
Business 259
Inventory 216, 218, 221, 223, 232
Investments 244, 245, 248, 250
Manufacturing 256, 258
Rentals 233
Small Business 251, 253, 267

Life Skills
Academics 223
Consumer Economics 223
Fund-raising 264

Sports and Leisure
Entertainment 249
Sports 225, 231, 232, 267
Travel 259

Other
Jewelry 263

QUADRATIC FUNCTIONS

Ancient clay tablet believed to contain Pythagorean triples

MATH CONNECTIONS

Coordinate Geometry 318, 321
Geometry 284, 285, 286, 287, 288, 296, 297, 305, 345
Maximum/Minimum 276, 277, 278, 312, 335

Patterns in Data 328
Statistics 323, 325
Transformations 279, 289, 302, 304, 306, 321, 345

APPLICATIONS

Science
Architecture 290, 295
Aviation 286, 344
Chemistry 347
Engineering 285, 288, 299, 303, 314, 345
Navigation 288
Physics 274, 288, 305, 328, 329, 336, 337, 345, 347
Rescue 281, 283

Language Arts
Communicate 277, 286, 295, 303, 310, 319, 326, 334

Business and Economics
Advertising 298
Business 312, 321, 328, 336, 347
Construction 279, 286, 289, 307, 309, 311
Manufacturing 312
Small Business 330, 332, 336, 337
Telecommunications 288

Life Skills
Fund-raising 279, 305

Highway Safety 322, 325, 327
Recycling 321

Sports and Leisure
Art 312
Recreation 288, 344
Sports 280, 288, 289, 297, 298, 304, 306, 313, 329, 336, 337

EXPONENTIAL AND LOGARITHMIC FUNCTIONS 352

MATH CONNECTIONS

Geometry 415
Patterns in Data 355, 359

Statistics 366, 368
Transformations 363, 364, 368, 373, 375, 386, 398

APPLICATIONS

Science
Agriculture 399
Archeology 396, 397, 398, 408
Biology 354, 408, 414
Chemistry 360, 373, 374, 375, 391, 413
Earth Science 415
Geology 402, 403, 407, 408
Health 357, 358, 359, 383, 414
Physical Science 360

Physics 376, 383, 386, 387, 389, 390, 398, 405, 407, 414
Space Science 360

Social Studies
Demographics 356, 358, 359, 360, 408, 415
Psychology 408

Language Arts
Communicate 358, 366, 374, 381, 389, 396, 406

Business and Economics
Business 399, 417
Depreciation 412
Economics 398
Investments 361, 365, 367, 368, 384, 392, 394, 396, 397, 398, 399, 409, 412, 414, 415, 417

7 POLYNOMIAL FUNCTIONS

MATH CONNECTIONS

Geometry 430, 448   **Transformations** 462
Statistics 436, 438

APPLICATIONS

Science
Agriculture 453
Archaeology 473
Medicine 454
Thermodynamics 465

Social Studies
Education 432
Geography 464

Language Arts
Communicate 429, 437, 445, 452, 463

Business and Economics
Business 430
Investments 424, 426, 458, 470, 473

Manufacturing 447, 454, 461, 470
Packaging 447, 471
Real Estate 438

Sports and Leisure
Travel 439

MATH CONNECTIONS

APPLICATIONS

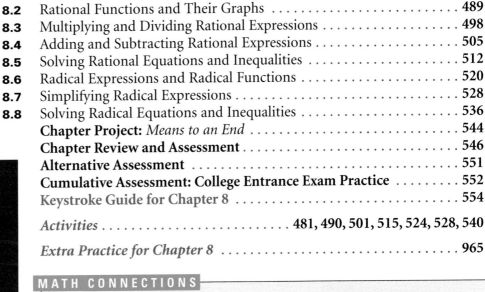

CONIC SECTIONS

MATH CONNECTIONS

Coordinate Geometry 563, 564, 568, 569, 577, 584

Geometry 566, 568, 569, 612
Transformations 577, 584, 593, 602

APPLICATIONS

Science
Architecture 593
Astronomy 588, 591, 593, 618
Biology 618
Forestry 610
Geology 585, 618
Lighting 577, 593
Physics 618
Radio Navigation 595
Space Science 585

Language Arts
Communicate 566, 576, 582, 591, 600, 610

Business and Economics
Business 608, 612, 613
Communications 570, 573, 577, 579, 581, 582, 585

Sports and Leisure
Sports 576, 577, 621

Other
Emergency Services 564, 567
Law Enforcement 602

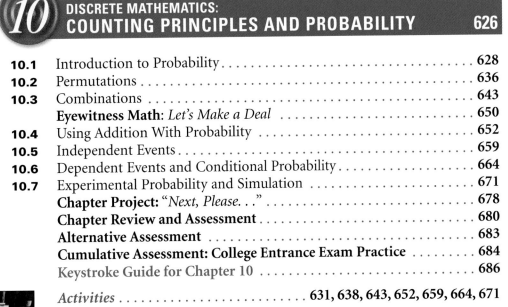

10 DISCRETE MATHEMATICS: COUNTING PRINCIPLES AND PROBABILITY — 626

MATH CONNECTIONS

Geometry 630, 634, 641, 657, 669, 674,   **Maximum/Minimum** 642
675, 677

APPLICATIONS

Science
Computers 630, 632
Health 648, 664, 667, 668,
  670, 682
Nutrition 642
Security 635, 663

Language Arts
Communicate 632, 640,
  647, 655, 661, 667, 675

Social Studies
Demographics 634, 669
Politics 657
Surveys 646, 654
Voting 645, 670

**Business and
Economics**
Advertising 670
Business 649
Catering 639
Management 673, 675
Production 658
Publishing 634
Quality Control 658
Small Business 641, 642

Life Skills
Academics 634
Education 656
Shopping 644, 645
Transportation 632, 634,
  672, 675

Sports and Leisure
Entertainment 661
Extracurricular Activities
  652, 655, 660, 665, 685
Lottery 649
Music 637
Sports 641, 642, 671
Travel 663

MATH CONNECTIONS

Geometry 697, 705, 725, 726, 733, 744, 745, 746
Maximum/Minimum 747

Patterns in Data 707, 708
Probability 735, 738, 739

APPLICATIONS

Science
Astronomy 690, 692
Biology 697
Genetics 740
Health 705
Meteorology 745, 747
Physics 726, 734, 754, 757

Social Studies
Demographics 726

Language Arts
Communicate 695, 703, 710, 717, 724, 732, 738, 745

Business and Economics
Construction 734
Depreciation 699, 701, 703, 705, 713, 714, 717, 726
Inventory 711
Investments 721, 724, 726, 733, 754
Merchandising 710, 712, 754
Real Estate 718, 754

Life Skills
Academics 740
Income 697, 705

Sports and Leisure
Art 728
Entertainment 712, 747, 754
Music 719, 727
Recreation 698
Sports 719, 741, 743, 746, 747

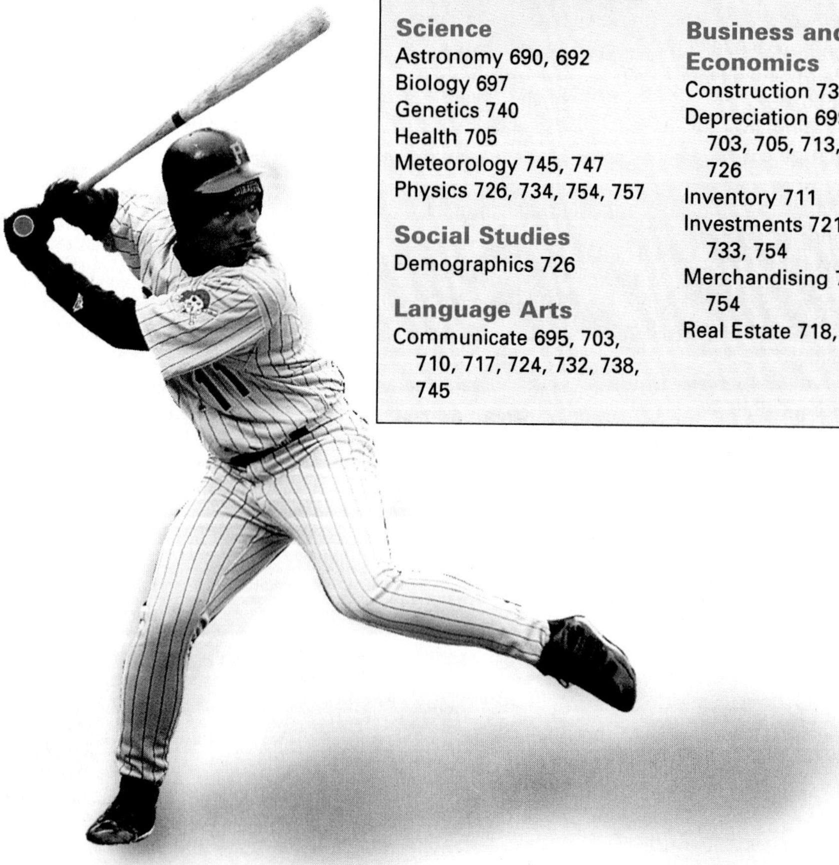

DISCRETE MATHEMATICS: STATISTICS

762

MATH CONNECTIONS

Patterns in Data 779, 786   **Transformations** 780, 795, 797
Probability 775, 777

APPLICATIONS

Science
Aviation 805
Climate 781, 784, 785, 792
Ecology 766, 767, 785
Meteorology 806
Veterinary Medicine 803

Social Studies
Demographics 786, 787, 819
Geography 787
Government 788
Social Services 782
Surveys 797, 804
Workforce 770

Language Arts
Communicate 768, 777, 785, 796, 803, 811

Business and Economics
Accounting 771
Automobile Distribution 818
Broadcasting 764, 765
Business 765, 770, 774, 777, 778, 779, 797
Inventory 770
Manufacturing 793, 794, 797, 811
Marketing 769, 772, 779
Quality Control 812, 813

Life Skills
Academics 771, 809
Awards 804
Education 778, 796, 805, 813

Income 779
Mortgage 812
Transportation 811, 812

Sports and Leisure
Entertainment 821
Gardening 800
Music 768
Recreation 773
Sports 784, 797
Travel 810

Other
Armed Forces 779
Emergency Services 799, 801
Hospital Statistics 804
Law Enforcement 778
Public Safety 776, 803
Security 789

MATH CONNECTIONS

Coordinate Geometry 850	**Probability** 842, 881
Geometry 832, 834, 843, 849, 851, 856	**Transformations** 860, 861, 862, 863

APPLICATIONS

Science
Acoustics 858, 862
Architecture 872
Astronomy 872
Aviation 834, 836, 837, 841, 867, 871
Bicycle Design 849
Engineering 842, 856
Forestry 872
Machinery 857
Meteorology 851, 854
Navigation 842, 879
Robotics 843, 845, 848, 849

Surveying 833
Technology 856
Temperature 865
Wildlife 828, 831

Language Arts
Communicate 832, 840, 847, 854, 864, 871

Social Studies
Employment 865
Map Making 878
Public Safety 873

Business and Economics
Carpentry 872
Construction 834, 849

Life Skills
Home Improvement 834
Income 866

Sports and Leisure
Auto Racing 856
Entertainment 855
Hiking 873

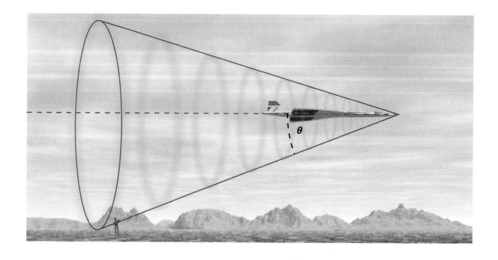

14 FURTHER TOPICS IN TRIGONOMETRY — 884

MATH CONNECTIONS

Geometry 886, 887, 889, 892, 898, 900,
906, 926, 933
Maximum/Minimum 900

Probability 935
Transformations 904, 912, 914, 915,
921

APPLICATIONS

Science
Architecture 917, 919
Forestry 892
Geology 908
Navigation 894, 896, 899
Physics 893, 902, 905, 906,
907, 915, 926, 927
Space Science 932
Surveying 888, 892, 893,
901, 932

Language Arts
Communicate 890, 898,
906, 913, 920, 925

**Business and
Economics**
Legal Investigation 916
Manufacturing 901
Real Estate 932

Sports and Leisure
Recreation 932
Sports 921, 922, 925

Other
Design 909, 913, 914
Fire Fighting 892
Law Enforcement 916
Rescue 893

INFO BANK — 940

Data and Linear Representations

COLLECTING, ORGANIZING, AND REPRESENTING data are important skills in the real world. One example is the research of the annual migration of millions of monarch butterflies. Observers across North America collect data and share their information over the World Wide Web.

Lessons

Tagging a monarch butterfly

Spring and summer migration routes of monarch butterflies

About the Chapter Project

Algebra provides the power to model real-world data. In the Chapter Project, *Correlation Exploration,* you will investigate the correlations between many common variables. Throughout this book, you will learn about different types of algebraic models that can be used to investigate trends and make predictions. In this chapter, you will focus on linear models.

After completing the Chapter Project, you will be able to do the following:

- Represent real-world data by using scatter plots.

- Find and use linear models to predict other possible data values.

About the Portfolio Activities

Throughout the chapter, you will be given opportunities to complete Portfolio Activities that are designed to support your work on the Chapter Project.

- Creating a graph to represent your data is included in the Portfolio Activity on page 11.

- Estimating a linear model for your data is included in the Portfolio Activity on page 20.

- Using your linear model to predict other possible data values is included in the Portfolio Activity on page 36.

- Using technology to find a least-squares regression line for your data set is included in the Portfolio Activity on page 44.

- Using the least-squares regression line to predict other data values is included in the Portfolio Activity on page 51.

Tables and Graphs of Linear Equations

Why *Linear relationships between two variables occur in a wide variety of situations. For example, the wages of a salesperson who earns a commission are often linearly related to the dollar amount of his or her sales.*

A salesperson in a music store usually earns commission.

Objectives

- Represent a real-world linear relationship in a table, graph, or equation.

- Identify linear equations and linear relationships between variables in a table.

PROBLEM SOLVING

Activity
Investigating Commission

You will need: graph paper and a straightedge

Suppose that you work part-time in a music store. You earn $40 per week plus a 10% commission on all of the sales you make.

1. Discuss what it means to earn commission.

2. You can represent this relationship between weekly sales and weekly wages by **making a table.** Copy and complete the table below.

Weekly sales, s (in dollars)	Weekly wages, w (in dollars)
100	$40 + 0.10(100) = 50$
200	?
300	?
400	?
500	?

3. What observations can you make about successive entries in the weekly sales column? in the weekly wages column?

4. You can represent each row in the table as an ordered pair (s, w). Plot each ordered pair, and connect the first and last points with a straightedge. Does each point that you plotted appear to be contained in this line segment?

CHECKPOINT ✔ **5.** Write an equation to represent the relationship between s and w.

In the Activity on page 4, a linear relationship that can be modeled by a linear equation is described. Example 1 provides another instance of a linear relationship.

E X A M P L E ❶ **An attorney charges a fixed fee of $250 for an initial meeting and $150 per hour for all hours worked after that.**

    a. Make a table of the total charge for 1, 2, 3, and 4 hours worked.

    b. Graph the points represented by your table and connect them.

    c. Write a linear equation to model this situation.

    d. Find the charge for 25 hours of work.

A lawyer, or attorney, in court

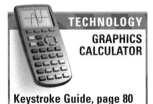

Keystroke Guide, page 80

⬤ **SOLUTION**

a.

Hours worked	1	2	3	4
Total charge	$400	$550	$700	$850

c. Translate the verbal description into an equation involving c and h.

$$\frac{\text{total}}{\text{charge}} = \frac{\text{variable}}{\text{charge}} + \frac{\text{fixed}}{\text{fee}}$$

$$c = 150h + 250$$

Thus, $c = 150h + 250$.

d. Use the equation. Substitute 25 for h in the equation.

$$c = 150h + 250$$
$$c = 150(25) + 250$$
$$c = 4000$$

CHECK

From the graph of $y = 150x + 250$, you can see that when $x = 25$, $y = 4000$.

Thus, the attorney charges $4000 for 25 hours of work.

b.

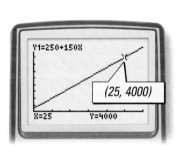

TRY THIS
A water tank already contains 55 gallons of water when Darius begins to fill it. Water flows into the tank at a rate of 9 gallons per minute.

    a. Make a table for the volume of water in the tank after 1, 2, 3, and 4 minutes.

    b. Graph the points represented by your table and connect them.

    c. Write a linear equation to model this situation.

    d. Find the volume of water in the tank 20 minutes after Darius begins filling the tank.

The equations in Example 1 and the Try This exercise above have a characteristic in common. Each has the form shown below.

total amount = variable amount + fixed amount

In general, if a relationship between x and y can be written as $y = mx + b$, where m and b are real numbers, then x and y are **linearly related**. The equation $y = mx + b$ is called a **linear equation**. The graph of a linear equation is a straight line.

CHECKPOINT ✔ What are the values of m and b in the equation $c = 150h + 250$ from Example 1?

E X A M P L E ❷ Graph $y = \frac{2}{3}x - 1$.

● **SOLUTION**

Because $y = \frac{2}{3}x - 1$ is of the form $y = mx + b$, where $m = \frac{2}{3}$ and $b = -1$, its graph is a straight line. A line is determined by two points, so you need to plot only two ordered pairs that satisfy $y = \frac{2}{3}x - 1$ and draw the line through them.

x	0	3
y	$y = \frac{2}{3}(0) - 1 = -1$	$y = \frac{2}{3}(3) - 1 = 1$

Plot $(0, -1)$ and $(3, 1)$, and draw a line through them.

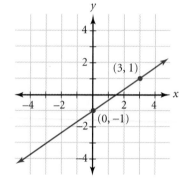

TECHNOLOGY

GRAPHICS CALCULATOR

Keystroke Guide, page 80

CHECK

Graph $y = \frac{2}{3}x - 1$ on a graphics calculator, and verify that the points $(0, -1)$ and $(3, 1)$ are on the line.

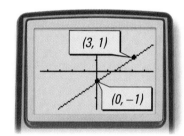

TRY THIS Graph $y = \frac{5}{4}x + 3$.

When variables represented in a table of values are linearly related and there is a constant difference in the x-values, there is also a constant difference in the y-values. For example, consider the linear equation $y = -2x + 5$.

Make a table of values by choosing x-values that have a constant difference, such as 1, 2, 3, 4, and so on.

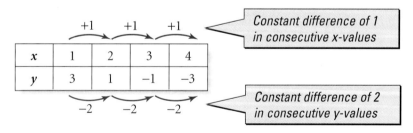

In a linear relationship, a constant difference in consecutive x-values results in a constant difference in consecutive y-values.

CHECKPOINT ✔ Suppose that you are making a table of values to determine whether the variables are linearly related. Describe the relationship. What must exist between the x-values that you choose?

E X A M P L E ③ Does the table of values at right represent a linear relationship between x and y? Explain. If the relationship is linear, write the next ordered pair that would appear in the table.

x	7	12	17	22	27	32
y	11	8	5	2	−1	−4

● **SOLUTION**

Find differences in consecutive x-values and consecutive y-values.

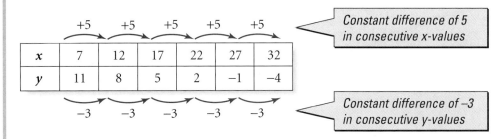

Constant difference of 5 in consecutive x-values

Constant difference of −3 in consecutive y-values

PROBLEM SOLVING   **Look for a pattern.** Because there is a constant difference in the x-values and a constant difference in the y-values, the relationship between x and y is linear.

The next table entry for x is 32 + 5, or 7.
The next table entry for y is −4 + (−3), or −7.

TRY THIS   Does the table of values at right represent a linear relationship between x and y? Explain. If the relationship is linear, write the next ordered pair that would appear in the table.

x	−2	2	6	10	14	18
y	1	2	4	8	16	32

CRITICAL THINKING   Does the table at right represent a linear relationship between x and y? Explain.

x	9	6	3	0	−3	−6
y	5	5	5	5	5	5

Exercises

● *Communicate*

1. Discuss the relationships among the table, equation, and graph shown here.

x	−4	−2	0	2	4
y	−7	−4	−1	2	5

$y = \frac{3}{2}x - 1$

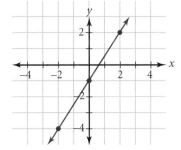

APPLICATION

2. SALES TAX Suppose that a state sales tax is 7%. Make a table showing the amount of tax on items with prices of $6, $8, $10, and $12. How can you find whether the price and amount of sales tax are linearly related?

3. Explain how to verify that the points (−1, 7), (0, 4), and (2, −2) are all on the same line.

Guided Skills Practice

4. INCOME Suppose that you work part-time at a department store, earning a base salary of $50 per week plus a 15% commission on all sales that you make.
(EXAMPLE 1)
  a. Copy and complete the table.
  b. Graph the points represented in the table and connect them.

Weekly sales, x	Weekly income, y
100	$50 + (0.15)(100) = 65$
200	?
300	?
400	?
x	?

  c. Write a linear equation to represent the relationship between the weekly sales, x, and the weekly income y.
  d. Find the weekly income, y, for weekly sales of $1200.

5. Graph $y = 3x - 2$. *(EXAMPLE 2)*

6. Does the table below represent a linear relationship between x and y? If the relationship is linear, write the next ordered pair that would appear in the table. *(EXAMPLE 3)*

x	-4	1	6	11	16	21
y	13	19	25	31	37	43

Practice and Apply

State whether each equation is a linear equation.

7. $y = -3x$ **8.** $y = -x$ **9.** $y = 12 + 2x$

10. $y = 5 - 4x$ **11.** $y = \frac{1}{2}x - 3$ **12.** $y = -\frac{2}{3}x$

13. $y = \frac{1}{x}$ **14.** $y = \frac{-4}{x}$ **15.** $y = -x^2 + 1$

16. $y = 2 + 5x^2$ **17.** $y = 5.5x - 2$ **18.** $y = 11 - 1.2x$

Graph each linear equation.

19. $y = 2x + 1$ **20.** $y = 4x + 3$ **21.** $y = 3x - 6$
22. $y = 6x - 3$ **23.** $y = 5 - 2x$ **24.** $y = 3 - 5x$
25. $y = -x + 5$ **26.** $y = -x - 2$ **27.** $y = \frac{2}{3}x + 4$
28. $y = \frac{1}{3}x - 5$ **29.** $y + 3 = x + 6$ **30.** $y + 4 = x - 3$

For Exercises 31–38, determine whether each table represents a linear relationship between x and y. If the relationship is linear, write the next ordered pair that would appear in the table.

31.

x	y
0	10
1	22
2	34
3	46

32.

x	y
0	-5
3	-1
6	3
9	7

33.

x	y
3	-5
4	1
5	6
6	11

34.

x	y
-2	1
-3	2
-4	4
-5	8

35.

x	y
8	28
6	22
4	16
2	10

36.

x	y
12	−3
9	−8
6	−13
3	−18

37.

x	y
6	115
9	100
12	85
15	75

38.

x	y
−6	58
−9	44
−12	32
−15	20

For each graph, make a table of values to represent the points. Does the table represent a linear relationship? Explain.

39.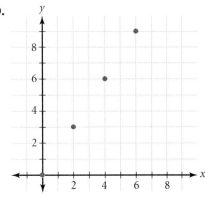

40.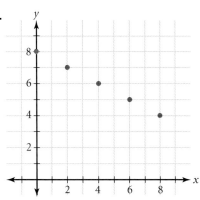

41. Make a table of values for the equation $y = 4x - 1$, and graph the line. Is the point $(2, 6)$ on this line? Explain how to answer this question by using the table, the graph, and the equation.

> *Calculator button indicates that a graphics calculator is recommended.*

Use a graphics calculator to graph each equation. Then sketch the graph on graph paper.

42 $y = -3x + 1.5$

43 $y = -x - 2.5$

44 $y = 12 - 2.5x$

45 $y = 4 - 0.5x$

46 $y = \frac{1}{2}x - \frac{3}{5}$

47 $y = -\frac{2}{3}x + \frac{1}{2}$

CHALLENGE

48. What can you determine about the graph of $y = mx + b$ when $x = 0$? What can you determine about the graph of $y = mx + b$ when $y = 0$?

APPLICATION

49. INCOME A video rental store charges a $6 membership fee and $3 for each video rented. In the graph at right, the *x*-axis represents the number of videos rented by a customer and the *y*-axis represents the store's revenue from that customer.

a. Make a table for the data points on the graph.

b. If 15 videos are rented, what is the revenue?

c. If a new member paid the store a total of $27, how many videos were rented?

d. Explain how to find answers to parts **b** and **c** by using an extended table and an extended graph.

Registration day at a community college

50. DEMOGRAPHICS City Community College plans to increase its enrollment capacity to keep up with an increasing number of student applicants. The college currently has an enrollment capacity of 2200 students and plans to increase its capacity by 70 students each year.

a. Let x represent the number of years from now, and let y represent the enrollment capacity. Make a table of values for x and y with x-values of 0, 1, 2, 3, and 4.

b. What will the enrollment capacity be 3 years from now?

c. Write a linear equation that could be used to find the enrollment capacity, y, after x years.

51. BUSINESS An airport parking lot charges a basic fee of $2 plus $1 per half-hour parked.

a. Copy and complete the table.

b. Graph the points represented in the table. Label each axis, and indicate your scale.

c. Write an equation for the total charge, c, in terms of the number of half-hours parked, h.

d. How many half-hours is 72 hours? What is the total charge for parking in the lot for 72 hours?

Half-hours	Total charge ($)
0	$2 + (1)(0) = 2$
1	?
2	?
3	?
?	12

52. METEOROLOGY At 6:00 A.M., the temperature was 67°F. As a cold front passed, the temperature began to drop at a steady rate of 4°F per hour.

a. Write a linear equation relating the temperature in degrees Fahrenheit, t, to the number of hours, h, after the initial temperature reading.

b. Estimate, to the nearest 15 minutes, how long it would take to reach freezing (32°F) if the drop in temperature continued at the same rate.

> **Supply** is the amount that manufacturers are willing to produce at a certain price.
> **Demand** is the amount that consumers are willing to buy at a certain price.

53. ECONOMICS This table gives the price, the *supply*, and the *demand* for a video game.

a. Graph the points representing (price, supply) and the points representing (price, demand) on the same coordinate plane.

b. Estimate the price at which the supply of video games meets the demand. Estimate the supply and demand at this price.

c. What happens to the supply and to the demand when the price of the video game is higher than the price in part **b**? lower than the price in part **b**?

Price ($)	Supply	Demand
20	150	500
30	250	400
50	450	200

54. BUSINESS Casey has a small business making dessert baskets. She estimates that her fixed weekly costs for rent, electricity, and salaries is $200. The ingredients for one dessert basket cost $2.50.

a. If Casey makes 40 dessert baskets in a given week, what will her total weekly costs be?

b. Casey's total costs for last week were $500. How many dessert baskets did she make?

 *Look Back*

The following *Rules of Divisibility* are useful in finding factors of numbers.
If a number is

- divisible by 3, the sum of the digits of the number is divisible by 3.
- divisible by 6, the number is divisible by 3 and is even.
- divisible by 9, the sum of the digits of the number is divisible by 9.
- divisible by 4, the number formed by the last two digits is divisible by 4.

Find numbers *a* and *b* that meet the following conditions:

55. $ab = 36$ and $a + b = 13$

56. $ab = 51$ and $a + b = 20$

57. $ab = 82$ and $a + b = 43$

58. $ab = 72$ and $a + b = 22$

59. $ab = 128$ and $a + b = 24$

60. $ab = 56$ and $a + b = 15$

61. $ab = 48$ and $a + b = 19$

62. $ab = 52$ and $a + b = 17$

Evaluate each expression. Write your answer in simplest form.

63. $\frac{1}{2} \times \frac{4}{7}$

64. $\frac{2}{3} \times \frac{6}{11}$

65. $3 \times \frac{2}{3}$

66. $\frac{13}{14} \times 7$

67. $7 \div \frac{7}{8}$

68. $5 \div \frac{5}{6}$

69. $21 \div \frac{7}{8}$

70. $10 \div \frac{5}{6}$

 *Look Beyond*

71. Graph the equations $y = 2x$, $y = 2x + 3$, and $y = 2x - 4$ on the same coordinate plane. How are the graphs alike? How are they different?

1. Describe three real-world situations in which a distance changes at a fairly constant rate over time. For example, the distance driven on an interstate highway or the distance walked in a walkathon changes at a fairly constant rate.

2. Choose one of your three real-world situations from Step 1, and determine a suitable way to collect some time and distance data. Collect and record a minimum of seven data values. This data will become your **portfolio data set**.

3. Organize the data from your portfolio data set in a table of values.

4. Use graph paper to graph your portfolio data set. Label the *x*-axis with units of time, and label the *y*-axis with units of distance. The point that represents the first distance measure that you took should have an *x*-coordinate of 0.

WORKING ON THE CHAPTER PROJECT

You should now be able to complete Activity 1 of the Chapter Project.

Slopes and Intercepts

Why *Trends in the real world, such as the increase in cellular phone use, can often be modeled by a linear equation, in which the slope indicates a rate of change.*

Objectives

● Graph a linear equation.

● Write a linear equation for a given line in the coordinate plane.

APPLICATION

COMMUNICATIONS

Every year more and more people in the United States become cellular phone subscribers. The table below represents the recent trend in cellular phone subscriptions. The third column in the table gives the change in the number of subscribers from one year to the next.

Year	Number of subscribers (in millions, rounded to the nearest 100,000)	Yearly change (in millions, rounded to the nearest 100,000)	
1990	5.3		
1991	7.6	1990–1991	2.3
1992	11.0	1991–1992	3.4
1993	16.0	1992–1993	5.0
1994	24.0	1993–1994	8.0
1995	33.8	1994–1995	9.8

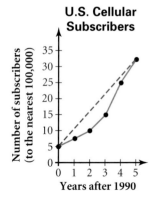

U.S. Cellular Subscribers

Number of subscribers (to the nearest 100,000)

Years after 1990

Notice in the highlighted row above that the number of new subscribers from 1990 to 1991 is 7.6 − 5.3, or 2.3. This difference can also be represented by the ratio shown below.

$$\frac{\text{Change in subscribers}}{\text{Change in years}} = \frac{7.6 - 5.3}{1991 - 1990} = \frac{2.3}{1} = 2.3$$

All entries in the third column can be found by using a ratio. Each of the ratios gives the *rate of change* from one year to the next.

You can also find the *average rate of change* from 1990 to 1995. On average, from 1990 to 1995, there were about 5.7 million new subscribers per year. This average rate of change is indicated by the red dashed line on the graph at left.

$$\frac{\text{Total change in subscribers}}{\text{Total change in years}} = \frac{33.8 - 5.3}{1995 - 1990} = \frac{28.5}{5} = 5.7$$

CHECKPOINT ✔ Estimate the average rate of change from 1990 to 1993 and from 1993 to 1995.

In a graph, the *slope* of a line is the change in vertical units divided by the corresponding change in horizontal units.

Slope of a Line

If points (x_1, y_1) and (x_2, y_2) lie on a line, then the slope, m, of the line is given by the ratio below.

$$m = \frac{\text{change in } y}{\text{corresponding change in } x} = \frac{y_2 - y_1}{x_2 - x_1}$$

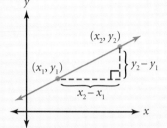

The slope of a line is sometimes referred to as $m = \frac{rise}{run}$.

You can find the slope of a line if you know the coordinates of two points on the line. This is shown in Example 1.

EXAMPLE **1** **Find the slope of the line containing the points (0, 4) and (3, 1).**

SOLUTION

PROBLEM SOLVING

Use a formula. Let $(x_1, y_1) = (0, 4)$ and $(x_2, y_2) = (3, 1)$. Apply the definition of slope.

$$m = \frac{y_2 - y_1}{x_2 - x_1} = \frac{1 - 4}{3 - 0} = \frac{-3}{3} = -1$$

The line containing $(0, 4)$ and $(3, 1)$ has a slope of -1.

TRY THIS Find the slope of the line containing the points $(-5, 3)$ and $(3, -4)$.

Activity
Exploring Slopes

TECHNOLOGY
GRAPHICS CALCULATOR

Keystroke Guide, page 80

You will need: a graphics calculator

1. Each equation below has the form $y = mx$, where m is the slope. Graph each pair of equations. Describe how the slopes for each pair of lines are alike and how they are different.

   a. $y = \frac{1}{5}x$ and $y = -\frac{1}{5}x$

   b. $y = \frac{2}{3}x$ and $y = -\frac{2}{3}x$

   c. $y = x$ and $y = -x$

   d. $y = \frac{3}{2}x$ and $y = -\frac{3}{2}x$

   e. $y = 5x$ and $y = -5x$

2. Make a conjecture about the slopes of $y = mx$ when $m < 0$ and when $m > 0$. Explain how the graphs of these lines are related.

CHECKPOINT ✔ 3. Verify your conjecture from Step 2 by writing and graphing another pair of equations with the relationship that you described in Step 2.

Intercepts

The *y*-coordinate of the point where the graph of a linear equation crosses the *y*-axis is called the **y-intercept** of the line. In the graph below, the *y*-intercept of **line r** is 3 and the *y*-intercept of **line s** is −2.

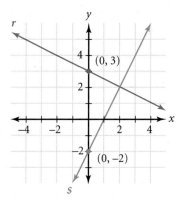

To find the *y*-intercept of a line, substitute 0 for *x* in an equation for the line.

Line s

$y = 2x - 2$

$y = 2(0) - 2$

$y = -2$ ◁ *The y-intercept of $y = 2x - 2$ is −2.*

Line r

$y = -\frac{1}{2}x + 3$

$y = -\frac{1}{2}(0) + 3$

$y = 3$ ◁ *The y-intercept of $y = -\frac{1}{2}x + 3$ is 3.*

Slope-Intercept Form

The **slope-intercept form** of a line is $y = mx + b$, where *m* is the slope and *b* is the *y*-intercept.

The slope of a line tells you about the steepness and direction of the line. The *y*-intercept tells you where the line crosses the *y*-axis.

Varying the slope
$y = mx + 1$

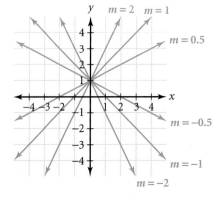

Varying the y intercept
$y = 2x + b$

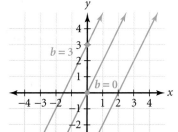

EXAMPLE ② **Use the slope and *y*-intercept to graph the equation $-2x + y = -3$.**

● **SOLUTION**

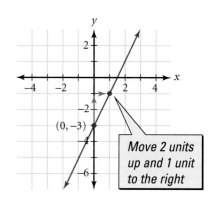

1. Write the equation in slope-intercept form, $y = mx + b$.

$$-2x + y = -3$$
$$y = 2x - 3$$

slope   *y-intercept*

The slope is 2 and the *y*-intercept is -3.

Move 2 units up and 1 unit to the right

2. Plot the point $(0, -3)$, and use the slope to find a second point.

$$m = \frac{\text{change in } y}{\text{corresponding change in } x} = \frac{2}{1}$$

3. Connect the two points to graph the line.

TRY THIS   Use the slope and *y*-intercept to graph the equation $2x + y = 3$.

Example 3 shows you how to write an equation for a line that is graphed.

EXAMPLE ③ **Write the equation, in slope-intercept form, for the line graphed.**

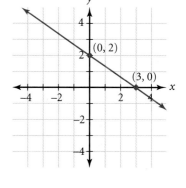

● **SOLUTION**

Because the point $(0, 2)$ is on the graph, the *y*-intercept is 2. Use another convenient point on the line, such as $(3, 0)$, to find the slope.

The same result occurs when $(x_1, y_1) = (3, 0)$ and when $(x_2, y_2) = (0, 2)$.

Let $(x_1, y_1) = (0, 2)$ and $(x_2, y_2) = (3, 0)$.

$$m = \frac{y_2 - y_1}{x_2 - x_1} = \frac{0 - 2}{3 - 0} = -\frac{2}{3}$$

The equation in slope-intercept form is $y = -\frac{2}{3}x + 2$.

TRY THIS   Write the equation, in slope-intercept form, for the line that passes through $(1, 4)$ and has a *y*-intercept of 3.

Standard Form

The **standard form** of a linear equation is $Ax + By = C$, where A, B, and C are real numbers and A and B are not *both* 0.

Example 4 on page 16 shows you how to use the *x*- and *y*-intercepts to sketch the graph of a linear equation. The ***x*-intercept** of a graph is the *x*-coordinate of the point where the graph crosses the *x*-axis.

E X A M P L E ④ Use intercepts to graph the equation $2x - 3y = 6$.

SOLUTION

To find the *x*-intercept, let $y = 0$.
$$2x - 3y = 6$$
$$2x - 3(0) = 6$$
$$x = 3$$

To find the *y*-intercept, let $x = 0$.
$$2x - 3y = 6$$
$$2(0) - 3y = 6$$
$$y = -2$$

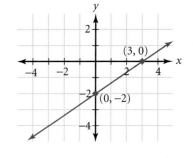

Graph the points $(3, 0)$ and $(0, -2)$. Draw the line through these two points.

TRY THIS   Use intercepts to graph the equation $5x + 3y = 15$.

Horizontal and Vertical Lines

For the **horizontal line** at right, the formula for slope gives $\frac{3 - 3}{2 - (-3)} = \frac{0}{5}$, which is 0.

A **horizontal line** is a line that has a slope of 0.

For the **vertical line** at right, the formula for slope gives $\frac{1 - (-3)}{-2 - (-2)} = \frac{4}{0}$, which is undefined.

A **vertical line** is a line that has an undefined slope.

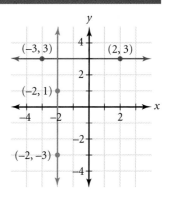

CHECKPOINT ✔ Which type of line has a *y*-intercept but no *x*-intercept? Which type of line has an *x*-intercept but no *y*-intercept?

E X A M P L E ⑤ Graph each equation.
   a. $y = -2$ **b.** $x = -3$

SOLUTION

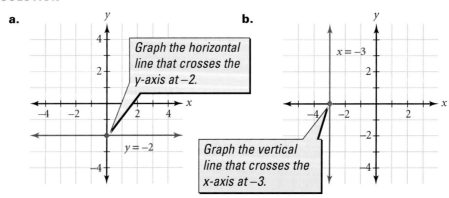

CRITICAL THINKING   Verify that every line of the form $By = C$ is horizontal and that every line of the form $Ax = C$ is vertical.

Exercises

Communicate

1. Explain how to arrange the linear equations given below in ascending order of steepness, that is, from least steep to most steep.

   a. $y = 3x - 5$ **b.** $y = \frac{1}{3}x + 5$ **c.** $y = \frac{1}{2}x + 5$

   d. $y = 5x + 5$ **e.** $y = 5$ **f.** $y = 3x + 5$

2. Describe how to sketch the graph of the line $3x + 2y = 4$.

3. Explain how to find the y-intercept for the graph of $2x - 5y = 10$.

4. Describe how to write the equation $x - y = 2$ in slope-intercept form.

Guided Skills Practice

5. Find the slope of the line containing the points $(-2, 4)$ and $(8, -3)$. **(EXAMPLE 1)**

6. Use the slope and y-intercept to graph the equation $\frac{1}{2}x + y = -4$. **(EXAMPLE 2)**

7. Write the equation in slope-intercept form for the line graphed at right. **(EXAMPLE 3)**

8. Use intercepts to graph $-2x - 4y = 8$. **(EXAMPLE 4)**

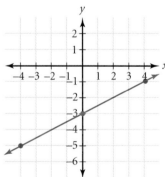

Graph each equation. (EXAMPLE 5)

9. $x = \frac{1}{2}$ 10. $y = \frac{3}{2}$

Practice and Apply

Write the equation in slope-intercept form for the line that has the indicated slope, *m*, and *y*-intercept, *b*.

11. $m = 2, b = 0.75$ 12. $m = -5, b = 0$

13. $m = 0, b = -3$ 14. $m = -\frac{1}{8}, b = 2$

15. $m = -3, b = 7$ 16. $m = -\frac{2}{3}, b = -1$

17. $m = \frac{1}{4}, b = -\frac{3}{4}$ 18. $m = 0.08, b = -2.91$

Find the slope of the line containing the indicated points.

19. $(0, 0)$ and $(3, 30)$ 20. $(1, -3)$ and $(3, -5)$

21. $(3, -2)$ and $(4, 5)$ 22. $(-10, -4)$ and $(-3, -3)$

23. $(-6, -6)$ and $(-3, 1)$ 24. $(-2, 8)$ and $(-2, -1)$

25. $\left(\frac{1}{2}, -3\right)$ and $\left(3, -\frac{1}{2}\right)$ 26. $(-4, 8)$ and $(-3, -6)$

Identify the slope, *m*, and the *y*-intercept, *b*, for each line. Then graph.

27. $y + 2x = 0$

28. $y = 2$

29. $-\frac{1}{3}x + y = -7$

30. $x + y = 6$

31. $y = x$

32. $-2x = 8 + 4y$

33. $-0.6x + y = -4$

34. $2x + y = 1$

35. $x = -3$

Write an equation in slope-intercept form for each line.

36.
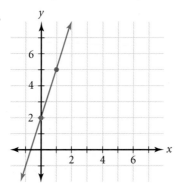

37.
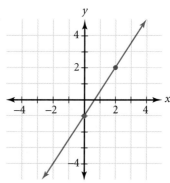

38.
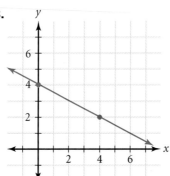

39.
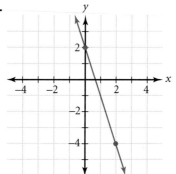

Use intercepts to graph each equation.

40. $4x + y = -4$

41. $x + 3y = 12$

42. $2x - y = 8$

43. $-x + 2y = 5$

44. $7x + 3y = 2$

45. $-x + 8y = -6$

46. $-3x + y = -9$

47. $-x - 7y = 3$

48. $x - y = -1$

49. $-\frac{1}{2}x + 3y = 7$

50. $5x - 8y = 16$

51. $x + \frac{1}{2}y = -2$

Find the slope of each line. Then graph.

52. $x = 5$

53. $x = -2$

54. $y = 8$

55. $y = -5$

56. $x = -1$

57. $x = 9$

58. $y = -8$

59. $y = 7$

60. $x = -\frac{1}{3}$

61. $x = -\frac{1}{4}$

62. $y = \frac{3}{4}$

63. $y = \frac{2}{3}$

CHALLENGE

64. The points $(-2, 4)$, $(0, 2)$, and $(3, a - 1)$ are on one line. Find *a*.

APPLICATION

65. TAXES Tristan buys a computer for $3600. For tax purposes, he declares a linear depreciation (loss of value) of $600 per year. Let *y* be the declared value of the computer after *x* years.
  a. What is the slope of the line that models this depreciation?
  b. Find the *y*-intercept of the line.
  c. Write a linear equation in slope-intercept form to model the value of the computer over time.
  d. Find the value of Tristan's computer after 4.5 years.

66. PHYSICS The graph at right shows data for the distance of an object from a motion detector.

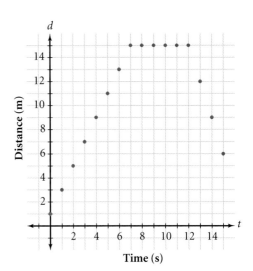

a. Describe how the motion of the object changes with time in the graph.

b. Model the distance of the object from the detector by using three linear equations.

c. For what times is each equation valid?

d. During which time interval is the object moving the fastest?

e. Is the slope of the segment representing the fastest movement positive or negative? Explain what the sign of the slope indicates about the motion of the object.

67. METEOROLOGY The thermometer at left shows temperatures in degrees Fahrenheit, *F*, and in degrees Celsius, *C*. Room temperature is 20°C, or 68°F.

a. Choose two other Fahrenheit temperatures, and use the thermometer at left to estimate the Celsius equivalents.

b. Let the temperature equivalents from part **a** represent points of the form (*F*, *C*). Graph the three points and draw a line through the points.

c. Find the slope and *y*-intercept of the line.

d. Write the equation of the line in slope-intercept form.

68. CONSTRUCTION The slope of a roof is called the pitch and is defined as follows:

$$\text{pitch} = \frac{\text{rise of roof}}{\frac{1}{2} \times \text{span of roof}}$$

a. Find the pitch of a roof if the rise is 12 feet and the span is 30 feet.

b. Find the pitch of a roof if the rise is 18 feet and the span is 60 feet.

c. Find the pitch of a roof if the rise is 4 feet and the span is 50 feet.

d. If the pitch is constant, is the relationship between the rise and span linear? Explain.

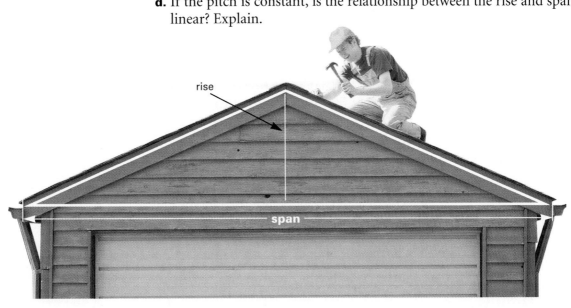

Shown above is a Jersey cow, one type of dairy cow.

69. AGRICULTURE The table at right shows the average milk production of dairy cows in the United States for the years from 1993 to 1996.

Year	Pounds of milk per day
1993	42.7
1994	44.3
1995	45.2
1996	45.2

[*Source: U.S. Dept. of Agriculture*]

a. Let $x = 0$ represent 1990. Make a line graph with years on the horizontal axis and pounds of milk on the vertical axis.

b. In what year did the average milk production increase the most? What is the slope of the graph for that year?

c. In what year did the average milk production increase the least? What is the slope of the graph for that year?

 Look Back

70. Find the value of V in the equation $V = lwh$ when $l = 2$, $w = 3$, and $h = 5$.

71. Use the formula $I = prt$ to find the interest, I, in dollars when the principal, p, is $1000; the annual interest rate, r, is 8%; and the time, t, is 2 years.

72. Use the formula $P = 4s$ to find the perimeter of a square, P, in feet when the length of a side, s, is 16 feet.

73. Does the table of values at right represent a linear relationship between x and y? Explain. If the relationship is linear, write the next ordered pair that would appear in the table. *(LESSON 1.1)*

x	−8	−5	−2	1	4	7
y	9	7	5	3	1	−1

74. Make a table of values for the equation $y = -3x + 7$, and graph the line. Is the point $(4, -4)$ on this line? Explain how to answer this question by using the table, the graph, and the equation. *(LESSON 1.1)*

Look Beyond

Calculator button indicates that a graphics calculator is recommended.

75 Graph the equations $y = 2.12x - 3.7$ and $y = x + 5.4$ on the same screen. Find the coordinates of any points of intersection.

Refer to your portfolio data set from the Portfolio Activity on page 11.

1. Choose two data points from your portfolio data set. Choose points that seem to fit the overall trend of your portfolio data set, not data points that contains values which may be far higher or lower than the others.

2. Use a straightedge to draw a line through the points on your graph. This line will be your linear model for your portfolio data set. Find the equation of your linear model.

3. What rate of change is indicated by your linear model? Include the appropriate units of measurement.

WORKING ON THE CHAPTER PROJECT

You should now be able to complete Activity 2 of the Chapter Project.

Linear Equations in Two Variables

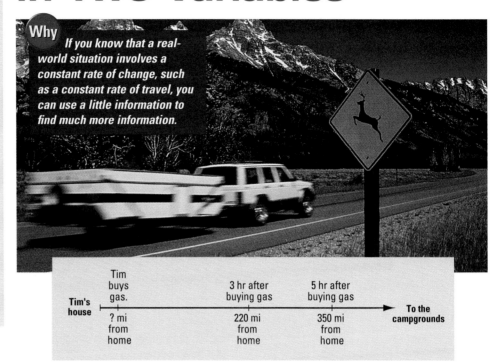

Why *If you know that a real-world situation involves a constant rate of change, such as a constant rate of travel, you can use a little information to find much more information.*

Objectives

- Write a linear equation in two variables given sufficient information.

- Write an equation for a line that is parallel or perpendicular to a given line.

APPLICATION
TRAVEL

Tim leaves his house and drives at a constant speed to go camping. On his way to the campgrounds, he stops to buy gasoline. Three hours after buying gas, Tim has traveled 220 miles from home, and 5 hours after buying gas he has traveled 350 miles from home. How far from home was Tim when he bought gas? To answer this question, you can use the information given to write a linear equation in two variables. *You will solve this problem in Example 3.*

Example 1 shows you how to write a linear equation given two points on the line.

E X A M P L E ① Write an equation in slope-intercept form for the line containing the points (4, −3) and (2, 1).

● **SOLUTION**

1. Find the slope of the line.

$$m = \frac{1 - (-3)}{2 - 4} = \frac{4}{-2} = -2$$

2. Find the *y*-intercept of the line.

Substitute −2 for *m* and the coordinates of either point into $y = mx + b$.

$$y = mx + b$$
$$1 = -2(2) + b \quad \text{The point (2, 1) is used.}$$
$$1 = -4 + b$$
$$5 = b$$

3. Write an equation.

$$y = mx + b$$
$$y = -2x + 5$$

You can use the *point-slope form* to write an equation of a line if you are given the slope and the coordinates of any point on the line.

Point-Slope Form

If a line has a slope of m and contains the point (x_1, y_1), then the **point-slope form** of its equation is $y - y_1 = m(x - x_1)$.

EXAMPLE ② Write an equation in slope-intercept form for the line that has a slope of $\frac{1}{2}$ and contains the point $(-8, 3)$.

● **SOLUTION**

$$y - y_1 = m(x - x_1) \qquad \text{\textit{Begin with point-slope form.}}$$

$$y - 3 = \frac{1}{2}[x - (-8)] \qquad \text{\textit{Substitute } } \frac{1}{2} \text{ \textit{for m, 3 for } } y_1, \text{ \textit{and} } -8 \text{ \textit{for} } x_1.$$

$$y - 3 = \frac{1}{2}x + 4$$

$$y = \frac{1}{2}x + 7 \qquad \text{\textit{Write the equation in slope-intercept form.}}$$

The distance traveled by a motorist driving at a constant speed can be modeled by a linear equation.

EXAMPLE ③ Refer to the travel problem described at the beginning of the lesson.

How far from home was Tim when he bought gas?

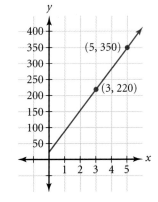

● **SOLUTION**

Write a linear equation to model Tim's distance, y, in terms of time, x. Three hours after buying gas, Tim has traveled 220 miles, and 5 hours after buying gas, he has traveled 350 miles.

The line contains $(3, 220)$ and $(5, 350)$.

Find the slope. $m = \dfrac{350 - 220}{5 - 3} = 65$

Write an equation. Begin with point-slope form.

$$y - y_1 = m(x - x_1)$$

$$y - 220 = 65(x - 3) \qquad \text{\textit{Use either point. The point (3, 220) is used here.}}$$

$$y - 220 = 65x - 195$$

$$y = 65x + 25 \qquad \text{\textit{Write the equation in slope-intercept form.}}$$

Thus, $y = 65x + 25$ models Tim's distance from home with respect to time. Since x represents the number of hours he traveled *after* he bought gas, he bought gas when $x = 0$. Thus, he bought gas when he was 25 miles from home.

CHECKPOINT ✔ What does the slope of the line $y = 65x + 25$ in Example 3 represent?

Parallel and Perpendicular Lines

CONNECTION

COORDINATE GEOMETRY

The graph at right shows line ℓ_2 parallel to ℓ_1 and ℓ_3 perpendicular to ℓ_1 at point P.

In the Activity below, you can explore how parallel lines and perpendicular lines are related.

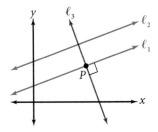

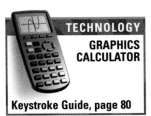

TECHNOLOGY

GRAPHICS CALCULATOR

Keystroke Guide, page 80

Activity
Exploring Parallel and Perpendicular Lines

You will need: a graphics calculator

1. Graph $y = 2x + 1$. On the same screen, graph $y = 2x$, $y = 2x - 2.5$, and $y = 3x + 1$. Which equations have graphs that appear to be parallel to that of $y = 2x + 1$? What do these equations have in common?

CHECKPOINT ✔ 2. Write an equation in slope-intercept form for a line whose graph you think will be parallel to that of $y = 2x + 1$. Verify by graphing.

3. Graph $y = 2x + 1$. On the same screen, graph $y = -\frac{1}{2}x + 2$, $y = \frac{1}{2}x + 2$, and $y = -\frac{1}{2}x + 3$. Which equations have graphs that appear to be perpendicular to that of $y = 2x + 1$? What do these equations have in common?

CHECKPOINT ✔ 4. Write an equation in slope-intercept form whose graph you think will be perpendicular to that of $y = 2x + 1$. Verify by graphing.

The relationships between the slopes of parallel lines are stated below.

Parallel Lines

If two lines have the same slope, they are parallel.

If two lines are parallel, they have the same slope.

All vertical lines have an undefined slope and are parallel to one another.

All horizontal lines have a slope of 0 and are parallel to one another.

The graphs of three parallel lines are shown at right.

$$y = 2x + 3$$
$$y = 2x - 1$$
$$y = 2x - 4$$

Notice that the lines do not intersect.

Because they are parallel, the lines will *never* intersect.

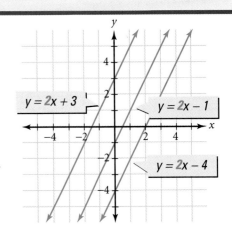

EXAMPLE **4** Write an equation in slope-intercept form for the line that contains the point (−1, 3) and is parallel to the graph of $y = -2x + 4$.

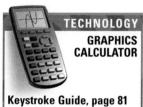

TECHNOLOGY
GRAPHICS CALCULATOR

Keystroke Guide, page 81

● **SOLUTION**

Because the line is parallel to the graph of $y = -2x + 4$, the slope is also −2.

$$y - y_1 = m(x - x_1)$$
$$y - 3 = -2[x - (-1)]$$
$$y - 3 = -2x - 2$$
$$y = -2x + 1$$

CHECK

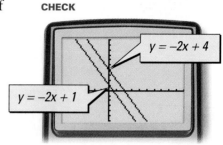

$y = -2x + 4$

$y = -2x + 1$

TRY THIS Write an equation in slope-intercept form for the line that contains the point (−3, −4) and is parallel to the graph of $y = -4x - 2$.

The relationships between the slopes of perpendicular lines are stated below.

Perpendicular Lines

If a nonvertical line is perpendicular to another line, the slopes of the lines are negative reciprocals of one another.

All vertical lines are perpendicular to all horizontal lines.

All horizontal lines are perpendicular to all vertical lines.

The graphs of two perpendicular lines are shown at right.

$$y = 2x + 1 \text{ and } y = -\frac{1}{2}x - 3$$

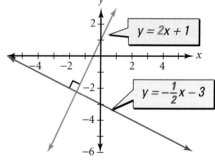

$y = 2x + 1$

$y = -\frac{1}{2}x - 3$

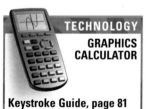

TECHNOLOGY
GRAPHICS CALCULATOR

Keystroke Guide, page 81

EXAMPLE **5** Write an equation in slope-intercept form for the line that contains the point (4, −3) and is perpendicular to the graph of $y = 4x + 5$.

● **SOLUTION**

Because the line is perpendicular to the graph of $y = 4x + 5$, the slope is $-\frac{1}{4}$.

$$y - y_1 = m(x - x_1)$$
$$y - (-3) = -\frac{1}{4}(x - 4)$$
$$y + 3 = -\frac{1}{4}x + 1$$
$$y = -\frac{1}{4}x - 2$$

CHECK

Use a square viewing window.

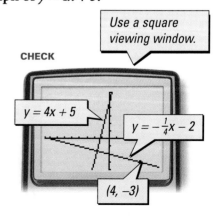

$y = 4x + 5$

$y = -\frac{1}{4}x - 2$

(4, −3)

TRY THIS Write an equation in slope-intercept form for the line that contains the point $(-1, 5)$ and is perpendicular to the graph of $y = -4x - 2$.

CRITICAL THINKING The graph of $3x - y = 4$ is perpendicular to the graph of $Ax + 2y = 8$ for some value of A. Find A.

Exercises

Communicate

1. Describe how to write an equation in slope-intercept form for the line containing two given points, such as $(1, 3)$ and $(4, -2)$.

2. Explain how to use the different forms of a linear equation to write the equation of the line graphed at right.

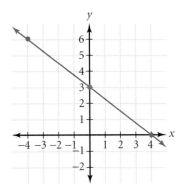

3. Describe how to determine whether the lines $5x + 6y = 12$ and $6x - 5y = 15$ are parallel, perpendicular, or neither.

4. Explain how to write the equation for the line that contains the point $(3, -1)$ and is perpendicular to the line $x + 2y = 4$.

Guided Skills Practice

5. Write an equation in slope-intercept form for the line containing the points $(3, 3)$ and $(-5, -1)$. *(EXAMPLE 1)*

6. Write an equation in slope-intercept form for the line that has a slope of 3 and contains the point $(4, 7)$. *(EXAMPLE 2)*

APPLICATION

7. **TRAVEL** Tina leaves home and drives at a constant speed to college. On her way to the campus, she stops at a restaurant to have lunch. Two hours after leaving the restaurant, Tina has traveled 130 miles, and 4 hours after leaving the restaurant, she has traveled 240 miles. How far from home was Tina when she had lunch? *(EXAMPLE 3)*

8. Write an equation in slope-intercept form for the line that contains the point $(6, -5)$ and is parallel to the line $2x - 5y = -3$. *(EXAMPLE 4)*

9. Write an equation in slope-intercept form for the line that contains the point $(-7, 3)$ and is perpendicular to the line $2x + 5y = 3$. *(EXAMPLE 5)*

Practice and Apply

Write an equation for the line containing the indicated points.

10. $(0, 0)$ and $(3, 30)$

11. $(1, -3)$ and $(3, -5)$

12. $(-4, -4)$ and $(-3, -3)$

13. $(-10, -4)$ and $(-3, -3)$

14. $(-6, -6)$ and $(-3, 1)$

15. $(-2, 8)$ and $(-2, -1)$

16. $(4, -8)$ and $(3, -6)$

17. $(8, -3)$ and $(-8, 3)$

18. $\left(-\frac{1}{2}, 7\right)$ and $\left(-4, \frac{1}{2}\right)$

19. $\left(\frac{1}{2}, -3\right)$ and $\left(3, -\frac{1}{2}\right)$

20. $(-9, 1)$ and $\left(-\frac{1}{2}, 1\right)$

21. $(-5, 4)$ and $\left(-5, -\frac{2}{3}\right)$

Write an equation in slope-intercept form for the line that has the indicated slope, *m*, and contains the given point.

22. $m = -\frac{1}{2}, (8, 1)$

23. $m = -\frac{2}{3}, (6, -5)$

24. $m = -4, (5, -3)$

25. $m = 5, (-1, -3)$

26. $m = 0, (2, 3)$

27. $m = 0, (-7, 8)$

28. $m = 4, (9, -3)$

29. $m = 3, (-4, 9)$

30. $m = -\frac{1}{5}, (8, -2)$

31. $m = -\frac{2}{3}, (5, -4)$

Write a linear equation to model each table of values. For each equation, state what the slope represents.

32.

Hours	Miles
3	135
5	225

33.

Items	Cost ($)
4	14.00
7	21.50

34.

Hours	Parking fee ($)
3	6.50
7	12.50

Write an equation in slope-intercept form for the line that contains the given point and is parallel to the given line.

35. $(-2, 3), y = -3x + 2$

36. $(5, -3), y = 4x + 2$

37. $(0, -4), y = \frac{1}{2}x - 1$

38. $(-6, 2), y = -\frac{2}{3}x - 3$

39. $(-1, -3), 2x + 5y = 15$

40. $(4, -3), 3x + 4y = 8$

41. $(3, 0), -x + 2y = 17$

42. $(4, -3), -4x + y = -7$

Write an equation in slope-intercept form for the line that contains the given point and is perpendicular to the given line.

43. $(-2, 5), y = -2x + 4$

44. $(1, -4), y = 3x - 2$

45. $(8, 5), y = -x + 2$

46. $(0, -5), y = x - 5$

47. $(2, 5), 6x + 2y = 24$

48. $(3, -1), 12x + 4y = 8$

49. $(-2, 4), x - 6y = 15$

50. $(5, -2), 2x - 5y = 15$

51. Write an equation for the line that is perpendicular to the line $2x + 5y = 15$ at the *y*-intercept.

52. Write an equation for the line that is perpendicular to the line $x - 3y = 9$ at the *x*-intercept.

COORDINATE GEOMETRY **For Exercises 53–58, refer to the lines graphed on the coordinate plane below.**

53. Use slopes to determine whether ℓ_1 is parallel to ℓ_2.

54. Use slopes to determine whether ℓ_3 is parallel to ℓ_4.

55. Use slopes to determine whether ℓ_1 is perpendicular to ℓ_3.

56. Use slopes to determine whether ℓ_2 is perpendicular to ℓ_3.

57. Use slopes to determine whether ℓ_2 is perpendicular to ℓ_4.

58. Use slopes to determine whether ℓ_1 is perpendicular to ℓ_4.

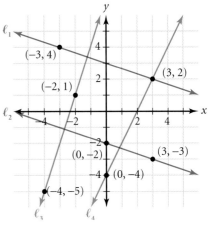

59. **COORDINATE GEOMETRY** Opposite sides of a parallelogram are parallel. Use slopes to determine whether the quadrilateral graphed in the coordinate plane at right is a parallelogram.

60. **COORDINATE GEOMETRY** A rectangle has opposite sides that are parallel and four right angles. Use slopes to determine whether the quadrilateral graphed in the coordinate plane at right is a rectangle.

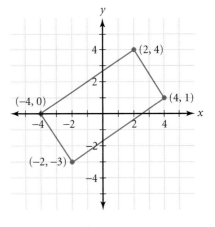

61. Use the diagram at right to prove that the diagonals of any square are perpendicular.

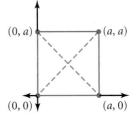

62. **TRAVEL** Mac bikes at a nonconstant rate of speed from home through town. When he begins his training ride, he bikes at a constant speed of 25 miles per hour. After 3 hours of biking at a constant speed, his odometer shows that he has traveled 83 miles since he left home.

  a. Write a linear equation in slope-intercept form for the distance, d, in miles that Mac has traveled in terms of the time, t, in hours since he began his training ride.

  b. When Mac began his training ride, how far from home was he?

63. ACADEMICS A professor gives a test, and the scores range from 40 to 80. The professor decides to *scale* the test in order to make the scores range from 60 to 90. Let x represent an original score, and let y represent a converted score.

   a. Use the ordered pairs (40, 60) and (80, 90) to write the equation that the professor will use to scale the test scores.

   b. What will an original score of 45 become?

   c. If a converted score is 84, what was the original score?

64. INCOME Trevor is a salesperson who earns a weekly salary and a commission that is 7% of his weekly sales. In one week Trevor's sales were $952.00 and his weekly income was $466.64. In another week his sales were $2515.00 and his weekly income was $576.05.

   a. Write a linear equation in slope-intercept form for Trevor's weekly income, y, in terms of his weekly sales, x.

   b. What is Trevor's weekly salary?

 Look Back

Copy and complete the table. Write the fractions in simplest form.

	Fraction	Decimal	Percent
65.		$0.0\overline{3}$	$33\frac{1}{3}\%$
66.		0.875	
67.			2%
68.	$\frac{1}{20}$		
69.			$12\frac{1}{2}\%$
70.	$\frac{2}{3}$		
71.	$\frac{1}{6}$		
72.			0.01%
73.		0.80	
74.	$\frac{2}{5}$		
75.		0.45	
76.	$\frac{5}{6}$		

77. Use the formula $d = rt$ to find the distance, d, in meters when the rate, r, is 50 meters per second and the time, t, is 4 seconds.

78. Use the formula $C = \pi d$ to find the circumference, C, in centimeters when the diameter, d, is 8 centimeters. Use 3.14 for π.

 Look Beyond

79. Let $y = 4x$.

   a. $\frac{y}{x} = $ ___?___

   b. If $y = 3$, then $x = $ ___?___.

80. Let $y = mx$. If $y = 4$ and $x = 2$, then $m = $ ___?___.

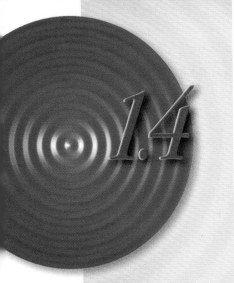

Direct Variation and Proportion

Why *Many events in the real world have a direct-variation relationship. For example, the distance you travel when bicycling can have a direct-variation relationship with time.*

Objectives

- Write and apply direct-variation equations.

- Write and solve proportions.

APPLICATION
RECREATION

Each day Johnathon rides his bicycle for exercise. When traveling at a constant rate, he rides 4 miles in about 20 minutes. At this rate, how long would it take Johnathon to travel 7 miles? To answer this question, you can use a *direct-variation equation* or a *proportion*. *You will solve this problem in Example 2.*

Recall that distance, *d*, rate, *r*, and elapsed time, *t*, are related by the equation $d = rt$. You can say that *d varies directly as t* because as time increases, the distance traveled increases proportionally.

Direct Variation

The variable *y* varies directly as *x* if there is a nonzero constant *k* such that $y = kx$. The equation $y = kx$ is called a **direct-variation equation** and the number *k* is called the **constant of variation**.

EXAMPLE ① Find the constant of variation, *k*, and the direct-variation equation if *y* varies directly as *x* and $y = -24$ when $x = 4$.

● **SOLUTION**

$$y = kx \qquad \textit{Use the direct-variation equation.}$$
$$-24 = k \cdot 4 \qquad \textit{Substitute 24 for y and 4 for x.}$$
$$\frac{-24}{4} = k \qquad \textit{Solve for k.}$$
$$-6 = k$$

The direct-variation equation is $y = -6x$.

TRY THIS Find the constant of variation, *k*, and the direct-variation equation if *y* varies directly as *x* and $y = 15$ when $x = 3$.

At the constant rate that Johnathon bikes, how long would it take him to travel 7 miles?

● SOLUTION

1. Write a direct-variation equation, $d = rt$, that models Johnathon's distance as it varies with time.

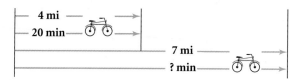

Find the constant of variation, r.

$$r = \frac{4 \text{ mi}}{20 \text{ min}} = \frac{1}{5} \text{ mile per minute}$$

Write the direct-variation equation.

distance in miles   *time in minutes*
↘   ↙
$$d = \frac{1}{5}t$$

2. Use the direct-variation equation to solve the problem.

$$d = \frac{1}{5}t$$

$7 = \frac{1}{5}t$ *Substitute 7 for d.*

$35 = t$ *Solve for t.*

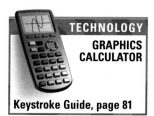

TECHNOLOGY

GRAPHICS
CALCULATOR

Keystroke Guide, page 81

CHECK

Graph the equation $y = \frac{1}{5}x$, and check to see that the point $(35, 7)$ is on the line.

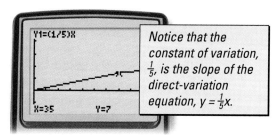

Notice that the constant of variation, $\frac{1}{5}$, is the slope of the direct-variation equation, $y = \frac{1}{5}x$.

Thus, at the rate given it will take Johnathon 35 minutes to travel 7 miles.

TRY THIS   Suppose that when Johnathon is riding, he travels 5 miles in about 30 minutes. At this rate, how long would it take Johnathon to travel 12 miles?

The *Proportion Property* given below applies to all direct-variation relationships.

Proportion Property of Direct Variation

For $x_1 \neq 0$ and $x_2 \neq 0$:

If (x_1, y_1) and (x_2, y_2) satisfy $y = kx$, then $\frac{y_1}{x_1} = k = \frac{y_2}{x_2}$.

In the Activity below, you can see a connection between the concepts of geometric similarity, proportion, and direct variation.

Exploring Similarity and Direct Variation

CONNECTION
GEOMETRY

You will need: a calculator

Recall from geometry that *similar* figures have the same shape. This means that the corresponding angles of similar polygons are congruent, and their corresponding sides are proportional.

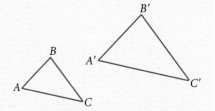

1. Copy and complete the table below to compare the lengths of the sides in $\triangle A'B'C'$ with the corresponding lengths in $\triangle ABC$.

Length in $\triangle ABC$	Length in $\triangle A'B'C'$	Ratio of $\triangle A'B'C'$ to $\triangle ABC$
$AB = 16$	$A'B' = 24$	$\frac{A'B'}{AB} = ?$
$BC = 20$	$B'C' = 30$	$\frac{B'C'}{BC} = ?$
$AC = 24$	$A'C' = 36$	$\frac{A'C'}{AC} = ?$

CHECKPOINT ✔ 2. Do your calculations in the third column indicate a direct-variation relationship between the lengths of the sides of $\triangle A'B'C'$ and those of $\triangle ABC$? Explain your response.

It is said that if y varies directly as x, then y is *proportional* to x.

A **proportion** is a statement that two *ratios* are equal. A ratio is the comparison of two quantities by division. A proportion of the form $\frac{a}{b} = \frac{c}{d}$ can be rearranged as follows:

$$\frac{a}{b} = \frac{c}{d}$$
$$\frac{a}{b} \cdot bd = \frac{c}{d} \cdot bd$$
$$ad = bc$$

The result is called the *Cross-Product Property of Proportions.*

Cross-Product Property of Proportions

For $b \neq 0$ and $d \neq 0$:

If $\frac{a}{b} = \frac{c}{d}$, then $ad = bc$.

In a proportion of the form $\frac{a}{b} = \frac{c}{d}$, a and d are the *extremes* and b and c are the *means*. By the Cross-Product Property, the product of the extremes equals the product of the means.

APPLICATION
PHYSICS

Using Newton's law of universal gravitation, ratios that compare the weight of an object on Earth with its weight on another planet can be calculated. For Mars and Earth, the ratio is shown below.

$$\text{weight on Mars} \rightarrow \frac{W_M}{W_E} \approx \frac{38}{100} \leftarrow \text{weight on Earth}$$

EXAMPLE ③ *Sojourner* is the name of the first rover (robotic roving vehicle) that was sent to Mars. *Sojourner* weighs 24.3 pounds on Earth and is about the size of a child's small wagon.

a. Find the weight of *Sojourner* on Mars to the nearest tenth of a pound.

b. Write a direct-variation equation that gives the weight of an object on Mars, W_M, in terms of its weight on Earth, W_E.

SOLUTION

a. Solve the proportion for the weight of *Sojourner* on Mars.

$$\frac{W_M}{24.3} \approx \frac{38}{100}$$

$$(W_M)(100) \approx (24.3)(38) \quad \textit{Use the Cross-Product Property.}$$

$$W_M \approx \frac{(24.3)(38)}{100} \quad \begin{array}{l}\leftarrow \textit{weight on Mars} \\ \leftarrow \textit{weight on Earth}\end{array}$$

$$W_M \approx 9.2$$

On Mars, Sojourner would weigh about 9.2 pounds.

The Sojourner

b.
$$\frac{W_M}{W_E} \approx \frac{38}{100}$$

$$W_M \approx \frac{38W_E}{100} \quad \begin{array}{l}\leftarrow \textit{weight on Mars} \\ \leftarrow \textit{weight on Earth}\end{array}$$

$$W_M \approx 0.38W_E$$

TECHNOLOGY
GRAPHICS CALCULATOR

Keystroke Guide, page 81

CHECK
Graph $y = 0.38x$, and confirm that a weight of 24.3 pounds on Earth, x, corresponds to a weight of about 9.2 pounds on Mars, y.

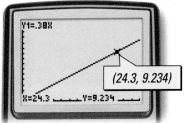

(24.3, 9.234)

EXAMPLE ④ Solve $\frac{3x-1}{5} = \frac{x}{2}$. Check your answer.

SOLUTION

$$\frac{3x-1}{5} = \frac{x}{2}$$

$$(3x-1)(2) = (5)(x) \quad \textit{Use the Cross-Product Property.}$$

$$6x - 2 = 5x$$

$$x - 2 = 0$$

$$x = 2$$

CHECK

$$\frac{3x-1}{5} = \frac{x}{2}$$

$$\frac{3(2)-1}{5} \stackrel{?}{=} \frac{2}{2}$$

$$1 = 1 \quad \textbf{True}$$

TRY THIS Solve $\frac{3x+2}{7} = \frac{x}{2}$. Check your answer.

CRITICAL THINKING Let $a > 0$. How many solutions does $\frac{x}{a} = \frac{a}{x}$ have? Find the solutions. Justify your answer.

Exercises

Communicate

1. Suppose that y varies directly as x and that $y = 18$ when $x = 9$. Describe how you would find an equation of direct variation that relates these two variables.

2. When are linear equations *not* direct variations? How do their graphs differ from those of direct variations?

3. Describe two methods for solving the following problem:

   If y varies directly as x and $y = 8$ when $x = -2$, what is the value of x when $y = 12$?

Determine whether each equation describes a direct variation. Explain your reasoning.

4. $y = x + 5$ **5.** $y = x - 5$ **6.** $y = 5x$ **7.** $y = \frac{x}{5}$

Guided Skills Practice

8. Find the constant of variation, k, and the direct-variation equation if y varies directly as x and $y = 1000$ when $x = 200$. *(EXAMPLE 1)*

APPLICATIONS

9. **PHYSICS** The speed of sound in air is about 335 feet per second. At this rate, how far would sound travel in 25 seconds? *(EXAMPLE 2)*

10. **INCOME** The wages for a worker at a particular store are hourly. A person who worked 18 hours earned $114.30. *(EXAMPLE 3)*
    a. How many hours must this person work to earn $127?
    b. Write a direct-variation equation that gives the income of this person in terms of the hours worked. What does the constant of variation represent?

Solve each equation for x. Check your answers. *(EXAMPLE 4)*

11. $\frac{4x - 1}{21} = \frac{x}{6}$ **12.** $\frac{x + 4}{-4} = \frac{3x}{36}$ **13.** $\frac{2x}{8} = \frac{x + 3}{7}$

Practice and Apply

In Exercises 14–29, y varies directly as x. Find the constant of variation, and write an equation of direct variation that relates the two variables.

14. $y = 21$ when $x = 7$ **15.** $y = 2$ when $x = 1$

16. $y = -16$ when $x = 2$ **17.** $y = 1$ when $x = \frac{1}{3}$

18. $y = \frac{4}{5}$ when $x = \frac{1}{5}$ **19.** $y = -\frac{6}{7}$ when $x = -\frac{18}{35}$

20. $y = -2$ when $x = 9$ **21.** $y = 5$ when $x = -0.1$

22. $y = 1.8$ when $x = 30$ **23.** $y = 0.4$ when $x = -1$

24. $y = 24$ when $x = 8$ **25.** $y = 12$ when $x = \frac{1}{4}$

26. $y = -\frac{5}{8}$ when $x = -1$ **27.** $y = 4$ when $x = 0.2$

28. $y = 0.6$ when $x = -3$ **29.** $y = -1.2$ when $x = 4$

Write an equation that describes each direct variation.

30. p varies directly as q.   **31.** a is directly proportional to b.

For Exercises 32–36, a varies directly as b.

32. If a is 2.8 when b is 7, find a when b is -4.

33. If a is 6.3 when b is 70, find b when a is 5.4.

34. If a is -5 when b is 2.5, find b when a is 6.

35. If b is $-\frac{3}{5}$ when a is $-\frac{9}{10}$, find a when b is $\frac{1}{3}$.

36. If b is $-\frac{1}{2}$ when a is $-\frac{3}{10}$, find a when b is $-\frac{5}{9}$.

Solve each proportion for the variable. Check your answers.

37. $\frac{w}{4} = \frac{10}{12}$ **38.** $\frac{5}{q} = \frac{7}{8}$ **39.** $\frac{1}{8} = \frac{x}{100}$

40. $\frac{9}{10} = \frac{6}{r}$ **41.** $\frac{x}{3} = \frac{-7}{10}$ **42.** $\frac{3}{5} = \frac{x}{2}$

43. $\frac{7}{x} = \frac{3}{4}$ **44.** $\frac{x+5}{2} = \frac{4}{3}$ **45.** $\frac{x}{-5} = x - 6$

46. $\frac{x-1}{56} = \frac{x}{64}$ **47.** $\frac{3x+1}{5} = \frac{x}{2}$ **48.** $\frac{-4x}{-7} = x - 3$

49. $\frac{x+1}{9} = \frac{5x}{40}$ **50.** $\frac{6x-3}{9} = \frac{8x}{8}$ **51.** $\frac{5x}{-30} = \frac{x-5}{4}$

Determine whether the values in each table represent a direct variation. If so, write an equation for the variation. If not, explain.

52.

x	2	3	4	5	6
y	-4	-9	-16	-25	-36

53.

x	5	6	7	8	9
y	0.10	0.12	0.14	0.16	0.18

54.

x	-1	0	1	2	3
y	8	10	12	14	16

55.

x	-2	-1	0	1	2
y	1	0.5	0	-0.5	-1

56.

x	-7	-3	1	5	9
y	133	57	-19	-95	-171

57.

x	1	-5	-11	-17	-23
y	-6	42	90	138	186

58. Show that if x varies directly as y, then y varies directly as x.

59. If a varies directly as c and b varies directly as c, show that $a + b$ varies directly as c.

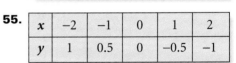

60. COORDINATE GEOMETRY Which of the lines shown in the graph at right represents a direct variation? Explain your reasoning.

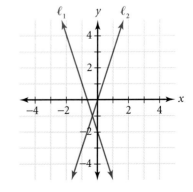

CULTURAL CONNECTION: ASIA The Harappan civilization flourished in an area near present-day Pakistan around 2500 B.C.E. They used balancing stones in their system of weights and measures. The Vedic civilization, which followed the Harappan civilization, used gunja seeds to weigh precious metals. The smallest Harappan stone has the same mass as 8 gunja seeds.

The scale is balanced with 16 gunja seeds on the left and the second smallest Harappan stone on the right.

61. The mass of a Harappan stone, m, varies directly as the number of gunja seeds, g. Find the constant of variation and the direct-variation equation for this relationship.

62. How many gunja seeds are equivalent to a Harappan stone whose mass is 3.52 grams?

63. The largest Harappan stone is equivalent to 320 gunja seeds. What is the mass of this stone?

Smallest Harappan stone

0.88 gram

1.76 grams

3.52 grams

*320 gunja seeds
Largest Harappan stone*

CONNECTIONS

64. GEOMETRY In the figure at right, the height of each object is directly proportional to the length of its shadow. The person is $5\frac{1}{2}$ feet tall and casts an 8-foot shadow, while the tree casts a 33-foot shadow. How tall is the tree?

65. GEOMETRY In an aerial photograph, a triangular plot of land has the dimensions given in the figure at right. If the actual length of the longest side of the plot is 50 kilometers, find the actual lengths of the two shorter sides.

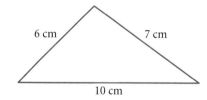

APPLICATION

PHYSICS In an electric circuit, Ohm's law states that the voltage, V, measured in volts varies directly as the electric current, I, measured in amperes according to the equation $V = IR$. The constant of variation is the electrical resistance of the circuit, R, measured in ohms.

66. An iron is plugged into a 110-volt electrical outlet, creating a current of 5.5 amperes in the iron. Find the electrical resistance of the iron.

67. A heater is plugged into a 110-volt outlet. If the resistance of the heater is 11 ohms, find the current in the heater.

68. Find the current, to the nearest hundredth of an ampere, in a night light with a resistance of 300 ohms that is plugged into a 110-volt outlet.

69. Find the current, to the nearest hundredth of an ampere, in a lamp that has a resistance of 385 ohms and is plugged into a 110-volt outlet.

70. PHYSICS As a scuba diver descends, the increase in water pressure varies directly as the increase in depth below the water's surface. However, the constant of variation is smaller in fresh water than in salt water. For example, at 80 feet below the surface of a typical freshwater lake, the pressure is 34.64 pounds per square inch greater than the pressure at the surface. In a typical ocean, where the water is salty, the pressure at 80 feet is 35.6 pounds per square inch greater than the pressure at the surface.

a. Find the constant of variation and the equation of direct variation for the increase in pressure in a typical freshwater lake.

b. Find the increase in pressure at 100 feet below the surface of a lake.

c. Find the constant of variation and the equation of direct variation for the increase in pressure in a typical ocean.

d. Find the increase in pressure at 100 feet below the surface of an ocean.

71. PHYSICS The distance a spring stretches varies directly as the amount of weight that is hanging on it. A weight of 32 pounds stretches the spring 6 inches, and a weight of 48 pounds stretches it 9 inches.

a. Find the constant of variation and the equation of direct variation for the stretch of the spring. What does the constant of variation represent?

b. How heavy is the weight hanging on the spring when it is stretched 3 inches?

c. Find the stretch of the spring when a weight of 40 pounds is hanging on it.

 *Look Back*

Write the prime factorization for each number.

72. 261   **73.** 860   **74.** 315   **75.** 180   **76.** 154   **77.** 490

Evaluate.

78. $\dfrac{\frac{11}{13}}{\frac{11}{26}}$ **79.** $\dfrac{\frac{5}{6}}{\frac{15}{12}}$ **80.** $\dfrac{-\frac{1}{3}}{\frac{4}{21}}$ **81.** $\dfrac{-\frac{2}{5}}{\frac{28}{25}}$

Calculator button indicates that a graphics calculator is recommended.

 Look Beyond

82 An equation of the form $xy = k$, where k is a constant greater than zero, is called an *inverse-variation equation*. Choose a positive value for k, and graph the equation. Describe the graph.

Refer to your portfolio data set from the Portfolio Activity on page 11.

1. In your portfolio data set, does one variable vary directly as the other variable? Explain.

2. Using data values from your portfolio data set, write a proportion of the form $\dfrac{y_1}{x_1} = \dfrac{y_2}{x_2}$. Is the proportion true for some values? Is the proportion true for all values? Explain.

3. Using points on your linear model from the Portfolio Activity on page 20, write a proportion of the form $\dfrac{y_1}{x_1} = \dfrac{y_2}{x_2}$. Is the proportion true for some values? Is the proportion true for all values? Explain.

Scatter Plots and Least-Squares Lines

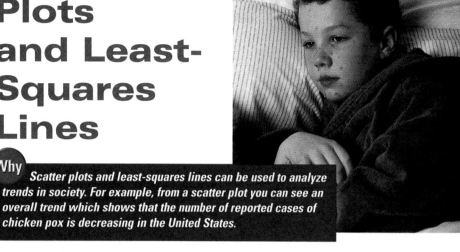

Why *Scatter plots and least-squares lines can be used to analyze trends in society. For example, from a scatter plot you can see an overall trend which shows that the number of reported cases of chicken pox is decreasing in the United States.*

Objectives

● Create a scatter plot and draw an informal inference about any correlation between the variables.

● Use a graphics calculator to find an equation for the least-squares line and use it to make predictions or estimates.

In many real-world problems, you will find data that relate two variables such as time and distance or age and height. You can view the relationship between two variables with a **scatter plot**.

The following data on the number of reported cases of chicken pox in thousands in the United States is graphed in a scatter plot. The variable x represents the number of years after 1988 ($x = 0$ represents 1988) and y represents the number of cases in thousands.

Chicken Pox in the United States	
Year	**Reported cases (in the thousands)**
1989	185.4
1990	173.1
1991	147.1
1992	158.4
1993	134.7
1994	151.2

[*Source: Centers for Disease Control and Prevention*]

Chicken Pox in the United States

Number of years after 1988

Activity

Investigating a Scatter Plot

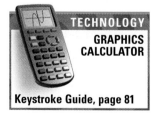

You will need: a graphics calculator

1. Create a scatter plot for the data on reported cases of chicken pox in the United States from 1989 to 1994. Let $x = 1$ represent the year 1989.

2. Write a linear equation in slope-intercept form that closely fits the data points. Graph your equation along with the data points.

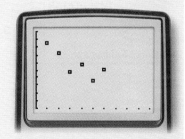

3. Adjust the slope and *y*-intercept of your equation until you think the graph best fits the data points. Record your *best-fit* equation.

4. What rate of change is indicated by the slope of your linear equation? Write a sentence that states what the slope indicates about the reported cases of chicken pox.

The chicken-pox data in the Activity involves a two-variable data set that has a *negative correlation*. In general, there is a *correlation* between two variables when there appears to be a line about which the data points cluster. The diagrams below show the three possible correlations.

Positive correlation

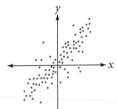

Negative correlation

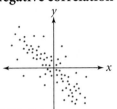

No reliable correlation

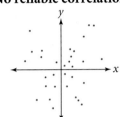

Finding the Least-Squares Line

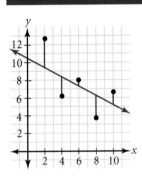

A scatter plot can help you see patterns in data involving two variables. If you think there may be a linear correlation between the variables, you can use a calculator to find a *linear-regression line*, also called the *least-squares line*, that best fits the data.

The graph at left shows the vertical distance from each point in a scatter plot to a fitted line. The fit of a **least-squares line** is based on *minimizing* these vertical distances for a data set. A least-squares line is one type of linear model for a data set.

E X A M P L E **1** Create a scatter plot for the data shown at right. Describe the correlation. Then find and graph an equation for the least-squares line.

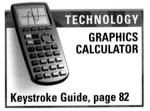

x	y
0	−3.2
2	1.2
4	5.0
6	8.8
7	11.6
8	13.0
10	17.5

SOLUTION

1. Create the scatter plot.

2. Describe the correlation.

Because the points rise from left to right, the correlation is positive.

3. Find and graph the least-squares line.

The equation of the least-squares line is $y \approx 2.05x - 3.13$.

Graph the least-squares line on the scatter plot with the data points.

Correlation and Prediction

CONNECTION

STATISTICS

Examine the graphics calculator display at left, which shows the linear-regression equation for Example 1. Notice that the display also shows a value of about 0.9993 for *r*. The **correlation coefficient,** denoted by *r*, indicates how closely the data points cluster around the least-squares line.

The correlation coefficient can vary from −1, which is a perfect fit for a negative correlation, to +1, which is a perfect fit for a positive correlation.

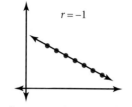

Perfect negative correlation

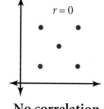

No correlation

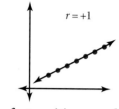

Perfect positive correlation

The closer the correlation coefficient is to −1 or +1, the better the least-squares line fits the data.

CHECKPOINT ✔ Refer to the data and the least-squares line found in Example 1. What is the correlation coefficient for this least-squares line? Is the correlation strong?

E X A M P L E ❷ The winning times for the men's Olympic 1500-meter freestyle swimming event are given in the table. Notice that there is not a winning time recorded for the year 1940 (the Olympic games were not held during World War II).

APPLICATION

SPORTS

Estimate what the winning time for this event could have been in 1940.

● **SOLUTION**

Let *x* represent the number of years after 1900. Let *y* represent the winning time in minutes. Enter the data into your calculator, and make a scatter plot.

TECHNOLOGY

GRAPHICS CALCULATOR

Keystroke Guide, page 82

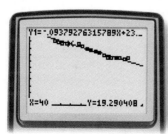

Year	Time (min:sec)	Time (min)
1908	22:48.4	22.81
1912	22:00.0	22.00
1920	22:23.2	22.39
1924	20:06.6	20.11
1928	19:51.8	19.86
1932	19:12.4	19.21
1936	19:13.7	19.23
1948	19:18.5	19.31
1952	18:30.3	18.51
1956	17:58.9	17.98
1960	17:19.6	17.33
1964	17:01.7	17.03
1968	16:38.9	16.65
1972	15:52.58	15.88
1976	15:02.40	15.04
1980	14:58.27	14.97
1984	15:05.20	15.09
1988	15:00.40	15.00
1992	14:43.48	14.72
1996	14:56.40	14.94

Using the equation for the least-squares line calculated from columns 1 and 2, the *y*-value that corresponds to *x* = 40 is about 19.29. Thus, for the men's Olympic 1500-meter freestyle in 1940, the winning time might have been about 19.29 minutes, or about 19:17.42.

TRY THIS   Use the least-squares line in Example 2 to estimate the winning time in this Olympic event in the year 2000.

CRITICAL THINKING   What assumption is made by using the least-squares line in the Try This exercise above?

Exercises

● *Communicate*

For Exercises 1–3, decide whether each statement is true or false. If it is false, explain why.

1. A correlation coefficient can be equal to 3.

2. For a given data set, if the slope of the least-squares line is positive, then the correlation coefficient is positive.

3. A data set with a correlation coefficient of 0.2 has a stronger linear relationship than a data set with a correlation coefficient of −0.9.

APPLICATIONS

4. **DEMOGRAPHICS** As a population increases, the area available per person decreases. Give another example of a situation that you would expect to have a strong negative correlation with population.

5. **TAXES** As a population increases, the government revenue from taxes tends to increase. Give another example of a situation that you would expect to have a strong positive correlation with population.

Describe the correlation among data that have the given correlation coefficient.

6. $r = 0.02$ 7. $r = -0.61$ 8. $r = 0.96$

● *Guided Skills Practice*

Create a scatter plot of the data in each table. Describe the correlation. Then find an equation for the least-squares line. *(EXAMPLE 1)*

Calculator button indicates that a graphics calculator is recommended.

9

x	5	0	2	6	9	4	5	3	6	4	2	6	1	7	5	2
y	6	8	7	5	2	5	7	8	3	6	8	4	9	3	5	8

10

x	4	4	0	5	2	9	7	6	1	8	2	7	8	3	9	5
y	2	6	1	6	1	7	5	7	2	7	2	9	9	5	8	7

11

x	1	6	9	8	2	7	4	9	1	3	6	5	0	5	8	3
y	2	5	8	2	8	1	7	9	9	1	9	4	9	5	1	2

APPLICATION

12 **SPORTS** The Indianapolis 500 auto race is held each year on Memorial Day. The table below gives the average speed, in miles per hour, of the winner for selected years from 1911 to 1996. In 1945, the race was not held. Estimate what could have been the average winning speed in 1945. Let $x = 0$ represent the year 1900. **(EXAMPLE 2)**

Ray Harroun, 1911

Jim Rathman, 1960

Arie Luyendyk, 1990

Year	Winner	Average speed	Year	Winner	Average speed
1911	Ray Harroun	74.602	1960	Jim Rathman	138.767
1915	Ralph DePalma	89.010	1965	Jimmy Clark	150.686
1920	Gaston Chevrolet	88.618	1970	Al Unser, Sr.	155.749
1925	Peter DePaolo	101.127	1975	Bobby Unser	149.213
1930	Billy Arnold	100.448	1980	Johnny Rutherford	142.862
1935	Kelly Petillo	106.240	1985	Danny Sullivan	152.982
1940	Wilbur Shaw	114.277	1990	Arie Luyendyk	185.984
1946	George Robson	114.820	1994	Al Unser, Jr.	160.872
1950	Johnnie Parsons	124.002	1995	Jacques Villenueve	153.616
1955	Bob Sweikert	128.209	1996	Buddy Lazier	147.956

[*Source: Sportsline USA, Inc., 1997*]

Practice and Apply

13 Create a scatter plot of the data in the table below. Describe the correlation. Then find an equation for the least-squares line.

x	8	4	1	5	4	4	9	8	5	2	7	1	6	3	2	4
y	7	6	2	5	6	4	8	8	6	3	8	3	6	4	1	3

14 Find an equation for the least-squares line of the data below. Use the equation to predict the x-value that corresponds to a y-value of 7.

x	9	5	8	6	2	4	7	3	1	2	6	5	7	2	4	6
y	8	4	9	5	1	4	8	3	2	1	5	5	6	2	5	6

Match each correlation coefficient with one of the data sets graphed.

$r = 1$ $r \approx 0.87$ $r \approx 0.63$ $r = -1$ $r \approx -0.91$ $r \approx -0.84$

15.
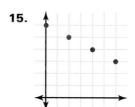

16.
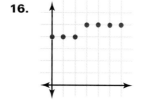

17.
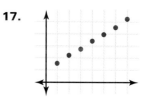

18.
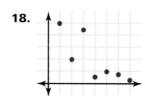

19.

20.
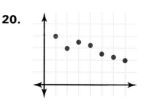

21. ETYMOLOGY Look for the words *interpolate* and *extrapolate* in a dictionary. For each word, write a definition that you think best applies to using a least-squares regression line to make predictions.

22 MARKETING Sixteen people of various ages were polled and asked to estimate the number of CDs they had bought in the previous year. The following table contains the collected data:

Age	18	20	20	22	24	25	25	26	28	30	30	31	32	33	35	45
CDs	12	15	18	12	10	8	6	6	4	4	4	2	2	3	6	1

a. Let *x* represent age, and let *y* represent the number of CDs purchased. Enter the data in a graphics calculator, and find the equation of the least-squares line.

b. Find the correlation coefficient, *r*, to the nearest tenth. Explain how the value of *r* describes the data.

c. Use the least-squares line to predict the number of CDs purchased by a person who is 27 years old.

d. Use the least-squares line to predict the age of a person who purchased 15 CDs in the previous year.

23 ANATOMY The following tables give the height and shoe size of some adults. Let *x* represent height, in inches, and let *y* represent shoe size.

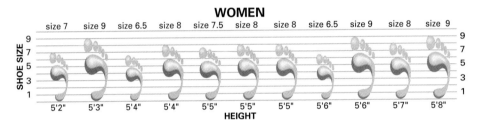

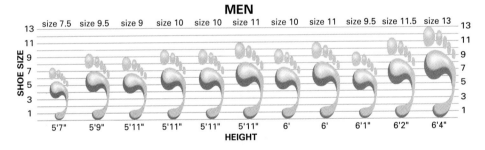

a. Enter the data for women, and find the equation of the least-squares line.

b. Enter the data for men, and find the equation of the least-squares line.

c. Find the correlation coefficients for the women's data and for the men's data. Explain how the different correlation coefficients describe the two data sets.

d. Use the appropriate least-squares line to predict the shoe size of a woman who is 5'1" tall.

e. Use the appropriate least-squares line to predict the shoe size of a man who is 6'2" tall.

f. Use the appropriate least-squares line to predict the height of a man who wears size 12 shoes.

g. Use the appropriate least-squares line to predict the height of a woman who wears size 8 shoes.

L. Douglas Wilder served as governor of Virginia from 1990 to 1994. He was the first elected African American governor in U.S. history.

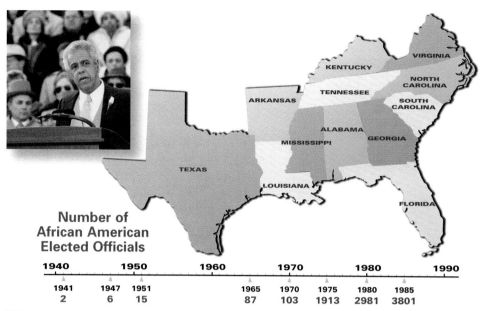

Number of African American Elected Officials

1940	1950	1960	1970	1980	1990

1941	1947	1951	1965	1970	1975	1980	1985
2	6	15	87	103	1913	2981	3801

APPLICATIONS

24 GOVERNMENT The time line above shows the number of African American elected officials in Southern states from 1941 to 1985.
  a. Create a scatter plot for this information, with the years on the x-axis. Let $x = 0$ represent 1900.
  b. Find the least-squares line for the data from 1941 to 1965.
  c. Find the least-squares line for the data from 1965 to 1985.
  d. Explain how the slopes of the two lines are different. What happened in the 1960s that might explain the extreme change?

25 HEALTH The table below gives information about cigarette smokers between the ages of 18 and 24 in the United States for selected years from 1965 to 1993.
  a. Enter the data for females, and find the equation of the least-squares line. Let $x = 0$ represent 1900.
  b. Enter the data for males, and find the equation of the least-squares line.
  c. Find the correlation coefficients for the female's data and for the male's data. Explain what the different correlation coefficients tell you about the two data sets.

Percent of Population That Are Cigarette Smokers in the United States

Year	Female (18–24)	Male (18–24)
1965	38.1	54.1
1974	34.1	42.1
1979	33.8	35.0
1983	35.5	32.9
1985	30.4	28.0
1987	26.1	28.2
1990	22.5	26.6
1992	24.9	28.0
1993	22.9	28.8

[*Source: Statistical Abstract of the United States, 1996*]

  d. Use the appropriate least-squares line to estimate the percent of females between the ages of 18 and 24 who were smokers in 1980.
  e. Use the appropriate least-squares line to estimate the percent of males between the ages of 18 and 24 who were smokers in 1970.
  f. Use the appropriate least-squares line to estimate the year in which 50% of males between the ages of 18 and 24 were smokers.
  g. Use the appropriate least-squares line to estimate the year in which 22% of males between the ages of 18 and 24 were smokers.

26 **AGRICULTURE** The table below gives the number of farms in the United States from 1940 to 1995.

Year	1940	1950	1960	1970	1980	1995
Number of U.S. farms	174	213	297	374	426	469

[*Source: The World Almanac, 1997*]

a. Let $x = 0$ represent the year 1900, and let y represent the number of farms in the United States. Enter the data, and find the equation of the least-squares line.

b. Find the correlation coefficient, r, to the nearest tenth. Explain what the value of r tells you about the data.

c. Use the least-squares line to estimate the number of farms in 1955.

d. Use the least-squares line to predict the year in which there were about 325 farms.

Look Back

Without using a calculator, write an equivalent decimal for each fraction.

27. $\frac{1}{3}$ **28.** $-\frac{3}{5}$ **29.** $\frac{17}{4}$ **30.** $\frac{5}{3}$ **31.** $\frac{7}{20}$

Without using a calculator, evaluate each expression. Write your answer as a decimal.

32. $5 \div 2$ **33.** $5 \div 0.2$ **34.** $5 \div 0.02$

35. The line whose equation is $y = -1.6x + 1$ is parallel to another line whose equation is $y = mx - 4$. Find m. *(LESSON 1.3)*

Look Beyond

Determine whether each equation is true when a, b, and x are real numbers.

36. $ax + bx = bx + ax$ **37.** $ax - bx = bx - ax$

38. $ax \cdot bx = bx \cdot ax$ **39.** $ax \div bx = bx \div ax$

PORTFOLIO ACTIVITY

1. Use a graphics calculator to find the equation of the least-squares line for your portfolio data set.

2. Plot the least-squares line on the same coordinate plane as your portfolio data points and with the linear model that you created in the Portfolio Activity on page 36.

3. Compare the slope of the least-squares line with the slope of your linear model.

4. What is the correlation coefficient for your least-squares line?

WORKING ON THE CHAPTER PROJECT

You should now be able to complete Activity 3 of the Chapter Project.

Introduction to Solving Equations

Why *You can solve many real-world problems by solving an equation. An equation is like a balanced scale. To keep both sides equal, any operation must be performed on each side.*

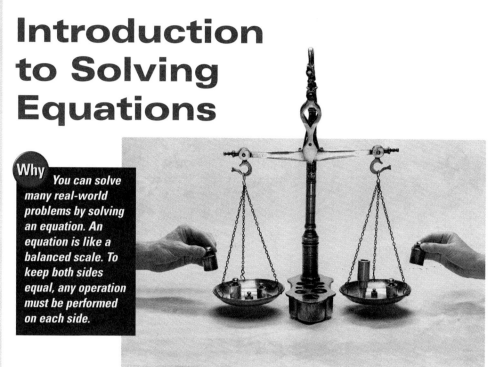

Objectives

• Write and solve a linear equation in one variable.

• Solve a literal equation for a specified variable.

An **equation** is a statement that two expressions are equal. An equation usually contains one or more variables. A **variable** is a symbol that represents many different numbers in a set of numbers.

Equation in *one* variable, *w*: $12w = 10$
Equation in *two* variables, *x* and *y*: $2x + 3y = 12$

Any value of a variable that makes an equation true is called a **solution of the equation.** For example, $12w = 10$ is an equation in one variable, *w*. Because $\frac{5}{6}$ satisfies the equation, $\frac{5}{6}$ is a solution.

$$12w = 10$$
$$12\left(\frac{5}{6}\right) \stackrel{?}{=} 10$$
$$10 = 10 \quad \textbf{True}$$

To solve equations, the *Properties of Equality,* shown below, or the *Substitution Property,* shown on page 46, may be used.

Properties of Equality

For real numbers *a*, *b*, and *c*:

Reflexive Property $a = a$

Symmetric Property   If $a = b$, then $b = a$.

Transitive Property   If $a = b$ and $b = c$, then $a = c$.

Addition Property   If $a = b$, then $a + c = b + c$.

Subtraction Property   If $a = b$, then $a - c = b - c$.

Multiplication Property If $a = b$, then $ac = bc$.

Division Property   If $a = b$, then $\frac{a}{c} = \frac{b}{c}$, where $c \neq 0$.

Substitution Property

If $a = b$, you may replace a with b in any true statement containing a and the resulting statement will still be true.

In an expression, such as $5 + 3x - x - 1$, the parts that are added or subtracted are called **terms**. The terms $3x$ and x are called **like terms** because they contain the *same form of the variable x*. The constant terms, 5 and 1, are also like terms. An expression is **simplified** when all the like terms have been combined and all the parentheses have been removed.

$$5 + 3x - x - 1$$
$$= 2x + 4 \quad \textit{simplified}$$

E X A M P L E 1 The relationship between the Celsius temperature, C, and the Fahrenheit temperature, F, is given by $F = \frac{9}{5}C + 32$.

APPLICATION
TEMPERATURE

Find the Celsius temperature that is equivalent to 86°F.

● **SOLUTION**

$$F = \frac{9}{5}C + 32$$
$$86 = \frac{9}{5}C + 32 \qquad \textit{Substitute 86 for F.}$$
$$86 - 32 = \frac{9}{5}C + 32 - 32 \qquad \textit{Use the Subtraction Property.}$$
$$54 = \frac{9}{5}C \qquad \textit{Simplify.}$$
$$\left(\frac{5}{9}\right)54 = \left(\frac{5}{9}\right)\left(\frac{9}{5}C\right) \qquad \textit{Use the Multiplication Property.}$$
$$30 = C \qquad \textit{Simplify.}$$

Thus, 30°C is equivalent to 86°F.

E X A M P L E 2 **Solve $2x + 7 = 5x - 9$. Check your solution by using substitution.**

● **SOLUTION**

$$2x + 7 = 5x - 9$$
$$2x + 7 - 7 = 5x - 9 - 7 \qquad \textit{Use the Subtraction Property.}$$
$$2x = 5x - 16 \qquad \textit{Simplify.}$$

> Combine $2x$ and $5x$.

$$2x - 5x = 5x - 16 - 5x \qquad \textit{Use the Subtraction Property.}$$
$$-3x = -16 \qquad \textit{Simplify.}$$
$$x = \frac{-16}{-3} = \frac{16}{3}, \text{ or } 5\frac{1}{3} \qquad \textit{Use the Division Property.}$$

CHECK
$$2x + 7 = 5x - 9$$
$$2\left(\frac{16}{3}\right) + 7 \stackrel{?}{=} 5\left(\frac{16}{3}\right) - 9$$
$$17\frac{2}{3} = 17\frac{2}{3} \qquad \textbf{True}$$

TRY THIS   Solve $3x + 12 = -5x + 24$. Check your solution by using substitution.

An algebraic solution method was shown in Example 2. In the Activity below, you can explore a graphic solution method for solving equations.

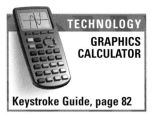

TECHNOLOGY
GRAPHICS CALCULATOR

Keystroke Guide, page 82

Exploring Graphic Solution Methods

You will need: a graphics calculator

1. In the equation $x + 3 = 9 - 2x$, what two expressions are equal?

2. Use a graphics calculator to graph $y = x + 3$ and $y = 9 - 2x$ on the same screen. For what value of x do $x + 3$ and $9 - 2x$ have the same value?

3. Check to see if this value is the solution to the original equation.

CHECKPOINT ✔   **4.** Describe how to solve $2x - 1 = 2 - x$ by using a graphics calculator.

E X A M P L E ③ **Solve $3.24x - 4.09 = -0.72x + 3.65$ by graphing.**

● **SOLUTION**

Write the original equation as the pair of equations below.

$$3.24x - 4.09 = -0.72x + 3.65$$
$$y = 3.24x - 4.09 \quad \text{and} \quad y = -0.72x + 3.65$$

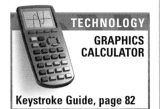

TECHNOLOGY
GRAPHICS CALCULATOR

Keystroke Guide, page 82

Graph the two equations on the same screen, and find the point of intersection.

Read the x-coordinate of the point where the graphs intersect.

From the calculator display, the solution is $x \approx 1.95$.

TRY THIS   Solve $2.24x - 6.24 = 4.26x - 8.76$ by graphing.

Literal Equations

A **literal equation** is an equation that contains two or more variables.

CONNECTION
GEOMETRY

Formulas are examples of literal equations. The following examples of literal equations are from geometry:

Volume of a cube, V:

$$V = s^3, \text{ where } s \text{ is the side length}$$

Area of a circle, A:

$$A = \pi r^2, \text{ where } r \text{ is the radius}$$

Volume of a square pyramid, V:

$$V = \frac{1}{3}s^2 h, \text{ where } s \text{ is the side length and } h \text{ is the altitude}$$

Young's formula is used to relate a child's dose of a medication to an adult's dose of the same medication. The formula applies to children from 1 to 12 years old.

$$\frac{a}{a + 12} \times d = c, \text{ where } \begin{cases} a \text{ represents the child's age} \\ d \text{ represents the adult's dose} \\ c \text{ represents the child's dose} \end{cases}$$

E X A M P L E **4** Solve $\frac{a}{a + 12} \times d = c$ **for** *d*.

SOLUTION

$$\frac{a}{a + 12} \times d = c$$

$$(a + 12)\frac{a}{a + 12} \times d = (a + 12)c \qquad \textit{Use the Multiplication Property.}$$

$$ad = c(a + 12) \qquad \textit{Simplify and use the Commutative Property.}$$

$$d = \frac{c(a + 12)}{a} \qquad \textit{Use the Division Property.}$$

CRITICAL THINKING Solve $\frac{a}{a + 12} \times d = c$ for *a*.

CHECKPOINT ✔ Two equations are **equivalent** if they have the same solution.

Use substitution to verify that the following equations are equivalent:

$$86 = \frac{9}{5}C + 32 \qquad\qquad 54 = \frac{9}{5}C \qquad\qquad C = 30$$

Exercises

Communicate

Tell which Properties of Equality you would use to solve each equation.

1. $52 = -2.7x - 3$ **2.** $\frac{x}{5} = x + 2.2$ **3.** $x - 5 = -2x - 2$

4. Describe one way to obtain an equation that is equivalent to $4x - 7 = 14$.

5. Describe how to solve $\frac{2(x + 3)}{7} = \frac{9(x - 3)}{5}$ by graphing.

Guided Skills Practice

Solve each equation. Check your solution. *(EXAMPLES 1 AND 2)*

6. $4x + 12 = 20$ **7.** $\frac{x}{5} + 3 = 4$

8. $-\frac{5}{2}x + \frac{5}{2} = 2 - 3x$ **9.** $7 - 6x = 2x - 9$

Calculator button indicates that a graphics calculator is recommended.

10 Solve $\frac{4(x + 5)}{3} = \frac{-3(x - 7)}{5}$ by graphing. *(EXAMPLE 3)*

11. Solve $Ax + By = C$ for *y*. *(EXAMPLE 4)*

Practice and Apply

Solve each equation.

12. $1 = 2x - 5$ **13.** $-2x - 7 = 9$ **14.** $2x - 1 = -5$

15. $3x - 3 = 5$ **16.** $2x - 5 = 19$ **17.** $5x - 3 = 12$

18. $20 = 6x - 10$ **19.** $4 - 5x = 19$ **20.** $3x + 1 = \frac{1}{2}$

21. $4x + 80 = -6x$ **22.** $5x + 15 = 2x$ **23.** $7x = -2x + 5$

24. $5x + 3 = 2x + 18$ **25.** $-4x - 3 = x + 7$ **26.** $3x - 8 = 2x + 2$

27. $\frac{1}{5}x + 3 = 2$ **28.** $\frac{1}{4}x - \frac{5}{2} = -2$ **29.** $\frac{1}{6}x + \frac{3}{2} = 2$

30. $0 = \frac{1}{2}x + 2$ **31.** $-\frac{3}{5}x + 12 = 4$ **32.** $-5 = \frac{3}{2}x - 2$

33. $\frac{1}{3}x = -x + 4$ **34.** $x - 5 = -\frac{3}{2}x + \frac{5}{2}$

35. $-\frac{1}{3}x + 1 = \frac{3}{2}x - 1$ **36.** $-2x + 5 = -\frac{1}{3}x - 6$

37. $\frac{2}{3}x - 9 = -\frac{1}{2}x + 4$ **38.** $\frac{1}{4}x - 3 = 6x$

39. $\frac{1}{3}x - \frac{4}{3} = -\frac{1}{6}x - 1$ **40.** $\frac{2}{5}x + \frac{6}{5} = x - 3$

Solve each equation by graphing. Give your answers to the nearest hundredth.

41 $0.24x + 1.1 = 2.56x - 1.5$ **42** $1.05x - 4.28 = -2.65x + 4.1$

43 $-0.75x + 12.42 = 4.36$ **44** $0.35x - 2.72 = 5.83x$

45 $0.67x - 8.75 = -0.48x + 3.99$ **46** $5.9(0.33x - 1.33) = -1.03x - 5.72$

Solve each literal equation for the indicated variable.

47. $\frac{1}{2}bh = A$ for b **48.** $P = 2l + 2w$ for w

49. $\frac{1}{R} = \frac{1}{r_1} + \frac{1}{r_2}$ for r_2 **50.** $A = \frac{1}{2}h(b_1 + b_2)$ for b_2

51. $A = \frac{1}{2}h(b_1 + b_2)$ for h **52.** $y = \frac{u+1}{u+2}$ for u

53. $ax + b = cx + d$ for x **54.** $ax + b = cx + d$ for d

55. $I = P(1 + rt)$ for r **56.** $I = P(1 + rt)$ for t

Solve each literal equation for v.

57. $x = vt$ **58.** $x = vt + \frac{1}{2}at^2$ **59.** $y = \frac{1}{2}xv$

60. Given the equation $y = 4x + 7$, use substitution to solve $-2x + y = 19$ for x.

61. Given the equation $x = -y + 9$, use substitution to solve $3x - 5y = 59$ for x.

CONNECTIONS

62. GEOMETRY The measure of one supplementary angle is 45° more than twice the measure of the other. Write an equation and find the measure of each angle. Recall that two angles are supplementary if the sum of their measures is equal to 180°.

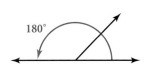

CHALLENGE

63. GEOMETRY The formula for the area of a cone in terms of the slant height, s, and the radius of the base, r, is $A = \pi rs + \pi r^2$. Write a formula for the slant height of a cone in terms of its area and the radius of its base.

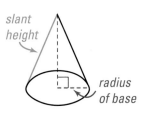

slant height

radius of base

Write and solve an appropriate equation for each situation.

64. RECREATION A summer carnival charges a $2 admission fee and $0.50 for each ride. If Tamara has $10 to spend, how many rides can she go on?

65. TAXES Aaron's mother purchases a new computer for $1750. If she claims a linear depreciation (loss of value) on the computer at a rate of $250 per year, how long will it take for the value of the computer to be $0?

66. CONSUMER ECONOMICS The receipt for repairs on Victor's car is shown at right.
  a. Write an equation to model the total bill in terms of parts and labor.
  b. What hourly rate does the repair shop charge for labor?

AUTO REPAIR
#111 Auto Lane
Lana, TX 78787

INVOICE

Date: July 7

ITEM	AMOUNT
Parts:	
Brake Fluid	$6.00
Wheel Cylinder	$28.50
Rear Brake Shoes	$20.00
Front Brake Pads	$15.00
Shop Supplies	$2.50
Labor	3.5 hours
TOTAL	$272.00

67. INCOME Louis has two different job offers for a position in shoe sales. One pays $25 per week plus a $2 commission for each pair of shoes sold. The second job pays $40 per week plus a $1.50 commission for each pair of shoes sold. How many shoes would Louis have to sell to make the same total salary in either job?

68. BANKING Carmen has taken out a loan for $800 to buy a car. She plans to pay back the loan at a rate of $40 per month. Ramona has borrowed $500 to buy a car, which she plans to pay back at a rate of $20 per month.
  a. How long will it take Carmen to pay back her loan?
  b. How long will it take Ramona to pay back her loan?
  c. If Carmen and Ramona take out their loans at the same time, how long will it take for their remaining balances to be equal? What are their remaining balances after this amount of time?

69. INCOME Amelia has a job baby-sitting for a neighbor. She is paid $20 per week plus $2.50 for each hour on the job. If Amelia wants to earn $40 to buy a new sweater, how many hours would she need to work?

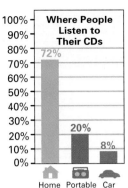

70. RECREATION The results of a survey of CD listeners in 1993 show that 72% usually listen to CDs at home, 20% usually listen to CDs on a portable player, and 8% usually listen to CDs in a car. If 180 of the respondents say that they usually listen to CDs on a portable player, how many people were surveyed?

71. INCOME Anthony wants to buy a used car that will cost $185.00 per month. If Anthony earns $5.35 per hour, how many hours must Anthony work each month in order to pay for the car?

 *Look Back*

Identify the slope, *m*, and *y*-intercept, *b*, for each line. Then graph the equation. *(LESSON 1.2)*

72. $y = 2x - 6$ **73.** $3x + 4y = 9$ **74.** $y = 2$

Write each number in decimal notation.

75. 5.736×10^4 **76.** 7.4609×10^3

77. 46.72×10^6 **78.** 6.72×10^{-6}

Write each number in scientific notation.

79. 25,000   **80.** 720,000   **81.** 260.07

82. 5.7002   **83.** 0.05   **84.** 0.0002046

 *Look Beyond*

Explain what each expression means.

85. $y > -5$ **86.** $-3 < x < 3$ **87.** $-1 \leq y \leq 1$ **88.** $x \leq -3$

1. Choose a *y*-value (distance) that is different from those in your portfolio data set. Substitute this *y*-value into the equation for the least-squares line, and make a prediction about the corresponding time.

2. Show your results from Step 1 on your graph.

WORKING ON THE CHAPTER PROJECT

You should now be able to complete the Chapter Project.

A Man & A Method

Predicting eclipses and planetary motions seems complicated, but imagine having no formal education and teaching yourself the mathematics needed to make such calculations. Imagine publishing an almanac of your results for farmers and astronomers across the nation. That is exactly what an African American named Benjamin Banneker did over 200 years ago. The almanac impressed Thomas Jefferson so much that he asked Banneker to help survey the land for the new nation's capital, Washington, D.C.

Benjamin Banneker also published math puzzles. Some he made up. Others, like the one below, were sent to him. He published the puzzle shown below in his *Manuscript Journal.*

> Divide 60 into four Such parts, that the first being increased by 4, the Second decreased by 4, the third multiplyed by 4, the fourth part divided by 4, that the Sum, the difference, the product, and the Quotient shall be one and the Same Number—

Banneker gave the answer but not his method for finding it. He may have used a method called *false position.* In the false position method, you guess the answer, see how far off your guess is, and then use that information in a proportion to get the correct answer.

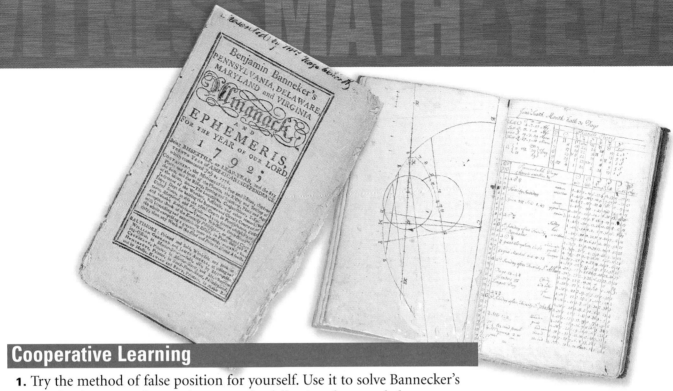

Cooperative Learning

1. Try the method of false position for yourself. Use it to solve Bannecker's puzzle, shown on the previous page, by following the steps below.

    a. Let x represent the answer, "one and the same number."

$$\text{first part} + 4 = x$$
$$\text{second part} - 4 = x$$
$$\text{third part} \times 4 = x$$
$$\text{fourth part} \div 4 = x$$

    Choose any number to be the answer, x. For instance, you can choose 5 or 10 or any other number you like.

    b. Substitute the number you chose for the answer, x, into each equation above, and solve for each of the four parts. For example, if you chose 5 for x, then the first part can be found as shown below.

$$\text{first part} + 4 = 5$$
$$\text{first part} = 1 \qquad \textit{Solve for the "first part."}$$

    c. Find the sum of the four parts.

    d. Use a proportion to find the correct answer, x, for the "one and the same number."

$$\frac{\text{Correct "one and the same number"}}{\text{Correct sum} = 60} = \frac{\text{Trial "one and the same number"}}{\text{Trial sum}}$$

    e. Use the correct answer for x, "one and the same number," from the proportion above to find the four parts. Is the sum of these parts really 60?

2. Now use algebra to solve the same puzzle. Follow the steps below.

    a. Write each of the four parts in terms of x, and represent the puzzle with one equation in one variable.

    b. Show that the solution to this equation gives the correct first, second, third, and fourth parts of the puzzle.

3. Use the graph at right to explain why the method of false position works for this puzzle.

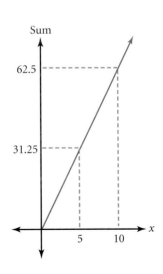

Introduction to Solving Inequalities

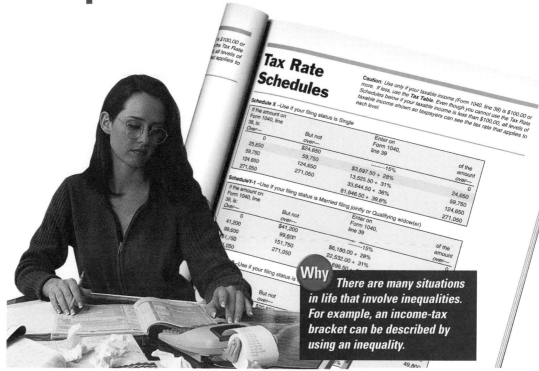

Objectives

- Write, solve, and graph linear inequalities in one variable.

- Solve and graph compound linear inequalities in one variable.

APPLICATION

TAXES

The federal tax calculation table above applies to single people filing a tax return in 1998 for the tax year 1997.

Suppose, for example, that your taxable income is x dollars and the tax due is t dollars. You can read the second row as follows:

If $x > 24{,}650$ *and* $x \leq 59{,}750$, then $t = 3697.50 + 0.28(x - 24{,}650)$.

The statements $x > 24{,}650$ *and* $x \leq 59{,}750$ are examples of *linear inequalities in one variable*. In general, an **inequality** is a mathematical statement involving $<$, $>$, $\leq$, $\geq$, or $\neq$.

Just as there are Properties of Equality that you can use to solve equations, there are *Properties of Inequality* that you can use to solve inequalities.

Properties of Inequality

For all real numbers a, b, and c, where $a \leq b$:

Addition Property	$a + c \leq b + c$
Subtraction Property	$a - c \leq b - c$
Multiplication Property	If $c \geq 0$, then $ac \leq bc$. If $c \leq 0$, then $ac \geq bc$.
Division Property	If $c > 0$, then $\dfrac{a}{c} \leq \dfrac{b}{c}$. If $c < 0$, then $\dfrac{a}{c} \geq \dfrac{b}{c}$.

Similar statements can be written for $a < b$, $a \geq b$, and $a > b$.

Any value of a variable that makes an inequality true is called a **solution of the inequality**. For example, $6x + 1 < 13$ is an inequality in one variable, x. Values such as $\frac{1}{2}$ and -1 are solutions of the inequality, as shown below.

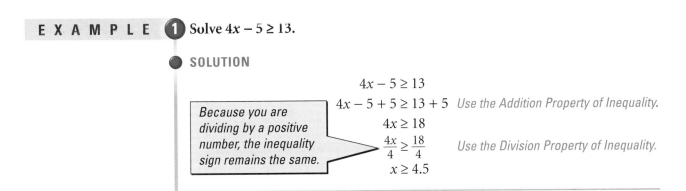

$$6x + 1 < 13 \qquad\qquad\qquad 6x + 1 < 13$$
$$6\left(\frac{1}{2}\right) + 1 \overset{?}{<} 13 \qquad\qquad\qquad 6(-1) + 1 \overset{?}{<} 13$$
$$4 < 13 \quad \textbf{True} \qquad\qquad\qquad -5 < 13 \quad \textbf{True}$$

CHECKPOINT ✔ Find two or more solutions of $6x + 1 < 13$, and show that they are solutions.

E X A M P L E ❶ Solve $4x - 5 \geq 13$.

● SOLUTION

$$4x - 5 \geq 13$$

Because you are dividing by a positive number, the inequality sign remains the same.

$$4x - 5 + 5 \geq 13 + 5 \quad \textit{Use the Addition Property of Inequality.}$$
$$4x \geq 18$$
$$\frac{4x}{4} \geq \frac{18}{4} \qquad\qquad \textit{Use the Division Property of Inequality.}$$
$$x \geq 4.5$$

TRY THIS Solve $-4 < 7 - 3x$.

You can represent the solution of an inequality in one variable on a number line. The number line shown below is the graph of $x \geq 4.5$.

Because the inequality symbol is $\geq$, a solid dot is used.

E X A M P L E ❷ Solve $4 - 3p > 16 - p$. Graph the solution on a number line.

● SOLUTION

$$4 - 3p > 16 - p$$
$$4 - 3p + p > 16 - p + p \quad \textit{Use the Addition Property of Inequality.}$$
$$4 - 2p > 16$$
$$4 - 2p - 4 > 16 - 4 \qquad \textit{Use the Subtraction Property of Inequality.}$$

Because you are dividing by a negative number, the inequality sign is reversed.

$$-2p > 12$$
$$\frac{-2p}{-2} < \frac{12}{-2} \qquad\qquad \textit{Use the Division Property of Inequality.}$$
$$p < -6$$

Because the inequality symbol is $<$, an open circle is used.

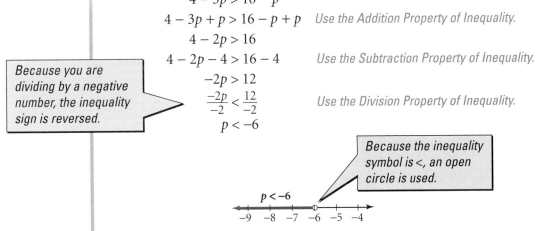

TRY THIS Solve $5 - 7t > 8 - 4t$. Graph the solution on a number line.

EXAMPLE ③

APPLICATION
ACADEMICS

Claire's test average in her world history class is 90. The test average is $\frac{2}{3}$ of the final grade and the homework average is $\frac{1}{3}$ of the final grade.

What homework average does Claire need in order to have a final grade of at least 93?

● SOLUTION

PROBLEM SOLVING

Write an equation.

$$\text{Final grade} = \frac{2}{3}\left(\text{Test average}\right) + \frac{1}{3}\left(\text{Homework average}\right)$$

$$f = \frac{2}{3}(90) + \frac{1}{3}h$$

Claire wants a final grade of at least 93, or $f \geq 93$.

$$f \geq 93$$

$$\frac{2}{3}(90) + \frac{1}{3}h \geq 93 \qquad \textit{Substitute } \frac{2}{3}(90) + \frac{1}{3}h \textit{ for f.}$$

$$60 + \frac{1}{3}h \geq 93 \qquad \textit{Simplify.}$$

$$\frac{1}{3}h \geq 33 \qquad \textit{Use the Subtraction Property of Inequality.}$$

$$h \geq 99 \qquad \textit{Use the Multiplication Property of Inequality.}$$

Claire's homework average must be at least 99 in order for her to have a final grade of at least 93.

Activity
Exploring Inequalities Graphically

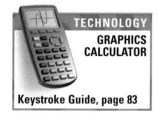

TECHNOLOGY
GRAPHICS CALCULATOR

Keystroke Guide, page 83

You will need: a graphics calculator

1. Solve $2x - 3 < 3$ for x.

2. Use a graphics calculator to graph $y = 2x - 3$ and $y = 3$ on the same screen.

3. For what values of x is the graph of $y = 2x - 3$ below the graph of $y = 3$?

4. Explain how the answer to Step 3 helps you to solve $2x - 3 < 3$.

CHECKPOINT ✔ 5. How would you use graphs to solve $3x + 2 > 5$? List and explain your steps.

CRITICAL THINKING Does the method you explored in the Activity above apply to solving inequalities such as $2x - 3 < x + 4$ and $4 \geq 3x + 1$? Justify your response.

The inequalities $x > 24{,}650$ *and* $x \leq 59{,}750$, which describe the income-tax bracket stated at the beginning of this lesson, form a compound inequality. A **compound inequality** is a pair of inequalities joined by *and* or *or*.

To solve an inequality involving *and*, find the values of the variable that satisfy *both* inequalities. This is shown in Example 4.

E X A M P L E ④ Solve $2x + 1 \geq 3$ *and* $3x - 4 \leq 17$. **Graph the solution.**

● **SOLUTION**

$$2x + 1 \geq 3 \quad and \quad 3x - 4 \leq 17$$
$$2x \geq 2 \qquad\qquad 3x \leq 21$$
$$x \geq 1 \qquad\qquad x \leq 7$$

The solution is all values of x between 1 and 7 inclusive.

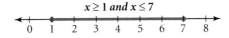

$x \geq 1$ *and* $x \leq 7$

TRY THIS Solve $-2x + 5 \geq 3$ *and* $x - 5 > -12$. Graph the solution.

The solution $x \geq 1$ *and* $x \leq 7$ in Example 4 can also be written as $1 \leq x \leq 7$. In general, the compound statement $x > a$ *and* $x < b$, where $a < b$, can be written as $a < x < b$.

CHECKPOINT ✔ What is another way to express the statement $x < 3$ *and* $x > -4$?

When you solve a compound inequality involving *or*, find those values of the variable that satisfy *at least one* of the inequalities. This is shown in Example 5.

E X A M P L E ⑤ Solve $5x + 1 > 21$ *or* $3x + 2 < -1$. **Graph the solution.**

● **SOLUTION**

$$5x + 1 > 21 \quad or \quad 3x + 2 < -1$$
$$5x > 20 \qquad\qquad 3x < -3$$
$$x > 4 \qquad\qquad x < -1$$

The solution is all values of x less than -1 or greater than 4.

$x < -1$ *or* $x > 4$

TRY THIS Solve $2x \leq 5$ *or* $7x + 1 > 36$. Graph the solution.

Exercises

● *Communicate*

1. Describe the steps you would take to graph $7x - 7 > 0$ on a number line.

2. How does the graph of $7x - 7 > 0$ differ from the graph of $7x - 7 \geq 0$? from the graph of $7x - 7 < 0$?

3. Is $x < 16$ is equivalent to $-x < -16$? Explain.

4. How can you express "x is nonnegative" by using an inequality?

5. Solve $3x + 1 < 13$. *(EXAMPLE 1)*

6. Solve $q + 4 < 4q - 11$. Graph the solution on a number line. *(EXAMPLE 2)*

APPLICATION

7. ACADEMICS Connor's homework average in English class is 92. The test average is $\frac{3}{4}$ of the final grade, and the homework average is $\frac{1}{4}$ of the final grade. What test average does Connor need in order to have a final grade of at least 80? *(EXAMPLE 3)*

8. Solve $3x - 7 \geq -13$ *and* $2x + 3 < 15$. Graph the solution. *(EXAMPLE 4)*

9. Solve $2x + 4 \geq -10$ *or* $4x - 6 > 14$. Graph the solution. *(EXAMPLE 5)*

● *Practice and Apply* ▬▬▬▬▬

Write an inequality that describes each graph.

10.

11.

12.

13.

14.

15.

16.

17.

18.

19.

Solve each inequality, and graph the solution on a number line.

20. $5x > 10$ **21.** $35x > 70$ **22.** $-5x > 10$

23. $-35x > 70$ **24.** $-5x > -10$ **25.** $-35x > -70$

26. $s - 2 > 10$ **27.** $y + 5 < -3$ **28.** $3x + 7 < 31$

29. $2x - 3 \geq 19$ **30.** $\frac{1}{2}d - 1 \geq -15$ **31.** $\frac{1}{5}x - 2 \leq 28$

32. $-2x > 14$ **33.** $-5x \leq 30$ **34.** $-x + 8 < 41$

35. $-5x - 15 > 60$ **36.** $-10 < -5x$ **37.** $-81 \leq -9x$

38. $\frac{-x}{3} \geq 10$ **39.** $\frac{-t}{32} < 2$ **40.** $-6(p + 4) < 12$

41. $6 - (4x - 3) \geq 8$ **42.** $4y - 12 > 7y - 15$ **43.** $8a - 11 < 4a + 9$

44. $3(4x - 5) < 8x + 3$ **45.** $6(x - 9) \geq 21 + x$ **46.** $-4x - 3 < -6x - 17$

47. $-x + 5 \geq -4x - 7$ **48.** $2(x - 5) < -4(3x + 2)$ **49.** $-5(3x + 2) \geq 4(x - 1)$

50. Graph each compound inequality on a number line.
    a. $x > -4$ *and* $x < 2$ **b.** $x > -4$ *and* $x > 2$
    c. $x > -4$ *or* $x < 2$ **d.** $x > -4$ *or* $x > 2$

51. Graph each compound inequality on a number line.
    a. $x < -4$ *and* $x < 2$ **b.** $x < -4$ *and* $x > 2$
    c. $x < -4$ *or* $x < 2$ **d.** $x < -4$ *or* $x > 2$

Graph the solution of each compound inequality on a number line.

52. $n + 4 < 16$ *and* $n - 3 > 12$

53. $y - 2 < 4$ *and* $y + 4 > 7$

54. $s + 7 > 4$ *or* $s - 2 < 2$

55. $x + 8 < 5$ *or* $x - 1 > 3$

56. $x + 9 \le 5$ *and* $4x \ge 12$

57. $5y \ge 15$ *and* $y + 8 \ge 2$

58. $c - 8 \le 2$ *or* $6c \ge -18$

59. $x + 9 \le 5$ *or* $4x \ge 12$

60. $5a + 12 < 2$ *and* $5a - 12 < 3$

61. $3t + 5 > 11$ *and* $4t - 1 < 15$

62. $-9x > -81$ *and* $2(x + 6) > -4$

63. $-5d < 40$ *and* $4(d - 3) < -8$

64. $20 - 3x \ge 11$ *or* $-4x \le -20$

65. $14 - 3x \le 2$ *or* $5 - 4x \ge 17$

66. $5 - 2b > -3$ *or* $-3(b - 3) < -6$

67. $-6x - 11 < 13$ *or* $3(x + 2) \le -9$

68. $\frac{1}{2}(x + 9) \le -3$ *and* $-10 < -5x$

69. $\frac{4m}{3} + 5 > 2$ *and* $4 \le -2(m - 3) - 7$

70. $2x < 7x - 10$ *or* $8x \le 3x - 15$

71. $2x - 7 < 5x + 8$ *or* $\frac{1}{2}(16 - 4x) \ge 0$

72. Solve $-2a \le 3x + a < 10a$ for x.

73. FUND-RAISING A charity is planning to raffle off a new car donated by a local car dealer. The charity wants to raise at least $70,000. It expects to sell between 1250 and 1500 tickets and to spend $5000 promoting the raffle. Find the possible ticket prices, p, by solving the inequality below.

$$1250p - 5000 \ge 70,000$$

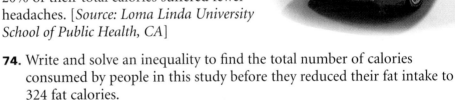

HEALTH One study has found that people who reduced their fat intake to less than 20% of their total calories suffered fewer headaches. [*Source: Loma Linda University School of Public Health, CA*]

74. Write and solve an inequality to find the total number of calories consumed by people in this study before they reduced their fat intake to 324 fat calories.

75. Write and solve an inequality to find the number of fat calories consumed by someone in this study who consumed a total of 1850 calories before reducing the fat intake.

Hamburger with french fries: about 46 grams of fat

Grilled chicken with rice and carrots: about 10 grams of fat

76. BUSINESS The money earned, or *revenue R*, from selling x units of a product is $R = 54x$. The cost of producing x units is $C = 40x + 868$. In order to make a profit, the revenue must be greater than the cost.
   a. Write and solve an inequality in one variable that describes this relationship between revenue and cost.
   b. How many units of the product must be sold in order to make a profit?
   c. Graph the solution on a number line.

 *Look Back*

Find the slope of each line. *(LESSON 1.2)*

77. $y + 2x = 3$ **78.** $3x - y = 6$

79. $x - 3y = -8$ **80.** $2x - 4y = 3(x - y) + 7$

Write the equation in slope-intercept form of a line that passes through the given points. *(LESSON 1.3)*

81. $(1, 2)$ and $(3, -1)$ **82.** $(5, -2)$ and $(-4, -9)$ **83.** $(8, -30)$ and $(-1, -6)$

84. TRAVEL Michelle finds that after 4 hours of driving at a constant speed, she is 220 miles from her starting point. After 6 more hours, she is 550 miles from her starting point. Write an equation in slope-intercept form for the distance traveled, d, in miles in terms of the elapsed time, t, in hours. *(LESSON 1.3)*

85. GOVERNMENT In order to determine how people feel about a school-bond proposal, a public opinion poll is taken. Of a sample of 300 registered voters, 240 favor the bond proposal. If the number of people who favor the bond proposal is directly proportional to the number of registered voters, how many of the 75,000 registered voters favor the bond proposal? *(LESSON 1.4)*

Calculator button indicates that a graphics calculator is recommended.

86 STATISTICS Enter the data from the table below in a graphics calculator. *(LESSON 1.5)*

x	1.0	1.3	1.5	1.6	1.8	1.9	2.0	2.2	2.3	2.5
y	58	47	50	39	40	35	41	31	34	36

   a. Create a scatter plot, identify the correlation as positive or negative, and find the equation of the least-squares line.
   b. Use the equation of the least-squares line that you found in part **a** to predict the value of y when x is 2.8.

Solve each literal equation for the indicated variable. *(LESSON 1.6)*

87. $A = p + prt$ for t **88.** $SA = 2ab + 2ac + 2bc$ for a

 *Look Beyond*

89. What two real numbers have an absolute value of 4?

Solving Absolute-Value Equations and Inequalities

Objective

- Write, solve, and graph absolute-value equations and inequalities in mathematical and real-world situations.

Why *Measurement usually involves an allowable amount of error, called measurement tolerance, which can be expressed by using absolute-value notation. Measurement tolerance is important in many fields, including manufacturing.*

APPLICATION
MANUFACTURING

A company manufactures a small gear for a car according to design specifications. If the gear is made too large, it will not fit. If it is made too small, the car will not run properly. What measurement tolerance is close enough for this gear? *You will solve this problem in Example 5.*

Definition of Absolute Value

$$|-3| = 3 \qquad\qquad |3| = 3$$

The absolute value of a negative number is its opposite.

The absolute value of a nonnegative number is itself.

Notice that both 3 and −3 are 3 units from 0 on the number line.

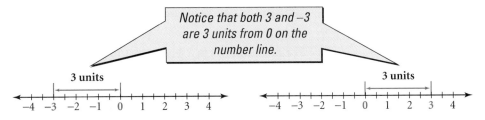

The algebraic and geometric definitions of absolute value are given below.

Absolute Value

Let x be any real number.

Algebraic definition:

The **absolute value** of x, denoted by $|x|$, is given by the following:

If $x \geq 0$, then $|x| = x$.

If $x < 0$, then $|x| = -x$.

Geometric definition:

The **absolute value** of x is the distance from x to 0 on the number line.

CHECKPOINT ✔ Verify for the following values of x that the algebraic definition and the geometric definition of absolute value give the same result:

$$\{-2, -1, 0, 1, 2\}$$

Absolute-Value Equations

You can use a graph to better understand absolute-value equations. Examine the graphs below.

$y = |x|$ and $y = 2$ **$y = |x|$ and $y = 3$**   **$y = |x|$ and $y = 4$**

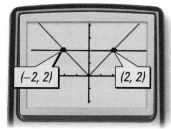   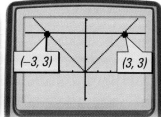   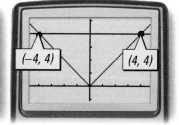

If $|x| = 2$, then   If $|x| = 3$, then   If $|x| = 4$, then
$x = -2$ or $x = 2$. $x = -3$ or $x = 3$. $x = -4$ or $x = 4$.

The graphs suggest the following fact:

Absolute-Value Equations

If $a > 0$ and $|x| = a$, then $x = a$ or $x = -a$.

By definition, $|x|$ is a distance and is therefore always nonnegative. Notice, however, that the solution to an absolute-value equation can be negative.

CHECKPOINT ✔ Solve the absolute-value equation $|x| = 5$.

EXAMPLE **1** **Solve |2x + 3| = 4. Graph the solution on a number line.**

SOLUTION

Solve the two related equations.

$$2x + 3 = 4 \qquad or \qquad 2x + 3 = -4$$
$$2x = 1 \qquad\qquad\qquad 2x = -7$$
$$x = 0.5 \qquad\qquad\qquad x = -\frac{7}{2}, \text{ or } -3.5$$

CHECK

Let $x = 0.5$.

$$|2x + 3| = 4$$
$$|2(0.5) + 3| \stackrel{?}{=} 4$$
$$|4| = 4 \ \textbf{True}$$

Let $x = -3.5$.

$$|2x + 3| = 4$$
$$|2(-3.5) + 3| \stackrel{?}{=} 4$$
$$|-4| = 4 \ \textbf{True}$$

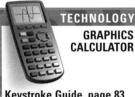

TECHNOLOGY
GRAPHICS CALCULATOR

Keystroke Guide, page 83

You can also check your solutions by graphing $y = |2x + 3|$ and $y = 4$ on the same screen.

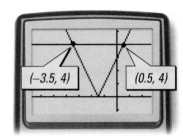

$(-3.5, 4)$ $(0.5, 4)$

The graph shows that if $|2x + 3| = 4$, then $x = -3.5$ or $x = 0.5$.

The solution is graphed on the number line at right.

$x = -3.5$ or $x = 0.5$

TRY THIS Solve $|3x + 5| = 7$. Graph the solution on a number line.

Activity

Exploring Solution Possibilities

TECHNOLOGY
GRAPHICS CALCULATOR

Keystroke Guide, page 83

You will need: a graphics calculator

The display at right shows the graphs of $y = |x|$ and $y = 2x - 2$. These equations model $|x| = mx + b$, where $m = 2$ and $b = -2$.

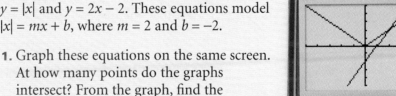

1. Graph these equations on the same screen. At how many points do the graphs intersect? From the graph, find the solution of $|x| = 2x - 2$.

PROBLEM SOLVING

2. **Guess and check.** Modify $y = 2x - 2$ so that the graph of the modified equation intersects the graph of $y = |x|$ at two points. Graph the equations to check. What are the solutions of $|x| = mx + b$ for your modified values of m and b?

3. Find values of m and b such that the graphs of $y = |x|$ and $y = mx + b$ have no points in common. Graph the equations to check.

4. Find values of m and b such that the graphs of $y = |x|$ and $y = mx + b$ have infinitely many points in common. Graph the equations to check.

CHECKPOINT ✔ 5. Summarize the possible solutions of $|x| = mx + b$.

E X A M P L E ❷ Solve $|x - 3| = 3x + 5$. Check your solution.

● **SOLUTION**

Graph the two related equations.

$$x - 3 = 3x + 5 \qquad or \qquad x - 3 = -(3x + 5)$$
$$-2x = 8 \qquad\qquad\qquad x - 3 = -3x - 5$$
$$x = -4 \qquad\qquad\qquad\quad 4x = -2$$
$$\qquad\qquad\qquad\qquad\qquad x = -\frac{1}{2}, \text{ or } -0.5$$

CHECK

Let $x = -4$.
$$|x - 3| = 3x + 5$$
$$|(-4) - 3| \stackrel{?}{=} 3(-4) + 5$$
$$|-7| = -7 \quad \textbf{False}$$

Let $x = -0.5$.
$$|x - 3| = 3x + 5$$
$$|(-0.5) - 3| \stackrel{?}{=} 3(-0.5) + 5$$
$$|-3.5| = 3.5 \quad \textbf{True}$$

Since -4 does not satisfy the given equation and -0.5 does satisfy the given equation, the only solution is -0.5.

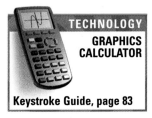

TECHNOLOGY
GRAPHICS CALCULATOR

Keystroke Guide, page 83

You can also check your solution by graphing $y = |x - 3|$ and $y = 3x + 5$ on the same screen and looking for any points of intersection.

The graph shows that $|x - 3| = 3x + 5$ is true only when $x = -0.5$.

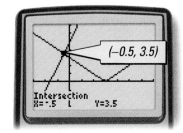

TRY THIS   Solve $|x - 4| = x + 1$. Check your solution.

Absolute-Value Inequalities

The red dots on the number line below illustrate the solution of $|x| = 3$. Notice that these solutions divide the number line into three distinct regions.

This suggests a fact that will help you solve absolute-value inequalities.

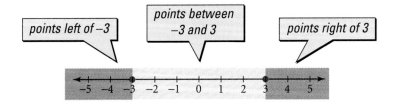

Absolute-Value Inequalities

If $a > 0$ and $|x| < a$, then $x > -a$ *and* $x < a$.

If $a > 0$ and $|x| > a$, then $x < -a$ *or* $x > a$.

You can write similar statements for $|x| \leq a$ and $|x| \geq a$.

Solve |5 − 3x| > 9. Graph the solution on a number line.

● **SOLUTION**

The inequality is of the form |x| > a, so solve an *or* statement.

$$5 - 3x > 9 \quad or \quad 5 - 3x < -9$$

Change the direction of the inequality symbol.

$$-3x > 4 \qquad\qquad -3x < -14$$
$$x < -1\frac{1}{3} \qquad\qquad x > 4\frac{2}{3}$$

Change the direction of the inequality symbol.

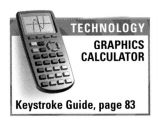

TECHNOLOGY
GRAPHICS CALCULATOR

Keystroke Guide, page 83

CHECK
Check your solution by graphing
$y = |5 - 3x|$ and $y = 9$ on the same screen.

The graph shows that if $|5 - 3x| > 9$, then
$x < -1\frac{1}{3}$ or $x > 4\frac{2}{3}$.

The solution is graphed on the number
line at right.

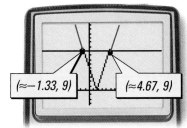

$(\approx -1.33, 9)$ $(\approx 4.67, 9)$

$x < -1\frac{1}{3}$ or $x > 4\frac{2}{3}$

-2 |-1 0 1 2 3 4 |5
   $-1\frac{1}{3}$ $4\frac{2}{3}$

TRY THIS   Solve |3x − 7| > 1. Graph the solution on a number line.

Solve |5 − 3x| < 9. Graph the solution on a number line.

● **SOLUTION**

The inequality is of the form |x| < a, so solve an *and* statement.

$$5 - 3x < 9 \quad and \quad 5 - 3x > -9$$

Change the direction of the inequality symbol.

$$-3x < 4 \qquad\qquad -3x > -14$$
$$x > -1\frac{1}{3} \qquad\qquad x < 4\frac{2}{3}$$

Change the direction of the inequality symbol.

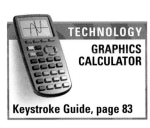

TECHNOLOGY
GRAPHICS CALCULATOR

Keystroke Guide, page 83

CHECK
Check your solution by graphing
$y = |5 - 3x|$ and $y = 9$ on the same screen.

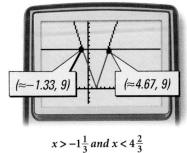

The graph shows that if $|5 - 3x| < 9$, then
$x > -1\frac{1}{3}$ and $x < 4\frac{2}{3}$, or $-1\frac{1}{3} < x < 4\frac{2}{3}$.

$(\approx -1.33, 9)$ $(\approx 4.67, 9)$

The solution is graphed on the number
line at right.

$x > -1\frac{1}{3}$ and $x < 4\frac{2}{3}$

-2 |-1 0 1 2 3 4 |5
   $-1\frac{1}{3}$ $4\frac{2}{3}$

TRY THIS   Solve |5x − 3| < 7. Graph the solution on a number line.

CHECKPOINT ✔ Compare and contrast the problems in Examples 3 and 4.

You can write an absolute-value inequality to describe the measurement tolerance for a machine part.

EXAMPLE 5

APPLICATION
MANUFACTURING

A gear is designed with a specification of 3.50 centimeters for the diameter. It will work if it is no more than ±0.01 centimeter of the specified measurement.

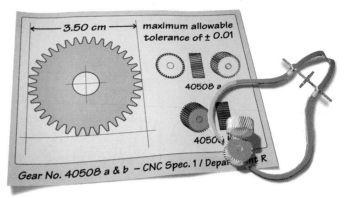

Write an absolute-value inequality to represent the measurement tolerance for the diameter of this gear.

● SOLUTION

Let d represent an acceptable gear diameter.
$$d \geq 3.50 - 0.01 \ and \ d \leq 3.50 + 0.01$$
Write this compound inequality as follows:
$$3.50 - 0.01 \leq d \leq 3.50 + 0.01$$
Solve the compound inequality.

$$3.50 - 0.01 \leq \qquad d \qquad \leq 3.50 + 0.01$$
$$3.50 - 0.01 - \mathbf{3.50} \leq d - \mathbf{3.50} \leq 3.50 + 0.01 - \mathbf{3.50}$$
$$-0.01 \leq d - 3.50 \leq 0.01$$

Thus, $|d - 3.50| \leq 0.01$ represents the tolerance for the diameter of this gear.

TRY THIS Write $12.00 - 0.01 \leq t \leq 12.00 + 0.01$ as an absolute-value inequality.

An absolute-value inequality may have no solution, or any real number may be a solution. Examine the graphs of $y = |2x - 1|$ and $y = -3$ below.

Notice that the graph of $y = |2x - 1|$ is never below the graph of $y = -3$. Thus, $|2x - 1| < -3$ has no solution. There is no value of x for which the absolute value, $|2x - 1|$, is less than -3.

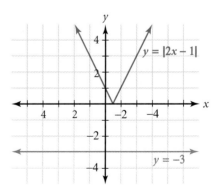

Notice also that the graph of $y = |2x - 1|$ is always above the graph of $y = -3$. Thus, any real number is a solution to $|2x - 1| > -3$. The absolute value of any real number is greater than -3.

CHECKPOINT ✔ Write an absolute-value inequality that contains $\leq$ and has no solution. Write an absolute-value inequality that contains $\geq$ and has all real numbers as its solution.

CRITICAL THINKING If $|x| \leq a$ has no solution, what can you conclude about the possible values of a and about the solution to $|x| > a$?

Exercises

Communicate

1. Explain why the equation $|3x - 5| + 4 = 3$ has no solution.

2. Discuss why it is necessary to always check your solution when solving absolute-value equations.

3. Explain why an absolute-value equation can have two solutions.

4. Discuss the meanings of the words *and* and *or*. Compare the mathematical meanings of these words with their common meanings.

5. Use a graph to describe the type of absolute-value inequality whose solution is any real number.

Guided Skills Practice

Solve each equation. Check your solution. *(EXAMPLES 1 AND 2)*

6. $|x - 10| = 4$ **7.** $|2x - 5| = 3$ **8.** $10 = |7 - 3x|$

9. $x + 4 = |x - 2|$ **10.** $\frac{1}{2}x + 1 = |x - 2| - 1$ **11.** $\frac{1}{2}x + 1 = |x + 3|$

Solve each inequality. Graph the solution on a number line.
(EXAMPLES 3 AND 4)

12. $2 < |4 - x|$ **13.** $|2x + 1| \geq 5$ **14.** $|5 + x| < \frac{1}{2}$

15. $\frac{1}{2}|2x + 1| \geq 2$ **16.** $3|x + 1| \leq 2$ **17.** $3|x + 1| + 3 > 2$

18. **RECREATION** Ashley tosses a horseshoe at a stake 25 feet away. The horseshoe lands no more than 2 feet from the stake.
(EXAMPLE 5)
   a. Write an absolute-value inequality that represents the range of distances that the horseshoe traveled.
   b. Solve this inequality and graph it on a number line.

Practice and Apply

Match each statement on the left with a statement or sentence on the right.

19. $|x + 2| = 4$

20. $|x + 2| < 4$

21. $|x + 2| < -4$

22. $|x + 2| > -4$

23. $|x + 2| > 4$

24. $|x + 2| = -4$

a. $x < 2$ *and* $x > -6$

b. $x = 2$ *or* $x = -6$

c. $x > 2$ *or* $x < -6$

d. There is no solution.

e. The solution is all real numbers.

f. none of the above

LESSON 1.8 SOLVING ABSOLUTE-VALUE EQUATIONS AND INEQUALITIES **67**

Solve each equation.

25. $|x + 4| = 8$ **26.** $|x - 5| = 12$ **27.** $|2 + x| = 10$

28. $|8 - x| = 1$ **29.** $|x - 2| = 9$ **30.** $|x + 5| = 11$

31. $|2x - 15| = 11$ **32.** $|3x + 12| = 18$ **33.** $|10 - 4x| = 28$

34. $|5 + 4x| = 17$ **35.** $|5x - 6| = 2$ **36.** $|10 - 3x| + 5 = 2$

37. $|10x + 2| - 18 = -12$ **38.** $|4 - 3x| - 9 = 3$ **39.** $|2x - 8| + 2 = 1$

Solve each inequality. Graph the solution on a number line. If the equation has no solution, write *no solution*.

40. $|x - 4| > 1$ **41.** $|x + 5| \leq 7$ **42.** $|3x| > 15$

43. $|-2x| \leq 12$ **44.** $|4x| \leq -8$ **45.** $|3 - x| \geq -5$

46. $|2 + 5x| \leq 3$ **47.** $|2x - 3| < 11$ **48.** $|4x + 6| \leq 14$

49. $\left|\dfrac{2x + 3}{-5}\right| < 3$ **50.** $|4x - 5| \geq 15$ **51.** $|2x - 1| \geq -5$

52. $|5x + 3| > -2$ **53.** $|7 - 6x| < -4$ **54.** $|9x + 4| \leq -11$

55. $-2|4x + 1| \leq -4$ **56.** $-2|4x + 1| \geq -4$ **57.** $\left|\dfrac{3}{2} - \dfrac{5}{2}x\right| < -\dfrac{7}{2}$

SUMMARY		
Three different representations of an inequality are given below.		
Verbal	**Algebraic**	**Graphic**
The distance between x and 3 is less than 5.	$\|x - 3\| < 5$	(number line from -4 to 8: open circles at -2 and 8; -4 -2 0 2 4 6 8, with 3 marked below)

Examine the summary box above. For Exercises 58–60, write the two missing representations for each inequality.

58. The distance between x and 7 is less than 4.

59. $|x - 4| < 1$

60. (number line: 2 4 6 8 10 12 14, with a segment marked from about 9 to 12)

CHALLENGE

61. Solve the inequality $\left|\dfrac{4x}{3}\right| \leq 2x + 5$.

For Exercises 62–65, write and solve an absolute-value inequality.

APPLICATIONS

62. **HEALTH** Antonio weighs 120 pounds, and his doctor said that his weight differs from his ideal body weight by less than 5 percent. What are the possible values, to the nearest pound, for Antonio's ideal body weight?

63. **ENTERTAINMENT** A tightrope walker is 10 feet from one end of the rope. If he then takes 3 steps and each step is 11 inches long, how far is he now from the same end of the rope? Give both possible answers.

64. METEOROLOGY An instrument called an *anemometer* measures a wind speed of 30 feet per second. The true wind speed is within 2 feet per second (inclusive) of the measured wind speed. What range is possible for the true wind speed?

65. RECREATION A recent poll reported that 68 percent of moviegoers eat popcorn during the movie. The margin of error for the poll was 3%. What are the minimum and maximum possible percents according to this poll?

An anemometer is used to measure wind speed.

 Look Back

66. REAL ESTATE A rental property is purchased for $90,000. For tax purposes, a depreciation of 5% of property's initial value, or $4500, is assumed per year. *(LESSON 1.1)*
a. Make a table of values for the value of the property, *v*, after *t* years.
b. Write a linear equation for the value of the property, *v*, after *t* years.
c. What is the value of the property after 15 years?

67. SPORTS A baseball pitcher allows 10 runs in 15 innings. At this rate, how many runs would you expect the pitcher to allow in a 9-inning game? *(LESSON 1.4)*

Solve each proportion for x. *(LESSON 1.4)*

68. $\frac{2}{x} = \frac{5}{8}$ **69.** $\frac{x-3}{4} = \frac{2x}{16}$ **70.** $\frac{10x}{-60} = \frac{2x-10}{8}$

71. Solve $\frac{1}{2}bh = A$ for *h*. *(LESSON 1.6)*

72. Solve $P = 2l + 2w$ for *l*. *(LESSON 1.6)*

Solve each inequality, and graph the solution on a number line. *(LESSON 1.7)*

73. $4x - 5 < \frac{1}{3}(8x + 3)$ **74.** $x - 9 \geq \frac{1}{6}(21 + x)$

Graph each compound inequality on a number line. *(LESSON 1.7)*

75. $x > -1$ *and* $x < 5$ **76.** $x < 3$ *and* $x > -3$

77. $x \leq -2$ *or* $x > 4$ **78.** $x > 2$ *or* $x \leq -1$

 **Look Beyond**

79. ETYMOLOGY Look up the word *rational* in the dictionary. Write the definition that is related to math. What is the meaning of the root word, *ratio*, that relates to the math usage?

PROJECT CHAPTER ONE

CORRELATION EXPLORATION

Activity ❶

Discuss the questions below, and record your hypotheses.

1. Do you think taller people have longer arm spans? Explain.

2. Do you think taller people have bigger hand spans? Explain.

3. Do you think the distance from the top of a person's head to the ceiling is related to his or her height? Explain.

4. Do you think the value of one's pocket change is related to his or her height? Explain.

Person	Height	Arm span	Hand span	Distance from head to ceiling	Value of change
1					
2					
3					
⋮					

5. Collect the information indicated in the table above for each student in the classroom. Record your data in a table like the one shown above. Create a scatter plot for the data identified below. Label the *x*-axis with units for height and the *y*-axis with units for the other variable in each case.

    a. height and arm span
    b. height and hand span
    c. height and distance from the top of one's head to the ceiling
    d. height and value of pocket change

Activity 2

1. Use a straightedge to estimate a linear model for each scatter plot.

2. Write an equation for each of your linear models.

3. Identify the slope and *y*-intercept for each of your linear models.

4. For each linear model, what does the slope tell you about the relationship between the variables?

5. For each linear model, what does the *y*-intercept tell you about the relationship between the variables?

Activity 3

1. Describe the correlation between the variables represented in each scatter plot.

2. Find the correlation coefficient for each scatter plot.

3. For each scatter plot, find and graph an equation for the least-squares line.

4. For each scatter plot, was your linear model reasonably close to the least-squares line? Explain.

5. Use the equations of the least-squares lines to make each prediction below.
   a. the arm span of a person who is 5 feet tall
   b. the hand span of a person who is 5 feet tall
   c. the distance to the ceiling from the head of a person who is 5 feet tall
   d. the value of the pocket change of a person who is 5 feet tall

Activity 4

Solve the equation of the appropriate least-squares line to make each prediction below. Name the Properties of Equality that you use to solve each equation.

1. the height of a person with an arm span of 62 inches

2. the height of a person with a hand span of $8\frac{1}{2}$ inches

3. the height of a person whose head is 28 inches from the ceiling

4. the height of a person with $1.26 in pocket change

Chapter Review and Assessment

VOCABULARY

Key Skills & Exercises

LESSON 1.1

Key Skills

Identify linear equations and linear relationships between variables in a table.

$y = 8x + 4$ is a linear equation in the form $y = mx + b$, where $m = 8$ and $b = 4$.

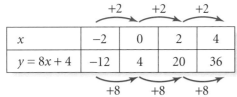

x	−2	0	2	4
$y = 8x + 4$	−12	4	20	36

Represent a real-world linear relationship in a table, graph, or equation.

Projected college enrollments are given below.

Year	Enrollment (in millions)
1998	14.3
2000	14.8
2002	15.3
2004	15.8

[*Source: U.S. Department of Education*]

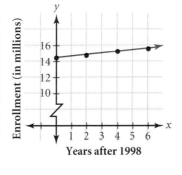

Years after 1998

The equation is $y = 0.5x + 14.3$, where $x = 0$ represents 1998 and y is the projected enrollment.

Exercises

State whether each relationship is linear; if so, write the next ordered pair that would appear in the table.

1.

x	3	6	9	12
y	3	6	12	24

2.

x	1	2	3	4
y	2	4	6	8

3.

x	7	14	21	28
y	5	10	15	20

PSYCHOLOGY Psychologists define intelligence quotient (IQ) as 100 times a person's mental age divided by his or her chronological age. The result is rounded to the nearest integer.

4. Find the IQ for an individual whose chronological age is 15 and whose mental age is the following: 10, 14, 15, 19, and 25.

5. Represent the linear relationship from Exercise 4 in a table, a graph, and an equation.

Key Skills

Graph a linear equation by using the slope and _y_-intercept.

Graph $y = -3x + 4$.

The y-intercept is 4.

The slope is -3.

$m = -3 = \dfrac{-3}{1}$ or $\dfrac{3}{-1}$

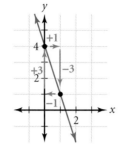

Exercises

Graph each equation.

6. $y = -\dfrac{1}{2}x$

7. $y = \dfrac{4}{5}x + 1$

8. $y = 3x - 1$

9. $y = -2x$

10. $2x + y - 3$

11. $3y - x = 1$

12. $y = 1$

13. $x = -2$

Key Skills

Write a linear equation in two variables given sufficient information.

slope of $\dfrac{2}{3}$ and contains the point $(6, 9)$

$$y - y_1 = m(x - x_1)$$
$$y - 9 = \tfrac{2}{3}(x - 6)$$
$$y = \tfrac{2}{3}x - 5$$

contains the points $(2, 500)$ and $(3, 1500)$

Find m.

$$m = \frac{1500 - 500}{3 - 2} = 1000$$

Find b.

$$y = 1000x + b$$
$$500 = 1000(2) + b$$
$$b = -1500$$

Thus, $y = 1000x - 1500$.

Write an equation in slope-intercept form for the line that contains a given point and is perpendicular or parallel to a given line.

perpendicular to $y = 4x + 10$ and contains $(60, 40)$

$$y - y_1 = m(x - x_1)$$
$$y - 40 = -\tfrac{1}{4}(x - 60)$$
$$y = -\tfrac{1}{4}x + 55$$

> Substitute the negative reciprocal of 4 for m.

parallel to $y = 4x + 10$ and contains $(60, 40)$

$$y - y_1 = m(x - x_1)$$
$$y - 40 = 4(x - 60)$$
$$y = 4x - 200$$

> Substitute 4 for m.

Exercises

Write an equation in slope-intercept form for the line that has the indicated slope, _m_, and contains the given point.

14. $m = -3$, $(5, 8)$

15. $m = 100$, $(-2, 198)$

16. $m = \dfrac{1}{20}$, $(0, 5)$

17. $m = 0$, $(-5, 4)$

Write an equation for the line that contains the indicated points.

18. $(3, 4)$ and $(5, 4)$

19. $(-2, 8)$ and $(-2, -1)$

20. $\left(-5\tfrac{3}{4}, 2\right)$ and $\left(-3\tfrac{1}{4}, 3\tfrac{1}{2}\right)$

21. $(6.8, 2)$ and $(3.6, 6)$

Write an equation for the line that contains the given point and is perpendicular or parallel to the given line.

22. $(3, 0)$, $y = -2x - 5$, perpendicular

23. $(-3, -2)$, $y = \tfrac{1}{3}x - 5$, parallel

24. $(4, -1)$, $y = -\tfrac{2}{3}x + 7$, parallel

25. $(4, -1)$, $y = -8$, perpendicular

Key Skills

Write a direct-variation equation for given variables.

Find the constant of variation and the direct-variation equation if y varies directly as x and $y = 2.25$ when $x = 9$.

$$k = \frac{2.25}{9} = 0.25$$
$$y = 0.25x$$

Write and solve proportions.

$$\frac{10}{12} = \frac{x}{24}$$
$$12x = 240$$
$$x = 20$$

Exercises

For Exercises 26–28, y varies directly as x. Find the constant of variation and the direct-variation equation.

26. $y = 750$ when $x = 25$

27. $y = 0.05$ when $x = 10$

28. $y = -2$ when $x = 14$

PHYSICS The bending of a beam varies directly as the mass of the load it supports. Suppose that a beam is bent 20 millimeters by a mass of 40 kilograms.

29. How much will the beam bend when it supports a mass of 100 kilograms?

30. If the beam bends 25 millimeters, what load is the beam supporting?

Key Skills

Make a scatter plot, and describe the correlation.

x	y
1	−6
2	−3
3	−4
4	0
5	−6
6	3
7	5
8	4
9	12
10	7

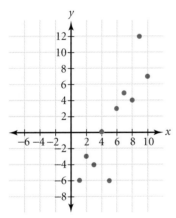

Because the data points go upward from left to right, the correlation is positive.

Find an equation for the least-squares line, and use it to make predictions.

The least-squares line for the data above is $y \approx 1.73x - 83$.

Exercises

31. STATISTICS Make a scatter plot of the data below. Describe the correlation.

x	−4	−3	−2	−1	0	1	2	3	4
y	30	25	24	25	17	10	13	5	−1

32. FREIGHT CHARGES A statistician for the Civil Aeronautics Board wants to be able to predict the freight charge for a standard-sized crate. The statistician takes a sample of 10 freight invoices from different companies. Let d represent the distance in miles and let c represent the freight charge in dollars. Make a scatter plot of the data below. Describe the correlation. Then find an equation for the least-squares line.

d	500	600	900	1000	1200	1400	1600	1700	2200
c	41	55	50	70	60	78	75	89	105

Key Skills

Write and solve a linear equation in one variable.

INCOME Johanna works as a waitress. Her wages are $2.50 per hour plus tips, which average $50 for each 4-hour shift. How many 4-hour shifts does she have to work to earn $300?

Let n represent the number of shifts.

$$(\text{hourly rate} \times \text{no. of hours} + \text{tips})n = 300$$
$$[2.5(4) + 50]n = 300$$
$$n = 5$$

Johanna must work 5 shifts to earn $300.

Solve each literal equation for the indicated variable.

Solve $A = \pi rs + \pi r^2$ for s.

$$A = \pi rs + \pi r^2$$
$$A - \pi r^2 = \pi rs$$
$$\frac{A - \pi r^2}{\pi r} = s$$
$$\frac{A}{\pi r} - r = s$$

Exercises

CONSUMER ECONOMICS Jorge's monthly bill from his Internet service provider was $25. The service provider charges a base rate of $15 per month plus $1 for each hour that the service is used.

33. Write a linear equation to represent the total monthly charges.

34. Find the number of hours that Jorge was charged for that month.

Solve each literal equation for the indicated variable.

35. $F = \frac{9}{5}C + 32$ for C

36. $S = s_0 + v_0 + \frac{1}{2}gt^2$ for v_0

37. $\frac{1}{f} = \frac{1}{f_1} + \frac{1}{f_2}$ for f

38. $A = \frac{h}{2}(b_1 + b_2)$ for b_2

Key Skills

Write, solve and graph linear inequalities in one variable.

> *Notice that the inequality sign is reversed.*

$$14 - 6t \geq 16$$
$$-6t \geq 2$$
$$t \leq -\frac{2}{6}$$

Solve and graph compound linear equalities in one variable.

$$5x + 7(x - 2) > 6 \quad or \quad 4x + 6 \leq -6$$
$$x > \frac{5}{3} \qquad\qquad x \leq -3$$

$$x > \tfrac{5}{3} \text{ or } x \leq -3$$

$$5x + 7(x - 2) < 6 \quad and \quad 4x + 6 \geq -6$$
$$x < \frac{5}{3} \qquad\qquad x \geq -3$$

$$-3 \leq x < \tfrac{5}{3}$$

Exercises

Write an inequality for each situation. Graph the solution.

39. GEOMETRY If the width of a rectangle is 10 meters and the perimeter is not to exceed 140 meters, how long can the length be?

40. BUSINESS An organization wants to sell tickets to a concert. It plans on selling 300 reserved-seat tickets and 150 general-admission tickets. The price of a reserved-seat ticket is $2 more than a general-admission ticket. If the organization wants to collect at least $3750, what is the minimum price it can charge for a reserved-seat ticket?

Solve and graph.

41. $4x - 3 < 29$ *and* $4 - 3x < -5$

42. $-3x - 8 \leq 7$ *and* $-4x > -18$

43. $4x - 3 < 29$ *or* $4 - 3x < -5$

44. $-3x - 8 \leq 7$ *or* $-4x > -18$

Key Skills

Solve and graph absolute-value equations.

a.
$$|5x| = 45$$
$$5x = 45 \quad or \quad 5x = -45$$
$$x = 9 \qquad\qquad x = -9$$

b.
$$\tfrac{1}{2}|5x| + 5 = 45$$
$$\tfrac{1}{2}|5x| = 40$$
$$5x = 80 \quad or \quad x = -80$$
$$x - 16 \qquad\qquad x = -16$$

Solve and graph absolute-value inequalities.

a.
$$|x + 5| \geq 45$$
$$x + 5 \geq 45 \quad or \quad x + 5 \leq -45$$
$$x \geq 40 \qquad\qquad x \leq -50$$

$$x \leq -50 \ or \ x \geq 40$$

b.
$$|x + 5| \leq 45$$
$$x + 5 \leq 45 \quad and \quad x + 5 \geq -45$$
$$x \leq 40 \qquad\qquad x \geq -50$$

$$-50 \leq x \leq 40$$

Exercises

Solve and graph on a number line.

45. $\left|\dfrac{1}{2}x\right| = 20$

46. $\left|\dfrac{4}{5}x\right| = 16$

47. $12|2x| = 108$

48. $\dfrac{2}{3}\left|x + 4\right| - 5 = 7$

Solve and graph on a number line.

49. $\left|\dfrac{1}{2}x\right| > 20$

50. $-\dfrac{1}{2}\left|\dfrac{1}{2}x\right| - 4 > 20$

51. $-5|6x - 7| \leq 35$

52. $|6x - 7| \leq -35$

Applications

GEOMETRY The length of the hypotenuse of a 30-60-90 triangle varies directly as the length of the side opposite the 30° angle. The length of the hypotenuse, h, is 45 units when the side opposite the 30° angle, s, is 22.5 units.

53. Find the constant of variation and the direct-variation equation.

54. Find the length of the side opposite the 30° angle when the hypotenuse is 13 inches long.

PERSONAL FINANCE The majority of American families save less than $\dfrac{1}{10}$ of their income. Suppose that an average American family saves $2850.

55. Write and solve an inequality that models this situation.

56. Graph the solution on a number line.

Alternative Assessment

Performance Assessment

1. SPORTS Some sports use handicaps to equalize the chances of winning between players of different abilities. In bowling, the handicap, h, that is added to a players score is calculated as follows:

$$h = 0.8(200 - \text{average bowling score})$$

a. Create some average bowling scores, and make a table of corresponding handicaps.

b. Graph the ordered pairs in your table. Which variable did you choose for the x-axis? Why?

c. Can a player have a negative handicap? How can a handicap worsen your score? Explain.

d. Make up scores for two bowlers, and explain how their handicaps would be used.

e. Describe the advantages of using an algebraic formula to express handicaps.

f. Research golf handicaps. Write an algebraic formula to represent them.

2. CONSTRUCTION To prepare ready-mix concrete, you must combine the proper ratios of dry mix and water. Suppose that a 40-pound bag of dry mix requires 2 quarts of water.

a. How much water does a 60-pound bag require?

b. Show all of the possible ways that the ratio of dry mix to water from Step 1 can be written. Which do you prefer? Why?

c. Find the constant of variation and the direct-variation equation for this situation. Explain what the constant of variation represents.

Portfolio Projects

1. CULTURAL CONNECTION: AFRICA A trial-and-error procedure for solving equations in one variable is given in the Rhind papyrus, written almost 4000 years ago in Egypt. Apply each step below to solve a variety of equations.

Solve $x + \frac{1}{4}x = 15$.

a. Guess a number, such as 4, and substitute it for x in the equation.

$$x + \frac{1}{4}x = 15$$
$$(4) + \frac{1}{4}(4) = 15$$
$$5 \neq 15$$

b. Find the correction factor by dividing the desired result, 15, by the actual result, 5.

$$\frac{15}{5} = 3$$

c. Multiply the correction factor, 3, by the original guess, 4, and substitute this new value in the equation. Thus, $x = 12$.

$$3 \times 4 = 12$$
$$(12) + \frac{1}{4}(12) = 15$$
$$15 = 15$$

2. LINEAR RELATIONSHIPS Use print or Internet sources to find five examples of linear relationships expressed in graphs or tables.

For each linear relationship, make a graph from the table or a table from the graph. Compare each table with the corresponding graph, and discuss the advantages of each representation. Write an equation to model each linear relationship.

---

internetconnect

The HRW Web site contains many resources to reinforce and expand your knowledge of linear representations. This Web site also provides Internet links to other sites where you can find information and real-world data for use in research projects, reports, and activities that involve linear representations. Visit the HRW Web site at **go.hrw.com**, and enter the keyword **MB1 CH1** to access the resources for this chapter.

College Entrance Exam Practice

QUANTITATIVE COMPARISON For Items 1–5, write
A if the quantity in Column A is greater than the quantity in Column B;
B if the quantity in Column B is greater than the quantity in Column A;
C if the quantities are equal; or
D if the relationship cannot be determined from the given information.

	Column A	Column B	Answers
1.	$2y - 3x = 4$ slope of the graph of the equation	y-intercept of the graph of the equation	(A) (B) (C) (D) [Lesson 1.2]
2.	slope of the line graphed 	y-intercept of the graph 	(A) (B) (C) (D) [Lesson 1.2]
3.	slope of the line containing (4, 3) and (−4, −3)	(−3, −4) and (1, −1)	(A) (B) (C) (D) [Lesson 1.2]
4.	the value of x $\dfrac{1 - 2x}{5} = \dfrac{x}{6}$	$\dfrac{2x - 4}{3} = \dfrac{x}{5}$	(A) (B) (C) (D) [Lesson 1.4]
5.	the value of x $|3x - 1| = 2$	$|5x| - 3 = 7$	(A) (B) (C) (D) [Lesson 1.8]

6. Which one of the following equations is not a linear equation? *(LESSON 1.1)*

a. $2x + 3y = 11$ b. $y = \dfrac{3 - 4x}{7}$

c. $y = \dfrac{7}{3 - 4x}$ d. $x = 3 - y$

7. Which gives the slope and y-intercept for the graph of $2x + 3y = 2$? *(LESSON 1.2)*

a. $m = -\dfrac{2}{3}, b = \dfrac{2}{3}$ b. $m = \dfrac{2}{3}, b = -\dfrac{2}{3}$

c. $m = 2, b = -2$ d. $m = -2, b = 2$

8. Find the slope of the line containing the points $(2, -1)$ and $(-5, 0)$. *(LESSON 1.2)*

a. -7 b. -3

c. $\dfrac{1}{7}$ d. $-\dfrac{1}{7}$

9. Which equation represents a line with no y-intercept? *(LESSON 1.2)*

a. $y = 4$ b. $x = -\dfrac{1}{4}$

c. $x + y = 2$ d. $y = 3x$

10. Which statement is *not* true? **(LESSON 1.2)**
    a. All horizontal lines are perpendicular to vertical lines.
    b. The slopes of two nonvertical lines that are perpendicular to each other are reciprocals.
    c. The slope of any horizontal line is 0.
    d. The slope of any vertical line is undefined.

11. Which equation contains the point $(-4, 6)$ and is parallel to the graph of $y = -2x - \frac{1}{4}$? **(LESSON 1.3)**
    a. $y = -2x + 2$ b. $y = 2x - 2$
    c. $y = 2x + 2$ d. $y = -2x - 2$

12. If x varies directly as y and $x = 4$ when $y = -5$, what is x when $y = 2.5$? **(LESSON 1.4)**
    a. $-\frac{1}{2}$ b. $\frac{1}{2}$ c. 2   d. -2

13. Solve $T = \frac{24I}{B(n+1)}$ for I. **(LESSON 1.6)**
    a. $I = \frac{24T}{B(n+1)}$ b. $I = \frac{24B}{T(n+1)}$
    c. $I = \frac{T(n+1)}{24B}$ d. $I = \frac{TB(n+1)}{24}$

14. Graph the equation $y = -5x - 12$. **(LESSON 1.1)**

15. Does the information in the table below represent a linear relationship between x and y? Explain your response. **(LESSON 1.1)**

x	0	1	2	3
y	13	17	21	25

16. Find the equation of the line containing the points $(-3, 6)$ and $(-5, 8)$. **(LESSON 1.3)**

17. Write the equation in slope-intercept form for the line that contains the point $(5, -8)$ and is perpendicular to the graph of $y = \frac{1}{3}x - 4$. **(LESSON 1.3)**

18. Write an equation in slope-intercept form for the line that contains the points $(2, -4)$ and $(3, -1)$. **(LESSON 1.3)**

ANATOMY The following table lists the heights and weights for 10 randomly selected young adult males with medium frames. The heights are in inches, and the weights are in pounds. **(LESSON 1.5)**

Heights, x	67	66	70	67	67	68	69	66	70	71
Weights, y	146	145	157	148	145	149	151	141	154	159

19. Create a scatter plot for this data. Is the correlation positive, negative, or none?

20. Find the correlation coefficient, r.

21. Graph the least-squares line with the scatter plot. Predict the weight (to the nearest pound) of a young adult male selected at random from this group who is 63 inches tall.

22. Solve and graph the inequality $5x - 6(x + 9) < 1$. **(LESSON 1.7)**

23. Solve $|2 + 3x| \geq 14$. **(LESSON 1.8)**

FREE RESPONSE GRID The following questions may be answered by using a free-response grid such as that commonly used by standardized-test services.

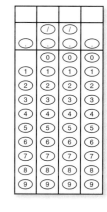

24. Find the slope of the line containing $(11, -3)$ and $(-3, 10)$. **(LESSON 1.2)**

25. Find the y-intercept of the graph of $3x - 5y = 2$. **(LESSON 1.2)**

26. Find the slope of the graph of $3x - 5y = 2$. **(LESSON 1.2)**

GEOMETRY The perimeter, p, of a square varies directly as the length, l, of a side. **(LESSON 1.4)**

27. What is the constant of variation that relates the perimeter to the length of a side?

28. If a square has a side length of 3.5 centimeters, how many centimeters long is its perimeter?

Keystroke Guide for Chapter 1

Essential keystroke sequences (using the model TI-82 or TI-83 graphics calculator) are presented below for all Activities and Examples found in this chapter that require or recommend the use of a graphics calculator.

internetconnect

HRW Keystrokes for other models of graphics calculators are found on the HRW Web site.

LESSON 1.1

E X A M P L E **①** Graph $y = 150x + 250$, and find the value of y when $x = 25$.

Page 5

Use viewing window [0, 30] by [−500, 5000].

Graph the equation:

| Y= | 150 | X,T,Θ,n | + | 250 | GRAPH |

Evaluate for $x = 25$:

| 2nd | TRACE | 1:value | ENTER | $(x =)$ 25 | ENTER |

(CALC above TRACE)

E X A M P L E **②** Graph $y = \frac{2}{3}x - 1$, and verify that $(0, -1)$ and $(3, 1)$ are on the line.

Page 6

Use viewing window [−4, 4] by [−3, 3].

(3, 1)

(0, −1)

Graph the equation:

| Y= | (| 2 | ÷ | 3 |) | X,T,Θ,n | − | 1 | GRAPH |

Evaluate for $x = 0$ and $x = 3$:
Use a keystroke sequence similar to that used in Example 1.

LESSON 1.2

Activity
Page 13

Graph each pair of equations in Step 1.

Use the standard viewing window [−10, 10] by [−10, 10]. Use a keystroke sequence similar to that used in Example 2 of Lesson 1.1.

LESSON 1.3

Activity
Page 23

For Steps 1 and 3, graph the given equations on the same screen.

Use viewing window [−3, 3] by [−3, 3].

Use a keystroke sequence similar to that used in Example 1 of Lesson 1.1.

Use keystrokes ZOOM 5:ZSquare ENTER to obtain a square viewing window.

E X A M P L E S **4** and **5** For Example 4, graph $y = -2x + 4$ and $y = -2x + 1$ on the same
Page 24   screen.

Use viewing window [–6, 10] by [–6, 10].

[Y=]   [(–)] 2 [X,T,θ,n]   [+] 4 [ENTER] (Y2=) [(–)] 2 [X,T,θ,n]   [+] 1 [GRAPH]

For Example 5, use viewing window [–6, 10] by [–6, 10].

Use a keystroke sequence similar to that used in Example 2 of Lesson 1.1.
Use keystrokes [ZOOM] [5:ZSquare] [ENTER] to obtain a square viewing window.

LESSON 1.4

E X A M P L E **2** Graph $y = \frac{1}{5}x$, and verify that the point (35, 7) is on the line.
Page 30

Use viewing window [0, 50] by [–4, 25].

Graph the equation:

[Y=]   [( ] 1 [÷] 5 [ )] [X,T,θ,n] [GRAPH]

Evaluate for $x = 35$:

Use a keystroke sequence similar to that used in Example 1 of Lesson 1.1.

E X A M P L E **3** Graph the equation $y = 0.38x$, and confirm that an x-value of 24.3
Page 32   corresponds to a y-value of about 9.2 kilograms.

Use viewing window [0, 30] by [0, 15].

To graph the equation and evaluate for $x = 24.3$, use a keystroke sequence
similar to that used in Example 1 of Lesson 1.1.

LESSON 1.5

Activity
Page 37

> First clear old data
> and equations.

For Step 1, create a scatter plot of the data.

Use viewing window [0, 10] by [100, 200].

Enter the data:

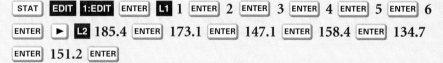

[STAT] [EDIT] [1:EDIT] [ENTER] [L1] 1 [ENTER] 2 [ENTER] 3 [ENTER] 4 [ENTER] 5 [ENTER] 6
[ENTER] [►] [L2] 185.4 [ENTER] 173.1 [ENTER] 147.1 [ENTER] 158.4 [ENTER] 134.7
[ENTER] 151.2 [ENTER]

Create a scatter plot:

[2nd] [Y=] STAT PLOT [STAT PLOTS] [1:Plot 1] [ENTER] [On] [ENTER] [▼] (Type:) [...] [ENTER]
[▼] (Xlist:) [2nd] [L1] [1] [▼] (Ylist:) [2nd] [L2] [2] [▼] (Mark:) [◻]
⇑ TI-82: [L1] [ENTER]   ⇑ TI-82: [L2] [ENTER]

[ENTER] [GRAPH]

EXAMPLE ❶

Page 38

Create a scatter plot for the data. Then graph the least-squares line.

Use viewing window [−1, 11] by [−10, 24].

Create a scatter plot:

Use a keystroke sequence similar to that in the Activity for this lesson.

Graph the least-squares line:

| STAT | | CALC | | 4:LinReg(ax+b) | | ENTER | | Y= |

⇑ TI-82: 5:LinReg(ax+b)

| VARS | | VARS | | 5:Statistics | | ENTER | | EQ | | 1:RegEQ | | ENTER | | GRAPH |

⇑ TI-82: 7:RegEQ

EXAMPLE ❷

Page 39

Create a scatter plot for the data, graph the least-squares line, and find the *y*-value that corresponds to *x* = 40.

Use viewing window [0, 100] by [0, 24].

Create a scatter plot, and graph the least-squares line:

Use a keystroke sequence similar to that in the Activity for this lesson and in Example 1 above.

Evaluate for *x* = 40:

| 2nd | | CALC TRACE | | 1: value | | ENTER | (X=) **40** | ENTER |

LESSON 1.6

Activity

Page 47

For Step 2, graph $y = x + 3$ and $y = 9 − 2x$ on the same screen. Find the value of *x* for which $y = x + 3$ and $y = 9 − 2x$ are equal.

Use the friendly viewing window [−4.7, 4.7] by [−10, 10].

| Y= | | X,T,θ,n | | + | **3** | ENTER | (Y2=) **9** | − | **2** | X,T,θ,n | GRAPH |

Press TRACE and move the cursor toward the point of intersection.

Use ▲ and ▼ to move the cursor from one line to the other.

EXAMPLE ❸

Page 47

Graph $y = 3.24x − 4.09$ and $y = −0.72x + 3.65$ on the same screen, and find any points of intersection.

Use viewing window [−5, 5] by [−5, 5].

Graph the equations:

Use a keystroke sequence similar to that in the Activity for this lesson.

Find any points of intersection:

Move your cursor as indicated.

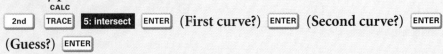

| 2nd | | CALC TRACE | | 5: intersect | | ENTER | (**First curve?**) | ENTER | (**Second curve?**) | ENTER |

(**Guess?**) | ENTER |

LESSON 1.7

Activity
Page 56

For Step 2, graph $y = 2x - 3$ and $y = 3$ on the same screen.

Use the friendly viewing window $[-4.7, 4.7]$ by $[-5, 5]$. Use a keystroke sequence similar to that in the Activity for Lesson 1.6.

LESSON 1.8

Activity
Page 63

For Step 1, graph $y = |x|$ and $y = 2x - 2$, and find any points of intersection.

Use viewing window $[-5, 5]$ by $[-5, 5]$.

Graph the equations:

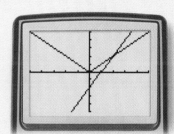

Find the point of intersection:
Use a keystroke sequence similar to that in
Example 3 of Lesson 1.6.

EXAMPLES ① and ② Graph the two equations on the same screen, and find any
Pages 63 and 64 points of intersection.

For Example 1, use viewing window $[-7, 3]$ by $[-1, 5]$.
For Example 2, use viewing window $[-3, 7]$ by $[-3, 7]$.

Use a keystroke sequence similar to that in the Activity for this lesson.

EXAMPLES ③ and ④ For Examples 3 and 4, graph $y = |5 - 3x|$ and $y = 9$ on the same
Page 65 screen, and find any points of intersection.

Use viewing window $[-11, 17]$ by $[-3, 15]$.

Use a keystroke sequence similar to that in
the Activity for this lesson.

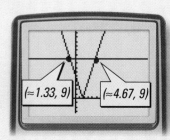

Numbers and Functions

FUNCTIONS ARE USED IN THE REAL WORLD to quantify trends and relationships between two variables. For example, the relationship between the *speed* at which an amusement park ride rotates and the *force* that holds riders in their seat can be described by a function.

Greetings

About the Chapter Project

Real-world situations are often very complex, with changing or unknown factors. Mathematical models can be used to represent such real-world situations and to predict probable outcomes. In the Chapter Project, *Space Trash,* you will use functions to model data related to the growing problem of space debris orbiting the Earth.

After completing the Chapter Project, you will be able to do the following:

- Use a table to represent the relationship between time in years and the number of space debris objects, and show that an appropriate function models this relationship.

- Find and discuss models for the accumulation of space debris.

- Determine the piecewise function that describes the relationship between altitude and number of orbital debris objects.

About the Portfolio Activities

Throughout the chapter, you will be given opportunities to complete Portfolio Activities that are designed to support your work on the Chapter Project.

- Finding the projected number of space debris objects at the end of each year through the year 2010 is included in the Portfolio Activity on page 93.

- Using exponents to project the number of space debris objects in a given year is included in the Portfolio Activity on page 101.

- Comparing regression models for the space debris data is included in the Portfolio Activity on page 110.

- Operating on function models is included in the Portfolio Activity on page 117.

- Using piecewise functions to model trends that change over time is included in the Portfolio Activity on page 132.

Operations With Numbers

Objectives

- Identify and use Properties of Real Numbers.

- Evaluate expressions by using the order of operations.

APPLICATION

METEOROLOGY

Why In everyday life, people use many different types of numbers. A weather reporter, for example, will use integers to give temperature measurements, and rational numbers to give barometric pressure readings.

A typical weather report might say that the temperature is 82°F, which is an integer, and that the barometric pressure is 29.98 inches of mercury, which is a positive rational number written as a decimal. These, as well as other types of numbers, typically belong to more than one *number set*.

Number Sets

Natural numbers	1, 2, 3, . . .
Whole numbers	0, 1, 2, 3, . . .
Integers	. . . , −3, −2, −1, 0, 1, 2, 3, . . .
Rational numbers	$\frac{p}{q}$, where p and q are integers and $q \neq 0$
Irrational numbers	numbers whose decimal part does not terminate or repeat
Real numbers	all rational and all irrational numbers

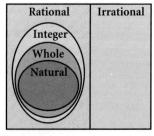

The *Venn diagram* at left shows the relationship between the various number sets. An important fact about rational numbers is stated in the following theorem, which will help you differentiate between rational and irrational numbers:

Every rational number can be written as a terminating or repeating decimal. Every terminating or repeating decimal represents a rational number.

When a repeating decimal is written, a bar is used to indicate the digit or digits that repeat. For example, $0.\overline{3}$ represents the repeating rational number $0.333333\ldots$

EXAMPLE **1** Classify each number in as many ways as possible.

a. −2.77   **b.** 178,000   **c.** 12.020002000002 . . .

● **SOLUTION**

a. Since −2.77 is a terminating decimal, it is a rational and a real number.
b. Since 178,000 is positive and has no decimal part, it is a natural number, a whole number, an integer, a rational number, and a real number.
c. The pattern of digits in the decimal part of 12.020002000002 . . . suggests that the decimal part does not terminate and does not repeat. This number is irrational and real.

Every real number corresponds to a point on the real-number line. Conversely, for every point on the number line, you can assign a real-number coordinate.

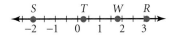

On the number line at left, point S corresponds to −2, point T corresponds to 0.5, point W corresponds to $1\frac{2}{3}$, and point R corresponds to the irrational number π, which is about 3.14.

Properties of Real Numbers

Properties for the fundamental operations of addition and multiplication with real numbers are listed below. Addition and multiplication are linked by the *Distributive Property*.

Properties of Addition and Multiplication

For all real numbers a, b, and c:

	Addition	Multiplication
Closure	$a + b$ is a real number.	ab is a real number.
Commutative	$a + b = b + a$	$ab = ba$
Associative	$(a + b) + c = a + (b + c)$	$(ab)c = a(bc)$
Identity	There is a number 0 such that $a + 0 = a$ and $0 + a = a$.	There is a number 1 such that $1 \cdot a = a$ and $a \cdot 1 = a$.
Inverse	For every real number a, there is a real number $-a$ such that $a + (-a) = 0$.	For every nonzero real number a, there is a real number $\frac{1}{a}$ such that $a\left(\frac{1}{a}\right) = 1$.

The Distributive Property

For all real numbers a, b, and c:

$$a(b + c) = ab + ac \text{ and } (b + c)a = ba + ca$$

Example 2 shows you how to use Properties of Real Numbers to rewrite an expression.

E X A M P L E ② **Write and justify each step in the simplification of $(z + x)(2 + w)$.**

● **SOLUTION**

$$
\begin{aligned}
(z + x)(2 + w) &= (z + x)(2) + (z + x)(w) \quad && \textit{Use the Distributive Property.} \\
&= z \cdot 2 + x \cdot 2 + zw + xw \quad && \textit{Use the Distributive Property.} \\
&= 2z + 2x + wz + wx \quad && \textit{Use the Commutative Property.}
\end{aligned}
$$

TRY THIS   Write and justify each step in the simplification of $(a + b)(c - d)$.

E X A M P L E ③ When you purchase an item costing c dollars in a state that has a sales tax of 5%, the total cost, T, is given by $T = c + 0.05c$.

APPLICATION

TAXES

Show that $T = 1.05c$. Justify each step.

● **SOLUTION**

$$
\begin{aligned}
T &= c + 0.05c \\
T &= 1c + 0.05c \quad && \textit{Use the Identity Property.} \\
T &= (1 + 0.05)c \quad && \textit{Use the Distributive Property.} \\
T &= 1.05c \quad && \textit{Add.}
\end{aligned}
$$

TRY THIS   If the sales tax is 6%, then $T = c + 0.06c$. Show that $T = 1.06c$. Justify each step.

CRITICAL THINKING   When you purchase an item costing c dollars in a state that has a sales tax of r%, show that $T = \left(1 + \frac{r}{100}\right)c$. Justify each step.

Order of Operations

If an expression involves only numbers and operations, you can evaluate the expression by using the *order of operations*.

Order of Operations

1. Perform operations within the innermost grouping symbols according to Steps 2–4 below.
2. Perform operations indicated by exponents (powers).
3. Perform multiplication and division in order from left to right.
4. Perform addition and subtraction in order from left to right.

Example 4 shows you how to evaluate an expression by using the order of operations.

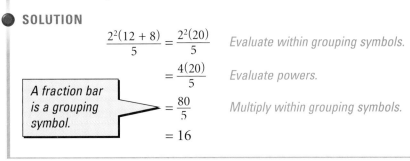

E X A M P L E ④ Evaluate $\frac{2^2(12+8)}{5}$ by using the order of operations.

● **SOLUTION**

$$\frac{2^2(12+8)}{5} = \frac{2^2(20)}{5}$$ *Evaluate within grouping symbols.*

$$= \frac{4(20)}{5}$$ *Evaluate powers.*

A fraction bar is a grouping symbol.

$$= \frac{80}{5}$$ *Multiply within grouping symbols.*

$$= 16$$

TRY THIS Evaluate $\frac{18-2\cdot 5}{15+3(-3)}$ by using the order of operations.

In the Activity below, you can explore how calculators use the order of operations.

Activity
Exploring the Order of Operations

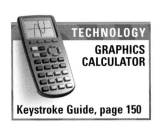

TECHNOLOGY
GRAPHICS CALCULATOR

Keystroke Guide, page 150

You will need: a scientific or graphics calculator

1. Evaluate $\frac{12+8}{5}$ on a calculator as follows:
   a. without any parentheses for grouping
   $$12 \boxed{+} 8 \boxed{\div} 5$$
   b. with parentheses to group the numerator
   $$\boxed{(}\, 12 \boxed{+} 8 \boxed{)} \boxed{\div} 5$$

CHECKPOINT ✔ 2. Explain why your results in parts **a** and **b** in Step 1 are not equal. Which result is correct?

3. The slope of the line containing the points (2, 3) and (5, 8) is $\frac{8-3}{5-2}$. Evaluate this expression on a calculator as follows:
   a. without any parentheses for grouping
   $$8 \boxed{-} 3 \boxed{\div} 5 \boxed{-} 2$$
   b. with parentheses to group the numerator but not the denominator
   $$\boxed{(}\, 8 \boxed{-} 3 \boxed{)} \boxed{\div} 5 \boxed{-} 2$$
   c. with parentheses to group the numerator and the denominator
   $$\boxed{(}\, 8 \boxed{-} 3 \boxed{)} \boxed{\div} \boxed{(} 5 \boxed{-} 2 \boxed{)}$$

CHECKPOINT ✔ 4. Discuss why there are three different results to Step 3. Which result is correct?

When you use a calculator to evaluate expressions such as $\frac{9-4}{7-5}$, you need to enclose the numerator and the denominator in separate sets of parentheses.

CHECKPOINT ✔ What keystrokes will give the correct answer for $\frac{9-4}{7-5}$?

Exercises

Communicate

1. Discuss two times in the past week when you added numbers. What type of numbers did you add? Can you think of occasions when you used any of the other types of numbers?

APPLICATIONS

2. **ETYMOLOGY** Explain what the Commutative Properties of Addition and Multiplication are. Why is the word *commutative* appropriate for these properties?

3. **ETYMOLOGY** Explain what the Associative Properties of Addition and Multiplication are. Why is the word *associative* appropriate for this property?

Guided Skills Practice

4. Classify $\frac{3}{2}$ and $-2.101001000\ldots$ in as many ways as possible. *(EXAMPLE 1)*

Write and justify each step in the simplification of each expression.
(EXAMPLE 2)

5. $2(b + d)$ 6. $-3a + 3a$ 7. $\frac{3(8 + 2)}{2}$

8. $\frac{7 - 1}{5 - 2}$ 9. $\frac{1}{4}(4 \cdot 5)$ 10. $-5(4t^2)$

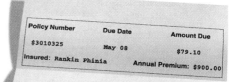

APPLICATION

11. **BUSINESS** A monthly automotive insurance payment, m, is given by $m = \frac{p}{12} + \frac{0.06p}{12}$, where p is the yearly premium and $0.06p$ represents the annual processing fee. Show that $m = \frac{1.06p}{12}$. Justify each step. *(EXAMPLE 3)*

Evaluate each expression by using the order of operations. *(EXAMPLE 4)*

12. $5^2 + 8 \div 4 - 2$ 13. $(7 - 3^2)2$

14. $\frac{5 \cdot 6 \div 3 \cdot 7}{12}$ 15. $2[14 - 3(6 - 1)^2]$

An insurance adjuster evaluates the damage to a car after an accident.

Practice and Apply

Classify each number in as many ways as possible.

16. -23 17. -5.1 18. $\sqrt{3}$ 19. $\sqrt{2}$

20. $\frac{2}{3}$ 21. $\frac{3}{9}$ 22. $-0.\overline{85}$ 23. $-1.0\overline{63}$

24. $-\frac{5}{7}$ 25. $\sqrt{25}$ 26. $\frac{\sqrt{36}}{2}$ 27. 1

28. 0 29. $-\pi$ 30. $5.010010001\ldots$ 31. $\sqrt{28}$

Graph each pair of numbers on a number line.

32. -3 and -2.5 33. -1.5 and -4 34. $\frac{13}{2}$ and 7

35. $4\frac{3}{8}$ and 2 36. $-3.\overline{6}$ and -4 37. $\sqrt{7}$ and 3

State the property that is illustrated in each statement. All variables represent real numbers.

38. $v(3t) = (3t)v$

39. $(25x)y = 25(xy)$

40. $4x + 13y = 13y + 4x$

41. $2.3 + x = x + 2.3$

42. $(2 + 3) + 5 = 2 + (3 + 5)$

43. $(3 + a) + b = 3 + (a + b)$

44. $x\left(\dfrac{1}{x}\right) = 1$, where $x \neq 0$

45. $\dfrac{x}{3} \cdot \dfrac{3}{x} = 1$, where $x \neq 0$

46. $-7 + 7 = 0$

47. $0 = 2x + (-2x)$

48. $1 \cdot (3x) = 3x$

49. $63 \cdot 1 = 63$

50. $5x + 0 = -5x$

51. $x + y = 0 + x + y$

52. $m(x^2 + x) = mx^2 + mx$

53. $2(3 - y) = 2 \cdot 3 - 2y$

54. $4yw = 4wy$

55. $5(127) = 127(5)$

Evaluate each expression by using the order of operations.

56. $3 \cdot 2^2 + 3$

57. $6 \div 3 \cdot 2$

58. $2^2(2 + 3) + 5$

59. $6 \div (3 - 1) \cdot 5$

60. $-3 \cdot 5^2 + 16$

61. $5(2 - 3)^2$

62. $(3 - 2) + (5 - 4) - 2$

63. $30 - 3 \times 2 + 6 \div 3$

64. $16 \div 2 \times 6 - 1$

65. $(2^2 + 1) + 4 \div 2$

66. $6 \div 3 - (10 - 3^2)$

67. $2^{(3-1)} + (3 - 1)$

68. $3 \cdot 4 - 2^{(4-1)}$

69. $\dfrac{8 - 2}{3} + (2 + 1)$

70. $2 \cdot 4 + \dfrac{14}{5 + 2}$

71. Complete the following investigation:
   a. Count the number of items in your home that display numbers.
   b. What types of numbers are represented?
   c. Name two examples of integers and two examples of rational numbers that you found.

72. Can a number be both rational and irrational? Explain your reasoning.

73. STATISTICS While trying to find the average of 8, 10, 14, and 16, Ron entered 8 $\boxed{+}$ 10 $\boxed{+}$ 14 $\boxed{+}$ 16 $\boxed{\div}$ 4 $\boxed{=}$ into a calculator and got 36 for an answer.
   a. Did Ron get the correct average of 8, 10, 14, and 16? Explain.
   b. What keystrokes should Ron have used?

74. CULTURAL CONNECTION: ASIA Ancient Babylonians used rational numbers as approximations of irrational numbers. For example, the Babylonians knew that the diagonal of a square was $\sqrt{2}$ times the length of a side. For the value of $\sqrt{2}$, the Babylonians used 1.4142. They thought this value was close enough for their practical purposes.

A Babylonian cuneiform tablet showing the calculation of areas

Use a calculator for the following exercises:
   a. Show that $\sqrt{2}$ does not equal exactly 1.4142.
   b. Find $\sqrt{2}$ on your calculator. Write down the result. Enter this number in your calculator, and square it. Is the result equal to 2? Explain why or why not.

75. BUSINESS A small business contributes $224 per month per worker for health insurance. This amount is half of the worker's monthly insurance premium and can be represented by $\frac{0.5p}{12} = 224$, where p is the yearly premium. Solve for p and justify each step.

76. CURRENT EVENTS Use your local newspaper to answer the following questions:
  a. Find three articles that include numerical data.
  b. Summarize each article. Include the reason that the article depends on numbers and the possible effect that each article may have on daily life.
  c. What types of numbers were included in each article? What units, if any, were used with the numbers?

DEMOGRAPHICS Read the article below and answer the questions that follow.

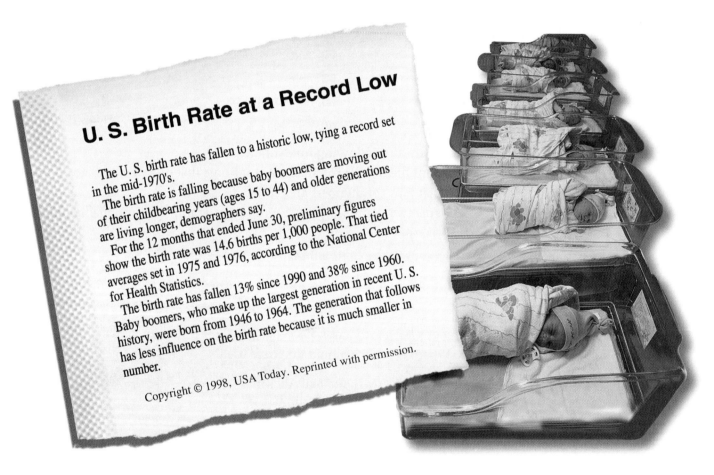

U. S. Birth Rate at a Record Low

The U. S. birth rate has fallen to a historic low, tying a record set in the mid-1970's.

The birth rate is falling because baby boomers are moving out of their childbearing years (ages 15 to 44) and older generations are living longer, demographers say.

For the 12 months that ended June 30, preliminary figures show the birth rate was 14.6 births per 1,000 people. That tied averages set in 1975 and 1976, according to the National Center for Health Statistics.

The birth rate has fallen 13% since 1990 and 38% since 1960. Baby boomers, who make up the largest generation in recent U. S. history, were born from 1946 to 1964. The generation that follows has less influence on the birth rate because it is much smaller in number.

Copyright © 1998, USA Today. Reprinted with permission.

77. Explain how rates such as 14.6 per 1000 can be considered rational numbers.

78. Explain how percents such as 13% can be considered rational numbers.

79. How much had the birth rate fallen since 1990 at the time of this article? Write this percent as a fraction, and classify it in as many ways as possible.

80. For the 12 months that ended June 30, 1998, what was the birth rate? Write this rate as a fraction, and classify it in as many ways as possible.

 ## Look Back

Find the slope of each line. *(LESSON 1.2)*

81. $y = -3x$ **82.** $y = 2x - 1$ **83.** $y = \dfrac{3x - 1}{4}$

84. $y = -\dfrac{x}{2} + 1$ **85.** $4y = 3x + 21$ **86.** $5x - 2y = 6$

Solve each equation. *(LESSON 1.6)*

87. $3(x - 5) = 4$ **88.** $-\dfrac{x}{3} + 9 = 2$

89. $-3x - 5 = x + 12$ **90.** $\dfrac{1}{5}x - 4 = 3(x - 5)$

Solve each absolute-value equation or inequality. Graph the solution on a number line. *(LESSON 1.8)*

91. $|5x| = 12$ **92.** $\left|\dfrac{4}{5}x\right| = 12$

93. $|4x + 2| > x + 3$ **94.** $|4x + 2| > 5x + 5$

 ## Look Beyond

95. The solutions to equations illustrate the need for different kinds of numbers. The equation $x + 7 = 5$ has the solution $x = -2$, which is a negative number, even though only nonnegative numbers appear in the equation. Similarly, only integers appear in the equation $2x = 5$, but the solution is $x = 2.5$, which is not an integer.

  a. Find another example of an equation that includes only nonnegative numbers and that has a negative-number solution.

  b. Find another example of an equation that includes only integers and that has a non-integer solution.

SPACE SCIENCE Scientists catalog only the space debris objects large enough to be repeatedly tracked by ground-based radar. At the end of 1993, the Air Force Space Command cataloged a total of 7000 debris objects in Earth orbit. At that time, it was projected that the number of cataloged space debris objects would grow at a rate of 3% per year.

Start with 7000 objects, the total number of space debris objects tracked at the end of 1993.

Using the annual growth rate of 3% (1.03 × the previous year's total), find the projected number of space debris objects at the end of each successive year through the year 2010. Round all results to the nearest whole number. Record your results in a table. Throughout the Portfolio Activities in this chapter, this will be your **Space Debris Table.**

2.2

Properties of Exponents

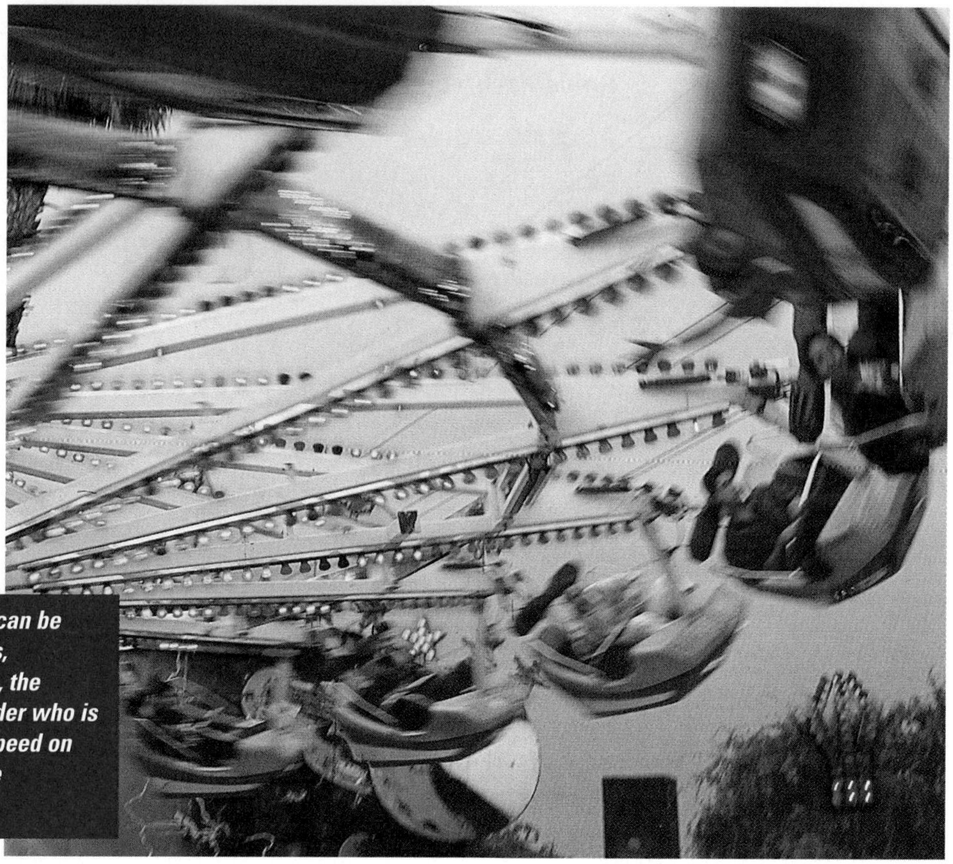

Objectives

- Evaluate expressions involving exponents.
- Simplify expressions involving exponents.

Why *Exponential expressions can be found in a wide variety of fields, including physics. For example, the centripetal acceleration of a rider who is traveling in a circle at a high speed on an amusement park ride can be described by using exponents.*

APPLICATION
PHYSICS

In an amusement park ride, a compartment with a rider travels in a circle at a high speed. The centripetal acceleration acting on the rider can be calculated by using the equation below. *You will use this equation in Example 1.*

$A_c = 4\pi^2 rT^{-2}$, where
- A_c represents the centripetal acceleration in feet per second squared
- r represents the radius of the circle in feet
- T represents the time for a full rotation in seconds

Recall that the expression a^n is called a **power** of a. In the expression, a is called the **base** and n is called the **exponent**.

Definition of Integer Exponents

Let a be a real number.

If n is a natural number, then $a^n = a \times a \times a \times \cdots \times a$, n times.

If a is nonzero, then $a^0 = 1$.

If n is a natural number, then $a^{-n} = \frac{1}{a^n}$.

In the expression a^0, a must be nonzero because 0^0 is undefined.

Example 1 shows how you can use the definition $a^{-n} = \frac{1}{a^n}$.

EXAMPLE **1** Refer to the equation for centripetal acceleration given at the beginning of the lesson.

Find the centripetal acceleration in feet per second squared of a rider who makes one rotation in 2 seconds and whose radius of rotation is 6 feet.

SOLUTION

Evaluate $A_c = 4\pi^2 r T^{-2}$ for $T = 2$ and $r = 6$.

$$A_c = 4\pi^2 r T^{-2}$$
$$= 4\pi^2(6)(2)^{-2}$$
$$= \frac{24\pi^2}{2^2} \qquad \textit{Use } a^{-n} = \frac{1}{a^n}.$$
$$= 6\pi^2 \approx 59.2$$

The centripetal acceleration is about 59 feet per second squared.

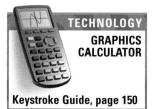

TECHNOLOGY
GRAPHICS CALCULATOR

Keystroke Guide, page 150

CHECK

4π²·6·(2^ 2)
              59.21762641

TRY THIS Find the centripetal acceleration of a rider that makes one rotation in 5 seconds and whose radius of rotation is 6 feet.

Exploring Properties of Exponents

You will need: no special materials

1. Rewrite $a^3 \cdot a^5$ by writing out all of the factors of a, counting them, and simplifying them as a power with a single exponent. What operation could you perform on the exponents in $a^3 \cdot a^5$ to obtain an equivalent expression with a single exponent?

2. Rewrite $(a^3)^5$ by writing out five sets of three factors of a, counting the factors of a, and simplifying them as a power with a single exponent. What operation could you perform on the exponents in $(a^3)^5$ to obtain an equivalent expression with a single exponent?

CHECKPOINT ✔ 3. Explain how to simplify $(a^7 \cdot a^3)^2$ by using addition and multiplication.

The results of the Activity suggest some *Properties of Exponents*.

Properties of Exponents

Let a and b be nonzero real numbers. Let m and n be integers.

Product of Powers	$(a)^m(a)^n = a^{m+n}$
Quotient of Powers	$\frac{a^m}{a^n} = a^{m-n}$
Power of a Power	$(a^m)^n = a^{mn}$
Power of a Product	$(ab)^n = a^n b^n$
Power of a Quotient	$\left(\frac{a}{b}\right)^n = \frac{a^n}{b^n}$

In this lesson, you may assume that variables with negative exponents represent nonzero numbers.

EXAMPLE ② Simplify $3x^2y^{-2}(-2x^3y^{-4})$. **Write your answer with positive exponents only.**

● **SOLUTION**

$$3x^2y^{-2}(-2x^3y^{-4}) = (3)(-2)x^2x^3y^{-2}y^{-4} \qquad \textit{Use the Commutative Property.}$$

$$= (3)(-2)x^{(2+3)}y^{[-2+(-4)]} \qquad \textit{Use the Product of Powers Property.}$$

$$= -6x^5y^{-6} \qquad \textit{Simplify.}$$

$$= -\frac{6x^5}{y^6} \qquad \textit{Use } a^{-n} = \frac{1}{a^n}.$$

TRY THIS Simplify $2z(3x^2)(5z^{-3})$. Write your answer with positive exponents only.

PROBLEM SOLVING **Look for a pattern.** Examine what happens to powers with a *negative* base:

$$(-2)^2 = (-2)(-2) = 4$$
$$(-2)^3 = (-2)(-2)(-2) = -8$$
$$(-2)^4 = (-2)(-2)(-2)(-2) = 16$$
$$(-2)^5 = (-2)(-2)(-2)(-2)(-2) = -32$$

When the exponent of a negative base is *even*, the result is positive. When the exponent of a negative base is *odd*, the result is negative.

When simplifying an expression, be careful not to confuse the results of a negative base with the results of a negative exponent.

Even Exponent	**Odd Exponent**
$(-2x)^{-2}$	$(-2x)^{-3}$
$= \dfrac{1}{(-2x)^2}$	$= \dfrac{1}{(-2x)^3}$
$= \dfrac{1}{(-2)^2x^2}$	$= \dfrac{1}{(-2)^3x^3}$
$= \dfrac{1}{4x^2}$	$= \dfrac{1}{-8x^3}$, or $-\dfrac{1}{8x^3}$

EXAMPLE ③ Simplify $\left(\dfrac{-y^7}{2z^{12}y^3}\right)^4$. **Write your answer with positive exponents only.**

● **SOLUTION**

$$\left(\frac{-y^7}{2z^{12}y^3}\right)^4 = \frac{(-y^7)^4}{(2z^{12}y^3)^4} \qquad \textit{Use the Power of a Quotient Property.}$$

$$= \frac{y^{28}}{16z^{48}y^{12}} \qquad \textit{Use the Power of a Power Property.}$$

$$= \frac{y^{28-12}}{16z^{48}} \qquad \textit{Use the Quotient of Powers Property.}$$

$$= \frac{y^{16}}{16z^{48}}$$

TRY THIS Simplify $\left(\dfrac{-3b^2c^5}{c^2b^7}\right)^3$. Write your answer with positive exponents only.

CRITICAL THINKING Find a, b, and c such that $(x^{-2}y^3z^2)(y^az^bx^c) = x^{-3}y^4$ for all nonzero values of x, y, and z.

Rational Exponents

An expression with rational exponents can be represented in an equivalent form that involves the radical symbol, $\sqrt{}$.

For example, $a^{\frac{1}{3}}$ equals $\sqrt[3]{a}$ because when $a^{\frac{1}{3}}$ is cubed, the result is a, as shown at right. This is the definition of $\sqrt[3]{a}$.

$$\left(a^{\frac{1}{3}}\right)^3 = a^{\frac{1}{3} \cdot 3} = a$$

This relationship is true for all rational exponents. An expression with an exponent of $\frac{2}{3}$ is rewritten at right.

$$a^{\frac{2}{3}} = a^{\frac{1}{3} \cdot 2} = \left(a^{\frac{1}{3}}\right)^2 = \left(\sqrt[3]{a}\right)^2$$

Definition of Rational Exponents

For all positive real numbers a:

If n is a nonzero integer, then $a^{\frac{1}{n}} = \sqrt[n]{a}$.

If m and n are integers and $n \neq 0$, then $a^{\frac{m}{n}} = \left(a^{\frac{1}{n}}\right)^m = \left(\sqrt[n]{a}\right)^m = \sqrt[n]{a^m}$.

Example 4 shows how you can use the definition of rational exponents.

E X A M P L E **4** Evaluate each expression.

   a. $16^{\frac{1}{4}}$ **b.** $27^{\frac{4}{3}}$

SOLUTION

a. $16^{\frac{1}{4}} = (2^4)^{\frac{1}{4}}$ **b.** $27^{\frac{4}{3}} = (3^3)^{\frac{4}{3}}$

    $= 2^{4 \cdot \frac{1}{4}}$ $= 3^{3 \cdot \frac{4}{3}}$

    $= 2^1 = 2$ $= 3^4 = 81$

CHECK   CHECK

TECHNOLOGY
GRAPHICS CALCULATOR

Keystroke Guide, page 150

TRY THIS Evaluate $64^{\frac{1}{3}}$ and $36^{\frac{3}{2}}$.

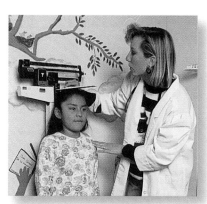

APPLICATION
MEDICINE

The formula below is used to estimate a person's surface area based on his or her weight and height. This formula is used to calculate dosages for certain medications.

$$S = 0.007184 \times W^{0.425} \times H^{0.725},$$

where $\begin{cases} S \text{ is the surface area in square meters} \\ W \text{ is the weight in kilograms} \\ H \text{ is the height in centimeters} \end{cases}$

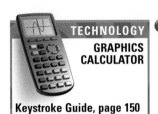

E X A M P L E **5** Estimate to the nearest tenth of a square meter the surface area of a person who stands 152.5 centimeters tall and weighs 57.2 kilograms.

TECHNOLOGY
GRAPHICS CALCULATOR

Keystroke Guide, page 150

● **SOLUTION**

Evaluate $S = 0.007184 \times W^{0.425} \times H^{0.725}$ for $W = 57.2$ and $H = 152.5$.

$$S = 0.007184 \times W^{0.425} \times H^{0.725}$$
$$= 0.007184 \times (57.2)^{0.425} \times (152.5)^{0.725}$$
$$\approx 1.54$$

The estimated surface area is about 1.5 square meters.

```
.007184*57.2^.42
5*152.5^.725
        1.535077381
```

TRY THIS Estimate to the nearest tenth of a square meter the surface area of a person who stands 180 centimeters tall and weighs 62.3 kilograms.

Exercises

● *Communicate*

1. Explain why x^5x^3 and $(x^5)^3$ are not equivalent expressions.

2. Explain why ax^2 and $(ax)^2$ are not equivalent expressions.

3. Describe how to evaluate 5^{-2}.

4. Describe how to evaluate $4^{\frac{3}{2}}$ by using the definition of rational exponents.

● *Guided Skills Practice*

APPLICATION

5. PHYSICS Find the centripetal acceleration in feet per second squared of a model airplane that makes one rotation in 1.5 seconds and whose radius of rotation is 8 feet. *(EXAMPLE 1)*

Simplify each expression, assuming that no variable equals zero. Write your answers with positive exponents only. *(EXAMPLES 2 AND 3)*

6. x^4x^2 **7.** $\dfrac{z^9}{z^3}$ **8.** $(y^3)^6$ **9.** $(a^3b^7)^4$

10. $(y^5y^{-2})^4$ **11.** $\left(\dfrac{-2x^3y}{5x^7}\right)^2$ **12.** $\left(\dfrac{a^3b^{-1}}{a^{-2}b^2}\right)^{-2}$ **13.** $\left(\dfrac{1}{x^{-1}y^3z^0}\right)^{-1}$

Evaluate each expression. *(EXAMPLE 4)*

14. $100^{\frac{1}{2}}$ **15.** $9^{\frac{3}{2}}$ **16.** $27^{\frac{1}{3}}$ **17.** $64^{\frac{2}{3}}$

APPLICATION

18. MEDICINE Estimate to the nearest hundredth of a square meter the surface area of a person who stands 167.64 centimeters tall and weighs 53.64 kilograms. *(EXAMPLE 5)*

Practice and Apply

Evaluate each expression.

19. 3^0 **20.** 9^0 **21.** $(5a)^0$ **22.** $(2^5 \cdot 2^3)^0$

23. 6^{-1} **24.** 4^{-2} **25.** $\left(\dfrac{3}{5}\right)^4$ **26.** $\left(\dfrac{4}{5}\right)^2$

27. $\left(\dfrac{1}{4}\right)^{-1}$ **28.** $\left(\dfrac{2}{5}\right)^{-2}$ **29.** $\left(-\dfrac{1}{3}\right)^{-3}$ **30.** $\left(-\dfrac{2}{3}\right)^{-3}$

31. $49^{\frac{1}{2}}$ **32.** $27^{\frac{2}{3}}$ **33.** $64^{\frac{4}{3}}$ **34.** $25^{\frac{3}{2}}$

35. $36^{\frac{6}{4}}$ **36.** $8^{\frac{2}{6}}$ **37.** $-64^{\frac{2}{3}}$ **38.** $81^{-\frac{3}{2}}$

Simplify each expression, assuming that no variable equals zero. Write your answer with positive exponents only.

39. y^5y^2 **40.** $-2z^3z^5$ **41.** $-2y^3(5xy^4)$ **42.** $6x^5 \cdot 3x^5 \cdot x^0$

43. $\dfrac{m^9}{m^5}$ **44.** $\dfrac{bb^4}{b^2}$ **45.** $\dfrac{x^2x^{-5}}{x^4}$ **46.** $\dfrac{s^5t^2}{st^{-4}}$

47. $(2x^4y)^3$ **48.** $(3st^{12})^3$ **49.** $(-5w^4v^5)^2$ **50.** $(-3x^2y^7)^3$

51. $\left(\dfrac{-2z^2}{x^3}\right)^7$ **52.** $\left(\dfrac{2b^4}{-a^2}\right)^3$ **53.** $\left(\dfrac{-2p^5q^{-4}}{q^3}\right)^3$ **54.** $\left(\dfrac{3m^2n^3}{m^{-1}}\right)^5$

55. $\left(\dfrac{3x^4}{y^{-2}}\right)^5$ **56.** $\left(\dfrac{-7y^{-2}}{-x^5}\right)^6$ **57.** $\left(\dfrac{5r^2s^{-2}}{s^{-3}}\right)^{-1}$ **58.** $\left(\dfrac{x^{-2}y}{y^{-1}}\right)^{-3}$

Simplify each expression, assuming that no variable equals zero. Write your answer with positive exponents only.

59. $\left(\dfrac{15xy^3}{3y^2}\right)^{-1}$ **60.** $\left[\dfrac{2x^{-3}}{(2x)^3}\right]^{-1}$ **61.** $\left(\dfrac{4a^3b^{-3}}{a^{-1}b^2}\right)^{-2}$

62. $\left(\dfrac{15a^2b^{-2}}{-3ab^{-3}}\right)^{-2}$ **63.** $(x^{-3}y^{-1})^{-1}(x^{-3}y^0)^2$ **64.** $(a^{-3}b^2)^4(-2a^3b^7)^{-3}$

65. $\left[\dfrac{(a^3b^5)^2}{a^5b^2}\right]^{-1}$ **66.** $\left(\dfrac{s^{-3}}{4t}\right)^{-3}\left(\dfrac{5t}{s^{-7}}\right)^{-2}$ **67.** $\left(\dfrac{3z}{x^{-4}}\right)^2\left(\dfrac{3x^{-12}yz^{-3}}{2xy^7}\right)^{-3}$

68. $\left[\left(\dfrac{x^5y^2}{x^{-3}y}\right)^{-2}\left(\dfrac{y^{-3}}{2x^5}\right)^3\right]^{-1}$ **69.** $\left[\dfrac{(a^{-5}b^2)^{-1}}{(-a^1b^4c^{-1})^2}\right]^{-3}$ **70.** $\left[\dfrac{(2s^{3x}t^{2y})^2}{(s^{3x}t^{-4})^{-1}}\right]^2$

Use a calculator to evaluate each expression to the nearest tenth.

71. $12^{6.05} + 8.8^{3.24}$ **72.** $3.3^{2.7} - 5^{1.9} + 0.63^{0.95}$

73. $0.005^{21.53} + 9.05^{0.034}$ **74.** $71.33^{0.44} + 478.2^{0.4}$

75. $11.7^{0.6} + 29.3^{1.23} - 6^{-2.2}$ **76.** $89^{3.5} - 5.25^{9.25} + 324^{0.05}$

CHALLENGES

77. Show that if $y \neq 0$, then $y^{a-b} = \dfrac{1}{y^{b-a}}$.

78. Show that $\dfrac{x^{-1} - y^{-1}}{x - y} = -\dfrac{1}{xy}$.

CONNECTION

79. GEOMETRY The height, h, of a right circular cone can be calculated from the equation $h = \dfrac{3}{\pi}Vr^{-2}$, where V is the volume of the cone and r is the radius of the circular base.

a. Find the height to the nearest tenth of a right circular cone whose volume is 200 cubic centimeters and whose radius is 4 centimeters.

b. Write the equation for the height of a right circular cone with positive exponents only.

80. ENGINEERING The maximum load in tons that a foundation column can withstand is represented by the equation $F_{max} = \frac{9}{4}d^4l^{-2}$, where d is the diameter of the column in inches and l is the length of the column in feet.

  a. Find the maximum load for a column that is 5 feet long and 10 inches in diameter.

  b. Write the equation $F_{max} = \frac{9}{4}d^4l^{-2}$ with positive exponents only.

Foundation columns are cylindrical weight-bearing supports for structures such as the bridge shown above.

81. PHYSICS The resistance caused by friction between the blood and vessels that carry it can be modeled by the equation $R = \frac{2}{3}lr^{-4}$, where R is the resistance, l is the length of the blood vessel, and r is the radius of the blood vessel.

  a. Find the resistance to the nearest tenth for a 0.2-meter long vessel with a 0.015-meter radius.

  b. Write the resistance equation, $R = \frac{2}{3}lr^{-4}$, with positive exponents only.

82. PHYSICS The rate at which an object emits radiant energy can be expressed as $P = 5 \times 10^{-8}\left(\frac{A}{T^{-4}}\right)$, where P is the power radiated by the object in watts, A is the surface area of the object in square meters, and T is the temperature of the object in kelvins.

  a. Write the equation $P = 5 \times 10^{-8}\left(\frac{A}{T^{-4}}\right)$ with positive exponents only.

  b. Find the power radiated by a heater with a surface area of 0.25 square meters and a temperature of 300 K.

CHEMISTRY Radioactive plutonium decays very slowly. The percent of plutonium remaining after x years can be represented by $A = 100\left(0.5^{\frac{x}{24,360}}\right)$. Find the percent of plutonium remaining after each number of years.

83. $x = 100$ **84.** $x = 500$ **85.** $x = 1000$ **86.** $x = 5000$

PHYSICS Air pressure decreases with altitude according to the formula $P = 14.7(10)^{-0.000014a}$, where P is the air pressure in pounds per square inch and a is the altitude measured in feet above sea level.

87. Find the air pressure for Denver, Colorado, where the altitude is 1 mile (5280 feet) above sea level.

88. Find the air pressure at the top of Mount Everest, where the altitude is 29,028 feet above sea level.

Mount Everest
29,028 ft

Denver
5280 ft

Sea level

 **Look Back**

Graph the solution to each compound inequality on a number line.
(LESSON 1.7)

89. $x > -3$ *and* $x < 1$ **90.** $x > -\frac{1}{4}$ *and* $x > \frac{1}{2}$

91. $x > -3$ *or* $x < 1$ **92.** $x > -\frac{1}{4}$ *or* $x > \frac{1}{2}$

Classify each number in as many ways as possible. *(LESSON 2.1)*

93. $9.373737\ldots$ **94.** $13\frac{1}{2}$

95. $5.38388388838888\ldots$ **96.** -7.9

Evaluate each expression by using the order of operations. *(LESSON 2.1)*

97. $2(3 - 1) + 6 \div 3 \div 2$ **98.** $-3(9 - 12) - 2(7 - 3) - 1$

99. $3 \cdot 5^2 - 4(5 - 8)^2 \div 3$ **100.** $(5 - 3)^{\frac{(10-8)}{(13-12)}}$

 Look Beyond

APPLICATION

101. GENEALOGY Your two parents are your first-generation ancestors, your four grandparents are your second-generation ancestors, and your eight great-grandparents are your third-generation ancestors. Make a table that represents these generations and the corresponding number of ancestors in each generation. Write an expression that represents the number of ancestors in the nth generation. (Hint: Use exponents in your expression.)

On January 22, 1997, the second-stage propellant tank of a Delta II launch vehicle landed near Georgetown, Texas, after spending nine months in Earth orbit.

SPACE SCIENCE Refer to the Space Debris Table from the Portfolio Activity on page 93.

1. For data in the table, let the years be represented by t (where $t = 0$ represents 1993) and let the total projected number of debris objects in orbit be represented by d.

Show that the data in the table can be modeled by the equation $d = 7000(1.03)^t$.

2. Use the equation in Step 1 to calculate the total projected number of debris objects in space at the end of the year 2020.

Introduction to Functions

Objectives

- Graph a relation, state its domain and range, and tell whether it is a function.

- Write a function in function notation and evaluate it.

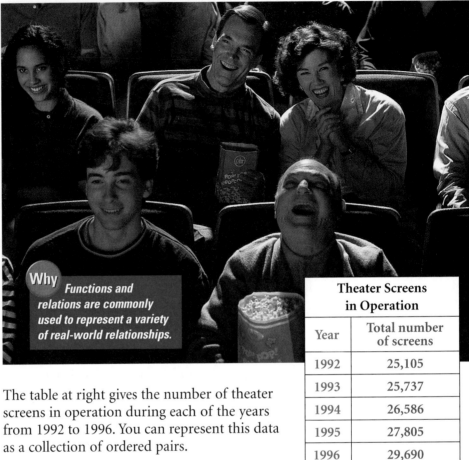

| Theater Screens in Operation ||
Year	Total number of screens
1992	25,105
1993	25,737
1994	26,586
1995	27,805
1996	29,690

[*Source: Motion Picture Association of America, Inc.*]

The table at right gives the number of theater screens in operation during each of the years from 1992 to 1996. You can represent this data as a collection of ordered pairs.

{(**1992, 25,105**), (**1993, 25,737**), (**1994, 26,586**), (**1995, 27,805**), (**1996, 29,690**)}

Notice that for each year, there is exactly one total number of screens. This relationship between years and the total number of screens is one example of a *function*.

Recall from geometry the formulas for the perimeter and the area of a square.

$$\text{Perimeter: } P = 4s \quad \text{Area: } A = s^2$$

Each value for *s* defines exactly one perimeter and exactly one area. These relationships are also examples of *functions*.

CONNECTION

GEOMETRY

Definition of Function

A **function** is a relationship between two variables such that each value of the first variable is paired with exactly one value of the second variable.

The **domain** of a function is the set of all possible values of the first variable. The **range** of a function is the set of all possible values of the second variable.

A function may also be represented by data in a table, as shown in Example 1.

E X A M P L E ❶ State whether the data in each table represents a function. Explain.

a.

Domain, x	Range, y
1	−3.6
2	−3.6
3	4.2
4	4.2
5	10.7
6	12.1
52	52

b.

Domain, x	Range, y
3	7
3	8
3	10
4	42
10	34
11	18
52	52

● **SOLUTION**

   a. For each value of x in the table, there is exactly one value of y. The data set represents a function.

   b. The data set does not represent a function because three different y-values 7, 8, and 10, are paired with one x-value, 3.

You can use the *vertical-line test* to determine if a graph represents a function.

Vertical-Line Test

If every vertical line intersects a given graph at no more than one point, then the graph represents a function.

Example 2 shows how you can use the vertical-line test to determine whether a graph represents a function.

E X A M P L E ❷ State whether each graph represents a function. Explain.

a.

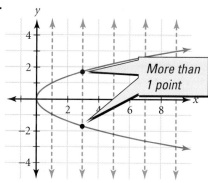

b.

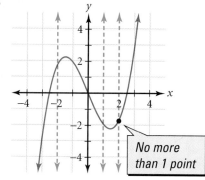

● **SOLUTION**

   a. The graph does not represent a function. There are many vertical lines that intersect the graph at two points.

   b. The graph represents a function. Every vertical line intersects the graph at no more than one point.

CONNECTION
GEOMETRY

Exploring Functions

You will need: no special tools

1. What variables influence how much water can be held in a cylindrical container? Discuss your responses.

2. Describe a real-world situation in which cost is a function of one or two variables. State the domain and range of your function.

3. The graph at right represents the volume, *V*, of water in a bathtub in gallons as a function of time, *t*, in minutes. Describe how *V* changes as *t* varies from 0 minutes to 16 minutes.

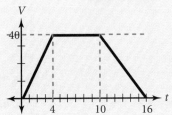

CHECKPOINT ✔ 4. Make up your own function like the one in Step 3. Describe your variables, and sketch a reasonable graph.

A function is a special type of *relation*.

Definition of Relation

A relationship between two variables such that each value of the first variable is paired with one or more values of the second variable is called a **relation**.

The **domain** is the set of all possible values of the first variable. The **range** is the set of all possible values of the second variable.

Example 3 gives an example of a real-world relation.

E X A M P L E ❸ Let the first variable, *R*, represent residents in Brownsville, Texas, who have telephone service. Let the second variable, *T*, represent telephone numbers of residents in Brownsville, Texas.

Is the relationship between *R* and *T* a relation? a function? Explain.

● **SOLUTION**

A resident with telephone service has at least one telephone number and may have more. Thus, the relationship is a relation.

Because some residents may have more than one telephone number, the relation is not a function.

TRY THIS Let the first variable, *R*, represent checking and savings account customers at a local bank. Let the second variable, *N*, represent checking and savings account numbers. Is the relationship between *R* and *N* a relation? a function? Explain.

CHECKPOINT ✔ Give two sets of ordered pairs that form a relation but not a function.

Example 4 shows you how to determine the domain and range of a function or relation from a graph.

E X A M P L E **4** State the domain and range of each function graphed.

a.
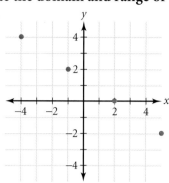

b.
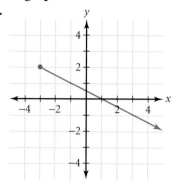

SOLUTION

The domain consists of the *x*-values, and the range consists of the *y*-values.

a. domain: {−4, −1, 2, 5}
   range: {−2, 0, 2, 4}

b. domain: $x \geq -3$
   range: $y \leq 2$

TRY THIS State the domain and range of each function graphed.

a.
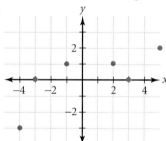

b.
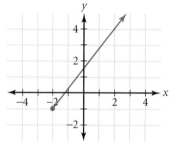

You can tell from a graph whether the function is *discrete* or *continuous*. The graph in part **a** of Example 4 illustrates a **discrete function**, whose graph is a set of individual points. The graph in part **b** of Example 4 illustrates a **continuous function**, whose graph is a line, ray, segment, or smooth curve.

CHECKPOINT ✔ Suppose that *x* is any real number. Is $y = 3x + 2$ a continuous function or a discrete function? Explain.

Functions and Function Notation

An equation can represent a function. The equation $y = 2x + 5$ represents a function. To express this equation as a function, use *function notation* and write $y = 2x + 5$ as $f(x) = 2x + 5$.

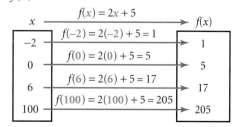

Function Notation

If there is a correspondence between values of the domain, x, and values of the range, y, that is a function, then $y = f(x)$, and (x, y) can be written as $(x, f(x))$. The notation $f(x)$ is read "f of x." The number represented by $f(x)$ is the value of the function f at x.

The variable x is called the **independent variable**.

The variable y, or $f(x)$, is called the **dependent variable**.

E X A M P L E Evaluate $f(x) = 0.5x^2 - 3x + 2$ for $x = 4$ and $x = 2.5$.

SOLUTION

$$f(x) = 0.5x^2 - 3x + 2 \qquad\qquad f(x) = 0.5x^2 - 3x + 2$$
$$f(4) = 0.5(4)^2 - 3(4) + 2 \qquad f(2.5) = 0.5(2.5)^2 - 3(2.5) + 2$$
$$f(4) = -2 \qquad\qquad\qquad f(2.5) = -2.375$$

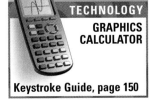

TECHNOLOGY

GRAPHICS CALCULATOR

Keystroke Guide, page 150

CHECK

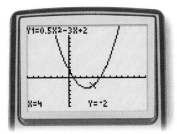

E X A M P L E 6 Monthly residential electric charges, c, are determined by adding a fixed fee of $6.00 to the product of the amount of electricity consumed each month, x, in kilowatt-hours and a rate factor of 0.035 cents per kilowatt-hour.

APPLICATION

CONSUMER ECONOMICS

  a. Write a linear function to model the monthly electric charge, c, as a function of the amount of electricity consumed each month, x.
  b. If a household uses 712 kilowatt-hours of electricity in a given month, how much is the monthly electric charge?

SOLUTION

a. $c(x) = $ **electricity used $+$ fixed fee**

$$c(x) = \quad 0.035x \quad + \quad 6.00$$

The linear function is $c(x) = 0.035x + 6.00$.

b. Evaluate the function for $x = 712$.

$$c(x) = 0.035x + 6.00$$
$$c(712) = 0.035(712) + 6.00$$
$$c(712) = 30.92$$

For 712 kilowatt-hours of electricity, the monthly charge is $30.92.

CHECKPOINT ✔ State the independent and dependent variables in Example 6. Explain your response.

Exercises

Communicate

1. Explain how functions are different from relations. Sketch a graph of a relation that is not a function to illustrate your explanation.

2. Describe three ways to represent a function.

3. Explain how to find the domain and range of a set of ordered pairs such as {(4, 2), (3, 5), (−2, 0), (2, 5)}.

4. **INCOME** Cleo wants to graph the relationship between the dollar value of the meals she served and the amount of tips she received. Identify a real-world domain and range for this relationship and draw a sample graph for Cleo.

Guided Skills Practice

State whether the data in each table represents *y* as a function of *x*. Explain. *(EXAMPLE 1)*

5.

x	y
5	3
8	4
5	7
9	2

6.

x	y
0	3
1	8
2	8
3	−7

7.

x	y
10	7
20	11
30	9
40	7

8.

x	y
3	9
2	2
8	−3
2	1

State whether each graph represents a function. Explain. *(EXAMPLE 2)*

9.
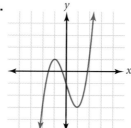

10.
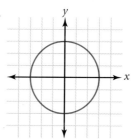

11. **TRANSPORTATION** If the first variable, *R*, represents registered automobiles in your state that may be legally driven and the second variable, *L*, represents license plate numbers for these automobiles, is the relationship between *R* and *L* a relation? a function? Explain. *(EXAMPLE 3)*

State the domain and range of each function graphed. *(EXAMPLE 4)*

12.
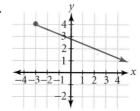

13.
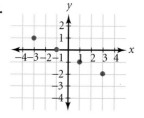

14. Evaluate $f(x) = x^2 + 2x - 1$ for $x = 3$ and $x = 1.5$. *(EXAMPLE 5)*

15. INCOME A plumber charges $24 per hour of work plus $20.00 to make a service call. *(EXAMPLE 6)*
   a. Write a linear function to model the plumber's wages, w, for the number of hours worked, h.
   b. Find the plumber's wages for 5.5 hours of work.

Practice and Apply

State whether each relation represents a function.

16. $\{(0, 0), (1, 1)\}$

17. $\{(1, 2), (2, 2), (3, 2)\}$

18. $\{(1, -1), (1, -2), (1, -3)\}$

19. $\{(4, 1), (5, 2), (6, 3)\}$

20. $\left\{\left(\frac{1}{2}, 1\right), \left(\frac{2}{5}, 2\right), \left(\frac{1}{3}, 1\right)\right\}$

21. $\left\{\left(\frac{1}{3}, \frac{1}{4}\right), \left(\frac{1}{5}, \frac{1}{5}\right), \left(\frac{1}{4}, \frac{3}{4}\right)\right\}$

22. $\{(11, 0), (12, -1), (21, -2)\}$

23. $\{(0, 0), (2, 5), (3, 3)\}$

24. $\{(1, 7), (-1, 7), (1, -7)\}$

25. $\{(-1, 8), (-1, 7), (0, 9)\}$

26.

x	y
0	3
2	-5
2	1
4	7

27.

x	y
1	6
2	6
3	9
4	9

28.

x	y
4	-2
4	2
6	-3
6	3

29.

x	y
-5	8
-3	8
-1	-2
1	-2

30.

x	y
-2	-5
-2	-3
0	4
2	6

State whether each relation graphed below is a function. Explain.

31.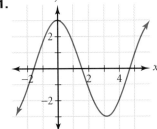

32.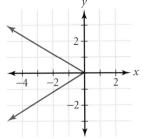

33.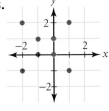

34.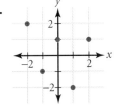

35.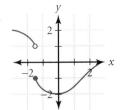

36.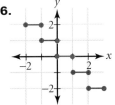

State the domain and range of each function.

37. $\{(0, 2), (3, 4)\}$

38. $\{(1, 5), (2, 5), (3, 5)\}$

39. $\{(9, -1), (8, -2), (7, -3)\}$

40. $\{(4, 1), (5, 2), (6, 3)\}$

41. $\{(6, -6), (5, -5), (4, -4)\}$

42. $\{(0, 0), (1.5, 0), (2.5, 0)\}$

Evaluate each function for the given values of *x*.

43. $f(x) = 2x - 6$ for $x = 1$ and $x = 3$

44. $f(x) = 5 - 3x$ for $x = 1$ and $x = 3$

45. $g(x) = \frac{2x - 1}{3}$ for $x = -1$ and $x = 1$

46. $g(x) = \frac{x - 4}{5}$ for $x = -9$ and $x = 9$

47. $f(x) = 2x^2 - 3x$ for $x = 3$ and $x = -2.5$

48. $f(x) = -x^2 + 4x - 1$ for $x = 2$ and $x = 1.5$

49. $f(x) = \frac{1}{3}x^2$ for $x = -1$ and $x - \frac{3}{4}$

50. $f(x) = -4x^2$ for $x = \frac{3}{2}$ and $x = -2$

Graph each function, and state the domain and range.

51. $y = -\frac{x}{2}$ 　　**52.** $y = \frac{2}{3}x - 5$ 　　**53.** $y = -2x^2$ 　　**54.** $y = x^2 + 2$

55. $y = 4$ 　　**56.** $y = -6$ 　　**57.** $y = x^3$ 　　**58.** $y = \left(\frac{x}{2}\right)^3$

59. Graph a function with a domain of $-3 \le x \le 3$ and a range of $-5 \le y \le 5$.

60. Graph a function with a domain of $-2 \le x \le 5$ and a range of $0 \le y \le 4$.

CHALLENGE

Given $f(t) = t^2 - 3$, find the indicated function value.

61. $f(\sqrt{2})$ 　　　　**62.** $f(\sqrt{2} - 1)$ 　　　　**63.** $f(a + \sqrt{2})$

CONNECTION

GEOMETRY The cube shown has volume *V*.

64. Express the volume of the cube as a function of *s*, the length of each side.

65. If the volume of the cube is 27 cubic meters, find the area of one face of the cube.

APPLICATIONS

66. CONSUMER ECONOMICS Computer equipment can depreciate very rapidly. Suppose a business assumes that a computer will depreciate linearly at a rate of 15% of its original price each year.
　a. If a computer is purchased for $3200, write an equation in which the value for the computer is a function of its age in years.
　b. Find the value of a computer after 3 years.

CONSUMER ECONOMICS A clothing store is selling all out-of-season clothing at 30% off the original price.

67. Write a function that gives the discounted price as a function of the original price.

68. Jason spent $47.25 on out-of-season items. Find the original cost of the items.

69. Helena purchased out-of-season items that originally cost $52. Find the sale price of these items.

 **Look Back**

Write the equation in slope-intercept form for the line that has the indicated slope, *m*, and contains the given point. *(LESSON 1.3)*

70. $m = 5, (2, 3)$

71. $m = -3, (4, 1)$

72. $m = \frac{1}{5}, (4, -11)$

73. $m = -\frac{2}{3}, (-8, -3)$

Write an equation in slope-intercept form of the line containing the indicated points. *(LESSON 1.3)*

74. $(1, 4)$ and $(-3, 0)$

75. $(0, 2)$ and $(-1, 1)$

76. $(2, 3)$ and $(0, 0)$

77. $(-2, -5)$ and $(5, -1)$

Write an equation in slope-intercept form of the line that contains the given point and is perpendicular to a line with the given slope. *(LESSON 1.3)*

78. $P(6, -1), m = \frac{4}{3}$

79. $P(-5, 3), m = -\frac{1}{2}$

Evaluate each expression by using the order of operations. *(LESSON 2.1)*

80. $3[2 - (5 - 3) - 7] \div 2$

81. $-(-5^2)^3$

 **Look Beyond**

82 Graph $y = x^2 - 3x - 10$. Explain why this is a function. Give the domain and range of this function.

83 Graph $y = 2^x$. Explain why this is a function. Give the domain and range of this function.

SPACE SCIENCE Refer to the Space Debris Table from the Portfolio Activity on page 93.

1. Graph the ordered pairs in the Space Debris Table that you created in the Portfolio Activity on page 93. Let the years be represented by x (where $x = 0$ represents 1993) and the total number of debris objects by y. Describe how your graph illustrates that the total number of debris objects in space, y, is a function of time, x.

2. Give the domain and range of the function you described in Step 1. Then state the independent and dependent variables for this function.

3. Using the linear regression feature on your calculator, find a linear function that models this data. Next, using the exponential regression feature, find an exponential function that models this data.

4. Graph your linear model and your exponential model, and compare how well or how poorly the models appear to fit the data.

WORKING ON THE CHAPTER PROJECT

You should now be able to complete Activities 1 and 2 of the Chapter Project.

Operations With Functions

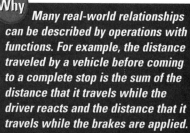

Why Many real-world relationships can be described by operations with functions. For example, the distance traveled by a vehicle before coming to a complete stop is the sum of the distance that it travels while the driver reacts and the distance that it travels while the brakes are applied.

Objectives

● Perform operations with functions to write new functions.

● Find the composite of two functions.

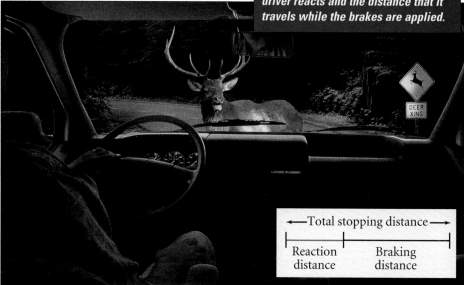

←——Total stopping distance——→

| Reaction | Braking |
| distance | distance |

APPLICATION

TRANSPORTATION

Common sense tells you that the faster you drive, the farther you will travel while reacting to an obstacle and while braking to a complete stop. In other words, the reaction distance and braking distance depend on the speed of the car at the moment the obstacle is observed.

Stopping Distance Data

Speed (mph)	Reaction distance (ft)	Braking distance (ft)	Stopping distance (ft)
10	11	5	16
20	22	21	43
30	33	47	80
40	44	84	128
50	55	132	187
60	66	189	255
70	77	258	335

Activity
Investigating Braking Distance

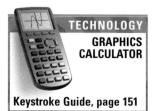

TECHNOLOGY

GRAPHICS CALCULATOR

Keystroke Guide, page 151

You will need: a graphics calculator

1. Using a graphics calculator, make a scatter plot of the data for speed and reaction distance. What type of function is represented by this data?

2. Using a graphics calculator, make a scatter plot of the data for speed and braking distance. What trend do you see in the graph?

3. Using the table above, identify a relationship between the stopping distance and the reaction and braking distances. Use this relationship to make predictions about the scatter plot of the data for speed and stopping distance.

CHECKPOINT ✔ 4. Using a graphics calculator, make a scatter plot of the data for speed and stopping distance. What trend do you see in the graph?

The functions at right relate speed, x, in miles per hour to the reaction distance, r, and to braking distance, b, both in feet.

$$r(x) = \frac{11}{10}x \qquad b(x) = \frac{1}{19}x^2$$

$$s(x) = r(x) + b(x)$$

You can relate speed, x, to the total stopping distance, s, as a *sum* of r and b.

$$s(x) = \frac{11}{10}x + \frac{1}{19}x^2$$

Functions can also be combined by subtraction, multiplication, and division.

Operations With Functions

For all functions f and g:

Sum	$(f + g)(x) = f(x) + g(x)$
Difference	$(f - g)(x) = f(x) - g(x)$
Product	$(f \cdot g)(x) = f(x) \cdot g(x)$
Quotient	$\left(\dfrac{f}{g}\right)(x) = \dfrac{f(x)}{g(x)}$, where $g(x) \neq 0$

EXAMPLE 1 Let $f(x) = 5x^2 - 2x + 3$ and $g(x) = 4x^2 + 7x - 5$.
  a. Find $f + g$. **b.** Find $f - g$.

SOLUTION

a. $(f + g)(x) = f(x) + g(x)$
  $= (5x^2 - 2x + 3) + (4x^2 + 7x - 5)$
  $= 5x^2 + 4x^2 - 2x + 7x + 3 - 5$ *Use the Commutative Property.*
  $= 9x^2 + 5x - 2$ *Combine like terms.*

b. $(f - g)(x) = f(x) - g(x)$
  $= (5x^2 - 2x + 3) - (4x^2 + 7x - 5)$
  $= 5x^2 - 4x^2 - 2x - 7x + 3 - (-5)$ *Use the Commutative Property.*
  $= x^2 - 9x + 8$ *Combine like terms.*

TRY THIS Let $f(x) = -7x^2 + 12x + 2.5$ and $g(x) = 7x^2 - 5$. Find $f + g$ and $f - g$.

EXAMPLE 2 Let $f(x) = 5x^2$ and $g(x) = 3x - 1$.
  a. Find $f \cdot g$. **b.** Find $\dfrac{f}{g}$, and state any domain restrictions.

SOLUTION

a. $(f \cdot g)(x) = f(x) \cdot g(x)$
  $= 5x^2(3x - 1)$
  $= 5x^2(3x) - 5x^2(1)$
  $= 15x^3 - 5x^2$

b. $\left(\dfrac{f}{g}\right)(x) = \dfrac{f(x)}{g(x)}$, where $g(x) \neq 0$
  $= \dfrac{5x^2}{3x - 1}$, where $x \neq \dfrac{1}{3}$

$3x - 1 \neq 0$
$3x \neq 1$
$x \neq \frac{1}{3}$

CHECKPOINT ✔ Which property of real numbers is used in part **a** of Example 2?

TRY THIS Let $f(x) = 3x^2 + 1$ and $g(x) = 5x - 2$. Find $f \cdot g$ and $\dfrac{f}{g}$.

Composition of Functions

When you apply a function rule on the result of another function rule, you *compose* the functions. The illustration below shows how the composition $f \circ g$, or $f(g(x))$, read "f of g of x," works.

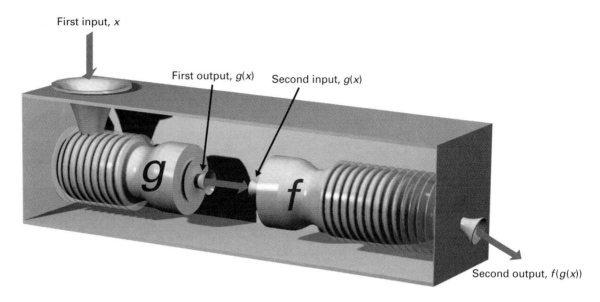

First input, x

First output, $g(x)$ Second input, $g(x)$

Second output, $f(g(x))$

Composition of Functions

Let f and g be functions of x.

The composition of f with g, denoted $f \circ g$, is defined by $f(g(x))$.

The domain of $y = f(g(x))$ is the set of domain values of g whose range values are in the domain of f. The function $f \circ g$ is called the **composite** function of f with g.

Example 3 shows you how to form the composition of two functions.

E X A M P L E **3** Let $f(x) = x^2 - 1$ and $g(x) = 3x$.

a. Find $f \circ g$.   **b.** Find $g \circ f$.

● **SOLUTION**

a. $(f \circ g)(x) = f(g(x))$ **b.** $(g \circ f)(x) = g(f(x))$
$= f(3x)$ $= g(x^2 - 1)$
$= (3x)^2 - 1$ $= 3(x^2 - 1)$
$= 9x^2 - 1$ $= 3x^2 - 3$ *Distributive Property*

TRY THIS   Let $f(x) = -2x^2 + 3$ and $g(x) = -2x$. Find $f \circ g$ and $g \circ f$.

In Example 3 and in most cases, $f \circ g$ and $g \circ f$ are not equivalent. That is, the composition of functions is not commutative.

CRITICAL THINKING   Write two functions, f and g, whose composite functions $f \circ g$ and $g \circ f$ are equivalent. Justify your response.

Example 4 shows you how composite functions can model problems that involve a series of actions.

E X A M P L E ④ **A local electronics store is offering a $100.00 rebate along with a 10% discount. Let x represent the original price of an item in the store.**

APPLICATION
CONSUMER ECONOMICS

a. Write the function D that represents the sale price after a 10% discount and the function R that represents the sale price after a $100 rebate.

b. Find the composite functions $(R \circ D)(x)$ and $(D \circ R)(x)$, and explain what they represent.

SOLUTION

a. Since a 10% discount on the original price is the same as paying 90% of the original price, $D(x) = x - 0.1x = 0.9x$.

The rebate function is $R(x) = x - 100$.

b. **10% discount first**

$$(R \circ D)(x) = R(D(x)) = R(0.9x)$$
$$= (0.9x) - 100$$
$$= 0.9x - 100$$

$100 rebate first

$$(D \circ R)(x) = D(R(x)) = D(x - 100)$$
$$= 0.9(x - 100)$$
$$= 0.9x - 90$$

Notice that taking the 10% discount first results in a lower sale price.

Exercises

Communicate

1. Explain how to write a function for reaction distance, r, in terms of the function for braking distance, b, and the function for stopping distance, s.

2. Explain how to find $f \circ g$ given $f(x) = 4x - 7$ and $g(x) = 2x^2 + 4$.

3. Show that $f \circ g$ and $g \circ f$ are not equivalent functions given $f(x) = 3x + 1$ and $g(x) = 2x$.

Guided Skills Practice

Let $f(x) = \frac{x}{2}$ and $g(x) = 3x + 1$. Perform each function operation. State any domain restrictions. *(EXAMPLES 1, 2, AND 3)*

4. $f + g$

5. $f - g$

6. $f \cdot g$

7. $\frac{f}{g}$

8. $f \circ g$

9. $g \circ f$

10. CONSUMER ECONOMICS A coupon for $5 off any meal states that a 15% tip will be added to the total check before the $5 is subtracted. Let x represent the total check amount. Write a function, R, for the price reduction and a function, T, for the tip. Find the composite functions $(R \circ T)(x)$ and $(T \circ R)(x)$, and explain which composite function represents the conditions of the coupon. *(EXAMPLE 4)*

Practice and Apply

Find $f + g$ and $f - g$.

11. $f(x) = 4x + 3; g(x) = 5$ **12.** $f(x) = 20x + 7; g(x) = -3x$

13. $f(x) = x^2 + 2x - 1; g(x) = 3x - 5$ **14.** $f(x) = -x^2 - 3x; g(x) = 6x^2 - 3$

15. $f(x) = x - 2; g(x) = 4 - 3x^2$ **16.** $f(x) = 3x^2 - x; g(x) = 6 - x^2$

Find $f \cdot g$ and $\frac{f}{g}$. State any domain restrictions.

17. $f(x) = 3x^2; g(x) = x - 8$ **18.** $f(x) = 2x^2; g(x) = 7 - x$

19. $f(x) = -x^2; g(x) = 3x$ **20.** $f(x) = 4x^2 - 2x + 1; g(x) = -5x$

21. $f(x) = 2x^2; g(x) = 7 - x$ **22.** $f(x) = 7x^2; g(x) = 2x - 6$

23. $f(x) = -3x^2 - x; g(x) = 5 - x$ **24.** $f(x) = 4x^2 + 3; g(x) = 3x - 9$

Let $f(x) = x^2 - 1$ and $g(x) = 2x - 3$. Find each new function and write it in simplest form. Justify each step in the simplification, and state any domain restrictions.

25. $f + g$ **26.** $f - g$ **27.** $g - f$ **28.** $f \cdot g$ **29.** $\frac{f}{g}$

Let $f(x) = x - 3$ and $g(x) = x^2 - 9$. Find each new function and write it in simplest form. Justify each step in the simplification, and state any domain restrictions.

30. $f + g$ **31.** $f - g$ **32.** $g - f$ **33.** $f \cdot g$ **34.** $\frac{g}{f}$

Find $f \circ g$ and $g \circ f$.

35. $f(x) = x + 1; g(x) = 2x$ **36.** $f(x) = 3x; g(x) = 2x + 3$

37. $f(x) = 3x - 2; g(x) = x + 2$ **38.** $f(x) = 2x - 3; g(x) = x + 4$

39. $f(x) = -3x^2 - 1; g(x) = -5x$ **40.** $f(x) = -2x; g(x) = -2x^2 + 3$

41. $f(x) = -4x^2 + 3x - 1; g(x) = 3$ **42.** $f(x) = 2x^2 + 3x - 5; g(x) = 4$

Let $f(x) = 3x - 4$ and $g(x) = -x^2$. Evaluate each composite function.

43. $(f \circ g)(2)$ **44.** $(f \circ g)(-2)$ **45.** $(f \circ f)(2)$ **46.** $(f \circ f)(-2)$

47. $(g \circ g)(2)$ **48.** $(g \circ g)(-2)$ **49.** $(g \circ f)(0)$ **50.** $(f \circ g)(0)$

Let $f(x) = 2x$, $g(x) = x^2 + 2$, and $h(x) = -4x + 3$. Find each composite function.

51. $f \circ g$ **52.** $g \circ f$ **53.** $f \circ h$ **54.** $h \circ g$

55. $f \circ f$ **56.** $h \circ f$ **57.** $h \circ (h \circ g)$ **58.** $(h \circ f) \circ g$

59. Let $h(x) = x^2 - 9$. Find two functions f and g such that $f \circ g = h$.

60. DEMOGRAPHICS College enrollments in the United States are projected to increase from 1995 to 2005 for public and private schools. The models below give the total projected college enrollments in thousands, where $t = 0$ represents the year 1995. [*Source: U.S. National Center for Education Statistics*]

Public: $f(t) = 160t + 11{,}157$
Private: $g(t) = 50t + 3114$

  a. Find $f + g$.
  b. Evaluate $f + g$ for the year 2000.

61. MANUFACTURING The function $C(x) = 4x + 850$ closely approximates the cost of a daily production run of x picture frames. The number of picture frames produced is represented by the function $x(t) = 90t$, where t is the time in hours since the beginning of the production run.
  a. Give the cost of a daily production run, C, as a function of time, t.
  b. Find the cost of the production run that lasts 5 hours.
  c. How many picture frames are produced in 5 hours?

62. TEMPERATURE A temperature given in kelvins is equivalent to the temperature given in degrees Celsius plus 273. A temperature given in degrees Celsius is equivalent to $\frac{9}{5}$ times the quantity given by the temperature in degrees Fahrenheit minus 32.
  a. Write a function expressing kelvins in terms of degrees Celsius.
  b. Write a function expressing degrees Celsius in terms of degrees Fahrenheit.
  c. Write a function expressing kelvins in terms of degrees Fahrenheit.
  d. Water freezes at 32°F. At what Kelvin temperature does water freeze?
  e. Are kelvins and degrees Fahrenheit linearly related? Explain.

63. BUSINESS Jovante decides to start a business by making buttons and selling them for 25 cents each. The button machine costs $125 dollars, and the materials for each button cost 10 cents.
  a. Write a cost function, C, that represents the cost in dollars of making n buttons.
  b. Write an income function, I, that represents the income in dollars generated by selling n buttons.
  c. Write a profit function, P, that represents the income, I, minus the cost, C.
  d. Find the number of buttons that Jovante must sell in order to make a $100 profit.

64. CONSUMER ECONOMICS A store is offering a discount of 30% on a suit. There is a sales tax of 6%.

   a Represent the situation in which the discount is taken before the sales tax is applied with a composition of functions.

   b. Represent the situation in which the sales tax is applied before the discount is taken with a composition of functions.

   c. Compare the composite functions from parts **a** and **b**. Does one of them result in a lower final cost? Explain why or why not.

 *Look Back*

Write an equation in slope-intercept form for each line described. *(LESSON 1.2)*

65. contains $(3, -2)$ and has a slope of $-\frac{1}{2}$

66. contains $(-1, 4)$ and $(-3, 8)$

Describe the correlation among data that have the given correlation coefficient. *(LESSON 1.5)*

67. $r = 0.09$ **68.** $r = -0.95$ **69.** $r = 0.52$

State the domain and range of each function. *(LESSON 2.3)*

70. $\{(1, 3), (2, 5), (3, 7)\}$ **71.** $y = -4x + 2$

 *Look Beyond*

72. Given $f(x) = 2x + 5$ and $g(x) = \frac{x-5}{2}$, find $f \circ g$ and $g \circ f$. Compare your results.

SPACE SCIENCE One source of space debris is nonfunctional spacecraft components. At the end of 1993, scientists tracked 1550 nonfunctional components in orbit and projected that 42 such objects are added each year. Suppose that an average of 15 of these are brought back to Earth each year.

1. Let t represent time in years. Write the function D that models the total number of cataloged nonfunctional components in orbit at the end of the year if 42 such objects are added each year to the initial 1550 objects in orbit.

2. Write the function R that models the total number of components that are brought back to Earth each year.

3. Write a function relating time, t, in years and the total number of nonfunctional components in orbit as a difference of D and R.

4. Graph the function from Step 3 on a graphics calculator. Examine the table of values for the function. Are there constant first differences in the x-values and in the y-values?

5. Identify the type of function that you graphed in Step 4 and justify your answer.

Inverses of Functions

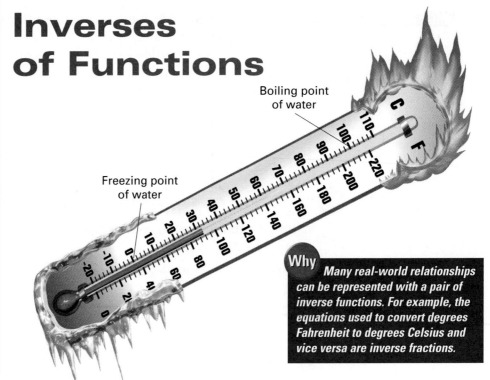

Boiling point of water

Freezing point of water

Why *Many real-world relationships can be represented with a pair of inverse functions. For example, the equations used to convert degrees Fahrenheit to degrees Celsius and vice versa are inverse fractions.*

Objectives

● Find the inverse of a relation or function.

● Determine whether the inverse of a function is a function.

APPLICATION

TEMPERATURE

In Lesson 1.6, you used the equation $F = \frac{9}{5}C + 32$ to find the Celsius temperature corresponding to 86°F. How can you find the Celsius temperatures that correspond to Fahrenheit temperatures? To answer this question, you need a function that gives C in terms of F. You will need to find the *inverse of a function*.

EXAMPLE **1** Solve $F = \frac{9}{5}C + 32$ for *C*.

● **SOLUTION**

$$F = \frac{9}{5}C + 32$$

$$F - 32 = \frac{9}{5}C + 32 - 32$$

$$\frac{5}{9}(F - 32) = \frac{5}{9}\left(\frac{9}{5}C\right)$$

$$\frac{5}{9}(F - 32) = C$$

Notice that subtraction of 32 and multiplication by $\frac{5}{9}$ are the inverse operations of those in $F = \frac{9}{5}C + 32$.

Thus, $C = \frac{5}{9}(F - 32)$.

Example 1 indicates that finding the inverse of a function involves changing an ordered pair of the form (C, F) to an ordered pair of the form (F, C).

Inverse of a Relation

The **inverse of a relation** consisting of the ordered pairs (x, y) is the set of all ordered pairs (y, x).

The domain of the inverse is the range of the original relation.

The range of the inverse is the domain of the original relation.

EXAMPLE 2 **Find the inverse of each relation. State whether the relation is a function. State whether the inverse is a function.**

a. $\{(1, 2), (2, 4), (3, 6), (4, 8)\}$ **b.** $\{(1, 5), (1, 6), (3, 6), (4, 9)\}$

SOLUTION

a. relation: $\{(1, 2), (2, 4), (3, 6), (4, 8)\}$
inverse: $\{(2, 1), (4, 2), (6, 3), (8, 4)\}$

The given relation is a function because each domain value is paired with exactly one range value. The inverse is also a function because each domain value is paired with exactly one range value.

b. relation: $\{(1, 5), (1, 6), (3, 6), (4, 9)\}$
inverse: $\{(6, 1), (5, 1), (6, 3), (9, 4)\}$

The given relation is not a function because the domain value 1 is paired with two range values, 5 and 6. The inverse is not a function because the domain value 6 is paired with two range values, 1 and 3.

Example 3 shows you how to find the inverse of a function by interchanging x and y and then solving for y.

EXAMPLE 3 **Find an equation for the inverse of $y = 3x - 2$.**

SOLUTION

In $y = 3x - 2$, interchange x and y. Then solve for y.

$$\begin{aligned} x &= 3y - 2 \\ x + 2 &= 3y \\ \frac{x+2}{3} &= y \\ y &= \frac{1}{3}x + \frac{2}{3} \end{aligned}$$

TRY THIS Find an equation for the inverse of $y = 4x - 5$.

In the Activity below, you can explore the relationship between the graph of a function and the graph of its inverse.

Activity

Exploring Functions and Their Inverses

TECHNOLOGY
GRAPHICS CALCULATOR
Keystroke Guide, page 151

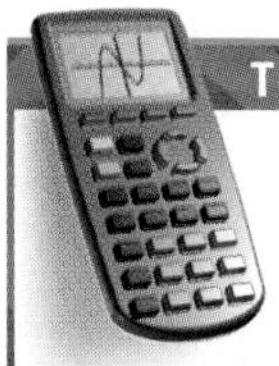

You will need: a graphics calculator

1. Graph $y = 2x - 1$, its inverse, and $y = x$ in a square viewing window. Use the inverse feature of the calculator. How do the graphs of these functions relate to one another? Consider symmetry in your response.
2. Repeat Step 1 for each function listed at right.

CHECKPOINT ✓ 3. Write a generalization about the relationship between the graph of a function and the graph of its inverse.

Function
$y = 3x - 2$
$y = 3x + 2$
$y = -2x + 5$
$y = x^2$

If a function f and its inverse are both functions, the inverse of f is denoted by f^{-1}.

The graph of $f(x) = 3x - 2$ and its inverse, $f^{-1}(x) = \frac{1}{3}x + \frac{2}{3}$, from Example 3 are shown at right. Notice that the ordered pairs $(-2, 0)$ and $(0, -2)$ are "mirror images" or *reflections* of one another across the line $y = x$. This means every point (a, b) on the graph of f corresponds to a point (b, a) on the graph of f^{-1}. This is true for any two relations that are inverses of each other.

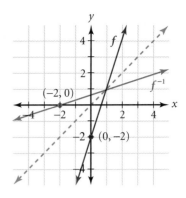

You can use the *horizontal-line test* to determine from a graph whether the inverse of a given function is a function.

Horizontal-Line Test

The inverse of a function is a function if and only if every horizontal line intersects the graph of the given function at no more than one point.

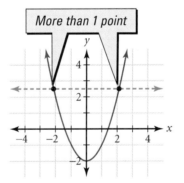

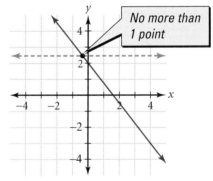

The horizontal-line test above shows that the inverse of this function is not a function.

The horizontal-line test above shows that the inverse of this function is a function.

If a function has an inverse that is also a function, then the function is **one-to-one**. Every one-to-one function passes the horizontal-line test and has an inverse that is a function.

Just as the graphs of f and f^{-1} are reflections of one another across the line $y = x$, the composition of a function and its inverse are related to the *identity function*. The **identity function**, I, is defined as $I(x) = x$.

Composition and Inverses

If f and g are functions and $(f \circ g)(x) = (g \circ f)(x) = I(x) = x$, then f and g are inverses of one another.

E X A M P L E ④ Show that $f(x) = 7x - 2$ and $g(x) = \frac{1}{7}x + \frac{2}{7}$ are inverses of each other.

SOLUTION

$(f \circ g)(x) = f(g(x)) = f\left(\frac{1}{7}x + \frac{2}{7}\right)$ $(g \circ f)(x) = g(f(x)) = g(7x - 2)$

$\qquad\qquad = 7\left(\frac{1}{7}x + \frac{2}{7}\right) - 2$ $\qquad\qquad = \frac{1}{7}(7x - 2) + \frac{2}{7}$

$\qquad\qquad = x + 2 - 2$ $\qquad\qquad\qquad = x - \frac{2}{7} + \frac{2}{7}$

$\qquad\qquad = x$ $\qquad\qquad\qquad\qquad = x$

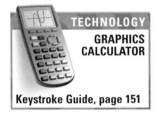

TECHNOLOGY

GRAPHICS CALCULATOR

Keystroke Guide, page 151

CHECK

Graph $f \circ g$ and $g \circ f$ to check that the two functions are inverses.

Because $(f \circ g)(x) = x$ and $(g \circ f)(x) = x$, the two functions are inverses of each other.

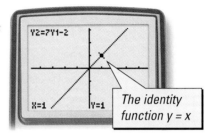

The identity function $y = x$

TRY THIS   Show that $f(x) = -5x + 7$ and $g(x) = -\frac{1}{5}x + \frac{7}{5}$ are inverses of each another.

CRITICAL THINKING   Let $f(x) = mx + b$, where $m \neq 0$. Find f^{-1}. Using composition, verify that f and f^{-1} are inverses of one another.

Exercises

Communicate

1. Explain what it means for a function to be a one-to-one function.

2. Describe when and why you would use the vertical-line test and the horizontal-line test.

3. Describe the procedure for finding the inverse of $y = 4x - 1$.

4. Explain how the graphs of a function and its inverse are related.

Guided Skills Practice

APPLICATION

5. **CHEMISTRY** A chemical reaction takes place at temperatures between 290 K and 300 K. The Fahrenheit and Kelvin temperature scales are related by the formula $K = \frac{5}{9}(F - 32) + 273$. Solve this equation for F. *(EXAMPLE 1)*

Find the inverse of each relation. State whether the relation is a function. State whether the inverse is a function. *(EXAMPLE 2)*

6. $\{(8, 3), (2, 2), (4, 3)\}$ 7. $\{(3, 2), (9, 5), (2, 3), (4, 7)\}$

Find an equation for the inverse of each function. *(EXAMPLE 3)*

8. $y = 3x + 9$

9. $y = 5 - 3x$

10. Verify that $f(x) = 6x - 5$ and $g(x) = \frac{1}{6}x + \frac{5}{6}$ are inverses of each other.
(EXAMPLE 4)

Practice and Apply

Find the inverse of each relation. State whether the relation is a function. State whether the inverse is a function.

11. $\{(3, 5), (6, 10), (9, 15)\}$

12. $\{(2, -3), (3, -4), (4, -2)\}$

13. $\{(5, 2), (4, 3), (3, 4), (2, 5)\}$

14. $\{(-1, -6), (0, 2), (1, 2), (3, 6)\}$

15. $\{(-3, -6), (-1, 2), (1, 2), (3, 6)\}$

16. $\{(2, 1), (4, 2), (2, 3), (8, 4)\}$

17. $\{(1, 2), (3, 4), (-3, 4), (-1, 2)\}$

18. $\{(9, -2), (4, -1), (1, 0), (3, 1), (7, 2)\}$

Find the inverse of each function. State whether the inverse is a function.

19. $\{(-1, 0), (-2, 1), (4, 3), (3, 4)\}$

20. $\{(1, 4), (2, 3), (3, 2), (4, 1)\}$

21. $\{(1, 2), (2, 3), (3, 2), (4, 1)\}$

22. $\{(3, -2), (2, -3), (1, -2), (0, -1)\}$

23. $\{(5, 2), (4, 3), (3, 5), (2, 3)\}$

24. $\{(3, 0), (2, -1), (1, 2), (0, 1), (-1, 2)\}$

25. $\{(0, 2), (2, 3), (3, 4), (1, 1)\}$

26. $\{(-1, 2), (-2, 3), (-3, 4), (0, 0)\}$

Determine whether the inverse of each function graphed is also a function.

27.

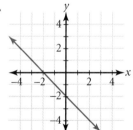

28.

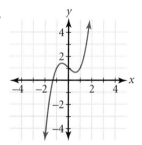

For each function, find an equation for the inverse. Then use composition to verify that the equation you wrote is the inverse.

29. $f(x) = 5x + 1$

30. $g(x) = -2x - 7$

31. $h(x) = -\frac{1}{2}x + 3$

32. $g(x) = \frac{x - 1}{4}$

33. $h(x) = \frac{x + 8}{3}$

34. $f(x) = \frac{x - 3}{2}$

35. $f(x) = \frac{2x - 3}{4}$

36. $f(x) = \frac{1}{3}x - 1$

37. $g(x) = 2x - \frac{3x}{4}$

38. $h(x) = \frac{1}{4}(x - 1)$

39. $g(x) = \frac{1}{2}(x + 2) - 3$

40. $h(x) = \frac{3}{2}(x - 3) + 2$

Graph each function, and use the horizontal-line test to determine whether the inverse is a function.

41 $f(x) = 1 - x^2$

42 $h(x) = -\frac{1}{3}x + 5$

43 $g(x) = \frac{7 - 2x}{5}$

44 $f(x) = 2x^3$

45 $g(x) = 3$

46 $h(x) = \frac{3}{x}$

47 $g(x) = x^4$

48 $f(x) = x^2 - 2x$

49 $f(x) = x^5$

CHALLENGE

50. If a relation is not a function, can its inverse be a function? Explain and give examples.

APPLICATIONS

51. CONSUMER ECONOMICS New carpeting can be purchased and installed for $17.50 per square yard plus a $50 delivery fee.
   a. Write an equation that gives the cost, c, of carpeting s square yards of a house.
   b. Find the inverse of the cost function.
   c. How many square yards can be carpeted for $1485?

52. REAL ESTATE New house prices depend on the cost of the property, or lot, and the size of the house. Suppose that a lot costs $60,000 and a builder charges $84 per square foot of living area in a house.
   a. Write the function p that represents the price of a house with x square feet of living area.
   b. Find the inverse of the price function, and discuss what it represents.
   c. How big, to the nearest square foot, is a house that can be purchased for $180,000?

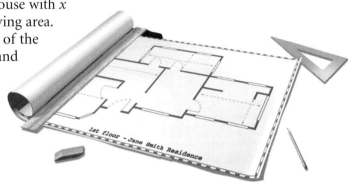

53. PUZZLES In a number puzzle, you are told to add 4 to your age, then multiply by 2, subtract 6, and finally divide by 2. You give the result, and you are immediately told your age. Use an inverse function to explain how the puzzle works.

 Look Back

APPLICATION

54. BUSINESS The total revenue, R, is directly proportional to the number of cameras, x, sold. When 500 cameras are sold, the revenue is $3800. *(LESSON 1.4)*
   a. Find the revenue when 600 cameras are sold.
   a. What is the constant of variation?
   c. In this situation, what does the constant of variation represent?

Evaluate each expression. *(LESSON 2.2)*

55. $2^3 \cdot 2^5$ **56.** $25^{-\frac{1}{2}}$ **57.** $(3^2)^3$

Let $f(x) = 3x - 2$ and $g(x) = 5x + 2$. *(LESSON 2.4)*

58. Find $f + g$.   **59.** Find $f \cdot g$.

60. Evaluate $(f + g)(-1)$.   **61.** Evaluate $(f \cdot g)(-3)$.

 *Look Beyond*

62 Graph $f(x) = 2^x$. Why would you expect this function to have an inverse that is a function? Graph the inverse and state its domain.

Special Functions

2.6

Objective

- Write, graph, and apply special functions: piecewise, step, and absolute value.

Why *Some real-world relationships can be modeled with special functions. For example, the total wages earned by working regular and overtime hours can be modeled with a piecewise function.*

Piecewise Functions

APPLICATION

INCOME

A truck driver earns $21.00 per hour for the first 40 hours worked in one week. The driver earns time-and-a-half, or $31.50, for each hour worked in excess of 40. The pair of function rules below represent the driver's wage, $w(h)$, as a function of the hours worked in one week, h.

$$w(h) = \begin{cases} 21h & \text{if } 0 < h \le 40 \\ 31.5h - 420 & \text{if } h > 40 \end{cases}$$

This function is an example of a *piecewise function*. A **piecewise function** consists of different function rules for different parts of the domain.

CRITICAL THINKING

Where does the number -420 in the piecewise function w come from?

Exploring Piecewise Functions

You will need: graph paper

1. Copy and complete the table below, using the function for the truck driver's wages given above.

Hours worked, h	10.0	30.0	35.0	40.0	52.5
Wage, $w(h)$					

2. Extend your table by choosing other values of h in the interval $0 < h \le 60$.

3. Plot the ordered pairs from your table and make a scatter plot.

CHECKPOINT ✔ 4. If you connect the consecutive points in the scatter plot, what observations can you make about the graph?

Example 1 shows you how to use the appropriate function rule for each domain of a piecewise function when graphing it.

EXAMPLE **1** Graph: $f(x) = \begin{cases} 2x & \text{if } 0 \le x < 2 \\ 4 & \text{if } 2 < x < 4 \\ -\dfrac{1}{4}x + 5 & \text{if } 4 \le x \le 6 \end{cases}$

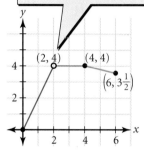

Notice that an open circle is graphed at (2, 4) because 2 is not included in the domain.

● **SOLUTION**

1. Graph $y = 2x$ for $0 \le x < 2$.
   $0 = 2(0)$ and $4 = 2(2)$
   Connect $(0, 0)$ and $(2, 4)$. Use an open circle at $(2, 4)$.

2. Graph $y = 4$ for $2 < x < 4$.
   Connect $(2, 4)$ and $(4, 4)$. Use an open circle at $(2, 4)$.

3. Graph $y = -\dfrac{1}{4}x + 5$ for $4 \le x \le 6$.
   $4 = -\dfrac{1}{4}(4) + 5$ and $3\dfrac{1}{2} = -\dfrac{1}{4}(6) + 5$ Connect $(4, 4)$ and $\left(6, 3\dfrac{1}{2}\right)$.

TRY THIS   Graph: $f(x) = \begin{cases} -2x + 3 & \text{if } 0 \le x < 5 \\ -3x + 8 & \text{if } 5 \le x \le 10 \end{cases}$

Step Functions

The graph of a linear function with a slope of 0 is a horizontal line. This type of function is called a **constant function** because every function value is the same number.

A **step function** is a piecewise function that consists of different constant range values for different intervals of the domain of the function. The two basic step functions are shown below.

Greatest-integer function, or rounding-down function

$f(x) = [x]$, or $f(x) = \lfloor x \rfloor$

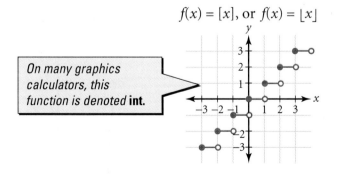

*On many graphics calculators, this function is denoted **int**.*

x	-3	-1.5	0	2.8
$f(x) = [x]$	-3	-2	0	2

Rounding-up function

$f(x) = \lceil x \rceil$

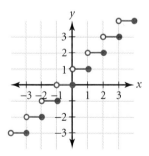

x	-3	-1.5	0	2.8
$f(x) = \lceil x \rceil$	-3	-1	0	3

The domain of both $f(x) = [x]$ and $f(x) = \lceil x \rceil$ is the set of all real numbers, and the range of both functions is the set of all integers.

CHECKPOINT ✔ Evaluate $[5]$, $[3.2]$, and $[-4.4]$. Evaluate $\lceil 5 \rceil$, $\lceil 3.2 \rceil$, and $\lceil -4.4 \rceil$.

Example 2 shows how first-class postage can be modeled with a rounding-up function.

E X A M P L E ② The cost of mailing a first-class letter (up to 11 ounces inclusive) in 1998 is given by the function $p(w) = 32 + 23\lceil w - 1 \rceil$, where w represents the weight in ounces and p represents the postage in cents.

Find the cost of mailing a first-class letter given each weight.
   a. 2.2 ounces   **b.** 4.8 ounces

● **SOLUTION**

a. $p(2.2) = 32 + 23\lceil 2.2 - 1 \rceil$
         $= 32 + 23\lceil 1.2 \rceil$
         $= 32 + 23(2)$
         $= 78$
  The cost is $0.78.

b. $p(4.8) = 32 + 23\lceil 4.8 - 1 \rceil$
         $= 32 + 23\lceil 3.8 \rceil$
         $= 32 + 23(4)$
         $= 124$
  The cost is $1.24.

TRY THIS Find the cost of mailing an 0.8-ounce and a 2.9-ounce first-class letter.

Example 3 shows you how to graph a variation, or transformation, of a basic step function.

E X A M P L E ③ Graph $g(x) = 2\lceil x \rceil$.

● **SOLUTION**

Make a table to compare values of $f(x) = \lceil x \rceil$ with values of $g(x)$.

Interval of x	$f(x) = \lceil x \rceil$	$g(x) = 2\lceil x \rceil$
$-4 < x \le -3$	-3	-6
$-3 < x \le -2$	-2	-4
$-2 < x \le -1$	-1	-2
$-1 < x \le 0$	0	0
$0 < x \le 1$	1	2
$1 < x \le 2$	2	4
$2 < x \le 3$	3	6

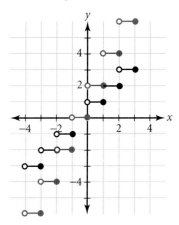

TRY THIS Graph $g(x) = \lceil x \rceil - 1$.

CRITICAL THINKING Let $f(x) = [x]$ and $g(x) = \lceil x \rceil$. Compare and contrast $f - g$ with $g - f$.

Absolute-Value Functions

The **absolute-value function**, denoted by $f(x) = |x|$, can be defined as a piecewise function as follows:

$$f(x) = \begin{cases} |x| = x & \text{if } x \geq 0 \\ |x| = -x & \text{if } x < 0 \end{cases}$$

The graph of the absolute-value function has a characteristic V shape, as shown. The domain of $f(x) = |x|$ is the set of all real numbers, and the range is the set of all nonnegative real numbers.

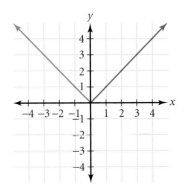

Example 4 involves a transformation of the absolute-value function.

E X A M P L E 4 Graph $g(x) = 3|x| - 1$ by making a table of values. Then graph the inverse of g on the same coordinate plane.

PROBLEM SOLVING

CONNECTION

TRANSFORMATIONS

SOLUTION

Make a table of values to compare values of g with values of $f(x) = |x|$.

x	$f(x) = |x|$	$g(x) = 3|x| - 1$
−2	2	$3|-2| - 1 = 5$
−1	1	$3|-1| - 1 = 2$
0	0	$3|0| - 1 = -1$
1	1	$3|1| - 1 = 2$
2	2	$3|2| - 1 = 5$

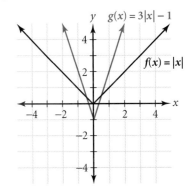

To graph the inverse of g, interchange the values of x and $g(x)$ given in the table above.

TECHNOLOGY

GRAPHICS CALCULATOR

Keystroke Guide, page 152

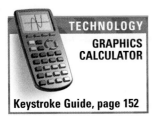

x	Inverse of g
5	−2
2	−1
−1	0
2	1
5	2

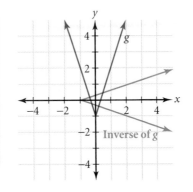

CHECK

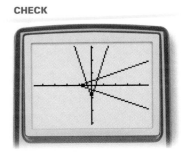

TRY THIS Graph $f(x) = \frac{1}{2}|x| + 1$ by making a table of values. Then graph the inverse of f on the same coordinate plane.

When a measurement is performed on an object, the measured value and the true value may be slightly different. This difference may be due to factors such as the quality of the measuring device or the skill of the individual using the measuring device.

The *relative error* in a measurement of an object gives the amount of error in the measurement relative to the *true measure* of the object. If an object's true measure is x_t units, then the **relative error**, r, in the measurement, x, is given by $r(x) = \left| \frac{x_t - x}{x_t} \right|$.

EXAMPLE 5

APPLICATION
MANUFACTURING

A certain machine part's true length is 25.50 centimeters. Its length is measured as 25.55 centimeters.

Find the relative error in the measurement.

SOLUTION

$$r(x) = \left| \frac{x_t - x}{x_t} \right|$$

$$r(25.55) = \left| \frac{25.50 - 25.55}{25.50} \right|$$

$$= \left| \frac{-0.05}{25.50} \right|$$

$$\approx 0.002$$

The relative error in the measurement, 25.55 centimeters, is about 0.002, or 0.2%.

TRY THIS

The true length of a second machine part is 40.00 centimeters. Its length is measured as 40.05 centimeters. Find the relative error in this measurement.

Exercises

Communicate

1. Describe the defining characteristics of piecewise functions.

2. Explain why $[1.5] = 1$ but $[-1.5] \neq -1$.

3. Compare and contrast the greatest-integer and rounding-up functions.

4. Is the inverse of $y = |x|$ a function? Explain.

Guided Skills Practice

Graph each piecewise function. *(EXAMPLE 1)*

5. $f(x) = \begin{cases} 3x + 5 & \text{if } -1 \leq x < 2 \\ -x + 9 & \text{if } 2 \leq x < 5 \end{cases}$

6. $g(x) = \begin{cases} x + 3 & \text{if } -3 \leq x < 3 \\ 2x & \text{if } x \geq 3 \end{cases}$

CONSUMER ECONOMICS Darren and Joel called their grandmother during winter break. In 1998, this daytime call from Austin, Texas, to Denver, Colorado, was charged at a rate of $0.14 per minute or fraction of a minute. The cost of this phone call can be modeled by $c(x) = 0.14\lceil x \rceil$, where c is the cost in dollars and x is the length of the call in minutes. Find the cost for each call. *(EXAMPLE 2)*

7. 21.25 minutes   **8.** 10 minutes
9. 33.5 minutes   **10.** 0.1 minutes

Graph each step function by making a table of values. *(EXAMPLE 3)*

11. $f(x) = 3\lceil x \rceil$

12. $g(x) = -4\lceil x \rceil$

Graph each absolute-value function by making a table of values. Then graph the inverse on the same coordinate plane. *(EXAMPLE 4)*

13. $f(x) = |x| + 2$

14. $g(x) = 2|x| - 1$

15. MANUFACTURING A certain machine part's true length is 16.000 centimeters. Its length is measured as 16.035 centimeters. Find the relative error in this measurement. *(EXAMPLE 5)*

Practice and Apply

Graph each piecewise function.

16. $f(x) = \begin{cases} x + 1 & \text{if } 0 \le x < 5 \\ 2x - 4 & \text{if } 5 \le x < 10 \end{cases}$

17. $g(x) = \begin{cases} 3x - 4 & \text{if } 0 \le x < 6 \\ 20 - x & \text{if } 6 \le x < 12 \end{cases}$

18. $m(x) = \begin{cases} 20 & \text{if } 0 \le x < 10 \\ \frac{x}{2} + 15 & \text{if } 10 \le x < 20 \end{cases}$

19. $f(x) = \begin{cases} 4x & \text{if } 0 \le x < 2 \\ -2x + 10 & \text{if } 2 \le x < 5 \\ 2 & \text{if } 5 \le x < 10 \end{cases}$

20. $h(x) = \begin{cases} -2 & \text{if } x < 0 \\ x + 1 & \text{if } 0 \le x \le 10 \\ -\frac{1}{2}x + 16 & \text{if } x > 10 \end{cases}$

21. $b(x) = \begin{cases} 2 & \text{if } x < 1 \\ 2x & \text{if } 1 \le x \le 3 \\ 7 - \frac{1}{3}x & \text{if } x > 3 \end{cases}$

22. $k(x) = \begin{cases} 2x + 3 & \text{if } x < 4 \\ x - 1 & \text{if } 4 \le x \le 9 \end{cases}$

23. $f(x) = \begin{cases} 5 - x & \text{if } x < 2 \\ x - 1 & \text{if } 2 \le x \le 10 \end{cases}$

Write the piecewise function represented by each graph.

24.

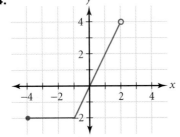

25.

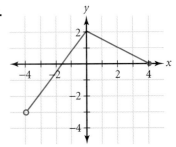

26.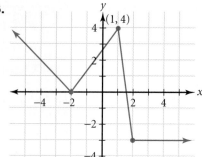

27.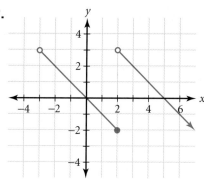

Evaluate.

28. $[3.9]$

29. $[-6.105]$

30. $\lceil 3.9 \rceil$

31. $\lceil -6.105 \rceil$

32. $[-4.1] - [-3.25]$

33. $[5.1] + [-2.01]$

34. $\lceil -4.1 \rceil - \lceil -3.25 \rceil$

35. $\lceil 5.1 \rceil + \lceil -2.01 \rceil$

36. $[-2.5] + [1.999]$

37. $[-2.99] + \lceil 2.99 \rceil$

38. $\lceil -5.1 \rceil - \lceil 5.1 \rceil$

39. $\lceil -2.5 \rceil - \lceil 1.999 \rceil$

40. $[-2.3] - \lceil 5.6 \rceil$

41. $-\lceil 0.9 \rceil + [-8.7]$

42. $[6.2] - \lceil -4.7 \rceil$

43. $\lceil -8.99 \rceil - [-5.1]$

44. $-[0.25] - \lceil 0.25 \rceil$

45. $\lceil 2.75 \rceil - [2.75]$

46. $|4| - |-5|$

47. $|-7| - |2.2|$

48. $|3| + |-4|$

49. $-|-1| - |1|$

50. $|-1| - |3|$

51. $|6| - |-2.67|$

Graph each function.

52. $f(x) = 2\lceil x \rceil$

53. $f(x) = 3\lceil x \rceil$

54. $g(x) = [x] + 3$

55. $g(x) = [x] - 3$

56. $g(x) = 2 - \lceil x \rceil$

57. $h(x) = 4 + \lceil x \rceil$

Graph each function and its inverse together on a coordinate plane.

58. $f(x) = 4|x| - 1$

59. $g(x) = \frac{1}{2}|x|$

60. $h(x) = 5|x| + 10$

Determine whether each statement is true or false. Explain.

61. $|x + y| = |x| + |y|$

62. $|x - y| = |x| - |y|$

63. $|xy| = |x| \cdot |y|$

64. $\left|\dfrac{x}{y}\right| = \dfrac{|x|}{|y|}$

65 Let $S(x) = \left| x - [x] - \frac{1}{2} \right|$ for $x \geq 0$. Graph S for $x \geq 0$. Describe the shape of the graph of S.

66. Compare and contrast $y = |[x]|$ with $y = [|x|]$. Include a discussion of the graphs of these functions.

67. Write a function f that rounds x up to the nearest tenth. Write another function g that rounds x down to the nearest hundredth.

68. TRANSFORMATIONS The absolute-value function can be used to reflect a portion of the graph of g across the x-axis by using composition. Given $f(x) = |x|$ and $g(x) = x^2 - 2$, find and graph $f \circ g$. Compare the graphs of g and $f \circ g$.

MANUFACTURING Find the relative error for each measurement of a machine part whose true length is 6.000 centimeters.

69. 6.035 centimeters

70. 6.025 centimeters

71. 6.150 centimeters

72. 6.300 centimeters

73. CONSUMER ECONOMICS A gourmet coffee store sells the house blend of coffee beans at $9.89 per pound for quantities up to and including 5 pounds. For each additional pound, the price is $7.98 per pound.

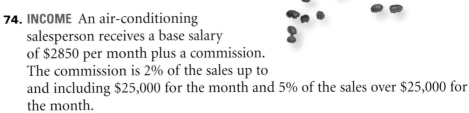

   a. Construct a table to represent the cost for the domain $0 < x \le 10$, where x is the number of pounds of coffee beans purchased.
   b. Graph the data in your table.
   c. Write a function that relates the cost and the number of pounds of coffee beans purchased.
   d. Determine the cost for 5.5 pounds of coffee beans.

74. INCOME An air-conditioning salesperson receives a base salary of $2850 per month plus a commission. The commission is 2% of the sales up to and including $25,000 for the month and 5% of the sales over $25,000 for the month.

   a. Construct a table to represent the salesperson's total monthly income for the domain $0 < s \le 50{,}000$, where s is the sales for the month.
   b. Graph the data in your table.
   c. Write a function that relates the salesperson's total monthly income with his or her sales for the month.
   d. Determine the salesperson's total monthly income if his or her sales were $43,000 for the month.

75. CONSUMER ECONOMICS The Break-n-Fix Repair Store charges $45 for a service call that involves up to and including one hour of labor. For each additional half-hour of labor or fraction thereof, the store charges $20.

   a. Construct a table to represent the charges for the domain $0 < t \le 5$, where t is the labor measured in hours.
   b. Graph the data in your table.
   c. Write a function that relates the cost and the amount of labor involved in the service call.
   d. Determine the cost of a service call that takes 3.75 hours.

76. CONSUMER ECONOMICS Residential water charges, c, are based on the monthly consumption of water, x, in thousands of gallons. Graph the piecewise function given below, which represents the rate schedule for monthly charges.

$$c(x) = \begin{cases} 1.25x + 4.50 & \text{if } 0 < x \le 3 \\ 2x + 2.25 & \text{if } 3 < x \le 7 \\ 2.60x - 7.25 & \text{if } 7 < x \le 15 \\ 3.80x - 22.75 & \text{if } x > 15 \end{cases}$$

 Look Back

APPLICATION

77. CONSUMER ECONOMICS A valet parking lot charges a fixed fee of $2.00 to park a car plus $1.50 per hour for covered parking. *(LESSON 2.3)*
   a. Write a linear function, c, to model the valet parking charge for h hours of covered parking.
   b. If a car is parked in covered parking for 3.5 hours, what is the charge?

Let $f(x) = x + 2$ and $g(x) = 3x$. Perform each function operation. State any domain restrictions. *(LESSON 2.4)*

78. Find $f \circ g$.   **79.** Find $g \circ f$.

80. Find $f \circ f$.   **81.** Find $g \circ g$.

82. Find $f - g$.   **83.** Find $f + g$.

84. Find $f \cdot g$.   **85.** Find $\frac{f}{g}$.

Find an equation for the inverse of each function. Then use composition to verify that the equation you wrote is the inverse. *(LESSON 2.5)*

86. $f(x) = 3x - \frac{1}{2}$ **87.** $a(x) = \frac{3}{4}(x - 2)$

88. $h(x) = -2(x - 4) + 1$ **89.** $g(x) = -x + 8$

 Look Beyond

CONNECTION

90 **TRANSFORMATIONS** Graph $f(x) = \frac{|x|}{x}$, $g(x) = \frac{2|x|}{x}$, and $h(x) = \frac{-2|x|}{x}$. State the domain and range for each function.

SPACE SCIENCE In future years, space technology is expected to improve to a point where many of the components presently left orbiting in space can be returned to Earth. This will greatly reduce the current rate of space debris accumulation.

   1. Your Space Debris Table specified an initial 7000 objects and an annual rate of increase of 3%. Now assume that the projected annual increase becomes a constant 200 objects each year, beginning in 2001. Write and graph a piecewise function that models the total number of debris objects at the end of t years.

   2. Determine the total number of debris objects in 2005 by using the function you wrote in Step 1.

   3. Using your piecewise function from Step 1, calculate how many years it would take for the number of debris objects to be double the number found at the end of 1993. (Refer to the table that you created in the Portfolio Activity on page 93.) Compare this with the number of years it would take to double without the change in Step 1. (Refer to the Portfolio Activity on page 110.)

   4. Using the piecewise function you wrote in Step 1, model the number of debris objects in space in 2010. Compare this with the number for the same year in the table that you created in the Portfolio Activity on page 93.

A Preview of Transformations

Objective

- Identify the transformation(s) from one function to another.

APPLICATION
HEALTH

Why *Many real-world situations are represented by using transformations. For example, translations are often used to graph data involving trends such as the decreasing number of reported cases of chickenpox over time.*

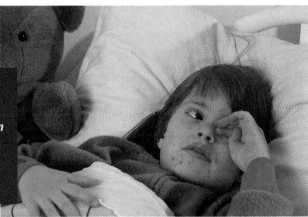

The table of data below gives the number of reported cases of chickenpox in the United States in thousands from 1989 to 1994. In Lesson 1.5, this data was used to create a scatter plot by *translating* the *x*-values from the actual year to the number of years after 1988. Columns 2 and 3 in the table below show two other possible translations.

Year	Number of years after 1960	Number of years after 1970	Cases reported (in thousands)
1989	29	19	185.4
1990	30	20	173.1
1991	31	21	147.1
1992	32	22	158.4
1993	33	23	134.7
1994	34	24	151.2

[*Source: U.S. Centers for Disease Control and Prevention*]

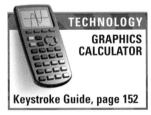

TECHNOLOGY
GRAPHICS CALCULATOR

Keystroke Guide, page 152

Activity
Exploring Translations of Data

You will need: a graphics calculator

1. Enter the data from columns 2 and 4 into your graphics calculator. Make a scatter plot. Then use linear regression to find an equation for the least-squares line.

2. Enter the data from columns 3 and 4 into your graphics calculator. Make a scatter plot. Then find an equation for the least-squares line.

CHECKPOINT ✔ 3. How are the equations for the least-squares lines different? How are the graphs of the least-squares lines similar?

Just as you translate data, you can translate a function. A translation is one type of *transformation*. A **transformation** of a function is an alteration of the function rule that results in an alteration of its graph.

Translation

Example 1 illustrates a *vertical translation* and a *horizontal translation*.

TECHNOLOGY
GRAPHICS CALCULATOR

Keystroke Guide, page 153

E X A M P L E ❶ **Graph each pair of functions, and identify the transformation from *f* to *g*.**
   a. $f(x) = x^2$ and $g(x) = x^2 + 3$ **b.** $f(x) = |x|$ and $g(x) = |x + 4|$

● **SOLUTION**

a.

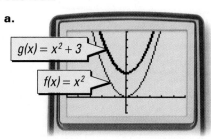

b.

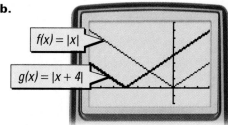

Notice that $g(x) = f(x) + 3$. The function $g(x) = x^2 + 3$ is a vertical translation of the graph of f 3 units up.

Notice that $g(x) = f(x + 4)$. The function $g(x) = |x + 4|$ is a horizontal translation of the graph of f 4 units to the left.

TRY THIS   Graph each pair of functions, and identify the transformation from *f* to *g*.
   a. $f(x) = x^2$ and $g(x) = x^2 - 2$ **b.** $f(x) = |x|$ and $g(x) = |x - 3|$

Notice that the shape of the transformed graphs in Example 1 do not change. Only the position of the graphs with respect to the coordinate axes changes.

Vertical and horizontal translations are generalized as follows:

Vertical and Horizontal Translations

If $y = f(x)$, then $y = f(x) + k$ gives a **vertical translation** of the graph of f. The translation is k units up for $k > 0$ and $|k|$ units down for $k < 0$.

If $y = f(x)$, then $y = f(x - h)$ gives a **horizontal translation** of the graph of f. The translation is h units to the right for $h > 0$ and $|h|$ units to the left for $h < 0$.

Vertical Translation

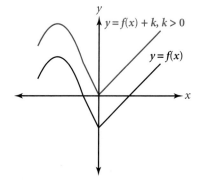

Horizontal Translation

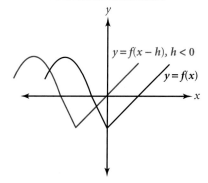

CHECKPOINT ✔ How does writing the function $j(x) = |x + 4|$ as $j(x) = |x - (-4)|$ help you to recognize that the translation is to the left?

Vertical Stretch and Compression

Example 2 illustrates a *vertical stretch* and a *vertical compression*.

E X A M P L E **2** Graph each pair of functions, and identify the transformation from *f* to *g*.

a. $f(x) = \sqrt{16 - x^2}$ and
$g(x) = 2\sqrt{16 - x^2}$

b. $f(x) = \sqrt{16 - x^2}$ and
$g(x) = \frac{1}{2}\sqrt{16 - x^2}$

● **SOLUTION**

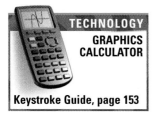

TECHNOLOGY
GRAPHICS CALCULATOR

Keystroke Guide, page 153

a.

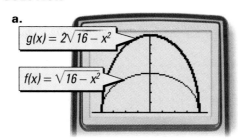

b.

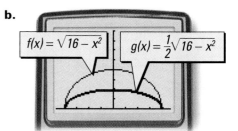

Notice that $g(x) = 2 \cdot f(x)$.
The function $g(x) = 2\sqrt{16 - x^2}$
is a vertical stretch of the graph
of *f* by a factor of 2.

Notice that $g(x) = \frac{1}{2} \cdot f(x)$.
The function $g(x) = \frac{1}{2}\sqrt{16 - x^2}$
is a vertical compression of the
graph of *f* by a by a factor of $\frac{1}{2}$.

TRY THIS Graph each pair of functions, and identify the transformation from *f* to *g*.
a. $f(x) = \sqrt{25 - x^2}$ and $g(x) = 3\sqrt{25 - x^2}$
b. $f(x) = \sqrt{25 - x^2}$ and $g(x) = \frac{1}{3}\sqrt{25 - x^2}$

A vertical stretch or compression moves the graph away from or toward the *x*-axis, respectively. It can be generalized as follows:

Vertical Stretch and Vertical Compression

If $y = f(x)$, then $y = af(x)$ gives a **vertical stretch** or **vertical compression** of the graph of *f*.

- If $a > 1$, the graph is stretched vertically by a factor of *a*.
- If $0 < a < 1$, the graph is compressed vertically by a factor of *a*.

Vertical Stretch

Vertical Compression

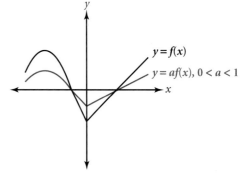

CRITICAL THINKING Let $0 < r < 1$ and $s > 1$. Compare the graphs of $f(x) = r|x|$ and $g(x) = s|x|$.

Horizontal Stretch and Compression

Example 3 illustrates a *horizontal stretch* and a *horizontal compression*.

EXAMPLE ③ Graph each pair of functions, and identify the transformation from f to g.

a. $f(x) = \sqrt{16 - x^2}$ and $g(x) = \sqrt{16 - (2x)^2}$

b. $f(x) = \sqrt{16 - x^2}$ and $g(x) = \sqrt{16 - \left(\frac{1}{2}x\right)^2}$

SOLUTION

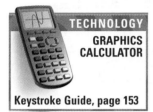
a.

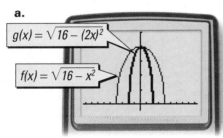

$g(x) = \sqrt{16 - (2x)^2}$

$f(x) = \sqrt{16 - x^2}$

b.

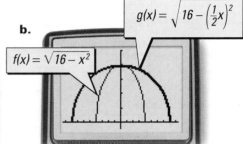

$g(x) = \sqrt{16 - \left(\frac{1}{2}x\right)^2}$

$f(x) = \sqrt{16 - x^2}$

Notice that $g(x) = f(2x)$.
The function $g(x) = \sqrt{16 - (2x)^2}$
is a horizontal compression of the
graph of f by a factor of $\frac{1}{2}$.

Notice that $g(x) = f\left(\frac{1}{2}x\right)$.

The function $g(x) = \sqrt{16 - \left(\frac{1}{2}x\right)^2}$

is a horizontal stretch of the
graph of f by a factor of 2.

TRY THIS   Graph each pair of functions, and identify the transformation from f to g.

a. $f(x) = \sqrt{25 - x^2}$ and $g(x) = \sqrt{25 - (3x)^2}$

b. $f(x) = \sqrt{25 - x^2}$ and $g(x) = \sqrt{25 - \left(\frac{1}{4}x\right)^2}$

A horizontal stretch or compression moves the graph away from or toward the
y-axis, respectively. It can be generalized as follows:

Horizontal Stretch and Horizontal Compression

If $y = f(x)$, then $y = f(bx)$ gives a **horizontal stretch** or **horizontal compression** of the graph of f.

- If $b > 1$, the graph is compressed horizontally by a factor of $\frac{1}{b}$.

- If $0 < b < 1$, the graph is stretched horizontally by a factor of $\frac{1}{b}$.

Horizontal Stretch

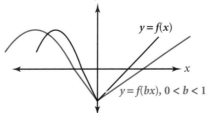

$y = f(x)$

$y = f(bx),\ 0 < b < 1$

Horizontal Compression

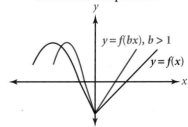

$y = f(bx),\ b > 1$

$y = f(x)$

Reflection

Example 4 illustrates reflections across the x-axis and across the y-axis.

E X A M P L E **4** **Graph each pair of functions, and identify the transformation from f to g.**

    a. $f(x) = x^2$ and $g(x) = -(x^2)$ **b.** $f(x) = 2x + 3$ and $g(x) = 2(-x) + 3$

SOLUTION

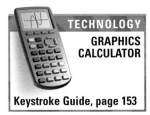

TECHNOLOGY
GRAPHICS CALCULATOR

Keystroke Guide, page 153

a.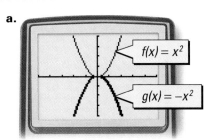

$f(x) = x^2$
$g(x) = -x^2$

Notice that $g(x) = -f(x)$. The function $g(x) = -(x^2)$ is a reflection of the graph of f across the x-axis.

b.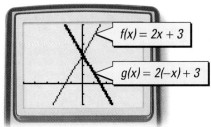

$f(x) = 2x + 3$
$g(x) = 2(-x) + 3$

Notice that $g(x) = f(-x)$. The function $g(x) = 2(-x) + 3$, or $g(x) = -2x + 3$, is a reflection of the graph of f across the y-axis.

TRY THIS   Graph each pair of functions, and identify the transformation from f to g.

    a. $f(x) = |x|$ and $g(x) = -|x|$ **b.** $f(x) = 2x - 1$ and $g(x) = 2(-x) - 1$

CRITICAL THINKING   Can the graph of a function be reflected across both the x- and y-axes simultaneously? Explain and give an example.

Reflections can be generalized as follows:

Reflections

If $y = f(x)$, then $y = -f(x)$ gives a **reflection** of the graph of f across the x-axis.

If $y = f(x)$, then $y = f(-x)$ gives a **reflection** of the graph of f across the y-axis.

Reflection Across the x-axis

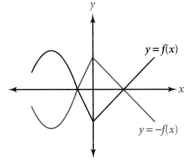

Reflection Across the y-axis

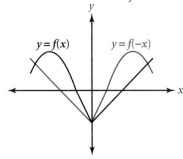

CRITICAL THINKING   Let $f(x) = x^2$. What does $f(-x) = (-x)^2 = x^2$ tell you about the graph of $f(-x)$? Justify your response.

Combining Transformations

The functions $f(x) = x^2$ and $h(x) = |x|$ are examples of *parent functions* because other functions are related to them by one or more transformations. Example 5 illustrates a combination of transformations.

EXAMPLE ⑤ Graph each pair of functions, and identify the transformations from f to g.
    a. $f(x) = x^2$ and $g(x) = (x + 2)^2 - 1$ **b.** $f(x) = |x|$ and $g(x) = -4|x| + 3$

● SOLUTION

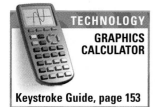

TECHNOLOGY
GRAPHICS
CALCULATOR

Keystroke Guide, page 153

a.

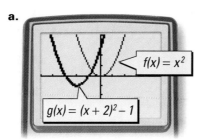

$f(x) = x^2$

$g(x) = (x + 2)^2 - 1$

b.

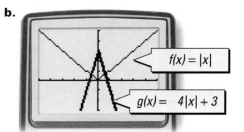

$f(x) = |x|$

$g(x) = -4|x| + 3$

Notice that $g(x) = f(x + 2) - 1$, or $g(x) = f(x - (-2)) - 1$. There are two transformations of the parent function $f(x) = x^2$: a translation of 2 units to the left and a translation of 1 unit down.

$$g(x) = [x - (-2)]^2 - 1$$

horizontal   vertical
translation   translation

Notice that $g(x) = -4 \cdot f(x) + 3$. There are three transformations of the parent function $f(x) = |x|$: a vertical stretch by a factor of 4, a reflection across the x-axis, and a vertical translation of 3 units up.

reflection⟍

$$g(x) = -4|x| + 3$$

vertical   vertical
stretch   translation

TRY THIS   Graph each pair of functions, and identify the transformations from f to g.
    a. $f(x) = x^2$ and $g(x) = 3(x - 1)^2$ **b.** $f(x) = |x|$ and $g(x) = \frac{1}{2}|x| - 2$

A summary of the transformations in this lesson is given below.

SUMMARY OF TRANSFORMATIONS	
Transformations of $y = f(x)$	**Transformed function**
Vertical translation of k units up	$y = f(x) + k$, where $k > 0$
Vertical translation of $|k|$ units down	$y = f(x) + k$, where $k < 0$
Horizontal translation of h units to the right	$y = f(x - h)$, where $h > 0$
Horizontal translation of $|h|$ units to the left	$y = f(x - h)$, where $h < 0$
Vertical stretch by a factor of a	$y = af(x)$, where $a > 1$
Vertical compression by a factor of a	$y = af(x)$, where $0 < a < 1$
Horizontal stretch by a factor of $\frac{1}{b}$	$y = f(bx)$, where $0 < b < 1$
Horizontal compression by a factor of $\frac{1}{b}$	$y = f(bx)$, where $b > 1$
Reflection across the x-axis	$y = -f(x)$
Reflection across the y-axis	$y = f(-x)$

Exercises

Communicate

1. Describe each transformation of $f(x) = x^2$.

a.
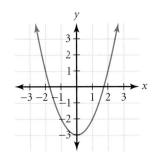

b.
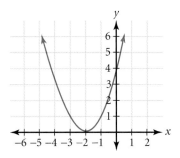

2. Describe the range of possible values of $\frac{1}{b}$ when $0 < b < 1$.

3. Compare and contrast reflections and translations.

4. For what values of h will the graph of $f(x - h)$ be translated to the right? to the left? Explain.

5. Differentiate between the effects of a vertical stretch and a horizontal stretch on the graph of a function.

Guided Skills Practice

Identify the transformations from _f_ to _g_.

6. $f(x) = x^2$ and $g(x) = x^2 - 3$ *(EXAMPLE 1)*

7. $f(x) = \sqrt{9 - x^2}$ and $g(x) = \frac{4}{3}\sqrt{9 - x^2}$ *(EXAMPLE 2)*

8. $f(x) = \sqrt{36 - x^2}$ and $g(x) = \sqrt{36 - (2x)^2}$ *(EXAMPLE 3)*

9. $f(x) = -3x + 1$ and $g(x) = -3(-x) + 1$ *(EXAMPLE 4)*

10. $f(x) = x^2$ and $g(x) = (x - 3)^2 + 1$ *(EXAMPLE 5)*

Practice and Apply

Identify each transformation from the parent function $f(x) = x^2$ to _g_.

11. $g(x) = 4x^2$

12. $g(x) = 5x^2$

13. $g(x) = (4x)^2$

14. $g(x) = (-5x)^2$

15. $g(x) = -\frac{1}{2}x^2$

16. $g(x) = -\frac{1}{5}x^2$

17. $g(x) = x^2 - 2$

18. $g(x) = x^2 + 3$

19. $g(x) = (x - 2)^2$

20. $g(x) = (x + 3)^2$

21. $g(x) = (-5x)^2 + 2$

22. $g(x) = 3(x - 1)^2$

23. $g(x) = \frac{1}{3}x^2 - 1$

24. $g(x) = -\frac{1}{4}x^2 + 3$

25. $g(x) = -2(x + 4)^2 + 1$

26. $g(x) = -5(x - 2)^2 - 4$

Identify each transformation from the parent function $f(x) = \sqrt{x}$ to g.

27. $g(x) = 4\sqrt{x}$ **28.** $g(x) = 3\sqrt{x}$ **29.** $g(x) = -\frac{1}{4}\sqrt{x}$

30. $g(x) = -\frac{1}{3}\sqrt{x}$ **31.** $g(x) = \sqrt{-4x}$ **32.** $g(x) = \sqrt{-3x}$

33. $g(x) = \sqrt{x} + 4$ **34.** $g(x) = \sqrt{x} - 3$ **35.** $g(x) = \sqrt{x+4}$

36. $g(x) = \sqrt{x-3}$ **37.** $g(x) = \sqrt{-2x} + 1$ **38.** $g(x) = -\sqrt{x} + 3$

39. $g(x) = -\sqrt{x-4} + 3$ **40.** $g(x) = -\sqrt{3x} - 1$ **41.** $g(x) = -\sqrt{-x}$

Write the function for each graph described below.

42. the graph of $f(x) = |x|$ translated 4 units to the left

43. the graph of $f(x) = x^2$ translated 2 units to the right

44. the graph of $f(x) = |x|$ translated 5 units up

45. the graph of $f(x) = x^2$ translated 6 units down

46. the graph of $f(x) = x^2$ vertically stretched by a factor of 3

47. the graph of $f(x) = \sqrt{x}$ vertically compressed by a factor of $\frac{1}{3}$

48. the graph of $f(x) = x^2$ horizontally compressed by a factor of $\frac{1}{5}$

49. the graph of $f(x) = \sqrt{x}$ horizontally stretched by a factor of 4

50. the graph of $f(x) = 3x + 1$ reflected across the x-axis

51. the graph of $f(x) = 2x - 1$ reflected across the y-axis

52. the graph of $f(x) = x^2$ vertically stretched by a factor of 2 and translated 1 unit to the right

53. the graph of $f(x) = |x|$ horizontally compressed by a factor of $\frac{1}{3}$, reflected across the x-axis, and translated 3 units down

54. the graph of $f(x) = x^2$ translated 7 units to the left

55. the graph of $f(x) = x^2$ translated 5 units up

56. the graph of $f(x) = x^2$ stretched vertically by a factor of 2

57. the graph of $f(x) = x^2$ reflected across the y-axis and stretched horizontally by a factor of 2

CHALLENGES

58. How are the domain and range of a function affected by a reflection across the y-axis? across the x-axis? Include examples in your explanation.

59. Show that a vertical compression can have the same effect on a graph as a horizontal stretch.

At right is the graph of the function f. Draw a careful sketch of each transformation of f.

60. $g(x) = f(2x)$ **61.** $g(x) = 2f(x)$

62. $g(x) = -f(x)$ **63.** $g(x) = f(x + 2)$

64. $g(x) = f(x) + 3$ **65.** $g(x) = f\left(\frac{1}{2}x\right)$

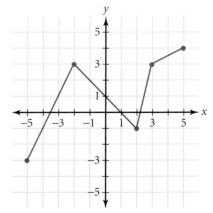

66. PHYSICS Let the function $h(t) = -16t^2 + 100$ model the altitude of an eagle in free fall when it dives from an initial altitude of 100 feet to catch a fish.

a. Describe the transformations from the graph of $f(t) = t^2$ to the graph of h.

b. Write a transformed function, h, that represents the altitude of an eagle diving from an initial altitude of 25 feet.

c. Graph f and h on the same coordinate plane, and describe the transformation from f to h by following the transformation of a point.

A bald eagle, the national bird of the United States

Look Back

67. Write an equation in slope-intercept form for the line that contains $(-3, 4)$ and is perpendicular to the graph of $y = -\frac{1}{2}x + 10$. *(LESSON 1.3)*

68. Solve $\frac{3}{5} = \frac{5}{x}$. *(LESSON 1.4)*

69. Solve the literal equation $D = \pi\left(\frac{b}{2}\right)^2 sn$ for s. *(LESSON 1.6)*

Classify each number in as many ways as possible. *(LESSON 2.1)*

70. 15.3849 **71.** 14.393939 . . . **72.** 17.1012012301234 . . .

Find the inverse of each relation. State whether the relation is a function. State whether the inverse is a function. *(LESSON 2.5)*

73. {(1, 100), (2, 200), (3, 300), (4, 400)}

74. {(1, 5), (2, 10), (3, 10), (4, 15)}

75. Graph the piecewise function below. *(LESSON 2.6)*

$$f(x) = \begin{cases} x & \text{if } -4 \leq x \leq -1 \\ x + 2 & \text{if } -1 < x < 3 \\ -3x + 18 & \text{if } 3 \leq x \leq 5 \end{cases}$$

Look Beyond

76 Graph the linear functions $x - 2y = -4$ and $3x + 2y = -4$ together. Find the coordinates of the point of intersection. Then add the corresponding sides of the two equations and solve the resulting equation for x. Is this x-value close to the x-value at the intersection of the two graphs?

Space Trash

More than 3600 space missions since 1957 have left thousands of large and millions of smaller debris objects in near-Earth space. Information about the orbital debris is needed to determine the current and future hazards that this debris may pose to space operations. Only the largest objects can be repeatedly tracked and cataloged.

The table at right shows the estimated number of cataloged rocket bodies and fragmentation debris from 1965 to 1990 in five-year periods.

Space Debris Table		
Year	Rocket bodies	Fragmentation debris
1965	175	900
1970	350	1850
1975	525	2250
1980	700	2600
1985	875	3200
1990	1050	2900

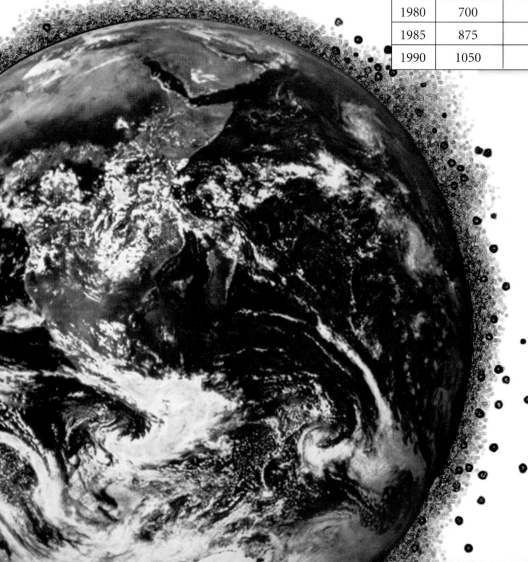

Activity 1

Skylab, *the United States' first space station*

1. Use the data from the Space Debris Table on the previous page, which shows the estimated number of cataloged rocket bodies and fragmentation debris for the years 1965 to 1990. Find the average annual rate of change in the number of rocket bodies and debris from 1965 to 1990. Then find the rate of change for each five-year interval. Compare the individual five-year rates with the average rate.

2. Find a linear model for all of the rocket body data from Step 1. Let the years be represented by x (where $x = 0$ represents 1965 and $x = 5$ represents 1970). Verify your equation by using data from the table.

Activity 2

1. Create a scatter plot for the number of other cataloged debris objects for the given years from 1965 to 1990 from the Space Debris Table on the previous page. Plot the years on the horizontal axis (where $x = 0$ represents 1965) and number of other debris objects on the vertical axis.

2. Sketch the curve on your scatter plot that you think best models your data. Describe the trend you see in the scatter plot. Do you think you can make reliable predictions by using the model you sketched? Explain.

3. Using a graphics calculator, find linear, quadratic, and exponential regression equations for this data. Discuss which model best approximates the data.

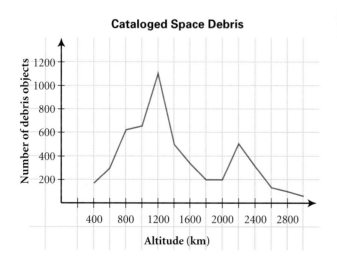

Cataloged Space Debris

Activity 3

1. Using the Cataloged Space Debris graph at left, which shows the distribution of cataloged debris objects by altitude, describe what happens to the number of debris objects as the altitude increases. Write an approximate step function that models the data in the graph.

2. Using the step function that you wrote in Step 1, estimate the number of objects at an altitude of 725 kilometers, 1450 kilometers, and 1900 kilometers. Discuss the usefulness of your model.

Chapter Review and Assessment

Key Skills & Exercises

LESSON 2.1

Key Skills

Identify and use Properties of Real Numbers.

The real numbers have the Closure, Commutative, Associative, Identity, Inverse, and Distributive Properties for addition and multiplication.

Evaluate expressions by using the order of operations.

$$\frac{-3 \times (6-4)^2}{6} = \frac{-3 \times 2^2}{6}$$
$$= \frac{-3 \times 4}{6}$$
$$= \frac{-12}{6}$$
$$= -2$$

Exercises

State the property that is illustrated in each statement. All variables represent real numbers.

1. $a(2b) = (2b)a$ **2.** $2 \times 1 = 2$

3. $a\left(\frac{1}{a}\right) = 1$ **4.** $(2s)t = 2(st)$

5. $4x + 0 = 4x$ **6.** $-2a + 2a = 0$

7. $(x + y) + 5 = 5 + (x + y)$

8. $5(2 - x) = 5(2) + 5(-x)$

Evaluate each expression.

9. $-1(5 + 3)^2 - 11$ **10.** $\frac{(11-5)^2}{3 \times 2}$

11. $\frac{(6-12)5}{3^3}$ **12.** $\frac{2^3 - (13+4)}{(-3)^2}$

LESSON 2.2

Key Skills

Simplify and evaluate expressions by using the Properties of Exponents.

$$\left(\frac{(5^3)(5^{-2})}{5^2}\right)^2 = \left(\frac{5^{3-2}}{5^2}\right)^2 = \left(\frac{5^1}{5^2}\right)^2 = (5^{1-2})^2$$
$$= (5^{-1})^2 = 5^{-2} = \frac{1}{5^2} = \frac{1}{25}$$

Exercises

Evaluate or simplify each expression. Assume that no variable equals zero.

13. $x^4(3x)^2$ **14.** $2a(5a^3b^5)^2$ **15.** $\frac{(u^2v)^3}{v^2}$

16. $\left(\frac{p^{-1}q^2}{p^{-1}}\right)^{-4}\left(\frac{-p^5q^{-3}}{p^{-3}q^{-1}}\right)^{-3}$ **17.** $\frac{(2x)^3}{y^2}\left(\frac{x^2}{3}\right)^3$

LESSON 2.3

Key Skills

State the domain and range of a relation, and state whether it is a function.

The relation $\{(1, 2), (2, 4), (3, 6), (4, 8)\}$ is a function because each x-coordinate is paired with one and only one y-coordinate.

domain: $\{1, 2, 3, 4\}$ range: $\{2, 4, 6, 8\}$

Evaluate functions.

Evaluate $f(x) = 2x^2 - x + 3$ for $x = 5$.

$$f(5) = 2(5)^2 - 5 + 3$$
$$f(5) = 50 - 5 + 3$$
$$f(5) = 48$$

Exercises

State whether each relation is a function.

18. $\{(1, 2), (2, 3), (3, 5), (4, 7), (5, 11)\}$
19. $\{(1, -1), (2, -2), (3, -3)\}$
20. $\{(1, -1), (1, 1), (2, -3)\}$
21. $\{(1, 1), (1, -1), (2, 2), (2, -2)\}$

State the domain and range for each function.

22. $\{(-1, -6), (5, 8), (9, -1), (2, 3)\}$
23. $\{(-1, 2), (0, 6), (2, 7), (4, -7)\}$

Evaluate each function for $x = 1$ and $x = -1$.

24. $f(x) = 3x^2 - 2x + 1$ 25. $g(x) = 11x - 2$
26. $f(x) = 3x^2 - 2$ 27. $h(x) = 2 - 3x$

LESSON 2.4

Key Skills

Add, subtract, multiply, and divide functions.

The sum, difference, product, and quotient of functions f and g are defined as follows:

$$(f + g)(x) = f(x) + g(x)$$
$$(f - g)(x) = f(x) - g(x)$$
$$(f \cdot g)(x) = f(x) \cdot g(x)$$
$$\left(\frac{f}{g}\right)(x) = \frac{f(x)}{g(x)}, \text{ where } g(x) \neq 0$$

Compose functions.

If f and g are functions with appropriate domains and ranges, then the composition of f with g, $f \circ g$, is defined by $f(g(x))$.

Exercises

Let $f(x) = 3x - 4$ and $g(x) = \frac{x}{2} - 5$. Find each new function, and state any domain restrictions.

28. $f + g$ 29. $f - g$ 30. $g - f$
31. $f \circ g$ 32. $\frac{f}{g}$ 33. $\frac{g}{f}$

Let $f(x) = 2x$ and $g(x) = -x + 2$. Find each composite function.

34. $f \circ g$ 35. $g \circ f$
36. $f \circ f$ 37. $g \circ g$

Let $f(x) = -3x - 5$ and $g(x) = 4x - 1$. Evaluate each composite function.

38. $(f \circ g)(3)$ 39. $(g \circ f)(2)$ 40. $(g \circ g)(-1)$

LESSON 2.5

Key Skills

Find the inverse of a function.

To find the inverse of the function $f = \{(1, 2), (2, 4), (3, 8), (4, 16)\}$, reverse the order of the coordinates in each ordered pair. The inverse of f is $\{(2, 1), (4, 2), (8, 3), (16, 4)\}$.

To find the inverse of a function f defined by a function rule, replace $f(x)$ with y, interchange x and y, and solve for y.

Exercises

Find the inverse of each function.

41. $f = \{(-2, 0), (-1, 1), (0, 0), (1, 1), (2, 0)\}$
42. $f = \{(1, 2), (2, 3), (3, 4), (4, 5)\}$

Find an equation for the inverse of each function. Then use composition to verify that the equation you wrote is the inverse.

43. $f(x) = -\frac{2}{3}x + 4$ 44. $f(x) = \frac{2 - x}{3}$

Use the horizontal-line test to determine whether the inverse relation is a function.

If a function, f, has an inverse that is a function, then any horizontal line that intersects the graph of f will do so at only one point.

Graph each function, and use the horizontal-line test to determine whether the inverse is a function.

45 $f(x) = \dfrac{3x + 3}{2}$ **46** $f(x) = x^2 - 1$

47 $f(x) = 2\left(\dfrac{2x}{3} + 1\right)$ **48** $f(x) = 3x + 5$

LESSON 2.6

Key Skills

Define and graph piecewise functions, step functions, and absolute-value functions.

The piecewise function $f(x) = \begin{cases} 2x + 1 & \text{if } x < 0 \\ 5x & \text{if } x \geq 0 \end{cases}$

is the function that assigns the function value $2x + 1$ to negative values of x and the function value $5x$ to nonnegative values of x.

A step function consists of different constant range values, and its graph resembles stair steps.

The absolute-value function $f(x) = |x|$ gives the distance from x to 0 on a number line and has a v-shaped graph.

Exercises

Graph each function.

49. $f(x) = \begin{cases} x & \text{if } x < 1 \\ -2x + 3 & \text{if } x \geq 1 \end{cases}$

50. $f(x) = \begin{cases} x^2 + 1 & \text{if } x < 0 \\ 1 & \text{if } x \geq 0 \end{cases}$

51. $f(x) = 3[x]$ **52.** $f(x) = \frac{1}{2}|x| - 1$

Evaluate.

53. $[-77.99]$ **54.** $[4] - [-7.1]$

55. $\lceil 3.5 \rceil$ **56.** $\lceil 4.0 \rceil - \lceil -7.001 \rceil$

57. $|-7| + [1.09]$ **58.** $|3.5| - \lceil 2.9 \rceil$

LESSON 2.7

Key Skills

Identify transformations of functions.

The graph of $g(x) = 2[3(x - 1)]^2 + 4$ is formed by the following transformations of the graph of $f(x) = x^2$:
- a horizontal translation of 1 unit to the right
- a horizontal compression by a factor of $\frac{1}{3}$
- a vertical stretch by a factor of 2
- a vertical translation of 4 units up

Exercises

Identify the transformations from f to g.

59. $f(x) = x^2$, $g(x) = (x - 2)^2$

60. $f(x) = \sqrt{x}$, $g(x) = \sqrt{-x} + 3$

61. $f(x) = |x|$, $g(x) = -|x + 3|$

Applications

62. CONSUMER ECONOMICS Hardwood flooring cost $4.75 per square foot for amounts up to and including 500 square feet and $4.50 for amounts of more than 500 square feet. Write and graph a function that describes the cost, c, of x square feet of hardwood flooring.

63. SPORTS The function $h(t) = -9.8t^2 + 1.5$ gives the height in meters of a basketball thrown from an initial height of 1.5 meters. Describe the transformations from $f(t) = t^2$ to h.

Alternative Assessment

Performance Assessment

1. **CHEMISTRY** A drop of water contains about 1.7×10^{21} water molecules.
   a. Find the number of molecules of water in a glass that has 2.5×10^4 drops.
   b. State each Property of Real Numbers and of Exponents that you used in Step 1.
   c. How many millions of molecules are in the glass? Write your answer without using exponents.

2. **CURRENCY EXCHANGE** Use a newspaper to obtain current exchange rates for U.S. dollars, British pounds, and Canadian dollars.
   a. Write a function that represents how many British pounds, B, you would receive for x U.S. dollars.
   b. Write a function that represents how many Canadian dollars, C, you would receive for x U.S. dollars.
   c. Find inverse relations for each exchange function, and describe what they represent.
   d. Create a new function that gives the number of Canadian dollars that you would receive for x British pounds.

3. **ORDER OF OPERATIONS GAME** In as many ways as possible, obtain a result of 10 by using each of the numbers 11, 1, 8, 3, and 14 only once and using any order of operations. For example:

$$(11 \times 3) - (14 + 8) - 1 = 10$$

Portfolio Projects

1. **PATTERNS IN EXPONENTS**
   a. Copy and complete the pattern for 2^4 through 2^1.

   $$2^5 = 2 \cdot 2 \cdot 2 \cdot 2 \cdot 2 = 32$$
   $$2^4 = 2 \cdot 2 \cdot 2 \cdot 2 = \underline{\quad ? \quad}$$
   $$2^3 = 2 \cdot 2 \cdot 2 = \underline{\quad ? \quad}$$
   $$2^2 = 2 \cdot 2 = \underline{\quad ? \quad}$$
   $$2^1 = 2 = \underline{\quad ? \quad}$$
   $$2^0 = \underline{\quad ? \quad}$$
   $$2^{-1} = \underline{\quad ? \quad}$$
   $$2^{-2} = \underline{\quad ? \quad}$$
   $$2^{-3} = \underline{\quad ? \quad}$$

   b. Look for a pattern in the values of 2^5 through 2^1. Use this pattern to find the values for 2^0 through 2^{-3}. Verify your values for 2^0 through 2^{-3} by using a calculator.
   c. Make area models to represent the value of each power of 2. For example, a 4-by-8 rectangle can represent 2^5.
   d. Discuss how your area models relate to one another. How would this relationship differ if the base of the powers were 10 instead of 2?

2. **MEASURING π** Measure the diameter and circumference of at least five different-size cans. Organize your data in a table. Add a column (or row) for the ratio of circumference to diameter. Calculate the average of the ratios, and discuss how your average compares with π.

---

internetconnect

The HRW Web site contains many resources to reinforce and expand your knowledge of numbers and functions. This Web site also provides Internet links to other sites where you can find information and real-world data for use in research projects, reports, and activities that involve numbers and functions. Visit the HRW Web site at **go.hrw.com,** and enter the keyword **MB1 CH2** to access the resources for this chapter.

College Entrance Exam Practice

QUANTITATIVE COMPARISON For Items 1–5, write
A if the quantity in Column A is greater than the quantity in Column B;
B if the quantity in Column B is greater than the quantity in Column A;
C if the quantities are equal; or
D if the relationship cannot be determined from the given information.

	Column A	Column B	Answers
1.	The value of x in $x - 2 = 3 + 4x$	The value of y in $-8y - 2 = 3 - 3y$	Ⓐ Ⓑ Ⓒ Ⓓ [Lesson 1.6]
2.	$3[4.95] - 2$	$3[3.95] - 2$	Ⓐ Ⓑ Ⓒ Ⓓ [Lesson 2.5]
3.	$\frac{x^3}{x} - x^2$, where $x \neq 0$	$x^2 \cdot x^{-2}$, where $x \neq 0$	Ⓐ Ⓑ Ⓒ Ⓓ [Lesson 2.2]
4.	$f(-1)$ $f(x) = x^2 - 2x + 3$	$f(3)$	Ⓐ Ⓑ Ⓒ Ⓓ [Lesson 2.3]
5.	The slope of a line perpendicular to the graph of $y = -\frac{1}{6}x + 5$	The slope of a line parallel to the graph of $y = -\frac{1}{6}x + 5$	Ⓐ Ⓑ Ⓒ Ⓓ [Lesson 1.3]

6. Which is the equation for the line whose slope, m, is -5 and y-intercept, b, is $-\frac{1}{2}$? **(LESSON 1.2)**

a. $y = -\frac{1}{2}x - 5$ **b.** $y = -\frac{1}{2}x + 5$

c. $y = -5x - \frac{1}{2}$ **d.** $y = -5x + \frac{1}{2}$

7. Solve $|2 + 3x| = 14$. **(LESSON 1.7)**
a. $x = -4$ **b.** $x = -\frac{16}{3}$
c. $x = -4$ or $x = \frac{16}{3}$ **d.** $x = 4$ or $x = -\frac{16}{3}$

8. Let $f(x) = -3x^2$ and $g(x) = 2 - x$. Which of the following function operations gives the new function $h(x) = 3x^3 - 6x^2$? **(LESSON 2.4)**
a. $f - g$ **b.** $f \cdot g$ **c.** $f \div g$ **d.** $f \circ g$

9. Solve $S = \frac{1780Ad}{r}$ for A. **(LESSON 1.6)**
a. $A = \frac{1780Sd}{r}$ **b.** $A = \frac{Sd}{1780r}$
c. $A = \frac{1780dr}{S}$ **d.** $A = \frac{Sr}{1780d}$

10. Which linear equation contains the points $(-1, -4)$ and $(3, 8)$? **(LESSON 1.3)**
a. $y = \frac{1}{3}x + 7$ **b.** $y = -\frac{1}{3}x + 9$
c. $y = 3x - 1$ **d.** $y = -3x - 7$

11. Which number is irrational? **(LESSON 2.1)**
a. -3 **b.** $\frac{1}{3}$ **c.** $0.\overline{5}$ **d.** π

12. Which is an equation for the line that contains the point $(10, 3)$ and is perpendicular to the graph of $y = 5x - 3$? **(LESSON 1.3)**
a. $y = -\frac{1}{5}x + 5$ **b.** $y = -\frac{1}{5}x - 3$
c. $y = -5x - 3$ **d.** $y = -5x + 5$

13. Which is the inverse of the function $y = -3x + 12$? **(LESSON 2.5)**
a. $y = -3x + 12$ **b.** $y = \frac{1}{3}x + 12$
c. $y = -\frac{1}{3}x + 4$ **d.** $y = -3x + 4$

14. Which description below identifies the transformations from f to $y = 3f(x - 2)$? *(LESSON 2.7)*

   a. a horizontal translation of 2 units to the right and a vertical stretch by a factor of 3

   b. a horizontal translation of 2 units to the left and a vertical stretch by a factor of 3

   c. a vertical translation of 2 units up and a vertical stretch by a factor of 3

   d. a vertical translation of 2 units down and a vertical stretch by a factor of 3

STATISTICS The following data set gives the resale price of a certain computer at monthly intervals. *(LESSON 1.5)*

Months	Price ($)	Months	Price ($)
1	3250	6	2700
2	3150	7	2700
3	3100	8	2450
4	2850	9	2350
5	2800	10	2300

15 Find the equation of the least-squares line.

16 Use the least-squares line to predict the price after 12 months.

17 Find the correlation coefficient, and explain how it describes the data.

Find the inverse of each function. State whether the inverse is a function. *(LESSON 2.5)*

18. $\{(3, 4)), (8, 4),(13, -4), (4, 0)\}$

19. $f(x) = \frac{x - 2}{4}$

20. Solve and graph the inequality $2(1 - 2x) \geq -x + 4$. *(LESSON 1.7)*

21. Write a relation that is not a function, and explain why it is not a function. *(LESSON 2.3)*

Let $f(x) = 2x - 2$ and $g(x) = 3x$. Perform each operation below, and write your answer in simplest form. *(LESSON 2.4)*

22. $f + g$ **23.** $f - g$ **24.** $f \cdot g$

25. $f \div g$ **26.** $f \circ g$ **27.** $g \circ f$

CONSUMER ECONOMICS Residential wastewater rates are based on a monthly customer charge of $4.00 plus $1.75 per 1000 gallons of water used up to and including 6900 gallons and $3.50 for each additional 1000 gallons of water. *(LESSON 2.6)*

28. Write a piecewise function to represent the monthly cost, c, in dollars for x gallons of water used.

29. Graph the function from Item 28. What is the monthly cost for using 8400 gallons of water in a month?

30. If the monthly wastewater bill is $25.00, how much water was used?

FREE RESPONSE GRID

The following questions may be answered by using a free-response grid such as that commonly used by standardized-test services.

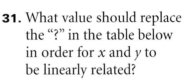

31. What value should replace the "?" in the table below in order for x and y to be linearly related? *(LESSON 1.1)*

x	3	5	7	9	11
y	2	?	-4	-7	-10

32. Evaluate $27^{\frac{2}{3}}$. *(LESSON 2.2)*

33. If a varies directly as b and $a = -3$ when $b = 12$, what is b when $a = 1.5$? *(LESSON 1.4)*

34. Evaluate $-[-32.90]$. *(LESSON 2.6)*

35. Evaluate $75 - \dfrac{3(4 + 12 \div 2)^2}{2 + 3}$. *(LESSON 2.1)*

36. Evaluate $\dfrac{6^2 \cdot 6^{-3}}{6^{-1}}$. *(LESSON 2.2)*

37. Find the slope of the line represented by $2x + 3y = 7$. *(LESSON 1.2)*

38. Find $f(0)$ for $f(x) = 5x^2 - x + 12$. *(LESSON 2.3)*

39. What value of x is the solution to the equation $\dfrac{3x - 15}{2} = 9 - 4x$? *(LESSON 1.5)*

40. Evaluate $\lceil -0.75 \rceil$. *(LESSON 2.6)*

Keystroke Guide for Chapter 2

Essential keystroke sequences (using the model TI-82 or TI-83 graphics calculator) are presented below for all Activities and Examples found in this chapter that require or recommend the use of a graphics calculator.

internetconnect

HRW Keystrokes for other models of graphics calculators are found on the HRW Web site.

LESSON 2.1

Page 89

For Step 1, evaluate $\frac{12+8}{5}$ without and with parentheses.

12 [+] 8 [÷] 5 [ENTER] [( ] 12 [+] 8 [ )] [÷] 5 [ENTER]

Use a similar keystroke sequence for Step 3.

LESSON 2.2

E X A M P L E **1** Evaluate $A_c = 4\pi^2 r T^{-2}$ for $T = 2$ and $r = 6$.

Page 95

4 [2nd] [$\overset{\pi}{\wedge}$] [x^2] [×] 6 [×] [( ] 2 [^] [(-)] 2 [ )] [ENTER]

E X A M P L E S **4** and **5** For Example 4, part a, evaluate the expression $16^{\frac{1}{4}}$.

Pages 97 and 98

16 [^] [( ] 1 [÷] 4 [ )] [ENTER]

Use a similar keystroke sequence for part **b** and for Example 5.

LESSON 2.3

E X A M P L E **5** Evaluate $f(x) = 0.5x^2 - 3x + 2$ for $x = 4$ and $x = 2.5$.

Page 106

Use viewing window [–7, 12] by [–7, 12].

Graph the function:

> First clear all equations and statplots.

[Y=] 0.5 [X,T,θ,n] [x^2] [–] 3 [X,T,θ,n]

[+] 2 [GRAPH]

Evaluate for $x = 4$ and $x = 2.5$:

[2nd] [TRACE] (CALC) [1: value] [ENTER] (X=) 4 [ENTER]

[2nd] [TRACE] (CALC) [1: value] [ENTER] (X=) 2.5 [ENTER]

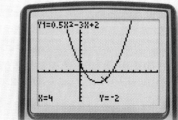

Activity

Page 111

First clear all data.

First clear all equations.

For Step 1, enter the data for the speed and the reaction distance, and create a scatter plot.

Use viewing window [0, 75] by [−15, 95].

Enter the data:

[STAT] [EDIT] [1:EDIT] [ENTER] [L1] 10 [ENTER] 20 [ENTER] 30 [ENTER] 40 [ENTER] 50 [ENTER] 60 [ENTER] 70 [ENTER] [▶] [L2] 11 [ENTER] 22 [ENTER] 33 [ENTER] 44 [ENTER] 55 [ENTER] 66 [ENTER] 77 [ENTER]

Create the scatter plot:

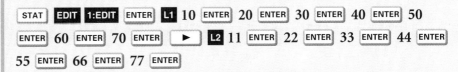

[2nd] [Y=] [STAT PLOT] [1:PLOT 1] [ENTER] [ON] [ENTER] [▼] (Type:) ⠿ [ENTER]
[▼] (Xlist:) [2nd] [1] [▼] (Ylist:) [2nd] [2nd] [▼] (Mark:) ▪
⇑TI-82: [L1] [ENTER]   ⇑TI-82: [L2] [ENTER]
[ENTER] [GRAPH]

Use a similar keystroke sequence for Steps 2 and 4.

Activity

Page 119

First clear all equations and statplots.

For Step 1, graph y = 2x − 1, its inverse, and y = x on the same screen.

Begin with viewing window [−10, 10] by [−10, 10].

Graph the given functions:

[Y=] 2 [X,T,θ,n] [−] 1 [ENTER] (Y2=) [X,T,θ,n] [ZOOM] [5:ZSquare] [ENTER]

Graph the inverse of y = 2x − 1:

[2nd] [PRGM] [8:DrawInv] [ENTER] [VARS] [Y-VARS] [1:Function] [ENTER] [1:Y1]
⇑TI-82: [2nd] [VARS]
[ENTER] [ENTER]

Use a similar keystroke sequence for Step 2.

E X A M P L E ④ Let f(x) = 7x − 2 and g(x) = $\frac{1}{7}x + \frac{2}{7}$. Graph f ∘ g.

Page 121

Use friendly viewing window [−4.7, 4.7] by [−3.1, 3.1].

Graph f ∘ g:

[Y=] [◄] [=] [ENTER] [▶] [(] 1 [÷] 7 [)] [X,T,θ,n] [+] [(] 2 [÷]
7 [)] [ENTER] (Y2=) 7 [VARS] [Y-VARS] [1:Function] [ENTER] [1:Y1] [ENTER] [−]
⇑TI-82: [2nd] [VARS]
2 [GRAPH]

To graph g ∘ f, change x in Y1 to Y2, and change Y1 in Y2 to x. Turn off Y2, turn on Y1, and graph.

E X A M P L E **4** Graph $y = 3|x| - 1$ and its inverse on the same screen.

Page 127

Use friendly viewing window [–4.7, 4.7] by [–3.1, 3.1].

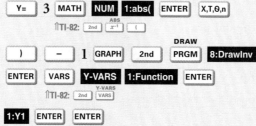

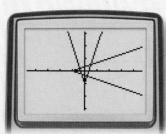

LESSON 2.7

Activity

Page 133

For Step 1, enter the data from columns 2 and 4, create a scatter plot, and graph the least-squares line for the data.

Use viewing window [25, 35] by [120, 200].

Enter the data:

STAT EDIT 1:Edit ENTER L1 29 ENTER 30 ENTER 31 ENTER 32 ENTER 33
ENTER 34 ENTER ▶ L2 185.4 ENTER 173.1 ENTER 147.1 ENTER 158.4
ENTER 134.7 ENTER 151.2 ENTER

Create the scatter plot:

2nd Y= STAT PLOT 1:Plot 1 ENTER ON ENTER ▼

(Type:) ⬝⬝⬝ ENTER ▼ (Xlist:) 2nd 1 ▼
⇑TI-82: L1 ENTER

(Ylist:) 2nd 2 ▼ (Mark:) ◻ ENTER GRAPH
⇑TI-82: L2 ENTER

Graph the regression line for the data:

STAT CALC 4:LinReg(ax+b) ENTER 2nd 1 , 2nd 2 ,
VARS Y-VARS 1:Function ENTER 1:Y1 ENTER ENTER GRAPH

TI-82:
STAT CALC 5:LinReg(ax + b) ENTER 2nd 1 , 2nd 2 2nd ENTER Y= VARS 5:Statistics
ENTER 7:REGEQ ENTER GRAPH

Use a similar keystroke sequence for Step 2.

E X A M P L E ❶ For part a, graph $y = x^2$ and $y = x^2 + 3$ on the same screen.

Page 134

Use friendly viewing window $[-4.7, 4.7]$ by $[-2, 8]$.

> The TI-82 model does not draw thick lines. Omit cursor keys and ENTER key in Y2.

For part b, graph $y = |x|$ and $y = |x + 4|$ on the same screen.

Use friendly viewing window $[-4.7, 4.7]$ by $[-2, 8]$.

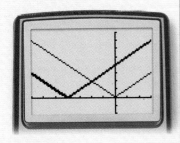 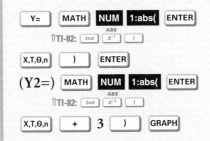 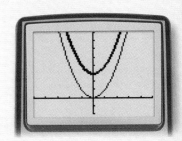

E X A M P L E ❷ For part a, graph $y = \sqrt{16 - x^2}$ and $y = 2\sqrt{16 - x^2}$ on the same screen.

Page 135

Use friendly viewing window $[-4.7, 4.7]$ by $[0, 8]$.

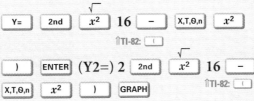 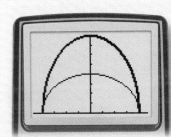

E X A M P L E S ❸ , ❹ , and ❺ For Example 3, part a, graph $y = \sqrt{(16 - x^2)}$ and $y = \sqrt{16 - (2x)^2}$ on the same screen.

Pages 136-138

Use friendly viewing window $[-9.4, 9.4]$ by $[0, 6.2]$.

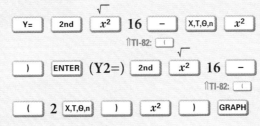 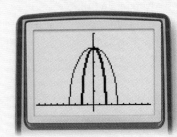

Use a similar keystroke sequence for part **b**.

Use a similar keystroke sequence for Examples 4 and 5.

3

Systems of Linear Equations and Inequalities

SYSTEMS OF LINEAR EQUATIONS AND INEQUALITIES are used to find optimal solutions to problems in business, finance, manufacturing, agriculture, and other fields such as photography.

For instance, the time required to develop a photograph involves both the *concentration* and the *temperature* of the developer fluid. Situations in which variables are related in more than one way can be represented with a system of equations.

Lessons

Supplies used to develop photographs.

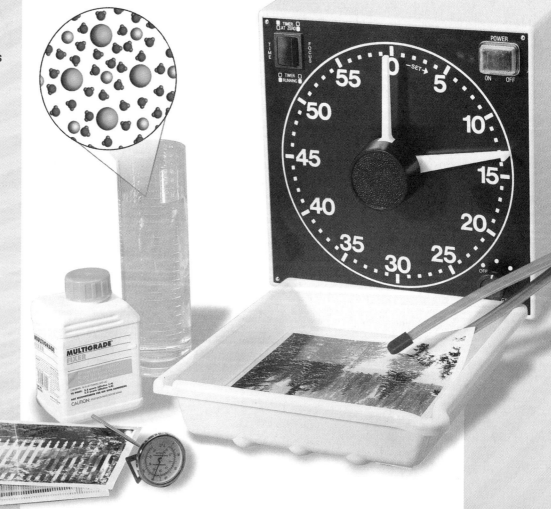

Students
in a photo
lab

About the Chapter Project

The Chapter Project, *Maximum Profit/Minimum Cost,* consists of two linear-programming problems. In one, you will be faced with a limited number of resources and will be asked to maximize profit. In the second, you will be asked to complete a job while minimizing the costs of labor. You will have an opportunity to use mathematics as it is often used in the real world to solve problems and make decisions.

After completing the Chapter Project, you will be able to do the following:

- Set up and solve linear-programming problems that involve finding maximums or minimums.

- Investigate how changes in the objective function or in the constraint inequalities affect the outcomes.

About the Portfolio Activities

Throughout the chapter, you will be given opportunities to complete Portfolio Activities that are designed to support your work on the Chapter Project.

- Writing and solving a system of equations to solve a production problem is included in the Portfolio Activity on page 171.

- Using a system of linear inequalities to find production limits and possibilities is included in the Portfolio Activity on page 186.

- Using linear programming to maximize the profits of a production company are included in the Portfolio Activity on page 194.

Solving Systems by Graphing or Substitution

Why *Systems of equations are frequently used to model events that occur in daily life. A system of equations can be used to determine business profits or create exact mixtures.*

Objectives

- Solve a system of linear equations in two variables by graphing.

- Solve a system of linear equations by substitution.

APPLICATION
CHEMISTRY

A laboratory technician is mixing a 10% saline solution with a 4% saline solution. How much of each solution is needed to make 500 milliliters of a 6% saline solution? *You will solve this problem in Example 3.*

A **system of equations** is a collection of equations in the same variables.

The solution of a system of two linear equations in x and y is any ordered pair, (x, y), that satisfies both equations. The solution (x, y) is also the point of intersection for the graphs of the lines in the system. For example, the ordered pair $(2, -1)$ is the solution of the system below.

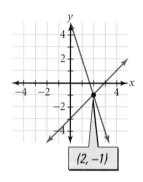

(2, –1)

$$\begin{cases} y = x - 3 \\ y = 5 - 3x \end{cases} \rightarrow \begin{cases} (-1) = (2) - 3 \\ (-1) = 5 - 3(2) \end{cases} \quad \begin{matrix} \textbf{True} \\ \textbf{True} \end{matrix}$$

Activity

Exploring Graphs of Systems

TECHNOLOGY
GRAPHICS CALCULATOR

Keystroke Guide, page 210

You will need: graph paper or a graphics calculator

1. Graph system I at right.

   a. Are there any points of intersection?

   b. Can you find exactly one solution to the system? If so, what is it? If not, modify the system so that it has exactly one solution and state that solution.

2. Repeat Step 1 for systems II and III.

CHECKPOINT ✔

3. Describe the slopes of the lines whose equations form a system with no solution, with infinitely many solutions, and with exactly one solution.

	System
I.	$\begin{cases} y = 2x - 1 \\ y = -x + 5 \end{cases}$
II.	$\begin{cases} y = 2x - 1 \\ y = 2x + 1 \end{cases}$
III.	$\begin{cases} y = \dfrac{8 - 3x}{4} \\ y = -\dfrac{3}{4}x + 2 \end{cases}$

You can graph a system of equations in two variables to find whether a solution for the system exists. The systems and graphs below illustrate the three possibilities for a system of two linear equations in two variables.

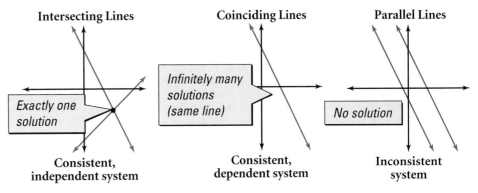

Intersecting Lines

Exactly one solution

Consistent, independent system

Coinciding Lines

Infinitely many solutions (same line)

Consistent, dependent system

Parallel Lines

No solution

Inconsistent system

Classifying Systems of Equations

If a system of equations has at least one solution, it is called **consistent**.
 • If a system has exactly one solution, it is called **independent**.
 • If a system has infinitely many solutions, it is called **dependent**.
If a system does not have a solution, it is called **inconsistent**.

EXAMPLE ① Graph and classify each system. Then find the solution from the graph.

a. $\begin{cases} x + y = 5 \\ x - 5y = -7 \end{cases}$

b. $\begin{cases} x - 2y = 3 \\ x + 5 = 2y \end{cases}$

● **SOLUTION**

Solve each equation for y.

a. $\begin{cases} x + y = 5 \\ x - 5y = -7 \end{cases} \rightarrow \begin{cases} y = -x + 5 \\ y = \dfrac{x + 7}{5} \end{cases}$

b. $\begin{cases} x - 2y = 3 \\ x + 5 = 2y \end{cases} \rightarrow \begin{cases} y = \dfrac{x - 3}{2} \\ y = \dfrac{x + 5}{2} \end{cases}$

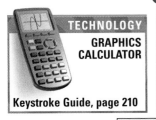

TECHNOLOGY
GRAPHICS CALCULATOR
Keystroke Guide, page 210

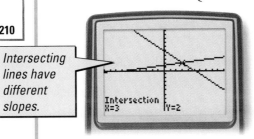

Intersecting lines have different slopes.

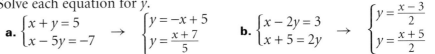

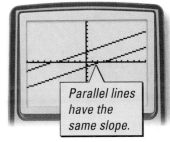

Parallel lines have the same slope.

Because the lines intersect at exactly one point, the system is consistent and independent. The solution is (3, 2).

The lines appear to be parallel. You can verify this by examining the slopes of the lines—both are $\frac{1}{2}$. Thus, the system is inconsistent, and there is no solution.

TRY THIS Graph and classify $\begin{cases} y = 3x + 4 \\ y = -2x + 4 \end{cases}$. Then find the solution from the graph.

CRITICAL THINKING Classify $\begin{cases} y = mx \\ y = nx \end{cases}$, where $m \neq 0$ and $n \neq 0$, as thoroughly as possible.

Example 2 shows you how to use substitution to solve a system in which a variable has a coefficient of 1.

E X A M P L E **2** **Use substitution to solve the system. Check your solution.** $\begin{cases} 2x + y = 3 \\ 3x - 2y = 8 \end{cases}$

● **SOLUTION**

Solve the first equation for y because it has a coefficient of 1.

$$2x + y = 3$$
$$y = 3 - 2x$$

Substitute $3 - 2x$ for y in the second equation.

$$3x - 2y = 8$$
$$3x - 2(3 - 2x) = 8 \quad \boxed{\text{This equation has only one variable.}}$$
$$3x - 6 + 4x = 8 \quad \textit{Use the Distributive Property.}$$
$$7x = 14$$
$$x = 2$$

Substitute 2 for x in either original equation to find y.

First equation: $\quad 2x + y = 3$ | Second equation: $\quad 3x - 2y = 8$
$$2(2) + y = 3 \qquad\qquad\qquad\qquad\qquad 3(2) - 2y = 8$$
$$y = -1 \qquad\qquad\qquad\qquad\qquad -2y = 8 - 6$$
$$\qquad\qquad\qquad\qquad\qquad\qquad\qquad\qquad y = -1$$

The solution is $(2, -1)$.

CHECK

$$\begin{cases} 2x + y = 3 \\ 3x - 2y = 8 \end{cases} \rightarrow \begin{cases} 2(2) + (-1) = 3 \quad \textbf{True} \\ 3(2) - 2(-1) = 8 \quad \textbf{True} \end{cases}$$

Always check your answers by substituting them into both original equations.

TRY THIS Use substitution to solve the system. Check your solution. $\begin{cases} 3x + y = 8 \\ 18x + 2y = 4 \end{cases}$

E X A M P L E **3** Refer to the saline solution mixture described at the beginning of the lesson.

How much of each solution, to the nearest milliliter, is needed to make 500 milliliters of a 6% saline solution?

● **SOLUTION**

Write two equations in x and y. Let x and y represent the amounts of the 10% and 4% solutions, respectively.

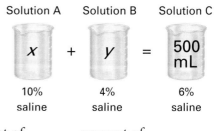

Solution A   Solution B   Solution C

10% saline   4% saline   6% saline

amount of 10% solution	+	amount of 4% solution	=	amount of 6% solution
x	+	y	=	500

saline in 10% solution	+	saline in 4% solution	=	saline in 6% solution
$0.10x$	+	$0.04y$	=	$0.06(500)$

Method 1 Use the substitution method.

1. Solve the first equation for y.

$$x + y = 500$$
$$y = 500 - x$$

> The first equation can be solved for either x or y.

2. Substitute $500 - x$ for y into the second equation, and solve for x.

$$0.10x + 0.04y = 0.06(500)$$
$$0.10x + 0.04(\textbf{500} - \textbf{x}) = 0.06(500) \quad \textit{Substitute.}$$
$$0.10x + 20 - 0.04x = 30 \quad \textit{Simplify.}$$
$$0.06x = 10$$
$$x \approx 167$$

3. Substitute 167 for x into the first equation.

$$x + y = 500$$
$$\textbf{167} + y \approx 500$$
$$y \approx 333$$

> You can use either original equation for this step.

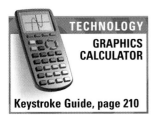

TECHNOLOGY

GRAPHICS CALCULATOR

Keystroke Guide, page 210

Method 2 Use the graphing method.

Graph the equations, and find any points of intersection.

To graph the system with a graphics calculator, solve for y and rewrite the system as shown below.

$$\begin{cases} y = 500 - x \\ y = \dfrac{0.06(500) - 0.10x}{0.04} \end{cases}$$

The technician needs to combine 167 milliliters of the 10% solution and 333 milliliters of the 4% solution.

TRY THIS If a 7% saline solution and a 4% saline solution are mixed to make 500 milliliters of a 5% saline solution, how much of each solution, to the nearest milliliter, is needed?

The solution of a system in three variables, such as in x, y, and z, is an *ordered triple* (x, y, z) that satisfies all three equations.

E X A M P L E **4** Use substitution to solve the system. Check your solution.
$$\begin{cases} x + y + z = 5 \\ 2x - 3y + z = -2 \\ 4z = 8 \end{cases}$$

● **SOLUTION**

1. Solve the third equation for z.
$$4z = 8$$
$$z = 2$$

2. Substitute 2 for z in the first and second equations. Then simplify.

$$\begin{cases} x + y + z = 5 \\ 2x - 3y + z = -2 \\ z = 2 \end{cases} \rightarrow \begin{cases} x + y + \textbf{2} = 5 \\ 2x - 3y + \textbf{2} = -2 \end{cases} \rightarrow \begin{cases} x + y = 3 \\ 2x - 3y = -4 \end{cases}$$

3. Use substitution to solve the resulting system. $\begin{cases} x + y = 3 \\ 2x - 3y = -4 \end{cases}$

$$x + y = 3$$
$$y = 3 - x \quad \rightarrow \quad \begin{aligned} 2x - 3y &= -4 \\ 2x - 3(3 - x) &= -4 \\ 2x - 9 + 3x &= -4 \\ 5x &= 5 \\ x &= 1 \end{aligned}$$

> Substitute $3 - x$ for y in $2x - 3y = -4$.

4. Now substitute 1 for x and 2 for z to find y.

$$\begin{aligned} x + y + z &= 5 \\ 1 + y + 2 &= 5 \\ y &= 2 \end{aligned}$$

> You can use either the first or second equation of the original system.

Thus, the solution for the system is $(1, 2, 2)$.

CHECK

$$\begin{cases} x + y + z = 5 \\ 2x - 3y + z = -2 \\ 4z = 8 \end{cases} \rightarrow \begin{cases} 1 + 2 + 2 = 5 & \textbf{True} \\ 2(1) - 3(2) + 2 = -2 & \textbf{True} \\ 4(2) = 8 & \textbf{True} \end{cases}$$

TRY THIS Use substitution to solve the system. Check your solution. $\begin{cases} x + y + z = 5 \\ 2x - 3y + z = -2 \\ 4z = -12 \end{cases}$

Exercises

Communicate

1. Describe the graphs of the three types of systems of linear equations.

2. Create three systems of linear equations, one to demonstrate each type of system: inconsistent, dependent, and independent.

3. Explain how to solve the system $\begin{cases} y = 2x - 5 \\ x + y = 13 \end{cases}$ by graphing.

4. Explain how to use substitution to solve the system. $\begin{cases} p - q = -7 \\ 2p + q = 17 \end{cases}$

Guided Skills Practice

Graph and classify each system. Then find the solution from the graph. (EXAMPLE 1)

5. $\begin{cases} x - y = -4 \\ 3x + y = 8 \end{cases}$

6. $\begin{cases} 3x + 4y = 12 \\ 4y - 12 = -3x \end{cases}$

7. Use substitution to solve the system. Check your solution. *(EXAMPLE 2)* $\begin{cases} 2x + y = 8 \\ 6x + 2y = -8 \end{cases}$

8. **SMALL BUSINESS** A candy manufacturer wishes to mix two candies as a sales promotion. One candy sells for \$2.00 per pound and the other candy sells for \$0.75 per pound. The manufacturer wishes to have 1000 pounds of the mixture and to sell the mixture for \$1.35 per pound. How many pounds of each type of candy should be used in the mixture? *(EXAMPLE 3)*

9. Use substitution to solve the system. Check your solution. *(EXAMPLE 4)*
$$\begin{cases} x + 6y + 2z = 1 \\ -2x + 3y - z = 4 \\ -1 = z + 2 \end{cases}$$

Practice and Apply

Classify the type of system of equations represented by each graph below. If the system has exactly one solution, write it.

10.
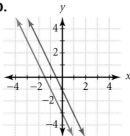

11.
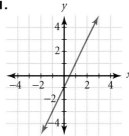

12.
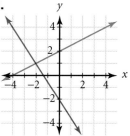

Graph and classify each system. Then find the solution from the graph.

13. $\begin{cases} 6x + 4y = 12 \\ 2y = 6 - 3x \end{cases}$

14. $\begin{cases} 2x + 3y = 1 \\ -3x + 4y = -10 \end{cases}$

15. $\begin{cases} y = 2x - 1 \\ 6x - y = 13 \end{cases}$

16. $\begin{cases} x + 3y = 13 \\ 2x - y = -9 \end{cases}$

17. $\begin{cases} y = -2x - 7 \\ 4x + 2y = 6 \end{cases}$

18. $\begin{cases} 2x + y = 5 \\ 4x + 2y = 6 \end{cases}$

19. $\begin{cases} -\frac{1}{2}x + y = 4 \\ x + 2y = 8 \end{cases}$

20. $\begin{cases} 3x - 6y = 9 \\ \frac{1}{2}x = y + \frac{3}{2} \end{cases}$

21. $\begin{cases} 4x + 5y = -7 \\ 3x - 6y = 24 \end{cases}$

22. $\begin{cases} -x + 2y = 3 \\ 2x - 4y = -6 \end{cases}$

23. $\begin{cases} 3x - y = 2 \\ -3x + y = 1 \end{cases}$

24. $\begin{cases} 6x - 3y = 9 \\ 3x + 7y = 47 \end{cases}$

Use substitution to solve each system of equations. Check your solution.

25. $\begin{cases} y = x + 3 \\ y = 2x - 4 \end{cases}$

26. $\begin{cases} x = y + 4 \\ 2x + 3y = 43 \end{cases}$

27. $\begin{cases} 4x + 2y = 20 \\ y = x - 2 \end{cases}$

28. $\begin{cases} x - y = 3 \\ 2x + 2y = 2 \end{cases}$

29. $\begin{cases} x - 2y = 0 \\ 2x - y = 6 \end{cases}$

30. $\begin{cases} x + y = 0 \\ y + 2x = 4 \end{cases}$

31. $\begin{cases} 2x + y = 8 \\ x - y = 3 \end{cases}$

32. $\begin{cases} x + 5y = 2 \\ x - 1 = 2y \end{cases}$

33. $\begin{cases} a = b + 2 \\ a = 5b - 6 \end{cases}$

34. $\begin{cases} p = 3q - 3 \\ 2p + 5q = -17 \end{cases}$

35. $\begin{cases} 3t - r = 9 \\ r = 2t + 8 \end{cases}$

36. $\begin{cases} 2x + y = -9 \\ 3x + y = 11 \end{cases}$

37. $\begin{cases} x - 5y = 2 \\ 9x + 8 = 15y \end{cases}$

38. $\begin{cases} s = 10 + 5t \\ 2s = 40 + 4t \end{cases}$

39. $\begin{cases} -3x - y = 2 \\ -6x + 2y = -2 \end{cases}$

40. Determine whether the given ordered pair is a solution of the given system.

a. $(1, 3)$ $\begin{cases} 5x + 2y = 11 \\ x - y = 7 \end{cases}$

b. $(5, -2)$ $\begin{cases} 4x - 3y = 26 \\ 2x + y = 8 \end{cases}$

c. $(2, 1)$ $\begin{cases} 2x - y = 8 \\ x + 3y = 5 \end{cases}$

d. $(5, 2)$ $\begin{cases} 4x - 2y = 16 \\ -8x + 4y = -32 \end{cases}$

e. Of the four systems given above, one is dependent. Identify that system and give three additional ordered pairs that satisfy the system.

Use substitution to solve each system of equations.

41. $\begin{cases} 2x - 3y - z = 12 \\ y + 3z = 10 \\ z = 4 \end{cases}$

42. $\begin{cases} 2x - 3y + 4z = 8 \\ 3x + 2y = 7 \\ x = 1 \end{cases}$

43. $\begin{cases} x + 3y - z = 8 \\ 2x - y + 2z = -9 \\ 3y = 9 \end{cases}$

44. $\begin{cases} 2x + 3y - 2z = 4 \\ 3x - 3y + 2z = 16 \\ 2z = -5 \end{cases}$

45. $\begin{cases} 3x + 5y = -3 \\ 10y - 2z = 2 \\ x = -z \end{cases}$

46. $\begin{cases} a + b + c = 6 \\ 3a - b + c = 8 \\ 2b = c \end{cases}$

Graph and classify each system. Then find the solution from the graph. Round your answers to the nearest hundredth when necessary.

47 $\begin{cases} y = 5x + 2.72 \\ y = 3.6x + 3.126 \end{cases}$

48 $\begin{cases} y = 4.3x - 0.44 \\ y = -2x + 4.6 \end{cases}$

49 $\begin{cases} -\frac{2}{5}x + y = -\frac{1}{10} \\ 3y - 2x = -\frac{5}{6} \end{cases}$

50 $\begin{cases} \frac{1}{7} = \frac{1}{14}x + 5\frac{1}{2}y \\ y = 4x + 14 \end{cases}$

51 $\begin{cases} 0.7y = 0.8x + 0.78 \\ -\frac{1}{5}x + \frac{1}{2}y = 2.1 \end{cases}$

52 $\begin{cases} 0.001y + \frac{4}{5}x = 0.2014 \\ 0.8x - 0.02y = 0.172 \end{cases}$

CHALLENGE

53. Solve $\begin{cases} ax + by = c \\ y = dx + e \end{cases}$ for x and y. Use the resulting expressions for x and y to solve a system in the same form, such as $\begin{cases} 2x + 3y = 21 \\ y = x + 2 \end{cases}$.

CONNECTION

GEOMETRY The perimeter of a rectangular swimming pool is 130 yards. Three times the length is equal to 10 times the width.

54. Find the length and the width of the pool.

55. Find the area of the pool.

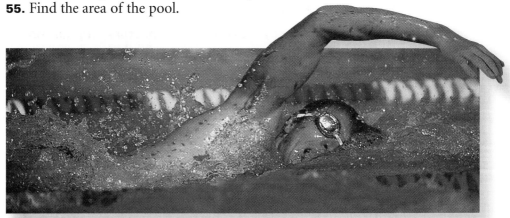

For Exercises 56–59, solve by writing a system of equations and using substitution. Check your answers.

APPLICATION

56. INCOME To earn money for college, Susan is making and selling earrings. Her weekly costs for advertising and phone calls are $36, and each pair of earrings costs $1.50 to produce. If Susan sells the earrings at $6 per pair, how many pairs must she sell per week to break even?

57. CONSUMER ECONOMICS Armando is comparing parking prices at a local concert. One option is a $7 entry fee plus $2 per hour. A second option is a $5 entry fee plus $3 per hour. What is the break-even point (intersection) for the two options? Which option do you think is better? Explain your reasoning.

58. CHEMISTRY To conduct a scientific experiment, students need to mix 90 milliliters of a 3% acid solution. They have a 1% and a 10% solution available. How many milliliters of the 1% solution and of the 10% solution should be combined to produce 90 milliliters of the 3% solution?

59. SPORTS Rebecca is the star forward on her high-school basketball team. In one game, her field-goal total was 23 points, made up of 2-point and 3-point baskets. If she made 4 more 2-point baskets than 3-point baskets, how many of each type of basket did she make?

Solve each equation or inequality, and graph the solution on a number line. *(LESSON 1.8)*

60. $|x - 4| = 9$ **61.** $|x - 2| \leq 5$ **62.** $|x + 3| \leq -1$

State the property that is illustrated in each statement. All variables represent real numbers. *(LESSON 2.1)*

63. $\frac{2}{3}(6x + 12) = \frac{2}{3} \cdot 6x + \frac{2}{3} \cdot 12$ **64.** $5a + (3a + 6) = (5a + 3a) + 6$

65. $-4a + 4a = 0$ **66.** $5x \cdot 9y = 9y \cdot 5x$

Evaluate each expression. *(LESSON 2.2)*

67. $5a^0$ **68.** $36^{\frac{1}{2}}$ **69.** $25^{-\frac{1}{2}}$ **70.** $9^{\frac{3}{2}}$

Simplify each expression, assuming that no variable equals zero. *(LESSON 2.2)*

71. $\left(\frac{2x^3}{x^{-2}}\right)^2$ **72.** $\left(\frac{m^{-1}n^2}{n^{-3}}\right)^{-3}$ **73.** $\left(\frac{2a^3b^{-2}}{-a^2b^{-3}}\right)^{-1}$ **74.** $\frac{(2y^2y)^{-2}}{3xy^{-4}}$

Find the inverse of each function. Graph the function and its inverse on the same coordinate plane, and state whether the inverse is a function. *(LESSON 2.5)*

75. $\{(1, 4), (-3, 4), (2, 0)\}$ **76.** $\{(7, 8), (6, 4), (5, 0), (4, 4)\}$

77. $\{(3, 4), (4, 3), (3, -1), (11, -3)\}$ **78.** $\{(8, 6), (9, 4), (-8, 6), (0, 0)\}$

Look Beyond

Use a graph to solve each nonlinear system of equations. Round your answers to the nearest hundredth when necessary.

79. $\begin{cases} y = x^2 + 3 \\ y = 4x \end{cases}$ **80.** $\begin{cases} x + y = 19 \\ y = 2^x \end{cases}$

Solving Systems by Elimination

Objective

- Solve a system of two linear equations in two variables by elimination.

Why *You can model real-world situations involving two variables, such as business cost and revenue, with a system of two equations in two variables.*

In business, makers and sellers of goods must relate the cost of making goods to their selling price. They must also keep production costs within budget and maintain realistic expectations of revenue.

This table gives production costs and selling prices per frame for two sizes of picture frames. How many of each size should be made and sold if the production budget is $930 and the expected revenue is $1920? *You will solve this problem in Example 2.*

	Small	Large
Production cost	$5.50	$7.50
Selling price	$12.00	$15.00

You have learned to solve systems of linear equations by graphing and by using substitution. Some systems are more easily solved by another method called the *elimination method*. The **elimination method** involves multiplying and combining the equations in a system in order to eliminate a variable.

Independent Systems

E X A M P L E ① Use elimination to solve the system. Check your solution.

$$\begin{cases} 2x + 5y = 15 \\ -4x + 7y = -13 \end{cases}$$

SOLUTION

1. To eliminate x, multiply each side of the first equation by 2, and combine the resulting equations.

$$\begin{cases} 2x + 5y = 15 \\ -4x + 7y = -13 \end{cases} \rightarrow \begin{cases} 2(2x + 5y) = 2(15) \\ -4x + 7y = -13 \end{cases} \rightarrow \begin{cases} 4x + 10y = 30 \\ -4x + 7y = -13 \end{cases}$$

$$\begin{aligned} 4x + 10y &= 30 \\ -4x + 7y &= -13 \\ \hline 17y &= 17 \end{aligned}$$ *Use the Addition Property of Equality.*

$$y = 1 \quad \text{Solve for } y.$$

2. Substitute 1 for y in either original equation to find x.

First equation:

$$2x + 5y = 15$$
$$2x + 5(1) = 15$$
$$x = 5$$

Second equation:

$$-4x + 7y = -13$$
$$-4x + 7(1) = -13$$
$$x = 5$$

The solution of the system is $x = 5$ and $y = 1$, or $(5, 1)$.

CHECK

$$\begin{cases} 2x + 5y = 15 \\ -4x + 7y = -13 \end{cases} \rightarrow \begin{cases} 2(5) + 5(1) = 15 \quad \textbf{True} \\ -4(5) + 7(1) = -13 \quad \textbf{True} \end{cases}$$

TRY THIS Use elimination to solve the system. Check your solution. $\begin{cases} 6r + 7s = -15 \\ -3r + s = -6 \end{cases}$

E X A M P L E ② Refer to the picture-frame problem described at the beginning of the lesson.

APPLICATION
BUSINESS

How many small frames and how many large frames can be made and sold if the production budget is \$930 and the expected revenue is \$1920?

● **SOLUTION**

1. Write a system of equations to represent the problem.

Let x represent the number of small picture frames, and let y represent the number of large picture frames.

	Small	Large	Total
Production cost	$5.5x$	$7.5y$	930
Selling price	$12x$	$15y$	1920

From the data in the table, write the system. $\begin{cases} 5.5x + 7.5y = 930 \\ 12x + 15y = 1920 \end{cases}$

2. To eliminate y, multiply each side of the first equation by -2, and combine the resulting equations.

$$\begin{cases} -2(5.5x + 7.5y) = -2(930) \\ 12x + 15y = 1920 \end{cases} \rightarrow \begin{cases} -11x - 15y = -1860 \\ 12x + 15y = 1920 \end{cases}$$

$$\begin{aligned} -11x - 15y &= -1860 \\ \underline{12x + 15y} &= \underline{1920} \\ x \quad\quad &= 60 \end{aligned}$$

Use the Addition Property of Equality.

3. Substitute 60 for x in either original equation to find y.

First equation:

$$5.5x + 7.5y = 930$$
$$5.5(60) + 7.5y = 930$$
$$7.5y = 600$$
$$y = 80$$

Second equation:

$$12x + 15y = 1920$$
$$12(60) + 15y = 1920$$
$$15y = 1200$$
$$y = 80$$

Thus, the solution is $(60, 80)$. To meet the required goals, 60 small picture frames and 80 large ones should be made.

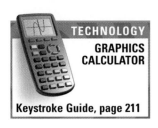

CHECK
You can use a graph, a table, or substitution to verify the solution.

To use a graphics calculator, solve each equation for y.

$$\begin{cases} 5.5x + 7.5y = 930 \\ 12x + 15y = 1920 \end{cases} \rightarrow \begin{cases} y = \dfrac{930 - 5.5x}{7.5} \\ y = \dfrac{1920 - 12x}{15} \end{cases}$$

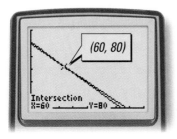

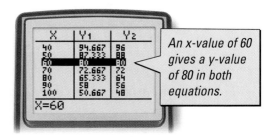

An x-value of 60 gives a y-value of 80 in both equations.

TRY THIS How does the solution to Example 2 change if the production budget is $1245 and the revenue goal is $2580?

CHECKPOINT ✔ Explain how you know that $5.5x + 7.5y$ and $12x + 15y$ are expressions that represent dollar amounts in Example 2.

CRITICAL THINKING The graph for the production budget and the graph for the revenue goal in Example 2 are quite similar. Describe what this means in terms of the number of small and large picture frames made and sold and in terms of the production budget and revenue goal.

Dependent and Inconsistent Systems

Investigating Systems

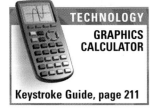

You will need: graph paper or a graphics calculator

1. Refer to system I in the first row.
   a. Graph the system and classify it as independent, dependent, or inconsistent.
   b. Solve the system by using elimination. Interpret the resulting mathematical statement.
2. Repeat parts **a** and **b** in Step 1 for system II.

System
I. $\begin{cases} x - y = -2 \\ -5x + 5y = 10 \end{cases}$
II. $\begin{cases} 3x + 3y = -5 \\ 2x + 2y = 7 \end{cases}$

CHECKPOINT ✔ 3. If an attempt to solve a system of equations results in the mathematical statement $0 = -3$, what can you say about this system?

CHECKPOINT ✔ 4. If an attempt to solve a system of equations results in the mathematical statement $0 = 0$, what can you say about this system?

You can use the elimination method to solve any system of two linear equations in two variables. Examples 3 and 4 show you how to interpret your results when the system is inconsistent or dependent.

E X A M P L E **3** Use elimination to solve the system. Check your solution. $\begin{cases} 2x + 5y = 12 \\ 2x + 5y = 15 \end{cases}$

● **SOLUTION**

Combine the equations to eliminate a variable.

$$2x + 5y = 12$$

This is a false statement. $\dfrac{2x + 5y = 15}{0 = -3}$ *Use the Subtraction Property of Equality.*

Because the result is a contradiction, the system is inconsistent. This means that the system has no solution.

CHECK

Graph the system. $\begin{cases} y = \dfrac{12 - 2x}{5} \\ y = \dfrac{15 - 2x}{5} \end{cases}$

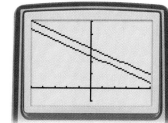

The graph indicates that the system is inconsistent. The slopes are equal.

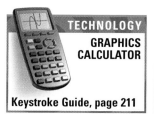
TECHNOLOGY
GRAPHICS CALCULATOR
Keystroke Guide, page 211

TRY THIS Use elimination to solve the system. Check your solution. $\begin{cases} 6x - 2y = 9 \\ 6x - 2y = 7 \end{cases}$

CHECKPOINT ✔ Find the slope of each equation in the system in Example 3. How do the slopes of those equations confirm the conclusion reached in Example 3?

E X A M P L E **4** Use elimination to solve the system. Check your solution. $\begin{cases} 2x + 5y = 15 \\ -3x - 7.5y = -22.5 \end{cases}$

● **SOLUTION**

Multiply each side of the first equation by 3, and multiply each side of the second equation by 2. Then combine the resulting equations to eliminate *x*.

$$\begin{cases} 3(2x + 5y) = 3(15) \\ 2(-3x - 7.5y) = 2(-22.5) \end{cases} \rightarrow \begin{cases} 6x + 15y = 45 \\ -6x - 15y = -45 \end{cases}$$

$$6x + 15y = 45$$

This is a true statement. $\dfrac{-6x - 15y = -45}{0 = 0}$ *Use the Addition Property of Equality.*

Because the result is true regardless of the values of the variables in the system, the system is consistent and dependent. This means that the solution of the system is all points on the graph of either equation.

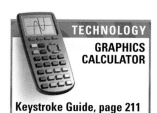
TECHNOLOGY
GRAPHICS CALCULATOR
Keystroke Guide, page 211

CHECK

Graph the system. $\begin{cases} y = \dfrac{15 - 2x}{5} \\ y = \dfrac{-22.5 + 3x}{-7.5} \end{cases}$

The two equations describe the same line.

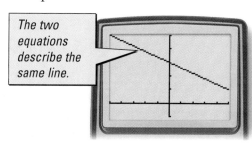

The graph indicates that the system is dependent.

TRY THIS Use elimination to solve the system. Check your solution. $\begin{cases} 8x + 4y = -16 \\ 2x + y = -4 \end{cases}$

CHECKPOINT ✔ Find the slope and y-intercept of each line represented in the system in Example 4. How do the slopes and y-intercepts of those lines confirm the conclusion reached in Example 4?

SUMMARY
THE ELIMINATION METHOD

1. Arrange each equation in standard form, $Ax + By = C$.

2. If the coefficients of x (or y) are the same number, use subtraction to eliminate the variable.

3. If the coefficients of x (or y) are opposites, use addition to eliminate the variable.

4. If the coefficients of x (or y) are different, multiply one or both equations by constants so that the coefficients of x (or y) are the same or opposite numbers. Then use Step 2 or 3 to eliminate the variable.

5. Use substitution to solve for the remaining variable.

Exercises

Communicate

1. Explain how to solve $\begin{cases} 3x - 4y = 3 \\ 2x + y = -5 \end{cases}$ by elimination.

2. When attempting to solve a system by elimination, what are the results for an inconsistent system? for a dependent system?

3. What property justifies adding the corresponding sides of two equations to create a new equation?

4. Compare the elimination method with the substitution method for solving systems of linear equations. What type of system is most easily solved by using substitution, and what type of system is most easily solved by using elimination?

Guided Skills Practice

5. Use elimination to solve the system. Check your solution. *(EXAMPLE 1)* $\begin{cases} 2x - 3y = 1 \\ 5x + 6y = 16 \end{cases}$

APPLICATION

6. BUSINESS How does the solution to Example 2 change if the production costs for large and small picture frames are \$7 and \$6, respectively? *(EXAMPLE 2)*

Use elimination to solve each system of equations. Check your solution. (EXAMPLES 3 AND 4)

7. $\begin{cases} 3x - y = -2 \\ 9x - 3y = 3 \end{cases}$

8. $\begin{cases} 3x + 2y = 5 \\ -6x - 4y = -10 \end{cases}$

Practice and Apply

Use elimination to solve each system of equations. Check your solution.

9. $\begin{cases} 2x + y = 8 \\ x - y = 10 \end{cases}$

10. $\begin{cases} 3x + 4y = 23 \\ -3x + y = 2 \end{cases}$

11. $\begin{cases} -2x + 3y = -14 \\ 2x + 2y = 4 \end{cases}$

12. $\begin{cases} 2p + 5q = 13 \\ p - q = -4 \end{cases}$

13. $\begin{cases} 2s - 5t = 22 \\ 2s - 3t = 6 \end{cases}$

14. $\begin{cases} 12y - 5z = 19 \\ 12y + 16z = 40 \end{cases}$

15. $\begin{cases} x + y = 4 \\ 2x + 3y = 9 \end{cases}$

16. $\begin{cases} 3a + 2b = 2 \\ a + 6b = 18 \end{cases}$

17. $\begin{cases} 2x - 7y = 3 \\ 5x - 4y = -6 \end{cases}$

18. $\begin{cases} 5x + 3y = 2 \\ 2x + 20 = 4y \end{cases}$

19. $\begin{cases} 7b - 5c = 11 \\ -4c - 2b = -14 \end{cases}$

20. $\begin{cases} 2y - 4x = 18 \\ -5x + 3y = 23 \end{cases}$

21. $\begin{cases} 5x - 8 = 3y \\ 10x - 6y = 18 \end{cases}$

22. $\begin{cases} 2x = 5 + 4y \\ 2y = 8 + x \end{cases}$

23. $\begin{cases} -8x + 4y = -2 \\ 4x - 2y = 1 \end{cases}$

24. $\begin{cases} 4y + 30 = 10x \\ 5x - 2y = 15 \end{cases}$

25. $\begin{cases} 3x - 4y = -1 \\ -10 + 8y = -6x \end{cases}$

26. $\begin{cases} 3x + 7y = 10 \\ 5x = 7 - 2y \end{cases}$

Use any method to solve each system of linear equations. Check your solution.

27. $\begin{cases} -4.5x + 7.5y = -9 \\ 3x - 5y = 6 \end{cases}$

28. $\begin{cases} 5x - 3y = 8 \\ x + 0.6y = 1.8 \end{cases}$

29. $\begin{cases} 3y = 5 - x \\ x + 4y = 8 \end{cases}$

30. $\begin{cases} 7y - \frac{1}{2}x = 2 \\ -2y = x + 4 \end{cases}$

31. $\begin{cases} \frac{5}{2}x - y = 5 \\ 4y = 3x - 6 \end{cases}$

32. $\begin{cases} 5x + 4y = 2 \\ 2x + 3y = 5 \end{cases}$

33. $\begin{cases} -2x + 5y = -23 \\ 24 + 4y = 3x \end{cases}$

34. $\begin{cases} \frac{x+3}{2} = x + 4y \\ x = 5y \end{cases}$

35. $\begin{cases} 16x - 6y = -1 + 6y \\ \frac{2}{3}x = 4y + 3 \end{cases}$

CHALLENGE

Find the value(s) of k that satisfy the given condition for each system.

36. The system $\begin{cases} kx - 5y = 8 \\ 7x + 5y = 10 \end{cases}$ is consistent.

37. The system $\begin{cases} kx - 5y = 8 \\ 7x + 5y = 10 \end{cases}$ has infinitely many solutions.

CONNECTION

38. COORDINATE GEOMETRY The ordered pairs (2, 9) and (6, 17) satisfy the linear equation $Ax + By = 5$, with coefficients A and B.
   a. Substitute each ordered pair into the equation to obtain two new equations in two variables, A and B.
   b. Solve the system of equations obtained in part a for A and B.
   c. Rewrite the linear equation $Ax + By = C$ with the values for A and B from part b.
   d. Solve the linear equation for y and identify the slope and y-intercept.
   e. Use the two ordered pairs and the slope formula to find the slope.
   f. Do your slopes from parts d and e agree?

39. CULTURAL CONNECTION: CHINA The *Jiuzhang,* or *Nine Chapters on the Mathematical Art,* was written around 250 B.C.E. in China. It includes problems with systems of linear equations, such as the one below. Solve the problem.

A family bought 100 acres of land and paid 10,000 pieces of gold. The price of good land is 300 pieces of gold per acre and the price of bad land is 500 pieces of gold for 7 acres. How many acres of good land and how many acres of bad land were purchased?

40. SPORTS Greg is a star player on the basketball team. In one game, his field-goal total was 20 points, made up of 2-point and 3-point baskets. If Greg made a total of 9 baskets, how many of each type did he make?

INVESTMENTS Beth has saved $4500. She would like to earn $250 per year by investing her money. She received advice about two different investments: a low-risk investment that pays a 5% annual interest and a high-risk investment that pays a 9% annual interest.

41. How much should Beth invest in each type of investment to earn her annual goal?

42. How much should Beth invest in each type of investment if she wishes to earn $325 per year?

43. BUSINESS A mail-order company charges for postage and handling according to the weight of the package. A package that weighs less than 3 pounds costs $2.00 for shipping and handling, and a package that weighs 3 pounds or more costs $3.00. An order of 12 packages had a total shipping and handling cost of $29.00. Find the number of packages that weighed less than 3 pounds and the number of packages that weighed 3 pounds or more.

NUTRITION One unit of whole-wheat flour has 13.6 grams of protein and 2.5 grams of fat. One unit of whole milk has 3.4 grams of protein and 3.7 grams of fat.

44. Write a system of equations that can be used to find the number of units of whole-wheat flour and the number of units of whole milk that must be mixed to make a dough that has 75 grams of protein and 15 grams of fat.

45. Solve the system and give the number of units, to the nearest tenth, of flour and of milk in the dough.

46. INCOME When Dale baby-sat for 8 hours and worked at a restaurant for 3 hours, he made a total of $58. When he baby-sat for 2 hours and worked at a restaurant for 5 hours, he made a total of $40. How much does Dale get paid for each type of work?

APPLICATION

47. LANDSCAPING The cost of plants is directly proportional to the area to be planted. Suppose that a nursery charges $78 for enough plants to cover an area of 50 square feet. How much would it cost to cover an area of 80 square feet? *(LESSON 1.4)*

Create a scatter plot of the data in each table. Then describe the correlation as positive or negative. *(LESSON 1.5)*

48.

x	3	5	6	0	8	5
y	9	4	3	11	1	3

49.

x	1	3	5	2	9	4
y	2	5	5	1	12	4

Solve each equation. *(LESSON 1.6)*

50. $3x - 12 = 24$　　**51.** $\frac{1}{5}x - 3 = x + 3$　　**52.** $5x - 2(3x - 1) = x - 10$

Solve each inequality, and graph the solution on a number line. *(LESSON 1.7)*

53. $4x > 6$　　**54.** $8x \le 24$　　**55.** $-\frac{1}{2}x \le 5$

Solve each compound inequality, and graph the solution on a number line. *(LESSON 1.7)*

56. $n + 1 < 9 \text{ and } n - 3 > 1$　　**57.** $2y - 10 \le -6 \text{ and } y + 8 \ge 2$

58. $x + 11 \ge 7 \text{ or } x - 4 \le 4$　　**59.** $-2a - 8 < 4 \text{ or } 3a - 9 < 21$

Evaluate each expression by using the order of operations. *(LESSON 2.1)*

60. $7(6 - 5^2)$　　**61.** $-(-3)^2 - 4^2$　　**62.** $21 - 7 \times 3 + 8 \div 3$

 Look Beyond

Solve each system of nonlinear equations by elimination.

63. $\begin{cases} x^2 + y^2 = 3 \\ x^2 + y^2 = 9 \end{cases}$　　　**64.** $\begin{cases} y^2 = 1 - x^2 \\ x^2 + y^2 = 1 \end{cases}$

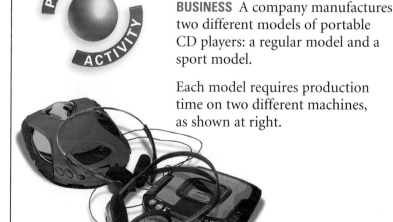

PORTFOLIO ACTIVITY

BUSINESS A company manufactures two different models of portable CD players: a regular model and a sport model.

Each model requires production time on two different machines, as shown at right.

	Regular model	Sport model
Machine A	2 minutes	1 minute
Machine B	1 minute	1 minute

Each machine is used for manufacturing many different items. In a given hour, machine A is used for CD-player production for 18 minutes and machine B is used for 10 minutes. How many CD players of each model are produced per hour?

3.3

Linear Inequalities in Two Variables

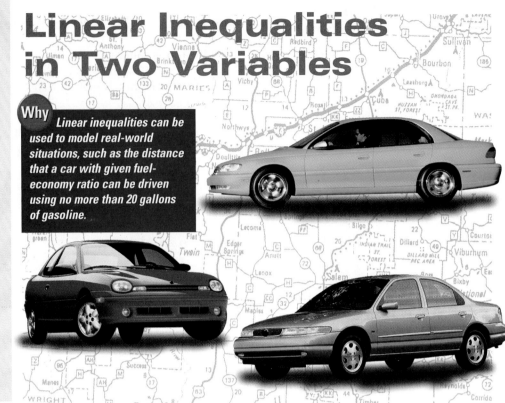

Why Linear inequalities can be used to model real-world situations, such as the distance that a car with given fuel-economy ratio can be driven using no more than 20 gallons of gasoline.

Objectives

● Solve and graph a linear inequality in two variables.

● Use a linear inequality in two variables to solve real-world problems.

The fuel-economy test results for three different automobiles are shown below.

EPA 1997 Fuel-Economy Program

Automobile	Fuel Economy (mpg)	
	City	Highway
Automobile A	28.1	33.3
Automobile B	25.6	31.5
Automobile C	20.2	31.7

[*Source: Environmental Protection Agency*]

Consider automobile A. If you let x represent miles driven in the city and y represent the miles driven on the highway, then $\frac{x}{28.1} + \frac{y}{33.3}$ represents the number of gallons of gasoline consumed. Solve $\frac{x}{28.1} + \frac{y}{33.3} \leq 20$ to find how far you can drive using no more than 20 gallons of gasoline. *You will solve this problem in Example 3.*

The inequality $\frac{x}{28.1} + \frac{y}{33.3} \leq 20$ is an example of a *linear inequality in two variables.*

Linear Inequality in Two Variables

A **linear inequality in two variables**, x and y, is any inequality that can be written in one of the forms below, where $A \neq 0$ and $B \neq 0$.

$$Ax + By \geq C \qquad Ax + By > C \qquad Ax + By \leq C \qquad Ax + By < C$$

A solution of a linear inequality in two variables, x and y, is an ordered pair (x, y) that satisfies the inequality. The solution to a linear inequality is a region of the coordinate plane and is called a *half-plane* bounded by a *boundary line*.

EXAMPLE ❶ **Graph each linear inequality.**

    a. $y < x + 2$ **b.** $y \geq -2x + 3$

● **SOLUTION**

a. Graph the boundary line $y = x + 2$. Use a dashed line because the values on this line are not included in the solution.

Choose a point such as $(0, 0)$ to test.

$$y \overset{?}{<} x + 2$$
$$0 < 0 + 2 \quad \textbf{True}$$

Since $(0, 0)$ satisfies the inequality, shade the region that contains this point.

b. Graph the boundary line $y = -2x + 3$. Use a solid line because the values on this line are included in the solution.

Choose a point such as $(0, 0)$ to test.

$$y \overset{?}{\geq} -2x + 3$$
$$0 \geq -2(0) + 3 \quad \textbf{False}$$

Since $(0, 0)$ does *not* satisfy the inequality, shade the region that does *not* contain this point.

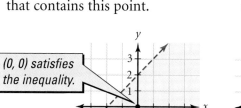

(0, 0) satisfies the inequality.

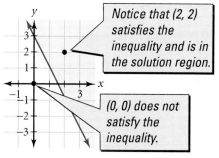

Notice that (2, 2) satisfies the inequality and is in the solution region.

(0, 0) does not satisfy the inequality.

TRY THIS   Graph each linear inequality.

    a. $y > -2x - 2$ **b.** $y \leq 2x + 5$

Sometimes you may need to solve for y before graphing a linear inequality, as shown in Example 2.

EXAMPLE ❷ **Graph $-2x - 3y \leq 3$.**

● **SOLUTION**

Solve for y in terms of x.

$$-2x - 3y \leq 3$$
$$-3y \leq 2x + 3$$
$$y \geq -\frac{2}{3}x - 1 \quad \text{Change } \leq \text{ to } \geq.$$

Then graph $y \geq -\frac{2}{3}x - 1$.

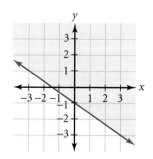

TRY THIS   Graph $3x - 4y \geq 4$.

CHECKPOINT ✔ Is the solution to $y < mx + b$ above or below the boundary line?
Is the solution to $y > mx + b$ above or below the boundary line?

3 Refer to the fuel-economy test results given at the beginning of the lesson.

a. Represent in a graph the possible distances that automobile A can travel using no more than 20 gallons of gasoline.

b. Can you drive 25 miles in the city and 400 miles on the highway in automobile A and use no more than 20 gallons of gasoline?

APPLICATION
FUEL ECONOMY

TECHNOLOGY
GRAPHICS CALCULATOR

Keystroke Guide, page 212

● **SOLUTION**

a. Solve for y, and graph.

$$\frac{x}{28.1} + \frac{y}{33.3} \le 20$$

$$y \le -\frac{33.3}{28.1}x + 20(33.3)$$

Distance cannot be negative, so both $x \ge 0$ and $y \ge 0$.

b. Test (25, 400) to see if the inequality is true.

$$\frac{25}{28.1} + \frac{400}{33.3} \overset{?}{\le} 20 \quad \rightarrow \quad 12.9 \le 20 \quad \textbf{True}$$

You can also plot the point (25, 400) to see whether the point is in the solution region.

Thus, you can drive 25 miles in the city and 400 miles on the highway and use no more than 20 gallons of gasoline in automobile A.

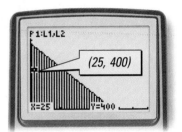

(25, 400)

The solution to a linear inequality in only one variable is also a half-plane when graphed in the coordinate plane.

4 Graph each linear inequality.

a. $x > -2$

b. $y \le -1$

● **SOLUTION**

a. Any ordered pair whose x-coordinate is greater than -2 is a solution. Graph the boundary line $x = -2$, using a dashed line, and shade the half-plane to the right of the line.

b. Any ordered pair whose y-coordinate is less than or equal to -1 is a solution. Graph the boundary line $y = -1$, using a solid line, and shade the half-plane below the line.

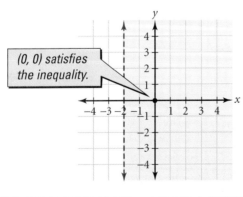

(0, 0) satisfies the inequality.

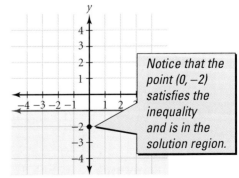

Notice that the point (0, −2) satisfies the inequality and is in the solution region.

TRY THIS   Graph $x \le 4$ and $y > 3$ separately.

CHECKPOINT ✔ On which side of the boundary line is the solution region for $x > c$ (or $x \geq c$)? On which side of the boundary line is the solution region for $x < c$ (or $x \leq c$)?

As you will notice in the Activity below, sometimes the solution to a linear inequality is a set of *discrete* points in a region instead of the entire region.

Activity
Exploring Discrete Solutions

You will need: no special materials

Daryll wants to buy some cassette tapes and CDs. A tape costs $8 and a CD costs $15. He can spend no more than $90 on tapes and CDs.

PROBLEM SOLVING

1. Let x represent the number of tapes he can buy. Let y represent the number of CDs he can buy. **Write a linear inequality** in x and y to represent his possible purchases.

CHECKPOINT ✔ 2. Explain why x and y must be whole numbers.

3. List four ordered pairs (x, y) that satisfy your inequality from Step 1.

4. How many tapes can Daryll buy if he chooses not to buy any CDs? How many CDs can Daryll buy if he chooses not to buy any tapes?

5. Graph all possible solutions to your inequality in Step 1 on a coordinate plane.

CHECKPOINT ✔ 6. Describe other situations that can be modeled by a linear inequality that has only nonnegative integer solutions.

The procedure for graphing linear inequalities is summarized below.

SUMMARY
GRAPHING LINEAR INEQUALITIES

1. Given a linear inequality in two variables, graph its related linear equation.

   - For inequalities involving $\leq$ or $\geq$, use a solid boundary line.

   - For inequalities involving $<$ or $>$, use a dashed boundary line.

2. Shade the appropriate region.

   - For inequalities of the form $y \leq mx + b$ or $y < mx + b$, shade below boundary line.

   - For inequalities of the form $y \geq mx + b$ or $y > mx + b$, shade above boundary line.

   - For inequalities of the form $x \leq c$ or $x < c$, shade to the left of the boundary line.

   - For inequalities of the form $x \geq c$ or $x > c$, shade to the right of the boundary line.

CRITICAL THINKING

Let $Ax + By \geq C$, where $A \neq 0$ and $B \neq 0$. Under what conditions is the solution region of the inequality above the boundary line? Under what conditions is the solution region below the boundary line?

Exercises

Communicate

1. Describe how to graph $7x - 5y > 0$ on graph paper.

2. When graphing a linear inequality, what determines whether the boundary line is dashed or solid?

3. Describe two ways to determine which region of the plane should be shaded for the different types of linear inequalities.

Guided Skills Practice

Graph each linear inequality. *(EXAMPLES 1 AND 2)*

4. $y < 2x + 6$ 5. $y \geq -\frac{1}{3}x + 6$ 6. $2y + 3x \geq 12$ 7. $4y - 5x < -8$

APPLICATION

8. **FUEL ECONOMY** Refer to the fuel-economy test results given on page 172. Can you drive 25 miles in the city and 400 miles on the highway in automobile B using no more than 20 gallons of gasoline? *(EXAMPLE 3)*

Graph each linear inequality. *(EXAMPLE 4)*

9. $x \leq 2$ 10. $y > -3$

Practice and Apply

Graph each linear inequality.

11. $y \geq 3x + 1$ 12. $y > 5x + 2$ 13. $y < 6x + 2$

14. $y \leq \frac{3}{2}x + 1$ 15. $y \geq -\frac{1}{2}x + \frac{2}{3}$ 16. $y > -3x - 4$

17. $y < -2x + \frac{1}{2}$ 18. $y \leq -10x + 3$ 19. $y - 5x \geq 2$

20. $2x + y > -2$ 21. $x + 3y < 1$ 22. $5x + 3y \leq 4$

23. $5x - y \geq 1$ 24. $-2x - y > 0$ 25. $6x - 4y > -2$

26. $3x - 2y > 5$ 27. $\frac{3}{2}x - \frac{5}{4}y - 1 \leq 0$ 28. $\frac{2}{3}x - \frac{1}{2}y \leq -2$

Write an inequality for each graph.

29.
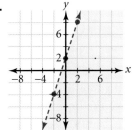

30.
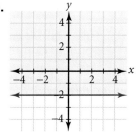

31.
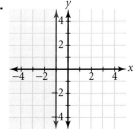

Graph each linear inequality.

32. $x < -1$ **33.** $x \le 2$ **34.** $y \ge 3$ **35.** $y > -2$

36. $2y < 5$ **37.** $2y \le -1$ **38.** $-x \le 4$ **39.** $-\frac{5}{4}x < -2$

40. $-7y < 21$ **41.** $\dfrac{3 - 12y}{7} < 0$ **42.** $\dfrac{6x + 5}{3} \ge 8$ **43.** $3(4 - 2x) \le -7$

44. Graph the inequality $y \ge \frac{1}{2}x + 5$.
- **a.** Does the ordered pair $(4, 1)$ satisfy the inequality? Support your answer by using both the inequality and the graph.
- **b.** Identify three ordered pairs that have an x-coordinate of 6 and satisfy the inequality.
- **c.** Identify three ordered pairs that have a y-coordinate of 8 and satisfy the inequality.

CHALLENGE

Describe the graphs in each *family* of inequalities for *n*-values of 1, 2, 3, and 4.

45. $x < n$ **46.** $y > (-1)^n x$ **47.** $ny \le 2x$

CONNECTION

48. GEOMETRY The perimeter of a rectangle with a length of x feet and a width of y feet cannot exceed 200 feet.
- **a.** Write three linear inequalities to describe the restrictions on the values of the perimeter, of x, and of y.
- **b.** Graph the solution region of the three inequalities from part **a.**

APPLICATIONS

SPORTS Michael is close to breaking his high-school record for field-goal points in a basketball game, needing 24 points to tie the record and 25 points to break the record. A field goal can be worth either 2 or 3 points. Michael will play in a game tonight. Write an equation or inequality for each situation below.

49. He fails to tie or break the record.

50. He ties the record.

51. He breaks the record.

52. FUND-RAISING The junior class is sponsoring a refreshment booth at home football games. They will earn a $0.25 profit on each soft drink sold and a $0.20 profit on each ice-cream bar sold. Their goal is to earn a profit of at least $50.
- **a.** Write an inequality that describes the profit goal.
- **b.** Graph the inequality.
- **c.** Give four ordered pairs that represent a profit of exactly $50.
- **d.** Give three ordered pairs that represent a profit more than $50.
- **e.** Give three ordered pairs that represent a profit less than $50.

53. RECREATION Amanda is planning a cookout. She has budgeted a maximum of $60 for hamburgers and turkey dogs. Hamburgers cost $3 per pound, and turkey dogs cost $2 per pound.
- **a.** Write an inequality to describe the possible number of pounds of hamburgers and of turkey dogs that she can purchase.
- **b.** Graph the inequality.
- **c.** What is the maximum number of pounds of hamburgers that she can purchase?
- **d.** What is the maximum number of pounds of turkey dogs that she can purchase?

54. SMALL BUSINESS A local bakery makes cakes for two special occasions: birthdays and holidays. A birthday cake requires 2 pounds of flour, and a holiday cake requires 1 pound of flour. The bakery currently has 20 pounds of flour available for making the two types of cakes.

    a. Write an inequality to show the possible numbers of birthday and holiday cakes that the bakery can make.

    b. Graph the inequality.

    c. Give three specific ordered pairs that satisfy the inequality.

55. CONSUMER ECONOMICS At the corner store, bags of popcorn cost $0.95 and bags of peanuts cost $1.25. Suppose that you want to buy x bags of popcorn and y bags of peanuts and that you have $5.75.

    a. Write an inequality to describe the number of bags of popcorn and the number of bags of peanuts you could buy.

    b. Solve the inequality for y.

    c. Graph the inequality.

Look Back

For Exercises 56–59, y varies directly as x. Find the constant of variation and the direct-variation equation that relates the two variable. *(LESSON 1.4)*

56. $x = 55$ when $y = 11$ **57.** $x = 4$ when $y = 32$

58. $x = -68$ when $y = \frac{1}{2}$ **59.** $x = \frac{1}{6}$ when $y = -45$

Solve each equation. *(LESSON 1.6)*

60. $3x - 5 = 1 - 4x$ **61.** $\frac{3}{2}x + 2 = 4 - 3x$ **62.** $-3(x - 2) = -x$

Graph and classify each system as independent, dependent, or inconsistent. Then find the solution from the graph. *(LESSON 3.1)*

63. $\begin{cases} x + 2y = -1 \\ 3x + 2y = 1 \end{cases}$ **64.** $\begin{cases} 2x - y = 3 \\ 3x + y = 7 \end{cases}$ **65.** $\begin{cases} 5x - 2y = 10 \\ x + 2y = 14 \end{cases}$

Use substitution to solve each system. *(LESSON 3.1)*

66. $\begin{cases} y = -2x - 4 \\ y = 2x + 5 \end{cases}$ **67.** $\begin{cases} y = 8 - x \\ \frac{1}{2}y - x = \frac{5}{2} \end{cases}$ **68.** $\begin{cases} y = 3x - 2 \\ 2y = 6x - 4 \end{cases}$

Use elimination to solve each system. *(LESSON 3.2)*

69. $\begin{cases} 8x + 5y = 22 \\ 6x + 2y = 13 \end{cases}$ **70.** $\begin{cases} 2x + 2y = 12 \\ 7x - 4y = -13 \end{cases}$ **71.** $\begin{cases} 2x - 3y = 3 \\ 4x + 2y = 14 \end{cases}$

Look Beyond

Graph each inequality.

72. $|x + y| \le 5$ **73.** $|x - y| \le 5$ **74.** $|x| + |y| \le 5$ **75.** $2|x| + |y| \le 5$

Systems of Linear Inequalities

Why *Systems of linear inequalities can be used to represent real-world situations such as the height and weight criteria that are needed for an actor.*

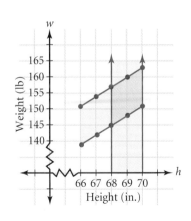

Objectives

- Write and graph a system of linear inequalities in two variables.

- Write a system of linear inequalities in two variables for a given solution region.

Suppose that an actor is needed for the lead character in a play. The search is on for a male actor between the ages of 25 and 35, standing between 5' 8" and 5' 10" tall, with a medium build, and within the weight ranges given below for males with medium builds.

Height (in.)	Weight (lb)
66	139–151
67	142–154
68	145–157
69	148–160
70	151–163

[*Source: Taber's Cyclopedic Medical Dictionary, 15th Edition*]

You can represent the height and weight criteria for this actor with the *system of linear inequalities* below.

$$\begin{cases} 68 \le h \le 70 \\ w \ge 3h - 59 \\ w \le 3h - 47 \end{cases}$$

The system of linear inequalities can be graphed as shown at right. The dark blue shaded region indicates the range of acceptable heights and weights for the lead actor.

A **system of linear inequalities** is a collection of linear inequalities in the same variables. The solution is any ordered pair that satisfies each of the inequalities in the system.

To graph a system of linear inequalities, shade the part of the plane that is the intersection of all of the individual solution regions.

E X A M P L E ❶ Graph the system. $\begin{cases} x \geq 0 \\ y \geq 0 \\ y > -2x + 5 \\ y \leq 3x + 1 \end{cases}$

● **SOLUTION**

The inequalities $x \geq 0$ and $y \geq 0$ tell you that the final solution region is in the first quadrant of a coordinate plane and may include points on the positive axes.

Graph $y > -2x + 5$ in the first quadrant. Use a dashed boundary line.

Graph $y \leq 3x + 1$ in the first quadrant. Use a solid boundary line.

The solution is the intersection of these two regions.

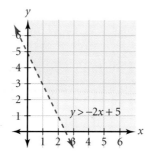

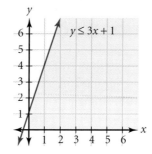

TRY THIS Graph the system. $\begin{cases} x \geq 0 \\ y \geq 0 \\ y < -x + 2 \\ y \geq -2x + 3 \end{cases}$

E X A M P L E ❷ Graph the system. $\begin{cases} y \geq -x - 1 \\ y \leq 2x + 1 \\ x < 1 \end{cases}$

● **SOLUTION**

Graph $y \geq -x - 1$. Use a solid boundary line.

Graph $y \leq 2x + 1$. Use a solid boundary line.

Graph the intersection of $y \geq -x - 1$ and $y \leq 2x + 1$ with $x < 1$.

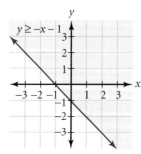

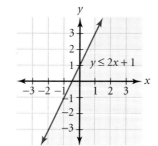

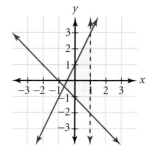

TRY THIS Graph the system. $\begin{cases} y > -x - 2 \\ y > x + 3 \\ y \leq 3 \end{cases}$

CRITICAL THINKING Find the coordinates of the vertices of the triangle graphed in Example 2. Do the coordinates of all three vertices satisfy the system? Justify your response.

In a coordinate plane, the graph of a compound inequality in one variable can be a vertical or horizontal strip, as shown in Example 3.

E X A M P L E ❸ Graph each inequality in a coordinate plane.

a. $-3 \le x \le 2$ **b.** $-1 < y < 3$

● SOLUTION

a. The solution is the set of all ordered pairs whose x-coordinate is between -3 and 2 inclusive. The solution is a vertical strip.

b. The solution is the set of all ordered pairs whose y-coordinate is between -1 and 3. The solution is a horizontal strip.

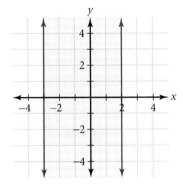 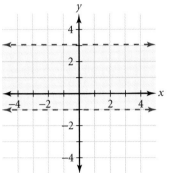

TRY THIS Graph each inequality in a coordinate plane.

a. $1 \le y < 4$ **b.** $0 < x \le 4$

CRITICAL THINKING In a coordinate plane, is the graph of a compound inequality in one variable always a vertical or horizontal strip? Explain.

E X A M P L E ❹ Write the system of inequalities graphed at right.

● SOLUTION

1. First find equations for the boundary lines.

$\overleftrightarrow{AB}$: $m = \frac{5-4}{3-0} = \frac{1}{3}$ and $b = 4$ → $y = \frac{1}{3}x + 4$

$\overleftrightarrow{BC}$: $m = \frac{0-5}{6-3} = -\frac{5}{3}$ → $y - 0 = -\frac{5}{3}(x-6)$

$\overleftrightarrow{OA}$: $x = 0$ $y = -\frac{5}{3}x + 10$

$\overleftrightarrow{OC}$: $y = 0$

2. Give each boundary line the appropriate inequality symbol. Because each boundary is solid, use $\ge$ or $\le$.

below $\overleftrightarrow{AB}$: $y \le \frac{1}{3}x + 4$ right of $\overleftrightarrow{OA}$: $x \ge 0$

below $\overleftrightarrow{BC}$: $y \le -\frac{5}{3}x + 10$ above $\overleftrightarrow{OC}$: $y \ge 0$

The system of inequalities is $\begin{cases} y \le \frac{1}{3}x + 4 \\ y \le -\frac{5}{3}x + 10 \\ x \le 0 \\ y \ge 0 \end{cases}$.

Activity

Exploring the Comfort Zone

You will need: no special materials

The region labeled "Comfort Zone" in the graph at right shows the temperatures and relative humidity levels at which the average person feels comfortable.

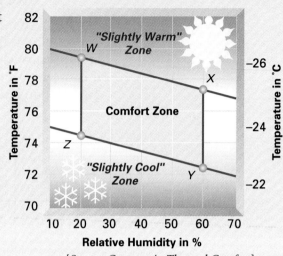

[*Source: Concepts in Thermal Comfort*]

1. What do $\overleftrightarrow{WX}$ and $\overleftrightarrow{ZY}$ represent? What do $\overleftrightarrow{WZ}$ and $\overleftrightarrow{XY}$ represent?

2. Record the coordinates of *W*, *X*, *Y*, and *Z*. Estimate the temperature at these points to the nearest one-half of a degree.

3. Write a system of linear inequalities that represents the comfort zone.

CHECKPOINT ✔ 4. What can you say about the temperature in the comfort zone as the relative humidity increases? Explain how this relates to the slope of one of the boundary lines.

Exercises

● Communicate

1. Describe when to use a solid line and when to use a dashed line to graph of a system of linear inequalities.

2. If the coordinates of a point above a boundary line make the inequality false, which side of the boundary line should be shaded?

3. Describe a system of linear inequalities that has no solution.

● Guided Skills Practice

Graph each system. *(EXAMPLES 1 AND 2)*

4. $\begin{cases} x \geq 0 \\ y \geq 0 \\ y \geq -x + 4 \\ y > x \end{cases}$

5. $\begin{cases} y \geq x \\ y \geq -x + 1 \\ y < 2 \end{cases}$

Graph each inequality in a coordinate plane. *(EXAMPLE 3)*

6. $2 < x < 4$

7. $-1 \leq y \leq 5$

8. Write the system of inequalities graphed at right.
(EXAMPLE 4)

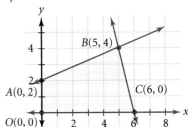

Practice and Apply

Graph each system of linear inequalities.

9. $\begin{cases} y \geq 2 \\ y < x + 1 \end{cases}$

10. $\begin{cases} x < 3 \\ y \leq 2x + 2 \end{cases}$

11. $\begin{cases} y < 3x - 4 \\ y \geq 6 - x \end{cases}$

12. $\begin{cases} y \leq 3 - x \\ y \geq x - 5 \end{cases}$

13. $\begin{cases} x \geq 0 \\ y \geq 0 \\ y > 2x + 1 \end{cases}$

14. $\begin{cases} x \geq 0 \\ y \leq 0 \\ y < -x \end{cases}$

15. $\begin{cases} x \geq 0 \\ y \leq 0 \\ y > 2x - 5 \end{cases}$

16. $\begin{cases} x \geq 0 \\ y \geq -1 \\ y < -2x + 3 \end{cases}$

17. $\begin{cases} y \geq 2x - 1 \\ x > 1 \\ y < 5 \end{cases}$

18. $\begin{cases} x \geq 0 \\ y \geq 1 \\ y \leq 5 - x \end{cases}$

19. $\begin{cases} y < x - 1 \\ y + 2x < 3 \\ y \geq -1 \end{cases}$

20. $\begin{cases} y + 2x \geq 0 \\ y \geq 2x - 4 \\ y \leq 3 \end{cases}$

Graph each compound inequality in a coordinate plane.

21. $-5 < y < 1$

22. $-1 \leq y \leq 3$

23. $2 \leq x \leq 8$

24. $-2 < x < 3$

25. $0 < y < 4$

26. $-6 \leq y \leq -2$

27. $-5 \leq x < -1$

28. $-\frac{2}{3} < x \leq \frac{1}{3}$

29. $-\frac{1}{4} \leq y < -\frac{1}{5}$

30. $-4.4 < y \leq -4$

31. $-1.5 \leq x < -0.5$

32. $-5.5 < x \leq -5.1$

Write the system of inequalities whose solution is graphed. Assume that each vertex has integer coordinates.

33.

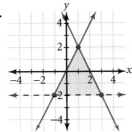

34.

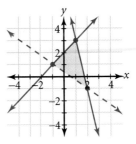

35.

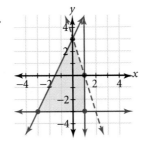

36.

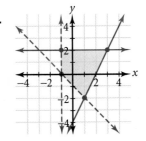

Graph each system of linear inequalities.

37. $\begin{cases} 3x + 2y \geq 1 \\ 2x + 3y < 2 \\ x < 3 \end{cases}$

38. $\begin{cases} x + y < 1 \\ 2x + 3y > 2 \\ x \geq -5 \end{cases}$

39. $\begin{cases} x + \frac{1}{2}y \leq 2 \\ 2x + 3y < 2 \end{cases}$

40. $\begin{cases} 2x + y \geq 2 \\ y \geq 3x + 2 \end{cases}$

41. $\begin{cases} x + y \leq 4 \\ 2x \leq y \end{cases}$

42. $\begin{cases} 2x - 2y < 1 \\ x + 2y \geq 2 \end{cases}$

43. $\begin{cases} 2x - y \leq 16 \\ x + y \leq 10 \\ x \geq 0 \\ y \geq 0 \end{cases}$

44. $\begin{cases} 3x - y \leq 15 \\ x + 2y \leq 10 \\ x \geq 0 \\ y \geq 0 \end{cases}$

45. $\begin{cases} 3x - 2y \geq 4 \\ x + y > 4 \\ x - y \leq 7 \\ x \geq 0 \\ y \geq 0 \end{cases}$

CONNECTIONS

46. GEOMETRY A parallelogram is a quadrilateral whose opposite sides are parallel. Create a graph of a parallelogram on a coordinate plane. Write a system of inequalities that represents the parallelogram and its interior.

CHALLENGE

47. GEOMETRY Classify the solution to $\begin{cases} y \leq a \\ y \geq |x| \end{cases}$, for $a > 0$, as a geometric figure.

APPLICATIONS

48. MANUFACTURING A small-appliance manufacturing company makes standard and deluxe models of a toaster oven. The company can make up to 200 ovens per week. The standard model costs $20 to produce, and the deluxe model costs $30 to produce. The company has budgeted no more than $3600 per week to produce the ovens.

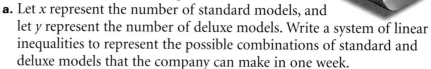

a. Let x represent the number of standard models, and let y represent the number of deluxe models. Write a system of linear inequalities to represent the possible combinations of standard and deluxe models that the company can make in one week.

b. Graph the system of inequalities.

c. Due to an increase in the rental costs for the company's factory, the company can budget no more that $3000 per week to make the toaster ovens. Explain how this changes the possible combinations of standard and deluxe models that the company can make in one week.

49. CRIMINOLOGY Officer Cheek is trying to solve a crime that was committed by a man with a shoe size from 9 to 10. According to witnesses, the man's height is between 5 feet and 5 feet 6 inches inclusive.

a. Let x represent the shoe size, and let y represent the height. Write a system of inequalities to represent the given information.

b. Graph the system of inequalities.

50. INCOME Angela works 40 hours or fewer per week programming computers and tutoring. She earns $20 per hour programming and $10 per hour tutoring. Angela needs to earn at least $500 per week.
  a. Write a system of linear inequalities that represents the possible combinations of hours spent tutoring and hours spent programming that will meet Angela's needs.
  b. Graph the system of linear inequalities. Is the solution a polygon?
  c. Find a point that is a solution to the system of linear inequalities. What are the coordinates of this point and what do the coordinates of this point represent?
  d. Which point in the solution region represents the best way for Angela to spend her time? Explain why you think this is the best solution.

51. ENTERTAINMENT A ticket office sells reserved tickets and general-admission tickets to a rock concert. The auditorium normally holds no more than 5000 people. There can be no more than 3000 reserved tickets and no more than 4000 general-admission tickets sold.
  a. Let x represent the number of reserved tickets, and let y represent the number of general-admission tickets. Write a system of three linear inequalities to represent the possible combinations of reserved and general-admission tickets that can be sold. (Note that x and y must be non-negative integers.)
  b. Graph the system of inequalities.
  c. In order to increase the number of people that come to the concert, the auditorium increases its seating capacity to 5500. Explain how this addition changes the possible ticket combinations.

52. BUSINESS A lawn and garden store sells gas-powered and electric hedge clippers. The store wants to sell at least 45 hedge clippers per month. The profit on each electric model is $50, and the profit on each gas-powered model is $40. The shop wants to earn at least $2000 per month on the sale of hedge clippers.
  a. Let x represent the number of electric hedge clippers, and let y represent the number of gas-powered hedge clippers. Write a system of linear inequalities to represent the possible combinations of each model sold.
  b. Graph the system of inequalities.
  c. If the shop sells 16 electric hedge clippers in one month, what is the minimum number of gas-powered hedge clippers that must be sold that month in order to meet their goals?

Look Back

53. Use intercepts to graph $5x - 3y = 7$. *(LESSON 1.2)*

54. Write the equation in slope-intercept form for the line that contains the point $(4, -3)$ and is parallel to $2x - 4y = 26$. *(LESSON 1.3)*

Solve each proportion for the variable. Check your answers.
(LESSON 1.4)

55. $\dfrac{3x}{2} = \dfrac{15}{12}$ **56.** $\dfrac{1 - 2x}{8} = \dfrac{7}{4}$ **57.** $\dfrac{3x + 5}{6} = \dfrac{x - 2}{5}$

Solve each equation. *(LESSON 1.6)*

58. $5x = 15 + 3x$ **59.** $7x - 13 = -2x$

Let $f(x) = 3x + 2$ and $g(x) = 5 - x$. Find each new function, and state any domain restrictions. *(LESSON 2.4)*

60. $f + g$ **61.** $f - g$ **62.** $f \cdot g$ **63.** $\dfrac{f}{g}$

Use any method to solve each system of equations. Then classify each system as independent, dependent, or inconsistent. *(LESSONS 3.1 AND 3.2)*

64. $\begin{cases} 4x - 2y = 3 \\ 8y - 6x = 24 \end{cases}$ **65.** $\begin{cases} 5x + y = -1 \\ 10x - y = 3 \end{cases}$

66. $\begin{cases} 2x + 5y = 10 \\ 2x - 5y = 0 \end{cases}$ **67.** $\begin{cases} 3x + y = 6 \\ 6x + 2y = 12 \end{cases}$

 *Look Beyond*

68. Evaluate $P = 20x + 30y$ for $(3, 5)$, $(4, 7)$, and $(5, 8)$. As x- and y-values increase, does the value of P increase or decrease?

69. Evaluate $C = 400p + 500q$ for $(1, 2)$, $(2, 5)$, and $(3, 8)$. As p- and q-values increase, does the value of C increase or decrease?

APPLICATION

70. SYNONYMS Define the word *feasible*. Use a dictionary or write your own definition. What is a synonym for *feasible*?

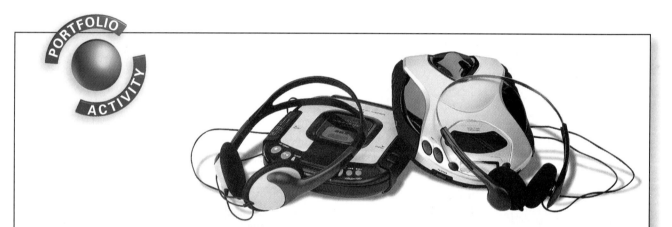

BUSINESS Another company also manufactures two different models of portable CD players: a regular model and a sport model. Each model requires time on three different machines, as shown below.

	Regular model	Sport model
Machine A	2 minutes	1 minute
Machine B	1 minute	3 minutes
Machine C	1 minute	1 minute

Each machine is used for manufacturing many different items, so in a given hour, machine A is available for CD-player production a maximum of 18 minutes, machine B for a maximum of 24 minutes, and machine C for a maximum of 10 minutes.

1. Is it possible for the company to produce 4 regular models and 5 sport models in one hour? Explain your reasoning.

2. Is it possible for the company to produce 6 regular models and 5 sport models in one hour? Explain your reasoning.

WORKING ON THE CHAPTER PROJECT

You should now be able to complete Activities 1 and 3 of the Chapter Project.

Linear Programming

Why *Linear programming is widely used in the management of business and agriculture to find optimal solutions to complex problems.*

Objectives

- Write and graph a set of constraints for a linear-programming problem.

- Use linear programming to find the maximum or minimum value of an objective function.

Max Desmond is a farmer who plants corn and wheat. In making planting decisions, he used the 1996 statistics at right from the United States Bureau of the Census.

Crop	Yield per acre	Average price
corn	113.5 bu	$3.15/bu
soybeans	34.9 bu	$6.80/bu
wheat	35.8 bu	$4.45/bu
cotton	540 lb	$0.759/lb
rice, rough	5621 lb	$0.0865/lb

(The abbreviation for bushel is bu.)

Mr. Desmond wants to plant according to the following *constraints*:
- no more than 120 acres of corn and wheat
- at least 20 and no more than 80 acres of corn
- at least 30 acres of wheat

How many acres of each crop should Mr. Desmond plant to maximize the revenue from his harvest? *You will answer this question in Example 2.*

A method called **linear programming** is used to find optimal solutions such as the maximum revenue from Mr. Desmond's harvest. Linear-programming problems have the following characteristics:
- The inequalities contained in the problem are called **constraints**.
- The solution to the set of constraints is called the **feasible region**.
- The function to be maximized or minimized is called the **objective function**.

Example 1 illustrates how to begin the method of linear programming.

EXAMPLE **1** **Refer to the planting problem described at the beginning of the lesson.**

APPLICATION

AGRICULTURE

a. Write a system of inequalities to represent the constraints.
b. Graph the feasible region.
c. Write an objective function for the revenue from Mr. Desmond's harvest.

SOLUTION

a. Let x represent the number of acres of corn. Let y represent the number of acres of wheat. Since x and y must be positive, $x \geq 0$ and $y \geq 0$.

Corn constraint: $20 \leq x \leq 80$
Wheat constraint: $y \geq 30$
Total acreage: $x + y \leq 120$

The system is: $\begin{cases} 20 \leq x \leq 80 \\ y \geq 30 \\ x + y \leq 120 \end{cases}$

b. The graph is shown below.

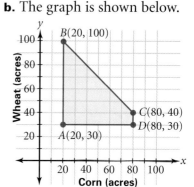

c. The objective function for the revenue is as follows:

$$R = \left(\begin{array}{c}\text{yield} \\ \text{per} \\ \text{acre}\end{array}\right)\left(\begin{array}{c}\text{average} \\ \text{price}\end{array}\right)x + \left(\begin{array}{c}\text{yield} \\ \text{per} \\ \text{acre}\end{array}\right)\left(\begin{array}{c}\text{average} \\ \text{price}\end{array}\right)y$$

$$R = (113.5)(3.15)x + (35.8)(4.45)y$$

$$R = 357.525x + 159.31y$$

For each point in the feasible region of a linear-programming problem, the objective function has a value. This value depends on both variables in the system that represents the feasible region.

In the Activity below, you will explore values in the feasible region for the objective function from Example 1.

CONNECTION

MAXIMUM/MINIMUM

Activity

Exploring the Objective Function

You will need: no special materials

1. Copy and complete the table to find the revenue at each of the four vertices of the feasible region from Example 1.

Vertex	Objective function
$A(20, 30)$	$R = 357.525(20) + 159.31(30) = 11{,}929.80$
$B(20, 100)$	?
$C(80, 40)$	?
$D(80, 30)$	?

2. Which vertex represents the greatest revenue? What do the coordinates of this vertex represent?

188 CHAPTER 3

3. Guess and check. Choose points on the boundary lines of the feasible region. Find the corresponding revenues for these points. Can you find a point that gives a greater revenue than the vertex you chose in Step 2?

4. Guess and check. Choose points inside the feasible region. Find the corresponding revenues for these points. Can you find a point that gives a greater revenue than the vertex you chose in Step 2?

5. Do your investigations suggest that the maximum value of the objective function occurs at a vertex? Justify your response.

6. Look for a pattern. Repeat Steps 2–5 for the minimum revenue instead of the maximum revenue. Explain how the points that correspond to the maximum and minimum revenues are related.

In the Activity, you may have examined several points in the feasible region and found that the maximum and minimum revenues occur at vertices of the feasible region. The *Corner-Point Principle* confirms that you need to examine only the vertices of the feasible region to find the maximum or minimum value of the objective function.

Corner-Point Principle

In linear programming, the maximum and minimum values of the objective function each occur at one of the vertices of the feasible region.

Using the information in Example 1, maximize the objective function. Then graph the objective function that represents the maximum revenues along with the feasible region.

● **SOLUTION**

Make a table containing the coordinates of the vertices of the feasible region. Evaluate $R = 357.525x + 159.31y$ for each ordered pair.

Vertex	Objective function
$A(20, 30)$	$R = 357.525(20) + 159.31(30) = 11{,}929.80$
$B(20, 100)$	$R = 357.525(20) + 159.31(100) = 23{,}081.50$
$C(80, 40)$	$R = 357.525(80) + 159.31(40) = 34{,}974.40$
$D(80, 30)$	$R = 357.525(80) + 159.31(30) = 33{,}381.30$

The maximum revenue of $34,974.40 occurs at $C(80, 40)$. Thus, Mr. Desmond should plant 80 acres of corn and 40 acres of wheat.

Write $357.525x + 159.31y = 34{,}974.4$ as $y = \dfrac{34{,}974.4 - 357.525x}{159.31}$, and graph it along with the boundaries of the feasible region.

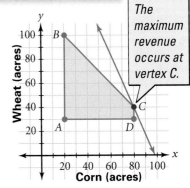

The maximum revenue occurs at vertex C.

CHECKPOINT ✔ How many acres of each crop give a minimum revenue?

EXAMPLE ③ Find the maximum and minimum values, if they exist, of the objective function $S = 2x + 3y$ given the set of constraints provided at right.

$$\begin{cases} x \geq 0,\, y \geq 0 \\ 5x + y \geq 20 \\ x + y \geq 12 \\ x + 2y \geq 16 \end{cases}$$

CONNECTION
MAXIMUM/MINIMUM

● **SOLUTION**

1. Graph the feasible region as shown.

2. The objective function is $S = 2x + 3y$.

3. Find the coordinates of each vertex by solving the appropriate system.

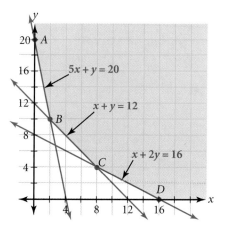

$$\begin{cases} 5x + y = 20 \\ x = 0 \end{cases} \text{ gives } A(0, 20)$$

$$\begin{cases} 5x + y = 20 \\ x + y = 12 \end{cases} \text{ gives } B(2, 10)$$

$$\begin{cases} x + y = 12 \\ x + 2y = 16 \end{cases} \text{ gives } C(8, 4)$$

$$\begin{cases} y = 0 \\ x + 2y = 16 \end{cases} \text{ gives } D(16, 0)$$

4. Evaluate $S = 2x + 3y$ for the coordinates of each vertex.

Vertex	Objective function
$A(0, 20)$	$S = 2(0) + 3(20) = 60$
$B(2, 10)$	$S = 2(2) + 3(10) = 34$
$C(8, 4)$	$S = 2(8) + 3(4) = 28$
$D(16, 0)$	$S = 2(16) + 3(0) = 32$

The feasible region is unbounded on the right of the vertices. Thus, there is no maximum value. The minimum value, 28, of $S = 2x + 3y$ occurs at $(8, 4)$.

CHECKPOINT ✔ Describe a real-world situation in which the feasible region would be unbounded on the right.

CRITICAL THINKING   Can there be a real-world situation in which the feasible region would be unbounded on the left? Explain.

SUMMARY

LINEAR-PROGRAMMING PROCEDURE

Step 1. Write a system of inequalities, and graph the feasible region.

Step 2. Write the objective function to be maximized or minimized.

Step 3. Find the coordinates of the vertices of the feasible region.

Step 4. Evaluate the objective function for the coordinates of the vertices of the feasible region. Then identify the coordinates that give the required maximum or minimum.

Exercises

Communicate

1. What is a *constraint* on a variable, such as *x*?

2. Discuss what the term *feasible* means when it is used to describe the possible solution region of a linear-programming problem.

3. In your own words, explain how to solve a linear-programming problem.

Guided Skills Practice

APPLICATION

AGRICULTURE Use the table of statistics at the beginning of the lesson to determine the constraints and to graph the feasible region for each situation below. Then write the corresponding objective function for the revenue. *(EXAMPLE 1)*

4. A farmer wants to plant corn and soybeans on 150 acres of land. The farmer wants to plant between 40 and 120 acres of corn and no more than 100 acres of soybeans.

5. A farmer wants to plant wheat and soybeans on 220 acres of land. The farmer wants to plant between 100 and 200 acres of wheat and no more than 75 acres of soybeans.

Find the number of acres of each crop that the farmer should plant to maximize the revenue for each situation. *(EXAMPLE 2)*

6. See Exercise 4.   7. See Exercise 5.

CONNECTION

MAXIMUM/MINIMUM **Find the maximum and minimum values, if they exist, of $C = 3x + 4y$ for each set of constraints.** *(EXAMPLE 3)*

8. $\begin{cases} 3 \leq x \leq 8 \\ 2 \leq y \leq 6 \\ 2x + y \geq 12 \end{cases}$

9. $\begin{cases} 2 \leq x \\ 4 \leq y \leq 8 \\ x + 2y \geq 16 \end{cases}$

Practice and Apply

Graph the feasible region for each set of constraints.

10. $\begin{cases} x + 2y \leq 8 \\ 2x + y \geq 10 \\ x \geq 0, y \geq 0 \end{cases}$

11. $\begin{cases} 3x + 2y \leq 12 \\ \frac{1}{2}x - y \leq -2 \\ x \geq 0, y \geq 0 \end{cases}$

12. $\begin{cases} x + 2y \leq 6 \\ 2x - y \leq 7 \\ x \geq 2, y \geq 0 \end{cases}$

13. $\begin{cases} 3x + y \leq 12 \\ 2x - 3y \geq -3 \\ x \leq 0, y \leq 6 \end{cases}$

Identify the vertices of the feasible region in

14. Exercise 10.   15. Exercise 11.

16. Exercise 12.   17. Exercise 13.

The feasible region for a set of constraints has vertices at (–2, 0), (3, 3), (6, 2), and (5, 1). Given this feasible region, find the maximum and minimum values of each objective function.

18. $C = 2x - y$

19. $M = 3y - x$

20. $I = 100x + 200y$

21. $P = 3x + 2.5y$

Find the maximum and minimum values, if they exist, of each objective function for the given constraints.

22. $P = 5y + 3x$
Constraints:
$$\begin{cases} x + y \le 6 \\ x - y \le 4 \\ x \ge 0 \\ y \ge 0 \end{cases}$$

23. $P = 3x + y$
Constraints:
$$\begin{cases} x + y \ge 3 \\ 3x + 4y \le 12 \\ x \ge 0 \\ y \ge 0 \end{cases}$$

24. $P = 4x + 7y$
Constraints:
$$\begin{cases} x + y \le 8 \\ y - x \le 2 \\ x \ge 0 \\ y \ge 0 \end{cases}$$

25. $P = 2x + 7y$
Constraints:
$$\begin{cases} 4x - 2y \le 8 \\ x \ge 1 \\ 0 \le y \le 4 \end{cases}$$

26. $E = 2x + y$
Constraints:
$$\begin{cases} x + y \ge 6 \\ x - y \le 4 \\ x \ge 0 \\ y \ge 0 \end{cases}$$

27. $E = x + y$
Constraints:
$$\begin{cases} x + 2y \ge 3 \\ 3x + 4y \ge 8 \\ x \ge 0 \\ y \ge 0 \end{cases}$$

28. $E = 3x + 5y$
Constraints:
$$\begin{cases} x - 2y \ge 0 \\ x + 2y \ge 8 \\ 1 \le x \le 6 \\ y \ge 0 \end{cases}$$

29. $E = 3x + 2y$
Constraints:
$$\begin{cases} x + y \le 5 \\ y - x \ge 5 \\ 4x + y \ge -10 \end{cases}$$

30. GEOMETRY If the feasible region for a linear-programming problem is bounded, it must form a *convex polygon*. Convex polygons cannot have "dents" and are defined as polygons in which any line segment connecting two points of the polygon has no part outside the polygon. Sketch two examples of convex polygons and two examples of polygons that are not convex (that is, concave).

31. MAXIMUM/MINIMUM An objective function can have a maximum (or minimum) value at two vertices if the graph of the objective function, equal to a constant function value, contains both vertices.
  a. Draw the graph of a feasible region that has maximum values of 6 at two vertices for the objective function $P = 2x + 3y$.
  b. Draw the graph of a feasible region that has minimum values of 6 at two vertices for the objective function $P = 2x + 3y$.

32. MANUFACTURING A ski manufacturer makes two types of skis and has a fabricating department and a finishing department. A pair of downhill skis requires 6 hours to fabricate and 1 hour to finish. A pair of cross-country skis requires 4 hours to fabricate and 1 hour to finish. The fabricating department has 108 hours of labor available per day. The finishing department has 24 hours of labor available per day. The company makes a profit of $40 on each pair of downhill skis and a profit of $30 on each pair of cross-country skis.
  a. Write a system of linear inequalities to represent the constraints.
  b. Graph the feasible region.
  c. Write the objective function for the profit, and find the maximum profit for the given constraints.

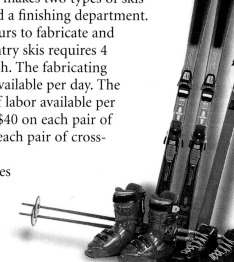

33. TRANSPORTATION Trenton, Michigan, a small community, is trying to establish a public transportation system of large and small vans. It can spend no more than $100,000 for both sizes of vehicles and no more than $500 per month for maintenance. The community can purchase a small van for $10,000 and maintain it for $100 per month. The large vans cost $20,000 each and can be maintained for $75 per month. Each large van carries a maximum of 15 passengers, and each small van carries a maximum of 7 passengers.
  a. Write a system of linear inequalities to represent the constraints.
  b. Graph the feasible region.
  c. Write the objective function for the number of passengers, and find the maximum number of passengers for the given constraints.

34. BUSINESS A tourist agency can sell up to 1200 travel packages for a football game. The package includes airfare, weekend accommodations, and the choice of two types of flights: a nonstop flight or a two-stop flight. The nonstop flight can carry up to 150 passengers, and the two-stop flight can carry up to 100 passengers. The agency can locate no more than 10 planes for the travel packages. Each package with a nonstop flight sells for $1200, and each package with a two-stop flight sells for $900. Assume that each plane will carry the maximum number of passengers.
  a. Write a system of linear inequalities to represent the constraints.
  b. Graph the feasible region.
  c. Write an objective function that maximizes the revenue for the tourist agency, and find the maximum revenue for the given constraints.

35. HEALTH A school dietitian wants to prepare a meal of meat and vegetables that has the lowest possible fat and that meets the Food and Drug Administration recommended daily allowances (RDA) of iron and protein. The RDA minimums are 20 milligrams of iron and 45 grams of protein. Each 3-ounce serving of meat contains 45 grams of protein, 10 milligrams of iron, and 4 grams of fat. Each 1-cup serving of vegetables contains 9 grams of protein, 6 milligrams of iron, and 2 grams of fat. Let x represent the number of 3-ounce servings of meat, and let y represent the number of 1-cup servings of vegetables.
  a. Write a system of linear inequalities to represent the constraints.
  b. Graph the feasible region.
  c. Write the objective function for the number of grams of fat, and find the minimum number of grams of fat for the given constraints.

36. AGRICULTURE A farmer has 90 acres available for planting millet and alfalfa. Seed costs $4 per acre for millet and $6 per acre for alfalfa. Labor costs are $20 per acre for millet and $10 per acre for alfalfa. The expected income is $110 per acre for millet and $150 per acre for alfalfa. The farmer intends to spend no more than $480 for seed and $1400 for labor.
  a. Write a system of linear inequalities to represent the constraints.
  b. Graph the feasible region.
  c. Write the objective function that maximizes the income, and find the maximum income for the given constraints.

37. SMALL BUSINESS A carpenter makes bookcases in two sizes, large and small. It takes 6 hours to make a large bookcase and 2 hours to make a small one. The profit on a large bookcase is $50, and the profit on a small bookcase is $20. The carpenter can spend only 24 hours per week making bookcases and must make at least 2 of each size per week.

  a. Write a system of linear inequalities to represent the constraints.

  b. Graph the feasible region.

  c. Write the objective function for the profit, and find the maximum profit for the given constraints.

 Look Back

Determine whether each table represents a linear relationship between *x* and *y*. If the relationship is linear, write the next ordered pair that would appear in the table. *(LESSON 1.1)*

38.

x	0	2	4	6
y	5	10	20	40

39.

x	−1	−2	−3	−4
y	2	4	6	8

Graph each function, and state the domain and the range. *(LESSON 2.3)*

40. $f(x) = 2x + 5$

41. $g(x) = 2x^2 - 3$

Find an equation for the inverse of each function. *(LESSON 2.5)*

42. $f(x) = 4x + 1$

43. $g(x) = -2x + \frac{1}{4}$

44. $f(x) = 5 - 2x$

45. $g(x) = \frac{1}{4}x - 6$

 Look Beyond

Find the *x*-intercepts for the graph of each function. Compare the factors of each function rule with the *x*-intercepts of the graph.

46 $f(x) = (x - 3)(x + 2)$

47 $f(x) = (x + 4)(x - 9)$

48 $f(x) = x(x + 12)$

BUSINESS Refer to the second company's CD-player production described in the Portfolio Activity on page 186.

  1. Determine the coordinates of the vertices of the feasible region.

  2. The second company estimates that it makes a $20 profit for every regular model produced and a $30 profit for every sport model produced. Write the objective function for the profit.

  3. How many regular models and sport models should the second company produce per hour in order to maximize their profit? What is the maximum profit?

WORKING ON THE CHAPTER PROJECT

You should now be able to complete the Chapter Project.

Parametric Equations

Why Parametric equations can be used to describe real-world situations involving two independent variables, such as the linear and vertical positions of an airplane during takeoff.

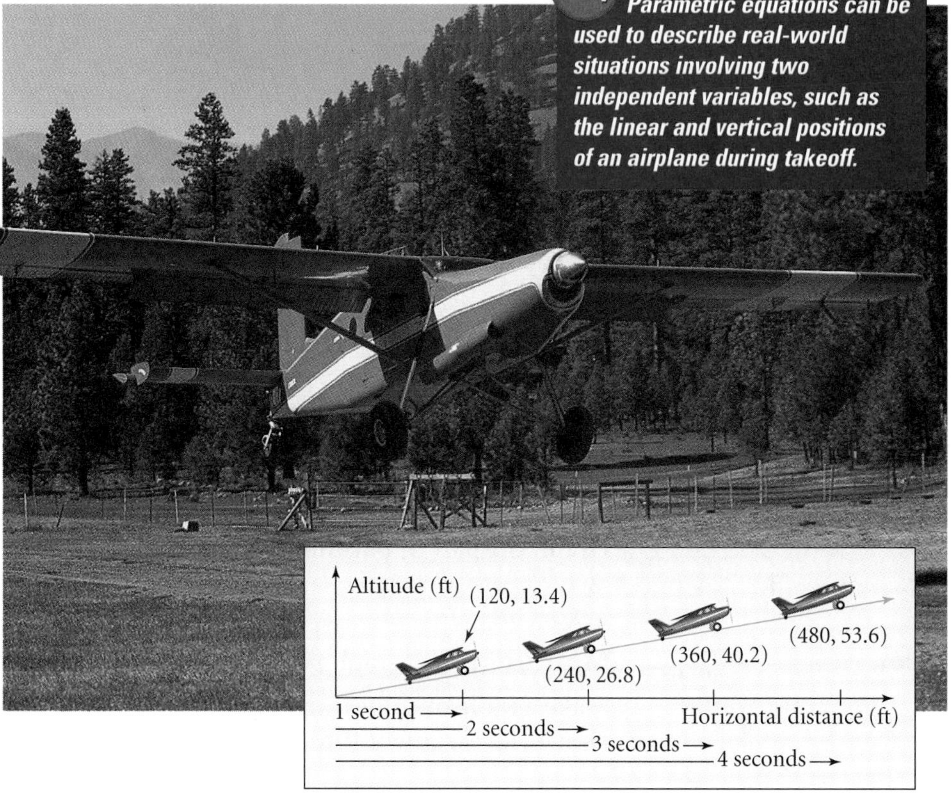

Objectives

- Graph a pair of parametric equations, and use them to model real-world applications.

- Write the function represented by a pair of parametric equations.

APPLICATION

AVIATION

A small airplane takes off from a field. One second after takeoff, the airplane is 120 feet down the runway and 13.4 feet above it. The airplane's ascent continues at a constant rate. To analyze the position of the airplane as a function of time, you can represent the horizontal and vertical distances traveled in terms of a third variable, the time after takeoff.

For the Activity below, use the information in the diagram above.

Activity

Exploring the Position of an Airplane

You will need: a graphics calculator

Refer to the airplane described above. Let t represent the time in seconds after takeoff, let x represent the horizontal distance in feet traveled in t seconds, and let y represent the vertical distance, or altitude, in feet traveled in t seconds.

1. Copy and complete each table of values below.

t	0	1	2	3	4
x					

t	0	1	2	3	4
y					

2. Verify that the relationships between x and t and between y and t are linear. Write a pair of *parametric equations*: an equation for x in terms of t and an equation for y in terms of t. Then write a linear function for the altitude, y, in terms of horizontal distance traveled, x.

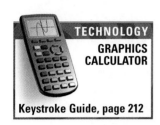
3. Use a graphics calculator in parametric mode to find how many seconds it will take for the airplane to achieve an altitude of 1500 feet. What is the horizontal distance that the airplane will have traveled from the point of takeoff when it reaches this altitude (assuming that the airplane continues along a straight path)?

4. Can you use the linear function that you wrote in Step 2 to answer the questions in Step 3? What additional information does the pair of parametric equations give you that the linear function does not?

CHECKPOINT ✔

In general, a pair of **parametric equations** is a pair of continuous functions that define the x- and y-coordinates of a point in a coordinate plane in terms of a third variable, such as t, called the **parameter**.

To graph a pair of parametric equations, you can make a table of values or use a graphics calculator, as shown in Example 1.

E X A M P L E ① Graph the pair of parametric equations for $-3 \le t \le 3$. $\begin{cases} x(t) = 2t - 1 \\ y(t) = -t + 2 \end{cases}$

● SOLUTION

Method 1 Use graph paper.

PROBLEM SOLVING

Make a table of values, and graph each ordered pair (x, y) in the table. Draw a line segment through the points graphed.

t	x	y
-3	$2(-3) - 1 = -7$	$-(-3) + 2 = 5$
-2	$2(-2) - 1 = -5$	$-(-2) + 2 = 4$
-1	$2(-1) - 1 = -3$	$-(-1) + 2 = 3$
0	$2(0) - 1 = -1$	$-(0) + 2 = 2$
1	$2(1) - 1 = 1$	$-(1) + 2 = 1$
2	$2(2) - 1 = 3$	$-(2) + 2 = 0$
3	$2(3) - 1 = 5$	$-(3) + 2 = -1$

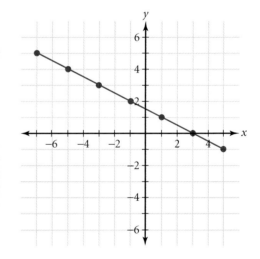

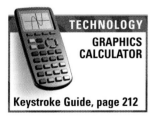
Method 2 Use a graphics calculator.

In parametric mode, enter the functions for x and for y in terms of t.

Define your viewing window, including minimum and maximum values for t. Then graph.

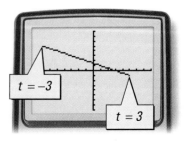

$t = -3$

$t = 3$

TRY THIS

Graph the pair of parametric equations $\begin{cases} x(t) = -2t + 2 \\ y(t) = -t - 2 \end{cases}$ for $-4 \le t \le 4$.

Let r and s be real numbers. Describe the line defined by each pair of parametric equations.

a. $\begin{cases} x(t) = r \\ y(t) = t \end{cases}$ **b.** $\begin{cases} x(t) = t \\ y(t) = s \end{cases}$

Example 2 shows how to describe a pair of parametric equations as an equation in two variables by eliminating the parameter.

E X A M P L E ❷ Write the pair of parametric equations as a single equation in x and y. $\begin{cases} x(t) = 2t + 4 \\ y(t) = 5t - 2 \end{cases}$

● **SOLUTION**

Method 1

1. Solve either equation for t.

$$x(t) = 2t + 4 \quad \rightarrow \quad x = 2t + 4$$

$$\frac{x - 4}{2} = t$$

2. Substitute the expression for t in the other equation, and simplify.

$$y(t) = 5t - 2 \quad \rightarrow \quad y = 5t - 2$$

$$y = 5\left(\frac{x - 4}{2}\right) - 2$$

$$y = \frac{5}{2}x - 10 - 2$$

$$y = \frac{5}{2}x - 12$$

Method 2

1. Solve both equations for t.

$$x(t) = 2t + 4 \quad \rightarrow \quad x = 2t + 4$$

$$\frac{x - 4}{2} = t$$

$$y(t) = 5t - 2 \quad \rightarrow \quad y = 5t - 2$$

$$\frac{y + 2}{5} = t$$

2. Set the resulting expressions for t equal to each other.

$$\frac{x - 4}{2} = \frac{y + 2}{5}$$

$$5(x - 4) = 2(y + 2)$$

$$5x - 20 = 2y + 4$$

$$y = \frac{5}{2}x - 12$$

TRY THIS Write the pair of parametric equations as a single equation in x and y. $\begin{cases} x(t) = -2t - 6 \\ y(t) = 3t - 1 \end{cases}$

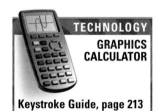

TECHNOLOGY
GRAPHICS CALCULATOR
Keystroke Guide, page 213

You can graph functions and their inverses by using parametric equations. If f is a function containing the point (x, y), then its inverse contains the point (y, x).

For example, $f(x) = x^2$ can be represented by $\begin{cases} x_1(t) = t \\ y_1(t) = t^2 \end{cases}$. The inverse of

$f(x) = x^2$ can be represented by $\begin{cases} x_2(t) = t^2 \\ y_2(t) = t \end{cases}$.

C O N N E C T I O N
TRANSFORMATIONS

Graph these two pairs of parametric equations for t-values from -5 to 5. Notice that the graphs are reflections of one another across the line $y = x$.

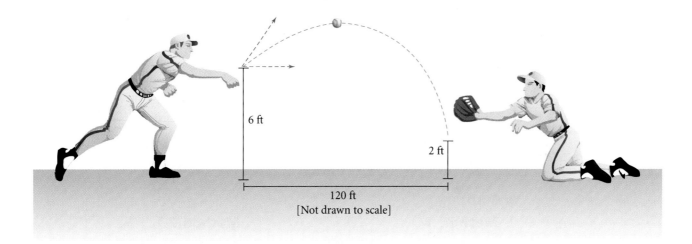

6 ft

2 ft

120 ft
[Not drawn to scale]

Keystroke Guide, page 213

EXAMPLE ③ An outfielder throws a baseball to the catcher 120 feet away to prevent a runner from scoring. The ball is released 6 feet above the ground with a horizontal speed of 70 feet per second and a vertical speed of 25 feet per second. The catcher holds his mitt 2 feet off the ground. The following parametric equations describe the path of the ball:

APPLICATION
SPORTS

$$\begin{cases} x(t) = 70t \\ y(t) = 6 + 25t - 16t^2 \end{cases}$$

x(t) gives the horizontal distance in feet after t seconds.
y(t) gives the vertical distance in feet after t seconds.

a. When does the ball reach its greatest altitude?
b. Can the catcher catch the ball?

TECHNOLOGY
GRAPHICS CALCULATOR

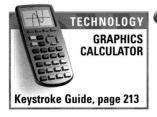

SOLUTION

a. Graph the pair of parametric equations. Using the trace feature, you can find that the ball reaches its maximum altitude of about 16 feet after about 0.8 second.

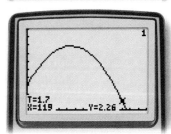

T=.8
X=56   Y=15.76

b. When the ball has traveled about 120 feet, the ball will be about 2.3 feet off the ground (and directly in front of the catcher). The catcher should be able to catch the ball.

T=1.7
X=119   Y=2.26

TRY THIS Suppose that an outfielder throws the ball to the catcher 100 feet away. The ball is released 6 feet above the ground, and the catcher holds his mitt 2 feet off the ground. The following parametric equations describe the path of the ball:

$$\begin{cases} x(t) = 60t \\ y(t) = 6 + 30t - 16t^2 \end{cases}$$

x(t) gives the horizontal distance in feet after t seconds.
y(t) gives the vertical distance in feet after t seconds.

a. When does the ball reach its greatest altitude?
b. Can the catcher catch the ball?

Exercises

● Communicate

1. Describe the procedure for eliminating the parameter t in the pair of parametric equations $x(t) = 2t + 3$ and $y(t) = -t + 1$.

2. Explain what is lost when a pair of parametric equations are rewritten as a function in two variables.

3. Describe what each variable in the parametric equations in Example 3 represents.

● Guided Skills Practice

Graph each pair of parametric equations for the given interval of t.
(EXAMPLE 1)

4. $\begin{cases} x(t) = t \\ y(t) = 3t + 2 \end{cases}$ for $-3 \le t \le 3$

5. $\begin{cases} x(t) = t + 7 \\ y(t) = 8 - t \end{cases}$ for $-4 \le t \le 4$

Write each pair of parametric equations as a single equation in x and y.
(EXAMPLE 2)

6. $\begin{cases} x(t) = 5t - 6 \\ y(t) = 3t + 1 \end{cases}$

7. $\begin{cases} x(t) = 2t + 5 \\ y(t) = 3 - 2t \end{cases}$

APPLICATION

8. **SPORTS** A batter hits a ball 3 feet above the ground with a horizontal speed of 98 feet per second and a vertical speed of 45 feet per second toward the outfield fence. The fence is 250 feet from the batter and 10 feet high. If $x(t)$ gives the horizontal distance in feet after t seconds and $y(t)$ gives the vertical distance in feet after t seconds, the following parametric equations describe the path of the ball. *(EXAMPLE 3)*

$$\begin{cases} x(t) = 98t \\ y(t) = 3 + 45t - 16t^2 \end{cases}$$

a. How long will it take the ball to reach the fence?
b. Will the ball go over the fence?

● Practice and Apply

Graph each pair of parametric equations for the given interval of t.

9. $\begin{cases} x(t) = 3t \\ y(t) = t - 2 \end{cases}$ for $-4 \le t \le 4$

10. $\begin{cases} x(t) = t + 5 \\ y(t) = 4t \end{cases}$ for $-3 \le t \le 3$

11. $\begin{cases} x(t) = 2t \\ y(t) = 6 - t \end{cases}$ for $-3 \le t \le 3$

12. $\begin{cases} x(t) = 5 - 2t \\ y(t) = \dfrac{t}{2} \end{cases}$ for $-4 \le t \le 4$

13. $\begin{cases} x(t) = 2t + 3 \\ y(t) = t^2 \end{cases}$ for $-3 \le t \le 3$

14. $\begin{cases} x(t) = t^2 \\ y(t) = 3t - 5 \end{cases}$ for $-4 \le t \le 4$

Write each pair of parametric equations as a single equation in *x* and *y*.

15. $\begin{cases} x(t) = 2t \\ y(t) = t - 1 \end{cases}$ **16.** $\begin{cases} x(t) = t + 3 \\ y(t) = 3t \end{cases}$ **17.** $\begin{cases} x(t) = 2t + 1 \\ y(t) = t + 5 \end{cases}$

18. $\begin{cases} x(t) = t - 2 \\ y(t) = t + 7 \end{cases}$ **19.** $\begin{cases} x(t) = 3t \\ y(t) = 1 - t \end{cases}$ **20.** $\begin{cases} x(t) = t \\ y(t) = 3 - 2t \end{cases}$

21. $\begin{cases} x(t) = 2t \\ y(t) = t^2 - 1 \end{cases}$ **22.** $\begin{cases} x(t) = t^2 \\ y(t) = \dfrac{t}{2} \end{cases}$ **23.** $\begin{cases} x(t) = \dfrac{1}{3}t \\ y(t) = t^2 \end{cases}$

24. $\begin{cases} x(t) = t^2 + 2t \\ y(t) = 2t \end{cases}$ **25.** $\begin{cases} x(t) = 5 - t^2 \\ y(t) = \dfrac{3}{2}t \end{cases}$ **26.** $\begin{cases} x(t) = 2 - 3t^2 \\ y(t) = -\dfrac{1}{3}t \end{cases}$

Graph the function represented by each pair of parametric equations. Then graph its inverse on the same coordinate plane.

27 $\begin{cases} x(t) = t^2 - 2 \\ y(t) = t \end{cases}$ **28** $\begin{cases} x(t) = t^2 \\ y(t) = t + 3 \end{cases}$ **29** $\begin{cases} x(t) = t \\ y(t) = 6 - t^2 \end{cases}$

30 $\begin{cases} x(t) = 4 - t \\ y(t) = t^2 - 1 \end{cases}$ **31** $\begin{cases} x(t) = t^2 + 5t - 1 \\ y(t) = t + 1 \end{cases}$ **32** $\begin{cases} x(t) = 4 + 5t - t^2 \\ y(t) = t - 1 \end{cases}$

CHALLENGE

33. Write a pair of parametric equations to represent a line that has a slope of 3 and contains the point (4, −5).

CONNECTION

34. TRANSFORMATIONS Write the pair of parametric equations that represent a transformation of $\begin{cases} x(t) = t \\ y(t) = t^2 \end{cases}$ 1 unit down and 2 units to the right.

APPLICATIONS

35 SPORTS Frannie throws a softball from one end of a 200-foot field. The ball leaves her hand at a height of 6.5 feet with an initial velocity of 60 feet per second in the horizontal direction and 40 feet per second in the vertical direction. If $x(t)$ gives the horizontal distance in feet after t seconds and $y(t)$ gives the vertical distance in feet after t seconds, the following parametric equations describe the ball's path:

$$\begin{cases} x(t) = 60t \\ y(t) = 6.5 + 40t - 16t^2 \end{cases}$$

a. How high does the ball get? How long does it take for the ball to reach this height?

b. What horizontal distance will the ball travel before it hits the ground? How long does it take for the ball to reach this point?

36 SPORTS The server in a volleyball game serves the ball at an angle of 35° with the ground and from a height of 2 meters. The server is 9 meters from the 2.2-meter high net. The ball must not touch the net when served and must land within 9 meters of the other side of the net. If $x(t)$ gives the horizontal distance in meters after t seconds and $y(t)$ gives the vertical distance in meters after t seconds, the following parametric equations describe the ball's path:

$$\begin{cases} x(t) = 8.2t \\ y(t) = 2 + 5.7t - 4.9t^2 \end{cases}$$

a. How high above the net will the ball travel?

b. According to the parametric equations, what horizontal distance will the ball travel before hitting the ground?

c. Will the ball land within the area described? Explain.

37 **AVIATION** An airplane at an altitude of 2000 feet is descending at a constant rate of 160 feet per second horizontally and 15 feet per second vertically.
    a. Write the pair of parametric equations that represent the airplane's flight path. Note that the vertical rate is negative.
    b. After how many seconds will the airplane touch down?
    c. What horizontal distance will the airplane have traveled when it touches down on the runway?

38 **HEALTH** A newborn baby weighs 7 pounds and is 21 inches long. During each of the first 6 months, the baby grows $\frac{1}{2}$ inch in length and gains 2 pounds.

    a. Write the parametric equations describing the height and weight for t months, where $0 < t < 6$.
    b. How many months will it take for the baby to weigh 14 pounds? How long is the baby at this time?
    c. How many months will it take for the baby to reach 23 inches? How much does the baby weigh at this time?

 **Look Back**

Let $f(x) = x + 2$ and $g(x) = 1 - x$. (LESSON 2.4)

39. Find $f \circ g$.   **40.** Find $g \circ f$.

41. Find $f \circ f$.   **42.** Find $g \circ g$.

TRANSFORMATIONS **Identify each transformation from the parent function $f(x) = x^2$ to g. (LESSON 2.7)**

43. $g(x) = 12x^2 + 3$ **44.** $g(x) = -\left(\frac{1}{3}x\right)^2$

45. $g(x) = -\frac{1}{2}x^2 + 4$ **46.** $g(x) = -0.25(4x - 1)^2$

TRANSFORMATIONS **Write the function for each graph described below. (LESSON 2.7)**

47. the graph of $f(x) = |x|$ translated 2 units to the right

48. the graph of $f(x) = |x|$ translated 1.5 units up

49. the graph of $f(x) = x^2$ compressed vertically by a factor of $\frac{1}{5}$

50. the graph of $f(x) = x^2$ reflected across the y-axis and stretched horizontally by a factor of 4

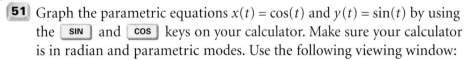 **Look Beyond**

51 Graph the parametric equations $x(t) = \cos(t)$ and $y(t) = \sin(t)$ by using the [SIN] and [COS] keys on your calculator. Make sure your calculator is in radian and parametric modes. Use the following viewing window:

Tmin = 0	Tmax = 10	Tstep = 0.01
Xmin = −4.7	Xmax = 4.8	Xscl = 1
Ymin = −3.1	Ymax = 3.2	Yscl = 1

Did the calculator draw the figure in a clockwise or counterclockwise direction? What is the shape of the graph?

MAXIMUM PROFIT/ MINIMUM COST

FLORAL ARRANGEMENTS FOR MAXIMUM PROFITS

A local florist is making two types of floral arrangements for Thanksgiving: regular and special. Each regular arrangement requires 3 mums, 3 daisies, and 2 roses, and each special arrangement requires 4 mums, 2 daisies, and 4 roses. The florist has set aside 60 mums, 54 daisies, and 52 roses for the two types of arrangements.

Activity ①

Let x represent the number of regular arrangements, and let y represent the number of special arrangements. Write a system of three equations to represent the florist's situation.

Activity ②

The florist will make a profit of $2 on each regular arrangement and $3 on each special arrangement.

1. Write an objective function for the profit.

2. Create a system of inequalities to represent the constraints. Graph the feasible region.

3. Identify the vertices of the feasible region.

4. How many of each type of arrangement should the florist make in order to maximize the profit? What is the maximum profit?

5. If the maximum profit is achieved, will there be any flowers left over? Explain your reasoning.

TILING AT MINIMUM LABOR COST

A construction firm employs two levels of tile installers: craftsmen and apprentices. Craftsmen install 500 square feet of specialty tile, 100 square feet of plain tile, and 100 linear feet of trim in one day. An apprentice installs 100 square feet of specialty tile, 200 square feet of plain tile, and 100 linear feet of trim in one day. The firm has a one-day job that requires 2000 square feet of specialty tile, 1600 square feet of plain tile, and 1200 linear feet of trim.

Activity 3

Let x represent the number of craftsmen, and let y represent the number of apprentices. Write a system of three equations to represent the construction firm's situation with this job.

Activity 4

The construction firm pays craftsmen $200 per day and pays apprentices $120 per day.

1. Write an objective function for the labor costs.

2. Create a system of inequalities to represent the constraints. Graph the feasible region.

3. Identify the vertices of the feasible region.

4. How many craftsmen and how many apprentices should be assigned to this job so that it can be completed in one day with the minimum labor cost? What is the minimum labor cost?

Activity 5

Suppose that each apprentice's wages are increased to $150 per day.

1. In this case, how many craftsmen and how many apprentices should be assigned to the job so that it can be completed in one day with the minimum labor cost? What is the minimum labor cost?

2. Do any points in the feasible region call for apprentices but no craftsmen? If so, is this a realistic scenario for the construction firm? What constraint could you add to ensure that every job has at least one craftsman assigned to it?

Activity 6

Suppose that union regulations require at least 1 craftsman for every 3 apprentices on a job.

1. Which of the vertices of the original feasible region (from Activity 4) satisfy this new constraint?

2. Write an inequality to represent the new constraint. Modify the feasible region on your graph by adding the boundary line for the new constraint.

3. Using the new constraints and the original labor cost of $120 per day for an apprentice, how many craftsmen and how many apprentices should be assigned to the job so that it can be completed in one day with the minimum labor cost? What is the minimum labor cost?

3 Chapter Review and Assessment

VOCABULARY

Key Skills & Exercises

LESSON 3.1

Key Skills

Solve a system of two linear equations in two variables graphically.

Classification of Systems of Equations	
Number of solutions	**Type**
0	inconsistent
1	consistent, independent
infinite	consistent, dependent

The solution to a consistent, independent system is given by the point of intersection of the graphs.

Use substitution to solve a system of linear equations.

Solve $\begin{cases} 3x - 5y = 28 \\ x + y = 4 \end{cases}$ by using substitution.

First solve $x + y = 4$ for one variable.

$$y = -x + 4$$

Then substitute $-x + 4$ for y in the other equation.

$$\begin{aligned} 3x - 5y &= 28 \\ 3x - 5(-x + 4) &= 28 \\ 8x &= 48 \\ x &= 6 \end{aligned}$$

Substitute 6 for x to find y.

$$\begin{aligned} x + y &= 4 \\ 6 + y &= 4 \\ y &= -2 \end{aligned}$$

Thus, the solution is $(6, -2)$.

Exercises

Graph and classify each system. Then find the solution from the graph.

1. $\begin{cases} x + y = 6 \\ 3x - 4y = 4 \end{cases}$

2. $\begin{cases} 3x + y = 11 \\ x - 2y = 6 \end{cases}$

3. $\begin{cases} y = 2x - 3 \\ -6x + 3y = -9 \end{cases}$

4. $\begin{cases} x + 2y = 4 \\ -3x - 6y = 12 \end{cases}$

5. $\begin{cases} 2x + 10y = -2 \\ 6x + 4y = 20 \end{cases}$

6. $\begin{cases} 5x + 6y = 14 \\ 3x + 5y = 7 \end{cases}$

Use substitution to solve each system. Check your solution.

7. $\begin{cases} y = 2x - 4 \\ 7x - 5y = 14 \end{cases}$

8. $\begin{cases} y = 3x - 12 \\ 2x + 3y = -3 \end{cases}$

9. $\begin{cases} 2x + 8y = 1 \\ x = 2y \end{cases}$

10. $\begin{cases} 4x + 3y = 13 \\ x + y = 4 \end{cases}$

11. $\begin{cases} 6y = x + 18 \\ 2y - x = 6 \end{cases}$

12. $\begin{cases} x + y = 7 \\ 2x + y = 5 \end{cases}$

LESSON 3.2

Key Skills

Use elimination to solve a system of linear equations.

Solve $\begin{cases} 2x - 3y = -17 \\ 5x = 15 - 4y \end{cases}$ by using elimination.

Write each equation in standard form.

$$\begin{cases} 2x - 3y = -17 \\ 5x + 4y = 15 \end{cases}$$

Multiply the equations as needed, and then combine to eliminate one of the variables.

$$\begin{cases} 5(2x - 3y) = 5(-17) \\ -2(5x + 4y) = -2(15) \end{cases} \rightarrow \begin{aligned} 10x - 15y &= -85 \\ \underline{-10x - 8y} &= \underline{-30} \\ -23y &= -115 \\ y &= 5 \end{aligned}$$

Then use substitution to solve for the other variable.

$$5x = 15 - 4y$$
$$5x = 15 - 4(5)$$
$$x = -1$$

Thus, the solution is $(-1, 5)$.

Exercises

Use elimination to solve each system. Check your solution.

13. $\begin{cases} 2x - 5y = 1 \\ 3x - 4y = -2 \end{cases}$ **14.** $\begin{cases} 9x + 2y = 2 \\ 21x + 6y = 4 \end{cases}$

15. $\begin{cases} -x + 2y = 12 \\ x + 6y = 20 \end{cases}$ **16.** $\begin{cases} 2x + 3y = 18 \\ 5x - y = 11 \end{cases}$

17. $\begin{cases} 3y = 3x - 6 \\ y = x - 2 \end{cases}$ **18.** $\begin{cases} y = \frac{3}{2}x + 4 \\ 2y - 8 = 3x \end{cases}$

19. $\begin{cases} y = \frac{1}{2}x + 9 \\ 2y - x = 1 \end{cases}$ **20.** $\begin{cases} y = -2x - 4 \\ 2x + y = 6 \end{cases}$

LESSON 3.3

Key Skills

Graph a linear inequality in two variables.

Solve the inequality for y, reversing the inequality symbol if multiplying or dividing by a negative number. Graph the boundary line, using a dashed line for < or > and a solid line for ≤ or ≥. Substitute a point into the inequality to determine whether to shade above or below the boundary line.

Exercises

Graph each linear inequality.

21. $y > 2x - 3$ **22.** $y - 3x < 4$

23. $2x - y \le 5$ **24.** $4x - 2y \le -3$

25. $\frac{y}{4} \ge -\frac{x}{3} + 1$ **26.** $\frac{3}{2}x \le \frac{1}{4}y - 3$

27. $y > -2$ **28.** $x \le 7$

LESSON 3.4

Key Skills

Graph the system of linear inequalities.

Graph. $\begin{cases} y \ge -1 \\ y \le \frac{4}{3}x + \frac{1}{3} \\ y < -4x + 11 \end{cases}$

Graph each boundary line, using a solid line or a dashed line. The solution is the shaded region shown.

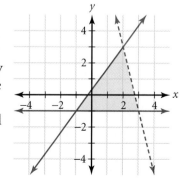

Exercises

Graph each system of linear inequalities.

29. $\begin{cases} y \ge 0 \\ x \ge 0 \\ y > -2x + 3 \\ y < 4x \end{cases}$ **30.** $\begin{cases} y \ge 0 \\ x \ge 0 \\ y \le x + 8 \\ y \ge -2x + 3 \end{cases}$

31. $\begin{cases} y < 2x + 3 \\ y \ge 3x - 1 \\ x > 1 \end{cases}$ **32.** $\begin{cases} y \ge -x - 3 \\ y < 4x + 2 \\ x > -2 \end{cases}$

Key Skills

Use linear programming to find the maximum or minimum value of an objective function.

Step 1 Write a system of inequalities, and graph the feasible region.

Step 2 Write the objective function to be maximized or minimized.

Step 3 Find the coordinates of the vertices of the feasible region.

Step 4 Evaluate the objective function for the coordinates of the vertices of the feasible region. Then identify the coordinates that give the required maximum or minimum.

Exercises

33. BROADCASTING At a radio station, 6 minutes of each hour are devoted to news, and the remaining 54 minutes are devoted to music and commercials. Station policy requires at least 30 minutes of music per hour and at least 3 minutes of music for each minute of commercials. Use linear programming to find the maximum number of minutes available for commercials each hour.

Key Skills

Graph a pair of parametric equations for a given interval of *t*.

Make a table, plot the ordered pairs (x, y), and draw a line or curve through the points. Or use a graphics calculator in parametric mode.

Write a pair of parametric equations as a single equation in *x* and *y*.

Given the parametric equations $\begin{cases} x(t) = 3t + 1 \\ y(t) = t - 5 \end{cases}$, solve either equation for t and substitute the expression for t in the other equation.

$$y = t - 5 \quad \rightarrow \quad t = y + 5$$
$$x = 3t + 1$$
$$x = 3(y + 5) + 1$$
$$x = 3y + 16, \text{ or } y = \frac{x - 16}{3}$$

Exercises

Graph each pair of parametric equations. Then write each pair of parametric equations as a single equation in *x* and *y*.

34. $\begin{cases} x(t) = 2t \\ y(t) = t - 1 \end{cases}$ **35.** $\begin{cases} x(t) = t + 3 \\ y(t) = 3t - 1 \end{cases}$

36. $\begin{cases} x(t) = t \\ y(t) = 3 - 2t \end{cases}$ **37.** $\begin{cases} x(t) = t + 5 \\ y(t) = 4t - 3 \end{cases}$

38. SPORTS A goalie kicks a soccer ball from a height of 2 feet above the ground toward the center of the field. The ball is kicked with a horizontal speed of 40 feet per second and a vertical speed of 65 feet per second. If $x(t)$ gives the horizontal distance in feet after t seconds and $y(t)$ gives the vertical distance in feet after t seconds, then the ball's path can be described by the parametric equations $\begin{cases} x(t) = 40t \\ y(t) = 2 + 65t - 16t^2 \end{cases}$. What horizontal distance does the ball travel before striking the ground?

Applications

39. MANUFACTURING A tire manufacturer has 1000 units of raw rubber to use for car and truck tires. Each car tire requires 5 units of rubber and each truck tire requires 12 units of rubber. Labor costs are $8 for a car tire and $12 for a truck tire. The manufacturer does not want to pay more than $1500 in labor costs. Write and graph a system of inequalities to represent this situation.

Alternative Assessment

Performance Assessment

1. BUSINESS PROFIT OR LOSS Suppose that a bagel bakery has fixed costs of $24,000, variable costs of $2 per dozen bagels, and revenues of $10 per dozen bagels. This scenario can be represented by the following system: $\begin{cases} y = 24{,}000 + 2x \\ y = 10x \end{cases}$

   a. Describe what each term in each equation represents.

   b. Graph the system.

   c. The solution to any cost-revenue system is the break-even point. Find this point for the system above. What does it mean?

   d. Write a system of inequalities for the region that represents a loss and for the region that represents a profit.

2. ECONOMICS Supply and demand equations describe the relationship between price, y, and quantity, x. Supply equations have positive slopes because as price increases, so does production. Demand equations have negative slopes because as price increases, demand decreases. The point of intersection in a supply and demand system is called the equilibrium price.

   a. Given $\begin{cases} 2y - x = 18 \\ 2y + 2x = 36 \end{cases}$, find the equilibrium price.

   b. Graph the system and indicate the equilibrium price.

   c. What are some of the factors that could cause the supply to fall below the equilibrium point?

   d. Describe what each of the four regions in the graph of the system represents.

Portfolio Projects

1. APPROXIMATING SOLUTIONS Using the trace and zoom features on a graphics calculator, you can approximate the solution to the system $\begin{cases} 2x - y = 1 \\ 3x + 5y = 5 \end{cases}$.

   a. Graph the system on a graphics calculator. Using the trace feature, find the approximate coordinates of the point of intersection. Estimate the error in the x- and y-values by finding the difference between the respective coordinates of points above and below the intersection point.

   b. Using the zoom feature and x- and y-zoom factors of 10, zoom in on the intersection point. Use the trace feature to find the approximate coordinates of the point of intersection. Estimate the error in the x- and y-values for the point.

   c. Repeat part **b** two more times.

   d. Solve the system by using elimination. Compare your exact solution with your approximate solution from part **b**.

   e. When is an approximate solution acceptable? Are the errors for the x- and y-values always the same? Explain.

2. RESEARCHING THE SIMPLEX METHOD The simplex method is a computer-based method for solving linear-programming problems. Research the simplex method and find how it differs from the graphing method used in Lesson 3.5. Try to solve a linear-programming problem in three variables by using the simplex method on symbolic algebra software or on a spreadsheet.

---

internet**connect**

The HRW Web site contains many resources to reinforce and expand your knowledge of systems of linear equations and inequalities. This Web site also provides Internet links to other sites where you can find information and real-world data for use in research projects, reports, and activities that involve systems of linear equations and inequalities. Visit the HRW Web site at **go.hrw.com,** and enter the keyword **MB1 CH3** to access the resources for this chapter.

QUANTITATIVE COMPARISON For Items 1–5, write
A if the quantity in Column A is greater than the quantity in Column B;
B if the quantity in Column B is greater than the quantity in Column A;
C if the two quantities are equal; or
D if the relationship cannot be determined from the given information.

	Column A	Column B	Answers
1.	$-0.7\overline{2}$	$-\dfrac{4}{5}$	Ⓐ Ⓑ Ⓒ Ⓓ [Lesson 2.1]
2.	The value of y when x is any real number $y = 4x$	$y = -4x$	Ⓐ Ⓑ Ⓒ Ⓓ [Lesson 2.3]
3.	The value of x $\dfrac{x}{4} = \dfrac{x+2}{5}$	$\dfrac{x}{2} = \dfrac{21-x}{4}$	Ⓐ Ⓑ Ⓒ Ⓓ [Lesson 1.4]
4.	$|x + 2|$	$|x - 2|$	Ⓐ Ⓑ Ⓒ Ⓓ [Lesson 1.8]
5.	$f(x) = -3x$ and $g(x) = x - 4$ $(f \circ g)(-5)$	$(g \circ f)(-5)$	Ⓐ Ⓑ Ⓒ Ⓓ [Lesson 2.4]

6. Which is a solution of the system?
$\begin{cases} -2x + y \le 8 \\ x - 3y > 9 \end{cases}$ *(LESSON 3.4)*
a. $(0, -3)$ **b.** $(0, 9)$
c. both **a** and **b**   **d.** neither **a** nor **b**

7. Which equation in x and y represents
$\begin{cases} x(t) = 3t - 1 \\ y(t) = 2 - 3t \end{cases}$? *(LESSON 3.6)*
a. $y = x - 1$ **b.** $y = 3x - 1$
c. $y = 1 - x$ **d.** $y = -3x - 1$

8. Evaluate $[3(2 + 1) + 3](2^2)$. *(LESSON 2.1)*
a. 36   **b.** 20
c. 32   **d.** 48

9. How many solutions does the system have?
$\begin{cases} 2x - 3y = 11 \\ 6x - 9y = 33 \end{cases}$ *(LESSON 3.1)*
a. 0   **b.** 1
c. 2   **d.** infinite

10. Which function represents the graph of $f(x) = x^2$ translated 5 units down?
(LESSON 2.7)
a. $f(x) = x^2 + 5$ **b.** $f(x) = x^2 - 5$
c. $f(x) = (x - 5)^2$ **d.** $f(x) = (x + 5)^2$

11. Which is the range of $f(x) = -\left(\dfrac{x}{3}\right)^2$?
(LESSON 2.3)
a. $f(x) \ge 0$ **b.** $f(x) \ge 3$
c. $f(x) \le 3$ **d.** $f(x) \le 0$

12. Simplify $\left(\dfrac{2x^{-2}y^3}{x^2y^{-3}}\right)^{-1}$. *(LESSON 2.2)*
a. 2   **b.** $\dfrac{2x^4}{y^6}$
c. $\dfrac{1}{2}$ **d.** $\dfrac{x^4}{2y^6}$

13. Which is the equation of the line that contains the point $(0, -2)$ and is parallel to the graph of $y = -\dfrac{1}{2}x - 1$? *(LESSON 1.3)*
a. $y = -\dfrac{1}{2}x - 2$ **b.** $y = -\dfrac{1}{2}x + 2$
c. $y = 2x - 2$ **d.** $y = 2x + 2$

Match each statement on the left with a solution on the right. *(LESSON 1.8)*

14. $|a - 5| < 3$

  a. $a = 2 \ \text{ or } \ a = 8$

15. $|a - 5| > 3$

  b. $a < 2 \ \text{ or } \ a > 8$

16. $|a - 5| = 3$

  c. $a > 2 \ \text{ and } \ a < 8$

17. $|a - 5| < -3$

  d. There is no solution.

18. Graph $2y > -1$. *(LESSON 3.3)*

19. Write the pair of parametric equations
$\begin{cases} x(t) = 2 + t \\ y(t) = 3 + t \end{cases}$ as a single equation in x and y.
(LESSON 3.6)

20. Classify $\begin{cases} 3y = 4x - 1 \\ x = \frac{4}{3}y \end{cases}$ as inconsistent, dependent, or independent. *(LESSON 3.1)*

21. Write the function for the graph of $f(x) = x^2$ translated 2 units up. *(LESSON 2.7)*

22. Solve. $\begin{cases} 3x - 3y = 1 \\ x + y = 4 \end{cases}$ *(LESSON 3.1)*

23. Graph the system. $\begin{cases} y \le x + 1 \\ y \ge 2x - 1 \end{cases}$ *(LESSON 3.4)*

24. Find the inverse of the function $f(x) = 3x - 2$. *(LESSON 2.5)*

25. Graph the ordered pairs below, and describe the correlation for the data as positive, negative, or none. *(LESSON 1.5)*

(10, 6), (20, 8), (20, 12), (30, 16), (40, 18), (50, 21), (60, 32), (80, 41), (100, 46), (110, 60), (120, 58)

26. Solve the literal equation $\frac{ax - b}{2} = c$ for x. *(LESSON 1.6)*

27. Graph the parametric equations for $-3 \le t \le 3$.
$\begin{cases} x(t) = t + 1 \\ y(t) = 2t - 1 \end{cases}$ *(LESSON 3.6)*

28. Let $f(x) = 2x + 1$ and $g(x) = 3x^2$. Find $f \circ g$. *(LESSON 2.4)*

Solve each inequality, and graph the solution on a number line. *(LESSON 1.7)*

29. $6(x - 4) \ge 6 + x$

30. $\frac{-x}{4} > 3$

Solve each equation. *(LESSON 1.8)*

31. $|x - 4| = 9$

32. $|3x + 12| = 18$

FREE-RESPONSE GRID The following questions may be answered by using a free-response grid such as that commonly used by standardized-test services.

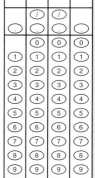

33. If a varies directly as b and $a = 16$ when $b = -8$, what is b when $a = 4$? *(LESSON 1.4)*

34. For what value of t does the graph of $\begin{cases} x(t) = t^2 + 1 \\ y(t) = t - 1 \end{cases}$ pass through the point (7.25, 1.5)? *(LESSON 3.6)*

35. The graph of $g(x) = x + 1$ can be formed by translating the graph of $f(x) = x + 3$ how many units to the right? *(LESSON 2.7)*

36. Evaluate $|-2| - |-2|$. *(LESSON 2.6)*

37. Let $f(x) = |x| + 2x$. Find $f(-2)$. *(LESSON 2.3)*

38. Find the slope of a line that contains the points $(-3, 4)$ and $(-1, -8)$. *(LESSON 1.2)*

39. ENGINEERING The equation $F = \frac{9}{4}d^4l^{-2}$, where d is the diameter in inches and l is the length in feet, gives the maximum load in tons that a foundation column can support. Find the maximum load, in tons, for a column that is 6 feet long and 12 inches in diameter. *(LESSON 2.2)*

40. MANUFACTURING The true diameter of a pipe is 7.25 inches. Its diameter is measured as 7.29 inches. Find the relative error in the measurement to the nearest thousandth. *(LESSON 2.6)*

41. INCOME Becky wants to buy a computer that costs $1590. If Becky earns $6.25 per hour, what is the minimum number of whole hours that she must work to earn enough money to buy the computer? *(LESSON 1.7)*

Keystroke Guide for Chapter 3

Essential keystroke sequences (using the model TI-82 or TI-83 graphics calculator) are presented below for all Activities and Examples found in this chapter that require or recommend the use of a graphics calculator.

internet connect

HRW **Keystrokes for other models of graphics calculators are found on the HRW Web site.**

LESSON 3.1

Page 156

For Step 1, graph $y = 2x - 1$ and $y = -x + 5$ on the same screen, and find any points of intersection.

Use friendly viewing window [−9.4, 9.4] by [−6.2, 6.2].

Graph the equations:

| Y= | 2 | X,T,θ,n | − | 1 | ENTER | (Y2=) | (−) | X,T,θ,n | + | 5 | GRAPH |

Move the cursor as indicated.

Find any points of intersection:

| 2nd | TRACE (CALC) | 5:intersect | ENTER | (First curve?) | ENTER | (Second curve?) |

| ENTER | (Guess?) | ENTER |

Use a similar keystroke sequence for Step 2.

E X A M P L E ❶
Page 157

For part a, graph $y = -x + 5$ and $y = \dfrac{x + 7}{5}$ on the same screen, and find any points of intersection.

Use standard viewing window [−10, 10] by [−10, 10].

Graph the equations:

| Y= | (−) | X,T,θ,n | + | 5 | ENTER | (Y2=) | (| X,T,θ,n | + | 7 |) |

| ÷ | 5 | GRAPH |

Find any points of intersection:
Use a keystroke sequence similar to that in the previous Activity.

Use a similar keystroke sequence for part **b.**

E X A M P L E ❸
Page 159

Graph $y = 500 - x$ and $y = \dfrac{0.06(500) - 0.10x}{0.04}$ on the same screen, and find any points of intersection.

Use viewing window [0, 400] by [0, 500].

Graph the equations:

[Y=] 500 [−] [X,T,θ,n] [ENTER] (Y2=) [(] [.] .06 [(] 500 [)] [−] .10
[X,T,θ,n] [)] [÷] [.] .04 [)]

Find any points of intersection:
Use a keystroke sequence similar to that in the previous Activity.

LESSON 3.2

E X A M P L E **②** Graph $y = \dfrac{930 - 5.5x}{7.5}$ and $y = \dfrac{1920 - 12x}{15}$ on the same screen, and find any

Page 166 points of intersection. Then verify with a table.

Use viewing window [0, 200] by [0, 150].

Graph the equations, and find any points of intersection:

Use a keystroke sequence similar to that in the Activity and Examples 1 and 3 in Lesson 3.1.

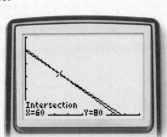

Verify the solution with a table:

         TBLSET
[2nd] [WINDOW] (TblStart =) 40 [ENTER]

⇑ TI-82: (Tbl Min =)

(△Tbl =) 10 [ENTER] (Indpnt:) [Auto] [▼]

                TABLE
(Depend:) [Auto] [2nd] [GRAPH]

> *Enter the equations before using the table.*

Page 166

For Step 1, graph $y = x + 2$ and $y = \dfrac{10 + 5x}{5}$ on the same screen.

Use standard viewing window [−10, 10] by [−10, 10].

Use a keystroke sequence similar to that in the Activity in Lesson 3.1.

For Step 2, use a keystroke sequence similar to that in the Activity in Lesson 3.1. Use standard viewing window [−10, 10] by [−10, 10].

E X A M P L E S **③** and **④** For Example 3, graph $y = \dfrac{12 - 2x}{5}$ and $y = \dfrac{15 - 2x}{5}$ on the same

Page 167 screen.

Use viewing window [−5, 5] by [−1, 5].

[Y=] [(] 12 [−] 2 [X,T,θ,n] [)] [÷] 5

[ENTER] (Y2=) [(] 15 [−] 2 [X,T,θ,n] [)]

[÷] 5 [GRAPH]

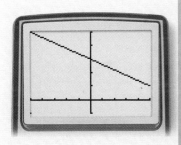

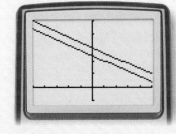

For Example 4, use a similar keystroke sequence. Use viewing window [−5, 5] by [−1, 5].

E X A M P L E  Graph $y \le \dfrac{-33.3}{28.1} x + 20(33.3)$, and see whether (25, 400) satisfies the inequality.

Page 174

Use viewing window [0, 800] by [0, 800].

Graph the inequality:

| Y= | ◄ | ◄ | ENTER | ENTER | ENTER |

(◣ Y1=) | ► | ► | (| (−) |

33.3 | ÷ | 28.1 |) | X,T,Θ,n | + |

20 | (| 33.3 |) | GRAPH |

TI-82: Graph the line and use the shade feature.

> First clear old data from L1 and L2.

Plot the point:

| STAT | EDIT | 1:Edit | ENTER | L1 | 25 | ENTER | ► | L2 |

STAT PLOT

| 400 | ENTER | 2nd | Y= | 1:Plot 1 | ENTER | ON |

| ENTER | ▼ | (Type:) | ⠂⠂⠂ | ENTER | ▼ |

L1

(Xlist:) | 2nd | 1 | ▼ | (Ylist:) | 2nd | 2 | L2

▼ | (Mark:) | + | ENTER | GRAPH |

> You can also move the cursor to find approximate coordinates.

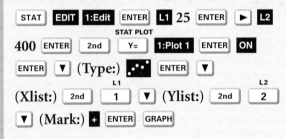

Activity

Page 196

For Step 3, graph the parametric equations for the horizontal and vertical distances, and find the values of t and x for $y = 1500$.

| MODE | Par | ENTER |

Use viewing window [0, 120, 1] by [0, 15,000] by [0, 1600].

| Y= | (X1T=) 120 | X,T,Θ,n | ENTER | (Y1T=) 13.4 | X,T,Θ,n | ENTER | TRACE |

> Move the cursor to the desired point.

E X A M P L E ① Graph the parametric equations $x(t) = 2t - 1$ and $y(t) = -t + 2$.

Page 196

Use viewing window [−3, 3, 0.1] by [−8, 8] by [−8, 8].

| Y= | (X1T=) 2 | X,T,Θ,n | − | 1 | ENTER |

(Y1T=) | (−) | X,T,Θ,n | + | 2 | GRAPH |

> Be sure that the calculator is in parametric mode.

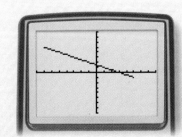

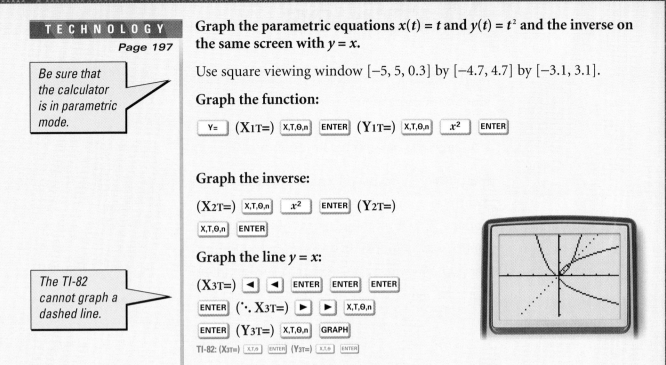

TECHNOLOGY

Page 197

Be sure that the calculator is in parametric mode.

Graph the parametric equations $x(t) = t$ and $y(t) = t^2$ and the inverse on the same screen with $y = x$.

Use square viewing window $[-5, 5, 0.3]$ by $[-4.7, 4.7]$ by $[-3.1, 3.1]$.

Graph the function:

$\boxed{Y=}$ $(X_1T=)$ $\boxed{X,T,\theta,n}$ $\boxed{ENTER}$ $(Y_1T=)$ $\boxed{X,T,\theta,n}$ $\boxed{x^2}$ $\boxed{ENTER}$

Graph the inverse:

$(X_2T=)$ $\boxed{X,T,\theta,n}$ $\boxed{x^2}$ $\boxed{ENTER}$ $(Y_2T=)$

$\boxed{X,T,\theta,n}$ $\boxed{ENTER}$

The TI-82 cannot graph a dashed line.

Graph the line $y = x$:

$(X_3T=)$ $\boxed{\blacktriangleleft}$ $\boxed{\blacktriangleleft}$ $\boxed{ENTER}$ $\boxed{ENTER}$ $\boxed{ENTER}$

$\boxed{ENTER}$ $(\therefore X_3T=)$ $\boxed{\blacktriangleright}$ $\boxed{\blacktriangleright}$ $\boxed{X,T,\theta,n}$

$\boxed{ENTER}$ $(Y_3T=)$ $\boxed{X,T,\theta,n}$ $\boxed{GRAPH}$

TI-82: $(X_3T=)$ $\boxed{X,T,\theta}$ $\boxed{ENTER}$ $(Y_3T=)$ $\boxed{X,T,\theta}$ $\boxed{ENTER}$

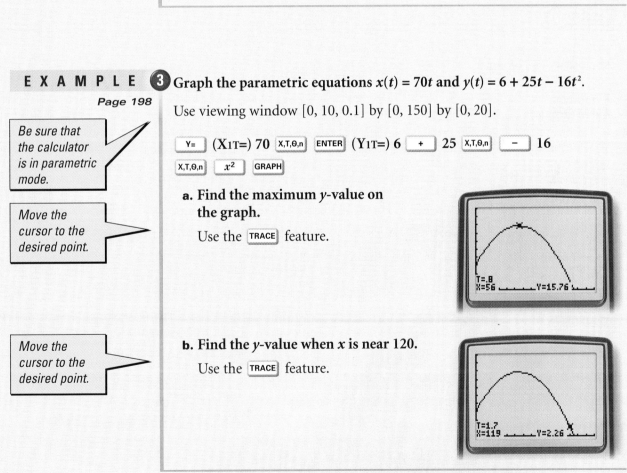

E X A M P L E ❸ Graph the parametric equations $x(t) = 70t$ and $y(t) = 6 + 25t - 16t^2$.

Page 198

Be sure that the calculator is in parametric mode.

Use viewing window $[0, 10, 0.1]$ by $[0, 150]$ by $[0, 20]$.

$\boxed{Y=}$ $(X_1T=)$ 70 $\boxed{X,T,\theta,n}$ $\boxed{ENTER}$ $(Y_1T=)$ 6 $\boxed{+}$ 25 $\boxed{X,T,\theta,n}$ $\boxed{-}$ 16

$\boxed{X,T,\theta,n}$ $\boxed{x^2}$ $\boxed{GRAPH}$

a. Find the maximum y-value on the graph.

Use the $\boxed{TRACE}$ feature.

Move the cursor to the desired point.

b. Find the y-value when x is near 120.

Use the $\boxed{TRACE}$ feature.

Move the cursor to the desired point.

Matrices

MATRICES CAN CONVENIENTLY ORGANIZE AND store data represented in tables. For example, an inventory of the number and types of plants in a large garden can be stored in a matrix.

Matrices are also used to manipulate data. For example, an updated inventory matrix can be obtained by combining the original inventory matrix with a matrix that represents the number and types of plants added to and removed from the garden.

Lessons

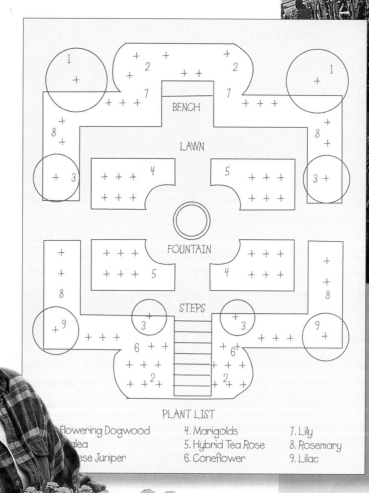

PLANT LIST

Flowering Dogwood	4. Marigolds	7. Lily
glea	5. Hybrid Tea Rose	8. Rosemary
ese Juniper	6. Coneflower	9. Lilac

About the Chapter Project

Mathematical models can apply to our everyday world in ways we rarely think about. By ordering seemingly random data into an organized format, models allow us to see underlying relations and to use them in fascinating ways.

In the Chapter Project, *Spell Check*, you will use the modeling process to examine spell-checking software.

After completing the Chapter Project, you will be able to do the following:

- Create a directed network and corresponding adjacency matrix to represent associated words in a spell-checking directory.

- Interpret powers of adjacency matrices.

About the Portfolio Activities

Throughout the chapter, you will be given opportunities to complete Portfolio Activities that are designed to support your work on the Chapter Project.

- Interpreting a directed network that represents paths between exhibits in the New York Museum of Natural History is included in the Portfolio Activity on page 224.

- Finding and interpreting powers of adjacency matrices that represent multistep paths between exhibits is included in the Portfolio Activity on page 233.

215

Using Matrices to Represent Data

Why Matrices can be used to organize data. For example, information about picnic tables and barbeque grills can be organized into matrices.

Objectives

- Represent mathematical and real-world data in a matrix.

- Find sums and differences of matrices and the scalar product of a number and a matrix.

INVENTORY

The table below shows business activity for one month in a home-improvement store. The table shows stock (inventory on June 1), sales (during June), and receipt of new goods (deliveries in June).

	Inventory (June 1)		Sales (June)		Deliveries (June)	
	Small	Large	Small	Large	Small	Large
Picnic tables	8	10	7	9	15	20
Barbeque grills	15	12	15	12	18	24

You can represent the inventory data in a *matrix*.

Small Large

Inventory matrix → Picnic tables $\begin{bmatrix} 8 & 10 \\ 15 & 12 \end{bmatrix} = M = \begin{bmatrix} m_{11} & m_{12} \\ m_{21} & m_{22} \end{bmatrix}$
Barbeque grills

m_{21}

2nd row   1st column

A **matrix** (plural, *matrices*) is a rectangular array of numbers enclosed in a single set of brackets. The **dimensions** of a matrix are the number of horizontal rows and the number of vertical columns it has. For example, if a matrix has 2 rows and 3 columns, its dimensions are 2×3, read as "2 by 3." The inventory matrix above, M, is a matrix with dimensions of 2×2.

Each number in the matrix is called an **entry**, or element. You can denote the *address* of the entry in row 2 and column 1 of the inventory matrix, M, as m_{21} and state that $m_{21} = 15$. This entry represents 15 small fans in stock on June 1.

EXAMPLE ❶ **Represent the June sales data in matrix S. Interpret the entry at s_{12}.**

● **SOLUTION**

Small Large
Sales matrix → Picnic tables $\begin{bmatrix} 7 & 9 \\ 15 & 12 \end{bmatrix} = S$
Barbeque grills

In matrix S, $s_{12} = 9$. In June, 9 large picnic tables were sold.

TRY THIS Represent the delivery data in matrix D. Interpret the entry at d_{21}.

Two matrices are *equal* if they have the same dimensions and if corresponding entries are equivalent.

E X A M P L E ② Solve $\begin{bmatrix} 2x+4 & 5 & 1 \\ -2 & -3y+5 & -4 \end{bmatrix} = \begin{bmatrix} 12 & 5 & 1 \\ -2 & 5y-3 & -4 \end{bmatrix}$ for *x* and *y*.

● **SOLUTION**

Because the matrices are equal, $2x+4=12$ and $-3y+5=5y-3$.

$$2x+4=12 \qquad\qquad -3y+5=5y-3$$
$$2x=8 \qquad\qquad\qquad -8y=-8$$
$$x=4 \qquad\qquad\qquad\quad y=1$$

Thus, $x=4$ and $y=1$.

TRY THIS Solve $\begin{bmatrix} -3 & -2x-3 \\ -2 & 3y-12 \end{bmatrix} = \begin{bmatrix} -3 & -15 \\ -2 & -2y+13 \end{bmatrix}$ for *x* and *y*.

Addition and Scalar Multiplication

To find the sum (or difference) of matrices *A* and *B* with the same dimensions, find the sums (or differences) of *corresponding* entries in *A* and *B*.

E X A M P L E ③ Let $A = \begin{bmatrix} -2 & 0 & 1 \\ 5 & -7 & 8 \end{bmatrix}$ and $B = \begin{bmatrix} 5 & 7 & -1 \\ 0 & 2 & -8 \end{bmatrix}$.

    a. Find $A + B$.   **b.** Find $A - B$.

● **SOLUTION**

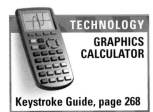
TECHNOLOGY
GRAPHICS CALCULATOR

Keystroke Guide, page 268

a.
$$A + B = \begin{bmatrix} -2 & 0 & 1 \\ 5 & -7 & 8 \end{bmatrix} + \begin{bmatrix} 5 & 7 & -1 \\ 0 & 2 & -8 \end{bmatrix}$$
$$= \begin{bmatrix} -2+5 & 0+7 & 1+(-1) \\ 5+0 & -7+2 & 8+(-8) \end{bmatrix}$$
$$= \begin{bmatrix} 3 & 7 & 0 \\ 5 & -5 & 0 \end{bmatrix}$$

CHECK

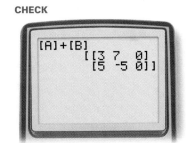

b.
$$A - B = \begin{bmatrix} -2 & 0 & 1 \\ 5 & -7 & 8 \end{bmatrix} - \begin{bmatrix} 5 & 7 & -1 \\ 0 & 2 & -8 \end{bmatrix}$$
$$= \begin{bmatrix} -2-5 & 0-7 & 1-(-1) \\ 5-0 & -7-2 & 8-(-8) \end{bmatrix}$$
$$= \begin{bmatrix} -7 & -7 & 2 \\ 5 & -9 & 16 \end{bmatrix}$$

CHECK

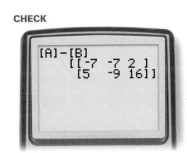

TRY THIS Let $A = \begin{bmatrix} 0 & 0 \\ 4 & 1 \\ -3 & -5 \end{bmatrix}$ and $B = \begin{bmatrix} -10 & 5 \\ 0 & 4 \\ -7 & 3 \end{bmatrix}$.

    a. Find $A - B$.   **b.** Find $A + B$.

CHECKPOINT ✔ Is it possible to find the sum $\begin{bmatrix} -2 & 5 & 6 \\ 1 & -8 & 0 \end{bmatrix} + \begin{bmatrix} 1 & -5 \\ 8 & -6 \\ -3 & 0 \end{bmatrix}$? Explain.

Example 4 below shows how matrix addition and subtraction can be used in inventory calculations. You can perform matrix addition and subtraction in one step.

EXAMPLE ④ Refer to the table of business activity at the beginning of the lesson. Let matrices M, S, and D represent the inventory, sales, and delivery data, respectively.

APPLICATION
INVENTORY

Find $M - S + D$. Interpret the final matrix.

● **SOLUTION**

$$M - S + D = \begin{bmatrix} 8 & 10 \\ 15 & 12 \end{bmatrix} - \begin{bmatrix} 7 & 9 \\ 15 & 12 \end{bmatrix} + \begin{bmatrix} 15 & 20 \\ 18 & 24 \end{bmatrix}$$

$$= \begin{bmatrix} 8 - 7 + 15 & 10 - 9 + 20 \\ 15 - 15 + 18 & 12 - 12 + 24 \end{bmatrix}$$

$$= \begin{matrix} & \text{Small} & \text{Large} \\ & \begin{bmatrix} 16 & 21 \\ 18 & 24 \end{bmatrix} & \begin{matrix} \textbf{Picnic tables} \\ \textbf{Barbeque grills} \end{matrix} \end{matrix}$$

At the end of June, the store has 16 small and 21 large picnic tables in stock. It also has 18 small and 24 large barbeque grills.

TRY THIS Find $\begin{bmatrix} 3 & 6 \\ -3 & -6 \end{bmatrix} + \begin{bmatrix} -4 & 5 \\ -7 & 8 \end{bmatrix} - \begin{bmatrix} 0 & 2 \\ -10 & 11 \end{bmatrix}$.

To multiply a matrix, A, by a real number, k, write a matrix whose entries are k times each of the entries in matrix A. This operation is called **scalar multiplication**.

EXAMPLE ⑤ Let $A = \begin{bmatrix} 3 & 2 & 0 \\ -1 & -3 & 6 \\ 2 & 0 & -10 \end{bmatrix}$. Find $-2A$.

● **SOLUTION**

$$-2A = \begin{bmatrix} -2(3) & -2(2) & -2(0) \\ -2(-1) & -2(-3) & -2(6) \\ -2(2) & -2(0) & -2(-10) \end{bmatrix} = \begin{bmatrix} -6 & -4 & 0 \\ 2 & 6 & -12 \\ -4 & 0 & 20 \end{bmatrix}$$

CHECKPOINT ✔ What are the entries in matrix kA if A is a 2×3 matrix and $k = 0$?

When $k = -1$, the scalar product kA is $-1A$, or simply $-A$, and is called the **additive inverse**, or *opposite*, of matrix A. For example,

if $A = \begin{bmatrix} 3 & -4 & 0 \\ 2 & -8 & 6 \\ 7 & 1 & -5 \end{bmatrix}$, then $-A = \begin{bmatrix} -3 & 4 & 0 \\ -2 & 8 & -6 \\ -7 & -1 & 5 \end{bmatrix}$ is the additive inverse of A.

CHECKPOINT ✔ Let $T = \begin{bmatrix} 3 & -5 \\ 0 & 2 \end{bmatrix}$. Write the sum of T and its additive inverse.

CRITICAL THINKING Let $k = 3$ and $A = \begin{bmatrix} 10 & -4 \\ -3 & 5 \end{bmatrix}$. Use matrix addition and scalar multiplication to show that $A + A + A = 3A$.

Properties of Matrix Addition

For matrices A, B, and C, each with dimensions of $m \times n$:

Commutative $A + B = B + A$

Associative $(A + B) + C = A + (B + C)$

Additive Identity   The $m \times n$ matrix having 0 as all of its entries is the $m \times n$ identity matrix for addition.

Additive Inverse   For every $m \times n$ matrix A, the matrix whose entries are the opposite of those in A is the additive inverse of A.

Geometric Transformations

Example 6 shows you how to represent a polygon in the coordinate plane as a matrix.

EXAMPLE **6** **Represent quadrilateral *ABCD* as matrix *P*.**

CONNECTION
COORDINATE GEOMETRY

● SOLUTION

Because each point has 2 coordinates and there are 4 points, create a 2×4 matrix.

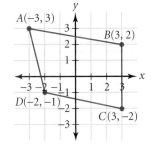

$$P = \begin{bmatrix} A & B & C & D \\ -3 & 3 & 3 & -2 \\ 3 & 2 & -2 & -1 \end{bmatrix} \begin{matrix} x\text{-coordinates} \\ y\text{-coordinates} \end{matrix}$$

When you perform a *transformation* on one geometric figure to get another geometric figure, the original figure is called the **pre-image** and the resulting figure is the **image**. When you apply scalar multiplication to a matrix that represents a polygon, the product represents either an enlarged image or a reduced image of the pre-image polygon. This is shown in Example 7 on page 220.

EXAMPLE ⑦ Refer to quadrilateral *ABCD* and matrix *P* in Example 6.

CONNECTION

TRANSFORMATIONS

Graph the polygon that is represented by each matrix.

a. $2P$ b. $\frac{1}{2}P$

● **SOLUTION**

a. Let quadrilateral $A'B'C'D'$ represent the image.

$$2P = \begin{matrix} A' & B' & C' & D' \\ \begin{bmatrix} -6 & 6 & 6 & -4 \\ 6 & 4 & -4 & -2 \end{bmatrix} \end{matrix}$$

Graph $A'B'C'D'$.

b. Let quadrilateral $A''B''C''D''$ represent the image.

$$\frac{1}{2}P = \begin{matrix} A'' & B'' & C'' & D'' \\ \begin{bmatrix} -\frac{3}{2} & \frac{3}{2} & \frac{3}{2} & -1 \\ \frac{3}{2} & 1 & -1 & -\frac{1}{2} \end{bmatrix} \end{matrix}$$

Graph $A''B''C''D''$.

> Quadrilateral $A'B'C'D'$ is an enlarged image, or dilation, of quadrilateral *ABCD* by a scale factor of 2.

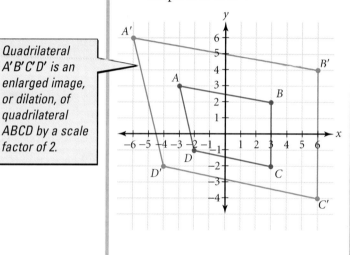

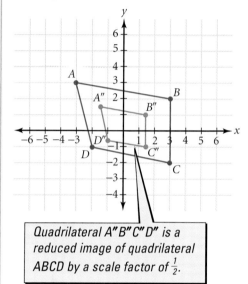

> Quadrilateral $A''B''C''D''$ is a reduced image of quadrilateral *ABCD* by a scale factor of $\frac{1}{2}$.

TRY THIS Refer to quadrilateral *ABCD* and matrix *P* in Example 6. Sketch the polygon that is represented by each matrix.

a. $4P$ b. $\frac{1}{4}P$

Exercises

Communicate

1. Describe the location of entry m_{52} in a matrix called *M*.

2. Describe the location of entries b_{21}, b_{22}, b_{23}, and b_{24} in a matrix called *B*. What are the smallest possible dimensions of matrix *B*?

3. Explain how to represent a polygon in the coordinate plane as a matrix.

4. Explain how to use scalar multiplication to transform a polygon (pre-image) in the coordinate plane into another polygon (image).

APPLICATION

5. INVENTORY Represent the inventory data at right in a matrix, M. Interpret the entry at m_{23}. *(EXAMPLE 1)*

	Inventory		
	Small	Medium	Large
Jerseys	12	28	17
T-shirts	15	32	45
Sweatshirts	6	20	30

6. Solve $\begin{bmatrix} 6 & 5 \\ x+8 & 4 \\ 0 & 2y-1 \end{bmatrix} = \begin{bmatrix} 6 & 5 \\ 14-x & 4 \\ 0 & -13-y \end{bmatrix}$ for x and y. *(EXAMPLE 2)*

7. Let $R = \begin{bmatrix} 3 & 2 \\ -5 & -1 \\ -7 & 9 \end{bmatrix}$ and $S = \begin{bmatrix} 8 & -9 \\ -2 & 6 \\ 7 & -3 \end{bmatrix}$. *(EXAMPLE 3)*

    a. Find $R + S$.   **b.** Find $R - S$.

8. Find $\begin{bmatrix} 2 & -9 & -5 \\ -6 & 1 & 3 \end{bmatrix} - \begin{bmatrix} 5 & -2 & 12 \\ 2 & -4 & -5 \end{bmatrix} + \begin{bmatrix} 0 & -2 & 8 \\ -4 & -6 & 7 \end{bmatrix}$. *(EXAMPLE 4)*

9. Let $A = \begin{bmatrix} -1 & 0 & 8 \\ 6 & -4 & 5 \end{bmatrix}$. Find $-\frac{1}{2}A$. *(EXAMPLE 5)*

CONNECTIONS

10. COORDINATE GEOMETRY Represent quadrilateral $ABCD$ at right as a matrix, Q. *(EXAMPLE 6)*

11. TRANSFORMATIONS Refer to quadrilateral $ABCD$ at right and matrix Q in Exercise 10. Graph the polygon that is represented by each matrix below. *(EXAMPLE 7)*

    a. $3Q$ **b.** $\frac{1}{3}Q$

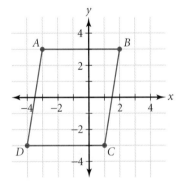

Practice and Apply

For Exercises 12–23,

let $A = \begin{bmatrix} 5 & 7 & -3 & 0 \\ -2 & 1 & 8 & 11 \end{bmatrix}$, $B = \begin{bmatrix} 8 & -5 & 2 \\ -1 & 4 & -2 \\ 0 & -5 & 3 \\ 5 & 7 & -6 \end{bmatrix}$, and $C = \begin{bmatrix} 7 \\ 2 \\ 6 \end{bmatrix}$.

Give the dimensions of each matrix.

12. A **13.** B **14.** C

Give the entry at the indicated address in matrix *A*, *B*, or *C*.

15. a_{23} **16.** b_{12} **17.** c_{31}

Find the indicated matrix.

18. $-A$ **19.** $-4C$ **20.** $-2B$

21. $-B$ **22.** $3A$ **23.** $\frac{1}{2}B$

Solve for *x* and *y*.

24. $\begin{bmatrix} 3 & 4y \\ 5 & 8 \end{bmatrix} = \begin{bmatrix} 3 & 2 \\ 2x-1 & 8 \end{bmatrix}$

25. $\begin{bmatrix} -6 & 5 \\ -1 & 0 \end{bmatrix} = \begin{bmatrix} y+12 & 5 \\ -1 & x+7 \end{bmatrix}$

26. $\begin{bmatrix} 18 & \frac{1}{24}x \\ -\frac{2}{9}y & 15 \end{bmatrix} = \begin{bmatrix} 2x+6 & \frac{1}{4} \\ \frac{2}{3} & -5y \end{bmatrix}$

27. $\begin{bmatrix} \frac{2}{3}x & 12 \\ -4 & \frac{1}{2}y+5 \end{bmatrix} = \begin{bmatrix} 6 & x+3 \\ -4 & y+1 \end{bmatrix}$

28. $\begin{bmatrix} 2.5x & 3y+5 \\ 4 & y \end{bmatrix} = \begin{bmatrix} -10 & 2 \\ -x & y \end{bmatrix}$

29. $\begin{bmatrix} 4.1x & x \\ -100 & -3.7y \end{bmatrix} = \begin{bmatrix} 16.4 & x \\ -25x & -11.1 \end{bmatrix}$

For Exercises 30–45, let $A = \begin{bmatrix} 7 & 3 & -1 & 5 \\ -2 & 8 & 0 & -4 \end{bmatrix}$ and $B = \begin{bmatrix} 6 & 0 & 11 & -3 \\ -5 & 2 & -8 & 9 \end{bmatrix}$.

Perform the indicated operations.

30. $A + B$
31. $A - B$
32. $2A$
33. $-3B$

34. $B - A$
35. $A + B - A$
36. $4(B - A)$
37. $(B + A) - (-A)$

38. $-(A - B)$
39. $2A - (-B - A)$
40. $-\left(\frac{1}{2}B - A\right)$
41. $-3(B + A) - A$

42. $-\frac{1}{2}A + (B - A)$
43. $3B + 2A$
44. $\frac{1}{4}(B - 2A)$
45. $4\left(\frac{1}{2}A + \frac{2}{3}A\right)$

CHALLENGE

46. Construct a 3×3 square matrix, A, where $a_{ij} = i^2 + 2j - 3$.

CONNECTION

TRANSFORMATIONS For Exercises 47–49, refer to the coordinate plane at left.

47. a. Represent $\triangle MNO$ as matrix A.
  b. Graph the polygon that is represented by $\frac{1}{2}A$.
  c. Graph the polygon that is represented by $-\frac{1}{2}A$.
  d. Graph the polygon that is represented by $4A$.

48. a. Represent $\triangle OPQ$ as matrix B.
  b. Graph the polygon that is represented by $2B$.
  c. Graph the polygon that is represented by $-4B$.
  d. Graph the polygon that is represented by $\frac{1}{4}B$.

49. a. Represent $\triangle ORS$ as matrix C.
  b. Graph the polygon that is represented by $2C$.
  c. Graph the polygon that is represented by $-C$.
  d. Graph the polygon that is represented by $-\frac{1}{2}C$.

APPLICATION

GEOGRAPHY Tracy and Renaldo both collect maps. Together they have a variety of maps from the 1960s to the 1990s. Matrix M shows the number of each type of map they have.

$$\begin{array}{r} \\ \text{Europe} \\ \text{Asia} \\ \text{North America} \\ \text{Africa} \end{array} \begin{array}{cccc} \text{'60s} & \text{'70s} & \text{'80s} & \text{'90s} \\ \begin{bmatrix} 3 & 1 & 4 & 2 \\ 5 & 3 & 6 & 3 \\ 2 & 7 & 9 & 5 \\ 8 & 5 & 4 & 6 \end{bmatrix} \end{array} = M$$

50. What are the dimensions of matrix M?

51. Describe the entry at m_{42}.

52. Describe the entry at m_{21}.

53. What is the total number of maps of Africa that Renaldo and Tracy have?

54. What is the total number of maps from the 1960s that Tracy and Renaldo have?

CONSUMER ECONOMICS At a local farmer's market, Jane sold 27 squash, 31 tomatoes, 24 peppers, and 18 melons. Jose sold 48 squash, 72 tomatoes, 61 peppers, and 25 melons.

55. Create a 2×4 matrix of this data. Name this matrix P.

56. What is the address of the number of peppers that Jane sold?

57. What is the address of the data stored in the second row and first column. What does this entry represent?

58. Could you have created a matrix with different dimensions from the one you created in Exercise 55?

ACADEMICS The matrix below shows the number of events during the fall semester for three extracurricular activities.

	Aug.	Sept.	Oct.	Nov.	Dec.
Drama productions	0	1	2	1	2
Soccer games	1	4	3	3	0
Journalism publications	1	2	3	3	2

59. What are the dimensions of this matrix?

60. Find the total number of events that occurred in September.

61. Find the total number of drama productions during the fall semester.

62. During which month did the most events occur?

INVENTORY A music store manager wishes to organize information about his inventory. The store carries records, tapes, and compact discs of country, jazz, rock, blues, and classical music.

63. Give possible numbers for each type of music in each type of format.

64. Create a matrix to store this information. Name this matrix M.

65. Indicate what the entry at m_{23} of the matrix you created in Exercise 64 represents.

 Look Back

Write an equation in slope-intercept form for the line containing the indicated points. *(LESSON 1.3)*

66. $(4, 0)$ and $(-9, 11)$

67. $(10, 3)$ and $(8, -5)$

68. If y varies directly as x and y is 49 when x is 14, find x when y is 63. *(LESSON 1.4)*

69. Find the inverse of $f(x) = 2x - 1$. *(LESSON 2.5)*

Write each pair of parametric equations as a single equation in x and y. *(LESSON 3.6)*

70. $\begin{cases} x(t) = 3t - 1 \\ y(t) = 2t \end{cases}$

71. $\begin{cases} x(t) = 5 - t \\ y(t) = 3t \end{cases}$

72. $\begin{cases} x(t) = -6t \\ y(t) = t^2 \end{cases}$

 Look Beyond

73. Write the system of linear equations represented by these equivalent matrices: $\begin{bmatrix} 5x - 2y \\ x + 4y \end{bmatrix} = \begin{bmatrix} 3 \\ 7 \end{bmatrix}$.

PORTFOLIO ACTIVITY

Finding your way around the exhibits in museums may appear to be a random process. However, to calculate the number of paths to and from exhibits requires a mathematical approach.

The exhibits on the fourth floor of the Museum of Natural History can be modeled by the network diagram below. The address n_{23} of matrix N below represents a path from the Evolution of Horses, H, to the Dinosaur Mummy, D.

Fourth Floor, NY Museum of Natural History

G: Glen Rose Trackway
T: Tyrannosaurus
D: Dinosaur Mummy
H: Evolution of Horses
M: Warren Mastodon

$$\text{From:} \quad \begin{array}{c} \\ M \\ H \\ D \\ T \\ G \end{array} \begin{bmatrix} 0 & 1 & 0 & 0 & 0 \\ 1 & 0 & 1 & 0 & 0 \\ 0 & 1 & 0 & 1 & 1 \\ 0 & 0 & 1 & 0 & 1 \\ 0 & 0 & 1 & 1 & 0 \end{bmatrix} = N$$

To: M H D T G

1. Describe the difference between locations n_{34} and n_{43} in matrix N.

2. Explain the meaning of the 1 at n_{54} and 0 at n_{14}.

3. Describe how to use matrix N to determine whether it is possible to reach Tyrannosaurus, T, directly from the Glen Rose Trackway, G.

4. Explain why each element of the main diagonal is 0.

5. Explain how to find the number of paths leading to each exhibit by using the matrix.

6. Explain how to find the number of paths going from each exhibit by using the matrix.

WORKING ON THE CHAPTER PROJECT

You should now be able to complete Activity 1 of the Chapter Project.

Matrix Multiplication

Why *Many simple calculations, such as keeping track of the score of a football game, involve a process of calculation that is very similar to matrix multiplication. Matrix multiplication can also be used for more complicated calculations.*

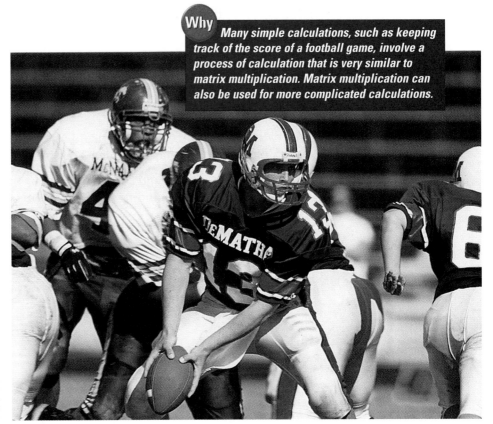

Objectives

● Multiply two matrices.

● Use matrix multiplication to solve mathematical and real-world problems.

A P P L I C A T I O N
SPORTS

Matrix multiplication involves multiplication and addition. The process of matrix multiplication can be demonstrated by using football scores.

A football team scores 5 touchdowns, 4 extra points, and 2 field goals. A touchdown is worth 6 points, an extra point is 1 point, and a field goal is 3 points. The final score is evaluated as follows:

(5 touchdowns)(6 pts) + (4 extra points)(1 pt) + (2 field goals)(3 pts)
=   30 points   +   4 points   +   6 points
=   40 points total

Matrix multiplication is performed in the same way.

$$\begin{array}{cccccc} \text{Touch-} & \text{Extra} & \text{Field} & \text{Point} & & \text{Total} \\ \text{downs} & \text{points} & \text{goals} & \text{values} & & \text{score} \end{array}$$

$$[5 \quad 4 \quad 2] \times \begin{bmatrix} 6 \\ 1 \\ 3 \end{bmatrix} = [(5)(6) + (4)(1) + (2)(3)] = [40]$$

Notice that a 1×3 matrix multiplied by a 3×1 matrix results in a 1×1 matrix. To multiply any two matrices, the *inner dimensions* must be the same. Then the *outer dimensions* become the dimensions of the resulting product matrix.

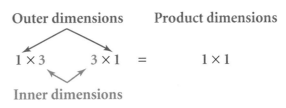

Outer dimensions   Product dimensions

1×3 3×1 = 1×1

Inner dimensions

CHECKPOINT ✔ Let $A = \begin{bmatrix} 2 & -1 & 3 \\ 0 & 5 & 1 \end{bmatrix}$ and $B = \begin{bmatrix} 1 & 0 \\ 2 & -1 \end{bmatrix}$. Is it possible to find the product AB? Is it possible to find the product BA? Explain.

The procedure for finding the product of two matrices is given below.

Matrix Multiplication

If matrix A has dimensions $m \times n$ and matrix B has dimensions $n \times r$, then the product AB has dimensions $m \times r$.

Find the entry in row i and column j of AB by finding the sum of the products of the corresponding entries in row i of A and column j of B.

EXAMPLE **1** Let $H = \begin{bmatrix} 2 & -3 \\ 1 & 5 \end{bmatrix}$ and $G = \begin{bmatrix} 6 & 0 \\ 4 & 7 \end{bmatrix}$.

a. Find HG, if it exists.   **b.** Find GH, if it exists.

● **SOLUTION**

a. The product HG has dimensions of 2×2.

$$\underset{H}{\begin{bmatrix} 2 & -3 \\ 1 & 5 \end{bmatrix}} \underset{G}{\begin{bmatrix} 6 & 0 \\ 4 & 7 \end{bmatrix}} = \begin{bmatrix} (2)(6) + (-3)(4) & (2)(0) + (-3)(7) \\ (1)(6) + (5)(4) & (1)(0) + (5)(7) \end{bmatrix} = \underset{HG}{\begin{bmatrix} 0 & -21 \\ 26 & 35 \end{bmatrix}}$$

row 1 of H, column 1 of G; row 1 of H, column 2 of G; row 2 of H, column 1 of G; row 2 of H, column 2 of G

b. The product GH has dimensions of 2×2.

$$\underset{G}{\begin{bmatrix} 6 & 0 \\ 4 & 7 \end{bmatrix}} \underset{H}{\begin{bmatrix} 2 & -3 \\ 1 & 5 \end{bmatrix}} = \begin{bmatrix} (6)(2) + (0)(1) & (6)(-3) + (0)(5) \\ (4)(2) + (7)(1) & (4)(-3) + (7)(5) \end{bmatrix} = \underset{GH}{\begin{bmatrix} 12 & -18 \\ 15 & 23 \end{bmatrix}}$$

row 1 of G, column 1 of H; row 1 of G, column 2 of H; row 2 of G, column 1 of H; row 2 of G, column 2 of H

In Example 1, notice that although both HG and GH exist, the products are not equal; that is, $HG \neq GH$. Thus, matrix multiplication is *not* commutative.

TRY THIS Let $R = \begin{bmatrix} 2 & -3 \\ 0 & 5 \\ -2 & 0 \end{bmatrix}$ and $W = \begin{bmatrix} 5 & 0 \\ 4 & 7 \end{bmatrix}$.

a. Find RW, if it exists.   **b.** Find WR, if it exists.

CRITICAL THINKING Find any matrices A and B such that $AB = A + B$. What can you say about the dimensions of any matrices A and B for which $AB = A + B$ is true?

EXAMPLE **2**

Karl and Kayla are making two snack mixes by mixing dried fruit and nuts. The amounts of protein, carbohydrates, and fat, in grams per serving, for the dried fruit and nuts are given in Table 1. The number of servings of dried fruit and nuts in each mix is given in Table 2.

Table 1

	Dried fruit	Nuts
Protein	3	20
Carbohydrates	65	21
Fat	1	52

Table 2

	Sports mix	Camp mix
Dried fruit	4	3
Nuts	2	3

a. Represent the information from Table 1 in a matrix called *N*. Represent the information from Table 2 in a matrix called *G*.

b. Find the product *NG*, and determine which mix has more protein and which mix has less fat.

● **SOLUTION**

Notice that three distinct categories are represented: nutrients, ingredients, and type of mix. The categories that correspond to the *inner* dimensions of the matrices must be the same. The categories that correspond to the outer dimensions are different from one another and will become the labels of the product matrix.

a.
$$\begin{array}{c} \\ \text{Protein} \\ \text{Carbohydrates} \\ \text{Fat} \end{array}\begin{array}{cc}\text{Dried} & \\ \text{fruit} & \text{Nuts} \end{array}\begin{bmatrix} 3 & 20 \\ 65 & 21 \\ 1 & 52 \end{bmatrix} = N \qquad \begin{array}{c} \\ \text{Dried fruit} \\ \text{Nuts} \end{array}\begin{array}{cc}\text{Sport} & \text{Camp} \\ \text{mix} & \text{mix} \end{array}\begin{bmatrix} 4 & 3 \\ 2 & 3 \end{bmatrix} = G$$

b.
$$NG = \begin{bmatrix} 3 & 20 \\ 65 & 21 \\ 1 & 52 \end{bmatrix}\begin{bmatrix} 4 & 3 \\ 2 & 3 \end{bmatrix} = \begin{bmatrix} 3(4) + 20(2) & 3(3) + 20(3) \\ 65(4) + 21(2) & 65(3) + 21(3) \\ 1(4) + 52(2) & 1(3) + 52(3) \end{bmatrix}$$

$$= \begin{array}{cc}\text{Sport} & \text{Camp} \\ \text{mix} & \text{mix} \end{array}\begin{bmatrix} 52 & 69 \\ 302 & 258 \\ 108 & 159 \end{bmatrix}\begin{array}{l} \text{Protein} \\ \text{Carbohydrates} \\ \text{Fat} \end{array}$$

The camp mix has more protein, 69 grams. The sport mix has less fat, 108 grams.

Activity
Exploring Rotations in the Plane

You will need: no special tools

You are given △*KLM* with vertices *K*(0, 0), *L*(4, 0), and *M*(4, 3).

Let $A = \begin{bmatrix} 0 & -1 \\ 1 & 0 \end{bmatrix}$ and $B = \begin{bmatrix} 0 & 1 \\ -1 & 0 \end{bmatrix}$.

1. Sketch △*KLM* on graph paper. Then represent △*KLM* as matrix *C*.

2. Find *AC*. Graph the triangle represented by *AC*, △*K′L′M′*, on the coordinate plane with △*KLM*. How are △*KLM* and △*K′L′M′* related?

3. Find *BC*. Graph triangle △*K″L″M″*, represented by *BC*, on the coordinate plane with △*KLM*. How are △*KLM* and △*K″L″M″* related?

CHECKPOINT ✔ 4. Make and verify a conjecture about the effect of matrix *A* on a geometric figure in the coordinate plane.

CHECKPOINT ✔ 5. Make and verify a conjecture about the effect of matrix *B* on a geometric figure in the coordinate plane.

APPLICATION

NETWORKS

Computer network connections

A *network* is a finite set of connected points. Each point is called a **vertex** (plural, *vertices*). A **directed network** is a network in which permissible directions of travel between the vertices are indicated.

You can represent a network in an **adjacency matrix**, which indicates how many one-stage (direct) paths are possible from one vertex to another. A directed network and corresponding adjacency matrix are shown below.

Directed network

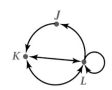

Adjacency matrix

$$\text{From: } \begin{matrix} \\ J \\ K \\ L \end{matrix} \begin{matrix} \text{To:} \\ \begin{matrix} J & K & L \end{matrix} \\ \begin{bmatrix} 0 & 1 & 0 \\ 0 & 0 & 2 \\ 1 & 2 & 1 \end{bmatrix} \end{matrix} = A$$

With the points traveled from naming the rows and the points traveled to naming the columns, the matrix shows that there is no path from *J* to itself (a_{11}), but there is a path from *L* to itself (a_{33}). There are two paths from *K* to *L* (a_{23}).

If *A* is the adjacency matrix of a network, then the product $A \times A = A^2$ gives the number of two-stage paths from one vertex to another vertex by means of one intermediate vertex, such as from *L* to *K* by means of *J*.

E X A M P L E ③ Refer to the directed network and adjacency matrix *A* above.
   a. Find the matrix that gives the number of two-stage paths.
   b. Interpret a_{32} in matrix A^2. List the corresponding paths.

TECHNOLOGY

GRAPHICS CALCULATOR

Keystroke Guide, page 268

● **SOLUTION**

   a. The matrix product A^2 gives the number of two-stage paths. Find A^2 or $A \times A$.
   b. The entry in row 3 column 2 is 3.

$$\text{From: } \begin{matrix} \\ J \\ K \\ L \end{matrix} \begin{matrix} \text{To:} \\ \begin{matrix} J & K & L \end{matrix} \\ \begin{bmatrix} 0 & 0 & 2 \\ 2 & 4 & 2 \\ 1 & ③ & 5 \end{bmatrix} \end{matrix} = A^2$$

This number 3 represents the number of two-stage paths from *L* to *K*. From the directed network above you can see that these paths are as follows:

$L \to L \to K$ (using one path to *K*)
$L \to L \to K$ (using another path to *K*)
$L \to J \to K$

Exercises

Communicate

1. What is necessary in order for two matrices to be multiplied?

2. Explain the steps you would use to multiply $\begin{bmatrix} 3 & -2 \\ 5 & 7 \end{bmatrix}$ and $\begin{bmatrix} 5 & -3 & 1 \\ -2 & -1 & 4 \end{bmatrix}$.

3. Explain how to represent a directed network with an adjacency matrix.

Guided Skills Practice

4. Let $A = [-1 \quad 3 \quad 5]$ and $B = \begin{bmatrix} -4 \\ 2 \\ -5 \end{bmatrix}$. **(EXAMPLE 1)**

    a. Find AB, if it exists.   **b.** Find BA, if it exists.

APPLICATIONS

5. NUTRITION Refer to Example 2 on page 227. Add a third kind of snack mix called trail mix, to matrix G. Let the trail mix contain 2 servings of dried fruit and 4 servings of nuts. **(EXAMPLE 2)**
    a. What will be the entries in the new version of matrix G?
    b. Find the new product NG.
    c. Which of the three mixes has the greatest amount of protein? Which has the greatest amount of carbohydrates?

6. NETWORKS Represent the directed network at right in an adjacency matrix, M. **(EXAMPLE 3)**
    a. Find the matrix that gives the number of two-stage paths.
    b. Interpret m_{22} in the resulting matrix, and list the corresponding paths.

Practice and Apply

Find each product, if it exists.

7. $\begin{bmatrix} 2 \\ 0 \\ 6 \end{bmatrix} [1 \quad -3 \quad 4]$

8. $[2 \quad 5 \quad 0] \begin{bmatrix} 8 & 1 \\ 0 & 4 \\ 2 & 5 \end{bmatrix}$

9. $\begin{bmatrix} 5 & 3 \\ 0 & 1 \end{bmatrix} \begin{bmatrix} 4 & 2 & -1 \\ 0 & 1 & 3 \end{bmatrix}$

10. $\begin{bmatrix} 1 & 5 \\ -3 & 0 \end{bmatrix} \begin{bmatrix} 3 & -2 \\ -4 & 6 \end{bmatrix}$

11. $\begin{bmatrix} 3 & 9 \\ 2 & -1 \end{bmatrix} \begin{bmatrix} 7 & 0 \\ 1 & 3 \end{bmatrix}$

12. $\begin{bmatrix} -1 & 4 & 3 & 5 \\ 2 & 0 & -6 & 1 \end{bmatrix} \begin{bmatrix} 2 & 0 \\ 1 & 4 \\ 3 & -2 \\ -5 & 1 \end{bmatrix}$

13. $\begin{bmatrix} 4 & -6 & 5 \\ 2 & 4 & -1 \end{bmatrix} \begin{bmatrix} 2 & 7 & 1 \\ -1 & 5 & 2 \\ 1 & 4 & 1 \end{bmatrix}$

14. $\begin{bmatrix} 1 & 1 & -1 \\ 2 & 1 & 1 \\ 1 & -2 & 3 \end{bmatrix} \begin{bmatrix} 1 & -0.2 & 0.4 \\ -1 & 0.8 & -0.6 \\ -1 & 0.6 & -0.2 \end{bmatrix}$

Let $A = \begin{bmatrix} 4 & -2 & 8 & 0 \\ 1 & 3 & -6 & 9 \\ -5 & 7 & 2 & 1 \end{bmatrix}$, $B = \begin{bmatrix} 7 & 6 \\ 2 & -3 \\ -1 & 8 \\ 9 & 5 \end{bmatrix}$, and $C = \begin{bmatrix} 0 & 8 \\ -2 & 1 \end{bmatrix}$. Find each product, if it exists.

15. BC **16.** CB **17.** BA

18. CA **19.** $A(BC)$ **20.** $(AB)C$

CONNECTIONS

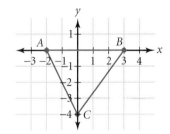

21. TRANSFORMATIONS Matrix $\begin{bmatrix} -2 & 3 & 0 \\ 0 & 0 & -4 \end{bmatrix}$ represents $\triangle ABC$ graphed at left.

a. Find the coordinates of the vertices of the image, $\triangle A'B'C'$, after multiplying the matrix above by the transformation matrix $\begin{bmatrix} \frac{1}{2} & 0 \\ 0 & \frac{1}{2} \end{bmatrix}$.

b. Sketch the image, $\triangle A'B'C'$, on the same plane as the pre-image, $\triangle ABC$.

c. Compare this transformation with the transformation resulting in an enlarged image or reduced image, which you learned in Lesson 4.1.

CHALLENGE

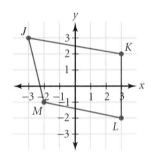

COORDINATE GEOMETRY For Exercises 22 and 23, let $A = \begin{bmatrix} -1 & 0 \\ 0 & 1 \end{bmatrix}$ and $B = \begin{bmatrix} 1 & 0 \\ 0 & -1 \end{bmatrix}$. Matrix $Q = \begin{bmatrix} -3 & 3 & 3 & -2 \\ 3 & 2 & -2 & -1 \end{bmatrix}$ represents the vertices of quadrilateral *JKLM* at left.

22. a. Find the product AQ.

b. Graph $J'K'L'M'$, the quadrilateral represented by AQ, on a coordinate plane with $JKLM$.

c. Make and verify a conjecture about the effect of matrix A on a geometric figure in the plane. (Hint: Describe the movement of the vertices from $JKLM$ to $J'K'L'M'$.)

23. a. Find the product BQ.

b. Graph $J''K''L''M''$, the quadrilateral represented by BQ.

c. Make and verify a conjecture about the effect of matrix B on a geometric figure in the coordinate plane.

APPLICATION

24. NUTRITION Jackson High School serves breakfast and lunch, each in two shifts. The cafeteria manager needs to estimate the number of meals needed during the first week of school. Table 1 gives the percentage of students who prefer meals with meat and of those who prefer meals with no meat at the first and second shifts. Table 2 shows the average number of students who come to first and second shifts of breakfast and of lunch.

Table 1

	1st shift	2nd shift
With meat	55%	62%
Without meat	45%	38%

Table 2

	Breakfast	Lunch
1st shift	72	102
2nd shift	85	130

a. Put the information from the tables into matrices.

b. Use matrix multiplication to find how many meals without meat are needed for breakfast and for lunch.

25. SPORTS A high-school football team has played four games this season. Matrix *S* shows the number of touchdowns, extra points, and field goals scored in each game. Use matrix *S* and the point-values matrix, *P*, to answer parts **a–c**.

$$\begin{array}{c} \\ \text{Game 1} \\ \text{Game 2} \\ \text{Game 3} \\ \text{Game 4} \end{array} \begin{array}{ccc} \text{Touchdowns} & \begin{array}{c}\text{Extra}\\\text{points}\end{array} & \begin{array}{c}\text{Field}\\\text{goals}\end{array} \\ \left[\begin{array}{ccc} 2 & 2 & 1 \\ 4 & 4 & 3 \\ 3 & 1 & 3 \\ 5 & 4 & 2 \end{array}\right] = S \end{array} \qquad \begin{array}{cc} & \begin{array}{c}\text{Point}\\\text{values}\end{array} \\ \begin{array}{c}\text{Touchdowns}\\\text{Extra points}\\\text{Field goals}\end{array} & \left[\begin{array}{c} 6 \\ 1 \\ 3 \end{array}\right] = P \end{array}$$

a. Find the product *SP*. What is the total number of points scored in game 3? in all four games?

b. Find the difference between the number of points scored in games 2 and 3. In which of these two games were the most points scored?

c. Suppose that matrix *S* included the information for all nine games of the season. How many rows and columns would the new product *SP* have?

26. NUTRITION A veterinarian has created formulas for producing her own mixtures of pet food. Using these formulas, she produces 3 mixtures from the 3 varieties of brand A food (regular, lite, and growth). She does the same for brand B. These mixtures are numbered 1, 2, and 3.
- The amounts of protein, fiber, and fat (in percent per serving) are given in matrix *G* for brand A and in matrix *H* for brand B.
- The three formulas that she is using, with the ingredients given in parts per serving, are stated in matrix *J*.

$$\begin{array}{c} \textbf{Brand A} \\ \begin{array}{c} \\ \text{Protein} \\ \text{Fiber} \\ \text{Fat} \end{array} \begin{array}{ccc} \text{Regular} & \text{Lite} & \text{Growth} \\ \left[\begin{array}{ccc} 22 & 14 & 26 \\ 3 & 15 & 3 \\ 13 & 4 & 17 \end{array}\right] = G \end{array} \end{array}$$

$$\begin{array}{c} \textbf{Brand B} \\ \begin{array}{c} \\ \text{Protein} \\ \text{Fiber} \\ \text{Fat} \end{array} \begin{array}{ccc} \text{Regular} & \text{Lite} & \text{Growth} \\ \left[\begin{array}{ccc} 26 & 22 & 17 \\ 5 & 5 & 4 \\ 15 & 12 & 28 \end{array}\right] = H \end{array} \end{array}$$

$$\begin{array}{c} \begin{array}{c}\textbf{Formulas for}\\\textbf{mixtures}\end{array} \\ \begin{array}{c} \\ \text{Regular} \\ \text{Lite} \\ \text{Growth} \end{array} \begin{array}{ccc} 1 & 2 & 3 \\ \left[\begin{array}{ccc} 1 & 2 & 1 \\ 2 & 1 & 1 \\ 1 & 1 & 2 \end{array}\right] = J \end{array} \end{array}$$

a. Which two matrices must be multiplied to determine the nutritional content of mixtures 1, 2, and 3 from brand A? Find the product.

b. Which two matrices would be multiplied to determine the nutritional content of mixtures 1, 2, and 3 from brand B? Find the product.

c. The veterinarian wants mixture 3 to have the highest percentage of protein and fiber per serving. Should she use brand A or brand B for the mixture?

d. The veterinarian wants mixture 1 to have the lowest percentage of fat per serving. Determine whether brand A or brand B should be used in this mixture.

27. INVENTORY A car rental agency has offices in New York and Los Angeles. Each month, $\frac{1}{2}$ of the cars in New York go to Los Angeles and $\frac{1}{3}$ of the cars in Los Angeles go to New York. If the company starts with 1000 cars at each office, how many cars are at each office n months later?

$$\text{Number of cars } \begin{matrix} \text{NY} & \text{LA} \\ [1000 & 1000] \end{matrix} = N \qquad \text{Origin: } \begin{matrix} & \text{NY} & \text{LA} \\ \text{NY} & \begin{bmatrix} \frac{1}{2} & \frac{1}{2} \\ \frac{1}{3} & \frac{2}{3} \end{bmatrix} \end{matrix} = P$$

Destination:

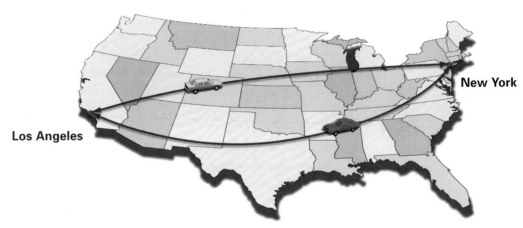

a. The product NP represents the number of cars in each location after one month. Find NP. How many rental cars are in each location after 1 month?

b. Multiply matrix NP by P to find the number of cars in each location after 2 months. (Hint: Round up the entry in column one, and round down the entry in column two of the product.)

c. Continue to multiply each new product matrix by P until the product (with entries rounded to the nearest whole number) no longer changes. What is the final distribution of cars? How many months have passed?

NETWORKS For Exercises 28 and 29, refer to the directed network at left.

28. a. Create an adjacency matrix that represents the number of one-stage paths between the vertices.
   b. How many one-stage paths does this directed network contain?
   c. List the one-stage paths.

29. a. Create an adjacency matrix for the two-stage paths between the vertices.
   b. How many two-stage paths does this directed network contain?
   c. List the two-stage paths.

30. SPORTS Suppose that a football team scores 5 touchdowns, 4 extra points, and 2 field goals in one game. A touchdown is worth 6 points, an extra point is 1 point, and a field goal is 3 points.
   a. Construct a matrix, S, to represent the team's scoring events and a matrix, P, to represent the point values for each scoring event.
   b. Multiply the two matrices to determine the team's total score for the game.

 *Look Back*

Find the slope and the *y*-intercept for each line. *(LESSON 1.2)*

31. $4(2x - 7) = -6$ **32.** $y = -2\left(\frac{1}{3}x + 5\right)$ **33.** $6 - \frac{2}{3}(y + 9) = 12x$

Which of the following are true for all nonzero real numbers *a* and *b*?
(LESSON 2.1)

34. $a \div b = b \div a$ **35.** $a + b = b + a$

36. $a - b = b - a$ **37.** $a \cdot b = b \cdot a$

Let $f(x) = 2x + 3$ and $g(x) = 5x - 2$. *(LESSON 2.4)*

38. Find $f \circ g$.   **39.** Find $g \circ f$.

40. Is $f \circ g$ equal to $g \circ f$?   **41.** Find $(f \circ g)(6)$.

APPLICATION

42. RENTALS An apartment building contains 200 apartments. Some apartments have only one bedroom and rent for $435 per month. The rest have two bedrooms and rent for $575 per month. When all the units are rented, the total monthly income is $97,500. How many one- and two-bedroom apartments are there? *(LESSON 3.2)*

 *Look Beyond*

43. Write the system of two equations represented by this matrix equation.

$$\begin{bmatrix} -3 & 4 \\ -6 & 8 \end{bmatrix} \begin{bmatrix} x \\ y \end{bmatrix} = \begin{bmatrix} 3 \\ 6 \end{bmatrix}$$

NETWORKS Refer to the adjacency matrix *N* below, taken from the Portfolio Activity on page 224.

Matrix powers can be used to give the number of *n*-stage paths from one vertex to another. Matrix powers can also be used to locate circuits, which are paths that start and end at the same vertex.

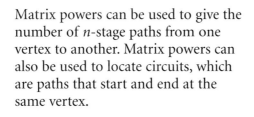

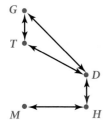

Matrix N^3 gives the number of three-stage paths from one vertex to another.

1. Find N^3. Interpret n_{54} in matrix N^3. List the corresponding paths.

2. Interpret n_{43} in matrix N^3. List the corresponding paths.

3. Find the sums of the rows of N^3. Use the sums to determine which exhibits have the greatest number of three-stage paths to themselves or other exhibits.

4. Find N^4. Interpret n_{13} in matrix N^4.

5. Find the number of four-stage paths from vertex *D* to itself. List the corresponding paths.

WORKING ON THE CHAPTER PROJECT

You should now be able to complete the Chapter Project.

The Inverse of a Matrix

Objectives

- Find and use the inverse of a matrix, if it exists.

- Find and use the determinant of a matrix.

Why *Just as inverse operations can be used to solve equations, inverse matrices can be used to decode messages.*

During World War II, Navaho code talkers, 29 members of the Navaho Nation, developed a code that was used by the United States Armed Forces.

APPLICATION

CRYPTOGRAPHY

The table at right is an assignment table for a code. Each letter of the alphabet is assigned a number. For example, the letter A is assigned the number 1 and Z is assigned the number 26. The dash, which represents the space between words in a message, is assigned the number 0. The question mark is assigned the number 27. For example, the phrase HELP ME would be encoded as 8 | 5 | 12 | 16 | 0 | 13 | 5.

– 0	G 7	N 14	U 21
A 1	H 8	O 15	V 22
B 2	I 9	P 16	W 23
C 3	J 10	Q 17	X 24
D 4	K 11	R 18	Y 25
E 5	L 12	S 19	Z 26
F 6	M 13	T 20	? 27

A matrix can be used to encode a message and another matrix, its inverse, is used to decode the message once it is received. *You will use a matrix to decode a message in Example 3.*

A **square matrix** is a matrix that has the same number of columns and rows. The following matrices are examples of square matrices:

$$\begin{bmatrix} 2 & -3 \\ \frac{1}{2} & 4 \end{bmatrix} \qquad \begin{bmatrix} -1 & 5 & 3 \\ 4 & -8 & 1 \\ 3 & 7 & 0 \end{bmatrix} \qquad \begin{bmatrix} -2 & -8 & 4 & 11 \\ 1 & -4 & 3 & -15 \\ 3 & 5 & 2 & 6 \\ 7 & 1 & 8 & 3 \end{bmatrix}$$

$$2 \times 2 \qquad\qquad 3 \times 3 \qquad\qquad\qquad 4 \times 4$$

The *identity matrix for multiplication* for all 2×2 square matrices is $\begin{bmatrix} 1 & 0 \\ 0 & 1 \end{bmatrix}$.

An identity matrix, called I, has 1s on its *main diagonal* and 0s elsewhere.

$$I_{2 \times 2} = \begin{bmatrix} 1 & 0 \\ 0 & 1 \end{bmatrix} \qquad I_{3 \times 3} = \begin{bmatrix} 1 & 0 & 0 \\ 0 & 1 & 0 \\ 0 & 0 & 1 \end{bmatrix} \qquad I_{4 \times 4} = \begin{bmatrix} 1 & 0 & 0 & 0 \\ 0 & 1 & 0 & 0 \\ 0 & 0 & 1 & 0 \\ 0 & 0 & 0 & 1 \end{bmatrix}$$

The Identity Matrix for Multiplication

Let A be a square matrix with n rows and n columns. Let I be a matrix with the same dimensions and with 1s on the main diagonal and 0s elsewhere. Then $AI = IA = A$.

The product of a real number and 1 is the same number. The product of a square matrix, A, and I is the same matrix, A.

$$\begin{bmatrix} 3 & 1 \\ 2 & 1 \end{bmatrix} \begin{bmatrix} 1 & 0 \\ 0 & 1 \end{bmatrix} = \begin{bmatrix} 3(1) + 1(0) & 3(0) + 1(1) \\ 2(1) + 1(0) & 2(0) + 1(1) \end{bmatrix} = \begin{bmatrix} 3 & 1 \\ 2 & 1 \end{bmatrix}$$

$A \quad \times \quad I \qquad\qquad\qquad\qquad\qquad\qquad\qquad = \quad A$

CHECKPOINT ✔ What is the product of $\begin{bmatrix} a & b \\ c & d \end{bmatrix}$ and $\begin{bmatrix} 1 & 0 \\ 0 & 1 \end{bmatrix}$?

The product of a real number and its multiplicative inverse is 1. The product of a square matrix and its *inverse* is the identity matrix I.

$$\begin{bmatrix} 3 & 1 \\ 2 & 1 \end{bmatrix} \begin{bmatrix} 1 & -1 \\ -2 & 3 \end{bmatrix} = \begin{bmatrix} 3(1) + 1(-2) & 3(-1) + 1(3) \\ 2(1) + 1(-2) & 2(-1) + 1(3) \end{bmatrix} = \begin{bmatrix} 1 & 0 \\ 0 & 1 \end{bmatrix}$$

$A \quad \times \quad \begin{matrix}\text{inverse} \\ \text{of } A\end{matrix} \qquad\qquad\qquad\qquad\qquad\qquad = \quad I$

The Inverse of a Matrix

Let A be a square matrix with n rows and n columns. If there is an $n \times n$ matrix B such that $AB = I$ and $BA = I$, then A and B are inverses of one another. The inverse of matrix A is denoted by A^{-1}. $\left(\text{Note: } A^{-1} \neq \dfrac{1}{A}\right)$

In general, to show that matrices are inverses of one another, you need to show that the multiplication of the matrices is commutative and results in the identity matrix.

E X A M P L E ❶ Let $A = \begin{bmatrix} 2 & 3 \\ 3 & 5 \end{bmatrix}$ and $B = \begin{bmatrix} 5 & -3 \\ -3 & 2 \end{bmatrix}$.

Show that A and B are inverses of one another.

● **SOLUTION**

$AB = \begin{bmatrix} 2 & 3 \\ 3 & 5 \end{bmatrix} \begin{bmatrix} 5 & -3 \\ -3 & 2 \end{bmatrix}$ $\qquad\qquad BA = \begin{bmatrix} 5 & -3 \\ -3 & 2 \end{bmatrix} \begin{bmatrix} 2 & 3 \\ 3 & 5 \end{bmatrix}$

$\quad = \begin{bmatrix} 2(5) + 3(-3) & 2(-3) + 3(2) \\ 3(5) + 5(-3) & 3(-3) + 5(2) \end{bmatrix}$ $\qquad = \begin{bmatrix} 5(2) + (-3)(3) & 5(3) + (-3)(5) \\ -3(2) + 2(3) & -3(3) + 2(5) \end{bmatrix}$

$\quad = \begin{bmatrix} 1 & 0 \\ 0 & 1 \end{bmatrix}$ $\qquad\qquad\qquad\qquad\quad = \begin{bmatrix} 1 & 0 \\ 0 & 1 \end{bmatrix}$

Since both product matrices are the 2×2 identity matrix for multiplication, A and B are inverses of one another.

You can use the equation $AB = I$ to find the inverse of a matrix. For example, let $A = \begin{bmatrix} 1 & 2 \\ 3 & 5 \end{bmatrix}$ and $B = \begin{bmatrix} a & b \\ c & d \end{bmatrix}$. Then write the equation $AB = I$, and proceed as follows:

$$\begin{bmatrix} 1 & 2 \\ 3 & 5 \end{bmatrix} \begin{bmatrix} a & b \\ c & d \end{bmatrix} = \begin{bmatrix} 1 & 0 \\ 0 & 1 \end{bmatrix}$$

$$\begin{bmatrix} a + 2c & b + 2d \\ 3a + 5c & 3b + 5d \end{bmatrix} = \begin{bmatrix} 1 & 0 \\ 0 & 1 \end{bmatrix}$$

Set the corresponding entries equal to each other, and solve the two resulting systems.

$$\begin{cases} a + 2c = 1 \\ 3a + 5c = 0 \end{cases} \qquad\qquad \begin{cases} b + 2d = 0 \\ 3b + 5d = 1 \end{cases}$$

$$a = -5 \text{ and } c = 3 \qquad\qquad b = 2 \text{ and } d = -1$$

Thus, the inverse of matrix A does exist. $B = A^{-1} = \begin{bmatrix} -5 & 2 \\ 3 & -1 \end{bmatrix}$.

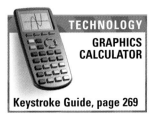

TECHNOLOGY
GRAPHICS CALCULATOR

Keystroke Guide, page 269

You can find the inverse of $A = \begin{bmatrix} 1 & 2 \\ 3 & 5 \end{bmatrix}$ on most graphics calculators. Enter the matrix, and use the x^{-1} key. The display at right shows matrices A and A^{-1}, the inverse of A.

Finding the inverse of a 3×3 matrix or verifying that there is one is a very lengthy process. For matrices larger than 2×2, you will find that a graphics calculator especially useful.

E X A M P L E ② Use a graphics calculator to find the inverse of each matrix.

a. $A = \begin{bmatrix} 6 & 8 \\ 5 & 7 \end{bmatrix}$ **b.** $B = \begin{bmatrix} 2 & -1 & 1 \\ -1 & 3 & 4 \\ -2 & 1 & 0 \end{bmatrix}$ **c.** $C = \begin{bmatrix} 8 & 4 \\ 6 & 3 \end{bmatrix}$

● **SOLUTION**

To find each inverse, enter the matrix and use the x^{-1} key.

TECHNOLOGY
GRAPHICS CALCULATOR

Keystroke Guide, page 269

a.   **b.**   **c.**

 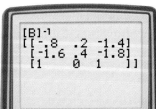 

$$A^{-1} = \begin{bmatrix} 3.5 & -4 \\ -2.5 & 3 \end{bmatrix} \qquad B^{-1} = \begin{bmatrix} -0.8 & 0.2 & -1.4 \\ -1.6 & 0.4 & -1.8 \\ 1 & 0 & 1 \end{bmatrix} \qquad$$ Matrix C does not have an inverse.

Matrix C in Example 2 is called *non-invertible* because it *does not* have an inverse. An *invertible* matrix *does* have an inverse.

CRITICAL THINKING

If $A^{-1} = \begin{bmatrix} 2 & 3 \\ 5 & 7 \end{bmatrix}$, find A. Then find $(A^{-1})^{-1}$. Explain how the three matrices are related.

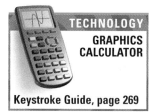

APPLICATION

CRYPTOGRAPHY

Using the table at the beginning of the lesson, assign a number to each letter and space in a message. If the message has an uneven number of characters, then add a zero to the end. Then choose an invertible matrix, A, that can multiply B to encode the message. A^{-1} can then be used to decode the message.

For example, the message GO BOB, represented by 7 | 15 | 0 | 2 | 15 | 2, would be translated into the 2×3 matrix B shown below:

$$B = \begin{bmatrix} 7 & 15 & 0 \\ 2 & 15 & 2 \end{bmatrix}$$

TECHNOLOGY

GRAPHICS CALCULATOR

Keystroke Guide, page 269

You can use an invertible matrix, such as $A = \begin{bmatrix} 6 & 5 \\ 7 & 6 \end{bmatrix}$, to encode the message by multiplying A and B.

During World War II, the United States used a rotor machine called the ECM Mark II, also known as SIGABA, to encrypt messages. The SIGABA was so well designed that its codes were never broken.

Example 3 shows how you can then use A^{-1} to decode a message that was encoded by A.

EXAMPLE ③ Use A^{-1} to decode the message 52 | 165 | 10 | 61 | 195 | 12 which was encoded by matrix $A = \begin{bmatrix} 6 & 5 \\ 7 & 6 \end{bmatrix}$.

APPLICATION

CRYPTOGRAPHY

PROBLEM SOLVING

SOLUTION

Work backward. To decode the message, insert the code numbers into a 2×3 matrix C. Multiply this matrix by A^{-1}.

$$C = \begin{bmatrix} 52 & 165 & 10 \\ 61 & 195 & 12 \end{bmatrix}$$

Enter the coding matrix A. Then find $A^{-1}C$.

$$A^{-1}C = \begin{bmatrix} 7 & 15 & 0 \\ 2 & 15 & 2 \end{bmatrix}$$

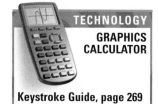

TECHNOLOGY

GRAPHICS CALCULATOR

Keystroke Guide, page 269

The matrix product gives the decoded message 7 | 15 | 0 | 2 | 15 | 2. These numbers translate to the original message, GO BOB.

Determinants

Each square matrix can be assigned a real number called the *determinant of the matrix*. The determinant of a 2×2 matrix is defined below.

Determinant of a 2 × 2 Matrix

Let $A = \begin{bmatrix} a & b \\ c & d \end{bmatrix}$. The **determinant** of A, denoted by $\det(A)$ or $\begin{vmatrix} a & b \\ c & d \end{vmatrix}$,

is defined as $\det(A) = \begin{vmatrix} a & b \\ c & d \end{vmatrix} = ad - bc$.

Matrix A has an inverse if and only if $\det(A) \neq 0$.

E X A M P L E ④ Find the determinant, and tell whether each matrix has an inverse.

a. $G = \begin{bmatrix} 7 & 8 \\ 6 & 7 \end{bmatrix}$ **b.** $H = \begin{bmatrix} 1 & 1 \\ 2 & 2 \end{bmatrix}$

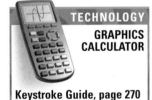

TECHNOLOGY

GRAPHICS CALCULATOR

Keystroke Guide, page 270

● **SOLUTION**

a. $\det(G) = (7)(7) - (8)(6)$
$= 1$
Since $\det(G) \neq 0$, matrix G has an inverse.

b. $\det(H) = (1)(2) - (1)(2)$
$= 0$
Since $\det(H) = 0$, matrix H has no inverse.

TRY THIS Find the determinant, and tell whether each matrix has an inverse.

a. $S = \begin{bmatrix} -3 & 4 \\ -2 & 9 \end{bmatrix}$ **b.** $T = \begin{bmatrix} -6 & 12 \\ 2 & -4 \end{bmatrix}$

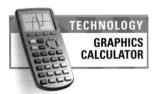

TECHNOLOGY

GRAPHICS CALCULATOR

PROBLEM SOLVING

Activity
Exploring Codes

You will need: a graphics calculator

1. Create a 2×2 matrix that you would like to use to encode messages.

2. **Guess and check.** Use your calculator to verify that your matrix has an inverse. If it does not, modify your matrix so that it does. (Hint: Create your matrix so that its determinant does not equal 0.)

3. Write a brief message. Use the assignment table from page 234 to translate it into numbers.

4. Use your matrix to encode the message. Write the coded message.

CHECKPOINT ✔ 5. Use your inverse to decode your message.

6. Explain why a matrix must be square and invertible in order to be an encoding matrix.

Exercises

Communicate

1. Look up the words *encryption* and *decryption* in a dictionary, and explain how matrices are used to encrypt and decrypt messages.

2. Describe each product matrix without multiplying.

   a. $\begin{bmatrix} 1 & 3 \\ 2 & -1 \end{bmatrix} \begin{bmatrix} 1 & 0 \\ 0 & 1 \end{bmatrix}$ **b.** $\begin{bmatrix} 1 & 0 \\ 0 & 1 \end{bmatrix} \begin{bmatrix} -2 & 1 \\ 5 & 3 \end{bmatrix}$

3. How do you find the inverse of a matrix with a graphics calculator?

4. Explain one way in which determinants can be used.

Guided Skills Practice

5. Show that the matrices $\begin{bmatrix} 2 & 1 \\ 1 & 1 \end{bmatrix}$ and $\begin{bmatrix} 1 & -1 \\ -1 & 2 \end{bmatrix}$ are inverses. *(EXAMPLE 1)*

6. Find the inverse of $\begin{bmatrix} 9 & 5 \\ 7 & 4 \end{bmatrix}$. *(EXAMPLE 2)*

APPLICATION

7. **CRYPTOGRAPHY** Use the inverse matrix you found in Exercise 6 to decode the message 282 | 9 | 260 | 75 | 180 | 221 | 7 | 203 | 60 | 140. *(EXAMPLE 3)*

Find the determinant, and tell whether each matrix has an inverse. (EXAMPLE 4)

8. $\begin{bmatrix} 2 & 1 \\ 6 & 3 \end{bmatrix}$ 9. $\begin{bmatrix} -5 & 2 \\ 3 & -2 \end{bmatrix}$

Practice and Apply

Determine whether each pair of matrices are inverses of each other.

10. $\begin{bmatrix} 4 & 0 \\ 0 & 3 \end{bmatrix}, \begin{bmatrix} \frac{1}{4} & 0 \\ 0 & \frac{1}{3} \end{bmatrix}$ 11. $\begin{bmatrix} 1 & 2 \\ 3 & 4 \end{bmatrix}, \begin{bmatrix} -2 & 1 \\ \frac{3}{2} & -\frac{1}{2} \end{bmatrix}$ 12. $\begin{bmatrix} 4 & 3 \\ 4 & 2 \end{bmatrix}, \begin{bmatrix} 2 & -3 \\ -4 & 6 \end{bmatrix}$

Find the determinant, and tell whether each matrix has an inverse.

13. $\begin{bmatrix} 2 & -5 \\ -1 & 3 \end{bmatrix}$ 14. $\begin{bmatrix} 1 & 2 \\ 1 & 3 \end{bmatrix}$ 15. $\begin{bmatrix} 2 & 3 \\ 4 & 6 \end{bmatrix}$ 16. $\begin{bmatrix} -3 & 2 \\ 9 & -6 \end{bmatrix}$

17. $\begin{bmatrix} 3 & 4 \\ 6 & 8 \end{bmatrix}$ 18. $\begin{bmatrix} 5 & 6 \\ 2 & 2 \end{bmatrix}$ 19. $\begin{bmatrix} 2 & 2 \\ 3 & 4 \end{bmatrix}$ 20. $\begin{bmatrix} 7 & 6 \\ 9 & 8 \end{bmatrix}$

Find the inverse matrix, if it exists. If the inverse matrix does not exist, write *no inverse*.

21. $\begin{bmatrix} -2 & 2 & -1 \\ 3 & -5 & 4 \\ 5 & -6 & 4 \end{bmatrix}$ 22. $\begin{bmatrix} 1 & 6 & 2 \\ -2 & 3 & 5 \\ 7 & 12 & -4 \end{bmatrix}$ 23. $\begin{bmatrix} 1 & -2 & 1 \\ -2 & 4 & -2 \\ 3 & 5 & 3 \end{bmatrix}$

If $A = \begin{bmatrix} a & b \\ c & d \end{bmatrix}$ and det(A) ≠ 0, then A^{-1} is given by the formula

$A^{-1} = \dfrac{1}{\det(A)} \begin{bmatrix} d & -b \\ -c & a \end{bmatrix}$. Use this formula to find the inverse of each

matrix, if it exists. If the inverse does not exist, write *no inverse*.

24. $\begin{bmatrix} 1 & 3 \\ 1 & 1 \end{bmatrix}$ **25.** $\begin{bmatrix} 2 & 1 \\ 0 & 3 \end{bmatrix}$ **26.** $\begin{bmatrix} -4 & 8 \\ 2 & -4 \end{bmatrix}$ **27.** $\begin{bmatrix} 6 & 3 \\ 9 & 10 \end{bmatrix}$

28. $\begin{bmatrix} 2 & 3 \\ 1 & 2 \end{bmatrix}$ **29.** $\begin{bmatrix} 3 & 7 \\ 2 & 5 \end{bmatrix}$ **30.** $\begin{bmatrix} 2 & -6 \\ 1 & -2 \end{bmatrix}$ **31.** $\begin{bmatrix} 2 & 1 \\ 1 & 1 \end{bmatrix}$

32. $\begin{bmatrix} 1 & 3 \\ 2 & 7 \end{bmatrix}$ **33.** $\begin{bmatrix} 5 & -7 \\ -2 & 3 \end{bmatrix}$ **34.** $\begin{bmatrix} \frac{1}{2} & \frac{3}{8} \\ 1 & \frac{1}{4} \end{bmatrix}$ **35.** $\begin{bmatrix} \frac{1}{3} & \frac{1}{6} \\ \frac{5}{6} & \frac{2}{3} \end{bmatrix}$

Find the inverse matrix, if it exists. Round entries to the nearest hundredth. If the inverse matrix does not exist, write *no inverse*.

36 $\begin{bmatrix} 2 & -4 \\ -3 & 6 \end{bmatrix}$ **37** $\begin{bmatrix} \frac{1}{2} & 0 \\ 1 & \frac{1}{4} \end{bmatrix}$ **38** $\begin{bmatrix} \frac{1}{2} & \frac{1}{10} \\ \frac{3}{2} & \frac{1}{5} \end{bmatrix}$

39 $\begin{bmatrix} \frac{1}{3} & \frac{1}{2} \\ \frac{1}{2} & \frac{1}{6} \end{bmatrix}$ **40** $\begin{bmatrix} 2 & -10 \\ -1 & 10 \end{bmatrix}$ **41** $\begin{bmatrix} -2 & -1 & 1 \\ 1 & -2 & 3 \\ 4 & 1 & 2 \end{bmatrix}$

42 $\begin{bmatrix} 2 & 0 & 5 \\ -3 & 1 & -5 \\ 0 & 2 & 4 \end{bmatrix}$ **43** $\begin{bmatrix} \pi & 2 & -1 \\ 1 & 5 & \pi \\ 2 & -3 & 4 \end{bmatrix}$ **44** $\begin{bmatrix} 2\pi & 3 & -1 \\ 0 & -2 & \pi \\ 3 & 0 & -5 \end{bmatrix}$

45. The determinant of a 3 × 3 matrix, $A = \begin{bmatrix} a & b & c \\ d & e & f \\ g & h & i \end{bmatrix}$, can be found by using the formula shown below.

$$\det(A) = \begin{vmatrix} a & b & c \\ d & e & f \\ g & h & i \end{vmatrix} = a\begin{vmatrix} e & f \\ h & i \end{vmatrix} - b\begin{vmatrix} d & f \\ g & i \end{vmatrix} + c\begin{vmatrix} d & e \\ g & h \end{vmatrix}$$

Use this formula to find the determinant of each 3 × 3 matrix.

a. $\begin{bmatrix} 2 & -1 & 3 \\ 4 & 0 & 1 \\ 2 & 0 & 3 \end{bmatrix}$ **b.** $\begin{bmatrix} 3 & 1 & -6 \\ -5 & 2 & 10 \\ 4 & 2 & -8 \end{bmatrix}$ **c.** $\begin{bmatrix} 1 & 2 & 0 \\ -3 & 7 & -2 \\ 2 & 1 & 5 \end{bmatrix}$

CHALLENGE

46. a. Find x, y, u, and v in terms of a, b, c, and d such that

$$\begin{bmatrix} a & b \\ c & d \end{bmatrix}\begin{bmatrix} x & u \\ y & v \end{bmatrix} = I.$$

b. Substitute the values of x, y, u, and v from part **a** in $\begin{bmatrix} x & u \\ y & v \end{bmatrix}$.

Divide out the common factor (a rational expression) from each term, and place it in front of the matrix as a scalar multiplier. How does this expression compare with the formula for A^{-1} given for Exercises 24–35?

47. COORDINATE GEOMETRY The matrix $A = \begin{bmatrix} 2 & 0 \\ 0 & 1 \end{bmatrix}$ horizontally stretches an object in the coordinate plane by a factor of 2. Find A^{-1}. Verify that A^{-1} horizontally compresses an object in the coordinate plane by a factor of $\frac{1}{2}$ by applying A^{-1} to the square with vertices at the points $(2, 2)$, $(2, -2)$, $(-2, -2)$, and $(-2, 2)$. Graph your results.

APPLICATION

CRYPTOGRAPHY Let $A = \begin{bmatrix} 5 & 3 \\ 3 & 2 \end{bmatrix}$. Use matrix A to encode each message.

48. MOVE OUT

49. HEAD NORTH

50. FALL IN

51. CEASE FIRE

Given $A = \begin{bmatrix} 5 & 3 \\ 3 & 2 \end{bmatrix}$, find A^{-1} and decode each message.

52. 97 | 70 | 68 | 80 | 24 | 62 | 45 | 45 | 52 | 16

53. 77 | 50 | 139 | 42 | 47 | 33 | 88 | 28

54. 8 | 160 | 100 | 17 | 18 | 124 | 42 | 5 | 100 | 60 | 11 | 11 | 79 | 28

55. 18 | 100 | 5 | 132 | 80 | 70 | 42 | 11 | 64 | 3 | 82 | 51 | 45 | 28

Look Back

Write an equation in slope-intercept form for the line containing the indicated points. (LESSON 1.3)

56. $(2, -2)$ and $(0, -1)$

57. $(0, 3)$ and $(-2, -6)$

Solve each equation. (LESSON 1.6)

58. $8.91 + x = 11.09$

59. $\frac{1}{4} = \frac{3}{4} + x$

60. $5\frac{1}{2}x = -62$

61. $\frac{1}{5}x = 0.3$

62. $\frac{2}{3}x + 1 = x + 3$

63. $\frac{1}{2}x + \frac{1}{4} = 2\frac{3}{4} - \frac{1}{3}x$

64. Evaluate $f(x) = 2 - 5x + x^2$ for $x = 3$ and $x = -4$. **(LESSON 2.3)**

65. Use any method to solve the system. $\begin{cases} 5x + 7y = 32 \\ 2x - 14y = 6 \end{cases}$ **(LESSONS 3.1 AND 3.2)**

Graph the solution to each system of linear inequalities. (LESSON 3.4)

66. $\begin{cases} 2x + y \geq 2 \\ y \geq 3x + 2 \end{cases}$

67. $\begin{cases} x + \frac{1}{2}y \leq 2 \\ 2x + 3y < 2 \end{cases}$

68. $\begin{cases} 3x + 2y \geq 1 \\ 2x + 3y < 2 \\ x < 3 \end{cases}$

Look Beyond

69. a. Write the system of equations $\begin{cases} 3x + 7y = 4 \\ 2x + 5y = 1 \end{cases}$ in matrix form.

$\left(\text{Hint: } \begin{bmatrix} ? & ? \\ ? & ? \end{bmatrix} \begin{bmatrix} x \\ y \end{bmatrix} = \begin{bmatrix} 4 \\ 1 \end{bmatrix} . \right)$

b. Let $A = \begin{bmatrix} 3 & 7 \\ 2 & 5 \end{bmatrix}$. Find A^{-1}. Find the product on each side of the equation $A^{-1} \begin{bmatrix} 3 & 7 \\ 2 & 5 \end{bmatrix} \begin{bmatrix} x \\ y \end{bmatrix} = A^{-1} \begin{bmatrix} 4 \\ 1 \end{bmatrix}$. What is the resulting equation?

c. Explain the connection between parts **a** and **b** of this exercise.

HOW SECRET IS SECRET?

Biggest Division a Giant Leap in Math

BY GINA KOLATA

In a mathematical feat that seemed impossible a year ago, a group of several hundred researchers using about 1,000 computers has broken a 155-digit number down into three smaller numbers that cannot be further divided.

The latest finding could be the first serious threat to systems used by banks and other organizations to encode secret data before transmission, cryptography experts said yesterday.

These systems are based on huge numbers that cannot be easily factored, or divided into two numbers that cannot be divided further.

In 1977, a group of three mathematicians devised a way of making secret codes that involves scrambling messages according to a mathematical formula based on factoring. Now, such codes are used in banking, for secure telephone lines and by the Defense Department.

In making these codes, engineers have to strike a delicate balance when they select the numbers used to scramble messages. If they choose a number that is easy to factor, the code can be broken. If they make the number much larger, and much harder to

factor, it takes much longer for the calculations used to scramble a message.

For most applications outside the realm of national security, cryptographers have settled on numbers that are about 150 digits long.

Dr. Mark Manasse of the Digital Equipment Corporation's Systems Research Center in Palo Alto, Calif., calculates that if a computer could perform a billion divisions a second, it would take 10 to the 60th years, or 1 with 60 zeros after it, to factor the number simply by trying out every smaller number that might divide into it easily. But with a newly discovered factoring method and with a world-wide collaborative effort, the number was cracked in a few months.

Connection Machine® is one of the most powerful high-performance computers in the world.

Factoring a 155-Digit Number:
13,407,807,929,942, 597,099,574,024,998, 205,846,127,479,365, 820,592,393,377,723, 561,443,721,764,030, 073,546,976,801,874, 298,166,903,427,690, 031,858,186,486,050, 853,753,882,811,946, 569,946,433,649,006, 084,097

equals

2,424,833

times

7,455,602,825,647, 884,208,337,395,736, 200,454,918,783,366, 342,657

times

741,640,062,627,530, 801,524,787,141,901, 937,474,059,940,781, 097,519,023,905,821, 306,144,415,759,504, 705,008,092,818,711, 693,940,737

[*Source:* New York Times, *June 20, 1990*]

You can use small numbers to get an idea of how code systems like the one described in the article work. Before you begin, you need a key (a number, p, that is not prime). You will use p to encode a secret message and then use p and its factors to decode the message.

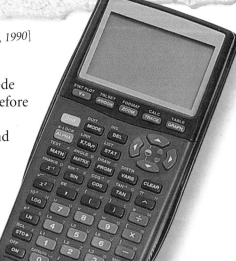

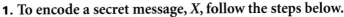

X secret message → Sender uses *p* to encode the secret message. → Y coded message → Receiver uses *p* and its factors to decode the message. → X secret message

Cooperative Learning

For this activity, use 55 for *p*. You will use a special algorithm to encode and decode the message. To keep things simple, let your secret message, *X*, be a two-digit number between 11 and 50.

1. To encode a secret message, *X*, follow the steps below.

   a. Calculate X^3.

   b. Divide X^3 by 55. Multiply the whole-number part of the quotient by 55. Subtract that product from X^3. The difference is the remainder. Use the remainder as the coded message *Y*.

Let *X* be 42. → X^3 = 74,088

74,088 ÷ 55 = 1347.054545 . . .

1347 × 55 = 74,085

74,088 − 74,085 = 3 → *Y* = 3

   c. If your calculator can display only 8 digits, then *Y* cannot be greater than 13. If it can display 10 digits, then *Y* cannot be greater than 26. If *Y* is too large, start over at part **a** with a different value for *X*.

The enigma machine was used in World War II for breaking coded messages.

2. To decode your secret message, use the factors of 55. Follow these steps.

   a. Find Y^3. Divide Y^3 by 5. Multiply the whole-number part of the quotient by 5, and subtract this product from Y^3. Call the remainder *a*.

Y is 3. → Y^3 = 27

27 ÷ 5 = 5.4

5 × 5 = 25

27 − 25 = 2 → *a* = 3

   b. Find Y^7. Divide Y^7 by 11. Multiply the whole-number part of the quotient by 11, and subtract this product from Y^7. Call the remainder *b*.

Y is 3. → Y^7 = 2187

2187 ÷ 11 = 198.8181 . . .

198 × 11 = 2178

2187 − 2178 = 9 → *b* = 9

   c. Evaluate $11a + 45b$, and divide the result by 55. Multiply the whole-number part of the quotient by 55, and subtract this product from the value of $11a + 45b$. How does the remainder compare with *X*, the secret message?

11*a* + 45*b* = 11(3) + 45(9) = 427

427 ÷ 55 = 7.736 . . .

7 × 55 = 385

427 − 385 = 42

3. Explain how you used the factors of *p* to encode or decode the message. Why would it be important for the factors of *p* to be secret?

4. How do you think coding systems may be affected if efficient methods for factoring very large numbers are found?

Solving Systems With Matrix Equations

Objective

- Use matrices to solve systems of linear equations in mathematical and real-world situations.

Why *Many real-world situations, such as investment options, can be represented by a system of linear equations that can be solved quite efficiently by solving a matrix equation.*

APPLICATION

INVESTMENTS

A financial manager wants to invest $50,000 for a client by putting some of the money in a low-risk investment that earns 5% per year and some of the money in a high-risk investment that earns 14% per year. How much money should be invested at each interest rate to earn $5000 in interest per year? *You will answer this question in Example 1.*

PROBLEM SOLVING

Let x represent the amount invested at 5%, and let y represent the amount invested at 14%. **Write a system of linear equations** to represent the situation.

$$\begin{cases} x + y = 50{,}000 \\ 0.05x + 0.14y = 5000 \end{cases}$$

The system $\begin{cases} x + y = 50{,}000 \\ 0.05x + 0.14y = 5000 \end{cases}$ can be written as a **matrix equation**, $AX = B$.

Coefficient matrix, A	Variable matrix, X	Constant matrix, B

Let $A = \begin{bmatrix} 1 & 1 \\ 0.05 & 0.14 \end{bmatrix}$, $X = \begin{bmatrix} x \\ y \end{bmatrix}$, and $B = \begin{bmatrix} 50{,}000 \\ 5000 \end{bmatrix}$.

Then $AX = B$ is $\begin{bmatrix} 1 & 1 \\ 0.05 & 0.14 \end{bmatrix} \begin{bmatrix} x \\ y \end{bmatrix} = \begin{bmatrix} 50{,}000 \\ 5000 \end{bmatrix}$.

CHECKPOINT ✔ Use the interest rates mentioned above. If the client wants to invest $100,000 and earn $10,000 in interest, what system of linear equations and corresponding matrix equation represent this investment?

Solving a matrix equation of the form $AX = B$, where $X = \begin{bmatrix} x \\ y \end{bmatrix}$, is similar to solving a linear equation of the form $ax = b$, where a, b, and x are real numbers and $a \neq 0$.

Real Numbers	Matrices
$ax = b$	$AX = B$
$\frac{1}{a}(ax) = \frac{1}{a}(b)$	$A^{-1}(AX) = A^{-1}B$
$\left(\frac{1}{a} \cdot a\right)x = \frac{b}{a}$	$(A^{-1}A)\,X = A^{-1}B$
	$IX = A^{-1}B$
$x = \frac{b}{a}$	$X - A^{-1}B$

Just as $\frac{1}{a}$ must exist in order to solve $ax = b$ (where $a \neq 0$), A^{-1} must exist to solve $AX = B$.

CHECKPOINT ✔ When solving the matrix equation $AX = B$, does it matter whether you calculate $A^{-1}B$ or BA^{-1}? Explain.

E X A M P L E ❶ Refer to the investment options described at the beginning of the lesson.

APPLICATION
INVESTMENTS

How much money should the manager invest at each interest rate to earn $5000 in interest per year?

● SOLUTION

Solve $\begin{bmatrix} 1 & 1 \\ 0.05 & 0.14 \end{bmatrix} \begin{bmatrix} x \\ y \end{bmatrix} = \begin{bmatrix} 50{,}000 \\ 5000 \end{bmatrix}$ for $\begin{bmatrix} x \\ y \end{bmatrix}$.

Enter the coefficient matrix, $A = \begin{bmatrix} 1 & 1 \\ 0.05 & 0.14 \end{bmatrix}$, and the constant matrix,

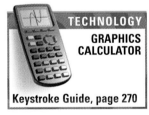

TECHNOLOGY
GRAPHICS CALCULATOR
Keystroke Guide, page 270

$B = \begin{bmatrix} 50{,}000 \\ 5000 \end{bmatrix}$, into your calculator. Solve for the variable matrix, X, by finding the product $A^{-1}B$.

$$X = A^{-1}B$$
$$\begin{bmatrix} x \\ y \end{bmatrix} = \begin{bmatrix} \$22{,}222.22 \\ \$27{,}777.78 \end{bmatrix}$$

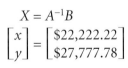

The manager should invest $22,222.22 at 5% and $27,777.78 at 14% to achieve the earned interest goal of $5000 per year.

TRY THIS How much money should the manager invest at each interest rate to earn $4000 in interest per year?

CRITICAL THINKING Suppose that the earned interest goal is $10,000 per year for an investment of $50,000. What happens when you try to find how much to invest at 5% and how much to invest at 14%? Explain your response.

Just as you can use a 2×2 matrix and its inverse to solve a system of two linear equations in two variables, you can use a 3×3 matrix and its inverse to solve a system of three equations in three variables, as shown in Example 2.

 E X A M P L E ❷ **Refer to the system of equations at right.**
  a. Write the system as a matrix equation.
  b. Solve the matrix equation.

$$\begin{cases} 2y - z = -7 - 5x \\ x - 2y + 2z = 0 \\ 3y = 17 - z \end{cases}$$

● **SOLUTION**

a. First write the equations of the system in *standard form*.

> In the third equation, use *0* as the coefficient of *x*.

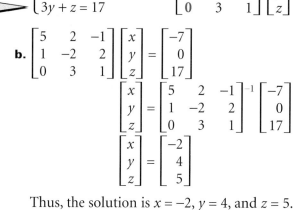

$$\begin{cases} 5x + 2y - z = -7 \\ x - 2y + 2z = 0 \\ 3y + z = 17 \end{cases} \rightarrow \begin{bmatrix} 5 & 2 & -1 \\ 1 & -2 & 2 \\ 0 & 3 & 1 \end{bmatrix}\begin{bmatrix} x \\ y \\ z \end{bmatrix} = \begin{bmatrix} -7 \\ 0 \\ 17 \end{bmatrix}$$

b. $\begin{bmatrix} 5 & 2 & -1 \\ 1 & -2 & 2 \\ 0 & 3 & 1 \end{bmatrix}\begin{bmatrix} x \\ y \\ z \end{bmatrix} = \begin{bmatrix} -7 \\ 0 \\ 17 \end{bmatrix}$

$$\begin{bmatrix} x \\ y \\ z \end{bmatrix} = \begin{bmatrix} 5 & 2 & -1 \\ 1 & -2 & 2 \\ 0 & 3 & 1 \end{bmatrix}^{-1}\begin{bmatrix} -7 \\ 0 \\ 17 \end{bmatrix}$$

$$\begin{bmatrix} x \\ y \\ z \end{bmatrix} = \begin{bmatrix} -2 \\ 4 \\ 5 \end{bmatrix}$$

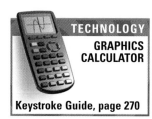

TECHNOLOGY

GRAPHICS CALCULATOR

Keystroke Guide, page 270

Thus, the solution is $x = -2$, $y = 4$, and $z = 5$.

TRY THIS Refer to the system at right.
a. Write the system as a matrix equation.
b. Solve the matrix equation.

$$\begin{cases} 2y - z = 4x - 3 \\ 2x + 3z = y - 6 \\ 3y - 1 = 2x + 2z \end{cases}$$

 Activity

Exploring Slopes and Solutions

TECHNOLOGY

GRAPHICS CALCULATOR

Keystroke Guide, page 270

You will need: a graphics calculator

Let $A = \begin{bmatrix} 4 & 9 \\ 2 & 5 \end{bmatrix}$ be the coefficient matrix for the system $\begin{cases} 4x + 9y = r \\ 2x + 5y = s \end{cases}$.

1. Find the determinant of matrix A. Does the matrix have an inverse? Justify your response.

2. Choose values for r and s. Write a matrix equation and use the inverse of matrix A to find x and y.

3. Find the slopes of the lines represented by the equations with your values for r and s. Do the slopes depend on the values of r and s?

4. Graph these lines. Based on the slopes and graphs, what can you conclude about any solution(s) of the system?

PROBLEM SOLVING 5. **Guess and check.** Choose other values for r and s, and graph the new equation. Do you think that this system will have a unique solution regardless of the values for r and s?

CHECKPOINT ✔ 6. Summarize what you know about the solutions of this system.

As you have learned, not all systems of linear equations have solutions. In a matrix equation of the form $AX = B$, if the coefficient matrix, A, does not have an inverse, then the system represented by the matrix equation does not have a unique solution. This is shown in Example 3.

E X A M P L E ③ Solve $\begin{cases} -3x + 4y = 3 \\ -6x + 8y = 18 \end{cases}$, if possible, by using a matrix equation. If not possible, classify the system.

● **SOLUTION**

The given system is represented by $\underbrace{\begin{bmatrix} -3 & 4 \\ -6 & 8 \end{bmatrix}}_{A} \underbrace{\begin{bmatrix} x \\ y \end{bmatrix}}_{X} = \underbrace{\begin{bmatrix} 3 \\ 18 \end{bmatrix}}_{B}$.

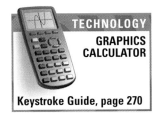
TECHNOLOGY
GRAPHICS CALCULATOR

Keystroke Guide, page 270

When you try to find $A^{-1}B$ on a graphics calculator, you will get an error. The inverse of A does not exist. Notice that $\det(A) = (-3)(8) - (4)(-6) = 0$, which also indicates that the inverse of A does not exist.

Therefore, there is no *unique* solution for the system, and the system is either dependent or inconsistent.

In this case, the system is inconsistent because the lines are parallel.

$$\begin{cases} -3x + 4y = 3 \\ -6x + 8y = 18 \end{cases} \rightarrow \begin{cases} y = \frac{3}{4}x + \frac{3}{4} \\ y = \frac{3}{4}x + 3 \end{cases}$$

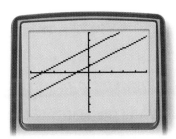

TRY THIS   Solve $\begin{bmatrix} -3 & 4 \\ -6 & 8 \end{bmatrix} \begin{bmatrix} x \\ y \end{bmatrix} = \begin{bmatrix} 3 \\ 6 \end{bmatrix}$, if possible, by using a matrix equation. If not possible, classify the system.

CRITICAL THINKING   Consider the system $\begin{cases} ax + by = e \\ (na)x + (nb)y = f \end{cases}$, where b and n are nonzero. Find the slope of each equation. Find the determinant of the coefficient matrix. How are the slopes and the determinant related?

Exercises

Communicate

1. Explain how to write a system of equations as a matrix equation.

2. Describe how to represent the system at right by using a matrix equation.
$$\begin{cases} x - y = 5 \\ -z + y = -6 \\ 2x - z = 2 \end{cases}$$

3. Discuss how solving the matrix equation $AX = B$ is similar to solving the linear equation $ax = b$, where a, b, and x are real numbers and $a \neq 0$.

4. Describe the steps involved in using a matrix equation to solve a system of linear equations such as $\begin{cases} 2x - 5y = 0 \\ x + y = -2 \end{cases}$.

5. How can you verify that $\begin{bmatrix} -1 \\ -3 \\ 2 \end{bmatrix}$ is a solution of $\begin{bmatrix} 1 & 1 & 3 \\ 2 & -1 & -2 \\ 3 & 2 & -2 \end{bmatrix} \begin{bmatrix} x \\ y \\ z \end{bmatrix} = \begin{bmatrix} 2 \\ -3 \\ -13 \end{bmatrix}$?

6. If coefficient matrix A in the matrix equation $AX = B$ does not have an inverse, what do you know about the related system of equations?

Guided Skills Practice

7. INVESTMENTS A total of $10,000 was invested in two certificates of deposit that earned 6% per year and 8% per year. If the investments earned $750 in interest each year, find the amount invested at each rate. *(EXAMPLE 1)*

Write each system of equations as a matrix equation. Then solve the system, if possible, by using a matrix equation. If not possible, classify the system. *(EXAMPLES 2 AND 3)*

8. $\begin{cases} x + y = 8 \\ 2x + y = 1 \end{cases}$

9. $\begin{cases} x + 3y = 7 \\ x + 3y = -2 \end{cases}$

10. $\begin{cases} 3x - 2y = 11 \\ 6x - 4y = 5 \end{cases}$

Practice and Apply

Write the matrix equation that represents each system.

11. $\begin{cases} 3x - 5y = 1 \\ 2x + y = -2 \end{cases}$

12. $\begin{cases} -3x + y = -3 \\ 6x - 12y = 6 \end{cases}$

13. $\begin{cases} 2a + 4b = -3 \\ a - b = 9 \end{cases}$

14. $\begin{cases} 4x + y - 2z = 10 \\ 3x + 5z = 14 \\ 8x + 3y - z = 23 \end{cases}$

15. $\begin{cases} y + 5z = -14 \\ -2x + 3y - z = 2 \\ 6x - 3z = 21 \end{cases}$

16. $\begin{cases} 12x + y - z = -7 \\ 11x + 2y = -2 \\ -x + 9y = -9 \end{cases}$

Write the system of equations represented by each matrix equation.

17. $\begin{bmatrix} 2 & -1 & 3 \\ -3 & 0 & -1 \\ 1 & -3 & 1 \end{bmatrix} \begin{bmatrix} x \\ y \\ z \end{bmatrix} = \begin{bmatrix} 4 \\ 1 \\ 5 \end{bmatrix}$

18. $\begin{bmatrix} -2 & 2 & 8 \\ 4 & 3 & 5 \\ 5 & 1 & 0 \end{bmatrix} \begin{bmatrix} x \\ y \\ z \end{bmatrix} = \begin{bmatrix} 3 \\ -2 \\ 1 \end{bmatrix}$

Write the matrix equation that represents each system, and solve the system, if possible, by using a matrix equation.

19 $\begin{cases} x + y - z = 14 \\ 4x - y + 5z = -22 \\ 2x + 2y - 3z = 35 \end{cases}$

20 $\begin{cases} -2x + y + 6z = 18 \\ 5x + 8z = -16 \\ 3x + 2y - 10z = -3 \end{cases}$

21 $\begin{cases} 3x + 6y - 6z = 9 \\ 2x - 5y + 4z = 6 \\ -x + 16y + 14z = -3 \end{cases}$

22 $\begin{cases} x + 3y - 2z = 4 \\ 4x - y + z = -1 \\ 3x - 4y + 3z = -5 \end{cases}$

23 $\begin{cases} x - 2y + 3z = 11 \\ 4x - z = 4 \\ 2x - y + 3z = 10 \end{cases}$

24 $\begin{cases} x + 2y - z = 5 \\ 3x + 9y - z = 8 \\ 2x + 10y - 2z = -2 \end{cases}$

25 $\begin{cases} x + y - 2z = -2 \\ 2x - 3y + z = 1 \\ 2x + y - 3z = -2 \end{cases}$

26 $\begin{cases} x - \frac{1}{2}y - 3z = -9 \\ 8z = -16 - 5x \\ \frac{3}{5}x + \frac{2}{5}y - 2z = -\frac{3}{5} \end{cases}$

27 $\begin{cases} 2.5x + y - z = -6 \\ -3.5y + 2.5z = 2.5 \\ 5x + 4y - 2z = -12 \end{cases}$

28 $\begin{cases} x + 2y = -6 \\ y + 2z = 11 \\ 2x + z = 16 \end{cases}$

Write the matrix equation that represents each system, and solve the system, if possible, by using a matrix equation.

29 $\begin{cases} x + y + z + w = 10 \\ 2x - y + z - 3w = -9 \\ 3x + y - z - w = -2 \\ 2x - 3y + z - w = -5 \end{cases}$

30 $\begin{cases} x + 2y - 6z + w = 12 \\ -2x - 3y + 9z + w = -19 \\ x + 2y - 5z + 2w = 15 \\ 2x + 4y - 12z + 3w = 24 \end{cases}$

CHALLENGE

31. The matrix $\begin{bmatrix} -1 & 0 \\ 0 & 1 \end{bmatrix}$ is its own inverse. Find another matrix, other than the identity matrix, which is its own inverse.

CONNECTION

32 GEOMETRY The measure of the largest angle of a certain triangle is 3 times the measure of the smallest angle. The measure of the remaining angle of the triangle is the average of the measures of the largest and smallest angles. Write the system of equations that describes the measure of each angle of the triangle. Then solve the system by using a matrix equation.

APPLICATION

33 ENTERTAINMENT One hundred and twenty people attended a musical. The total amount of money collected for tickets was $1515. Prices were $15 for regular adult admission, $12 for children, and $10 for senior citizens. Twice as many children's tickets as regular adult tickets were sold. Write a system of equations to find the number of children, adults, and senior citizens that attended the musical. Then solve the system by using a matrix equation and the inverse matrix.

APPLICATIONS

34 **CHEMISTRY** A nurse is mixing a 3% saline solution and an 8% saline solution to get 2 liters of a 5% saline solution. How many liters of each solution must be combined?

35 **CHEMISTRY** A solution of 4% acid and a solution of 7% acid are to be mixed to create 3 liters of a 6% acid solution. How many liters of the 3% solution and 7% solution must be combined?

36 **INVESTMENTS** A brokerage firm invested in three mutual-fund companies, A, B, and C. The firm invested $16,110 in low-risk funds, $9016.25 in medium-risk funds, and $5698.75 in high-risk funds, distributed among the three companies as shown below.

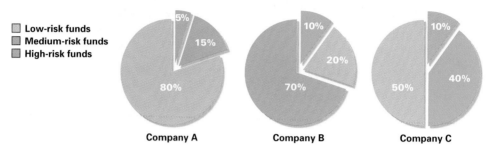

Low-risk funds
Medium-risk funds
High-risk funds

Company A   Company B   Company C

a. Write a system of equations to find the amount that the firm invested in each type of fund.
b. Write the matrix equation that represents this system.
c. Solve the matrix equation by using the inverse matrix.

 Look Back

37. State the domain and range of $f(x) = |x - 5| + 2$. *(LESSON 2.3)*

Let $f(x) = 2x + 3$ and $g(x) = x^2 - 3x + 1$. *(LESSONS 2.3 AND 2.4)*

38. Find $g(-3)$.   **39.** Find $g \circ f$.   **40.** Find $f \circ g$.

Graph each function. *(LESSON 2.6)*

41. $f(x) = 3[x]$ **42.** $f(x) = 2\lceil x \rceil - 3$

 Look Beyond

A method called *Cramer's rule* allows you to solve systems of equations by using determinants. Cramer's rule states that if $\begin{cases} ax + by = e \\ cx + dy = f \end{cases}$ is a system

of equations and $\begin{vmatrix} a & b \\ c & d \end{vmatrix} \neq 0$, then the solution of the system can be found

as follows:

$$x = \frac{\begin{vmatrix} e & b \\ f & d \end{vmatrix}}{\begin{vmatrix} a & b \\ c & d \end{vmatrix}} \quad \text{and} \quad y = \frac{\begin{vmatrix} a & e \\ c & f \end{vmatrix}}{\begin{vmatrix} a & b \\ c & d \end{vmatrix}}$$

Use Cramer's rule to solve each system.

43. $\begin{cases} 2x + y = 6 \\ x + 2y = 9 \end{cases}$ **44.** $\begin{cases} x + y = 3 \\ 3x + 2y = 4 \end{cases}$ **45.** $\begin{cases} x - 2y = 5 \\ 2x + 2y = 4 \end{cases}$ **46.** $\begin{cases} 2x + y = 10 \\ 3x + 3y = 21 \end{cases}$

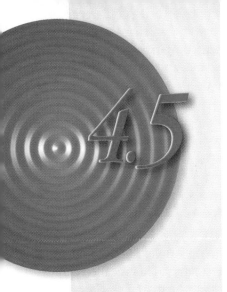

Using Matrix Row Operations

Objectives

- Represent a system of equations as an augmented matrix.

- Solve a system of linear equations by using elementary row operations.

APPLICATION

SMALL BUSINESS

Maya and her friends Amit and Nina have a lawn care business offering three services:

- lawn mowing and edging
- fertilizing and weeding
- trimming shrubs and small trees

They charge a flat rate for each service. The three partners divide up the work for a particular customer as shown below.

Service	Workers and Hours	Cost
Mowing	Maya—1 hr Amit—1 hr Nina—1 hr	$21
Fertilizing	Maya—2 hr Amit—1 hr	$23
Trimming	Amit—1 hr Nina—3 hr	$25

How much does each partner earn per hour and how much will each partner earn in total for his or her work for this customer? *You will solve this problem in Example 1.*

Recall from Lesson 4.4 that if the coefficient matrix of a matrix equation has an inverse, the system represented by the matrix equation is consistent and independent. If there is no inverse, the system is either dependent or inconsistent, but you cannot determine which one.

The **row-reduction method** of solving a system allows you to determine whether the system is independent, dependent, or inconsistent.

The row-reduction method is performed on an *augmented matrix*. An **augmented matrix** consists of the coefficients and constant terms in the system of equations.

The system of equations and the corresponding augmented matrix that represent the lawn-care problem are shown below. Let m, a, and n represent the hourly wages for Maya, Amit, and Nina, respectively.

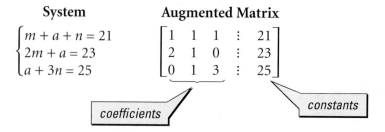

System

$$\begin{cases} m + a + n = 21 \\ 2m + a = 23 \\ a + 3n = 25 \end{cases}$$

Augmented Matrix

$$\left[\begin{array}{ccc:c} 1 & 1 & 1 & 21 \\ 2 & 1 & 0 & 23 \\ 0 & 1 & 3 & 25 \end{array}\right]$$

coefficients   constants

The goal of the row-reduction method is to transform, if possible, the coefficient columns into columns that form an identity matrix. This is called the **reduced row-echelon form** of an augmented matrix if the matrix represents an independent system. If the identity matrix can be formed, then the resulting constants will represent the unique solution to the system.

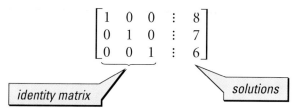

$$\left[\begin{array}{ccc:c} 1 & 0 & 0 & 8 \\ 0 & 1 & 0 & 7 \\ 0 & 0 & 1 & 6 \end{array}\right]$$

identity matrix   solutions

This final matrix is said to be in *reduced row-echelon* form.

To transform an augmented matrix into reduced row-echelon form, use the elementary row operations described below.

Elementary Row Operations

The following operations produce equivalent matrices, and may be used in any order and as many times as necessary to obtain reduced row-echelon form.

• Interchange two rows.

• Multiply all entries in one row by a nonzero number.

• Add a multiple of one row to another row.

You may use *row operation notation* to keep a record of the row operations that you perform.

ROW OPERATION	NOTATION
• Interchange rows 1 and 2.	$R_1 \leftrightarrow R_2$
• Multiply each entry in row 3 by -2.	$-2R_3 \rightarrow R_3$
• Replace row 1 with the sum of row 1 and 4 times each entry in row 2.	$4R_2 + R_1 \rightarrow R_1$

CRITICAL THINKING   Explain why the row operation $R_2 - 4R_1 \rightarrow R_1$ results in an equivalent matrix.

E X A M P L E ① Refer to the lawn-care problem described at the beginning of the lesson.
a. Use the row-reduction method to solve the system.
b. Find the hourly wages for Maya, Amit, and Nina. Then find the total amount that each partner earns for this job.

APPLICATION
SMALL BUSINESS

SOLUTION

System	Augmented Matrix
$\begin{cases} m + a + n = 21 \\ 2m + a = 23 \\ a + 3n = 25 \end{cases}$	$\begin{bmatrix} 1 & 1 & 1 & \vdots & 21 \\ 2 & 1 & 0 & \vdots & 23 \\ 0 & 1 & 3 & \vdots & 25 \end{bmatrix}$

a. Perform row operations.

• Inspect column 1.

The first row begins with 1, but the 2 in the second row needs to become 0.

$$-2R_1 + R_2 \rightarrow R_2$$

> Replace row 2 with the sum of row 2 and −2 times row 1.

$$\begin{bmatrix} 1 & 1 & 1 & \vdots & 21 \\ ⓪ & -1 & -2 & \vdots & -19 \\ 0 & 1 & 3 & \vdots & 25 \end{bmatrix}$$

• Inspect column 2.

Row 1:	Row 2:	Row 3:
Change the entry to 0.	Change the entry to 1.	Change the entry to 0.
$R_2 + R_1 \rightarrow R_1$	$-1R_2 \rightarrow R_2$	$-1R_2 + R_3 \rightarrow R_3$

$$\begin{bmatrix} 1 & ⓪ & -1 & \vdots & 2 \\ 0 & -1 & -2 & \vdots & -19 \\ 0 & 1 & 3 & \vdots & 25 \end{bmatrix} \begin{bmatrix} 1 & 0 & -1 & \vdots & 2 \\ 0 & ① & 2 & \vdots & 19 \\ 0 & 1 & 3 & \vdots & 25 \end{bmatrix} \begin{bmatrix} 1 & 0 & -1 & \vdots & 2 \\ 0 & 1 & 2 & \vdots & 19 \\ 0 & ⓪ & 1 & \vdots & 6 \end{bmatrix}$$

• Inspect column 3.

Row 1:	Row 2:
Change the entry to 0.	Change the entry to 0.
$R_3 + R_1 \rightarrow R_1$	$-2R_3 + R_2 \rightarrow R_2$

$$\begin{bmatrix} 1 & 0 & ⓪ & \vdots & 8 \\ 0 & 1 & 2 & \vdots & 19 \\ 0 & 0 & 1 & \vdots & 6 \end{bmatrix} \begin{bmatrix} 1 & 0 & 0 & \vdots & 8 \\ 0 & 1 & ⓪ & \vdots & 7 \\ 0 & 0 & 1 & \vdots & 6 \end{bmatrix}$$

The matrix is now in reduced row-echelon form.

$$\begin{bmatrix} 1 & 0 & 0 & \vdots & 8 \\ 0 & 1 & 0 & \vdots & 7 \\ 0 & 0 & 1 & \vdots & 6 \end{bmatrix} \quad \begin{matrix} m = 8 \\ a = 7 \\ n = 6 \end{matrix}$$

b. Maya receives $8 an hour; since she works 3 hours, she will earn $24.
Amit receives $7 an hour and works 3 hours, so he will earn $21.
Nina receives $6 an hour and works 4 hours, so she will earn $24.

CHECKPOINT ✔ Check the solution to Example 1 by using substitution.

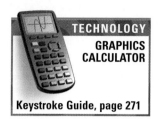
On many graphics calculators, you can enter an augmented matrix, and the calculator will give you the reduced row-echelon form. The displays below show the augmented matrix and the reduced row-echelon form for the system in Example 1.

Sometimes row operations do not result in an identity matrix in the coefficient columns. Examples 2 and 3 illustrate two possible alternative results and how they show that the system is inconsistent or dependent.

E X A M P L E ② Use the row-reduction method to solve the system below. Then classify the system as independent, dependent, or inconsistent.

$$\begin{cases} x - 2y - 2z = 6 \\ 3x - 4y + z = -1 \\ 5x - 8y - 3z = 11 \end{cases}$$

● **SOLUTION**

For the given system, the augmented matrix is shown below.

$$\begin{bmatrix} 1 & -2 & -2 & \vdots & 6 \\ 3 & -4 & 1 & \vdots & -1 \\ 5 & -8 & -3 & \vdots & 11 \end{bmatrix}$$

The reduced row-echelon form of the matrix and the corresponding simplified system of equations are shown below.

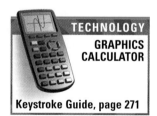
$$\rightarrow \begin{cases} x + 5z = -13 \\ y + 3.5z = -9.5 \\ 0z = 0 \end{cases} \rightarrow \begin{cases} x = -13 - 5z \\ y = -9.5 - 3.5z \\ 0z = 0 \end{cases}$$

This equation tells you that z can be any real number.

The system is dependent because it has infinitely many solutions. You can describe the solution as $(-13 - 5z, -9.5 - 3.5z, z)$, where z can be any real number.

TRY THIS Use the row-reduction method to solve the system below. Then classify the system as independent, dependent, or inconsistent.

$$\begin{cases} 2x + 3y - z = -2 \\ x + 2y + 2z = 8 \\ 5x + 9y + 5z = 22 \end{cases}$$

3 Use the row-reduction method to solve the system below. Then classify the system as independent, dependent, or inconsistent.

$$\begin{cases} 2x + 6y - 4z = 1 \\ x + 3y - 2z = 4 \\ 2x + y - 3z = -7 \end{cases}$$

● SOLUTION

Write the augmented matrix.

$$\begin{bmatrix} 2 & 6 & -4 & : & 1 \\ 1 & 3 & -2 & : & 4 \\ 2 & 1 & -3 & : & -7 \end{bmatrix}$$

Find the reduced row-echelon form and the simplified system as shown below.

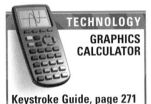

TECHNOLOGY

GRAPHICS CALCULATOR

Keystroke Guide, page 271

```
rref([A])
  [[1 0 -1.4 0]
   [0 1 -.2  0]
   [0 0 0    1]]
```

$$\rightarrow \begin{cases} x - 1.4z = 0 \\ y - 0.2z = 0 \\ 0 = 1 \end{cases}$$

This false statement tells you that there is no solution.

The system is inconsistent.

TRY THIS Use the row-reduction method to solve the system below. Then classify the system as independent, dependent, or inconsistent.

$$\begin{cases} 4x - 4y - 3z = 2 \\ 4x + 3z = 3 \\ 4y + 6z = 3 \end{cases}$$

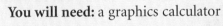

Activity

Exploring Systems of Three Equations

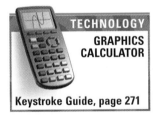

TECHNOLOGY

GRAPHICS CALCULATOR

Keystroke Guide, page 271

CONNECTION

GEOMETRY

You will need: a graphics calculator

The graphics calculator display at right shows the graph of the system below.

$$\begin{cases} -5x + 2y = 6 \\ x + 2y = -8 \\ x + 2y = 8 \end{cases}$$

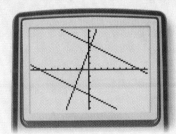

1. How can you tell from the system of equations that two of the lines are parallel?

2. Modify the equations in the system so that the intersections of the graphs form the vertices of a triangle. Graph the new system on a graphics calculator. What must be true of the system you wrote in order for the vertices of a triangle to be formed?

CHECKPOINT ✔ 3. Modify the equations in the original system so that the intersections of the graphs form the vertices of a right triangle. Graph the new system on a graphics calculator. Explain your strategy for changing the equations.

● *Communicate*

1. Describe how the second and third elementary row operations listed on page 252 may correspond to the operations you perform on equations in a system when using the elimination method.

2. Explain how to write the augmented matrix for the system of equations at right.

$$\begin{cases} x - 4y + 7z = 17 \\ 2x + y - z = -5 \\ x + 4z = 13 \end{cases}$$

3. Write the system of equations represented by the augmented matrix at right.

$$\begin{bmatrix} -3 & -4 & 0 & \vdots & 2 \\ 4 & 2 & -3 & \vdots & 6 \\ -2 & 0 & 1 & \vdots & -6 \end{bmatrix}$$

4. State which row operations were applied to the first matrix to obtain the second matrix.

$$\begin{bmatrix} 1 & 2 & 3 & \vdots & 1 \\ 2 & 5 & 7 & \vdots & 3 \\ 3 & 2 & 1 & \vdots & 1 \end{bmatrix} \rightarrow \begin{bmatrix} 2 & 4 & 6 & \vdots & 2 \\ 2 & 5 & 7 & \vdots & 3 \\ 5 & 7 & 8 & \vdots & 4 \end{bmatrix}$$

● *Guided Skills Practice*

APPLICATION

5. MANUFACTURING A company makes a total of 120 leather and imitation-leather jackets per week. The leather jackets cost the company $200 each to produce and the imitation-leather cost the company $50 each to produce. The company spends $12,750 per week on costs for producing jackets. *(EXAMPLE 1)*

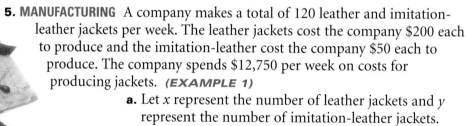

a. Let x represent the number of leather jackets and y represent the number of imitation-leather jackets. Write a system of linear equations to represent this situation.

b. Write an augmented matrix and use the row-reduction method to solve the system and find the number of each type of jacket made each week.

Use the row-reduction method to solve each system. Then classify each system as independent, dependent, or inconsistent.
(EXAMPLES 2 AND 3)

6. $\begin{cases} x + 2y + z = 3 \\ y + 2z = 3 \\ y + 2z = 5 \end{cases}$

7. $\begin{cases} x + y = 3 \\ 3x + y = 15 \\ 5x + y + z = 25 \end{cases}$

● *Practice and Apply*

Write the augmented matrix for each system of equations.

8. $\begin{cases} x + 3y = 23 \\ 4x - 2y = -6 \end{cases}$

9. $\begin{cases} -x + 2y - 5z = 23 \\ 2x + 7z = 19 \\ 5x - 2y + z = -10 \end{cases}$

10. $\begin{cases} 2x - 5y - z = -32 \\ -x + 4y + 2z = 34 \\ 3x + 7y - 3z = -2 \end{cases}$

Perform the indicated row operations on matrix *A*.

11. $3R_1 + R_2 \rightarrow R_2$

12. $-8R_1 + R_3 \rightarrow R_3$

$$A = \begin{bmatrix} -1 & 2 & -5 & \vdots & 4 \\ 3 & 7 & -2 & \vdots & 3 \\ -8 & 4 & 1 & \vdots & -7 \end{bmatrix}$$

Find the reduced row-echelon form of each matrix.

13. $\begin{bmatrix} 2 & -2 & \vdots & -2 \\ 0 & 1 & \vdots & 3 \end{bmatrix}$

14. $\begin{bmatrix} 3 & 3 & 6 & \vdots & 30 \\ 0 & 1 & 0 & \vdots & 3 \\ 0 & 0 & 2 & \vdots & 2 \end{bmatrix}$

15. $\begin{bmatrix} 4 & 4 & \vdots & 32 \\ 1 & 3 & \vdots & 16 \end{bmatrix}$

16. $\begin{bmatrix} 3 & 0 & 3 & \vdots & 24 \\ 1 & 2 & 3 & \vdots & 28 \\ 0 & 0 & 2 & \vdots & 12 \end{bmatrix}$

17. $\begin{bmatrix} 5 & 2 & 1 & \vdots & -4 \\ 7 & 4 & 1 & \vdots & -4 \\ 3 & 2 & 1 & \vdots & 0 \end{bmatrix}$

18. $\begin{bmatrix} 2 & 1 & 2 & \vdots & 19 \\ 3 & 3 & 3 & \vdots & 33 \\ 2 & 2 & 4 & \vdots & 30 \end{bmatrix}$

Solve each system of equations by using the row-reduction method. Show each step.

19. $\begin{cases} 4x + 3y = 1 \\ 3x - 2y = 5 \end{cases}$

20. $\begin{cases} x + 2y = 16 \\ 2x + y = 11 \end{cases}$

21. $\begin{cases} 3x - y = 4 \\ x + 4y = -3 \end{cases}$

22. $\begin{cases} x + 4y - 3z = -13 \\ -2y + z = 1 \\ -6z = -30 \end{cases}$

23. $\begin{cases} 4x - 7y + 5z = -52 \\ 3y + 8z = 7 \\ -z = 1 \end{cases}$

24. $\begin{cases} 2x - 3y + z = 2 \\ x - y + 2z = 2 \\ x + 2y - 3z = 4 \end{cases}$

25. $\begin{cases} 2x + y + 3z = 2 \\ x + y + 8z = 2 \\ x + y + z = 3 \end{cases}$

26. $\begin{cases} 2x - y + z = 1 \\ 2x + 2z = 4 \\ x + y + z = 4 \end{cases}$

27. $\begin{cases} 2x + 5z = 5 \\ x - 3y + 2z = 2 \\ 3x + y + 3z = 3 \end{cases}$

28. $\begin{cases} y + 2z = \dfrac{3}{2} \\ 2x + 2y + 2z = 4 \\ x + y = 2 \end{cases}$

29. $\begin{cases} 3x + 3y = -2 \\ x + z = 4 \\ 2x + y = 0 \end{cases}$

30. $\begin{cases} 2x + y + 4z = 4 \\ x - 3y + 2z = 2 \\ 3x + y + 6z = 6 \end{cases}$

Classify each system as inconsistent, dependent, or independent.

31 $\begin{cases} x + y = 3 \\ 2x + 2y = 6 \end{cases}$

32 $\begin{cases} x + y = 0 \\ x + y = 1 \end{cases}$

33 $\begin{cases} 2x + 3y = 8 \\ 3x + 2y = 7 \end{cases}$

34 $\begin{cases} 2x + y + 4z = 1 \\ 3x - y + z = 2 \\ x + 2y - z = -1 \end{cases}$

35 $\begin{cases} x + y + z = 2 \\ 3x + 2y + z = 3 \\ 6x + 4y + 2z = 6 \end{cases}$

36 $\begin{cases} 3x + 2y + z = 1 \\ x - y - z = -5 \\ 6x + 4y + 2z = 2 \end{cases}$

CHALLENGE

37. To perform a row operation on an $n \times n$ matrix *A*, you can perform the row operations on the identity matrix I_n to obtain a matrix *E*. The product *EA* is same as the product obtained by performing the row operations on *A* directly.

Let $A = \begin{bmatrix} 1 & 2 \\ 3 & 4 \end{bmatrix}$. Perform each operation below by using this technique.

First find matrix *E*. Then find *EA*. Verify that *EA* is equivalent to the matrix that results from performing the operations on *A* directly.

a. Multiply the entries in row 1 by 2.

b. Interchange rows 1 and 2.

c. Replace row 2 with the sum of 2 times the entries in row 1 and the entries in row 2.

38. CULTURAL CONNECTION: CHINA Over 2000 years ago, the Chinese used a counting board to solve systems of equations. The counting board later evolved into the abacus.

The sticks, or rod numerals, arranged on the counting board at right represent the system of equations below.

$$\begin{cases} 3x + 2y + z = 39 \\ 2x + 3y + z = 34 \\ x + 2y + 3z = 26 \end{cases}$$

a. How are numbers greater than 5 represented?

b. How are the numerals in the tens place represented?

c. How is the Chinese counting board similar to an augmented matrix?

d. Write the system of equations represented on the Chinese counting board at right.

e. Write the system of equations represented on the Chinese counting board at right.

39. PROBABILITY Suppose that a certain experiment has three possible outcomes with probabilities p_1, p_2, and p_3. The sum of p_1, p_2, and p_3 is 1. If $3p_1 + 18p_2 - 12p_3 = 3$ and $p_1 - 2p_2 - 2p_3 = 0$, find the probabilities of the three outcomes by solving a system of 3 equations.

40. MANUFACTURING A tool company manufactures pliers and scissors. In one hour the company uses 140 units of steel and 290 units of aluminum. Each pair of scissors requires 1 unit of steel and 3 units of aluminum. Each pair of pliers contains 2 units of steel and 4 units of aluminum. How many scissors and how many pliers can the tool company make in one hour?

41. TRAVEL A traveler is going south along the west coast of South America through the Andes mountain range. While in Peru, the traveler spent $20 per day on housing and $30 per day on food and travel. Passing through Bolivia, the traveler spent $30 per day on housing and $20 per day on food and travel. Finally, while following the long coast of Chile, the traveler spent $20 per day both for housing and for food and travel. In each country, the traveler spent $10 per day on miscellaneous items. The traveler spent a total of $220 on housing, $230 on food and travel, and $100 on miscellaneous items. Write and solve a system of linear equations in three variables to find the number of days the traveler spent in each country.

Look Back

Tell whether each equation is linear. *(LESSON 1.1)*

42. $y + 1 = 5$ **43.** $y + x^2 = 6$ **44.** $y + x = 5$

State whether each relation represents a function. Explain. *(LESSON 2.3)*

45. $\{(-1, 6), (0, 6), (1, 6), (2, 6)\}$ **46.** $\{(0, 14), (1, 12), (2, 10), (3, 8)\}$

47. $\{(-2, 0), (0, 0), (2, 0), (4, 0)\}$ **48.** $\{(-1, 0), (0, -1), (0, 1), (1, 0)\}$

49. Graph the piecewise function $f(x) = \begin{cases} x^2 - 1 & \text{if } 0 \le x < 5 \\ 3x + 9 & \text{if } 5 \le x < 10 \end{cases}$. *(LESSON 2.6)*

BUSINESS A movie theater charges $5 for an adult ticket and $3 for a child's ticket. The theater needs to sell at least $2500 worth of tickets to cover its expenses. Graph the solution to each scenario. *(LESSON 3.3)*

50. The theater sells less than $2500 worth of tickets.

51. The theater breaks even, selling exactly $2500 worth of tickets.

52. The theater makes a profit, selling more than $2500 worth of tickets.

53. Let $A = \begin{bmatrix} 3 & 2 & -2 \\ 1 & 1 & 4 \\ -1 & 2 & 3 \end{bmatrix}$ and $B = \begin{bmatrix} 2 & 3 & 1 \\ -1 & -2 & 2 \\ 4 & 1 & -4 \end{bmatrix}$. *(LESSON 4.2)*

    a. Find AB.   **b.** Find BA.   **c.** Is AB equal to BA?

Look Beyond

54. Let the points $(0, 0)$, $(1, 4)$ and $(2, 12)$ be on the graph of the function $f(x) = ax^2 + bx + c$. Write a system of three equations in terms of a, b, and c. Solve the system and use the values to write the function f.

PROJECT CHAPTER FOUR

SPELL CHECK

When you write a term paper on your word processor or computer, how do you make sure that your spelling is correct? Do you use spell-checker software? Have you ever wondered how it works? The basis for a spell-checker is a modeling process that uses a directed network.

Spelling

Not in Dictionary: classs

Change To: | class

Suggestions: | class
clasps
classes
claps

Add Words To: Custom Dictionary ▼

[Ignore] [Ignore All]
[Change] [Change All]
[Add] [Close]
[Suggest] [Options...]

Activity 1

1. Place the six words below in a circular arrangement. Each word will represent a vertex in a directed network.

   glass   clams   class   clays   clasp   claps

2. With a double-headed arrow, connect the words in which 4 of the 5 letter positions match exactly, while 1 of the 5 positions contains a non-matching letter. For example, *clays* and *claps* can be joined with a double-headed arrow, but *clays* and *clasp* cannot be.

3. Represent the directed network in an adjacency matrix, W. Record a 1 if there is an arrow joining two words, or vertices. Otherwise record a 0.

4. Which row or column in W represents the paths leading to the word *clasp*?

5. Which row or column in W represents the paths going from the word *clays*?

Activity 2

1. Using your results from Activity 1, find the number of two-stage paths from *class* to *clams*. List these paths.

2. Find the number of two-stage paths from *clams* to *clams*. List these paths.

Activity 3

The matrix $W + W^2$ gives the total number of one-stage and two-stage paths from one word to another.

1. Find $W + W^2$.

2. In how many ways can *clays* be connected to *claps* by using only a one-stage or a two-stage path? Which entry in the matrix gives this number? List the paths.

4

Chapter Review and Assessment

Key Skills & Exercises

LESSON 4.1

Key Skills

Add and subtract matrices, and find the scalar product of a number and a matrix.

$$\begin{bmatrix} 0 & 7 \\ 1 & 2 \end{bmatrix} - \begin{bmatrix} -2 & 1 \\ 3 & 9 \end{bmatrix} + 2\begin{bmatrix} 2 & 8 \\ 0 & -1 \end{bmatrix}$$

$$= \begin{bmatrix} 0-(-2) & 7-1 \\ 1-3 & 2-9 \end{bmatrix} + \begin{bmatrix} 2(2) & 2(8) \\ 2(0) & 2(-1) \end{bmatrix}$$

$$= \begin{bmatrix} 2 & 6 \\ -2 & -7 \end{bmatrix} + \begin{bmatrix} 4 & 16 \\ 0 & -2 \end{bmatrix}$$

$$= \begin{bmatrix} 2+6 & 4+16 \\ -2+0 & -7-2 \end{bmatrix}$$

$$= \begin{bmatrix} 8 & 20 \\ -2 & -9 \end{bmatrix}$$

Exercises

Let $A = \begin{bmatrix} -1 & 2 & 1 \\ 0 & 5 & 3 \end{bmatrix}$, $B = \begin{bmatrix} 6 & -9 & 4 \\ 1 & 0 & 7 \end{bmatrix}$, and

$C = \begin{bmatrix} 0 & -1 & -2 \\ 2 & 4 & 7 \end{bmatrix}$. Perform the indicated

operations.

1. $A + B$ 2. $B - A$
3. $C - C$ 4. $B + A - C$
5. $11C$ 6. $-3B$
7. $C - 3A$ 8. $0.5A - 3B$
9. $-C - 2B$ 10. $A + 2C - B$

LESSON 4.2

Key Skills

Multiply matrices.

In order to multiply matrices, the inner dimensions must be the same. The dimensions of the product matrix are the result of the outer dimensions. For example, the product of a 3×2 matrix and a 2×1 matrix is a 3×1 matrix.

$$\begin{bmatrix} 4 & 0 \\ -1 & 3 \\ 2 & -5 \end{bmatrix}\begin{bmatrix} 1 \\ -3 \end{bmatrix} = \begin{bmatrix} 4(1) + 0(-3) \\ -1(1) + 3(-3) \\ 2(1) + (-5)(-3) \end{bmatrix}$$

$$= \begin{bmatrix} 4 \\ -10 \\ 17 \end{bmatrix}$$

Exercises

Let $A = \begin{bmatrix} -9 & 2 \\ 4 & 1 \end{bmatrix}$, $B = \begin{bmatrix} 4 & 5 \\ -2 & 1 \\ 3 & 0 \end{bmatrix}$, and

$C = \begin{bmatrix} 1 & -2 & 1 \\ 0 & 3 & -4 \end{bmatrix}$. Find each product, if

possible.

11. AB 12. BC
13. BA 14. AC
15. CA 16. CB

Key Skills

Find the inverse and the determinant of a matrix.

Let $C = \begin{bmatrix} 4 & 2 \\ -1 & -3 \end{bmatrix}$. Find the determinant and the inverse of the matrix, if it exists.

$$\det(C) = (4)(-3) - (2)(-1) = -10$$

If $\det(C) \neq 0$, then C^{-1} exists.

Use a graphics calculator to find the inverse of the matrix.

$C^{-1} = \begin{bmatrix} 0.3 & 0.2 \\ -0.1 & -0.4 \end{bmatrix}$

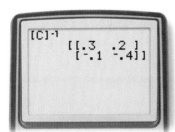

Exercises

Find the determinant and inverse of each matrix. If the inverse matrix does not exist, write *no inverse*.

17. $\begin{bmatrix} -2 & 3 \\ 5 & 0 \end{bmatrix}$ 18. $\begin{bmatrix} 3 & 1 \\ 7 & 9 \end{bmatrix}$ 19. $\begin{bmatrix} 2 & 2 \\ 2 & 2 \end{bmatrix}$

20. $\begin{bmatrix} 3 & 3 \\ 1 & 1 \end{bmatrix}$ 21. $\begin{bmatrix} 5 & -1 \\ -1 & 5 \end{bmatrix}$ 22. $\begin{bmatrix} 0 & 7 \\ -2 & 0 \end{bmatrix}$

23. $\begin{bmatrix} -3 & -4 \\ -1 & -3 \end{bmatrix}$ 24. $\begin{bmatrix} 5 & 6 \\ 7 & 8 \end{bmatrix}$ 25. $\begin{bmatrix} -9 & 12 \\ 3 & -4 \end{bmatrix}$

26. Let $A = \begin{bmatrix} 5 & 7 \\ 7 & 10 \end{bmatrix}$ and $B = \begin{bmatrix} 10 & -7 \\ -7 & 5 \end{bmatrix}$. Show that A and B are inverses of one another.

Key Skills

Use matrices to solve systems of linear equations.

Write the system as a matrix equation, $AX = B$. Insert 0 for any missing variables in an equation.

$$\begin{cases} x + 2y - z = -3 \\ -2x + y - 3z = -9 \\ y + 2z = 3 \end{cases} \rightarrow \underset{A}{\begin{bmatrix} 1 & 2 & -1 \\ -2 & 1 & -3 \\ 0 & 1 & 2 \end{bmatrix}} \underset{X}{\begin{bmatrix} x \\ y \\ z \end{bmatrix}} = \underset{B}{\begin{bmatrix} -3 \\ -9 \\ 3 \end{bmatrix}}$$

Solve the matrix equation by using an inverse matrix.

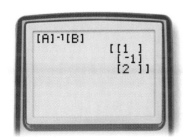

$$X = A^{-1}B \rightarrow \begin{bmatrix} x \\ y \\ z \end{bmatrix} = \begin{bmatrix} 1 \\ -1 \\ 2 \end{bmatrix}$$

$x = 1$, $y = -1$, and $z = 2$

Exercises

Use a matrix equation to solve each system of linear equations, if possible.

27. $\begin{cases} 6x + 4y = 12 \\ 3x + 2y = 6 \end{cases}$

28. $\begin{cases} 2x + y = 3 \\ 3x - 2y = 8 \end{cases}$

29. $\begin{cases} 3x - y = -1 \\ 2x - y + z = -6 \\ x + 4y - z = 9 \end{cases}$

30. $\begin{cases} 2x - 3y + 5z = 5 \\ x - y - 2z = 2 \\ -3x + 3y + 6z = 5 \end{cases}$

31. $\begin{cases} -\frac{1}{6}y = -\frac{1}{6} - \frac{1}{3}x \\ x + \frac{1}{2}z = -3 + \frac{1}{2}y \\ \frac{1}{5}x + \frac{4}{5}y = \frac{9}{5} + \frac{1}{5}z \end{cases}$

32. **JEWELRY** A jeweler plans to combine two silver alloys to make 50 grams of a new alloy that is 75% silver and contains 37.5 grams of pure silver (75% of 50 grams). If one silver alloy is 80% silver and the other is 60% silver, how many grams of each are needed?

Key Skills

Solve a system of linear equations by using elementary row operations.

Write the system as an augmented matrix.

$$\begin{cases} 2x + 3y - z = -7 \\ x + y - z = -4 \\ 3x - 2y - 3z = -7 \end{cases} \rightarrow \begin{bmatrix} 2 & 3 & -1 & : & -7 \\ 1 & 1 & -1 & : & -4 \\ 3 & -2 & -3 & : & -7 \end{bmatrix}$$

Use a calculator to obtain the reduced row-echelon form.

The solution for this independent system is $x = -1$, $y = -1$, and $z = 2$.

From the reduced row-echelon form of an augmented matrix, you can classify the system as dependent or inconsistent.

Dependent system

$$\begin{bmatrix} 1 & 0 & 5 & : & -13 \\ 0 & 1 & 3.5 & : & -9.5 \\ 0 & 0 & 0 & : & 0 \end{bmatrix}$$

$0 = 0$ is always a true statement.

Inconsistent system

$$\begin{bmatrix} 1 & 0 & 1 & : & 0 \\ 0 & 1 & 3 & : & 0 \\ 0 & 0 & 0 & : & 1 \end{bmatrix}$$

$0 = 1$ is always a false statement.

Exercises

Use the row-reduction method to solve each system, if possible. Then classify each system as independent, dependent, or inconsistent.

33. $\begin{cases} 3x - 2y + z = -5 \\ -2x + 3y - 3z = 12 \\ 3x - 2y - 2z = 4 \end{cases}$

34. $\begin{cases} 3x - y + 2z = 9 \\ x - 2y - 3z = -1 \\ 2x - 3y + z = 10 \end{cases}$

35. $\begin{cases} x - 2y + z = -2 \\ 2x + 6y = 12 \\ 3x - y + 2z = 4 \end{cases}$

36. $\begin{cases} 3x - y - 2z = 0 \\ x + 2y - 4z = 0 \\ 2x - 10y + 12z = 0 \end{cases}$

37. $\begin{cases} x - 3y - z = 0 \\ 2x - y - 4z = 0 \\ -2x + 6y - 4z = 0 \end{cases}$

38. $\begin{cases} 4x + 6y - 2z = 10 \\ 4x - 5y + 5z = -3 \\ 3x - y + 2z = 1 \end{cases}$

Application

39. FUND-RAISING Two hundred and ten people attended a school carnival. The total amount of money collected for tickets was $710. Prices were $5 for regular admission, $3 for students, and $1 for children. The number of regular tickets sold was 10 more than twice the number of child tickets sold. Write a system of equations to find the number of regular tickets, student tickets, and child tickets sold. Solve the system by using a matrix equation.

Alternative Assessment

Performance Assessment

1. ORGANIZING INFORMATION The hours worked each day for each employee is recorded in the table below.

	M	Tu	W	Th	F	S
Jones	7	7	6	8	8	0
Gutierrez	6	6	6	0	0	4
Rodman	8	8	8	7	8	0
McDonald	4	3	4	6	0	4

a. Represent this information in a 4×6 matrix called A. What does a_{32} represent? What does a_{23} represent?

b. If all of the employees earn the same hourly wage, what matrix operation can you use to obtain a matrix for the daily earnings for each employee?

c. If all of the employees earn the same hourly wage, how can you use the matrix to calculate the weekly earnings for each employee?

2. TRANSFORMATIONS

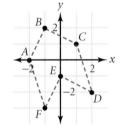

a. Write a matrix, T, to represent the 6-vertex polygon shown at right.

b. Find $3T$ and graph the polygon that it represents. Describe the transformation.

c. Use matrix row operations to multiply every x-coordinate of the original polygon by 2 and every y-coordinate by -3. Graph the resulting polygon and describe the transformation.

Portfolio Projects

1. TRANSFORMATIONS Create your own design by performing stretches, compressions, or other combinations of transformations on a figure, such as the example below.

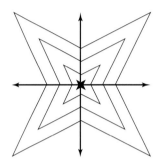

The original figure for this design is shown below:

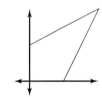

2. CRAMER'S RULE Research Cramer's rule for solving systems of equations. How does it involve determinants? Apply Cramer's rule to an independent system of three equations in three variables. What happens when Cramer's rule is applied to dependent or inconsistent systems? What are some of the advantages of this method? When is it most useful?

3. SOLVING LINEAR SYSTEMS Make a summary chart that lists all five methods of solving linear systems that you have learned so far. Provide a solved example for each method. Include the advantages and disadvantages of each method.

College Entrance Exam Practice

QUANTITATIVE COMPARISON For Items 1–4, write

A if the quantity in Column A is greater than the quantity in Column B;
B if the quantity in Column B is greater than the quantity in Column A;
C if the two quantities are equal; or
D if the relationship cannot be determined from the given information.

	Column A	Column B	Answers
1.	$\begin{bmatrix} 2 & 3x+1 \\ 2y-1 & 5 \end{bmatrix} = \begin{bmatrix} 2x-2 & -3y+1 \\ -5 & 5 \end{bmatrix}$ $\boxed{x}$	$\boxed{y}$	Ⓐ Ⓑ Ⓒ Ⓓ [Lesson 4.1]
2.	$\boxed{\lfloor 5.001 \rfloor - \lceil 3.125 \rceil}$	$\boxed{\lceil 1.75 \rceil - \lfloor 0.99 \rfloor}$	Ⓐ Ⓑ Ⓒ Ⓓ [Lesson 2.6]
3.	The value of x $\boxed{\dfrac{x}{2} - 1 = 3}$	$\boxed{1 - 2x = 5}$	Ⓐ Ⓑ Ⓒ Ⓓ [Lesson 1.6]
4.	$\begin{cases} y = 10 - 3x \\ 2x + 3y = -5 \end{cases}$ $\boxed{x}$	$\boxed{y}$	Ⓐ Ⓑ Ⓒ Ⓓ [Lesson 3.1]

5. Find the slope of the line containing the points $(4, 5)$ and $(6, 3)$. *(LESSON 1.3)*

   a. -2 **b.** 2 **c.** 1 **d.** -1

6. Simplify $\left(\dfrac{-2x^4 y^{-1}}{5x^{-2}y^4}\right)^3$. *(LESSON 2.2)*

   a. $\dfrac{8}{5}x^{14}y^{-7}$ **b.** $-\dfrac{8}{125}x^{18}y^{-15}$

   c. $\dfrac{8}{125}x^{-18}y^{15}$ **d.** $\dfrac{8}{5}x^{18}y^{-9}$

7. If $A = \begin{bmatrix} 3 & 0 & -2 \\ -1 & 2 & 1 \\ 1 & 5 & -1 \end{bmatrix}$ and $B = \begin{bmatrix} 0 & -3 & -1 \\ -1 & 4 & 3 \\ 2 & 2 & 2 \end{bmatrix}$, what is $A - B$? *(LESSON 4.1)*

   a. $\begin{bmatrix} 3 & 3 & -1 \\ 0 & -2 & -2 \\ -1 & 3 & -3 \end{bmatrix}$ **b.** $\begin{bmatrix} 3 & -3 & -3 \\ -2 & 6 & 4 \\ 3 & 7 & 1 \end{bmatrix}$

   c. $\begin{bmatrix} 3 & -3 & -3 \\ 0 & -2 & 4 \\ -1 & 7 & 1 \end{bmatrix}$ **d.** $\begin{bmatrix} 3 & 3 & -1 \\ -2 & -2 & -2 \\ 3 & 3 & -3 \end{bmatrix}$

8. Which equation in x and y represents this system of parametric equations? *(LESSON 3.6)*

$\begin{cases} x(t) = 2t + 1 \\ y(t) = t - 2 \end{cases}$

   a. $y = x - 5$

   b. $y = \dfrac{1}{2}x - \dfrac{5}{2}$

   c. $y = x - t - 3$

   d. $y = \dfrac{1}{2}x + 3$

9. Which set of ordered pairs represents a function? *(LESSON 2.3)*

   a. $\{(8, -9), (-9, 8), (8, 9)\}$
   b. $\{(0.1, 5), (0.2, 5), (0.1, 0)\}$
   c. $\{(-1, 4), (3, -2), (3, 2), (4, -1)\}$
   d. $\{(0, 1), (2, -2), (-2, 2), (1, 0)\}$

10. What is the inverse of $\{(0, 1), (2, -1), (3, 2), (4, -1)\}$? Is the inverse a function? *(LESSON 2.5)*

   a. $\{(0, 1), (2, -1), (3, 2), (4, -1)\}$; yes
   b. $\{(0, 1), (2, -1), (3, 2), (4, -1)\}$; no
   c. $\{(1, 0), (-1, 2), (2, 3), (-1, 4)\}$; yes
   d. $\{(1, 0), (-1, 2), (2, 3), (-1, 4)\}$; no

11 Let $A = \begin{bmatrix} 3 & -1 \\ -4 & 2 \end{bmatrix}$. Find A^{-1}. *(LESSON 4.3)*

a. $\begin{bmatrix} 3 & 1 \\ 4 & 2 \end{bmatrix}$ **b.** $\begin{bmatrix} 1 & 0.5 \\ 2 & 1.5 \end{bmatrix}$

c. $\begin{bmatrix} 2 & 1 \\ 4 & 3 \end{bmatrix}$ **d.** $\begin{bmatrix} 1.5 & 0.5 \\ 2 & 1 \end{bmatrix}$

ANATOMY The table below lists the height and weight of 10 young adult males with medium frames. The heights are in inches, and the weights are in pounds. *(LESSON 1.5)*

Height	65	66	70	69	67	68	67	66	68	71
Weight	146	145	157	158	145	149	155	141	154	159

12. Create a scatter plot, and identify the correlation as positive, negative, or none.

13 Use the least-squares line to estimate the weight of a 74-inch-tall male with a medium frame.

14. Solve $3 - 2x \geq -x + 2$, and graph the solution on a number line. *(LESSON 1.7)*

For Items 15 and 16, find $f \circ g$ and $g \circ f$. *(LESSON 2.4)*

15. $f(x) = 3x$, $g(x) = 2x - 1$

16. $f(x) = 2 - x$, $g(x) = x + 3$

17. Find the inverse of $f(x) = -5x + 3$. Is the inverse a function? *(LESSON 2.5)*

18. Graph the piecewise function below.
$$f(x) = \begin{cases} x - 6 & \text{if } 0 \leq x < 4 \\ -2x & \text{if } 4 \leq x < 10 \end{cases}$$ *(LESSON 2.6)*

19. Identify the transformation from the parent function $f(x) = |x|$ to $g(x) = -2|x - 4|$. *(LESSON 2.7)*

20. Graph the solution to $2(1 - 2x) \geq -y + 4$. *(LESSON 3.3)*

21. Graph the solution to the system of linear inequalities below. *(LESSON 3.4)*
$$\begin{cases} x + 2y \leq 4 \\ -2x + 3y \geq 6 \end{cases}$$

22. Solve the system below, if possible, by using a matrix equation. *(LESSON 4.4)*
$$\begin{cases} x + y - 2z = -1 \\ 2x + 2y + z = 3 \\ -3x - 2y - 3z = -4 \end{cases}$$

FREE-RESPONSE GRID The following questions may be answered by using a free-response grid such as that commonly used by standardized test services.

23. If the inverse function for $f(x) = \frac{2}{3}x - 7$ is written in the form $g(x) = ax + b$, what is the value of a? *(LESSON 2.5)*

24. Find the maximum value of the objective function $P = 2x + 3y$ given the constraints below. *(LESSON 3.5)*
$$\begin{cases} x + y \leq 4 \\ 2x + y \geq 2 \\ x \geq 0, y \geq 0 \end{cases}$$

25. Find the constant of variation, k, if y varies directly as x and $y = 102$ when $x = 3$. *(LESSON 1.4)*

SMALL BUSINESS Joshua wants to mix two types of candy. Candy A costs $2.50 per pound and candy B costs $4.50 per pound. Ten pounds of the combined candy mixture cost $37.00. *(LESSON 3.1)*

26. How many pounds of candy A are in the mixture?

27. How many pounds of candy B are in the mixture?

SPORTS The cost of an adult ticket to a football game is $4.00, and a student ticket is $2.50. The total amount received from 174 tickets was $1830. *(LESSON 3.2)*

28. How many adult tickets were sold?

29. How many student tickets were sold?

Keystroke Guide for Chapter 4

Essential keystroke sequences (using the model TI-82 or TI-83 graphics calculator) are presented below for all Activities and Examples found in this chapter that require or recommend the use of a graphics calculator.

> **🗗 internetconnect**
>
> **HRW** Keystrokes for other models of graphics calculators are found on the HRW Web site.

LESSON 4.1

E X A M P L E ③
Page 217

Let $A = \begin{bmatrix} -2 & 0 & 1 \\ 5 & -7 & 8 \end{bmatrix}$ and $B = \begin{bmatrix} 5 & 7 & -1 \\ 0 & 2 & -8 \end{bmatrix}$. For part a, find $A + B$.

For TI-83 Plus, press 2nd x^{-1} (MATRX) to access the matrix menu.

Enter the matrices:

> *Matrix A has dimensions of 2 × 3.*

MATRX **EDIT** **1:[A]** ENTER (Matrix[A]) 2 ENTER 3 ENTER (–) 2 ENTER 0 ENTER 1 ENTER 5 ENTER (–) 7 ENTER 8 ENTER MATRX **EDIT** **2:[B]** ENTER (Matrix[B]) 2 ENTER 3 ENTER 5 ENTER 7 ENTER (–) 1 ENTER 0 ENTER 2 ENTER (–) 8 ENTER 2nd MODE (QUIT)

Add the matrices:

MATRX **NAMES** **1:[A]** ENTER + MATRX **NAMES** **2:[B]** ENTER ENTER

For part **b**, find $A - B$ by using a similar keystroke sequence to subtract the matrices.

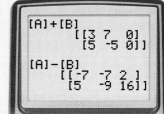

```
[A]+[B]
          [[3  7   0]
           [5  -5  0]]
[A]-[B]
          [[-7  -7  2 ]
           [5   -9  16]]
```

LESSON 4.2

E X A M P L E ③
Page 228

Enter matrix A, and find A^2.

Enter the matrix:

Use a keystroke sequence similar to that in Example 3 of Lesson 4.1.

Square the matrix:

MATRX **NAMES** **1:[A]** ENTER x^2 ENTER

```
[A]²
        [[0  0  2]
         [2  4  2]
         [1  3  5]]
```

TECHNOLOGY
Page 236

Enter matrix $A = \begin{bmatrix} 1 & 2 \\ 3 & 5 \end{bmatrix}$, and find its inverse.

Enter the matrix:

Use a keystroke sequence similar to that in Example 3 of Lesson 4.1.

Find the inverse of matrix A:

MATRX NAMES 1:[A] ENTER x^{-1} ENTER

E X A M P L E **2** For part a, enter matrix $A = \begin{bmatrix} 6 & 8 \\ 5 & 7 \end{bmatrix}$, and find its inverse.

Page 236

Enter the matrix:

Use a keystroke sequence similar to that in Example 3 of Lesson 4.1.

Find the inverse of matrix A:

MATRX NAMES 1:[A] ENTER x^{-1} ENTER

For parts **b** and **c**, use a similar keystroke sequence.

TECHNOLOGY

Page 237

Let $A = \begin{bmatrix} 6 & 5 \\ 7 & 6 \end{bmatrix}$ and $B = \begin{bmatrix} 7 & 15 & 0 \\ 2 & 15 & 2 \end{bmatrix}$. Find the product AB.

Enter the matrices:

Use a keystroke sequence similar to that in Example 3 of Lesson 4.1.

Find the product AB:

MATRX NAMES 1:[A] ENTER × MATRX NAMES

2:[B] ENTER ENTER

E X A M P L E **3** Let $A = \begin{bmatrix} 6 & 5 \\ 7 & 6 \end{bmatrix}$ and $C = \begin{bmatrix} 52 & 165 & 10 \\ 61 & 195 & 12 \end{bmatrix}$. Find $A^{-1}C$.

Page 237

Enter the matrices:

Use a keystroke sequence similar to that in Example 3 of Lesson 4.1.

Find the product $A^{-1}C$:

MATRX NAMES 1:[A] ENTER x^{-1} × MATRX NAMES 2:[C] ENTER ENTER

E X A M P L E **4**

Page 238

For part a, find the determinant of $\begin{bmatrix} 7 & 8 \\ 6 & 7 \end{bmatrix}$.

Enter the matrix:

Use a keystroke sequence similar to that in Example 3 of Lesson 4.1.

Find the determinant:

[MATRX] [MATH] [1:det(] [ENTER] [MATRX] [NAMES] [1:[A]] [ENTER] [ENTER]

LESSON 4.4

E X A M P L E **1**

Page 245

Solve $\begin{bmatrix} 1 & 1 \\ 0.05 & 0.14 \end{bmatrix}\begin{bmatrix} x \\ y \end{bmatrix} = \begin{bmatrix} 50{,}000 \\ 5000 \end{bmatrix}$ for $\begin{bmatrix} x \\ y \end{bmatrix}$.

Enter the matrices:

Enter the coefficient matrix, $A = \begin{bmatrix} 1 & 1 \\ 0.05 & 0.14 \end{bmatrix}$, and the constant matrix,

> *Do not enter the comma when you enter the number 50,000.*

$B = \begin{bmatrix} 50{,}000 \\ 5000 \end{bmatrix}$. Use a keystroke sequence

similar to that in Example 3 of Lesson 4.1.

Find the product $A^{-1}B$:

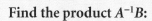

[MATRX] [NAMES] [1:[A]] [ENTER] [x⁻¹] [×]
[MATRX] [NAMES] [2:[B]] [ENTER] [ENTER]

E X A M P L E **2**

Page 246

Solve $\begin{bmatrix} 5 & 2 & -1 \\ 1 & -2 & 2 \\ 0 & 3 & 1 \end{bmatrix}\begin{bmatrix} x \\ y \\ z \end{bmatrix} = \begin{bmatrix} -7 \\ 0 \\ 17 \end{bmatrix}$ for $\begin{bmatrix} x \\ y \\ z \end{bmatrix}$.

Enter the matrices:

Enter matrix $A = \begin{bmatrix} 5 & 2 & -1 \\ 1 & -2 & 2 \\ 0 & 3 & 1 \end{bmatrix}$ and matrix $B = \begin{bmatrix} -7 \\ 0 \\ 17 \end{bmatrix}$.

Use a keystroke sequence similar to that in Example 3 of Lesson 4.1.

Find the product $A^{-1}B$:

Use a keystroke sequence similar to that in Example 1 of Lesson 4.4.

Activity

Page 246

For Step 1, find the determinant of matrix $A = \begin{bmatrix} 4 & 9 \\ 2 & 5 \end{bmatrix}$.

Enter the matrix:

Use a keystroke sequence similar to that in Example 3 of Lesson 4.1.

Find the determinant:

[MATRX] [MATH] [1:det(] [ENTER] [MATRX] [NAMES] [1:[A]] [ENTER] [ENTER]

E X A M P L E ❸ Solve $\begin{bmatrix} -3 & 4 \\ -6 & 8 \end{bmatrix}\begin{bmatrix} x \\ y \end{bmatrix} = \begin{bmatrix} 3 \\ 18 \end{bmatrix}$ for $\begin{bmatrix} x \\ y \end{bmatrix}$.

Page 247

Enter matrix $A = \begin{bmatrix} -3 & 4 \\ -6 & 8 \end{bmatrix}$ and matrix

$B = \begin{bmatrix} 3 \\ 18 \end{bmatrix}$, and find $A^{-1}B$. Use a keystroke

sequence similar to that in Example 1 of Lesson 4.4.

Solve $-3x + 4y = 3$ and $-6x + 8y = 18$ for y, and graph the lines:

Use viewing window $[-5, 5]$ by $[-5, 5]$.

[Y=] [( ] 3 [÷] 4 [ )] [X,T,θ,n] [+]

[( ] 3 [÷] 4 [ )] [ENTER] **(Y2=)**

[( ] 3 [÷] 4 [ )] [X,T,θ,n] [+] 3 [GRAPH]

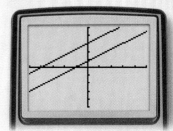

LESSON 4.5

T E C H N O L O G Y

Page 254

Find the reduced row-echelon form of the matrix $\begin{bmatrix} 1 & 1 & 1 & \vdots & 21 \\ 2 & 1 & 0 & \vdots & 23 \\ 0 & 1 & 3 & \vdots & 25 \end{bmatrix}$.

Enter the matrix:

Enter the augmented matrix as a 3×4 matrix without the column of dots. Use a keystroke sequence similar to that in Example 3 of Lesson 4.1.

> *The reduced row-echelon form can not be computed with one command on the TI-82.*

Find the reduced row-echelon form:

[MATRX] [MATH] [B:rref( ] [ENTER] [MATRX]

[NAMES] [1:[A]] [ENTER] [ )] [ENTER]

E X A M P L E S ❷ and ❸ **Find the reduced row-echelon form of the augmented matrix in each example.**

Pages 254 and 255

Use a keystroke sequence similar to that in the Technology example above.

Activity

Page 255

Graph the system of equations $\begin{cases} -5x + 2y = 6 \\ x + 2y = -8 \\ x + 2y = 8 \end{cases}$.

Use square viewing window $[-9.4, 9.4]$ by $[-6.2, 6.2]$.

Solve each equation for y, and use a keystroke sequence similar to that in Example 3 of Lesson 4.4.

Quadratic Functions

QUADRATIC FUNCTIONS HAVE IMPORTANT applications in science and engineering. For example, the parabolic path of a bouncing ball is described by a quadratic function. In fact, the motion of all falling objects can be described by quadratic functions. In this chapter, various techniques for solving quadratic equations are included, such as factoring and the quadratic formula.

Lessons

A basketball game is about to begin. The referee tosses the ball vertically into the air. A video camera follows the motion of the ball as it rises to its maximum height and then begins to fall.

The following table and graph represent the height of the ball in feet at 0.1-second intervals. After 1.1 seconds, one of the players makes contact with the ball by tapping it out of its vertical path to a teammate.

Time, x	Height, y
0.0	6.00
0.1	7.84
0.2	9.36
0.3	10.61
0.4	11.47
0.5	12.00
0.6	12.30
0.7	12.19
0.8	11.83
0.9	11.12
1.0	9.98
1.1	8.64

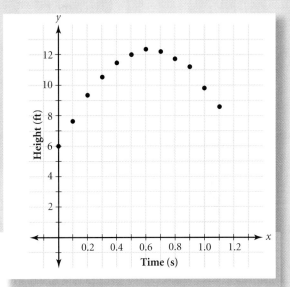

About the Chapter Project

The Chapter Project, *Out of This World*, extends the idea presented in the Portfolio Activities. By using different accelerations caused by the gravity on other planets, the height of the ball after a vertical toss on different planets can be compared with its height after a similar toss on Earth.

After completing the Chapter Project, you will be able to do the following:

- Use the function $h(t) = \frac{1}{2}gt^2 + v_0t + h_0$ to model the vertical motion of a basketball.
- Compare and contrast algebraic models of the form $h(t) = \frac{1}{2}gt^2 + v_0t + h_0$ for the vertical motion of the basketball on different planets.

About the Portfolio Activities

Throughout the chapter, you will be given opportunities to complete Portfolio Activities that are designed to support your work on the Chapter Project.

- Finding a reasonable model for the basketball data is included in the Portfolio Activity on page 280.
- Using various algebraic methods to answer questions about the height of the basketball along its path is in the Portfolio Activities on pages 298, 306, and 313.
- Comparing the algebraic model from physics with the quadratic regression model for the basketball data is included in the Portfolio Activity on page 329.
- Solving quadratic inequalities to answer questions about the height of the basketball along its path is in the Portfolio Activity on page 337.

Introduction to Quadratic Functions

Objectives

- Define, identify, and graph quadratic functions.

- Multiply linear binomials to produce a quadratic expression.

Why *Many real-world situations, such as the total stopping distance for a car, can be modeled by quadratic functions.*

APPLICATION

PHYSICS

Recall from Lesson 2.4 that the total stopping distance of a car on certain types of road surfaces is modeled by the function

$$d(x) = \frac{11}{10}x + \frac{1}{19}x^2,$$

where x is the speed of the car in miles per hour at the moment the hazard is observed and $d(x)$ is the distance in feet required to bring the car to a complete stop.

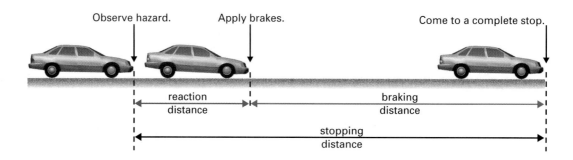

Observe hazard.   Apply brakes.   Come to a complete stop.

reaction distance

braking distance

stopping distance

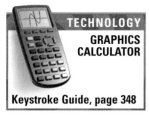

TECHNOLOGY

GRAPHICS CALCULATOR

Keystroke Guide, page 348

A table of values for the function d shows that a motorist driving at 20 miles per hour requires about 43 feet to come to a complete stop. However, a motorist traveling at 60 miles per hour requires over 255 feet to stop. Although the speed tripled, the total stopping distance increased by about 6 times. Clearly, the function for stopping distance is not a linear function.

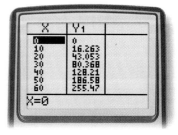

X	Y₁
0	0
10	16.263
20	43.053
30	80.368
40	128.21
50	186.58
60	255.47

X=0

Investigating Quadratic Functions

TECHNOLOGY
GRAPHICS CALCULATOR

You will need: a graphics calculator

1. Graph functions f and g from the first row of the table below on the same screen. Describe f and g and their graphs.

2. Graph $f \cdot g$ with f and g from the first row of the table on the same screen. Describe $f \cdot g$ and its graph. Then clear all three functions.

f	g	$f \cdot g$
$f(x) = 2x - 2$	$g(x) = 2x + 1$	$(f \cdot g)(x) = (2x - 2)(2x + 1)$
$f(x) = x + 1$	$g(x) = x + 1$	$(f \cdot g)(x) = (x + 1)(x + 1)$
$f(x) = 2x$	$g(x) = -2x + 1$	$(f \cdot g)(x) = 2x(-2x + 1)$
$f(x) = -x + 2$	$g(x) = 0.5x + 1$	$(f \cdot g)(x) = (-x + 2)(0.5x + 1)$

3. Repeat Steps 1 and 2 for the functions in the other rows of the table.

CHECKPOINT ✔ 4. In what ways do the graphs of f and g differ from the graph of $f \cdot g$?

CHECKPOINT ✔ 5. How are the x-intercepts of the graphs of f and g related to the x-intercepts of the graph of $f \cdot g$? Explain.

As the Activity suggests, when you multiply two linear functions with nonzero slopes, the result is a *quadratic function*.

In general, a **quadratic function** is any function that can be written in the form $f(x) = ax^2 + bx + c$, where $a \neq 0$. It is defined by a **quadratic expression**, which is an expression of the form $ax^2 + bx + c$, where $a \neq 0$. The stopping-distance function $d(x) = \frac{11}{10}x + \frac{1}{19}x^2$, or $d(x) = \frac{1}{19}x^2 + \frac{11}{10}x$, is an example of a quadratic function.

CHECKPOINT ✔ Identify a, b, and c for the stopping-distance function, d, on page 274.

E X A M P L E **1** Let $f(x) = (2x - 1)(3x + 5)$. Show that f represents a quadratic function. Identify a, b, and c when the function is written in the form $f(x) = ax^2 + bx + c$.

● **SOLUTION**

Method 1

$\begin{aligned} f(x) &= (2x - 1)(3x + 5) \\ &= (2x - 1)3x + (2x - 1)5 \\ &= 6x^2 - 3x + 10x - 5 \\ &= 6x^2 + 7x - 5 \end{aligned}$

Method 2

$\begin{aligned} f(x) &= (2x - 1)(3x + 5) \\ &= 2x(3x + 5) + (-1)(3x + 5) \\ &= 6x^2 + 10x - 3x - 5 \\ &= 6x^2 + 7x - 5 \end{aligned}$

Since $f(x) = 6x^2 + 7x - 5$ has the form $f(x) = ax^2 + bx + c$, f is a quadratic function with $a = 6$, $b = 7$, and $c = -5$.

TRY THIS Let $g(x) = (2x - 5)(x - 2)$. Show that g represents a quadratic function. Identify a, b, and c when the function is written in the form $g(x) = ax^2 + bx + c$.

The graph of a quadratic function is called a **parabola.** Two types of parabolas are graphed below. Notice that each parabola has an **axis of symmetry**, a line that divides the parabola into two parts that are mirror images of each other. The **vertex of a parabola** is either the lowest point on the graph or the highest point on the graph.

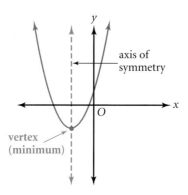

Notice that the axis of symmetry passes through the vertex of the parabola.

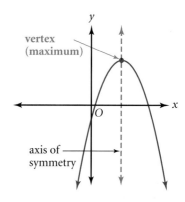

The domain of any quadratic function is the set of all real numbers. The range is either the set of all real numbers greater than or equal to the minimum value of the function (when the graph opens up) or the set of all real numbers less than or equal to the maximum value of the function (when the graph opens down).

E X A M P L E ② **Identify whether $f(x) = x^2 - x + 1$ has a maximum value or a minimum value at the vertex. Then give the approximate coordinates of the vertex.**

CONNECTION

MAXIMUM/MINIMUM

● **SOLUTION**

Method 1 Use a graph.
From the graph, you can see that the function has a minimum value.

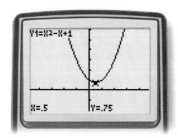

Tracing the graph, the coordinates of the vertex appear to be (0.5, 0.75).

Method 2 Use a table.
From a table of values you can see that an *x*-value between 0 and 1 gives the minimum value of the function.

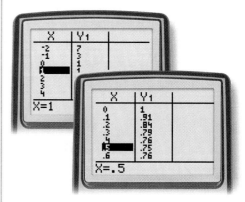

The coordinates of the vertex appear to be (0.5, 0.75).

TECHNOLOGY

GRAPHICS CALCULATOR

Keystroke Guide, page 348

TRY THIS Identify whether $f(x) = -2x^2 - 4x + 1$ has a maximum value or a minimum value at the vertex. Then give the approximate coordinates of the vertex.

CRITICAL THINKING Refer to solution Methods 1 and 2 in Example 2. If you know that $f(0) = f(1)$ for $f(x) = x^2 - x + 1$, describe how you can find the equation for the axis of symmetry.

By examining a in $f(x) = ax^2 + bx + c$, you can identify whether the function has a maximum or a minimum value.

Minimum and Maximum Values

Let $f(x) = ax^2 + bx + c$, where $a \neq 0$. The graph of f is a parabola.

If $a > 0$, the parabola opens up and the vertex is the lowest point. The y-coordinate of the vertex is the **minimum value** of f.

If $a < 0$, the parabola opens down and the vertex is the highest point. The y-coordinate of the vertex is the **maximum value** of f.

E X A M P L E ❸ State whether the parabola opens up or down and whether the y-coordinate of the vertex is the minimum value or the maximum value of the function. Then check by graphing.

CONNECTION

MAXIMUM/MINIMUM

a. $f(x) = x^2 + x - 6$ **b.** $g(x) = 5 + 4x - x^2$

● **SOLUTION**

a. In $f(x) = x^2 + x - 6$, the coefficient of x^2 is 1. Because $a > 0$, the parabola opens up and the function has a minimum value at the vertex.

b. In $g(x) = 5 + 4x - x^2$, the coefficient of x^2 is -1. Because $a < 0$, the parabola opens down and the function has a maximum value at the vertex.

TECHNOLOGY

GRAPHICS CALCULATOR

Keystroke Guide, page 348

CHECK

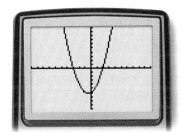

CHECK

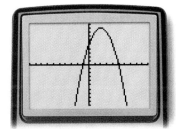

Exercises

● *Communicate*

1. Describe differences between the graphs of linear and quadratic functions.

2. Explain the difference between the expressions that define linear and quadratic functions.

3. How can you determine whether a quadratic function has a minimum value or a maximum value?

Guided Skills Practice

Show that each function is a quadratic function by writing it in the form $f(x) = ax^2 + bx + c$ and identifying a, b, and c. *(EXAMPLE 1)*

4. $f(x) = (x + 1)(x - 7)$ **5.** $g(x) = (x + 2)(x + 5)$ **6.** $f(x) = (2x + 5)(3x + 1)$

CONNECTIONS

MAXIMUM/MINIMUM Identify whether each function has a maximum or minimum value. Then give the approximate coordinates of the vertex. *(EXAMPLE 2)*

7. $g(x) = x^2 - 3x + 5$ **8.** $f(x) = 2 - 3x - x^2$ **9.** $g(x) = x^2 + 5x + 3$

MAXIMUM/MINIMUM State whether the parabola opens up or down and whether the y-coordinate of the vertex is the maximum value or the minimum value of the function. Then check by graphing. *(EXAMPLE 3)*

10. $f(x) = x^2 - 2x + 7$ **11.** $g(x) = -x^2 + 8x + 14$ **12.** $g(x) = -2x^2 - 5x + 1$

Practice and Apply

Show that each function is a quadratic function by writing it in the form $f(x) = ax^2 + bx + c$ and identifying a, b, and c.

13. $f(x) = (x - 3)(x + 8)$

14. $k(x) = (x + 3)(x - 5)$

15. $g(x) = (4 - x)(7 + x)$

16. $g(x) = (10 - x)(x + 4)$

17. $g(x) = -(x - 2)(x + 6)$

18. $f(x) = -(x + 3)(x - 9)$

19. $f(x) = 3(x - 2)(x + 1)$

20. $h(x) = 2(x + 1)(3x - 4)$

21. $h(x) = x(x - 3)$

22. $f(x) = 2x(x + 5)$

23. $g(x) = (2x + 3)(4 - x)$

24. $f(x) = (4x + 1)(4 - x)$

25. $h(x) = (x - 4)(x + 4)$

26. $f(x) = (x - 6)(x + 6)$

Identify whether each function is a quadratic function. Use a graph to check your answers.

27. $f(x) = 3 - x^2$

28. $g(s) = 3 - s$

29. $f(t) = \frac{1}{4}t^2 + \frac{1}{2}t - \frac{2}{3}$

30. $h(x) = \frac{3x^2 + 4x + 1}{x + 1}$

31. $g(t) = t^2 - t^2(t + 7)$

32. $h(x) = |x^2 + 5x - 2|$

State whether the parabola opens up or down and whether the y-coordinate of the vertex is the minimum value or the maximum value of the function.

33. $f(x) = -2x^2 - 2x$

34. $f(x) = 8x^2 - x$

35. $g(x) = -(3x^2 - x + 3)$

36. $f(x) = 2 + 3x - 5x^2$

37. $h(x) = 1 - 9x - x^2$

38. $g(x) = -(x^2 + x - 12)$

39. $g(x) = 3(x + 8)(-x + 9)$

40. $h(x) = -(4x + 1)(x + 4)$

Graph each function and give the approximate coordinates of the vertex.

41. $f(x) = x^2 - x + 9$

42. $g(x) = 9 - 2x - x^2$

43. $g(x) = 4x^2 - 2x + 2$

44. $f(x) = -0.5(x + 4)^2$

45. $f(x) = (x - 2)^2 - 1$

46. $f(x) = -(x - 2)(x + 6)$

47. Describe a way to find the exact coordinates of the vertex of a parabola given by $f(x) = (x + a)(x - a)$.

48. TRANSFORMATIONS **Graph each function.**

$$f(x) = (x + 2)(x - 4) \qquad g(x) = 2(x + 2)(x - 4) \qquad h(x) = \frac{1}{2}(x + 2)(x - 4)$$

$$i(x) = -(x + 2)(x - 4) \qquad j(x) = -2(x + 2)(x - 4) \qquad k(x) = -\frac{1}{2}(x + 2)(x - 4)$$

a. What do all of the graphs have in common?
b. Which of the functions have a maximum value?
c. Which of the functions have a minimum value?

49. CONSTRUCTION Carly plans to build a rectangular pen against an existing fence for her dog. She will buy 20 yards of fence material.

Width (yd)	Length (yd)	Area (yd²)
1	18	18
2	16	32
3	14	
4		
⋮	⋮	⋮
x		

a. The table at left shows some different widths, lengths, and resulting areas that are possible with 20 yards of fence material. Complete the table.
b. Let w be the width function. Graph $w(x) = x$. What domain for w is possible in this situation?
c. Based on the completed table, write and graph a linear function, l, for the length. What domain for l is possible in this situation?
d. Let $A(x) = w(x) \cdot l(x)$ be the area function. Show that the area function is quadratic.
e. What domain for A is possible in this situation? What range is possible?
f. What is the maximum area possible for the pen? What width and length will produce the maximum area?

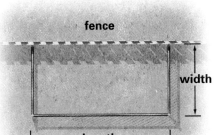

fence

width

length

x	Ticket price ($)	Attendance	Revenue ($)
−2			
−1			
0	5	300	1500
1	6	280	1680
2			
3			
4			
⋮			
x			

50. FUND-RAISING The student council plans to run a talent show to raise money. Last year tickets sold for $5 each and 300 people attended. This year, the student council wants to make an even bigger profit than last year. They estimate that for each $1 increase in the ticket price, attendance will drop by 20 people, and for each $1 decrease in the ticket price, attendance will increase by 20 people.

a. Let x be the change in the ticket price, in dollars. Copy and complete the table at left.

b. Write the function for the ticket price, $t(x)$. What type of function is t? What domain for t is possible in this situation?

c. Write the function for the attendance, $a(x)$. What type of function is a? What domain for a is possible in this situation?

d. Let $R(x) = t(x) \cdot a(x)$ be the function for the revenue. Show that this function is quadratic.

e. What domain for R is possible in this situation?

f. What is the maximum revenue possible for the talent show? What ticket price and attendance will produce the maximum revenue?

 *Look Back*

For Exercises 51–54, let $y = -4x + 11$. *(LESSON 1.2)*

51. Identify the slope m.

52. What is the x-intercept?

53. What is the y-intercept?

54. Graph the line.

 *Look Beyond*

55 Graph $y = x^2 - 3x + 5$, $y = x^2 + 7x + 6$, and $y = x^2 - 14x + 49$ on the same screen. How many x-intercepts are possible for the graph of a quadratic function?

SPORTS Refer to the basketball toss described on page 273.

1. Create a scatter plot of the data.

2. The height of a basketball thrown vertically into the air can be modeled by the function $h(t) = \frac{1}{2}gt^2 + v_0 t + h_0$, where g is the acceleration due to gravity (-32 feet per second squared), v_0 is the initial velocity in feet per second, and h_0 is the initial height in feet of the ball. Thus, $h(t) = -16t^2 + v_0 t + h_0$. Substitute 6 for the initial height, h_0, of the ball into $h(t) = -16t^2 + v_0 t + h_0$. Then graph the function on the same screen as the scatter plot, using different values for the initial velocity, v_0, until you find a model that provides a reasonably good fit for the data.

3. Use your best model to answer the questions below.

   a. What is the value of v_0?

   b. What is the maximum height achieved by the basketball?

   c. At what time does the basketball reach its maximum height?

4. Solve for v_0 algebraically by substituting the coordinates of one of the data points into $h(t) = -16t^2 + v_0 t + h_0$. Graph the resulting function on the same screen as the scatter plot. Use this model to answer the questions below.

   a. What is the value of v_0?

   b. What is the maximum height achieved by the basketball?

   c. At what time does the basketball reach its maximum height?

WORKING ON THE CHAPTER PROJECT

You should now be able to complete Activity 1 of the Chapter Project.

Introduction to Solving Quadratic Equations

6522

U.S. COAST GUARD

> **Why** *You can solve many real-world problems, such as those involving the force of gravity on a falling object, by solving a quadratic equation.*

Objectives

- Solve quadratic equations by taking square roots.

- Use the Pythagorean Theorem to solve problems involving right triangles.

APPLICATION
RESCUE

A rescue helicopter hovering 68 feet above a boat in distress drops a life raft. The height in feet of the raft above the water can be modeled by $h(t) = -16t^2 + 68$, where t is the time in seconds after it is dropped. How many seconds after the raft is dropped will it hit the water? Solving this problem involves finding square roots. *You will answer this question in Example 3.*

If $x^2 = a$ and $a \geq 0$, then x is called a square root of a. If $a > 0$, the number a has two square roots, $\sqrt{a}$ and $-\sqrt{a}$. The positive square root of a, $\sqrt{a}$, is called the **principal square root** of a. If $a = 0$, then $\sqrt{0} = 0$. When you solve a quadratic equation of the form $x^2 = a$, you can use the rule below.

Solving Equations of the Form $x^2 = a$

If $x^2 = a$ and $a \geq 0$, then $x = \sqrt{a}$ or $x = -\sqrt{a}$, or simply $x = \pm\sqrt{a}$.

The expression $\pm\sqrt{a}$ is read as "plus or minus the square root of a." To use the rule above, you may need to transform a given equation so that it is in the form $x^2 = a$. You can also use the *Properties of Square Roots* below to simplify the resulting square root.

Properties of Square Roots

Product Property of Square Roots   If $a \geq 0$ and $b \geq 0$: $\sqrt{ab} = \sqrt{a} \cdot \sqrt{b}$

Quotient Property of Square Roots   If $a \geq 0$ and $b > 0$: $\sqrt{\dfrac{a}{b}} = \dfrac{\sqrt{a}}{\sqrt{b}}$

EXAMPLE 1

Solve $4x^2 + 13 = 253$. Give exact solutions. Then approximate the solutions to the nearest hundredth.

SOLUTION

$$4x^2 + 13 = 253$$
$$4x^2 = 240 \qquad \text{Subtract 13 from each side.}$$
$$x^2 = 60 \qquad \text{Divide each side by 4.}$$
$$x = \pm\sqrt{60} \qquad \text{Take the square root of each side.}$$
$$x = \sqrt{60} \quad or \quad x = -\sqrt{60} \qquad \text{Exact solution}$$
$$x \approx 7.75 \qquad\quad x \approx -7.75 \qquad \text{Approximate solution}$$

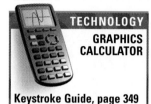

TECHNOLOGY
GRAPHICS CALCULATOR

Keystroke Guide, page 349

CHECK

Graph $y = 4x^2 + 13$ and $y = 253$ on the same screen, and find any points of intersection.

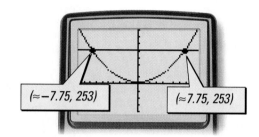

(≈ -7.75, 253)   (≈ 7.75, 253)

TRY THIS   Solve $5x^2 - 19 = 231$. Give exact solutions. Then approximate the solutions to the nearest hundredth.

CHECKPOINT ✔ Use the Product Property of Square Roots to show that $\sqrt{60} = 2\sqrt{15}$. Then use a calculator to approximate $2\sqrt{15}$.

EXAMPLE 2

Solve $9(x - 2)^2 = 121$.

SOLUTION

$$9(x - 2)^2 = 121$$
$$(x - 2)^2 = \frac{121}{9} \qquad \text{Divide each side by 9.}$$
$$x - 2 = \pm\sqrt{\frac{121}{9}} \qquad \text{Take the square root of each side.}$$
$$x = 2 + \sqrt{\frac{121}{9}} \quad or \quad x = 2 - \sqrt{\frac{121}{9}}$$
$$x = 2 + \frac{\sqrt{121}}{\sqrt{9}} \qquad\quad x = 2 - \frac{\sqrt{121}}{\sqrt{9}} \qquad \text{Use the Quotient Property of Square Roots.}$$
$$x = 2 + \frac{11}{3} \qquad\qquad x = 2 - \frac{11}{3}$$
$$x = \frac{17}{3}, \text{ or } 5\frac{2}{3} \qquad x = -\frac{5}{3}, \text{ or } -1\frac{2}{3}$$

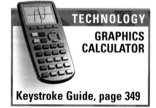

TECHNOLOGY
GRAPHICS CALCULATOR

Keystroke Guide, page 349

CHECK

Graph $y = 9(x - 2)^2$ and $y = 121$ on the same screen, and find any points of intersection.

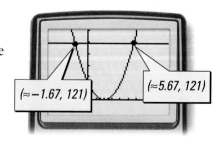

(≈ -1.67, 121)   (≈ 5.67, 121)

TRY THIS   Solve $4(x + 2)^2 = 49$.

Exploring Solutions to Quadratic Equations

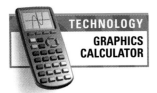

TECHNOLOGY
GRAPHICS CALCULATOR

You will need: a graphics calculator or graph paper

1. Copy and complete the second and third columns of the table below.

Equation	Exact solution(s)	Number of solutions	Related function	Number of x-intercepts
$x^2 - 7 = 0$	$x = \pm\sqrt{7}$	2	$f(x) = x^2 - 7$	2
$x^2 - 2 = 0$			$f(x) = x^2 - 2$	
$x^2 = 0$			$f(x) = x^2$	
$-x^2 + 2 = 0$			$f(x) = -x^2 + 2$	
$-x^2 + 7 = 0$			$f(x) = -x^2 + 7$	
$-x^2 = 0$			$f(x) = -x^2$	

2. Graph the related quadratic function for each equation, and complete the last column of the table.

CHECKPOINT ✔

3. What is the relationship between the number of solutions to a quadratic equation and the number of x-intercepts of the related function?

EXAMPLE 3

APPLICATION
RESCUE

Refer to the rescue-helicopter problem described at the beginning of the lesson.

After how many seconds will the raft dropped from the helicopter hit the water?

● **SOLUTION**

The raft will hit the water when its height above the water is 0 feet, or when $h(t) = 0$.

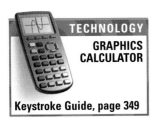

TECHNOLOGY
GRAPHICS CALCULATOR

Keystroke Guide, page 349

Method 1 Use algebra.
Let $h(t) = 0$.
$$-16t^2 + 68 = 0$$
$$-16t^2 = -68$$
$$t^2 = \frac{-68}{-16}$$
$$t^2 = \frac{17}{4}$$
$$t = \pm\sqrt{\frac{17}{4}}$$
$$t \approx \pm 2.1$$

Method 2 Use the graph.
Graph $h(t) = -16t^2 + 68$, and find the reasonable t-value for which $h(t) = 0$.

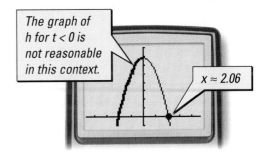

The graph of h for t < 0 is not reasonable in this context.

$x \approx 2.06$

Since t must be greater than 0, the raft will hit the water about 2.1 seconds after it is dropped.

TRY THIS

How many seconds will it take the raft to hit the water if the helicopter drops the raft from a height of 34 feet?

Using the Pythagorean Theorem

Greek mathematician Pythagoras (around 580–500 B.C.E.)

CULTURAL CONNECTION: ASIA

Sometime between 1900 B.C.E. and 1600 B.C.E. in ancient Babylonia (now Iraq), a table of numbers was inscribed on a clay tablet. When archeologists discovered the tablet, part of it was missing, so the meaning of the numbers on it remained a mystery. The sets of numbers on the tablet are believed to be triples, called *Pythagorean triples*, that form a special right-triangle relationship. This relationship, named after the Greek mathematician Pythagoras, is commonly called the *Pythagorean Theorem*.

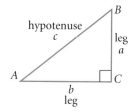

Ancient tablet believed to contain Pythagorean triples

When you sketch a right triangle, use capital letters to name the angles and corresponding lowercase letters to name the lengths of the sides opposite the angles. For example, $\overline{BC}$ is labeled a because it is opposite angle A.

Pythagorean Theorem

If $\triangle ABC$ is a right triangle with the right angle at C, then $a^2 + b^2 = c^2$.

When you apply the Pythagorean Theorem, use the principal square root because distance and length cannot be negative.

EXAMPLE ④ **Find the unknown length in each right triangle. Give answers to the nearest tenth.**

CONNECTION

GEOMETRY

a.

b.
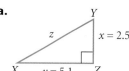

● **SOLUTION**

PROBLEM SOLVING

Use a formula.

a.
$$x^2 + y^2 = z^2$$
$$2.5^2 + 5.1^2 = z^2$$
$$z^2 = 5.1^2 + 2.5^2$$
$$z = \sqrt{5.1^2 + 2.5^2}$$
$$z \approx 5.68$$

z is about 5.7 units.

b.
$$p^2 + q^2 = r^2$$
$$p^2 + 4.0^2 = 8.2^2$$
$$p^2 = 8.2^2 - 4.0^2$$
$$p = \sqrt{8.2^2 - 4.0^2}$$
$$p \approx 7.16$$

p is about 7.2 units.

TRY THIS

Find the unknown length in each right triangle. Give answers to the nearest tenth.

a.

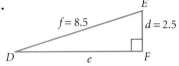

b.

CRITICAL THINKING

Suppose that $\triangle ABC$ is a right triangle with the right angle at C. Write a formula for b in terms of a and c, assuming that a and c are known. Then write a formula for a in terms of b and c, assuming that b and c are known.

Sometimes you may need to apply the Pythagorean Theorem twice in order to find the solution to a problem. This is shown in Example 5.

E X A M P L E ⑤ The diagram shows support wires $\overline{AD}$ and $\overline{BD}$ for a tower.

APPLICATION
ENGINEERING

How far apart are the support wires where they contact the ground? Give your answer to the nearest whole foot.

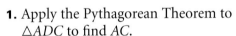

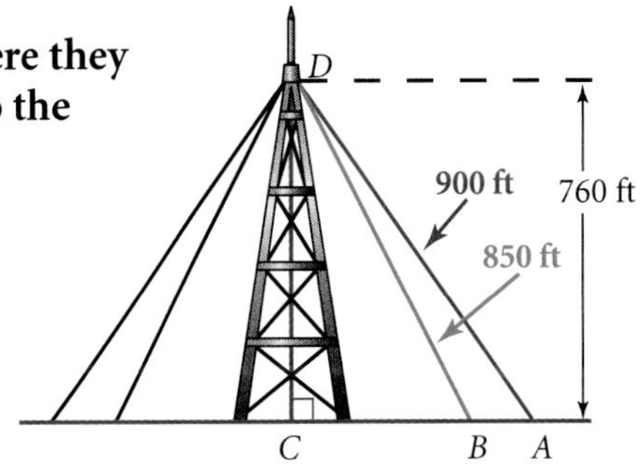

● **SOLUTION**

The distance between the support wires where they contact the ground is AB.

1. Apply the Pythagorean Theorem to $\triangle ADC$ to find AC.

$$(AC)^2 + (CD)^2 = (AD)^2$$
$$(AC)^2 + 760^2 = \mathbf{900^2}$$
$$(AC)^2 = 900^2 - 760^2$$
$$AC = \sqrt{900^2 - 760^2}$$
$$AC \approx 482.08$$

CONNECTION
GEOMETRY

2. Apply the Pythagorean Theorem to $\triangle BDC$ to find BC.

$$(BC)^2 + (CD)^2 = (BD)^2$$
$$(BC)^2 + 760^2 = \mathbf{850^2}$$
$$(BC)^2 = 850^2 - 760^2$$
$$BC = \sqrt{850^2 - 760^2}$$
$$BC \approx 380.66$$

TECHNOLOGY
SCIENTIFIC
CALCULATOR

You can edit the previous entry by replacing 900 with 850.

3. Find $AC - BC = AB$.

$$482.08 - 380.66 = 101.42$$

The wires are about 101 feet apart at ground level.

TRY THIS

In the diagram below, find PQ. Give your answer to the nearest whole meter.

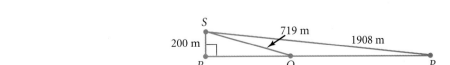

Exercises

● *Communicate*

1. Describe the procedure you would use to solve $5(x + 3)^2 = 12$.

2. Describe three situations in which it makes sense to consider only the principal root as a solution.

3. How can you find the length of the hypotenuse of a right triangle with legs that are 3 and 4 units long?

● *Guided Skills Practice*

Solve each equation. Give exact solutions. Then approximate each solution to the nearest hundredth, if necessary. *(EXAMPLES 1 AND 2)*

4. $x^2 = 29$ **5.** $2x^2 - 4 = 18$ **6.** $(x + 1)^2 = 9$

7. $3(x - 2)^2 = 21$ **8.** $2(x^2 - 4) + 3 = 15$ **9.** $\frac{1}{2}(x^2 + 6) - 5 = 10$

APPLICATION

10. AVIATION A crate of blankets and clothing is dropped without a parachute from a helicopter hovering at an altitude of 110 feet. The crate's height in feet above the ground is modeled by $h(t) = -16t^2 + 110$, where t is the time in seconds after it is dropped. How long will it take for the crate to reach the ground? *(EXAMPLE 3)*

CONNECTION

GEOMETRY Find the unknown length in each right triangle. Give your answer to the nearest tenth. *(EXAMPLE 4)*

11.

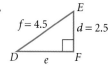

12.

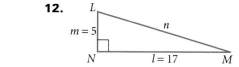

APPLICATION

13. CONSTRUCTION Two support wires and their lengths are shown in the diagram below. What is the distance in meters between the wires, represented by $\overline{CD}$, where they are attached to the ground? Give your answer to the nearest tenth of a meter. *(EXAMPLE 5)*

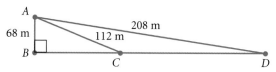

● *Practice and Apply*

Solve each equation. Give exact solutions. Then approximate each solution to the nearest hundredth, if necessary.

14. $x^2 = 121$ **15.** $x^2 = 32$ **16.** $3x^2 = 49$

17. $4x^2 = 20$ **18.** $4t^2 = 1$ **19.** $\frac{1}{2}x^2 = 6$

20. $\frac{2}{3}a^2 = 13$ **21.** $x^2 + 5 = 41$ **22.** $x^2 - 37 = 0$

23. $2t^2 - 5 = 6$ **24.** $4x^2 + 5 = 20$ **25.** $10 - 3x^2 = 4$

26. $8 - 2x^2 = -3$ **27.** $(x - 5)^2 = 16$ **28.** $(t + 2)^2 = 7$

29. $\frac{1}{3}(t^2 - 15) = 37$ **30.** $4(s^2 + 7) - 9 = 39$ **31.** $7 = 2(r + 1)^2 - 3$

Find the unknown length in each right triangle. Give answers to the nearest tenth.

32.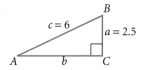

33.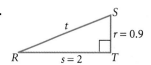

34.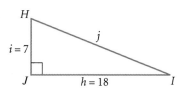

35.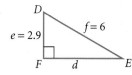

36.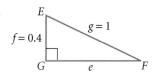

37.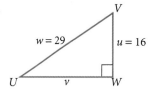

Find the missing side length in right triangle _ABC_. Give answers to the nearest tenth, if necessary.

38. a is 9 and b is 2.   **39.** a is 8 and b is 4.

40. c is 5 and b is 3.   **41.** c is $\sqrt{29}$ and b is 5.

42. a is 9 and c is $\sqrt{90}$.   **43.** a is 7 and c is $\sqrt{74}$.

CHALLENGE

Write a quadratic equation for each pair of solutions.

44. 7 and -7 **45.** $\sqrt{17}$ and $-\sqrt{17}$ **46.** $\sqrt{2001}$ and $-\sqrt{2001}$

CONNECTIONS

47. GEOMETRY The area of a circle is 20π square inches. Find the radius of the circle. (Hint: The area of a circle is given by $A = \pi r^2$.)

48. GEOMETRY Copy and complete the table.

Area of square	4	5	6	7	8	...	A
Side of square	2					...	
Diagonal of square	$\sqrt{8}$					...	

49. GEOMETRY A cube measures 3 feet on each edge.

  a. What is the length of a diagonal, such as a, along one of the faces of the cube?

  b. What is the length of a diagonal, such as b, that passes through the interior of the cube?

50. GEOMETRY A right pyramid that is 12 feet tall has a square base whose side length is 5 feet.
 a. What is its slant height?
 b. What is the length of its lateral edges?

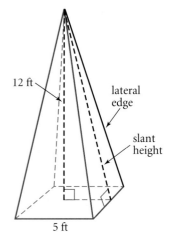

12 ft

lateral edge

slant height

5 ft

51. PHYSICS A worker drops a hammer from a second-story roof that is 10 meters above the ground. If the hammer's height in meters above the ground is modeled by $h(t) = -4.9t^2 + 10$, where t represents time in seconds after the hammer is dropped, about how long will it take the hammer to reach the ground?

52. RECREATION A child at a swimming pool jumps off a 12-foot platform into the pool. The child's height in feet above the water is modeled by $h(t) = -16t^2 + 12$, where t is the time in seconds after the child jumps. How long will it take the child to reach the water?

53. SPORTS A baseball diamond is a square with sides of 90 feet. To the nearest foot, how long is a throw to first base from third base?

54. NAVIGATION A hiker leaves camp and walks 5 miles east. Then he walks 10 miles south. How far from camp is the hiker?

55. TELECOMMUNICATIONS The cable company buries a line diagonally across a rectangular lot. The lot measures 105 feet by 60 feet. How long is the cable line?

56. ENGINEERING The velocity, v, in centimeters per second, of a fluid flowing in a pipe varies with respect to the distance in centimeters, x, from the center of the pipe according to the equation $v(x) = 16 - x^2$.
 a. Find x for $v = 7$.
 b. Find x for $v = 12$.

APPLICATIONS

57. CONSTRUCTION The bottom of a 20-foot ladder is placed $4\frac{1}{2}$ feet from the base of a house, as shown at right. At what height does the ladder touch the house?

58. SPORTS A cliff diver stands on a cliff overlooking water. To approximate his height above the water, he drops a pebble and times its fall. If the pebble takes about 3 seconds to strike the water, approximately how high is the diver above the water? Use the model $h(t) = -4.9t^2 + h_0$, where h is the pebble's height in meters above the ground, t is the time in seconds after the pebble is dropped, and h_0 is the height of the cliff in meters.

59. CONSTRUCTION Find the length of the rafter that provides for a rise of 5 feet over a run of 24 feet. Allow for a 1-foot overhang in the length of the rafter.

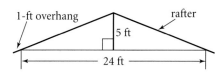

Look Back

Determine whether each table represents a linear relationship between *x* and *y*. If the relationship is linear, write the next ordered pair that would appear in the table. *(LESSON 1.1)*

60.

x	−5	−3	−1	0	2	4
y	2	1	0	−1	−2	−3

61.

x	−3	−1	1	3	5	7
y	−9	−5	−1	3	7	11

Find the slope of the line passing through the given points, and write the equation of the line in slope-intercept form. *(LESSON 1.2)*

62. $(-4, -2)$ and $(6, -7)$ **63.** $(3, 5)$ and $(-6, 1)$

Evaluate each expression. *(LESSON 2.2)*

64. $4^5 \cdot 4^{-3}$ **65.** $(5^4)^{-\frac{1}{2}}$ **66.** $(6^4 \cdot 6)^0$

Give the domain and range of each function. *(LESSON 2.3)*

67. $f(x) = 3x^2 - 7$ **68.** $f(x) = \frac{x-6}{5}$ **69.** $f(x) = 3\left(\frac{x}{2}\right)^2$

Look Beyond

CONNECTION

TRANSFORMATIONS Graph each pair of functions, find the vertices, and describe how the graphs are related.

70. $f(x) = (x-3)^2 - 5$ and $g(x) = (x-3)^2 + 5$

71. $f(x) = (x+5)^2 - 4$ and $g(x) = (x-2)^2 - 4$

72. $f(x) = x^2$ and $g(x) = (x-3)^2 - 4$

Factoring Quadratic Expressions

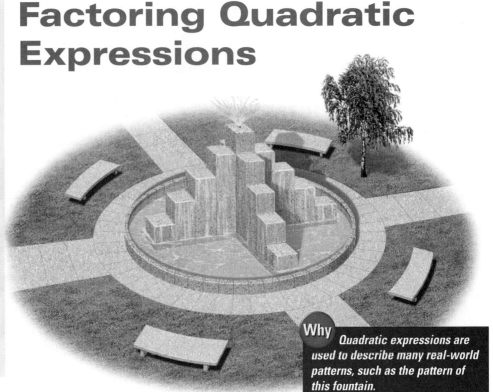

Why *Quadratic expressions are used to describe many real-world patterns, such as the pattern of this fountain.*

Objectives

- Factor a quadratic expression.

- Use factoring to solve a quadratic equation and find the zeros of a quadratic function.

APPLICATION

ARCHITECTURE

An architect created a proposal for the fountain shown above. Each level (except the top one) is an **X** formed by cubes. The number of cubes in each of the four parts of the **X** is one less than the number on the level below. A formula for the total number of cubes, c, in the fountain is given by $c = 2n^2 - n$, where n is the number of levels in the fountain. How many levels would a fountain consisting of 66 cubes have? *You will answer this question in Example 7.*

Factoring Quadratic Expressions

Multiplying

$$2x(x + 3) = 2x^2 + 6x$$

Factoring

When you learned to multiply two expressions like $2x$ and $x + 3$, you learned how to write a product as a sum. **Factoring** reverses the process, allowing you to write a sum as a product.

To factor an expression containing two or more terms, factor out the *greatest common factor* (GCF) of the two expressions, as shown in Example 1.

EXAMPLE ❶ Factor each quadratic expression.

    a. $3a^2 - 12a$ **b.** $3x(4x + 5) - 5(4x + 5)$

● **SOLUTION**

Factor out the GCF for all of the terms.

a. $3a^2 = 3a \cdot a$ and $12a = 3a \cdot 4$ **b.** The GCF is $4x + 5$.
The GCF is $3a$. $3x(4x + 5) - 5(4x + 5)$
$3a^2 - 12a = 3a(a) - 3a(4)$ $= (3x - 5)(4x + 5)$
             $= (3a)(a - 4)$

TRY THIS   Factor $5x^2 + 15x$ and $(2x - 1)4 + (2x - 1)x$.

An expression of the form $ax^2 + bx + c$, where $a \neq 0$, is often called a quadratic *trinomial.* In the Activity below, you will investigate how to factor this type of expression.

Factoring With Algebra Tiles

You will need: algebra tiles

You can model a quadratic expression that can be factored with algebra tiles, as shown below.

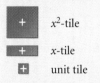

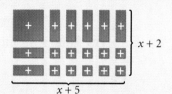

The rectangular region formed by algebra tiles above illustrates that the total area, $x^2 + 7x + 10$, can be represented as the product $(x + 5)(x + 2)$.

1. Use tiles to determine whether $x^2 + 4x + 4$ can be represented as the product of two linear factors. Justify and illustrate your response.

2. Use tiles to determine whether $x^2 + 6x + 8$ can be represented as the product of two linear factors. Justify and illustrate your response.

3. Use tiles to determine whether $x^2 + 7x + 12$ can be represented as the product of two linear factors. Justify and illustrate your response.

CHECKPOINT ✔   4. Describe how algebra tiles can be used to factor a quadratic trinomial.

Many quadratic expressions can be factored algebraically. Examine the factored expressions below.

PROBLEM SOLVING

Look for a pattern. Notice how the sums and products of the constants in the *binomial* factors are related to the last two terms in the unfactored expression.

$x^2 + 7x + 10 = (x + 5)(x + 2)$
$\boxed{5 + 2 = 7}$ $\boxed{5 \times 2 = 10}$

$x^2 - 7x + 10 = (x - 5)(x - 2)$
$\boxed{-5 - 2 = -7}$ $\boxed{-5 \times (-2) = 10}$

$x^2 + 3x - 10 = (x + 5)(x - 2)$
$\boxed{5 - 2 = 3}$ $\boxed{5 \times (-2) = -10}$

$x^2 - 3x - 10 = (x - 5)(x + 2)$
$\boxed{-5 + 2 = -3}$ $\boxed{-5 \times 2 = -10}$

The patterns shown above suggest a rule for factoring quadratic expressions of the form $x^2 + bx + c$.

Factoring $x^2 + bx + c$

To factor an expression of the form $ax^2 + bx + c$ where $a = 1$, look for integers r and s such that $r \cdot s = c$ and $r + s = b$. Then factor the expression.
$$x^2 + bx + c = (x + r)(x + s)$$

When c is positive in $x^2 + bx + c$ $(c > 0)$, test factors with the same sign.

EXAMPLE 2 Factor $x^2 + 5x + 6$.

● SOLUTION

PROBLEM SOLVING **Guess and check.** Begin with $(x\quad)(x\quad)$. Find the factors of 6 that result in $5x$ for the bx-term.

$(x + 1)(x + 6)$ $(x + 2)(x + 3)$ $(x - 1)(x - 6)$ $(x - 2)(x - 3)$

$1x + 6x = 5x$ $2x + 3x = 5x$ $-1x + (-6x) = 5x$ $-2x + (-3x) = 5x$
False   **True**   **False**   **False**

Thus, $x^2 + 5x + 6 = (x + 2)(x + 3)$.

TRY THIS   Factor $x^2 + 9x + 20$.

When c is negative in $x^2 + bx + c$ $(c < 0)$, test factors with opposite signs.

EXAMPLE 3 Factor $x^2 - 7x - 30$.

● SOLUTION

PROBLEM SOLVING **Guess and check.** Begin with $(x\quad)(x\quad)$. Find the factors of -30 that result in $-7x$ for the bx-term.

$(x - 1)(x + 30)$ $(x + 1)(x - 30)$ $(x - 2)(x + 15)$

$-1x + 30x = -7x$ $1x + (-30x) = -7x$ $-2x + 15x = -7x$
False   **False**   **False**

$(x + 2)(x - 15)$ $(x - 3)(x + 10)$ $(x + 3)(x - 10)$

$2x + (-15x) = -7x$ $-2x + 10x = -7x$ $3x + (-10x) = -7x$
False   **False**   **True**

Thus, $x^2 - 7x - 30 = (x + 3)(x - 10)$.

TRY THIS   Factor $x^2 - 10x - 11$.

You can use guess-and-check to factor an expression of the form $ax^2 + bx + c$, where $a \neq 1$.

EXAMPLE 4 Factor $6x^2 + 11x + 3$. Check by graphing.

● SOLUTION

PROBLEM SOLVING **Guess and check.** The positive factors of a, are 1, 6, 3, and 2. Begin with $(6x\quad)(x\quad)$ or $(3x\quad)(2x\quad)$. Find the factors of 3 that produce $11x$ for the bx-term.

$(6x + 3)(x + 1)$ $(6x + 1)(x + 3)$ $(3x + 3)(2x + 1)$ $(3x + 1)(2x + 3)$

$3x + 6x = 11x$ $1x + 18x = 11x$ $6x + 3x = 11x$ $2x + 9x = 11x$
False   **False**   **False**   **True**

Thus, $6x^2 + 11x + 3 = (3x + 1)(2x + 3)$.

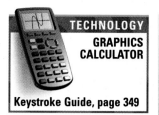

TECHNOLOGY

GRAPHICS
CALCULATOR

Keystroke Guide, page 349

CHECK
Graph $y = 6x^2 + 11x + 3$ and $y = (3x + 1)(2x + 3)$.

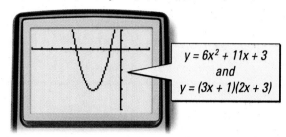

$y = 6x^2 + 11x + 3$
and
$y = (3x + 1)(2x + 3)$

The graphs appear to coincide. Thus, $6x^2 + 11x + 3 = (3x + 1)(2x + 3)$.

TRY THIS   Factor $3x^2 + 11x - 20$. Check by graphing.

Examine the product when $x + 3$ and $x - 3$ are multiplied.
$$(x + 3)(x - 3) = x^2 + 3x - 3x + 9$$
$$= x^2 - 9$$
$$= x^2 - 3^2 \quad \text{difference of two squares}$$

Factoring the Difference of Two Squares

$$a^2 - b^2 = (a + b)(a - b)$$

Examine the products when $x + 3$ and $x - 3$ are squared.

$$(x + 3)^2 = (x + 3)(x + 3) \qquad\qquad (x - 3)^2 = (x - 3)(x - 3)$$
$$= x^2 + 3x + 3x + 9 \qquad\qquad = x^2 - 3x - 3x + 9$$
$$= x^2 + 2(3x) + 9 \quad \text{perfect-square trinomials} \quad = x^2 - 2(3x) + 9$$

Factoring Perfect-Square Trinomials

$$a^2 + 2ab + b^2 = (a + b)^2 \qquad\qquad a^2 - 2ab + b^2 = (a - b)^2$$

E X A M P L E ❺ Factor each expression.

   a. $x^4 - 16$ **b.** $4x^2 - 24x + 36$

● **SOLUTION**

   a. $x^4 - 16 = (x^2 + 4)(x^2 - 4)$ **b.** $4x^2 - 24x + 36 = 4(x^2 - 6x + 9)$
   $$= (x^2 + 4)(x + 2)(x - 2) \qquad\qquad = 4[x^2 - 2(3)x + 3^2]$$
   $$= 4(x - 3)^2$$

TRY THIS   Factor $9x^2 - 49$ and $3x^2 + 6x + 3$.

LESSON 5.3 FACTORING QUADRATIC EXPRESSIONS   **293**

Using Factoring to Solve Quadratic Equations

You can sometimes use factoring to solve an equation and to find zeros of a function. A **zero of a function** f is any number r such that $f(r) = 0$.

Zero-Product Property

If $pq = 0$, then $p = 0$ *or* $q = 0$.

The form $ax^2 + bx + c = 0$ is called the **standard form of a quadratic equation.** Once a quadratic equation is in standard form, if the expression $ax^2 + bx + c$ can be factored, then the Zero-Product Property can be applied to solve the equation. To apply the Zero-Product Property, write the equation as a factored expression equal to zero. For example, the equation $x^2 + 6x = -5$ must first be rewritten in standard form as $x^2 + 6x + 5 = 0$ and then factored as $(x + 5)(x + 1) = 0$.

CHECKPOINT ✔ What is the solution to the equation $(x + 5)(x + 1) = 0$?

Example 6 shows you how to use the Zero-Product Property to find the zeros of a quadratic function.

E X A M P L E **6** Use the Zero-Product Property to find the zeros of each quadratic function.
 a. $f(x) = 2x^2 - 11x$ **b.** $g(x) = x^2 - 14x + 45$

● **SOLUTION**

Set each function equal to zero, and use the Zero-Product Property to solve the resulting equation.

a.
$$2x^2 - 11x = 0$$
$$x(2x - 11) = 0$$
$$x = 0 \quad or \quad 2x - 11 = 0$$
$$x = 0 \qquad\qquad x = \frac{11}{2}$$

b.
$$x^2 - 14x + 45 = 0$$
$$(x - 5)(x - 9) = 0$$
$$x - 5 = 0 \quad or \quad x - 9 = 0$$
$$x = 5 \qquad\qquad x = 9$$

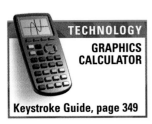

TECHNOLOGY
GRAPHICS
CALCULATOR

Keystroke Guide, page 349

CHECK

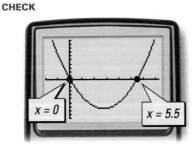

$x = 0$ $x = 5.5$

CHECK

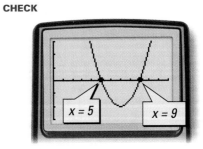

$x = 5$ $x = 9$

TRY THIS Use the Zero-Product Property to find the zeros of each function.
 a. $h(x) = 3x^2 + 12x$ **b.** $j(x) = x^2 + 4x - 21$

CRITICAL THINKING Show that $f(x) = ax^2 + bx$, where $a \neq 0$, has two zeros, namely 0 and $-\frac{b}{a}$.

Refer to the fountain problem discussed at the beginning of the lesson.

How many levels would a fountain consisting of 66 cubes have?

SOLUTION

Method 1 Use algebra.
Solve $2n^2 - n = 66$ by factoring.

$2n^2 - n - 66 = 0$ *Write in standard form.*

$(2n + 11)(n - 6) = 0$ *Factor $2n^2 - n - 66$.*

$2n + 11 = 0$ *or* $n - 6 = 0$

$n = -5.5$ $n = 6$

Because the number of levels must be a positive integer, −5.5 cannot be a solution. The fountain would have 6 levels.

TECHNOLOGY
GRAPHICS CALCULATOR

Keystroke Guide, page 349

Method 2 Use a table.
Make a table of values for $y = 2x^2 - x - 66$. From the table at right you can see that the function has a zero at $x = 6$.

Therefore, the fountain would have 6 levels.

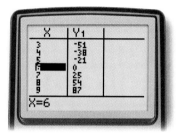

Exercises

Communicate

1. If $x^2 + 34x + 285$ is factored as $(x + q)(x + s)$, how do you find q and s?

2. What do you know about the factors of $x^2 + bx + c$ when c is positive? when c is negative? What information does the sign of b give you in each case?

3. State what must be true about the numbers p and q if $pq = 0$.

Guided Skills Practice

Factor each quadratic expression. *(EXAMPLE 1)*

4. $2x^2 - 8x$ **5.** $2y^2 - 6y$ **6.** $5ax^2 - 15a^2x$

7. $4x(x + 3) - 7(x + 3)$ **8.** $(4r + 7)3 - (4r + 7)2r$ **9.** $(9s - 5)8s + 3(9s - 5)$

Factor each quadratic expression. *(EXAMPLES 2, 3, AND 4)*

10. $x^2 + 5x + 6$ **11.** $x^2 + 8x + 7$ **12.** $y^2 - 5y + 4$

13. $x^2 - 4x - 12$ **14.** $y^2 - 9y - 36$ **15.** $x^2 + 10x - 24$

16. $2x^2 + 9x + 10$ **17.** $3x^2 + 5x + 2$ **18.** $5x^2 + 13x - 6$

19. $8x^2 + 24x - 14x - 42$ **20.** $12r^2 + 21r - 8r - 14$ **21.** $72s^2 - 56s - 36s + 28$

Factor each quadratic expression. *(EXAMPLE 5)*

22. $x^4 - 81$ **23.** $2x^2 - 8$ **24.** $16x^2 - 25$ **25.** $x^2 + 8x + 16$

Use the Zero-Product Property to find the zeros of each quadratic function. *(EXAMPLE 6)*

26. $f(x) = x^2 + 7x$ **27.** $g(x) = x^2 + 6x + 9$ **28.** $f(t) = t^2 + 3t - 10$

CONNECTION

29. GEOMETRY Line segments are drawn to connect n points with one another. The number of connecting segments is described by the function $h(n) = \frac{n(n-1)}{2}$. If 36 connecting segments are drawn, how many points are there? *(EXAMPLE 7)*

Practice and Apply

Factor each expression.

30. $3x + 6$

31. $3x^2 + 18$

32. $10n - n^2$

33. $x - 4x^2$

34. $6x - 2x^2$

35. $-3y^2 - 15y$

36. $5x(x - 2) - 3(x - 2)$

37. $(x + 3)(2x) + (x + 3)(7)$

38. $a^2x + 5a^2x^2 - 2ax$

39. $4ab^2 - 6a^2b$

Factor each quadratic expression.

40. $x^2 - 16x + 15$

41. $x^2 + 8x + 16$

42. $x^2 - 26x + 48$

43. $x^2 + 4x - 32$

44. $x^2 + 7x - 30$

45. $x^2 - 10x - 24$

46. $-22x - 48 + x^2$

47. $2x + x^2 - 24$

48. $x^2 - 56 - 10x$

49. $56 + 10x - x^2$

50. $30 + x - x^2$

51. $24 + 10x - x^2$

52. $3x^2 + 10x + 3$

53. $2x^2 + 5x + 2$

54. $2x^2 + 3x + 1$

55. $3x^2 + 7x + 2$

56. $12x^2 - 3x - 9$

57. $3x^2 - 5x - 2$

Solve each equation by factoring and applying the Zero-Product Property.

58. $15x^2 = 7x + 2$

59. $3x^2 - 5x = 2$

60. $4x - 4 = -15x^2$

61. $3x^2 + 3 = 10x$

62. $2x^2 - 15 = -7x$

63. $6x^2 - 17x = -12$

64. $x^2 - 36 = 0$

65. $t^2 - 9 = 0$

66. $x^4 - 81 = 0$

67. $x^4 - 1 = 0$

68. $4x^2 - 9 = 0$

69. $25x^2 - 16 = 0$

70. $x^2 - 2x + 1 = 0$

71. $x^2 + 4x + 4 = 0$

72. $9x^2 = -6x - 1$

73. $4x^2 + 1 = 4x$

74. $-4 + 20x - 25x^2 = 0$

75. $40x + 25 = -16x^2$

76. $64 + 16x + x^2 = 0$

77. $9 - 6x + x^2 = 0$

Use factoring and the Zero-Product Property to find the zeros of each quadratic function.

78. $f(x) = x^2 - 7x + 10$

79. $g(t) = t^2 - 2t - 15$

80. $f(x) = 4x^2 + 4x - 24$

81. $g(x) = 6x^2 + 3x - 9$

82. $f(t) = t^2 + 7t - 60$

83. $h(x) = x^2 - 15x + 56$

84. $f(x) = x^2 + 8x + 12$

85. $g(x) = x^2 - 3x - 40$

86. $g(x) = 6x^2 + 20x - 16$

87. $h(x) = 4x^2 - 8x + 3$

Use graphing to find the zeros of each function.

88. $f(n) = n^2 - n - 30$

89. $g(t) = 24 + 8t - 2t^2$

90. $f(x) = 2x^2 + 13x + 15$

91. $f(x) = 5x^2 + 30x + 40$

92. $g(a) = 24a^2 + 36a - 24$

93. $h(x) = 6x^2 - 33x - 18$

CHALLENGE

Factor each expression.

94. $(a + b)^4 - (a - b)^4$

95. $x^{2n} - 1$

96. $x^{2n} - 2x^n + 1$

CONNECTIONS

GEOMETRY The area of a triangle is $A = \frac{1}{2}bh$, where b is the base and h is the altitude. Use this information for Exercises 97 and 98.

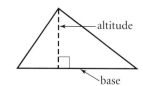

97. The base of a triangle is 5 centimeters longer than its altitude. If the area of the triangle is 42 square centimeters, what is its altitude?

98. The altitude of a triangle is 5 centimeters shorter than its base. If the area of the triangle is 12 square centimeters, what is its base?

99. **GEOMETRY** The area of a circle is given by $A = \pi r^2$, where r is the radius. If the radius of a circle is increased by 4 inches, the area of the resulting circle is 100π square inches. Find the radius of the original circle.

100. **GEOMETRY** The length of one leg of a right triangle is 7 centimeters longer than the other leg, and the hypotenuse is 13 centimeters. Find the lengths of the two legs.

APPLICATIONS

101. **SPORTS** A soccer ball is kicked from the ground, and its height in meters above ground is modeled by the function $h(t) = -4.9t^2 + 19.6t$, where t represents the time in seconds after the ball is kicked. How long is the ball in the air?

102. **SPORTS** A golf ball is hit from the ground, and its height in feet above the ground is modeled by the function $h(t) = -16t^2 + 180t$, where t represents the time in seconds after the ball is hit. How long is the ball in the air?

Look Back

Solve each inequality, and graph the solution on a number line.
(LESSON 1.7)

103. $2x - 4 > 12 + 5x$

104. $2x - \frac{3}{4} \geq 7$

105. $3(3x + 7) - 12 \leq 8 - \left(\frac{1}{2}x + 9\right)$

106. $-2\left(\frac{2}{3}x + 5\right) - 13 < -6$

APPLICATION

107. ADVERTISING An advertising agency can spend no more than $1,270,000 for television advertising. The two available time slots for commercials cost $40,000 and $25,000, and at least 40 commercials are desired.
(LESSON 3.4)

a. Write a system of linear inequalities to represent how many commercials at each price can be purchased.

b. Graph the region in which the solution to the system of inequalities can be found.

c. Find the coordinates of a point that is a solution to the system. What do the coordinates represent?

For Exercises 108–111, let $A = \begin{bmatrix} -3 & 1 & 0 \\ 2 & 6 & -4 \\ 5 & -2 & 1 \end{bmatrix}$ and $B = \begin{bmatrix} 0 & 2 & 8 \\ 1 & 4 & 3 \\ -2 & 0 & -1 \end{bmatrix}$.

Evaluate each expression. *(LESSON 4.1)*

108. $3A$

109. $-\frac{1}{2}B$

110. $A - B$

111. $2B + A$

Find each product. *(LESSON 5.1)*

112. $(3x + 4)(-x - 5)$

113. $(-2x + 9)(-4x + 7)$

114. $\left(\frac{1}{3}x + \frac{1}{4}\right)(-5x - 2)$

Look Beyond

Factor each quadratic expression, if possible.

115. $(x + 2)^2 - 4$

116. $(x + 9)^2 + 36$

117. $(x - 1)^2 - 16$

SPORTS Refer to the height function given in the Portfolio Activity on page 280.

1. Find the time when the basketball will return to a height of 6 feet by solving the related quadratic equation for $h(t) = 6$.

2. Use the data on page 273 to estimate the equation of the axis of symmetry of the

function. Using symmetry, estimate when the basketball will return to a height of 6 feet.

3. Compare your answers to Steps 1 and 2 above. Explain any difference you find.

Completing the Square

Why You can solve many real-world problems, such as finding the lowest point on the cable of a suspension bridge, by using a method called "completing the square" to solve quadratic equations.

Objectives

- Use completing the square to solve a quadratic equation.

- Use the vertex form of a quadratic function to locate the axis of symmetry of its graph.

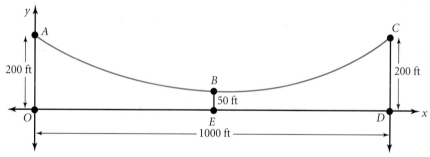

APPLICATION

ENGINEERING

Engineers are planning to build a cable suspension bridge like the one shown in the diagram above. The cable forms a *catenary* curve, which can be approximated by the quadratic function $f(x) = \frac{3}{5000}x^2 - \frac{3}{5}x + 200$, where $0 \leq x \leq 1000$. Write this quadratic function in a form that allows the coordinates of the lowest point on the cable to be easily identified. *You will solve this problem in Example 5.*

Completing the Square

Activity
Completing the Square With Tiles

You will need: algebra tiles

1. Can you arrange 1 x^2-tile and 4 x-tiles to form a square? Explain your response.

2. What is the smallest number of unit tiles you need to add to your tiles to form a square?

3. Write an expression in both standard and factored form for the complete set of tiles that form the square.

4. Repeat Steps 1–3 with 1 x^2-tile and 6 x-tiles.

5. Repeat Steps 1–3 with 1 x^2-tile and 8 x-tiles.

CHECKPOINT ✔ **6.** Explain how to find the smallest number of unit tiles needed to complete a square with 1 x^2-tile and 8 x-tiles.

Recall from Lesson 5.2 that you can solve equations of the form $x^2 = k$ by taking the square root of each side.

$$x^2 = 9$$
$$\sqrt{x^2} = \pm\sqrt{9}$$
$$x = \pm 3$$

The same is true for equations of the form $(x + a)^2 = k$.

$$(x + 3)^2 = 16$$
$$\sqrt{(x + 3)^2} = \pm\sqrt{16}$$
$$x + 3 = \pm 4$$
$$x = 1 \quad or \quad x = -7$$

When a quadratic equation does not contain a perfect square, you can create a perfect square in the equation by *completing the square*. **Completing the square** is a process by which you can force a quadratic expression to factor.

Examine the relationship between terms in a perfect-square trinomial.

Specific case

$$x^2 + 8x + 16 = (x + 4)^2$$
$$\tfrac{1}{2}(8) = 4 \rightarrow 4^2 = 16$$

General case

$$x^2 + bx + \left(\frac{b}{2}\right)^2 = \left(x + \frac{b}{2}\right)^2$$
$$\tfrac{1}{2}(b) = \frac{b}{2} \rightarrow \left(\frac{b}{2}\right)^2$$

In general, the constant term in a perfect square trinomial is the square of one-half the coefficient of the second term.

E X A M P L E ① Complete the square for each quadratic expression to form a perfect-square trinomial. Then write the new expression as a binomial squared.
   a. $x^2 - 6x$ **b.** $x^2 + 15x$

● **SOLUTION**

a. The coefficient of x is -6.
$$\tfrac{1}{2}(-6) = -3 \rightarrow (-3)^2 = 9$$

Thus, the perfect-square trinomial is $x^2 - 6x + 9$.

$$x^2 - 6x + 9 = (x - 3)^2$$

b. The coefficient of x is 15.
$$\tfrac{1}{2}(15) = \frac{15}{2} \rightarrow \left(\frac{15}{2}\right)^2$$

Thus, the perfect-square trinomial is $x^2 + 15x + \left(\frac{15}{2}\right)^2$.

$$x^2 + 15x + \left(\frac{15}{2}\right)^2 = \left(x + \frac{15}{2}\right)^2$$

TRY THIS Complete the square for each quadratic expression to form a perfect-square trinomial. Then write the new expression as a binomial squared.
   a. $x^2 - 7x$ **b.** $x^2 + 16x$

Solving Equations by Completing the Square

Examples 2 and 3 show you how to solve a quadratic equation by completing the square and by using square roots.

E X A M P L E **2** Solve $x^2 + 6x - 16 = 0$ by completing the square.

● **SOLUTION**

$$x^2 + 6x - 16 = 0$$
$$x^2 + 6x = 16$$
$$x^2 + 6x + \left(\frac{6}{2}\right)^2 = 16 + \left(\frac{6}{2}\right)^2 \quad \text{Add } \left(\frac{6}{2}\right)^2 \text{ to each side of the equation.}$$
$$x^2 + 6x + 9 = 25$$
$$(x + 3)^2 = 25$$
$$x + 3 = \pm\sqrt{25} \quad \text{Take the square root of each side.}$$
$$x + 3 = \pm 5$$
$$x = 5 - 3 \quad \text{or} \quad x = -5 - 3$$
$$x = 2 \qquad\qquad x = -8$$

TRY THIS Solve $x^2 + 10x - 24 = 0$ by completing the square.

E X A M P L E **3** Solve $2x^2 + 6x = 7$.

● **SOLUTION**

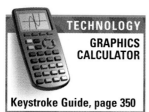

TECHNOLOGY
GRAPHICS CALCULATOR

Keystroke Guide, page 350

Method 1 Use algebra.
Solve by completing the square.
$$2x^2 + 6x = 7$$
$$2(x^2 + 3x) = 7$$
$$x^2 + 3x = \frac{7}{2}$$
$$x^2 + 3x + \left(\frac{3}{2}\right)^2 = \frac{7}{2} + \left(\frac{3}{2}\right)^2$$
$$\left(x + \frac{3}{2}\right)^2 = \frac{7}{2} + \frac{9}{4}$$
$$x + \frac{3}{2} = \pm\sqrt{\frac{23}{4}}$$
$$x = -\frac{3}{2} + \sqrt{\frac{23}{4}} \quad \text{or} \quad x = -\frac{3}{2} - \sqrt{\frac{23}{4}}$$
$$x \approx 0.90 \qquad\qquad x \approx -3.90$$

Thus, the exact solution is
$$x = -\frac{3}{2} + \sqrt{\frac{23}{4}} \text{ or } x = -\frac{3}{2} - \sqrt{\frac{23}{4}}.$$

Method 2 Use a graph.
Graph $y = 2x^2 + 6x$ and $y = 7$, and find the x-coordinates of any points of intersection.

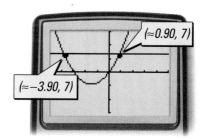

Or graph $y = 2x^2 + 6x - 7$, and find any zeros.

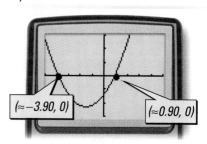

TRY THIS Solve $2x^2 + 10x = 6$.

Vertex Form

You know that the graph of $y = ax^2 + bx + c$, where $a \neq 0$, is a parabola. Using the method of completing the square, you can write the quadratic function in a form that contains the coordinates (h, k) of the vertex of the parabola.

Vertex Form

If the coordinates of the vertex of the graph of $y = ax^2 + bx + c$, where $a \neq 0$, are (h, k), then you can represent the parabola as $y = a(x - h)^2 + k$, which is the **vertex form** of a quadratic function.

CONNECTION

TRANSFORMATIONS

Recall from Lesson 2.7 that if $y = f(x)$, then
- $y = af(x)$ gives a vertical stretch or compression of f,
- $y = f(bx)$ gives a horizontal stretch or compression of f,
- $y = f(x) + k$ gives a vertical translation of f, and
- $y = f(x - h)$ gives a horizontal translation of f.

E X A M P L E **4** Given $g(x) = 2x^2 + 12x + 13$, write the function in vertex form, and give the coordinates of the vertex and the equation of the axis of symmetry. Then describe the transformations from $f(x) = x^2$ to g.

SOLUTION

$g(x) = 2x^2 + 12x + 13$
$\quad = 2(x^2 + 6x) + 13$ *Factor 2 from the x^2- and x-terms.*
$\quad = 2(x^2 + 6x + 9) + 13 - 2(9)$ *Complete the square.*
$\quad = 2(x + 3)^2 - 5$ *Simplify.*
$\quad = 2[x - (-3)]^2 + (-5)$ *Write in vertex form.*

The coordinates (h, k) of the vertex are $(-3, -5)$, and the equation for the axis of symmetry is $x = -3$.

Notice from the vertex form of the function that $g(x) = 2f(x + 3) - 5$. There are three transformations from f to g:
- a vertical stretch by a factor of 2
- a horizontal translation of 3 units to the left
- a vertical translation of 5 units down

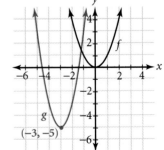

TRY THIS   Given $g(x) = 3x^2 - 9x - 2$, write the function in vertex form, and give the coordinates of the vertex and the equation of the axis of symmetry. Then describe the transformations from $f(x) = x^2$ to g.

5 Refer to the suspension bridge described at the beginning of the lesson.

APPLICATION
ENGINEERING

Complete the square, and write $f(x) = \frac{3}{5000}x^2 - \frac{3}{5}x + 200$ in vertex form. Then find the coordinates of the lowest point on the cable.

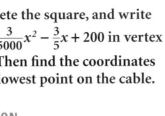

● SOLUTION

Method 1 Use algebra.

$f(x) = \frac{3}{5000}x^2 - \frac{3}{5}x + 200$

$\qquad = \frac{3}{5000}(x^2 - 1000x) + 200$

$\qquad = \frac{3}{5000}\left[x^2 - 1000x + \left(\frac{1000}{2}\right)^2\right] + 200 - \frac{3}{5000}\left(\frac{1000}{2}\right)^2$

$\qquad = \frac{3}{5000}(x^2 - 1000x + 500^2) + 200 - \frac{3}{5000}(500^2)$

$\qquad = \frac{3}{5000}(x - 500)^2 + 50$

Thus, $f(x) = \frac{3}{5000}(x - 500)^2 + 50$ is a function containing a perfect square.

The lowest point on the cable is represented by the vertex (500, 50).

TECHNOLOGY

GRAPHICS
CALCULATOR

Keystroke Guide, page 350

Method 2 Use a graph.

Graph $y = \frac{3}{5000}x^2 - \frac{3}{5}x + 200$, and find the coordinates of the lowest point.

From the graph of the function, the lowest point on the cable appears to be (500, 50).

Minimum
X=500.00006 Y=50

CRITICAL THINKING   Explain why you cannot write an equation for a parabola when given only the coordinates of the vertex.

Exercises

● *Communicate*

1. Explain how to solve the equation $x^2 + 4x - 13 = 0$ by completing the square.

2. Explain how to solve the equation $2x^2 + 4x = 15$ by completing the square.

3. Refer to Example 3. Describe two ways of solving $2x^2 + 4x = 15$ by graphing.

4. Explain what h and k represent in the vertex form of a parabola.

Guided Skills Practice

Complete the square for each quadratic expression to form a perfect-square trinomial. Then write the new expression as a binomial squared. *(EXAMPLE 1)*

5. $x^2 - 12x$ **6.** $x^2 + 5x$

7. Solve $x^2 - 4x - 21 = 0$ by completing the square. *(EXAMPLE 2)*

8. Solve $2x^2 + 5x = 3$. *(EXAMPLE 3)*

CONNECTION

9. **TRANSFORMATIONS** Given $g(x) = x^2 + 12x + 20$, write the function in vertex form, and give the coordinates of the vertex and the equation of the axis of symmetry. Then describe the transformations from $f(x) = x^2$ to g. *(EXAMPLE 4)*

APPLICATION

10. **SPORTS** A softball is thrown upward with an initial velocity of 32 feet per second from 5 feet above ground. The ball's height in feet above the ground is modeled by $h(t) = -16t^2 + 32t + 5$, where t is the time in seconds after the ball is released. Complete the square and rewrite h in vertex form. Then find the the maximum height of the ball. *(EXAMPLE 5)*

Practice and Apply

Complete the square for each quadratic expression to form a perfect-square trinomial. Then write the new expression as a binomial squared.

11. $x^2 + 10x$ **12.** $x^2 - 14x$ **13.** $x^2 - 8x$

14. $x^2 + 2x$ **15.** $x^2 + 13x$ **16.** $x^2 + 7x$

Solve each equation by completing the square. Give exact solutions.

17. $x^2 - 8x = 3$ **18.** $x^2 + 2x = 13$ **19.** $x^2 - 5x - 1 = 4 - 3x$

20. $0 = x^2 - 6x + 3$ **21.** $0 = x^2 + 7x - 26$ **22.** $0 = x^2 - 3x - 6$

23. $x^2 + 7x + 10 = 0$ **24.** $x^2 + 10x + 16 = 0$ **25.** $x^2 - x = 30$

26. $0 = 3x^2 - 2x - 12$ **27.** $-2x^2 + 14x + 60 = 0$ **28.** $0 = 3x^2 - 11x + 6$

29. $-10 = x^2 - 8x + 2$ **30.** $x^2 + 16x = 2$ **31.** $4 - x^2 = 10x$

32. $x^2 = 23 - 15x$ **33.** $8x - 2 = x^2 + 15x$ **34.** $-32x = 16 - x^2$

35. $2x^2 = 22x - 11$ **36.** $4x^2 - 8 = -13x$ **37.** $2x^2 - 12 = 3x$

Write each quadratic function in vertex form. Give the coordinates of the vertex and the equation of the axis of symmetry. Then describe the transformations from $f(x) = x^2$ to g.

38. $g(x) = 3x^2$ **39.** $g(x) = -x^2 + 2$ **40.** $g(x) = x^2 - 5x$

41. $g(x) = x^2 + 8x + 11$ **42.** $g(x) = x^2 - 6x - 2$ **43.** $g(x) = -x^2 + 4x + 2$

44. $g(x) = x^2 + 7x + 3$ **45.** $g(x) = -3x^2 + 6x - 9$ **46.** $g(x) = -2x^2 + 12x + 13$

47. Write three different quadratic functions that each have a vertex at $(2, 5)$.

304 CHAPTER 5

CHALLENGE

48. Write an equation for the quadratic function that has a vertex at $(2, 5)$ and contains the point $(1, 8)$.

CONNECTIONS

For Exercises 49 and 50, give both an exact answer and an approximate answer rounded to the nearest tenth.

49. GEOMETRY Each side of a square is increased by 2 centimeters, producing a new square whose area is 30 square centimeters. Find the length of the sides of the original square. width:

50. GEOMETRY The length of a rectangle is 6 feet longer than its width. If the area is 50 square feet, find the length and the width of the rectangle.

APPLICATIONS

51. PHYSICS The power, in megawatts, produced between midnight and noon by a power plant is given by $P = h^2 - 12h + 210$, where h is the hour of the day.
  a. At what time does the minimum power production occur?
  b. What is the minimum power production?
  c. During what hour(s) is the power production 187 megawatts?

52. FUND-RAISING Each year a school's booster club holds a dance to raise funds. In the past, the profit the club made after paying for the band and other costs has been modeled by the function $P(t) = -16t^2 + 800t - 4000$, where t represents the ticket price in dollars.
  a. What ticket price gives the maximum profit?
  b. What is the maximum profit?
  c. What ticket price(s) would generate a profit of $5424?

 Look Back

Solve each equation. *(LESSON 1.6)*

53. $5x + 3 = 2x + 18$ **54.** $\frac{2(x + 3)}{5} = x - 3$ **55.** $20 = 6x - 10$

For Exercises 56–59, determine whether each set of ordered pairs represents a function. *(LESSON 2.3)*

56. $\{(11, 0), (12, -1), (21, -2)\}$ **57.** $\{(0, 0), (2, 5), (3, 3)\}$

58. $\{(1, -1), (1, -2), (1, -3)\}$ **59.** $\{(4, 1), (5, 2), (6, 3)\}$

60. Evaluate $f(x) = \frac{1}{3}x - 2$ for $x = 2$ and $x = -3$. *(LESSON 2.3)*

61. Evaluate $g(x) = 7 - 4x$ for $x = 2$ and $x = -3$. *(LESSON 2.3)*

TRANSFORMATIONS **For Exercises 62–65, write the equation for the graph described.** *(LESSON 2.7)*

62. the graph of $f(x) = |x|$ translated 7 units to the left
63. the graph of $f(x) = x^2$ translated 6 units down
64. the graph of $f(x) = x^2$ stretched vertically by a factor of 8
65. the graph of $f(x) = |x|$ reflected through the x-axis and stretched horizontally by a factor of 3

66. Write a quadratic function whose zeros are −2 and 6. *(LESSON 5.1)*

Look Beyond

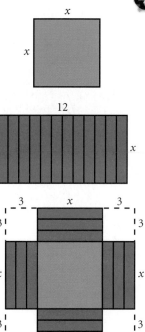

CULTURAL CONNECTION: AFRICA One of the first algebra books was written in Arabic by al-Khowarizmi around 800 C.E. This book used a method similar to algebra tiles to complete the square and solve for x.

To complete the square for the equation $x^2 + 12x = 45$, the al-Khowarizmi method begins with one square that is x units long on each side and 12 rectangles that are 1 unit wide and x units long.

Step 1 Divide the **12 rectangles** into 4 groups, and arrange them on the sides of the square. From the equation $x^2 + 12x = 45$, you know that the area of this shape is still 45 square units.

Step 2 To complete the square, add 3 × 3, or 9 units to each of the 4 corners:

$$9 \text{ units} \times 4 = 36 \text{ units}$$

The new area is $45 + 36 = 81$. If the area is 81, then the side length is 9. To find the length of x, solve $3 + x + 3 = 9$. Thus, $x = 3$.

67. Solve $x^2 + 20x = 125$ by using the al-Khowarizmi method.
68. Solve $x^2 + 32x = 33$ by using the al-Khowarizmi method.
69. Solve $x^2 + 56x = 116$ by using the al-Khowarizmi method.

SPORTS Refer to the height function in the Portfolio Activity on page 280.

Complete the square for the height function and answer the questions below.

1. What is the maximum height achieved by the basketball?

2. How long does it take the basketball to reach its maximum height?

3. What is the equation of the axis of symmetry for the height function?

4. How long would it take the basketball to drop to the ground if it were not tapped by a player?

5. Compare your answers to the questions above with those obtained in Portfolio Activities on page 280 and 298.

The Quadratic Formula

Objectives

● Use the quadratic formula to find real roots of quadratic equations.

● Use the roots of a quadratic equation to locate the axis of symmetry of a parabola.

Why *You can solve many real-world problems, such as finding the dimensions of this patio, by using the quadratic formula to solve quadratic equations.*

After watching a home-improvement show, the Wilkersons decided to build a patio along two sides of their home, as shown here. The patio will have the same width along both sides.

Find the width of the patio if the Wilkersons have enough material to cover a surface area of 650 square feet. You can use the *quadratic formula* to solve this problem. *You will solve this problem in Example 3.*

Using the method of completing the square, you can derive a formula that can be used to solve any quadratic equation in standard form.

$$ax^2 + bx + c = 0 \qquad \textit{Assume that } a \neq 0.$$

$$x^2 + \frac{b}{a}x + \frac{c}{a} = 0 \qquad \textit{Divide each side by a.}$$

$$x^2 + \frac{b}{a}x = -\frac{c}{a} \qquad \textit{Subtract } \tfrac{c}{a} \textit{ from each side.}$$

$$x^2 + \frac{b}{a}x + \left(\frac{b}{2a}\right)^2 = -\frac{c}{a} + \left(\frac{b}{2a}\right)^2 \qquad \textit{Complete the square.}$$

$$\left(x + \frac{b}{2a}\right)^2 = \frac{-4ac + b^2}{4a^2} \qquad \textit{Simplify.}$$

$$\sqrt{\left(x + \frac{b}{2a}\right)^2} = \pm\sqrt{\frac{b^2 - 4ac}{4a^2}} \qquad \textit{Take the square root of each side.}$$

$$x + \frac{b}{2a} = \pm\frac{\sqrt{b^2 - 4ac}}{2a} \qquad \textit{Simplify.}$$

$$x = -\frac{b}{2a} \pm \frac{\sqrt{b^2 - 4ac}}{2a} \qquad \textit{Subtract } \tfrac{b}{2a} \textit{ from each side.}$$

$$x = \frac{-b \pm \sqrt{b^2 - 4ac}}{2a} \qquad \textit{Simplify.}$$

Quadratic Formula

If $ax^2 + bx + c = 0$ and $a \neq 0$, then the solutions, or roots, are

$$x = \frac{-b \pm \sqrt{b^2 - 4ac}}{2a}.$$

Example 1 shows how to use the quadratic formula to solve a quadratic equation that is in standard form.

EXAMPLE ① Use the quadratic formula to find the roots of $x^2 + 5x - 14 = 0$.

● **SOLUTION**

In $x^2 + 5x - 14 = 0$, $a = 1$, $b = 5$, and $c = -14$.

$$x = \frac{-b \pm \sqrt{b^2 - 4ac}}{2a}$$

$$x = \frac{-5 \pm \sqrt{5^2 - 4(1)(-14)}}{2(1)} \qquad \textit{Use the quadratic formula.}$$

$$x = \frac{-5 + \sqrt{81}}{2} \quad or \quad x = \frac{-5 - \sqrt{81}}{2}$$

$$x = \frac{-5 + 9}{2} \qquad\qquad x = \frac{-5 - 9}{2} \qquad \textit{Substitute 9 for } \sqrt{81}.$$

$$x = 2 \qquad\qquad\qquad x = -7$$

TRY THIS   Use the quadratic formula to solve $x^2 - 7x + 6 = 0$.

CHECKPOINT ✔ Solve $x^2 + 5x - 14 = 0$ by factoring to check the solution to Example 1.

The solutions to a quadratic equation can be irrational numbers. This is shown in Example 2.

EXAMPLE ② Use the quadratic formula to solve $4x^2 = 8 - 3x$. Give exact solutions and approximate solutions to the nearest tenth.

● **SOLUTION**

PROBLEM SOLVING   **Use a formula.** Write the equation in standard form. Then use the quadratic formula.

$$4x^2 = 8 - 3x$$

$$4x^2 + 3x - 8 = 0$$

$$x = \frac{-3 \pm \sqrt{3^2 - 4(4)(-8)}}{2(4)}$$

$$x = \frac{-3 \pm \sqrt{137}}{8}$$

$$x = \frac{-3 + \sqrt{137}}{8} \quad or \quad x = \frac{-3 - \sqrt{137}}{8} \qquad \textit{Exact solution}$$

$$x \approx 1.1 \qquad\qquad\qquad x \approx -1.8 \qquad \textit{Approximate solution}$$

TRY THIS   Use the quadratic formula to solve $2x^2 - 6x = -3$. Give exact solutions and approximate solutions to the nearest tenth.

EXAMPLE **3** Refer to the patio described at the beginning of the lesson.

APPLICATION
CONSTRUCTION

Find the width of the patio if there is enough material to cover a surface area of 650 square feet.

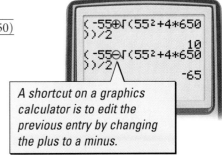

SOLUTION

PROBLEM SOLVING

Write an equation.

$$A(x) = 25x + 30x + x^2$$
$$= x^2 + 55x$$

Solve $x^2 + 55x = 650$ for x.

TECHNOLOGY
SCIENTIFIC
CALCULATOR

$$x^2 + 55x = 650$$
$$x^2 + 55x - 650 = 0$$
$$x = \frac{-55 \pm \sqrt{55^2 - 4(1)(-650)}}{2(1)}$$
$$x = \frac{-55 \pm 75}{2}$$
$$x = 10 \quad or \quad x = -65$$

Since the width must be positive, −65 cannot be a solution. The patio should be 10 feet wide.

A shortcut on a graphics calculator is to edit the previous entry by changing the plus to a minus.

TRY THIS
Find the width of the patio described at the beginning of the lesson if there is enough cement to cover a surface area of 500 square feet.

Recall from Lesson 5.3 that real-number solutions of a quadratic equation $ax^2 + bx + c = 0$ are also the x-intercepts of the related quadratic function $f(x) = ax^2 + bx + c$. You can examine this in the Activity below.

Activity
Exploring Roots of Equations

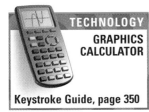

TECHNOLOGY
GRAPHICS
CALCULATOR

Keystroke Guide, page 350

You will need: a graphics calculator

1. Copy the table below. Complete the second and third columns of the table by using any method to find the roots of each equation.

2. Graph each related function and find the x-coordinate of the vertex. Then complete the last two columns of the table.

Equation	Roots	Average of roots	Related function	x-coordinate of vertex
$x^2 + 2x = 0$	0, −2	−1	$f(x) = x^2 + 2x$	−1
$-x^2 + 4 = 0$				
$x^2 + 4x + 4 = 0$				
$2x^2 + 5x - 3 = 0$				
$-x^2 - 3x + 4 = 0$				

CHECKPOINT ✔

3. Write a brief explanation that tells how to find the x-coordinate of the vertex for the graph of a quadratic function.

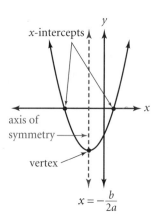

x-intercepts

y

x

axis of symmetry

vertex

$x = -\dfrac{b}{2a}$

Recall from Lesson 5.1 that the equation of the axis of symmetry of a parabola is obtained from the x-coordinate of the vertex of the parabola. Using the symmetry of the parabola, an equation for the axis of symmetry can be found by taking the average of the two roots found with the quadratic formula.

$$\dfrac{\left(\dfrac{-b + \sqrt{b^2 - 4ac}}{2a}\right) + \left(\dfrac{-b - \sqrt{b^2 - 4ac}}{2a}\right)}{2} = -\dfrac{b}{2a}$$

Axis of Symmetry of a Parabola

If $y = ax^2 + bx + c$, where $a \neq 0$, then the equation for the axis of symmetry of the parabola is $x = -\dfrac{b}{2a}$.

E X A M P L E **4** Let $f(x) = 19 + 8x + 2x^2$. Write the equation for the axis of symmetry of the graph, and find the coordinates of the vertex.

● **SOLUTION**

To find a and b, rewrite the function as $f(x) = 2x^2 + 8x + 19$. Then $a = 2$ and $b = 8$.

PROBLEM SOLVING

Use a formula. The axis of symmetry is $x = -\dfrac{b}{2a}$.

$x = -\dfrac{8}{2(2)} = -2$ → $f(x) = 19 + 8x + 2x^2$

→ $f(-2) = 19 + 8(-2) + 2(-2)^2$ *Substitute −2 for x.*

$f(-2) = 11$

Thus, the equation for the axis of symmetry is $x = -2$, and the coordinates of the vertex are $(-2, 11)$.

TRY THIS Let $g(x) = x^2 - 4x + 1$. Write the equation for the axis of symmetry of the graph, and find the coordinates of the vertex.

CRITICAL THINKING What do you know about an equation that has integer solutions when it is solved by using the quadratic formula?

Exercises

● *Communicate*

1. Describe at least three methods you can use to find the x-intercepts of the parabola described by $f(x) = x^2 + 2x - 3$.

2. Describe two ways to find the vertex of a parabola.

3. How is the axis of symmetry related to the vertex of a parabola?

Use the quadratic formula to find the roots of each equation.
(EXAMPLE 1)

4. $x^2 - 5x + 4 = 0$ **5.** $2x^2 - 5x = 3$

6. Use the quadratic formula to solve $3x^2 - 3x = 4$. Give exact solutions and approximate solutions to the nearest tenth. **(EXAMPLE 2)**

APPLICATION

7. CONSTRUCTION If the Wilkersons have enough material to cover a surface area of 700 square feet, then the equation becomes $x^2 + 55x = 700$. Find the width of the patio, to the nearest tenth of a foot, from this equation. **(EXAMPLE 3)**

For each function, write the equation for the axis of symmetry of the graph, and find the coordinates of the vertex. **(EXAMPLE 4)**

8. $f(x) = x^2 - x - 2$ **9.** $f(x) = 2x^2 - 12x + 11$

● *Practice and Apply* ━━━━━━━━

Use the quadratic formula to solve each equation. Give exact solutions.

10. $x^2 + 7x + 9 = 0$ **11.** $x^2 + 6x = 0$

12. $(x + 1)(x - 2) = 5$ **13.** $(x - 4)(x + 5) = 7$

14. $t^2 - 9t + 5 = 0$ **15.** $x^2 - 3x - 1 = 0$

16. $x^2 + 9x - 2 = -16$ **17.** $x^2 - 5x - 6 = 18$

18. $5x^2 + 16x - 6 = 3$ **19.** $4x^2 = -8x - 3$

20. $3x^2 - 3 = -5x - 1$ **21.** $x^2 + 3x = 2 - 2x$

22. $x^2 + 6x + 5 = 0$ **23.** $x^2 + 10x = 5$

24. $-2x^2 + 4x = -2$ **25.** $5x^2 - 2x - 3 = 0$

26. $-6x^2 + 3x + 19 = 0$ **27.** $-x^2 - 3x + 1 = 0$

For each quadratic function, write the equation for the axis of symmetry, and find the coordinates of the vertex.

28. $y = 7x^2 + 6x - 5$ **29.** $y = x^2 + 9x + 14$

30. $y = 3 + 7x + 2x^2$ **31.** $y = 10 - 5x^2 - 15x$

32. $y = 3x^2 + 6x - 18$ **33.** $y = 14 + 8x - 2x^2$

34. $y = 4 - 10x + 5x^2$ **35.** $y = -x^2 - 6x + 2$

36. $y = 3x^2 + 21x - 4$ **37.** $y = -2x^2 + 3x - 1$

38. $y = 3x^2 - 18x + 22$ **39.** $y = -2x^2 + 8x + 13$

40. $y = 3x - 2x^2 + 2$ **41.** $y = -1 - 8x + 12x^2$

42. $y = 7x^2 - 12x + 2$ **43.** $y = 2x - 2 + x^2$

44. $y = 4x^2 - 3x - 8$ **45.** $y = 9 - 3x^2$

46. $y = 5x - x^2$ **47.** $y = 5x^2 + 2x - 3$

CHALLENGE

48. Prove that if the roots of $ax^2 + bx + c = 0$, where $a \neq 0$, are reciprocals, then $a = c$.

MAXIMUM/MINIMUM A professional pyrotechnician shoots fireworks vertically into the air from the ground with an initial velocity of 192 feet per second. The height in feet of the fireworks is given by $h(t) = -16t^2 + 192t$.

49. How long does it take for the fireworks to reach the maximum height?

50. What is the maximum height reached by the fireworks?

51. Certain fireworks shoot sparks for 2.5 seconds, leaving a trail. After how many seconds might the pyrotechnician want the fireworks to begin firing in order for the sparks to be at the maximum height? Explain.

APPLICATIONS

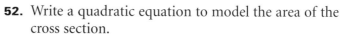

MANUFACTURING To form a rectangular rain gutter from a flat sheet of aluminum that is 12 inches wide, an equal amount of aluminum, x, is bent up on each side, as shown at left. The area of the cross section is 18 square inches.

52. Write a quadratic equation to model the area of the cross section.

53. Find the depth of the gutter.

BUSINESS The owner of a company that produces handcrafted music stands hires a consultant to help set the selling price for the product. The consultant analyzes the production costs and consumer demand for the stands and arrives at a function for the profit, $P(x) = -0.3x^2 + 75x - 2000$, where x represents the selling price of the stands.

54. At what price should the stands be sold to earn the maximum profit?

55. According to the function given, what is the maximum profit that the company can make?

56. What are the break-even points (the selling prices for which the profit is 0)? Give your answers to the nearest cent.

57. For what values of x does the company make a profit?

58. For what values of x does the company suffer a loss?

CHALLENGE

59. ART In the art of many cultures, a ratio called the *golden ratio*, or *golden mean*, has been used as an organizing principle because it produces designs that are deemed naturally pleasing to the eye. The golden mean is based on the division of a line segment into two parts, a and b, such that the ratio of the longer segment, a, to the shorter segment, b, equals the ratio of the whole segment, $a + b$, to the longer segment, a.
  a. Solve the golden ratio for a in terms of b.
  b. Find the value of the golden ratio. Give the exact value and the approximate value to the nearest hundredth. (Hint: Divide each side of the equation from part **a** by b, and simplify.)

 *Look Back*

Write an equation in slope-intercept form for the line that contains the given point and is perpendicular to the given line. *(LESSON 1.3)*

60. $(-2, 3), y = x - 5$ **61.** $(4, -6), 2x - y = 1$

Write an equation in slope-intercept form for the line that contains the given point and is parallel to the given line. *(LESSON 1.3)*

62. $(8, -1), y = -3x + 12$ **63.** $(-4, -2), 5x = 4 - y$

Solve each absolute-value inequality. Graph the solution on a number line. *(LESSON 1.8)*

64. $|x + 6| > 2$ **65.** $|x - 3| < 5$ **66.** $|-4x| \leq 8$ **67.** $|8 - 2x| \geq 6$

Find the inverse of each matrix, if it exists. Round numbers to the nearest hundredth. Indicate if the matrix does not have an inverse. *(LESSON 4.3)*

68. $\begin{bmatrix} -3 & 2 \\ 12 & 9 \end{bmatrix}$ **69.** $\begin{bmatrix} -1 & 8 \\ 4 & -7 \end{bmatrix}$ **70.** $\begin{bmatrix} 6 & -4 & 18 \\ 21 & -3 & 19 \\ 4 & 5 & -2 \end{bmatrix}$

Solve each equation. *(LESSON 5.2)*

71. $-2x^2 = -16$ **72.** $-3x^2 + 15 = -6$ **73.** $32 = 2x^2 - 4$

 *Look Beyond*

74. Use the quadratic formula to solve $2x^2 + 5x + 6 = 0$. Can you find a real-number solution? Explain.

SPORTS Use the quadratic formula and the formula for the axis of symmetry of a parabola to answer the questions below based on the height function from the Portfolio Activity on page 280.

1. What is the equation of the axis of symmetry for the model?

2. What is the maximum height achieved by the basketball?

3. How long does it take the basketball to reach its maximum height?

4. How much time would it take the basketball to drop to the ground if it were not tapped?

5. Compare your answers to the questions above with those obtained in the Portfolio Activities on pages 280, 298, and 306.

WORKING ON THE CHAPTER PROJECT

You should now be able to complete Activity 2 of the Chapter Project.

Quadratic Equations and Complex Numbers

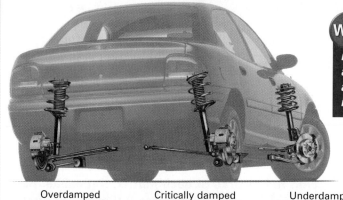

Why *Solutions to many real-world problems, such as classifying a shock absorber spring system, involve complex numbers.*

Overdamped	Critically damped	Underdamped
2 real roots	1 real root	0 real roots

Each diagram represents the motion of a shock absorber spring over a period of 2 seconds from left to right.

Objectives

- Classify and find all roots of a quadratic equation.
- Graph and perform operations on complex numbers.

APPLICATION

ENGINEERING

Carlos and Keiko are mechanical engineers who are analyzing car shock absorbers. They know that the motion of the spring is affected by a damping force. Three situations are possible depending on how the mass of the car, the spring, and the damping force are related. The roots of $x^2 + mx + n = 0$, where m and n depend on the car's mass, the spring, and the damping force, help them to classify a spring system. *You will classify a spring system after Example 1.*

The Discriminant

When you apply the quadratic formula to any quadratic equation, you will find that the value of $b^2 - 4ac$ is either positive, negative, or 0. The expression $b^2 - 4ac$ is called the **discriminant** of a quadratic equation.

You can see from the quadratic formula that if $b^2 - 4ac > 0$, the formula will give two different answers. If $b^2 - 4ac = 0$, there will be one answer, called a **double root**. If $b^2 - 4ac < 0$, the radical will be undefined for real numbers, so the formula gives no real solutions.

Solutions of a Quadratic Equation

Let $ax^2 + bx + c = 0$, where $a \neq 0$.

- If $b^2 - 4ac > 0$, then the quadratic equation has 2 distinct real solutions.
- If $b^2 - 4ac = 0$, then the equation has 1 real solution, a double root.
- If $b^2 - 4ac < 0$, then the equation has 0 real solutions.

EXAMPLE ❶ **Find the discriminant for each equation. Then determine the number of real solutions for each equation by using the discriminant.**

a. $2x^2 + 4x + 1 = 0$ **b.** $2x^2 + 4x + 2 = 0$ **c.** $2x^2 + 4x + 3 = 0$

● **SOLUTION**

a. $2x^2 + 4x + 1 = 0$

$b^2 - 4ac$

$= 4^2 - 4(2)(1)$

$= 8$

Because $b^2 - 4ac > 0$, the equation has 2 real solutions.

b. $2x^2 + 4x + 2 = 0$

$b^2 - 4ac$

$= 4^2 - 4(2)(2)$

$= 0$

Because $b^2 - 4ac = 0$, the equation has 1 real solution.

c. $2x^2 + 4x + 3 = 0$

$b^2 - 4ac$

$= 4^2 - 4(2)(3)$

$= -8$

Because $b^2 - 4ac < 0$, the equation has no real solutions.

CHECK

Graph the related functions to check.

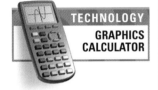

TECHNOLOGY

GRAPHICS CALCULATOR

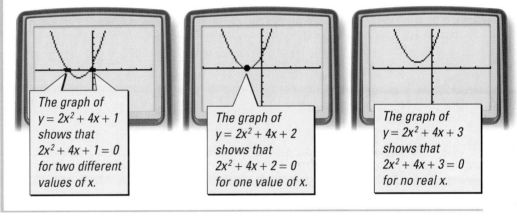

The graph of $y = 2x^2 + 4x + 1$ shows that $2x^2 + 4x + 1 = 0$ for two different values of x.

The graph of $y = 2x^2 + 4x + 2$ shows that $2x^2 + 4x + 2 = 0$ for one value of x.

The graph of $y = 2x^2 + 4x + 3$ shows that $2x^2 + 4x + 3 = 0$ for no real x.

TRY THIS Identify the number of real solutions to $-3x^2 - 6x + 15 = 0$.

CHECKPOINT ✔ Refer to the shock-absorber situation described on page 314. Classify a spring system in which $m = 8$ and $n = 24$.

Complex Numbers

Leonhard Euler

CULTURAL CONNECTION: EUROPE Whether it is possible to take the square root of a negative number is a question that puzzled mathematicians for a long time. In the sixteenth century, Italian mathematician Girolamo Cardano (1501–1576) was the first to use complex numbers to solve quadratic equations. Leonhard Euler (1707–1783) defined the **imaginary unit**, *i*, such that $i = \sqrt{-1}$ and $i^2 = -1$. In the nineteenth century, the theoretical basis of complex numbers was rigorously developed.

Girolamo Cardano

Imaginary Numbers

If $r > 0$, then the **imaginary number** $\sqrt{-r}$ is defined as follows:
$$\sqrt{-r} = \sqrt{-1} \cdot \sqrt{r} = i\sqrt{r}$$

For example, $\sqrt{-4} = \sqrt{-1} \cdot \sqrt{4} = 2i$ and $\sqrt{-6} = \sqrt{-1} \cdot \sqrt{6} = i\sqrt{6}$.

With the quadratic formula and the imaginary unit, i, you can find solutions to any quadratic equation. This is shown in Example 2.

E X A M P L E ❷ Use the quadratic formula to solve $3x^2 - 7x + 5 = 0$.

● **SOLUTION**

$$x = \frac{-(-7) \pm \sqrt{(-7)^2 - 4(3)(5)}}{2(3)} \qquad \textit{Substitute } a = 3, \ b = -7, \text{ and } c = 5.$$

$$x = \frac{7 \pm \sqrt{-11}}{6}$$

$$x = \frac{7}{6} + \frac{\sqrt{-11}}{6} \quad \textit{or} \quad x = \frac{7}{6} - \frac{\sqrt{-11}}{6}$$

$$x = \frac{7}{6} + \frac{i\sqrt{11}}{6} \qquad\qquad x = \frac{7}{6} - \frac{i\sqrt{11}}{6} \qquad \textit{Replace } \sqrt{-11} \text{ with } i\sqrt{11}.$$

> The numbers $\frac{7}{6} + \frac{i\sqrt{11}}{6}$ and $\frac{7}{6} - \frac{i\sqrt{11}}{6}$ are complex numbers.

TRY THIS Use the quadratic formula to solve $-4x^2 + 5x - 3 = 0$.

Complex Numbers

A **complex number** is any number that can be written as $a + bi$, where a and b are real numbers and $i = \sqrt{-1}$; a is called the **real part** and b is called the **imaginary part**.

The form $a + bi$ is called the *standard form* of a complex number. Real numbers are complex numbers for which $b = 0$. A complex number is called a *pure* imaginary number if its real part, a, is 0.

E X A M P L E ❸ Find x and y such that $7x - 2iy = 14 + 6i$.

● **SOLUTION**

Two complex numbers are equal if their real parts are equal and their imaginary parts are equal.

Real parts	Imaginary parts
$7x = 14$	$-2y = 6$
$x = 2$	$y = -3$

Thus, $x = 2$ and $y = -3$.

TRY THIS Find x and y such that $2x + 3iy = -8 + 10i$.

Operations With Complex Numbers

EXAMPLE 4 **Find each sum or difference.**

a. $(-3 + 5i) + (7 - 6i)$ **b.** $(-3 - 8i) - (-2 - 9i)$

SOLUTION

Add or subtract the corresponding real parts and imaginary parts.

a. $(-3 + 5i) + (7 - 6i)$
$= (-3 + 7) + (5i - 6i)$
$= 4 - 1i$
$= 4 - i$

b. $(-3 - 8i) - (-2 - 9i)$
$= (-3 + 2) - (8i - 9i)$
$= -1 + 1i$
$= -1 + i$

Two complex numbers whose real parts are opposites and whose imaginary parts are opposites are called *additive inverses.*

$$(4 + 3i) + (-4 - 3i) = 0 + 0i = 0$$

CHECKPOINT ✔ What is the additive inverse of $2i - 12$?

EXAMPLE 5 **Multiply $(2 + i)(-5 - 3i)$.**

SOLUTION

$(2 + i)(-5 - 3i) = 2(-5 - 3i) + i(-5 - 3i)$ *Apply the Distributive Property.*
$= -10 - 6i - 5i - 3i^2$
$= -10 - 11i - 3(-1)$ *Replace i^2 with -1.*
$= -7 - 11i$

TRY THIS Multiply $(6 - 4i)(5 - 4i)$.

Activity

Exploring Powers of *i*

You will need: no special materials

1. Copy and complete the table below. (Hint: Recall that $i^2 = -1$.)

i	$i^2 =$	$i^3 =$	$i^4 =$
$i^5 =$	$i^6 =$	$i^7 =$	$i^8 =$

2. Observe the patterns in the table above. Use your observations to complete the table below.

$i^9 =$	$i^{10} =$	$i^{11} =$	$i^{12} =$
$i^{13} =$	$i^{14} =$	$i^{15} =$	$i^{16} =$

CHECKPOINT ✔ 3. Describe the pattern that occurs in the powers of i. Explain how to use the pattern to evaluate i^{41}, i^{66}, i^{75}, and i^{100}.

In order to simplify a fraction containing complex numbers, you often need to use the *conjugate of a complex number*. For example, the conjugate of $2 + 5i$ is $2 - 5i$ and the conjugate of $1 - 3i$ is $1 + 3i$.

Conjugate of a Complex Number

The **conjugate** of a complex number $a + bi$ is $a - bi$. The conjugate of $a + bi$ is denoted $\overline{a + bi}$.

To simplify a quotient with an imaginary number in the denominator, multiply by a fraction equal to 1, using the conjugate of the denominator, as shown in Example 6. This process is called **rationalizing the denominator.**

E X A M P L E **6** Simplify $\frac{2 + 5i}{2 - 3i}$. **Write your answer in standard form.**

● **SOLUTION**

$\frac{2 + 5i}{2 - 3i} = \frac{2 + 5i}{2 - 3i} \cdot \frac{2 + 3i}{2 + 3i}$ *Multiply by 1, using the conjugate of the denominator.*

CHECK

In complex mode, enter the expression. Then express the answer with fractions.

$= \frac{(2 + 5i)(2 + 3i)}{(2 - 3i)(2 + 3i)}$

$= \frac{4 + 10i + 6i + 15i^2}{4 - 6i + 6i - 9i^2}$

$= \frac{-11 + 16i}{13}$

$= -\frac{11}{13} + \frac{16}{13}i$

TECHNOLOGY

GRAPHICS CALCULATOR

Keystroke Guide, page 350

Note that the last term is $\frac{16}{13}i$, not $\frac{16}{13i}$.

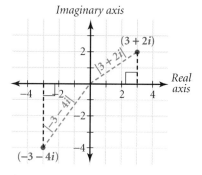

TRY THIS   Simplify $\frac{3 - 4i}{2 + i}$. Write your answer in standard form.

CRITICAL THINKING   Show that if a complex number is equal to its conjugate, the number is real.

C O N N E C T I O N

COORDINATE GEOMETRY

Complex numbers are graphed in the *complex plane*. In the **complex plane**, the horizontal axis is called the **real axis** and the vertical axis is called the **imaginary axis.** To graph the complex number $a + bi$, plot the point (a, b). For example, the point $(3, 2)$ represents the complex number $3 + 2i$ and the point $(-3, -4)$ represents the complex number $-3 - 4i$.

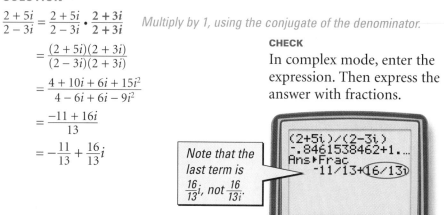

The absolute value of a real number is its distance from zero on the number line. Likewise, the **absolute value of a complex number** $a + bi$, denoted by $|a + bi|$, is its distance from the origin in the complex plane. By the Pythagorean Theorem, $|a + bi| = \sqrt{a^2 + b^2}$. For example, $|3 + 2i| = \sqrt{3^2 + 2^2} = \sqrt{13}$ and $|-3 - 4i| = \sqrt{(-3)^2 + (-4)^2} = 5$.

EXAMPLE **7** Evaluate $|-2 - 3i|$. Sketch a diagram that shows $-2 - 3i$ and $|-2 - 3i|$.

SOLUTION

$$|-2 - 3i| = \sqrt{(-2)^2 + (-3)^2}$$
$$= \sqrt{4 + 9}$$
$$= \sqrt{13}$$

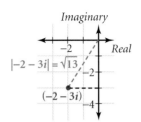

TRY THIS   Evaluate $|-3 + 5i|$. Sketch a diagram that shows $-3 + 5i$ and $|-3 + 5i|$.

CRITICAL THINKING   The real numbers are said to be "well-ordered," meaning that any real number is either larger or smaller than any other given real number. Are the complex numbers well-ordered? Explain.

Exercises

Communicate

1. What can the discriminant tell you about the solutions of a quadratic equation?

2. How do you simplify a rational expression that contains a complex number in the denominator?

3. How do you graph a real number in the complex plane? a pure imaginary number?

Guided Skills Practice

Determine the number of real solutions for each equation. *(EXAMPLE 1)*

4. $x^2 + 2x + 1 = 0$ 5. $2x^2 + 4x + 5 = 0$ 6. $x^2 + 3x + 1 = 0$

7. Solve the equation $2x^2 + 5x + 4 = 0$. *(EXAMPLE 2)*

8. Find x and y such that $-2x + 3yi = 2 + 6i$. *(EXAMPLE 3)*

Simplify each expression.

9. $(2 + 3i) + (4 + 7i)$ *(EXAMPLE 4)*

10. $(8 + 4i) - (3 + 2i)$ *(EXAMPLE 4)*

11. $(-1 + 2i)(3 + 4i)$ *(EXAMPLE 5)*

12. $\dfrac{-1 + 4i}{2 + 3i}$ *(EXAMPLE 6)*

13. Evaluate $|3 + 4i|$. Sketch a diagram that shows $3 + 4i$ and $|3 + 4i|$. *(EXAMPLE 7)*

Identify the real and imaginary parts of each complex number.

14. $-5 + 6i$ **15.** $2 + i$ **16.** 6 **17.** $4i$

Simplify.

18. $\sqrt{-36}$ **19.** $\sqrt{-100}$ **20.** $\sqrt{-13}$

21. $\sqrt{-17}$ **22.** $(-3i)^2$ **23.** $(-7i)^2$

Find the discriminant, and determine the number of real solutions. Then solve.

24. $x^2 + 5x + 8 = 0$ **25.** $3x^2 - 5x + 4 = 0$ **26.** $x^2 - 7x = -10$

27. $5x^2 - 5x + 2 = 0$ **28.** $-x^2 + 8x - 19 = 0$ **29.** $x^2 - 3x = 7$

30. $-2x^2 + 10x = 15$ **31.** $2x^2 - 6x = -5$ **32.** $4x^2 + x - 2 = 0$

33. $2x^2 + 3x = 0$ **34.** $5x^2 + 4x = -5$ **35.** $2x^2 + 2x + 2 = 0$

36. $16 - 8x = -x^2$ **37.** $x^2 + 49 = 14x$ **38.** $-x^2 + 4x - 5 = 0$

39. $8x^2 + 5x + 2 = 0$ **40.** $4x^2 + 9 = 12x$ **41.** $1 + 9x^2 = 6x$

Find *x* and *y*.

42. $6x + 7iy = 18 - 21i$ **43.** $3x - 4iy = 4 + 4i$ **44.** $2x + 5i = 8 + 20yi$

Perform the indicated addition or subtraction.

45. $(-2 + 3i) + (-1 - 4i)$ **46.** $(1 + 2i) - (1 + 5i)$ **47.** $\left(\frac{1}{2} + \frac{2}{5}i\right) + \left(\frac{1}{2} - \frac{1}{5}i\right)$

48. $\left(\frac{3}{8} + \frac{2}{3}i\right) - \left(\frac{1}{4} - \frac{1}{3}i\right)$ **49.** $(3 + i) + (6 - 2i)$ **50.** $(8 - 6i) - (4 - 3i)$

Multiply.

51. $i(2 + i)$ **52.** $(1 + i)(1 - i)$ **53.** $(-5 - i)(-2 + 2i)$

54. $(-5 + 3i)(2 - 3i)$ **55.** $(6 - 7i)^2$ **56.** $(2 - 4i)^2$

57. $(-1 + i\sqrt{5})^2$ **58.** $(2 + i\sqrt{3})^2$ **59.** $(2 - 3i\sqrt{2})^2$

Write the conjugate of each complex number.

60. $2 + 3i$ **61.** 8 **62.** $-4 - i$ **63.** $8 - 3i$

Simplify.

64. $\frac{4 + 2i}{2 + i}$ **65.** $\frac{3 + 2i}{5 + i}$ **66.** $\left(\frac{1}{2} + i\right)\left(\frac{2}{3} + \frac{1}{4}i\right)$

67. $\frac{4 + 2i}{\frac{2}{3} + \frac{1}{2}i}$ **68.** $2(3 - 2i) + 5(1 + i)$ **69.** $\frac{1}{4}(1 + i\sqrt{3})(1 - i\sqrt{3})$

70. $(1 + i)^2 + \frac{2 + 2i}{2 + i}$ **71.** $\frac{3 + i}{4 + i} + 1 + i$ **72.** $(-3i)(3i) - (2 + 2i)$

73. $i(1 + i) - (3 + i)$ **74.** $i^3(5 + i) + 7i$ **75.** $\left(\frac{\sqrt{2}}{2} + \frac{\sqrt{2}}{2}i\right)^2$

Graph each number and its conjugate in the complex plane.

76. $5 + 3i$ **77.** $-2 + 4i$ **78.** $-3 - 5i$ **79.** $2 - 3i$

80. $-2i$ **81.** $6i$ **82.** $-2 + 7i$ **83.** $-7 - 2i$

84. -4 **85.** $5 + i$ **86.** $3 - 5i$ **87.** 3

Evaluate. Then sketch a diagram that shows the absolute value.

88. $|1 + i|$ **89.** $|i|$ **90.** $\left|\dfrac{3}{5} + \dfrac{4}{5}i\right|$ **91.** $\left|1 + 0.01i\right|$

92. $|2i|$ **93.** $|2 + 3i|$ **94.** $\left|\dfrac{1}{\sqrt{2}} + \dfrac{1}{\sqrt{2}}i\right|$ **95.** $\left|\dfrac{1}{\sqrt{3}} + \dfrac{\sqrt{2}}{\sqrt{3}}i\right|$

96. Identify the complex numbers graphed on the complex plane at right.

97. Identify the coordinates of the conjugate of each complex number graphed at right.

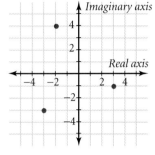

CHALLENGES

98. If $\overline{c + di} = -(c + di)$, what can you say about the complex number $c + di$? (Hint: Solve for c.)

99. Let $a > 0$ and $b > 0$. Plot $a + bi$, $a - bi$, $-(a + bi)$, and $-a + bi$ in the complex plane. Connect the points with vertical and horizontal lines. What is the result?

CONNECTION

100. TRANSFORMATIONS Describe the relationship between the graph of a complex number and the graph of its conjugate as a translation, rotation, or reflection.

 Look Back

Graph each function and its inverse on the same coordinate plane. (LESSON 2.5)

101. $f(x) = 2x - 3$ **102.** $f(x) = -3x + 5$ **103.** $f(x) = 2x$

Let $f(x) = 3x - 5$. Find the indicated function. (LESSONS 2.4 AND 2.5)

104. $f^{-1}(x)$ **105.** $(f \circ f^{-1})(x)$ **106.** $(f^{-1} \circ f)(x)$

APPLICATIONS

107. BUSINESS Gene ordered 8 prints for his new restaurant. Each unframed print cost $50, and each framed print cost $98. The total cost of the prints was $640. How many framed prints did Gene buy? *(LESSONS 3.1 AND 3.2)*

108. RECYCLING A recycling center pays $1.25 for 100 pounds of newspaper and $0.40 for 1 pound of aluminum. Linda took a 460-pound load of aluminum and newspaper to the recycling center and was paid $21.82. How many pounds of aluminum and how many pounds of newspaper did Linda have? *(LESSONS 3.1 AND 3.2)*

 *Look Beyond*

Graph each function, and estimate the zeros.

109 $f(x) = (x - 2)(x + 3)(x + 5)$ **110** $f(x) = x(x - 6)(x + 1)$

111 $f(x) = x^3 + x^2 - 2x$ **112** $f(x) = x^3 + 2x^2 + x$

Curve Fitting With Quadratic Models

Objectives

● Find a quadratic function that exactly fits three data points.

● Find a quadratic model to represent a data set.

Why *You can model real-world situations, such as the total stopping distance of a car, by using a process called curve fitting to find an appropriate model.*

Traffic speeds are reduced in school zones for improved safety of students.

APPLICATION

HIGHWAY SAFETY

Fitting a set of data with a quadratic model is an example of *curve fitting*. In Lesson 5.1, you examined a quadratic model for the total stopping distance, d, in feet as a function of a car's speed, x, in miles per hour.

$$d(x) = \frac{11}{10}x + \frac{1}{19}x^2$$

This function models actual data that is provided in Lesson 2.4. Another set of data for speed and stopping distance is shown at right. How can you find a quadratic model for this data? *You will answer this question in Example 3.*

Speed (mph)	Stopping distance (ft)
10	12.5
20	36.0
30	69.5
40	114.0
50	169.5
60	249.0
70	325.5

Some graphics calculators can fit a parabola to three noncollinear points. Example 1 illustrates another method that you can use.

EXAMPLE ❶ Find a quadratic function whose graph contains the points $(1, 3)$, $(2, -3)$, and $(6, 13)$.

● **SOLUTION**

1. To find a, b, and c in $f(x) = ax^2 + bx + c$, write and solve a system of three linear equations in three variables, a, b, and c.

Point	Substitution	Equation
$(1, 3)$	$a(1)^2 + b(1) + c = 3$	$a + b + c = 3$
$(2, -3)$	$a(2)^2 + b(2) + c = -3$	$4a + 2b + c = -3$
$(6, 13)$	$a(6)^2 + b(6) + c = 13$	$36a + 6b + c = 13$

$$\begin{cases} a + b + c = 3 \\ 4a + 2b + c = -3 \\ 36a + 6b + c = 13 \end{cases}$$

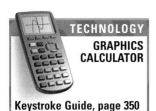

TECHNOLOGY
GRAPHICS
CALCULATOR

Keystroke Guide, page 350

2. Use a matrix equation to solve the system.

$$\begin{bmatrix} 1 & 1 & 1 \\ 4 & 2 & 1 \\ 36 & 6 & 1 \end{bmatrix} \begin{bmatrix} a \\ b \\ c \end{bmatrix} = \begin{bmatrix} 3 \\ -3 \\ 13 \end{bmatrix} \rightarrow \begin{bmatrix} a \\ b \\ c \end{bmatrix} = \begin{bmatrix} 2 \\ -12 \\ 13 \end{bmatrix}$$

The solution is $a = 2$, $b = -12$, and $c = 13$.

3. Write the quadratic function.

$$f(x) = ax^2 + bx + c$$
$$f(x) = 2x^2 - 12x + 13$$

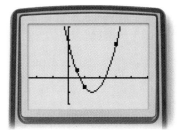

CHECK
Create a scatter plot of the three data points.
Graph $f(x) = 2x^2 - 12x + 13$ on the same screen.
The graph should contain the data points.

TRY THIS Find a quadratic function whose graph contains the points $(2, -3)$, $(4, 3)$, and $(6, 1)$.

When variables in a table represent a quadratic relationship, a constant difference in the consecutive x-values results in a constant *second difference* in the respective y-values. This fact is used in Example 2 to help determine whether a quadratic model is appropriate for a set of data.

E X A M P L E ❷ Refer to the pattern of dots below, in which each set of dots except the first is formed by adding a bottom row containing 1 more dot than the previous bottom row.

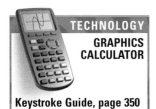

TECHNOLOGY
GRAPHICS
CALCULATOR

Keystroke Guide, page 350

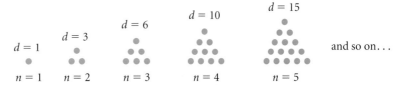

a. Explain why a quadratic model is suitable for relating the number of dots, d, in the triangle to the number of dots, n, on each side of the triangle.
b. Find a quadratic function for d in terms of n.
c. Use the model to predict the number of dots in a triangle with 10 dots on each side.

● **SOLUTION**

CONNECTION
STATISTICS

a. Make a scatter plot of points, (n, d). Use $(1, 1)$, $(2, 3)$, $(3, 6)$, $(4, 10)$, and $(5, 15)$. It appears that a curve rather than a straight line will fit the data.

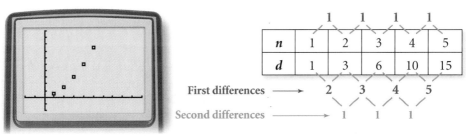

PROBLEM SOLVING

Look for a pattern. Because the second differences are constant, there will be a quadratic equation that models the data exactly.

LESSON 5.7 CURVE FITTING WITH QUADRATIC MODELS **323**

b. To find a, b, and c in $d = an^2 + bn + c$, write and solve a system of three linear equations in three variables a, b, and c.

Point	Evaluation	Equation
$(1, 1)$	$a(1)^2 + b(1) + c = 1$	$a + b + c = 1$
$(2, 3)$	$a(2)^2 + b(2) + c = 3$	$4a + 2b + c = 3$
$(3, 6)$	$a(3)^2 + b(3) + c = 6$	$9a + 3b + c = 6$

$$\begin{cases} a + b + c = 1 \\ 4a + 2b + c = 3 \\ 9a + 3b + c = 6 \end{cases}$$

TECHNOLOGY

GRAPHICS CALCULATOR

Keystroke Guide, page 351

Use a matrix equation to solve the system.

$$\begin{bmatrix} 1 & 1 & 1 \\ 4 & 2 & 1 \\ 9 & 3 & 1 \end{bmatrix} \begin{bmatrix} a \\ b \\ c \end{bmatrix} = \begin{bmatrix} 1 \\ 3 \\ 6 \end{bmatrix} \rightarrow \begin{bmatrix} a \\ b \\ c \end{bmatrix} = \begin{bmatrix} 0.5 \\ 0.5 \\ 0 \end{bmatrix}$$

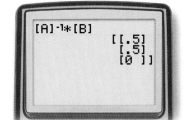

The solution is $a = 0.5$, $b = 0.5$, and $c = 0$.

Write the quadratic function.

$$d(n) = 0.5n^2 + 0.5n$$

CHECK

Check that the fourth and fifth data points satisfy $d(n) = 0.5n^2 + 0.5n$.

$d(n) = 0.5n^2 + 0.5n$ $d(n) = 0.5n^2 + 0.5n$

$10 \stackrel{?}{=} 0.5(4)^2 + 0.5(4)$ $15 \stackrel{?}{=} 0.5(5)^2 + 0.5(5)$

$10 = 8 + 2$ **True** $15 = 12.5 + 2.5$ **True**

Thus, $d(n) = 0.5n^2 + 0.5n$ models the pattern of dots.

c. Evaluate d for $n = 10$.

$$d(n) = 0.5n^2 + 0.5n$$
$$d(10) = 0.5(10)^2 + 0.5(10)$$
$$= 55$$

Thus, a triangle with 10 dots on each side would contain a total of 55 dots.

TECHNOLOGY

GRAPHICS CALCULATOR

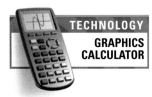

In Example 1, part **b**, you can also use a statistical model to find a quadratic function for d in terms of n. Enter the data, and use the keystrokes below to find a quadratic regression model for the dot pattern.

The quadratic regression equation is also $d(n) = 0.5n^2 + 0.5n$. Because the second differences for the number of dots in the triangle pattern are constant, this quadratic model fits the data exactly.

CRITICAL THINKING

Explain why you can always find a quadratic function to fit any three noncollinear points in the coordinate plane.

Modeling Real-World Data

Real-world data typically do not conform perfectly to a particular mathematical model. Just as you can use a linear function to represent data that show a linear pattern, you can use a quadratic function to model data that follow a parabolic pattern. In Example 3, you find a quadratic regression model to represent real-world data.

EXAMPLE **3** Make a scatter plot of the data below. Find a quadratic model to represent this data.

APPLICATION
HIGHWAY SAFETY

Speed (mph)	Stopping distance (ft)
10	12.5
20	36.0
30	69.5
40	114.0
50	169.5
60	249.0
70	325.5

● SOLUTION

The scatter plot is shown at right.

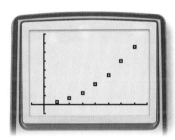

The data appear to follow a parabolic pattern. Use the quadratic regression feature of a graphics calculator to find a quadratic model.

TECHNOLOGY
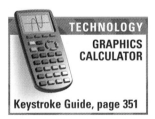
GRAPHICS CALCULATOR

Keystroke Guide, page 351

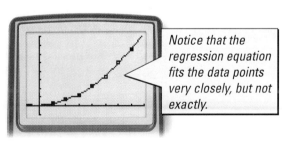

Notice that the regression equation fits the data points very closely, but not exactly.

According to this data, the quadratic model for the stopping distance, y, in terms of the car's speed, x, is $y \approx 0.06x^2 + 0.31x + 4$.

CHECKPOINT ✔ Explain why a quadratic model for stopping distance depends on the actual data from which it is obtained. Discuss the circumstances of the situation, such as the road conditions, the reaction time of the driver, and the condition of the brakes.

Collecting and Modeling Data Electronically

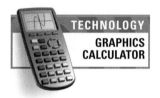

TECHNOLOGY

GRAPHICS CALCULATOR

You will need: a graphics calculator and a motion detector

This Activity involves tossing a ball vertically into the air, using a motion detector to measure its height over the elapsed time, using a graph to represent the data, and finding a quadratic model for the data.

1. Using a graphics calculator with a motion detector, collect data (elapsed time and height) for the vertical toss of a ball, such as a beach ball.

2. Make a scatter plot for the data. Do the data indicate a linear or quadratic relationship? Explain your response.

CHECKPOINT ✔ 3. Find a quadratic model for the data. Give values of *a*, *b*, and *c* to the nearest hundredth.

4. Acceleration due to gravity is about 32 feet per second squared. The value of *a* in your model represents half of the ball's acceleration due to gravity. Is the value of *a* in your model reasonable? Explain.

Exercises

Communicate

1. Let the points (1, 6), (−3, 8), and (5, −2) be on a parabola.
   a. Explain how to write a system of equations representing these points.
   b. Explain how to find a quadratic function that fits these points.

2. Describe how to find first and second differences of a data set. What type of function is indicated by a constant first difference? a constant second difference?

Guided Skills Practice

3. Find a quadratic function whose graph contains the points (2, −8), (5, 1), and (0, 6). *(EXAMPLE 1)*

4. Suppose that everyone in a room is required to shake hands with everyone else in the room. *(EXAMPLE 2)*

Number of people, *n*	Number of handshakes, *h*
2	1
3	3
4	6
5	
6	

a. Copy and complete the table at left. Explain why a quadratic model is suitable for relating the number of handshakes, *h*, to the number of people, *n*.

b. Find a quadratic function for *h* in terms of *n*.

c. Use the model to predict the number of handshakes when there are 10 people in the room.

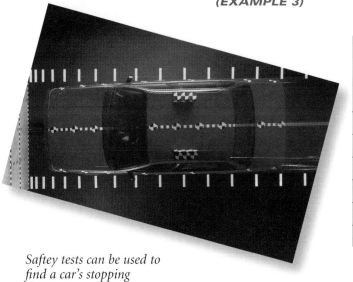

APPLICATION

5. HIGHWAY SAFETY The table below appears in a driver's manual.
(EXAMPLE 3)

Stopping Distance on Dry Concrete

Speed (mph)	Reaction distance before applying brakes (ft)*	Braking distance (ft)	Stopping distance (ft)
20	22	22	44
30	33	50	83
40	44	88	132
50	55	138	193
60	66	198	264
70	77	270	347

Safety tests can be used to find a car's stopping distance.

*Assume that perception time is zero seconds and reaction time is $\frac{3}{4}$ seconds. This is optimistic.

a. Make a scatter plot for stopping distance versus time.
b. Does it appear that a quadratic function would fit the data? If so, find a quadratic function for the stopping distance, d, in terms of the speed, x.

Practice and Apply

6. If the point $(2, 3)$ is on a parabola whose equation is in the form $y = ax^2 + bx + c$, which linear equation in three variables represents the parabola?

$$y = 2x^2 + 3x + c \qquad y = 4a + 2b + c \qquad 2 = 9a + 3b + c$$
$$3 = 4x^2 + 2x + c \qquad 3 = 4a + 2b + c$$

Solve a system of equations in order to find a quadratic function that fits each set of data points exactly.

7. $(1, -1), (2, 5), (3, 13)$ **8.** $(1, 13), (4, 7), (5, -3)$

9. $(2, 18), (6, 10), (8, -6)$ **10.** $(-2, -7), (1, 8), (2, 21)$

11. $(0, 4), (1, 5), (3, 25)$ **12.** $(-3, 7), (-1, -5), (6, 16)$

13. $(0, 15), (2, 5), (3, 6)$ **14.** $(1, 7), (-2, 4), (3, 19)$

15. $(5, 9), (2, 21), (4, 9)$ **16.** $(-1, 5), (4, 5), (8, -13)$

17. $(0, 7), (-2, -3), (2, 13)$ **18.** $(0, 4), (2, 1), (-2, 3)$

19. $(-2, 7), (4, 10), (1, 4)$ **20.** $(4, -4), (-2, 5), (0, 6)$

21. Find a quadratic model for the data points $(1, 4)$, $(2, 5)$, and $(3, 10)$ by using two methods: (1) writing a system of three equations in three variables and solving it and (2) using a graphics calculator to find a quadratic regression equation.

LESSON 5.7   CURVE FITTING WITH QUADRATIC MODELS **327**

22. PATTERNS IN DATA Cubes of various sizes are to be built from unit cubes. The surfaces of the resulting figures are to be painted green.

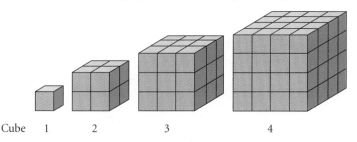

Cube   1   2   3   4

a. Copy and complete the table below.

Cube	Unit cubes with exactly 3 green faces	Unit cubes with exactly 2 green faces	Unit cubes with exactly 1 green face
2	8	0	0
3	8	12	6
4			
5			
6			

b. Find an appropriate model for the data in each column.

c. Use your models to add rows to the table for cubes 7, 8, and 20.

PHYSICS Imagine that an experiment is conducted on Mars in which an object is launched vertically from a height of h_0 above the surface of the planet and with an initial velocity of v_0 in feet per second. The height of the object is measured at three different points in time, and the data are recorded in the table shown at right.

Time (s)	Height (ft)
1	19
2	21
3	11

23. Find a quadratic function that fits the data by solving a system.

24. Find the initial height and the initial velocity of the object.

25. How long will it take for the object to reach its maximum height?

26. What is the maximum height reached by the object?

27. How long after the object is launched will it return to the surface of Mars?

28. Use your function to predict the height of the object when t is 2.5 seconds.

29. Use your function to predict the time(s) when the object is 16 feet above the surface of Mars.

30. BUSINESS A small computer company keeps track of its monthly production and profit over three months. The data are shown in the table at left.

  a. Use the data in the table to find a quadratic function that describes the profit as a function of the number of computers produced.

  b. Use your function to predict the level of production that will maximize the profit.

  c. Use your function to predict the maximum profit, assuming that all business conditions stay the same.

Number of computers produced	Profit
50	$5100
100	$5600
150	$1100

31. PHYSICS With the use of a regulation-size girls' basketball, a graphics calculator, a CBL, and a motion detector, the data below was collected and rounded to the nearest hundredth. Find a quadratic model to represent the data.

Time (s)	0.01	0.11	0.21	0.31	0.41	0.51	0.61	0.71	0.81	0.91
Height (ft)	1.88	3.05	4.13	4.91	5.37	5.50	5.31	4.82	4.00	2.97

Look Back

Determine whether the inverse of each function below is also a function. *(LESSON 2.5)*

32. $f(x) = 1 - 2x^2$ **33.** $g(x) = x - 2$ **34.** $h(x) = -\frac{1}{2}x + 3$

35. $f(x) = \frac{1}{3}x - 3$ **36.** $g(x) = \frac{3 - x}{2}$ **37.** $h(x) = \frac{2}{x}$

Evaluate. *(LESSON 2.6)*

38. $[-0.99] + [1.99]$ **39.** $[-2.1 - 1.1]$ **40.** $[-0.3] - [3.7]$

Find the determinant and tell whether each matrix has an inverse. *(LESSON 4.3)*

41. $\begin{bmatrix} 6 & -4 \\ -1 & 2 \end{bmatrix}$ **42.** $\begin{bmatrix} \frac{1}{3} & 0 \\ 1 & \frac{1}{2} \end{bmatrix}$ **43.** $\begin{bmatrix} \frac{1}{2} & \frac{1}{5} \\ \frac{2}{3} & \frac{1}{10} \end{bmatrix}$ **44.** $\begin{bmatrix} 1 & 0 \\ 0 & 1 \end{bmatrix}$

Look Beyond

45. Which is the solution to the inequality $x^2 - 16 < 0$?
    a. $x < 4$ **b.** $x > -4$
    c. $-4 < x < 4$ **d.** $x > 4 \quad or \quad x < -4$

46. Which is the solution to the inequality $x^2 - 2x - 15 < 0$?
    a. $-3 < x < 5$ **b.** $x < -3 \quad or \quad x > 5$
    c. $-5 < x < 3$ **d.** $x < -5 \quad or \quad x > 3$

SPORTS Refer to the basketball data given on page 273 to answer the questions below.

  1. Write and solve a system of equations to find a quadratic function whose graph contains any three points from the basketball data.

  2. Use your calculator to find a quadratic regression model for the three data points.

  3. Do your quadratic models from Steps 1 and 2 agree? How do these models compare with the models used in the Portfolio Activities on pages 280, 298, 306, and 313? Explain.

WORKING ON THE CHAPTER PROJECT

You should now be able to complete the Chapter Project.

Solving Quadratic Inequalities

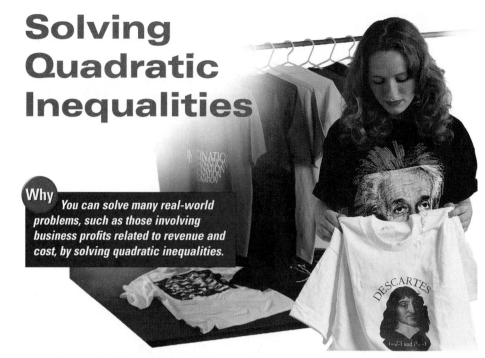

Why *You can solve many real-world problems, such as those involving business profits related to revenue and cost, by solving quadratic inequalities.*

Objectives

- Write, solve, and graph a quadratic inequality in one variable.

- Write, solve, and graph a quadratic inequality in two variables.

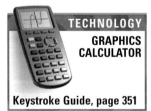

APPLICATION
SMALL BUSINESS

Katie makes and sells T-shirts. A consultant found that her monthly costs, C, are related to the selling price, p, of the shirts by the function $C(p) = 75p + 2500$. The revenue, R, from the sale of the shirts is represented by $R(p) = -25p^2 + 700p$. Her profit, P, is the difference between the revenue and the costs each month.

$$P(p) = R(p) - C(p)$$
$$= -25p^2 + 700p - (75p + 2500)$$
$$= -25p^2 + 625p - 2500$$

For what range of prices can Katie sell the shirts in order to make a profit? That is, for what values of p will $-25p^2 + 625p - 2500 > 0$? *You will answer this question in Example 2.*

One-Variable Quadratic Inequalities

Activity
Exploring Quadratic Inequalities

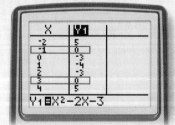

TECHNOLOGY
GRAPHICS CALCULATOR

Keystroke Guide, page 351

You will need: a graphics calculator

The display at right shows the values of $f(x) = x^2 - 2x - 3$ for integer values of x between -2 and 4 inclusive.

The table suggests the following three cases:
- When $x = -1$ or $x = 3$, $f(x) = 0$.
- When $x < -1$ or $x > 3$, $f(x) > 0$.
- When $-1 < x < 3$, $f(x) < 0$.

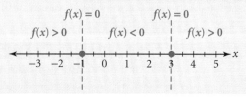

1. Copy and complete the table below. What values of x satisfy each equation or inequality?

Function	Number of x-intercepts	$f(x) = 0$	$f(x) > 0$	$f(x) < 0$
$f(x) = x^2 - 4$	2			
$f(x) = -x^2 + 2x + 3$				

2. Repeat Step 1 for the functions in the table below.

Function	Number of x-intercepts	$f(x) = 0$	$f(x) > 0$	$f(x) < 0$
$f(x) = x^2$	1			
$f(x) = -x^2$				

3. Repeat Step 1 for the functions in the table below.

Function	Number of x-intercepts	$f(x) = 0$	$f(x) > 0$	$f(x) < 0$
$f(x) = -x^2 + x - 1$	0			
$f(x) = x^2 + x + 3$				

CHECKPOINT ✔ 4. **a.** If the graph of a quadratic function crosses the x-axis at 2 distinct points, the graph separates the x-axis into __?__ distinct interval(s).
b. If the graph of a quadratic function crosses or touches the x-axis at 1 point, the graph separates the x-axis into __?__ distinct interval(s).
c. If the graph of a quadratic function does not cross the x-axis, the graph separates the x-axis into __?__ distinct interval(s).

You can determine the solution to a given inequality by finding the roots of the related quadratic equation or by using the graph of the related quadratic equation.

EXAMPLE ① Solve $x^2 - 2x - 15 \geq 0$. Graph the solution on a number line.

TECHNOLOGY
GRAPHICS CALCULATOR
Keystroke Guide, page 351

SOLUTION

The graph of $y = x^2 - 2x - 15$ indicates that the solution has two parts.

$x \leq$ smaller root *or* $x \geq$ larger root

$$x^2 - 2x - 15 = 0$$
$$(x + 3)(x - 5) = 0$$
$$x = -3 \quad or \quad x = 5$$

Therefore, the solution to the given inequality is $x \leq -3$ or $x \geq 5$.

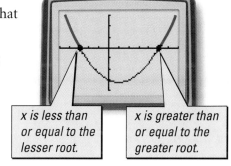
x is less than or equal to the lesser root.
x is greater than or equal to the greater root.

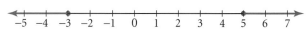

TRY THIS Solve $x^2 - 8x + 12 \leq 0$. Graph the solution on a number line.

E X A M P L E ❷ Refer to Katie's T-shirt business from the beginning of the lesson.

At what price range can Katie sell her T-shirts in order to make a profit?

APPLICATION

SMALL BUSINESS

TECHNOLOGY

GRAPHICS CALCULATOR

Keystroke Guide, page 351

● **SOLUTION**

Use the quadratic formula to find the roots of $-25x^2 + 625x - 2500 = 0$.

$$p = \frac{-b \pm \sqrt{b^2 - 4ac}}{2a}$$

$$p = \frac{-625 \pm \sqrt{625^2 - 4(-25)(-2500)}}{2(-25)}$$

$$p = 5 \quad or \quad p = 20$$

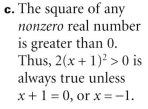

(5, 0)   (20, 0)

The graph of $y = -25x^2 + 625x - 2500$ indicates that the profit is positive *between* the roots of the related equation. If Katie sells her shirts at a price between \$5 and \$20, she will make a profit.

Special types of solutions to quadratic inequalities are shown in Example 3.

E X A M P L E ❸ **Solve each inequality.**

    a. $(x - 2)^2 \geq 0$ **b.** $(x + 3)^2 < 0$ **c.** $2(x + 1)^2 > 0$

● **SOLUTION**

a. The square of every real number is greater than or equal to 0. Therefore, the solution is all real numbers.

b. The square of a real number cannot be negative. Therefore, there is no solution.

c. The square of any *nonzero* real number is greater than 0. Thus, $2(x + 1)^2 > 0$ is always true unless $x + 1 = 0$, or $x = -1$.

$y = (x - 2)^2$

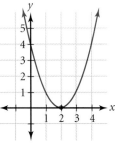

$y = (x + 3)^2$

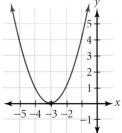

$y = 2(x + 1)^2$

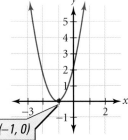

(−1, 0)

The graph of $y = (x - 2)^2$ indicates that all y-values of $y = (x - 2)^2$ are greater than or equal to zero for all real numbers x.

The graph of $y = (x + 3)^2$ indicates that no y-values of $y = (x + 3)^2$ are less than zero.

The graph of $y = 2(x + 1)^2$ indicates that the y-values of $y = 2(x + 1)^2$ are greater than zero for all real numbers x except $x = -1$.

TRY THIS   Find all solutions of $-(x + 1)^2 > 0$, if any exist.

Two-Variable Quadratic Inequalities

A **quadratic inequality in two variables** is an inequality that can be written in one of the forms below, where a, b, and c are real numbers and $a \neq 0$.

$$y \geq ax^2 + bx + c \qquad y > ax^2 + bx + c$$
$$y \leq ax^2 + bx + c \qquad y < ax^2 + bx + c$$

Example 4 shows how to graph a quadratic inequality in two variables.

E X A M P L E **4** Graph the solution to $y \geq (x-2)^2 + 1$.

SOLUTION

1. Graph the related equation, $y = (x-2)^2 + 1$. Use a solid curve because the inequality symbol is $\geq$.

2. Test $(0, 0)$ to see if this point satisfies the given inequality.

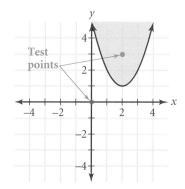

$$y \geq (x-2)^2 + 1$$
$$0 \overset{?}{\geq} (0-2)^2 + 1$$
$$0 \geq 5 \quad \textbf{False}$$

Test a point inside the parabola, such as $(2, 3)$.

$$y \geq (x-2)^2 + 1$$
$$3 \overset{?}{\geq} (2-2)^2 + 1$$
$$3 \geq 1 \quad \textbf{True}$$

3. Shade the region *inside* the graph of $y = (x-2)^2 + 1$ because this region contains the test point that satisfies $y \geq (x-2)^2 + 1$.

TRY THIS   Graph the solution to $y < (x+2)^2 - 3$.

CRITICAL THINKING   Explain why you should not use $(0, 0)$ as a test point when graphing the solution to an inequality such as $y > x^2 + 2x$.

TECHNOLOGY
GRAPHICS CALCULATOR

On most graphics calculators, you can graph a quadratic inequality in two variables. The graph of $y \geq (x-2)^2 + 1$ from Example 4 is shown below. The keystrokes for a TI-83 model are also given.

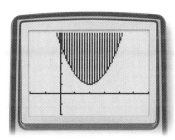

Use viewing window $[-2, 6]$ by $[-2, 6]$.

   (▼ Y1=) ▶ ▶ (X,T,Θ,n − 2)
 x^2 + 1 GRAPH

LESSON 5.8 SOLVING QUADRATIC INEQUALITIES **333**

Exercises

Communicate

1. Explain how to solve $x^2 - 2x - 8 > 0$.

2. Explain how a graph can assist you when solving $x^2 - 2x - 8 > 0$.

3. Explain how to graph an inequality such as $y < (x - 2)^2 + 2$.

4. Explain how to test whether the correct area has been shaded in the graph of an inequality.

5. Explain how to determine the possible solutions to $(x + 7)^2 < 0$ without solving the inequality.

Guided Skills Practice

6. Solve $x^2 - 7x + 12 \geq 0$. Graph the solution on a number line. **(EXAMPLE 1)**

7. For what integer values of x is $-2x^2 + 25x - 72 > 0$ true? **(EXAMPLE 2)**

Solve each inequality. (EXAMPLE 3)

8. $(x - 3)^2 < 0$ 9. $(x - 5)^2 > 0$ 10. $(x - 1)^2 < 0$

11. Graph the solution to $y \leq 2(x - 3)^2 - 2$. **(EXAMPLE 4)**

Practice and Apply

Solve each inequality. Graph the solution on a number line.

12. $x^2 - 1 \geq 0$ 13. $-x^2 + 5x - 6 > 0$ 14. $x^2 - 8x + 12 \leq 0$

15. $x^2 - 4x - 5 < 0$ 16. $x^2 - 7x + 10 \leq 0$ 17. $50 - 15x > -x^2$

18. $x^2 \leq \frac{3}{4} + x$ 19. $x^2 - x - 12 \leq 0$ 20. $-x^2 + \frac{4}{3}x - \frac{5}{9} > 0$

21. $x^2 - 4x - 12 > 0$ 22. $x^2 - 2x - 99 > 0$ 23. $x^2 + x - 6 \leq 0$

24. $-x^2 - x + 20 < 0$ 25. $x^2 \leq 7x - 6$ 26. $x^2 + 35 > -12x$

27. $10 - x^2 \geq 9x$ 28. $x^2 + 10x + 25 > 0$ 29. $x^2 + 3x - 18 > 0$

30. $x^2 - 2 > x$ 31. $x^2 + 6x \geq 7$ 32. $15 - 8x \leq -x^2$

33. $-x^2 + 3x + 6 < 0$ 34. $4x - 1 > 8 - x^2$ 35. $x^2 + 5x - 7 < 4x$

Sketch the graph of each inequality. Then decide which of the given points are in the solution region.

36. $y \geq (x - 1)^2 + 5$; $A(4, 1)$, $B(4, 14)$, $C(4, 20)$

37. $y > -(x - 3)^2 + 8$; $A(5, 1)$, $B(5, 4)$, $C(5, 6)$

38. $y < (x - 2)^2 + 6$; $A(3, 1)$, $B(3, 7)$, $C(3, 10)$

39. $y \leq -(x - 4)^2 + 7$; $A(6, 1)$, $B(6, 3)$, $C(6, 5)$

Graph each inequality.

40. $y \le (x - 2)^2 + 2$ **41.** $y \ge (x + 2)^2$ **42.** $y < (x - 5)^2 + 1$

43. $y > 2(x + 3)^2 - 5$ **44.** $y \le \left(x - \frac{1}{2}\right)^2 + 1$ **45.** $y \ge (x + 1)^2 + 2$

46. $y \le x^2 + 2x + 1$ **47.** $y < x^2 - 3x + 2$ **48.** $y \ge 2x^2 + 5x + 1$

49. $y > x^2 + 4x + 2$ **50.** $y - 3 \le x^2 - 6x$ **51.** $y - 1 < x^2 - 4x$

52. $y \le (x - \pi)^2 + 1$ **53.** $y \le -\left(x - \frac{5}{7}\right)^2 + 2$ **54.** $y + 3 < (x - 1)^2$

55. $y > x^2 + 12x + 35$ **56.** $x + y > x^2 - 6$ **57.** $y - 2x \le x^2 - 8$

CHALLENGES

58. Create a quadratic function in which $f(x) \ge 0$ for values of x between 2 and 6 inclusive.

59. Write a quadratic inequality whose solution is $x < 3$ *or* $x > 7$.

CONNECTION

60. MAXIMUM/MINIMUM Jon is a sales representative for a winter sports equipment wholesaler. The price per snowboard varies based on the number of snowboards purchased in each order. Beginning with a price of $124 for one snowboard, the price per snowboard is reduced by $1 for each additional snowboard purchased.

a. Copy and complete the table.

b. What is the function for the revenue?

c. What is the maximum revenue per order?

d. How many snowboards must be sold per order to attain the maximum revenue?

e. Assume that it costs the wholesaler $68 to produce each snowboard and that John spends an average of $128 in fixed costs (travel expenses, phone calls, and so on) per order. Based on these two factors alone, what is the function for the costs? Is the function linear or quadratic?

Number of snowboards purchased	Price per board ($)	Revenue per order ($)
1	124	124
2	123	246
3	122	366
4	121	484
5	120	600
⋮	⋮	⋮
x		

f. Graph the revenue and cost functions on the same coordinate plane. In order for the revenue to be greater than the costs, how many snowboards does Jon need to sell?

g. What is the function for profit per order?

h. Graph the profit function on the same coordinate plane as the functions for revenue per order and cost per order. How many snowboards does Jon need to sell per order to make a profit?

i. What is the maximum profit per order? How many snowboards must be sold to earn the maximum profit per order?

61. SPORTS At the beginning of a basketball game, the referee tosses the ball vertically into the air. Its height, h, in feet after t seconds is given by $h(t) = -16t^2 + 24t + 5$. During what time interval (to the nearest tenth of a second) is the height of the ball greater than 9 feet?

62. SMALL BUSINESS Suppose that the profit, p, for selling x bumper stickers is given by $p(x) = -0.1x^2 + 8x - 50$.
  a. What is the minimum number of bumper stickers that must be sold to make a profit?
  b. Is it possible for the profit to be greater than $100? Justify your answer algebraically and graphically.

63. BUSINESS A camping supplies company has determined cost and revenue information for the production of their backpacks.

The cost is given by $C(x) = 50 + 30x$, and the revenue is given by $R(x) = 5x(40 - x)$, where x is the number of backpacks sold in thousands. Both the cost and revenue are given in thousands of dollars.

The profit is given by $P(x) = R(x) - C(x)$.

Use the graph at right to give approximate answers to the questions below.

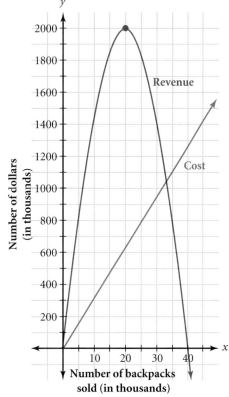

  a. To make a profit, revenue must be greater than cost. What is the range for the quantity of backpacks that the company must sell in order to make a profit?
  b. At what number of backpacks sold is the revenue maximized?
  c. Is there a greatest cost? Why or why not?
  d. Graph the profit function.

  e. What is the range for the quantity of backpacks that the company must sell to make a profit? Compare this answer to your answer from part **a.** Would you expect the answers to be the same? Why or why not?
  f. For what number of backpacks sold is the profit maximized? Compare this answer to your answer from part **b.** Would you expect the answers to be the same? Why or why not?
  g. At what point will the company start to lose money by producing too many backpacks?

PHYSICS The approximate length of a pendulum, l, in feet is related to the time, t, in seconds required for one complete swing as given by the formula $l \approx 0.81t^2$.

64. For what values of t is $l > 2$?   **65.** For what values of t is $l < 5$?

PHYSICS An object is dropped from a height of 1000 feet. Its height, h, in feet after t seconds is given by the function $h(t) = -16t^2 + 1000$.

66. For approximately how long, to the nearest hundredth of a second, will the height of the object be above 500 feet?

67. About how long, to the nearest hundredth of a second, does it take the object to fall from 500 feet to the ground?

SMALL BUSINESS A small company can produce up to 200 handmade sandals a month. The monthly cost, C, of producing x sandals is $C(x) = 1000 + 5x$. The monthly revenue, R, is given by $R(x) = 75x - 0.4x^2$.

68. For what values of x is the revenue greater than the cost?

69. At what production levels will the company make a profit?

70. At what production levels will the company lose money?

 Look Back

Graph each equation, and state whether y is a function of x.
(LESSON 2.3)

71. $y = |x|$ **72.** $x = |y|$ **73.** $y = -|x|$ **74.** $x = y^2$

Solve each equation. Give exact solutions. *(LESSON 5.2)*

75. $-2x^2 = -16$ **76.** $-3x^2 + 15 = -6$ **77.** $32 = 2x^2 - 4$

Simplify each expression, where $i = \sqrt{-1}$. *(LESSON 5.6)*

78. $(8 - 2i)(6 + 3i)$ **79.** $(1 + 5i) - (2 + i)$

80. $\dfrac{2 + i}{2 + 3i}$ **81.** $(3 + 2i) + (3 - i)$

 Look Beyond

82 Let $f(x) = x^3 - 2x^2 + 3x + d$. If the graph of f contains the point $(1, 9)$, find the value of d. Verify your answer by substituting this value for d in the function and graphing it. **7**

SPORTS Refer to the basketball data on page 273.

1. At what point(s) in time is the basketball at a height of 10 feet?

2. During what period(s) of time is the height of the basketball above 10 feet?

3. During what period(s) of time is the height of the basketball below 10 feet?

4. Use a graph to show that your answers to Steps 1–3 are correct.

OUT OF THIS WORLD!

The vertical motion of a basketball at the beginning of a game was described on page 273. The referee holds the ball at a height of 3 feet above the floor. He tosses the ball upward with a velocity of 24 feet per second. The ball is subject to the acceleration due to gravity at the Earth's surface, which is approximately 32 feet per second squared.

The vertical motion of the basketball can be described by the quadratic model below.

$$h(t) = -\tfrac{1}{2}gt^2 + v_0t + h_0$$

In this project, you will compare the vertical motion of the basketball on Earth with its vertical motion on each of the other 8 planets. On each planet, assume that the initial vertical height of the ball is 3 feet and that the initial velocity of the ball is 24 feet per second. However, the acceleration due to gravity near the surface of each planet is different from that on Earth.

The table below contains the acceleration due to gravity near the surface of each planet as a fraction of that on Earth.

Complete the table.

Planet	Gravity at surface (as a fraction of Earth's)	Gravity at surface, g (ft/s^2)	Vertical height model: $h(t) = -\tfrac{1}{2}gt^2 + v_0t + h_0$
Mercury	0.37		
Venus	0.88		
Earth	1.00	32	$h(t) = -16t^2 + 24t + 3$
Mars	0.38		
Jupiter	2.64		
Saturn	1.15		
Uranus	1.15		
Neptune	1.12		
Pluto	0.04		

Activity ❷

1. Complete the table below by using the quadratic functions obtained in Activity 1. Use a graphics calculator to obtain approximate values.

Planet	Maximum height of basketball	Time required to reach maximum height	Time required to return to planet's surface	Time required to reach a height of 10 feet
Mercury				
Venus				
Earth				
Mars				
Jupiter				
Saturn				
Uranus				
Neptune				
Pluto				

2. Are there any planets on which the ball would never reach a height of 10 feet? If so, name them.

❸

Refer to the table from Activity 2.

1. On which planet would the basketball achieve the highest maximum height?

2. On which planet would the basketball achieve the lowest maximum height?

3. Make a generalization about the relationship between the acceleration due to gravity, g, and the maximum height, h, that is reached.

Chapter Review and Assessment

Key Skills & Exercises

LESSON 5.1

Key Skills

Multiply linear binomials, and identify and graph a quadratic function.

$$f(x) = (x + 4)(x - 1)$$
$$= x(x - 1) + 4(x - 1)$$
$$= x^2 + 3x - 4$$

The function f is a quadratic function because it can be written in the form $f(x) = ax^2 + bx + c$, where $a = 1$, $b = 3$, and $c = -4$.

Since $a > 0$ in $f(x) = x^2 + 3x - 4$, the parabola opens up and the vertex contains the minimum value of the function.

The coordinates of the vertex are $(-1.5, -6.25)$.

The equation of the axis of symmetry is $x = -1.5$.

Exercises

Show that each function is a quadratic function by writing it in the form $f(x) = ax^2 + bx + c$ and identifying a, b, and c.

1. $f(x) = -(x + 1)(x - 4)$

2. $f(x) = 5(2x - 1)(3x + 2)$

Graph each function and give the approximate coordinates of the vertex.

3. $f(x) = -x^2 + 3x - 1$

4. $f(x) = 5x^2 - x - 12$

State whether the parabola opens up or down and whether the y-coordinate of the vertex is the maximum or the minimum value of the function.

5. $f(x) = -x^2 - x - 1$

6. $f(x) = (x - 3)(x + 2)$

Key Skills

Solve quadratic equations by taking square roots.

$$16(x + 3)^2 = 81$$
$$(x + 3)^2 = \frac{81}{16}$$
$$x + 3 = \pm\sqrt{\frac{81}{16}}$$
$$x = -3 + \frac{9}{4} \quad or \quad x = -3 - \frac{9}{4}$$
$$x = -\frac{3}{4} \qquad\qquad x = -5\frac{1}{4}$$

Use the Pythagorean Theorem to solve problems involving right triangles.

Find the unknown length, b, in right triangle ABC.

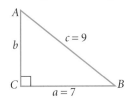

$$a^2 + b^2 = c^2$$
$$7^2 + b^2 = 9^2$$
$$b = \sqrt{9^2 - 7^2}$$
$$b = \sqrt{32}$$
$$b \approx 5.66$$

Exercises

Solve each equation, giving both exact solutions and approximate solutions to the nearest hundredth.

7. $x^2 = 8$

8. $3x^2 = 60$

9. $x^2 - 3 = 46$

10. $x^2 + 4 = 9$

11. $(x - 3)^2 = 64$

12. $(x - 5)^2 = 48$

13. $7(x + 1)^2 = 54$

14. $6(x + 2)^2 = 30$

Find the unknown length in right triangle *ABC*. Give your answers to the nearest tenth.

15. $a = 4$, $b = 5$

16. $c = 4$, $a = 1$

17. $b = 7$, $c = 12$

18. $a = 12$, $c = 15$

19. $c = 25$, $b = 5$

20. $b = 6$, $a = 6$

21. $a = 0.2$, $c = 0.75$

22. $b = 3.2$, $c = 5.8$

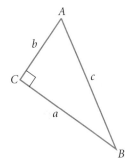

Key Skills

Use factoring to solve a quadratic equation and to find the zeros of a quadratic function.

$$6x^2 + 9x = 6$$
$$6x^2 + 9x - 6 = 0$$
$$3(2x^2 + 3x - 2) = 0$$
$$3(2x - 1)(x + 2) = 0$$
$$x = \frac{1}{2} \quad or \quad x = -2$$

The zeros of the related quadratic function, $f(x) = 6x^2 + 9x - 6$, are $\frac{1}{2}$ and -2.

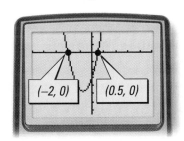

Exercises

Factor each expression.

23. $7x^2 - 21x$

24. $6n - 4n^2$

25. $x^2 + 7x + 10$

26. $x^2 + 11x + 28$

27. $t^2 - 5t - 24$

28. $x^2 - 7x + 12$

29. $x^2 - 8x - 20$

30. $y^2 - 6y - 27$

31. $x^2 + x - 20$

32. $x^2 + 4x - 21$

33. $3y^2 - y - 2$

34. $2x^2 - 5x - 25$

35. $16 - 9x^2$

36. $4x^2 - 49$

37. $x^2 - 16x + 64$

38. $4a^2 + 4a + 1$

Use the Zero-Product Property to find the zeros of each function.

39. $f(x) = x^2 - 10x + 24$

40. $g(x) = 2x^2 - 3x - 2$

41. $h(t) = 6t^2 + 11t - 10$

LESSON 5.4

Key Skills

Use completing the square to solve a quadratic equation.

$$3x^2 - 8x = 48$$
$$x^2 - \frac{8}{3}x = 16$$
$$x^2 - \frac{8}{3}x + \left(\frac{8}{6}\right)^2 = 16 + \left(\frac{8}{6}\right)^2$$
$$\left(x - \frac{8}{6}\right)^2 = \frac{160}{9}$$
$$x = \frac{8}{6} \pm \frac{\sqrt{160}}{3}$$
$$x = \frac{4 + \sqrt{160}}{3} \quad or \quad x = \frac{4 - \sqrt{160}}{3}$$

The coordinates of the vertex of the graph of a quadratic function in vertex form, $y = a(x - h)^2 + k$, are (h, k).

Exercises

Solve each quadratic equation by completing the square.

42. $x^2 - 6x = 27$ **43.** $5x^2 = 2x + 1$

44. $x^2 - 10x + 21 = 0$ **45.** $x^2 + 5x = 84$

46. $x^2 - 7x - 8 = 0$ **47.** $2x^2 + 7x = 4$

48. $4x^2 + 4 = 17x$ **49.** $2x + 8 = 3x^2$

Write each function in vertex form, and identify the coordinates of the vertex.

50. $y = 2x^2 - 16x + 33$ **51.** $y = -3x^2 - 6x - 7$

52. $y = -x^2 - 5x - 2$ **53.** $y = 4x^2 - 9x + 2$

LESSON 5.5

Key Skills

Use the quadratic formula to find the real roots of quadratic equations.

Solve $2x^2 + x = 10$.
$$2x^2 + x - 10 = 0 \rightarrow a = 2, b = 1, c = -10$$
$$x = \frac{-b \pm \sqrt{b^2 - 4ac}}{2a}$$
$$x = \frac{-1 \pm \sqrt{1^2 - 4(2)(-10)}}{2(2)}$$
$$x = \frac{-1 \pm \sqrt{81}}{4}$$
$$x = 2 \quad or \quad x = -\frac{10}{4}$$

The coordinates of the vertex of the graph of $f(x) = ax^2 + bx + c$ are $\left(-\frac{b}{2a}, f\left(-\frac{b}{2a}\right)\right)$.

Exercises

Use the quadratic formula to solve each equation.

54. $2x + 1 = 2x^2$ **55.** $6x = 2 - 5x^2$

56. $x^2 - 7x = -10$ **57.** $x^2 + 6x = -8$

58. $11x = 5x^2 - 3$ **59.** $x = 6x^2 - 3$

60. $3 = x^2 + 5x$ **61.** $x^2 = 1 - x$

For each function, find the coordinates of the vertex of the graph.

62. $f(x) = x^2 + 7x + 6$ **63.** $f(x) = x^2 - x - 12$

64. $g(x) = x^2 + 2x - 3$ **65.** $f(n) = n^2 + 12n + 5$

LESSON 5.6

Key Skills

Find and classify all roots of a quadratic equation.

Solve $x^2 + 8 = 0$. $a = 1, b = 0,$ and $c = 8$

$$b^2 - 4ac = 0^2 - 4(1)(8) = -32$$

Because the discriminant is less than zero, the solutions are imaginary.

$$x^2 + 8 = 0$$
$$x = \pm\sqrt{-8}$$
$$x = \pm i\sqrt{8}, \text{ or } \pm 2i\sqrt{2}$$

Exercises

Determine the number of real solutions for each equation by using the discriminant.

66. $4x^2 - 20x = -25$ **67.** $9x^2 + 12x = -2$

68. $x^2 = 21x - 110$ **69.** $-x^2 + 6x = 10$

Solve each equation. Write your answers in the form $a + bi$.

70. $x^2 - 6x + 25 = 0$ **71.** $x^2 + 10x + 34 = 0$

72. $x^2 + 8x + 20 = 0$ **73.** $x^2 - 6x + 11 = 0$

74. $4x^2 = 2x - 1$ **75.** $3x^2 + 2 = 2x$

342 CHAPTER 5

Graph and perform operations on complex numbers.

a. $(3 + 2i) + (-4 + i)$
$= -1 + 3i$

b. $(3 + 2i) - (-4 + i)$
$= 7 + i$

c. $(3 + 2i)(-4 + i)$
$= -12 - 8i + 3i + 2i^2$
$= -14 - 5i - 2$
$= -16 - 5i$

d. $\dfrac{(3 + 2i)}{-4 + i} = \dfrac{(3 + 2i)(-4 - i)}{(-4 + i)(-4 - i)}$
$= -\dfrac{10}{17} - \dfrac{11}{17}i$

e. $|3 - 3i| = \sqrt{3^2 + (-3)^2}$
$= \sqrt{18}$

The graph of $|3 - 3i|$ is shown at right.

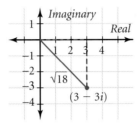

Perform the indicated operation.

76. $(3 - 4i) + (-1 - 8i)$ **77.** $(-2 - i)(1 + 3i)$

78. $\dfrac{5 - 2i}{-4 + i}$ **79.** $\dfrac{-3 + 3i}{3 - 3i}$

80. $(2 + 7i) - (-2 - 6i)$ **81.** $(9 - 3i) + (-3 - 6i)$

82. $(2 + i)(4 - 8i)$ **83.** $(8 - 2i) - (6 + 2i)$

Find each value. Then sketch a diagram that shows the absolute value.

84. $|4 - 2i|$ **85.** $|-3 - i|$

86. $|5 - 2i|$ **87.** $|1 + i|$

LESSON 5.7

Key Skills

Find a quadratic function that exactly fits three data points.

Find a quadratic function whose graph contains the points $(-1, 2)$, $(0, 3)$, and $(3, -6)$.

$$
\begin{aligned}
a(-1)^2 + b(-1) + c &= 2 \\
a(0)^2 + b(0) + c &= 3 \\
a(3)^2 + b(3) + c &= -6
\end{aligned}
\quad \rightarrow \quad
\begin{cases}
a - b + c = 2 \\
c = 3 \\
9a + 3b + c = -6
\end{cases}
$$

$$
\begin{bmatrix} 1 & -1 & 1 \\ 0 & 0 & 1 \\ 9 & 3 & 1 \end{bmatrix}
\begin{bmatrix} a \\ b \\ c \end{bmatrix}
=
\begin{bmatrix} 2 \\ 3 \\ -6 \end{bmatrix}
\quad \rightarrow \quad
\begin{bmatrix} a \\ b \\ c \end{bmatrix}
=
\begin{bmatrix} -1 \\ 0 \\ 3 \end{bmatrix}
$$

The quadratic function is $f(x) = -x^2 + 3$.

Find a quadratic model to represent a data set.

If the points of a given data set form an approximately parabolic shape, find the quadratic regression equation.

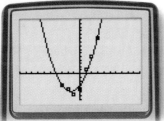

The quadratic regression equation shown above is $f(x) \approx 0.8x^2 + 2.3x - 3.1$.

Exercises

Find a quadratic function that fits each set of data points exactly.

88. $(-10, 185), (-5, 70), (1, -2)$

89. $(0, -9), (3, 42), (-5, 106)$

90. $(-2, -7), (1, 2), (-1, -2)$

91. $(0, 6), (1, 0), (-2, -12)$

92. $(-1, 4), (0, 4), (4, 84)$

93. $(-1, 3), (1, -3), (0, -3)$

94. $(-2, -1), (3, -6), (0, 9)$

95. $(-1, 6), (1, 6), (0, -1)$

Find a quadratic model to represent each data set.

96

x	−3	−2	−1	0	1	2	3
y	50	28	10	−2	20	33	80

97

x	−3	−2	−1	0	1	2	3
y	−12	−10	−8	−2	−1	−1	−6

98

x	−25	−10	0	15	30
y	1500	275	49	800	2015

Key Skills

Solve and graph quadratic inequalities in one variable.

$$x^2 - x < 12$$
$$x^2 - x - 12 < 0$$
$$(x + 3)(x - 4) < 0$$

The roots of the related equation, $x^2 - x - 12 = 0$, are -3 and 4.

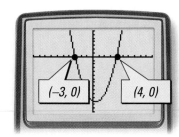

(−3, 0)   (4, 0)

The graph of $y = x^2 - x - 12$ indicates that $x^2 - x - 12$ is negative when x is between the roots. The solution is $-3 < x < 4$.

Solve and graph quadratic inequalities in two variables.

To graph $y \leq x^2 - 2x - 3$, graph $y = x^2 - 2x - 3$, and test a point, such as $(0, 0)$.

$$y \leq x^2 - 2x - 3$$
$$0 \stackrel{?}{\leq} 0^2 - 2(0) - 3$$

$$0 \leq -3 \quad \textbf{False}$$

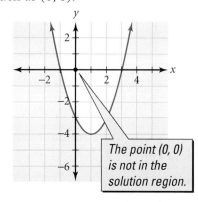

The point (0, 0) is not in the solution region.

Exercises

Solve each quadratic inequality, and graph the solution on a number line.

99. $x^2 - 8x + 12 > 0$

100. $x^2 - 3x - 10 < 0$

101. $x^2 + 7x + 10 \geq 0$

102. $2x^2 + x < 15$

103. $4x^2 > 9x + 9$

104. $2x^2 \geq 9x$

105. $4x^2 \leq 10x$

106. $-x^2 + 6x \geq 8$

Graph each quadratic inequality on a coordinate plane.

107. $y > x^2 - 6x + 8$

108. $y \leq x^2 + 3x - 10$

109. $y - 2x^2 < -x - 1$

110. $y - 5x \leq 2x^2 - 3$

111. $y + 4x + 21 \geq x^2$

112. $y - 5x > 6x^2 + 1$

Applications

113. AVIATION A crate of blankets and clothing is dropped without a parachute from a helicopter hovering at a height of 125 feet. The altitude of the crate, a, in feet, is modeled by $a(t) = -16t^2 + 125$, where t is the time, in seconds, after it is released. How long will it take for the crate to reach the ground?

114. RECREATION Students are designing an archery target with one ring around the bull's-eye. The bull's-eye has a radius of 6 inches. The area of the outer ring should be 5 times that of the bull's-eye. What should be the radius of the outer circle?

Alternative Assessment

Performance Assessment

1. PHYSICS The distance that an object travels as it falls is given below.

Time (s)	0	0.25	0.50	0.75	1.00	1.25
Distance (ft)	0	1	4	9	16	25

  a. Draw an accurate diagram to illustrate the data in the table.
  b. Find the differences between the successive distances. Describe the pattern in the differences.
  c. What do the second differences in the distance values indicate?
  d. Predict the value of *d* after 2.5 seconds.

2. TRANSFORMATIONS The graph of a function *g* has the same size and shape as the graph of $f(x) = -2x^2 - 8x + 3$. The graph of *g* is translated 2 units to the right and 4 units up from the graph of *f*. The graph of *g* also opens in the opposite direction from the graph of *f*. Write *g* in standard form.

3. ENGINEERING The wind pressure in pounds per square inch (psi) on the side of a building is related to the wind speed in miles per hour (mph) as shown in the table below.

Wind speed (mph)	50	75	100
Pressure (psi)	7.5	16.9	30

  a. What happens to the pressure, *p*, when the wind speed, *w*, doubles?
  b. Find a quadratic function to model the relationship between *w* and *p*.
  c. Predict the pressure for a 70-mph wind.

Portfolio Projects

1. GEOMETRY The Greeks used dots in the form of geometric shapes to represent numbers. Below are *pentagonal numbers*.

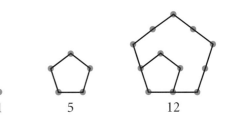

1   5   12

  a. Make a table of values for the pentagonal numbers, *p*, and the number of dots on each side, *s*.
  b. Find a quadratic function for *p* in terms of *s*.
  c. Use your function to predict *p* for *s* = 10.
  d. Do *octagonal numbers* follow a similar pattern?

2. QUADRATIC FORMULA Write a program that uses the quadratic formula to calculate the solutions of a quadratic equation expressed in standard form. Use input commands to enter the coefficients, *a*, *b*, and *c*. How does your program handle non-real solutions?

3. TRANSFORMATIONS Describe how the shape and position of the graph of the quadratic parent function, $y = ax^2 + bx + c$, depends on the coefficients, *a*, *b*, and *c*. Illustrate your description by graphing functions with different values for *a*, *b*, and *c*. Examine positive, negative, large, and small values for each coefficient.

⊿ internetconnect

The HRW Web site contains many resources to reinforce and expand your knowledge of quadratic functions. This Web site also provides Internet links to other sites where you can find information and real-world data for use in research projects, reports, and activities that involve quadratic functions. Visit the HRW Web site at **go.hrw.com,** and enter the keyword **MB1 CH5** to access the resources for this chapter.

College Entrance Exam Practice

QUANTITATIVE COMPARISON For Items 1–6, write
A if the quantity in Column A is greater than the quantity in Column B;
B if the quantity in Column B is greater than the quantity in Column A;
C if the quantities are equal; or
D if the relationship cannot be determined from the given information.

	Column A	Column B	Answers
1.	$27^{\frac{1}{3}}$	4	(A) (B) (C) (D) [Lesson 2.2]
2.	$\lvert 2i \rvert$	$\lvert -3i \rvert$	(A) (B) (C) (D) [Lesson 5.6]
3.	$\left(\frac{1}{2}\right)^{-2}$	$(-2)^2$	(A) (B) (C) (D) [Lesson 2.2]
4.	Entry m_{11} of the matrix product $M = \begin{bmatrix} 1 & 2 \\ 3 & 1 \end{bmatrix} \begin{bmatrix} 1 & 2 \\ 1 & 2 \end{bmatrix}$	$M = \begin{bmatrix} 2 & 3 \\ 3 & 2 \end{bmatrix} \begin{bmatrix} 1 & 2 \\ 1 & 2 \end{bmatrix}$	(A) (B) (C) (D) [Lesson 4.2]
5.	The largest root of the equation $x^2 - 3x + 2 = 0$	$x^2 - 4x + 3 = 0$	(A) (B) (C) (D) [Lesson 5.3]
6.	The value that completes the square for $x^2 + 16x$	8	(A) (B) (C) (D) [Lesson 5.4]

7. Find $2R - N$ given $R = \begin{bmatrix} 3 & 5 \\ -2 & 0 \end{bmatrix}$ and $N = \begin{bmatrix} 1 & -1 \\ 3 & 1 \end{bmatrix}$. *(LESSON 4.1)*

a. $\begin{bmatrix} -2 & 6 \\ -5 & -1 \end{bmatrix}$ b. $\begin{bmatrix} 2 & 4 \\ 1 & -1 \end{bmatrix}$

c. $\begin{bmatrix} 2 & 6 \\ -5 & -1 \end{bmatrix}$ d. $\begin{bmatrix} 5 & 11 \\ -7 & -1 \end{bmatrix}$

8. How many roots does the equation $5x^2 + 2x + 1 = 0$ have? *(LESSON 5.6)*
   a. 2 real roots   b. no real roots
   c. 1 real root   d. 2 complex roots

9. Which is the value of i^{13}? *(LESSON 5.6)*
   a. 1   b. -1
   c. i d. $-i$

10. Simplify: $\frac{a^2 b^{-1}}{a^{-3} b^2}$. *(LESSON 2.2)*
   a. $\frac{a}{b}$ b. $\frac{a^5}{b^3}$
   c. $\frac{b^2}{a}$ d. $\frac{b^3}{a^5}$

11. Which is the solution of the system?
   $\begin{cases} 5x + y = 11 \\ 3x + 2y = 8 \end{cases}$ *(LESSON 3.2)*
   a. $(3, 2)$ b. $(2, 1)$
   c. $(-1, 2)$ d. $(5, 6)$

12. Which is a correct factorization of $x^2 + 5x + 6$? *(LESSON 5.3)*

 a. $(x + 1)(x + 6)$ **b.** $(x + 2)(x + 3)$
 c. $(x - 1)(x - 6)$ **d.** $(x - 2)(x - 3)$

13. Which term describes the system?
$\begin{cases} 2x + 5y = 3 \\ 4x + 10y = 6 \end{cases}$ *(LESSON 3.1)*

 a. inconsistent **b.** dependent
 c. independent **d.** incompatible

14. Which is the inverse of the function $f(x) = 3x + 2$? *(LESSON 2.5)*

 a. $g(x) = 6x$ **b.** $g(x) = \dfrac{x - 3}{2}$

 c. $g(x) = 3 + \dfrac{x}{2}$ **d.** $g(x) = \dfrac{x - 2}{3}$

15. Graph $-\frac{1}{3}x \le 6$. *(LESSON 3.3)*

16. Find $(2 + i)(3 + 2i)$. *(LESSON 5.6)*

17. Solve $\begin{cases} 3x - 2y = 2 \\ x + y = 4 \end{cases}$. *(LESSON 3.1)*

18. Let $A = \begin{bmatrix} 3 & 2 \\ 1 & 4 \end{bmatrix}$ and $B = \begin{bmatrix} 1 & 4 \\ 2 & 3 \end{bmatrix}$. Find $A + B$.
 (LESSON 4.1)

19. Solve $x^2 + 3x + 1 = 0$. *(LESSON 5.5)*

20. Let $A = \begin{bmatrix} 1 & 4 \\ 3 & 1 \end{bmatrix}$ and $B = \begin{bmatrix} 0 & 1 \\ 2 & 3 \end{bmatrix}$. Find $A + B$.
 (LESSON 4.1)

21. Write the pair of parametric equations
$\begin{cases} x(t) = 1 - t \\ y(t) = 2 - t \end{cases}$ as a single equation in x and y.
 (LESSON 3.6)

22. Write the function for the graph of $f(x) = x^2$ translated 3 units to the left. *(LESSON 2.7)*

23. Let $f(x) = 3x + 1$ and $g(x) = x^2$. Find $(f \cdot g)(x)$.
 (LESSON 2.4)

24. Find the product $\begin{bmatrix} 2 & 3 \\ 2 & 1 \end{bmatrix} \begin{bmatrix} 3 & 2 \\ 1 & 0 \end{bmatrix}$. *(LESSON 4.2)*

25. Find the value of $i^2 + i^4$. *(LESSON 5.6)*

26. Evaluate $h(x) = 11 - \frac{1}{2}x$ for $x = -6$.
 (LESSON 2.3)

27. Given $5\begin{bmatrix} 1 & x \\ x - y & 5 \end{bmatrix} = \begin{bmatrix} 5 & 15 \\ 20 & 25 \end{bmatrix}$, find x and y.
 (LESSON 4.1)

28. CHEMISTRY A scientist wants to create 60 milliliters of a 5% salt solution from a 2% salt solution and a 12% salt solution. How much of each should be used? *(LESSON 3.1)*

FREE RESPONSE GRID The following questions may be answered by using a free-response grid such as that commonly used by standardized-test services.

29. Evaluate $8^{\frac{2}{3}}$. *(LESSON 2.2)*

30. Simplify $\dfrac{(3^2 - 7)^2}{3^{(2^2 - 2)}}$.
 (LESSON 2.1)

31. Find $\left| \dfrac{\sqrt{2}}{4} + \dfrac{\sqrt{2}}{4}i \right|$.
 (LESSON 5.6)

32. Find the discriminant for $x^2 + 4x + 1 = 0$.
 (LESSON 5.6)

33. What is the maximum value of $f(x) = -x^2 + 2x + 1$? *(LESSON 5.1)*

34. Let $A = \begin{bmatrix} 3 & 2 \\ 4 & 1 \end{bmatrix}$ and $B = \begin{bmatrix} 2x & 2 \\ 4 & 1 \end{bmatrix}$. For what value of x does $A = B$? *(LESSON 4.1)*

35. Find the maximum value of the objective function $P = 2x + 3y$ that satisfies the given constraints. *(LESSON 3.5)*
$$\begin{cases} x \ge 0, y \ge 0 \\ x + y \le 4 \\ 2x + y \ge 2 \end{cases}$$

36. PHYSICS A ball is dropped from a height of 10 feet. If the ball's height is modeled by $h(t) = -16t^2 + 10$, where h represents the height of the ball in feet and t represents time in seconds, how many seconds, to the nearest tenth, will it take the ball to reach the ground? *(LESSON 5.2)*

37. BUSINESS A company's profit on sales of digital pagers is modeled by the function $P(x) = -x^2 + 90x + 497{,}975$, where x represents the price of a pager in dollars. To the nearest dollar, what price gives the maximum profit? *(LESSON 5.4)*

Keystroke Guide for Chapter 5

Essential keystroke sequences (using the model TI-82 or TI-83 graphics calculator) are presented below for Activities and Examples found in this chapter that require or recommend the use of a graphics calculator.

Keystrokes for other models of graphics calculators are found on the HRW Web site.

LESSON 5.1

TECHNOLOGY
Page 274

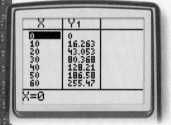

Create a table of values for $y = \frac{11}{10}x + \frac{1}{19}x^2$.

Enter the function:

| Y= | (| 11 | ÷ | 10 |) | X,T,Θ,n | + | (| 1 | ÷ | 19 |) |

| X,T,Θ,n | x^2 |

Create a table of values:

| 2nd | WINDOW | (TblStart=) 0 | ENTER | (ΔTbl=) 10 | ENTER | (Indpnt:) AUTO | ENTER |

⇑ TI-82: (TblMin=)

| ▼ | (Depend:) AUTO | ENTER | 2nd | GRAPH |

EXAMPLES ② and ③ For Example 2, graph $y = x^2 - x + 1$, and find the maximum or minimum value at the vertex.

Pages 276 and 277

Use friendly viewing window [−4.7, 4.7] by [−2, 6].

Graph the function:

| Y= | X,T,Θ,n | x^2 | − | X,T,Θ,n | + | 1 | GRAPH |

Find the minimum value:
Press TRACE, and use your cursor.

Create a table of values:
Use a keystroke sequence similar to that used in the Technology example above. First use TblStart = −2 and ΔTbl = 1. Then refine the table by using TblStart = 0 and ΔTbl = 0.1.

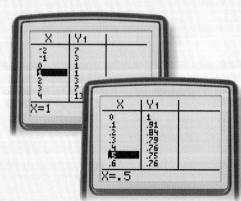

For Example 3, use a keystroke sequence similar to that above to graph each function. Use viewing window [−10, 10] by [−10, 10].

E X A M P L E S ➊ and ➋ **For Example 1, graph $y = 4x^2 + 13$ and $y = 253$ on the same screen, and find any points of intersection.**

Page 282

Use viewing window [–10, 10] by [–150, 400].

Graph the functions:
Use a keystroke sequence similar to that in Example 2 of Lesson 5.1.

Find any points of intersection:

> *Move your cursor as indicated.*

| 2nd | TRACE | 5:intersect | (**First curve?**)

CALC

| ENTER | (**Second curve?**) | ENTER |

(**Guess?**) | ENTER |

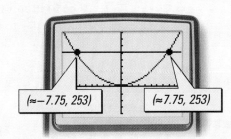

($\approx$–7.75, 253)   ($\approx$7.75, 253)

For Example 2, use viewing window [–5, 10] by [–25, 150]. Use a keystroke sequence similar to that above.

E X A M P L E ➌ **Graph $y = -16x^2 + 68$, and find the reasonable x-intercept.**

Page 283

Use viewing window [–5, 5] by [–10, 80].

Graph the functions:
Use a keystroke sequence similar to that in Example 2 of Lesson 5.1.

Find the x-intercepts:

> *Move your cursor as indicated.*

| 2nd | TRACE | 2:zero | (**Left Bound?**) | ENTER |

CALC

⇑ TI-82: 2:root

(**Right Bound?**) | ENTER | (**Guess?**) | ENTER |

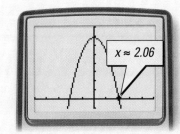

$x \approx 2.06$

E X A M P L E S ➍ and ➏ **For Example 4, use viewing window [–9, 3] by [–7, 2].**

Pages 293 and 294

For part **a** of Example 6, use viewing window [–2, 7] by [–20, 8].
For part **b** of Example 6, use viewing window [0, 12] by [–6, 6].

To graph the functions, use a keystroke sequence similar to that in Example 2 of Lesson 5.1. To find the zeros for Example 6, use a keystroke sequence similar to finding the x-intercepts in Example 3 of Lesson 5.2. Repeat for each zero.

E X A M P L E ➐ **Make a table of values for $y = 2x^2 - x - 66$.**

Page 295

Use a keystroke sequence similar to that used in the Technology example of Lesson 5.1. Use TblStart = 3 and ΔTbl = 1.

E X A M P L E ③ **Solve $2x^2 + 6x = 7$ by graphing.**

Page 301

Use viewing window $[-5, 5]$ by $[-12, 12]$.

To graph $y = 2x^2 - 6x$ and $y = 7$ and find the x-coordinates of any points of intersection, use keystroke sequences similar to those in Example 2 of Lesson 5.1 and Example 1 of Lesson 5.2.

To graph $y = 2x^2 - 6x - 7$ and find any zeros, use keystroke sequences similar to those in Example 2 of Lesson 5.1 and Example 6 of Lesson 5.3.

E X A M P L E ⑤ **Graph $y = \frac{3}{5000}x^2 - \frac{3}{5}x + 200$, and find the coordinates of the lowest point.**

Page 303

Use viewing window $[-100, 1000]$ by $[-150, 400]$.

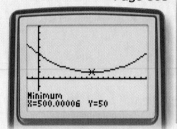

Find the minimum value:

CALC
[2nd] [TRACE] [3:minimum] **(Left Bound?)** [ENTER] **(Right Bound?)** [ENTER]

⇑ TI-82: (Lower Bound?)   ⇑ TI-82: (Upper Bound?)

(Guess)? [ENTER]

LESSON 5.5

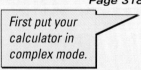

Page 309

For Step 2, use friendly viewing window $[-9.4, 9.4]$ by $[-7, 7]$. Press [TRACE], and use your cursor to find the coordinates of each vertex.

LESSON 5.6

E X A M P L E ⑥ **Evaluate the expression $\frac{2 + 5i}{2 - 3i}$, and express the answer with fractions.**

Page 318

First put your calculator in complex mode.

QUIT   *i*
[MODE] [a+bi] [ENTER] [2nd] [MODE] [( ] [2] [+] [5] [2nd] [.] [ )] [÷]

i
[( ] [2] [–] [3] [2nd] [.] [ )] [ENTER] [MATH] [1:▷Frac] [ENTER] [ENTER]

The TI-82 does not have a complex mode.

LESSON 5.7

E X A M P L E S ① and ② For Step 2 of Example 1, solve $\begin{bmatrix} 1 & 1 & 1 \\ 4 & 2 & 1 \\ 36 & 6 & 1 \end{bmatrix} \begin{bmatrix} a \\ b \\ c \end{bmatrix} = \begin{bmatrix} 3 \\ -3 \\ 13 \end{bmatrix}$.

Pages 323 and 324

Enter the coefficient matrix and the constant matrix:

[MATRX] [EDIT] [1:[A]] [ENTER] (MATRIX[A]) 3 [ENTER] 3 [ENTER] 1 [ENTER] 1 [ENTER] 1 [ENTER]

4 [ENTER] 2 [ENTER] 1 [ENTER] 36 [ENTER] 6 [ENTER] 1 [ENTER] [MATRX] [EDIT] [2:[B]] [ENTER]

QUIT
(MATRIX[B]) 3 [ENTER] 1 [ENTER] 3 [ENTER] [(–)] 3 [ENTER] 13 [ENTER] [2nd] [MODE]

Find the product $A^{-1}B$:

[MATRX] [NAMES] [1:[A]] [ENTER] [x^{-1}] [×] [MATRX] [NAMES] [2:[B]] [ENTER] [ENTER]

Plot points (1, 3), (2, –3), and (6, 13), and make a scatter plot:

Use viewing window [–5, 10] by [–10, 20].

[STAT] [EDIT] [1:EDIT] [ENTER] [L1] 1 [ENTER] 2 [ENTER] 6 [ENTER] [▶] [L2] 3

[ENTER] [(–)] 3 [ENTER] 13 [ENTER] [2nd] [Y=] **STAT PLOT** [STAT PLOT] [1:Plot 1]

[ENTER] [ON] [ENTER] [▼] (Type:) [⠂⠂⠂] [ENTER] [▼] (Xlist:) [2nd] **L1** [1]

⇑ TI-82: [L1] [ENTER]

[▼] (Ylist:) [2nd] **L2** [2] [▼] (Mark:) [▫] [ENTER] [GRAPH]

⇑ TI-82: [L2] [ENTER]

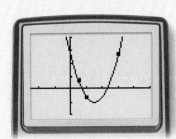

To graph $f(x) = 2x^2 - 12x + 13$, use a keystroke sequence similar to that in Example 2 of Lesson 5.1.

For Example 2, use a similar keystroke sequence. Use viewing window [–2, 10] by [–5, 20].

E X A M P L E ③ **Create a scatter plot of the given data, and find a quadratic model to represent the data.**

Page 325

Create the scatter plot:
Use a keystroke sequence similar to that in Example 2 of this lesson.

Find a quadratic model:
Use a keystroke sequence similar to that given on page 324.

LESSON 5.8

Activity

Page 330

For Step 2, use a keystroke sequence similar to that used in the Technology example of Lesson 5.1. Use TblStart = –2 and ΔTbl = 1.

E X A M P L E S ① **and** ② **For Example 1, graph $y = x^2 - 2x - 15$ and find the zeros of the**

Pages 331 and 332 **function.**

Use viewing window [–5, 7] by [–20, 15].

Graph the function:
Use a keystroke sequence similar to that in Example 2 of Lesson 5.1.

Find the zeros of the function:
Use a keystroke sequence similar to that used to find the *x*-intercepts in Example 3 of Lesson 5.2.

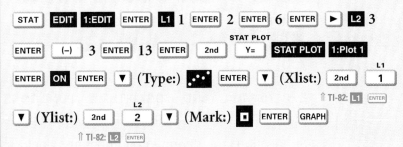

For Example 2, use a similar keystroke sequence. Use viewing window [0, 25] by [–100, 1500].

6

Exponential and Logarithmic Functions

EXPONENTIAL AND LOGARITHMIC FUNCTIONS model many scientific phenomena. Some applications of exponential functions include population growth, compound interest, and radioactive decay. Radioactive decay is used dating ancient objects found at archeological sites. Applications of logarithmic functions include the pH scale in chemistry, sound intensity, and Newton's law of cooling.

Background: Prehistoric rock art from the Canyon de Chelly National Monument, Arizona;

Right: Anasazi sandal, 700–900 years old, found at Navajo National Monument, Arizona

CHAPTER PORTFOLIO ACTIVITIES PROJECT

About the Chapter Project

The heating and cooling of objects can be modeled by functions. Throughout this chapter and in the Chapter Project, *Warm Ups*, you will model the heating and cooling of a temperature probe over several temperature ranges in order to find an appropriate general model for these phenomena.

After completing the Chapter Project, you will be able to do the following:

- Collect real-world data on the heating and cooling of an object, and determine an appropriate exponential function to model the heating and cooling of an object.

- Make predictions about the temperature of an object that is heating or cooling to a constant surrounding temperature.

- Verify Newton's law of cooling.

In the Portfolio Activities for Lessons 6.1 and 6.4 and in the Chapter Project, you will need to use a program like the one shown on the calculator screen at right to collect temperature data with a CBL.

About the Portfolio Activities

Throughout the chapter, you will be given opportunities to complete Portfolio Activities that are designed to support your work on the Chapter Project.

- Using a CBL to collect cooling temperature data in a laboratory setting is included in the Portfolio Activity on page 361.

- Comparing different models for the cooling temperature data is included in the Portfolio Activity on page 369.

- Using a CBL to collect warming temperature data and performing appropriate transformations on regression equations are included in the Portfolio Activity on page 384.

- Comparing Newton's law of cooling with regression models from empirical data is included in the Portfolio Activity on page 409.

Exponential Growth and Decay

6.1

Why Exponential growth and decay can be used to model a number of real-world situations, such as population growth of bacteria and the elimination of medicine from the bloodstream.

Objectives

- Determine the multiplier for exponential growth and decay.

- Write and evaluate exponential expressions to model growth and decay situations.

Bacteria are very small single-celled organisms that live almost everywhere on Earth. Most bacteria are not harmful to humans, and some are helpful, such as the bacteria in yogurt.

Bacteria reproduce, or grow in number, by dividing. The total number of bacteria at a given time is referred to as the population of bacteria. When each bacterium in a population of bacteria divides, the population doubles.

Activity
Modeling Bacterial Growth

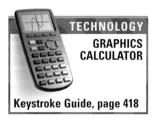

TECHNOLOGY
GRAPHICS CALCULATOR

Keystroke Guide, page 418

You will need: a calculator

You can use a calculator to model the growth of 25 bacteria, assuming that the entire population doubles every hour.

First enter 25. Then multiply this number by 2 to find the population of bacteria after 1 hour. Repeat this doubling procedure to find the population after 2 hours.

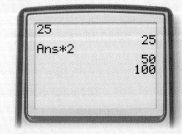

1. Copy and complete the table below.

Time (hr)	0	1	2	3	4	5	6
Population	25	50	100				

2. Write an algebraic expression that represents the population of bacteria after n hours. (Hint: Factor out 25 from each population figure.)

3. Use your algebraic expression to find the population of bacteria after 10 hours and after 20 hours.

CHECKPOINT ✔ **4.** Suppose that the initial population of bacteria was 75 instead of 25. Find the population after 10 hours and after 20 hours.

You can represent the growth of an initial population of 100 bacteria that doubles every hour by creating a table.

	+1	+1	+1	+1		
Time (hr)	0	1	2	3	4	$\cdots$	n
Population	100	200	400	800	1600	$\cdots$	$100(2)^n$
	×2	×2	×2	×2		

CONNECTION

PATTERNS IN DATA

The bar chart at right illustrates how the doubling pattern of growth quickly leads to large numbers.

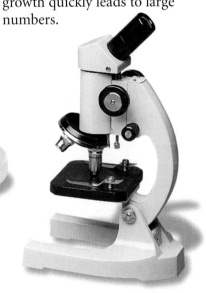

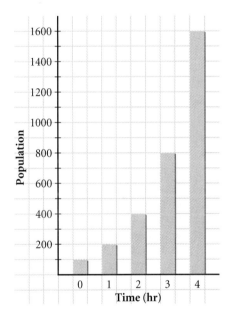

CHECKPOINT ✔ Assuming an initial population of 100 bacteria, predict the population of bacteria after 5 hours and after 6 hours.

The population after n hours can be represented by the following *exponential expression*:

$$\overbrace{100 \times 2 \times 2 \times 2 \times \cdots \times 2}^{n \text{ times}} = 100 \times 2^n$$

This expression, $100 \cdot 2^n$, is called an **exponential expression** because the exponent, n, is a variable and the base, 2, is a fixed number. The base of an exponential expression is commonly referred to as the **multiplier**.

Modeling Human Population Growth

Human populations grow much more slowly than bacterial populations. Bacterial populations that double each hour have a growth rate of 100% per hour. The population of the United States in 1990 was growing at a rate of about 8% per decade.

In Example 1, you will use this growth rate to make predictions.

E X A M P L E ❶ The population of the United States was 248,718,301 in 1990 and was projected to grow at a rate of about 8% per decade. [*Source: U.S. Census Bureau*]

Predict the population, to the nearest hundred thousand, for the years 2010 and 2025.

● **SOLUTION**

1. To obtain the multiplier for exponential growth, add the growth rate to 100%.

$$100\% + 8\% = 108\%, \text{ or } 1.08$$

2. Write the expression for the population n decades after 1990.

$$248{,}718{,}301 \cdot (1.08)^n$$

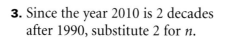

TECHNOLOGY
SCIENTIFIC CALCULATOR

3. Since the year 2010 is 2 decades after 1990, substitute 2 for n.

$$248{,}718{,}301(1.08)^n$$
$$= 248{,}718{,}301(1.08)^2$$
$$= 290{,}105{,}026.3$$

To the nearest hundred thousand, the predicted population for 2010 is 290,100,000.

Since the year 2025 is 3.5 decades after 1990, substitute 3.5 for n.

$$248{,}718{,}301(1.08)^n$$
$$= 248{,}718{,}301(1.08)^{3.5}$$
$$= 325{,}604{,}866$$

To the nearest hundred thousand, the predicted population for 2025 is 325,600,000.

These predictions are based on the assumption that the growth rate remains a constant 8% per decade.

TRY THIS The population of Brazil was about 162,661,000 in 1996 and was projected to grow at a rate of about 7.7% per decade. Predict the population, to the nearest hundred thousand, of Brazil for 2016 and 2020. [*Source: U.S. Census Bureau*]

CRITICAL THINKING If a population's growth rate is 1% per *year*, what is the population's growth rate per *decade*?

Modeling Biological Decay

Caffeine is eliminated from the bloodstream of a child at a rate of about 25% per hour. This exponential decrease in caffeine in a child's bloodstream is shown in the bar chart.

Caffeine Elimination in Children

A *rate of decay* can be thought of as a negative growth rate. To obtain the multiplier for the decrease in caffeine in the bloodstream of a child, subtract the rate of decay from 100%. Thus, the multiplier is 0.75, as calculated below.

$$100\% - 25\% = 75\%, \text{ or } 0.75$$

E X A M P L E **2** The rate at which caffeine is eliminated from the bloodstream of an adult is about 15% per hour. An adult drinks a caffeinated soda, and the caffeine in his or her bloodstream reaches a peak level of 30 milligrams.

Predict the amount, to the nearest tenth of a milligram, of caffeine remaining 1 hour after the peak level and 4 hours after the peak level.

Caffeine is an ingredient in coffee, tea, chocolate, and some soft drinks.

● **SOLUTION**

1. To obtain the multiplier for exponential decay, subtract the rate of decay from 100%. The multiplier is found as follows:

$$100\% - 15\% = 85\%, \text{ or } 0.85$$

2. Write the expression for the caffeine level x hours after the peak level.

$$30(0.85)^x$$

3. Substitute 1 for x.

$$30(0.85)^x$$
$$= 30(0.85)^1$$
$$= 25.5$$

The amount of caffeine remaining 1 hour after the peak level is 25.5 milligrams.

Substitute 4 for x.

$$30(0.85)^x$$
$$= 30(0.85)^4$$
$$\approx 15.7$$

The amount of caffeine remaining 4 hours after the peak level is about 15.7 milligrams.

TRY THIS A vitamin is eliminated from the bloodstream at a rate of about 20% per hour. The vitamin reaches a peak level in the bloodstream of 300 milligrams. Predict the amount, to the nearest tenth of a milligram, of the vitamin remaining 2 hours after the peak level and 7 hours after the peak level.

Exercises

● *Communicate*

1. What type of values of n are possible in the bacterial growth expression $25 \cdot 2^n$ and in the United States population growth expression $248{,}718{,}301 \cdot (1.08)^n$?

2. Explain how the United States population growth expression $248{,}718{,}301 \cdot (1.08)^n$ incorporates the growth rate of 8% per decade.

3. What assumption(s) do you make about a population's growth when you make predictions by using an exponential expression?

4. Describe the difference between the procedures for finding the multiplier for a growth rate of 5% and for a decay rate of 5%.

● *Guided Skills Practice*

Find the multiplier for each rate of exponential growth or decay.
(EXAMPLES 1 AND 2)

5. 5.5% growth   **6.** 0.25% growth   **7.** 3% decay   **8.** 0.5% decay

Evaluate each expression for $x = 3$. (EXAMPLES 1 AND 2)

9. 2^x **10.** $50(3)^x$ **11.** 0.8^x **12.** $100(0.75)^x$

APPLICATIONS

13. **DEMOGRAPHICS** The population of Tokyo-Yokohama, Japan, was about 28,447,000 in 1995 and was projected to grow at an annual rate of 1.1%. Predict the population, to the nearest hundred thousand, for the year 2004. [*Source: U.S. Census Bureau*] **(EXAMPLE 1)**

14. **HEALTH** A certain medication is eliminated from the bloodstream at a rate of about 12% per hour. The medication reaches a peak level in the bloodstream of 40 milligrams. Predict the amount, to the nearest tenth of a milligram, of the medication remaining 2 hours after the peak level and 3 hours after the peak level. **(EXAMPLE 2)**

● *Practice and Apply*

Find the multiplier for each rate of exponential growth or decay.

15. 7% growth   **16.** 9% growth   **17.** 6% decay

18. 2% decay   **19.** 6.5% growth   **20.** 8.2% decay

21. 0.05% decay   **22.** 0.08% growth   **23.** 0.075% growth

Given $x = 5$, $y = \dfrac{3}{5}$, and $z = 3.3$, evaluate each expression.

24. 2^x **25.** 3^y **26.** 2^{2x}

27. $50(2)^{3x}$ **28.** $25(2)^z$ **29.** $25(2)^y$

30. $100(3)^{x-1}$ **31.** $10(2)^{z+2}$ **32.** 2^{2y-1}

33. $100(2)^{4z}$ **34.** $100(0.5)^{3z}$ **35.** $75(0.5)^{2y}$

Predict the population of bacteria for each situation and time period.

36. 55 bacteria that double every hour
    a. after 3 hours   **b.** after 5 hours

37. 125 bacteria that double every hour
    a. after 6 hours   **b.** after 8 hours

38. 33 *E. coli* bacteria that double every 30 minutes
    a. after 1 hour   **b.** after 6 hours

39. 75 *E. coli* bacteria that double every 30 minutes
    a. after 2 hours   **b.** after 3 hours

40. 225 bacteria that triple every hour
    a. after 1 hour   **b.** after 3 hours

41. 775 bacteria that triple every hour
    a. after 2 hours   **b.** after 4 hours

CHALLENGE

42. Suppose that you put $2500 into a retirement account that grows with an interest rate of 5.25% compounded once each year. After how many years will the balance of the account be at least $15,000?

CONNECTION

PATTERNS IN DATA **Determine whether each table represents a linear, quadratic, or exponential relationship between *x* and *y*.**

43.

x	y
0	2
1	4
2	8
3	16

44.

x	y
1	1
2	3
3	9
4	27

45.

x	y
0	6
2	10
4	14
6	18

46.

x	y
0	−2
3	7
6	34
9	79

APPLICATIONS

47. DEMOGRAPHICS The population of Indonesia was 191,256,000 in 1990 and was growing at a rate of 1.9% per year. Predict the population, to the nearest hundred thousand, of Indonesia in 2010. [*Source: U.S. Census Bureau*]

Bali, Indonesia

48. HEALTH A dye is injected into the pancreas during a certain medical procedure. A physician injects 0.3 grams of the dye, and a healthy pancreas will secrete 4% of the dye each minute. Predict the amount of dye remaining, to the nearest hundredth of a gram, in a healthy pancreas 30 minutes after the injection.

49. DEMOGRAPHICS The population of China was 1,210,005,000 in 1996 and was growing at a rate of about 6% per decade. Predict the population, to the nearest hundred thousand, of China in 2016 and in 2021. [*Source: U.S. Census Bureau*]

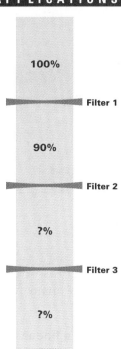

100%

Filter 1

90%

Filter 2

?%

Filter 3

?%

50. PHYSICAL SCIENCE Suppose that a camera filter transmits 90% of the light striking it, as illustrated at left.
  a. If a second filter of the same type is added, what portion of light is transmitted through the combination of the two filters?
  b. Write an expression to model the portion of light that is transmitted through n filters.
  c. Calculate the portion of light transmitted through 4, 5, and 6 filters.

51. DEMOGRAPHICS The population of India was 952,108,000 in 1996 and was growing at a rate of about 1.3% per year. [*Source: U.S. Census Bureau*]
  a. Predict the population, to the nearest hundred thousand, of India in 2000 and in 2010.
  b. Find the growth rate per decade that corresponds to the growth rate of 1.3% per year.
  c. Suppose that the population growth rate of India slows to 1% per year after the year 2000. What is the predicted population, to the nearest hundred thousand, of India in 2010?

52. CHEMISTRY A dilution is commonly used to obtain the desired concentration of a sample. For example, suppose that 1 milliliter of hydrochloric acid, or HCl, is combined with 9 milliliters of a buffer. The concentration of the resulting mixture is $\frac{1}{10}$ of the original concentration of HCl.
  a. Suppose that this dilution is performed again with 1 millimeter of the already diluted mixture and 9 milliliters of buffer. What is the concentration of the resulting mixture (compared with the original concentration)?
  b. Write an expression to model the concentration of HCl in the resulting mixture after repeated dilutions as described in part **a**.
  c. What is the concentration of the resulting mixture (compared to the original concentration) after 5 repeated dilutions?

53. SPACE SCIENCE The first stage of the *Saturn 5* rocket that propelled astronauts to the moon burned about 8% of its remaining fuel every 15 seconds and carried about 600,000 gallons of fuel at liftoff. Estimate the amount of fuel remaining, to the nearest ten thousand gallons, in the first stage 2 minutes after liftoff.

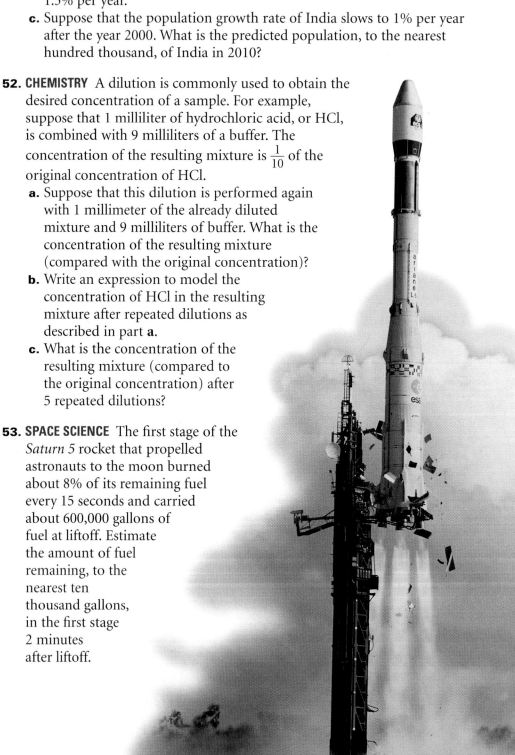

 **Look Back**

Evaluate each expression. *(LESSON 2.2)*

54. 4^{-2} **55.** $\left(\frac{1}{2}\right)^{-1}$ **56.** $25^{\frac{3}{2}}$ **57.** $49^{\frac{1}{2}}$

Simplify each expression, assuming that no variable equals zero. Write your answer with positive exponents only. *(LESSON 2.2)*

58. $\left(\frac{2x^3}{x^{-2}}\right)^2$ **59.** $\left(\frac{m^{-1}n^2}{n^{-3}}\right)^{-3}$ **60.** $\left(\frac{2a^3b^{-2}}{-a^2b^{-3}}\right)^{-1}$ **61.** $\frac{(2y^2y)^{-2}}{3xy^{-4}}$

Identify each transformation from the graph of $f(x) = x^2$ to the graph of g. *(LESSON 2.7)*

62. $g(x) = 6x^2$ **63.** $g(x) = (-2x)^2$ **64.** $g(x) = -\frac{1}{2}x^2 + 1$

65. $g(x) = -(0.5x)^2 + 3$ **66.** $g(x) = (x - 3)^2 + 2$ **67.** $g(x) = -5(x - 2)^2 - 4$

State whether each parabola opens up or down and whether the y-coordinate of the vertex is the maximum or minimum value of the function. *(LESSON 5.1)*

68. $f(x) = \frac{1}{2}x^2$ **69.** $f(x) = -2x^2 - x + 1$ **70.** $f(x) = 3 - 5x - x^2$

 Look Beyond

APPLICATION

71. INVESTMENTS Suppose that you want to invest $100 in a bank account that earns 5% interest *compounded once* at the end of each year. Determine the balance after 10 years.

Refer to the discussions of the Portfolio Activities and Chapter Project on page 353 for background on this activity.

You will need a CBL with a temperature probe, a glass of ice water, and a graphics calculator.

1. First use the CBL to find the temperature of the air. Then place the probe in the ice water for 2 minutes. Record 30 CBL readings taken at 2-second intervals. Take a final reading at the end of the 2 minutes.

2. a. Use the linear regression feature on your calculator to find a linear function that models your first 30 readings. (Use the variable t for the time in seconds).

b. Use your linear function to predict the temperature of the probe after 2 minutes, or 120 seconds. Compare this

prediction with your actual 2-minute reading.

c. Discuss the usefulness of your linear function for modeling the cooling process. (You may want to illustrate your answer with graphs.)

Save your data and results for use in the remaining Portfolio Activities.

WORKING ON THE CHAPTER PROJECT

You should now be able to complete Activity 1 of the Chapter Project.

6.2

Exponential Functions

Why You can use exponential functions to calculate the value of investments that earn compound interest and to compare different investments by calculating effective yields.

Objectives

- Classify an exponential function as representing exponential growth or exponential decay.

- Calculate the growth of investments under various conditions.

$$f(x) = b^{x} \quad \text{EXPONENT}$$

$$\text{BASE}$$

Consider the function $y = x^2$ and $y = 2^x$. Both functions have a base and an exponent. However, $y = x^2$ is a quadratic function, and $y = 2^x$ is an *exponential function*. In an exponential function, the base is fixed and the exponent is variable.

Exponential Function

The function $f(x) = b^x$ is an **exponential function** with **base** b, where b is a positive real number other than 1 and x is any real number.

---

x	$y = 2^x$
-3	$2^{-3} = \frac{1}{8}$
-2	$2^{-2} = \frac{1}{4}$
-1	$2^{-1} = \frac{1}{2}$
0	$2^0 = 1$
1	$2^1 = 2$
$\sqrt{2}$	$2^{\sqrt{2}} \approx 2.67$
2	$2^2 = 4$
3	$2^3 = 8$

Examine the table at left and the graph at right of the exponential function $y = 2^x$.

Notice that as x-values decrease, the y-values for $y = 2^x$ get closer and closer to 0, approaching the x-axis as an *asymptote*. An **asymptote** is a line that a graph approaches (but does not reach) as its x- or y-values become very large or very small.

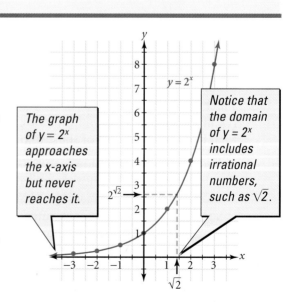

The graph of $y = 2^x$ approaches the x-axis but never reaches it.

Notice that the domain of $y = 2^x$ includes irrational numbers, such as $\sqrt{2}$.

Investigating Exponential Functions

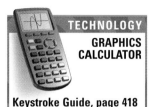

TECHNOLOGY

GRAPHICS CALCULATOR

Keystroke Guide, page 418

You will need: a graphics calculator

1. Graph $y_1 = 3^x$, $y_2 = 2^x$, and $y_3 = (1.5)^x$ on the same screen.

2. For what value of x is $y_1 = y_2 = y_3$ true?
   For what values of x is $y_1 > y_2 > y_3$ true?
   For what values of x is $y_1 < y_2 < y_3$ true?

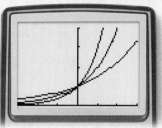

3. Graph $y_4 = \left(\frac{1}{3}\right)^x$, $y_5 = \left(\frac{1}{2}\right)^x$, and $y_6 = \left(\frac{1}{1.5}\right)^x$ on the same screen as y_1, y_2, and y_3.

PROBLEM SOLVING

4. **Look for a pattern.** Examine each corresponding pair of functions.

$$y_1 = 3 \text{ and } y_4 = \left(\frac{1}{3}\right)^x \qquad y_2 = 2^x \text{ and } y_5 = \left(\frac{1}{2}\right)^x$$

$$y_3 = (1.5)^x \text{ and } y_6 = \left(\frac{1}{1.5}\right)^x$$

How are the graphs of each corresponding pair of functions related?
How are the bases of each corresponding pair of functions related?

CHECKPOINT ✓

5. For what values of b does the graph of $y = b^x$ rise from left to right?
   For what values of b does the graph of $y = b^x$ fall from left to right?

The graphs of $f(x) = 2^x$ and $g(x) = \left(\frac{1}{2}\right)^x$ exhibit the two typical behaviors for exponential functions.

$g(x) = \left(\frac{1}{2}\right)^x$ *is a decreasing exponential function because its base is a positive number less than 1.*

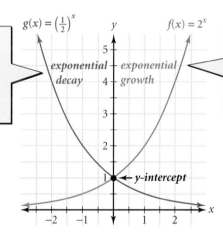

$f(x) = 2^x$ *is an increasing exponential function because its base is a positive number greater than 1.*

CONNECTION

TRANSFORMATIONS

Recall from Lesson 2.7 that the graphs of f and g are reflections of one another across the y-axis because $g(x) = f(-x) = 2^{-x} = \left(\frac{1}{2}\right)^x$.

Exponential Growth and Decay

When $b > 1$, the function $f(x) = b^x$ represents **exponential growth**.

When $0 < b < 1$, the function $f(x) = b^x$ represents **exponential decay**.

Exponential growth functions and exponential decay functions of the form $y = b^x$ have the same domain, range, and y-intercept. For example:

Function	Domain	Range	y-intercept
$f(x) = 2^x$	all real numbers	all positive real numbers	1
$g(x) = \left(\frac{1}{2}\right)^x$	all real numbers	all positive real numbers	1

Recall from Lesson 2.7 that $y = a \cdot f(x)$ represents a vertical stretch or compression of the graph of $y = f(x)$. This transformation is applied to exponential functions in Example 1.

E X A M P L E **1** Graph $f(x) = 2^x$ along with each function below. Tell whether each function represents exponential growth or exponential decay. Then give the y-intercept.

    a. $y = 3 \cdot f(x)$ **b.** $y = 5 \cdot f(-x)$

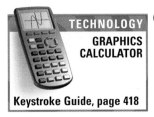
TECHNOLOGY
GRAPHICS CALCULATOR
Keystroke Guide, page 418

C O N N E C T I O N
TRANSFORMATIONS

SOLUTION

a. $y = 3 \cdot f(x) = 3 \cdot 2^x$

The function $y = 3 \cdot 2^x$ represents exponential growth because the base, 2, is greater than 1.

The y-intercept is 3 because the graph of $f(x) = 2^x$, which has a y-intercept of 1, is stretched by a factor of 3.

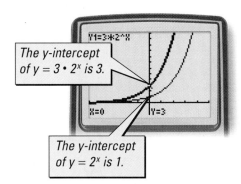

The y-intercept of $y = 3 \cdot 2^x$ is 3.

The y-intercept of $y = 2^x$ is 1.

b. $y = 5 \cdot f(-x) = 5 \cdot 2^{-x} = 5 \cdot \left(\frac{1}{2}\right)^x$

The function $y = 5 \cdot \left(\frac{1}{2}\right)^x$ represents exponential decay because the base, $\frac{1}{2}$, is less than 1.

The y-intercept is 5 because the graph of $f(x) = 2^x$, which has a y-intercept of 1, is stretched by a factor of 5.

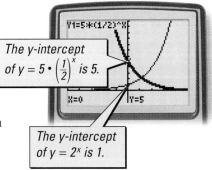

The y-intercept of $y = 5 \cdot \left(\frac{1}{2}\right)^x$ is 5.

The y-intercept of $y = 2^x$ is 1.

TRY THIS   Graph $f(x) = 2^x$ along with each function below. Tell whether each function represents exponential growth or exponential decay. Then give the y-intercept.

    a. $y = \frac{1}{3} \cdot f(x)$ **b.** $y = \frac{1}{4} \cdot f(-x)$

CHECKPOINT ✔   What transformation of f occurs when $a < 0$ in $y = a \cdot f(x)$?

CRITICAL THINKING   Describe the effect on the graph of $f(x) = b^x$ when $b > 1$ and b increases. Describe the effect on the graph of $f(x) = b^x$ when $0 < b < 1$ and b decreases.

Compound Interest

APPLICATION

INVESTMENTS

The growth in the value of investments earning compound interest is modeled by an exponential function.

Compound Interest Formula

The total amount of an investment, *A*, earning compound interest is

$$A(t) = P\left(1 + \frac{r}{n}\right)^{nt},$$

where *P* is the principal, *r* is the annual interest rate, *n* is the number of times interest is compounded per year, and *t* is the time in years.

E X A M P L E ➋ **Find the final amount of a $100 investment after 10 years at 5% interest compounded annually, quarterly, and daily.**

SOLUTION

In this situation, the principal is $100, the annual interest rate is 5%, and the time period is 10 years. Thus, $P = 100$, $r = 0.05$, and $t = 10$. The table shows calculations for $n = 1$, $n = 4$, and $n = 365$.

TECHNOLOGY

SCIENTIFIC CALCULATOR

Compounding period	n	$A(10) = 100\left(1 + \frac{0.05}{n}\right)^{n \cdot 10}$	Final amount
annually	1	$A(10) = 100\left(1 + \frac{0.05}{1}\right)^{1 \cdot 10}$	$162.89
quarterly	4	$A(10) = 100\left(1 + \frac{0.05}{4}\right)^{4 \cdot 10}$	$164.36
daily	365	$A(10) = 100\left(1 + \frac{0.05}{365}\right)^{365 \cdot 10}$	$164.87

CHECKPOINT ✔ Describe what happens to the final amount as the number of compounding periods increases.

Effective Yield

APPLICATION

INVESTMENTS

Suppose that you buy an item for $100 and sell the item one year later for $105. In this case, the *effective yield* of your investment is 5%. The **effective yield** is the annually compounded interest rate that yields the final amount of an investment. You can determine the effective yield by fitting an exponential regression equation to two points.

E X A M P L E ❸ A collector buys a painting for $100,000 at the beginning of 1995 and sells it for $150,000 at the beginning of 2000.

CONNECTION

STATISTICS

Use an exponential regression equation to find the effective yield.

● **SOLUTION**

1. Find the exponential equation that represents this situation.

   To find effective yield, the interest is compounded annually, so $n = 1$.

   From 1995 to 2000 is 5 years, so $t = 5$.

$$A(t) = P\left(1 = \frac{r}{n}\right)^{nt}$$

$$150{,}000 = 100{,}000\left(1 + \frac{r}{1}\right)^{1 \cdot 5}$$

$$150{,}000 = 100{,}000(1 + r)^5$$

TECHNOLOGY

GRAPHICS CALCULATOR

Keystroke Guide, page 419

2. Enter the two points that represent the given information, (0, 100,000) and (5, 150,000). Find and graph the exponential regression equation that fits the points.

3. The multiplier is about 1.084, so the effective yield, is about $1.084 - 1 = 0.084$, or 8.4%.

The exponential regression equation is $y \approx 100{,}000(1.084)^x$.

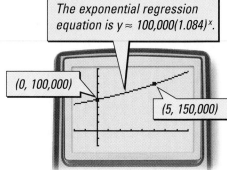

(0, 100,000)

(5, 150,000)

TRY THIS Find the effective yield for a painting bought for $100,000 at the end of 1994 and sold for $200,000 at the end of 2004.

Exercises

● *Communicate*

1. If $b > 0$ and the graph of $y = b^x$ falls from left to right, describe the possible values of b.

2. Compare the domain and range of $y = 3^x$ with the domain and range of $y = \left(\frac{1}{3}\right)^x$.

3. Describe how the y-intercept of the graph of $f(x) = 2(5)^x$ is related to the value of a in $f(x) = ab^x$.

4. How are the functions $y = x^2$ and $y = 2^x$ similar, and how are they different?

Tell whether each function represents exponential growth or exponential decay, and give the *y*-intercept. *(EXAMPLE 1)*

5. $f(x) = \left(\frac{1}{2}\right)^x$ **6.** $g(x) = 3(2)^x$ **7.** $k(x) = 5(0.5)^x$

APPLICATIONS

8. INVESTMENTS Find the final amount of a $250 investment after 5 years at 6% interest compounded annually, quarterly, and daily. *(EXAMPLE 2)*

9. INVESTMENTS Find the effective yield for a $2000 investment that is worth $4000 after 15 years. *(EXAMPLE 3)*

● *Practice and Apply*

Identify each function as linear, quadratic, or exponential.

10. $g(x) = 10x + 3$ **11.** $k(x) = (77 - x)x$ **12.** $f(x) = 12(2.5)^x$

13. $k(x) = 0.5^x - 3.5$ **14.** $g(x) = (2200)^{3.5x}$ **15.** $h(x) = 0.5x^2 + 7.5$

Tell whether each function represents exponential growth or decay.

16. $y(x) = 12(2.5)^x$ **17.** $k(x) = 500(1.5)^x$ **18.** $y(t) = 45\left(\frac{1}{4}\right)^t$

19. $d(x) = 0.125\left(\frac{1}{2}\right)^x$ **20.** $g(x) = 0.25(0.8)^x$ **21.** $s(k) = 0.5(0.5)^k$

22. $m(x) = 222(0.9)^x$ **23.** $f(k) = 722^{-k}$ **24.** $g(x) = 0.5(787)^{-x}$

Match each function with its graph.

25. $y = 2^x$ **26.** $y = 2(3)^x$

27. $y = 2\left(\frac{1}{3}\right)^x$ **28.** $y = \left(\frac{1}{2}\right)^x$

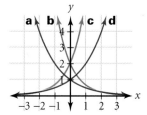

Find the final amount for each investment.

29. $1000 at 6% interest compounded annually for 20 years

30. $1000 at 6% interest compounded semiannually for 20 years

31. $750 at 10% interest compounded quarterly for 10 years

32. $750 at 5% interest compounded quarterly for 10 years

33. $1800 at 5.65% interest compounded daily for 3 years

34. $1800 at 5.65% interest compounded daily for 6 years

35. Graph $f(x) = 2^x$, $g(x) = 5^x$, and $h(x) = 8^x$.
   a. Which function exhibits the fastest growth? the slowest growth?
   b. What is the *y*-intercept of each function?
   c. State the domain and range of each function.

36. Graph $a(x) = \left(\frac{1}{2}\right)^x$, $b(x) = \left(\frac{1}{5}\right)^x$, and $c(x) = \left(\frac{1}{8}\right)^x$.
   a. Which function exhibits the fastest decay? the slowest decay?
   b. What is the *y*-intercept of each function?
   c. State the domain and range of each function.

CHALLENGE

37. Describe when the graph of $f(x) = ab^x$ is a horizontal line.

TRANSFORMATIONS Graph each pair of functions and describe the transformations from *f* to *g*.

38. $f(x) = \left(\frac{1}{2}\right)^x$ and $g(x) = 5\left(\frac{1}{2}\right)^x$

39. $f(x) = \left(\frac{1}{10}\right)^x$ and $g(x) = 0.5\left(\frac{1}{10}\right)^x$

40. $f(x) = 2^x$ and $g(x) = 3(2)^x + 1$

41. $f(x) = 10^x$ and $g(x) = 2(10)^x - 3$

42. $f(x) = 10^x$ and $g(x) = 3(10)^{x+2}$

43. $f(x) = 2^x$ and $g(x) = 5(2)^{x-1}$

44. $f(x) = 3\left(\frac{1}{2}\right)^x$ and $g(x) = 3(2^x)$

45. $f(x) = \left(\frac{1}{3}\right)^x$ and $g(x) = 2(3)^{-x}$

46. TRANSFORMATIONS Describe how each transformation of $f(x) = b^x$ affects the domain and range, the asymptotes, and the intercepts.
  a. a vertical stretch
  b. a vertical compression
  c. a horizontal translation
  d. a vertical translation
  e. a reflection across the *y*-axis

STATISTICS Use an exponential regression equation to find the effective yield for each investment. Assume that interest is compounded only once each year.

47 a $1000 mutual fund investment made at the beginning of 1990 that is worth $1450 at the beginning of 2000

48 a house that is bought for $75,000 at the end of 1995 and that is worth $95,000 at the end of 2005

STATISTICS Use an exponential regression equation to model the annual rate of inflation, or percent increase in price, for each item described.

49 a half-gallon of milk cost $1.37 in 1989 and $1.48 in 1995 [*Source: U.S. Bureau of Labor Statistics*]

50 a gallon of regular unleaded gasoline cost $0.93 in 1986 and $1.11 in 1993 [*Source: U.S. Bureau of Labor Statistics*]

51. INVESTMENTS Find the final amount of a $2000 certificate of deposit (CD) after 5 years at an annual interest rate of 5.51% compounded annually.

Certificate of Deposit

5.51%

Annual Percentage Yield*

$2,000 Minimum

52. INVESTMENTS Consider a $1000 investment that is compounded annually at three different interest rates: 5%, 5.5%, and 6%.
  a. Write and graph a function for each interest rate over a time period from 0 to 60 years.
  b. Compare the graphs of the three functions.
  c. Compare the shapes of the graphs for the first 10 years with the shapes of the graphs between 50 and 60 years.

53. INVESTMENTS The final amount for $5000 invested for 25 years at 10% annual interest compounded semiannually is $57,337.
  a. What is the effect of doubling the amount invested?
  b. What is the effect of doubling the annual interest rate?
  c. What is the effect of doubling the investment period?
  d. Which of the above has the greatest effect on the final amount of the investment?

Find the inverse of each function. State whether the inverse is a function. *(LESSON 2.5)*

54. $\{(-2, 4), (-3, -1), (2, 2), (3, 4)\}$

55. $\{(7, 2), (3, -1), (2, 2), (0, 0)\}$

56. $y = 2(x + 3)$ **57.** $y = 3x^2$ **58.** $y = x^2 + 2$ **59.** $y = -x^2$

Graph each piecewise function. *(LESSON 2.6)*

60. $f(x) = \begin{cases} 9 & \text{if } 0 \le x < 5 \\ 2x - 1 & \text{if } 5 \le x < 10 \end{cases}$
     61. $g(x) = \begin{cases} x & \text{if } 0 \le x < 2 \\ -3x + 8 & \text{if } 2 \le x < 5 \\ -5 & \text{if } 5 \le x < 10 \end{cases}$

Let $A = \begin{bmatrix} 3 & 4 & -1 \\ -2 & -8 & 6 \\ 10 & 8 & 0 \end{bmatrix}$, $B = \begin{bmatrix} 0 & 2 \\ 7 & -2 \\ -5 & 1 \end{bmatrix}$, and $C = \begin{bmatrix} 2 & -6 & -2 \\ 3 & -1 & 4 \end{bmatrix}$. **Find each**

product matrix, if it exists. *(LESSON 4.2)*

62. AB **63.** BA **64.** AC **65.** CA **66.** BC **67.** CB

Find a quadratic function to fit each set of points exactly. *(LESSON 5.7)*

68. $(1, -1), (2, -5), (3, 13)$ **69.** $(0, 4), (1, 5), (3, 25)$

 Look Beyond

70. Use guess-and-check to find x such that $10^x = 50$.

For this activity, use the data collected in the Portfolio Activity on page 361.

1. a. Use the quadratic regression feature on your calculator to find a quadratic function that models your first 30 readings.

  b. Use your linear function to predict the temperature of the probe after 2 minutes. Compare this prediction with your actual 2-minute reading.

  c. Discuss the usefulness of your quadratic function for modeling the cooling process.

2. Now use the exponential regression feature on your calculator to find an exponential function that models your first 30 readings, and repeat parts **b** and **c** of Step 1.

Save your data and results to use in the remaining Portfolio Activities.

WORKING ON THE CHAPTER PROJECT

You should now be able to complete Activity 2 of the Chapter Project.

Logarithmic Functions

Substance	pH
gastric fluid	1.8
lemon juice	2.2–2.4
vinegar	2.4–3.4
banana	4.8
saliva	6.5–7.5
water	7
egg white	7.6–8.0
Rolaids, Tums	9.9
milk of magnesia	10.5

The pH of an acidic solution is less than 7, the pH of a basic solution is greater than 7, and the pH of a neutral solution is 7.

Objectives

● Write equivalent forms for exponential and logarithmic equations.

● Use the definitions of exponential and logarithmic functions to solve equations.

Why *Logarithmic functions are widely used in measurement scales such as the pH scale, which ranges from 0 to 14.*

Logarithms are used to find unknown exponents in exponential models.

Logarithmic functions define many measurement scales in the sciences, including the pH, decibel, and Richter scales.

Activity
Approximating Exponents

TECHNOLOGY
GRAPHICS CALCULATOR

Keystroke Guide, page 419

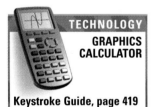

You will need: a graphics calculator

Use the table below to complete this Activity.

x	−3	−2	−1	0	1	2	3
$y = 10^x$	$\frac{1}{1000}$	$\frac{1}{100}$	$\frac{1}{10}$	1	10	100	1000

1. How are the *x*-values in the table related to the *y*-values?

CHECKPOINT ✔ 2. Use the table above to find the value of *x* in each equation below.

    a. $10^x = 1000$ **b.** $10^x = \frac{1}{100}$ **c.** $10^x = \frac{1}{1000}$ **d.** $10^x = 1$

PROBLEM SOLVING 3. **Make a table** of values for $y = 10^x$. Use the table to approximate the solution to $10^x = 7$ to the nearest hundredth.

CHECKPOINT ✔ 4. Use a table of values to approximate the solution to $10^x = 85$ to the nearest hundredth.

X	Y1
.83	6.7608
.84	6.9183
.85	7.0795
.86	7.2444
.87	7.4131
.88	7.5858
.89	7.7625
Y1=7.07945784384	

A table of values for $y = 10^x$ can be used to solve equations such as $10^x = 1000$ and $10^x = \frac{1}{100}$. However, to solve equations such as $10^x = 85$ or $10^x = 2.3$, a *logarithm* is needed. With logarithms, you can write an exponential equation in an equivalent logarithmic form.

Exponential form   **Logarithmic form**

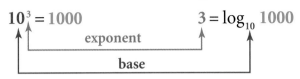

$10^3 = 1000$ $3 = \log_{10} 1000$

exponent

base

Equivalent Exponential and Logarithmic Forms

For any positive base b, where $b \neq 1$:
$$b^x = y \text{ if and only if } x = \log_b y$$

E X A M P L E **1**   **a.** Write $5^3 = 125$ in logarithmic form.
b. Write $\log_3 81 = 4$ in exponential form.

SOLUTION

a. $5^3 = 125 \quad \rightarrow \quad 3 = \log_5 125$ *3 is the exponent and 5 is the base.*
b. $\log_3 81 = 4 \quad \rightarrow \quad 3^4 = 81$ *3 is the base and 4 is the exponent.*

TRY THIS   Copy and complete each column in the table below.

Exponential form	$2^5 = 32$	?	$3^{-2} = \frac{1}{9}$	?
Logarithmic form	?	$\log_{10} 1000 = 3$	?	$\log_{16} 4 = \frac{1}{2}$

You can evaluate logarithms with a base of 10 by using the $\boxed{\text{LOG}}$ key on a calculator.

E X A M P L E **2**   **Solve for $10^x = 85$ for x. Round your answer to the nearest thousandth.**

SOLUTION

Write $10^x = 85$ in logarithmic form, and use the $\boxed{\text{LOG}}$ key.

Because $10^1 = 10$ and $10^2 = 100$, $x \approx 1.9294$ is a reasonable answer.

$10^x = 85$

$x = \log_{10} 85$

$x \approx 1.9294$ *Use a calculator.*

TRY THIS   Solve $10^x = \frac{1}{109}$ for x. Round your answer to the nearest thousandth.

Definition of Logarithmic Function

The inverse of the exponential function $y = 10^x$ is $x = 10^y$. To rewrite $x = 10^y$ in terms of y, use the equivalent logarithmic form, $y = \log_{10} x$.

Examine the tables and graphs below to see the inverse relationship between $y = 10^x$ and $y = \log_{10} x$.

x	$y = 10^x$
-3	$\frac{1}{1000}$
-2	$\frac{1}{100}$
-1	$\frac{1}{10}$
0	1
1	10
2	100
3	1000

x	$y = \log_{10} x$
$\frac{1}{1000}$	-3
$\frac{1}{100}$	-2
$\frac{1}{10}$	-1
1	0
10	1
100	2
1000	3

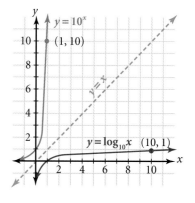

The table below summarizes the relationship between the domain and range of $y = 10^x$ and of $y = \log_{10} x$.

Function	Domain	Range
$y = 10^x$	all real numbers	all positive real numbers
$y = \log_{10} x$	all positive real numbers	all real numbers

Logarithmic Functions

The **logarithmic function** $y = \log_b x$ with base b, or $x = b^y$, is the inverse of the exponential function $y = b^x$, where $b \neq 1$ and $b > 0$.

CRITICAL THINKING Describe the graph that results if $b = 1$ in $y = \log_b x$. Is $y = \log_1 x$ a function?

Because $y = \log_b x$ is the inverse of the exponential function $y = b^x$ and $y = \log_b x$ is a function, the exponential function $y = b^x$ is a one-to-one function. This means that for each element in the domain of an exponential function, there is exactly one corresponding element in the range. For example, if $3^x = 3^2$, then $x = 2$. This is called the *One-to-One Property of Exponents*.

One-to-One Property of Exponents

If $b^x = b^y$, then $x = y$.

E X A M P L E ❸ Find the value of *v* in each equation.

    a. $v = \log_{125} 5$ **b.** $5 = \log_v 32$ **c.** $4 = \log_3 v$

● **SOLUTION**

Write the equivalent exponential form, and solve for *v*.

    a. $v = \log_{125} 5$ **b.** $5 = \log_v 32$ **c.** $4 = \log_3 v$

       $125^v = 5$ $v^5 = 32$ $3^4 = v$

      $(5^3)^v = 5$ $v^5 = 2^5$ $81 = v$

        $5^{3v} = 5^1$ $v = 2$

          $3v = 1$ ⟵ *Apply the One-to-One Property.*

            $v = \dfrac{1}{3}$

TRY THIS   Find the value of *v* in each equation.

    a. $v = \log_4 64$ **b.** $2 = \log_v 25$ **c.** $6 = \log_3 v$

C O N N E C T I O N

TRANSFORMATIONS

Recall from Lesson 2.7 that the graph of $y = -f(x)$ is the graph of $y = f(x)$ reflected across the *x*-axis. The graph of $y = \log_{10} x$ and of its reflection across the *x*-axis, $y = -\log_{10} x$, are shown at right.

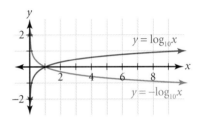

The function $y = -\log_{10} x$ is used in chemistry to measure pH levels. The pH of a solution describes its acidity. Substances that are more acidic have a lower pH, while substances that are less acidic, or basic, have a higher pH. The pH of a substance is defined as $\text{pH} = -\log_{10}[\text{H}^+]$, where $[\text{H}^+]$ is the hydrogen ion concentration of a solution in moles per liter.

E X A M P L E ❹ The pH of a carbonated soda is 3.

What is $[\text{H}^+]$ for this soda?

A P P L I C A T I O N

CHEMISTRY

● **SOLUTION**

    $\text{pH} = -\log_{10}[\text{H}^+]$

      $3 = -\log_{10}[\text{H}^+]$ *Substitute 3 for pH.*

    $-3 = \log_{10}[\text{H}^+]$

  $10^{-3} = [\text{H}^+]$ *Write the equivalent exponential equation.*

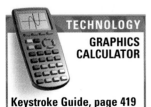

TECHNOLOGY

GRAPHICS CALCULATOR

Keystroke Guide, page 419

CHECK

Graph $y = -\log_{10} x$ and $y = 3$ on the same screen, and find the point of intersection. The window at right shows *x*-values between 0 and 0.01.

Thus, there is $\dfrac{1}{1000}$, or 0.001, moles of hydrogen ions in a liter of carbonated soda that has a pH of 3.

TRY THIS   Find $[\text{H}^+]$ for orange juice that has a pH of 3.75.

Exercises

Communicate

1. Describe the relationship between logarithmic functions and exponential functions.

2. State the domain and range of logarithmic functions. How are they related to the domain and range of exponential functions?

3. Explain how to approximate the value of x in $2^x = 58$ by using the table feature of a graphics calculator.

Guided Skills Practice

4. Write $4^2 = 16$ in logarithmic form. *(EXAMPLE 1)*

5. Write $\log_5 25 = 2$ in exponential form. *(EXAMPLE 1)*

Solve each equation for *x*. Round your answers to the nearest thousandth. *(EXAMPLE 2)*

6. $10^x = 568$

7. $10^x = \dfrac{1}{500}$

Find the value of *v* in each equation. *(EXAMPLE 3)*

8. $v = \log_7 49$

9. $2 = \log_v 144$

10. $2 = \log_4 v$

APPLICATION

11. **CHEMISTRY** The pH of black coffee is 5. What is $[\text{H}^+]$ for this coffee? *(EXAMPLE 4)*

Practice and Apply

Write each equation in logarithmic form.

12. $11^2 = 121$

13. $5^4 = 625$

14. $3^5 = 243$

15. $6^3 = 216$

16. $6^{-2} = \dfrac{1}{36}$

17. $7^{-2} = \dfrac{1}{49}$

18. $27^{\frac{1}{3}} = 3$

19. $16^{\frac{1}{4}} = 2$

20. $\left(\dfrac{1}{4}\right)^{-3} = 64$

21. $\left(\dfrac{1}{9}\right)^{-2} = 81$

22. $\left(\dfrac{1}{3}\right)^2 = \dfrac{1}{9}$

23. $\left(\dfrac{1}{2}\right)^3 = \dfrac{1}{8}$

Write each equation in exponential form.

24. $\log_6 36 = 2$

25. $\log_{10} 1000 = 3$

26. $\log_{10} 0.001 = -3$

27. $\log_{10} 0.1 = -1$

28. $3 = \log_9 729$

29. $3 = \log_7 343$

30. $\log_3 \dfrac{1}{81} = -4$

31. $\log_2 \dfrac{1}{32} = -5$

32. $-2 = \log_2 \dfrac{1}{4}$

33. $-3 = \log_3 \dfrac{1}{27}$

34. $\log_{121} 11 = \dfrac{1}{2}$

35. $\log_{144} 12 = \dfrac{1}{2}$

Find the approximate value of each logarithmic expression.

36. $\log_{10} 1026$

37. $\log_{10} 79$

38. $\log_{10} 8$

39. $\log_{10} 21{,}050$

40. $\log_{10} 0.08$

41. $\log_{10} 0.9$

42. $\log_{10} 0.002$

43. $\log_{10} 0.00013$

Solve each equation for x. Round your answers to the nearest hundredth.

44. $10^x = 31$
45. $10^x = 12$
46. $10^x = 7210$

47. $10^x = 3588$
48. $10^x = 1.498$
49. $10^x = 1.89$

50. $10^x = 0.0054$
51. $10^x = 0.035$
52. $10^x = \dfrac{3}{49}$

53. $10^x = \dfrac{1}{1085}$
54. $10^x = \sqrt{7.4}$
55. $10^x = \dfrac{1}{\sqrt{500}}$

Find the value of v in each equation.

56. $v = \log_{10} 1000$
57. $v = \log_4 64$
58. $v = \log_7 343$

59. $v = \log_{17} 289$
60. $v = \log_3 3$
61. $v = \log_7 7$

62. $v = \log_{10} 0.001$
63. $v = \log_{10} 0.01$
64. $v = \log_2 \dfrac{1}{4}$

65. $v = \log_{10} \dfrac{1}{100}$
66. $v = \log_4 1$
67. $v = \log_9 1$

68. $3 = \log_6 v$
69. $2 = \log_7 v$
70. $1 = \log_5 v$

71. $1 = \log_3 v$
72. $\dfrac{1}{2} = \log_9 v$
73. $\dfrac{1}{3} = \log_8 v$

74. $-2 = \log_6 v$
75. $-3 = \log_4 v$
76. $0 = \log_{13} v$

77. $0 = \log_2 v$
78. $\log_v 16 = 2$
79. $\log_v 125 = 3$

80. $\log_v 9 = \dfrac{1}{2}$
81. $\log_v 4 = \dfrac{1}{3}$
82. $\log_v \dfrac{1}{16} = -4$

83. $\log_v \dfrac{1}{8} = -3$
84. $\log_v 216 = 3$
85. $\log_v 243 = 5$

86. Graph $f(x) = 3^x$ along with f^{-1}. Make a table of values that illustrates the relationship between f and f^{-1}.

87. Graph $f(x) = 3^{-x}$ along with f^{-1}. Make a table of values that illustrates the relationship between f and f^{-1}.

CHALLENGE

Find the value of each expression.

88. $\log_{27} \sqrt{3}$
89. $\log_2 16\sqrt{2}$
90. $\log_{\frac{1}{2}} 8$

CONNECTIONS

TRANSFORMATIONS Let $f(x) = \log_{10} x$. For each function, identify the transformations from f to g.

91. $g(x) = 3 \log_{10} x$
92. $g(x) = -5 \log_{10} x$

93. $g(x) = \dfrac{1}{2} \log_{10} x + 1$
94. $g(x) = 0.25 \log_{10} x - 2$

95. $g(x) = -\log_{10}(x - 2)$
96. $g(x) = \log_{10}(x + 5) - 3$

APPLICATIONS

CHEMISTRY Calculate $[H^+]$ for each of the following:

97. household ammonia with a pH of about 10

98. distilled water with a pH of 7

99. human blood with a pH of about 7.4

100. CHEMISTRY How much greater is $[H^+]$ for lemon juice, which has a pH of 2.1, than $[H^+]$ for water, which has a pH of 7.0?

pH paper turns red in an acidic solution, 0 < pH < 7; the paper turns green in a neutral solution, indicating a pH of 7; and the paper turns blue in a basic solution, 7 < pH < 14.

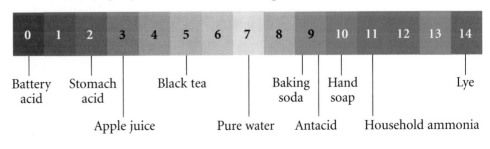

101. PHYSICS Earth's atmosphere is like an "ocean" of air with the upper layers of air pressing down on the lower layers of air. The weight of the layers of air creates atmospheric air pressure. At sea level (altitude of zero), the average air pressure is about 14.7 pounds per square inch. The air pressure, P, decreases with altitude, a, in feet according to the function $P = 14.7(10)^{-0.000018a}$. Find the altitude that corresponds to the air pressure commonly found in commercial airplanes, 11.82 pounds per square inch.

 Look Back

102. Write a linear equation for a line with a slope of 4 and a y-intercept of 3. **(LESSON 1.2)**

State the property that is illustrated in each statement. All variables represent real numbers. **(LESSON 2.1)**

103. $1 \cdot (5xy) = 5xy$

104. $(2 + z) + y = 2 + (z + y)$

105. $2(3x) = 3x(2)$

106. $-x + 0 = -x$

107. $\frac{a}{2} \cdot \frac{2}{a} = 1$, where $a \neq 0$

108. $-3 + x = x + (-3)$

109 Find the inverse of the matrix $\begin{bmatrix} 2 & 3 \\ 1 & -4 \end{bmatrix}$. **(LESSON 4.3)**

110. Solve the quadratic equation $x^2 - 6x + 9 = 0$. **(LESSONS 5.2 AND 5.4)**

111. State the two solutions of the equation $x^2 + 1 = 0$. **(LESSON 5.6)**

112. If an interest rate is 7.3%, what is the multiplier? **(LESSON 6.1)**

Look Beyond

113. Calculate $\log_2 2 + \log_2 8$ and $\log_2 32 - \log_2 2$. Then compare these values with the value of $\log_2 16$.

Properties of Logarithmic Functions

Why *The properties of logarithms allow you to simplify logarithmic expressions, which makes evaluating the expressions easier.*

Objectives

- Simplify and evaluate expressions involving logarithms.

- Solve equations involving logarithms.

John Napier (1550–1617)

Title page and calculations from Napier's Mirifici Logarithmorum Canonis Descriptio

In the seventeenth century, a Scottish mathematician named John Napier developed methods for efficiently performing calculations with large numbers. He found a method for finding the *product* of two numbers by *adding* two corresponding numbers, which he called logarithms.

John Napier's contributions to mathematics are contained in two essays: *Mirifici Logarithmorum Canonis Descriptio* (Description of the Marvelous Canon of Logarithms), published in 1614, and *Mirifici Logarithmorum Canonis Constructio* (Construction of the Marvelous Canon of Logarithms), published in 1619, two years after his death.

Product and Quotient Properties of Logarithms

The Product, Quotient, and Power Properties of Exponents are as follows:

$$a^m \cdot a^n = a^{m+n} \qquad \text{Product Property}$$
$$\frac{a^m}{a^n} = a^{m-n} \qquad \text{Quotient Property}$$
$$(a^m)^n = a^{m \cdot n} \qquad \text{Power Property}$$

Each property of exponents has a corresponding property of logarithms.

Activity
Exploring Properties of Logarithms

You will need: no special tools

Use the following table to complete the activity:

x	2	4	8	16	32	64	128
$y = \log_2 x$	1	2	3	4	5	6	7

1. The expression $\log_2(2 \cdot 4)$ can be written as $\log_2 8$. Use this fact and the table above to evaluate each expression below.

   a. $\log_2(2 \cdot 4) = \underline{\ ?\ }$ and $\log_2 2 + \log_2 4 = \underline{\ ?\ }$

   b. $\log_2(2 \cdot 8) = \underline{\ ?\ }$ and $\log_2 2 + \log_2 8 = \underline{\ ?\ }$

   c. $\log_2(2 \cdot 16) = \underline{\ ?\ }$ and $\log_2 2 + \log_2 16 = \underline{\ ?\ }$

   d. $\log_2(2 \cdot 32) = \underline{\ ?\ }$ and $\log_2 2 + \log_2 32 = \underline{\ ?\ }$

CHECKPOINT ✔ **2.** In Step 1, how is the first expression in each pair related to the second expression? Use this pattern to make a conjecture about $\log_2(a \cdot b)$.

3. The expression $\log_2 \frac{16}{2}$ can be written as $\log_2 8$. Use this fact and the table above to evaluate each expression below.

   a. $\log_2 \frac{16}{2} = \underline{\ ?\ }$ and $\log_2 16 - \log_2 2 = \underline{\ ?\ }$

   b. $\log_2 \frac{64}{32} = \underline{\ ?\ }$ and $\log_2 64 - \log_2 32 = \underline{\ ?\ }$

   c. $\log_2 \frac{32}{8} = \underline{\ ?\ }$ and $\log_2 32 - \log_2 8 = \underline{\ ?\ }$

   d. $\log_2 \frac{8}{4} = \underline{\ ?\ }$ and $\log_2 8 - \log_2 4 = \underline{\ ?\ }$

CHECKPOINT ✔ **4.** In Step 3, how is the first expression in each pair related to the second expression? Use this pattern to make a conjecture about $\log_2 \frac{a}{b}$.

The patterns explored in the Activity illustrate the *Product and Quotient Properties of Logarithms* given below.

Product and Quotient Properties of Logarithms

For $m > 0$, $n > 0$, $b > 0$, and $b \neq 1$:

Product Property	$\log_b(mn) = \log_b m + \log_b n$
Quotient Property	$\log_b \frac{m}{n} = \log_b m - \log_b n$

You can use the Product and Quotient Properties of Logarithms to evaluate logarithmic expressions. This is shown in Example 1.

EXAMPLE **1** Given $\log_2 3 \approx 1.5850$, approximate the value of each expression below by using the Product and Quotient Properties of Logarithms.

    a. $\log_2 12$ **b.** $\log_2 1.5$

SOLUTION

a.
$$\begin{aligned}
\log_2 12 &= \log_2 (2 \cdot 2 \cdot 3) \\
&= \log_2 2 + \log_2 2 + \log_2 3 \\
&\approx 1 + 1 + 1.5850 \\
&\approx 3.5850
\end{aligned}$$

b.
$$\begin{aligned}
\log_2 1.5 &= \log_2 \frac{3}{2} \\
&= \log_2 3 - \log_2 2 \\
&\approx 1.5850 - 1 \\
&\approx 0.5850
\end{aligned}$$

TRY THIS Given that $\log_2 3 = 1.5850$, approximate each expression below by using the Product and Quotient Properties of Logarithms.

    a. $\log_2 18$ **b.** $\log_2 \frac{3}{4}$

Example 2 demonstrates how to use the properties of logarithms to rewrite a logarithmic expression as a single logarithm.

EXAMPLE **2** Write each expression as a single logarithm. Then simplify, if possible.

    a. $\log_3 10 - \log_3 5$ **b.** $\log_b u + \log_b v - \log_b uw$

SOLUTION

a.
$$\begin{aligned}
\log_3 10 - \log_3 5 &= \log_3 \frac{10}{5} \\
&= \log_3 2
\end{aligned}$$

b.
$$\begin{aligned}
\log_b u + \log_b v - \log_b uw &= \log_b uv - \log_b uw \\
&= \log_b \frac{uv}{uw} \\
&= \log_b \frac{v}{w}
\end{aligned}$$

TRY THIS Write each expression as a single logarithm. Then simplify if possible.

    a. $\log_4 18 - \log_4 6$ **b.** $\log_b 4x - \log_b 3y + \log_b y$

The Power Property of Logarithms

Examine the process of rewriting the expression $\log_b(a^4)$.

$$\begin{aligned}
\log_b(a^4) &= \log_b(a \cdot a \cdot a \cdot a) \\
&= \log_b a + \log_b a + \log_b a + \log_b a \\
&= 4 \cdot \log_b a
\end{aligned}$$

This illustrates the *Power Property of Logarithms* given below.

Power Property of Logarithms

For $m > 0$, $b > 0$, $b \neq 1$, and any real number p:

$$\log_b m^p = p \log_b m$$

In Example 3, the Power Property of Logarithms is used to simplify powers.

EXAMPLE ③ Evaluate $\log_5 25^4$.

● **SOLUTION**

$$\log_5 25^4 = 4 \log_5 25 \quad \textit{Use the Power Property of Logarithms.}$$
$$= 4 \cdot 2$$
$$= 8$$

TRY THIS Evaluate $\log_3 27^{100}$.

Exponential-Logarithmic Inverse Properties

Recall from Lesson 2.5 that functions f and g are inverse functions if and only if $(f \circ g)(x) = x$ and $(g \circ f)(x) = x$. The functions $f(x) = \log_b x$ and $g(x) = b^x$ are inverses, so $(f \circ g)(x) = \log_b b^x = x$ and $(g \circ f)(x) = b^{\log_b x} = x$.

Exponential-Logarithmic Inverse Properties

For $b > 0$ and $b \neq 1$:
$$\log_b b^x = x \quad \text{and} \quad b^{\log_b x} = x \text{ for } x > 0$$

EXAMPLE ④ Evaluate each expression.

a. $3^{\log_3 4} + \log_5 25$ **b.** $\log_2 32 - 5^{\log_5 3}$

● **SOLUTION**

a. $3^{\log_3 4} + \log_5 25$ **b.** $\log_2 32 - 5^{\log_5 3}$
    $= 4 + \log_5 5^2$ $= \log_2 2^5 - 3$
    $= 4 + 2$ $= 5 - 3$
    $= 6$ $= 2$

TRY THIS Evaluate each expression.

a. $7^{\log_7 11} - \log_3 81$ **b.** $\log_8 8^5 + 3^{\log_3 8}$

CRITICAL THINKING Verify the Exponential-Logarithmic Inverse Properties by using only the equivalent exponential and logarithmic forms given on page 371.

Because exponential functions and logarithmic functions are one-to-one functions, for each element in the domain of $y = \log x$, there is exactly one corresponding element in the range of $y = \log x$.

One-to-One Property of Logarithms

If $\log_b x = \log_b y$, then $x = y$.

EXAMPLE ⑤ Solve $\log_3(x^2 + 7x - 5) = \log_3(6x + 1)$ for x. Check your answers.

SOLUTION

$$\log_3(x^2 + 7x - 5) = \log_3(6x + 1)$$
$$x^2 + 7x - 5 = 6x + 1 \qquad \text{\textit{Use the One-to-One Property of Logarithms.}}$$
$$x^2 + x - 6 = 0$$
$$(x - 2)(x + 3) = 0$$
$$x = 2 \quad \text{or} \quad x = -3 \qquad \text{\textit{Use the Zero Product Property.}}$$

CHECK

Let $x = 2$.
$$\log_3(x^2 + 7x - 5) \overset{?}{=} \log_3(6x + 1)$$
$$\log_3 13 = \log_3 13$$
True

Let $x = -3$.
$$\log_3(x^2 + 7x - 5) \overset{?}{=} \log_3(6x + 1)$$
$$\log_3(-17) = \log_3(-17)$$
Undefined

Since the domain of a logarithmic function excludes negative numbers, the solution cannot be -3. Therefore, the solution is 2.

Exercises

Communicate

1. Given that $\log_{10} 5 \approx 0.6990$, explain how to approximate the values of $\log_{10} 0.005$ and $\log_{10} 500$.

2. Explain how to write an expression such as $\log_7 32 - \log_7 4$ as a single logarithm.

3. Explain how to evaluate $4^{\log_4 8}$ and $\log_2 2^7$. Include the names of the properties you would use.

4. Explain why you must check your answers when solving an equation such as $\log_2 3x = \log_2(x + 4)$ for x.

Guided Skills Practice

Given $\log_3 7 \approx 1.7712$, approximate the value for each logarithm by using the Product and Quotient Properties of Logarithms. *(EXAMPLE 1)*

5. $\log_3 49$

6. $\log_3 \frac{3}{7}$

Write each expression as a single logarithm. Then simplify, if possible. *(EXAMPLE 2)*

7. $\log_3 x - \log_3 y + \log_3 z$

8. $\log_2 3 + \log_2 6 - \log_2 10$

Evaluate each expression. *(EXAMPLES 3 AND 4)*

9. $\log_4 16^8$

10. $3^{\log_3 12}$

11. $\log_7 7^3$

12. Solve $\log_3 x = \log_3(2x - 4)$ for x, and check your answers. *(EXAMPLE 5)*

Practice and Apply

Write each expression as a sum or difference of logarithms. Then simplify, if possible.

13. $\log_8(5 \cdot 8)$ **14.** $\log_2 8xy$ **15.** $\log_3 \frac{x}{9}$ **16.** $\log_4 \frac{x}{32}$

Use the values given below to approximate the value of each logarithmic expression in Exercises 17–28.

$\log_2 7 \approx 2.8074$	$\log_2 5 \approx 2.3219$	$\log_4 5 \approx 1.1610$
$\log_4 3 \approx 0.7925$	$\log_2 3 \approx 1.5850$	$\log_{10} 8.3 \approx 0.9191$

17. $\log_4 15$ **18.** $\log_2 35$ **19.** $\log_2 28$

20. $\log_4 12$ **21.** $\log_4 60$ **22.** $\log_2 105$

23. $\log_{10} 830$ **24.** $\log_{10} 0.0083$ **25.** $\log_4 \frac{3}{5}$

26. $\log_2 \frac{7}{10}$ **27.** $\log_4 \frac{5}{4}$ **28.** $\log_2 \frac{2}{7}$

Write each expression as a single logarithm. Then simplify, if possible.

29. $\log_2 5 + \log_2 7$ **30.** $\log_4 8 + \log_4 2$

31. $\log_3 45 - \log_3 9$ **32.** $\log_2 14 - \log_2 7$

33. $\log_2 5 + \log_2 x - \log_2 10$ **34.** $\log_3 x + \log_3 4 - \log_3 2$

35. $\log_7 3x - \log_7 9x + \log_7 6y$ **36.** $\log_5 6s - \log_5 s + \log_5 4t$

37. $5 \log_2 m - 2 \log_2 n$ **38.** $7 \log_3 y - 4 \log_3 x$

39. $4 \log_b m + \frac{1}{2} \log_b n - 3 \log_b 2p$ **40.** $\frac{1}{2} \log_b 3c + \frac{1}{2} \log_b 4d - 2 \log_b 5e$

41. $1 - 2 \log_7 x$ **42.** $2 + 4 \log_3 x$

Evaluate each expression.

43. $3^{\log_3 8}$ **44.** $9^{\log_9 2}$ **45.** $\log_4 4^5$

46. $\log_{10} 10^2$ **47.** $7^{\log_7 9} + \log_2 8$ **48.** $5^{\log_5 7} + \log_3 9$

49. $\log_9 9^{11} - \log_4 64$ **50.** $\log_3 3^5 + \log_5 125$ **51.** $6^{\log_6 3} - \log_5 \frac{1}{25}$

52. $2^{\log_2 3} + \log_6 \frac{1}{36}$ **53.** $\log_3 \frac{1}{9} - 2^{\log_2 3}$ **54.** $\log_2 \frac{1}{8} - 4^{\log_4 7}$

Solve for _x_, and check your answers. Justify each step in the solution process.

55. $\log_2 7x = \log_2(x^2 + 12)$ **56.** $\log_5(3x^2 - 1) = \log_5 2x$

57. $\log_b(x^2 - 15) = \log_b(6x + 1)$ **58.** $\log_{10}(5x - 3) - \log_{10}(x^2 + 1) = 0$

59. $2 \log_a x + \log_a 2 = \log_a(5x + 3)$ **60.** $\log_b(x^2 - 2) + 2 \log_b 6 = \log_b 6x$

61. $2 \log_3 x + \log_3 5 = \log_3(14x + 3)$ **62.** $\log_5 2 + 2 \log_5 t = \log_5(3 - t)$

State whether each equation is always true, sometimes true, or never true. Assume that _x_ is a positive real number.

63. $\log_3 9 = 2 \log_3 3$ **64.** $\log_2 8 - \log_2 2 = 2$ **65.** $\log x^2 = 2 \log x$

66. $\log x - \log 5 = \log \frac{x}{5}$ **67.** $\frac{\log 3}{\log x} = \log 3 - \log x$ **68.** $\log(x - 2) = \frac{\log x}{\log 2}$

69. $\frac{1}{2} \log x = \log \sqrt{x}$ **70.** $\log 12x = 12 \log x$ **71.** $\log_3 x + \log_3 x$

CHALLENGE

Solve each equation.

72. $\log_4(\log_3 x) = 0$

73. $\log_6[\log_5(\log_3 x)] = 0$

APPLICATIONS

74. HEALTH The surface area of a person is commonly used to calculate dosages of medicines. The surface area of a child is often calculated with the following formula, where S is the surface area in square centimeters, W is the child's weight in kilograms, and H is the child's height in centimeters.

$$\log_{10} S = 0.425 \log_{10} W + 0.725 \log_{10} H + \log_{10} 71.84$$

Use the properties of logarithms to write a formula for S without logarithms.

75. PHYSICS Atmospheric air pressure, P, in pounds per square inch and altitude, a, in feet are related by the logarithmic equation $a = -55{,}555.56 \log_{10} \dfrac{P}{14.7}$. Use properties of logarithms to find how much greater the air pressure at the top of Mount Whitney in the United States is compared with the air pressure at the top of Mount Everest on the border of Tibet and Nepal. The altitude of Mount Everest is 29,028 feet, and the altitude of Mount Whitney is 14,495 feet. (*Hint:* Find the ratio of the air pressures.)

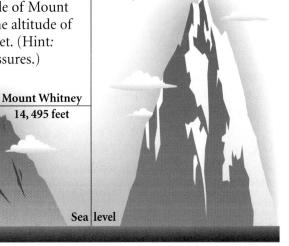

Mount Everest
29,028 feet

Mount Whitney
14,495 feet

Sea level

Look Back

Minimize each objective function under the given constraints.
(LESSON 3.5)

76. Objective function: $C = 2x + 5y$

Constraints: $\begin{cases} x + 5y \geq 8 \\ y - 3x \leq 14 \\ x \geq 0 \\ y \geq 0 \end{cases}$

77. Objective function: $C = x + 4y$

Constraints: $\begin{cases} x - y \geq 12 \\ 7y - x \leq 12 \\ x \geq 0 \\ y \geq 0 \end{cases}$

Write the matrix equation that represents each system. *(LESSON 4.4)*

78. $\begin{cases} 2x - y = 5 \\ 3x + 4y = -3 \end{cases}$

79. $\begin{cases} 3x + 2y - z = 7 \\ 5x + 3y - 2z = -12 \\ 3y - z + 2x = -5 \end{cases}$

80. $\begin{cases} x + y + z = 18 \\ \frac{1}{4}x + \frac{1}{2}y + \frac{1}{3}z = 6 \\ 2y + 3z = 33 \end{cases}$

Write the augmented matrix for each system of equations. *(LESSON 4.5)*

81. $\begin{cases} -3x + 2y = 11 \\ 4x = 5 - y \end{cases}$

82. $\begin{cases} 3x - 6y + 3z = 4 \\ x - 2y = 1 - z \\ 2x - 4y + 2z = 5 \end{cases}$

83. $\begin{cases} 0.5x + 0.3y = 2.2 \\ -8.5y + 1.2z = -24.4 \\ 3.3z + 1.3x = 29 \end{cases}$

APPLICATIONS

84. INVESTMENTS An investment of $100 earns an annual interest rate of 5%. Find the amount after 10 years if the interest is compounded annually, quarterly, and daily. *(LESSON 6.2)*

85. INVESTMENTS Find the final amount after 8 years of a $500 investment that is compounded semiannually at 6%, 7%, and 8% annual interest. *(LESSON 6.2)*

 *Look Beyond*

86 *e* is an irrational number between 2 and 3. The expression $\log_e x$ is commonly written as $\ln x$. Use the [LN] key to solve $2e^{3x} = 5$ for *x* to the nearest hundredth.

In this activity, you will use the CBL to collect data as a warm probe cools in air.

1. First record the air temperature for reference. Then place the temperature probe in hot water until it reaches a reading of at least 60°C. Remove the probe from the water and record the readings as in Step 1 of the Portfolio Activity on page 361.

2. a. Using the regression feature on your calculator, find linear, quadratic, and exponential functions that model this data. (Use the variable *t* for time in seconds.)

   b. Use each function to predict the temperature of the probe after 2 minutes (120 seconds). Compare the predictions with the actual 2-minute reading.

   c. Discuss the usefulness of each function for modeling the cooling process.

3. Create a new function to model the cooling process by performing the steps below.

   a. Subtract the air temperature from each temperature recorded in your data list. Store the resulting data values in a new list.

   b. Use the exponential regression feature on your calculator to find an exponential function of the form $y = a \cdot b^t$ that models this new data set.

   c. Add the air temperature to the function you found in part **b**. Graph the resulting function, $y = a \cdot b^t + c$, which will be called the approximating function.

   d. Repeat parts **b** and **c** from Step 2 with the approximating function.

Save your data and results to use in the last Portfolio Activity.

WORKING ON THE CHAPTER PROJECT

You should now be able to complete Activity 3 of the Chapter Project.

Applications of Common Logarithms

Objectives

- Define and use the common logarithmic function to solve exponential and logarithmic equations.

- Evaluate logarithmic expressions by using the change-of-base formula.

Why *Common logarithmic functions are used to define many real-world measurement scales, such as the decibel scale for the relative intensities of sounds.*

The human ear is sensitive to a wide range of sound intensities.

Type of sound	Relative intensity, R (in dB)
threshold of hearing	0
whisper	≈20
soft music	≈30
conversation	≈65
rock band	≈100
threshold of pain	120

The base-10 logarithm is called the *common logarithm*. The **common logarithm**, $\log_{10} x$, is usually written as $\log x$.

A table of values and a graph for $y = \log x$ are given below. Notice that the values in the domain increase quickly (by a factor of 10), while values in the range increase slowly (by adding 1). In general, logarithmic functions are used to assign large values in the domain to small values in the range.

x	10	100	1000	10,000	100,000	...
$y = \log x$	1	2	3	4	5	...

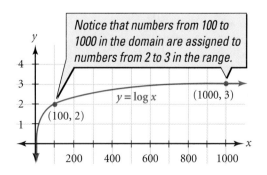

Notice that numbers from 100 to 1000 in the domain are assigned to numbers from 2 to 3 in the range.

$y = \log x$

$(100, 2)$

$(1000, 3)$

Recall from Lesson 2.7 that the graph of $y = a \cdot f(x)$ is the graph of $y = f(x)$ stretched by a factor of a. Therefore, the graph of $y = 10 \log x$ is the graph of $y = \log x$ stretched by a factor of 10.

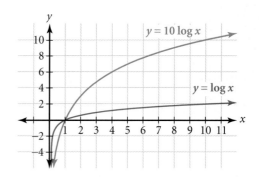

APPLICATION

PHYSICS

The function $y = 10 \log x$ models the relative intensities of sound. The intensity of the faintest sound audible to the human ear, called the *threshold of hearing*, is 10^{-12} watts per meters squared (W/m²). Sound intensities, I, which are between 0 and 1, are often compared with the threshold of hearing, I_0, yielding a ratio of sound intensities, $\frac{I}{I_0}$, between 1 and 10^{12}. On the decibel scale, the relative intensity, R, of a sound in decibels (dB) is given by the function $R = 10 \log \frac{I}{I_0}$.

The bel, the unit of measure for the intensity of sound, was named after Alexander Graham Bell, 1847–1922.

I (in W/m²)	$\frac{I}{I_0}$	$R = 10 \log \frac{I}{I_0}$ (in dB)
10^{-12}	1	0
10^{-11}	10	10
10^{-10}	100	20
⋮	⋮	⋮
10^{-2}	10^{10}	100
10^{-1}	10^{11}	110
$10^0 = 1$	10^{12}	120

Domain of R — column $\frac{I}{I_0}$

Range of R — column $R = 10 \log \frac{I}{I_0}$

EXAMPLE ① The intensity of a whisper is about 300 times as loud as the threshold of hearing, I_0.

Find the relative intensity, R, of this whisper in decibels.

● SOLUTION

PROBLEM SOLVING

Identify the wanted, given, and unknown information. In this problem, the ratio of I to I_0 is given and you need to find R.

$R = 10 \log \frac{I}{I_0}$

$R = 10 \log \frac{300 I_0}{I_0}$ *Substitute $300I_0$ for the intensity, I.*

$R = 10 \log 300$

$R \approx 25$ *Use the ☐ LOG ☐ key on a calculator.*

TECHNOLOGY

SCIENTIFIC CALCULATOR

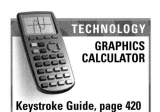

TECHNOLOGY

GRAPHICS CALCULATOR

Keystroke Guide, page 420

CHECK
Use a graphics calculator to graph $y = 10 \log x$. You find that when x is 300, y is about 25.

The relative intensity of this whisper is about 25 decibels.

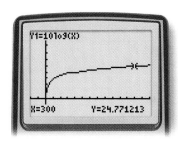

E X A M P L E ❷ The relative intensity, R, of a running vacuum cleaner is about 70 decibels.

Compare the intensity of this running vacuum cleaner with the threshold of hearing.

APPLICATION
PHYSICS

● **SOLUTION**

PROBLEM SOLVING

Identify the wanted, given, and unknown information. In this problem, R is given and you need to find the ratio of I to I_0.

$$R = 10 \log \frac{I}{I_0}$$

$$70 = 10 \log \frac{I}{I_0} \quad \text{\textit{Substitute 70 for the relative intensity, R.}}$$

$$7 = \log \frac{I}{I_0}$$

$$10^7 = \frac{I}{I_0} \quad \text{\textit{Write the equivalent exponential equation.}}$$

$$10^7 \cdot I_0 = I \quad \text{\textit{Write the intensity, I, in terms of }} I_0.$$

This running vacuum cleaner is about 10^7, or 10,000,000, times as loud as the threshold of hearing.

If x and y are positive real numbers and $x = y$, then $\log x = \log y$ by substitution. This is used to solve an equation in Example 3.

E X A M P L E ❸ **Solve $5^x = 62$ for x. Round your answer to the nearest hundredth.**

● **SOLUTION**

$$5^x = 62$$

$$\log 5^x = \log 62 \quad \text{\textit{Take the common logarithm of both sides.}}$$

$$x \log 5 = \log 62 \quad \text{\textit{Apply the Power Property of Logarithms.}}$$

$$x = \frac{\log 62}{\log 5}$$

$$x \approx 2.56 \quad \text{\textit{Use a calculator to evaluate.}}$$

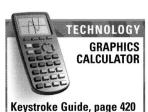

TECHNOLOGY

GRAPHICS CALCULATOR

Keystroke Guide, page 420

CHECK
Graph $y = 5^x$ and $y = 62$ in the same window, and find the point of intersection.

Thus, the solution to $5^x = 62$ is approximately 2.56.

TRY THIS Solve $8^x = 792$ for x. Round your answer to the nearest hundredth.

The Activity below leads to a method for evaluating logarithmic expressions with bases other than 10.

Exploring Change of Base

You will need: a scientific calculator

1. Write $3^x = 81$ as a logarithmic expression for x in base 3.

2. Write $3^x = 81$ as a logarithmic expression for x in base 10. (Hint: Refer to Example 3.)

3. Set your expressions for x from Steps 1 and 2 equal to each other.

CHECKPOINT ✔ 4. Write $b^x = y$ in logarithmic form. Then solve $b^x = y$ for x, and give the result as a quotient of logarithms. Set your two resulting expressions equal to each other.

The answer to Step 4 in the Activity suggests a *change-of-base formula*, shown below, for writing equivalent logarithmic expressions with different bases.

Change-of-Base Formula

For any positive real numbers $a \neq 1$, $b \neq 1$, and $x > 0$:

$$\log_b x = \frac{\log_a x}{\log_a b}$$

CHECKPOINT ✔ Write $\log_9 27$ as a base 3 expression.

You can use the change-of-base formula to change a logarithmic expression of any base to base 10 so that you can use the [LOG] key on a calculator. This is shown in Example 4.

E X A M P L E ④ **Evaluate $\log_7 56$. Round your answer to the nearest hundredth.**

● **SOLUTION**

TECHNOLOGY
SCIENTIFIC CALCULATOR

Use the change-of-base formula to change from base 7 to base 10.

$$\log_7 56 = \frac{\log 56}{\log 7}$$
$$\approx \frac{1.748}{0.845}$$
$$\approx 2.07 \qquad \textit{Use a calculator to evaluate.}$$

TRY THIS Evaluate $\log_8 36$. Round your answer to the nearest hundredth.

CRITICAL THINKING Use the change-of-base formula to justify each formula below.

a. $(\log_a b)(\log_b c) = \log_a c$ **b.** $\log_a b = \frac{1}{\log_b a}$

Exercises

Communicate

1. Explain why a common logarithmic function is appropriate to use for the decibel scale of sound intensities.

2. Describe the steps you would take to solve $6^x = 39$ for x.

3. Explain how to evaluate $\log_4 29$ by using a calculator.

Guided Skills Practice

APPLICATIONS

4. **PHYSICS** Suppose that a soft whisper is about 75 times as loud as the threshold of hearing, I_0. Find the relative intensity, R, of this whisper in decibels. *(EXAMPLE 1)*

5. **PHYSICS** The relative intensity, R, of a loud siren is about 130 decibels. Compare the intensity of this siren with the threshold of hearing, I_0. *(EXAMPLE 2)*

Solve each exponential equation for x. Round your answers to the nearest hundredth. *(EXAMPLE 3)*

6. $8^x = 4$
7. $4^x = 72$

Evaluate each logarithmic expression. Round your answers to the nearest hundredth. *(EXAMPLE 4)*

8. $\log_2 46$
9. $\log_5 2$

Practice and Apply

Solve each equation. Round your answers to the nearest hundredth.

10. $4^x = 17$
11. $2^x = 49$
12. $7^x = 908$

13. $8^x = 240$
14. $3.5^x = 28$
15. $7.6^x = 64$

16. $25^x = 0.04$
17. $3^x = 0.26$
18. $2^{-x} = 0.045$

19. $7^{-x} = 0.022$
20. $3^x = 0.45$
21. $5^x = 1.29$

22. $2^{x+1} = 30$
23. $3^{x-6} = 81$
24. $11 - 6^x = 3$

25. $67 - 2^x = 39$
26. $8 + 3^x = 10$
27. $1 + 5^x = 360$

Evaluate each logarithmic expression to the nearest hundredth.

28. $\log_4 92$

29. $\log_6 87$

30. $\log_6 18$

31. $\log_3 15$

32. $\log_6 3$

33. $\log_5 2$

34. $\log_9 4$

35. $\log_8 3$

36. $\log_4 0.37$

37. $\log_9 1.43$

38. $\log_{\frac{1}{3}} 9$

39. $\log_{\frac{1}{2}} 8$

40. $\log_8 \frac{1}{4}$

41. $\log_7 \frac{1}{50}$

42. $8 - \log_2 64$

43. $1 - \log_5 21$

44. $9 + \log_3 27$

45. $4 + \log_5 125$

CHALLENGE

46. Prove that $\log_{(b^n)} x = \frac{1}{n} \log_b x$ is true.

APPLICATIONS

47. PHYSICS The sound of a leaf blower is about $10^{10.5}$ times the intensity of the threshold of hearing, I_0. Find the relative intensity, R, of this leaf blower in decibels.

48. PHYSICS The sound of a conversation is about 350,000 times the intensity of the threshold of hearing, I_0. Find the relative intensity, R, of this conversation in decibels.

49. PHYSICS Suppose that the relative intensity, R, of a rock band is about 115 decibels. Compare the intensity of this band with that of the threshold of hearing, I_0.

50. PHYSICS The relative intensity, R, of an automobile engine is about 55 decibels. Compare the intensity of this engine with that of the threshold of hearing, I_0.

51. PHYSICS Suppose that background music is adjusted to an intensity that is 1000 times as loud as the threshold of hearing. What is the relative intensity of the music in decibels?

52. PHYSICS Suppose that a burglar alarm has a rating of 120 decibels. Compare the intensity of this decibel rating with that of the threshold of hearing, I_0.

53. PHYSICS Simon Robinson set the world record for the loudest scream by producing a scream of 128 decibels at a distance of 8 feet and 2 inches. Compare the intensity of this decibel rating with that of the threshold of hearing, I_0. [*Source: The Guinness Book of World Records, 1997*]

54. PHYSICS A small jet engine produces a sound whose intensity is one billion times as loud as the threshold of hearing. What is the relative intensity of the engine's sound in decibels?

CHEMISTRY In chemistry, pH is defined as pH = −log [H⁺], where [H⁺] is the hydrogen ion concentration in moles per liter.

55. An alkaline solution has a pH in the range 7 < pH < 14. Determine the corresponding range of [H⁺] for alkaline substances.

56. An acidic solution has a pH in the range 0 < pH < 7. Determine the corresponding range of [H⁺] for acidic substances.

57. For hydrochloric acid, [H⁺] is about 5×10^{-2} moles per liter. Find the pH for this strong acid to the nearest tenth.

58. For chicken eggs, [H⁺] is about 1.6×10^{-8} moles per liter. Find the pH of chicken eggs to the nearest tenth.

59. For milk of magnesia, [H⁺] is about 3.2×10^{-11} moles per liter. Find the pH of milk of magnesia to the nearest tenth.

60. CHEMISTRY Find the pH that corresponds to each hydrogen ion concentration.
  a. [H⁺] is about 6.3×10^{-5} moles per liter for tomato juice.
  b. [H⁺] is about 0.03 moles per liter for gastric juice.
  c. How much more concentrated is the gastric juice than the tomato juice? (Hint: Make a ratio of their hydrogen ion concentrations.)

 Look Back

Solve each system of equations. *(LESSONS 3.1 AND 3.2)*

61. $\begin{cases} x + y = 7 \\ 2x - 3y = 4 \end{cases}$

62. $\begin{cases} x + 3y = 23 \\ 4x - 2y = -6 \end{cases}$

63. $\begin{cases} -2x + 5y = -4 \\ 3x - y = -7 \end{cases}$

Show that each function is a quadratic function by writing it in the form $f(x) = ax^2 + bx + c$. *(LESSON 5.1)*

64. $h(x) = 11x(5 - x)$

65. $g(x) = (2x - 10)(x + 1)$

66. $k(x) = 4(x + 5)(x - 5)$

67. $f(x) = -(x + 1)(3x - 1)$

Solve each equation for x. *(LESSON 5.6)*

68. $x^2 + 5x = -6$

69. $x^2 + 2x - 15 = 0$

70. $(x - 2)(x + 3) = 5$

Identify each function as representing exponential growth or exponential decay. *(LESSON 6.2)*

71. $f(t) = 1000(2.5)^t$

72. $f(t) = 55(0.5)^t$

73. $f(t) = 0.005(8)^t$

 Look Beyond

74 Graph $y = 2^x$, $y = e^x$, and $y = 3^x$. Describe how the graph of e^x compares to the others. Use your calculator to find a value for e to four decimal places.

The Natural Base, e

The model below shows the embryo inside an 18-inch dinosaur egg, the largest known.

Objectives

- Evaluate natural exponential and natural logarithmic functions.
- Model exponential growth and decay processes.

Why *The exponential function with base e and its inverse, the natural logarithmic function, have a wide variety of real-world applications. For example, these functions are used to estimate the ages of artifacts found at archaeological digs.*

The natural base, e, is used to estimate the ages of artifacts and to calculate interest that is compounded continuously. Recall from Lesson 6.2 the compound interest formula, $A(t) = P\left(1 + \dfrac{r}{n}\right)^{nt}$, where P is the principal, r is the annual interest rate, n is the number of compounding periods per year, and t is the time in years. This formula is used in the Activity below.

Activity
Investigating the Growth of $1

You will need: a scientific calculator

1. Copy and complete the table below to investigate the growth of a $1 investment that earns 100% annual interest ($r = 1$) over 1 year ($t = 1$) as the number of compounding periods per year, n, increases. Use a calculator, and record the value of A to five places after the decimal point.

Compounding schedule	n	$1\left(1 + \frac{1}{n}\right)^{n}$	Value, A
annually	1	$1\left(1 + \frac{1}{1}\right)^{1}$	2.00000
semiannually	2	$1\left(1 + \frac{1}{2}\right)^{2}$	
quarterly	4		
monthly	12		
daily	365		
hourly			
every minute			
every second			

CHECKPOINT ✔ 2. Describe the behavior of the sequence of numbers in the *Value* column.

As n becomes very large, the value of $1\left(1 + \dfrac{1}{n}\right)^{n}$ approaches the number $2.71828\ldots$, named e. Because e is an irrational number like π, its decimal expansion continues forever without repeating patterns.

The Natural Exponential Function

The exponential function with base e, $f(x) = e^x$, is called the **natural exponential function** and e is called the **natural base**. The function $f(x) = e^x$ is graphed at right. Notice that the domain is all real numbers and the range is all positive real numbers.

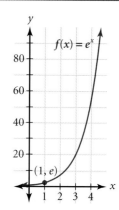

CHECKPOINT ✔ What is the y-intercept of the graph of $f(x) = e^x$?

Natural exponential functions model a variety of situations in which a quantity grows or decays continuously. Examples that you will solve in this lesson include continuous compounding interest and continuous radioactive decay.

EXAMPLE ① Evaluate $f(x) = e^x$ to the nearest thousandth for each value of x below.

a. $x = 2$ **b.** $x = \frac{1}{2}$ **c.** $x = -1$

● SOLUTION

a. $f(2) = e^2$
≈ 7.389

b. $f\left(\frac{1}{2}\right) = e^{\frac{1}{2}}$
≈ 1.649

c. $f(-1) = e^{-1}$
≈ 0.368

CHECK

Use a table of values for $y = e^x$ or a graph of $y = e^x$ to verify your answers.

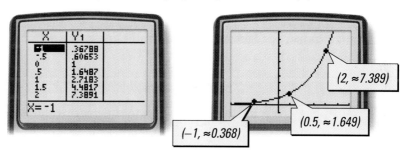

TECHNOLOGY
GRAPHICS CALCULATOR

Keystroke Guide, page 420

TRY THIS   Evaluate $f(x) = e^x$ to the nearest thousandth for $x = 6$ and $x = -\frac{1}{3}$.

Many banks compound the interest on accounts daily or monthly. However, some banks compound interest continuously, or at every instant, by using the *continuous compounding formula*, which includes the number e.

Continuous Compounding Formula

If P dollars are invested at an interest rate, r, that is compounded continuously, then the amount, A, of the investment at time t is given by

$$A = Pe^{rt}.$$

EXAMPLE ② An investment of $1000 earns an annual interest rate of 7.6%.

Compare the final amounts after 8 years for interest compounded quarterly and for interest compounded continuously.

APPLICATION
INVESTMENTS

● **SOLUTION**

Substitute 1000 for P, 0.076 for r, and 8 for t in the appropriate formulas.

Compounded quarterly	Compounded continuously
$A = P\left(1 + \frac{r}{n}\right)^{nt}$	$A = Pe^{rt}$
$A = 1000\left(1 + \frac{0.076}{4}\right)^{4 \cdot 8}$	$A = 1000e^{0.076 \cdot 8}$
$A \approx 1826.31$	$A \approx 1836.75$

Interest that is compounded continuously results in a final amount that is about $10 more than that for the interest that is compounded quarterly.

TRY THIS   Find the value of $500 after 4 years invested at an annual interest rate of 9% compounded continuously.

The Natural Logarithmic Function

The **natural logarithmic function**, $y = \log_e x$, abbreviated $y = \ln x$, is the inverse of the natural exponential function, $y = e^x$. The function $y = \ln x$ is graphed along with $y = e^x$ at right.

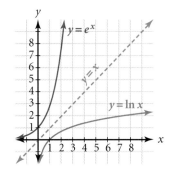

CHECKPOINT ✔ State the domain and range of $y = e^x$ and of $y = \ln x$.

EXAMPLE ③ **Evaluate $f(x) = \ln x$ to the nearest thousandth for each value of x below.**

a. $x = 2$ **b.** $x = \frac{1}{2}$ **c.** $x = -1$

● **SOLUTION**

a. $f(2) = \ln 2$
  ≈ 0.693

b. $f\left(\frac{1}{2}\right) = \ln \frac{1}{2}$
  ≈ -0.693

c. $f(-1) = \ln(-1)$ is undefined.

CHECK
Use a table of values for $y = \ln x$ or a graph of $y = \ln x$ to verify your answers.

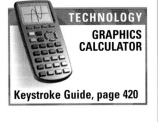

TECHNOLOGY
GRAPHICS CALCULATOR

Keystroke Guide, page 420

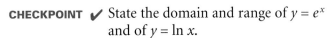

Nonpositive numbers are not in the domain of $y = \ln x$.

$(2, \approx 0.693)$

$(2, \approx -0.693)$

The natural logarithmic function can be used to solve an equation of the form $A = Pe^{rt}$ for the exponent t in order to find the time it takes for an investment that is compounded continuously to reach a specific amount. This is shown in Example 4.

EXAMPLE ④ **How long does it take for an investment to double at an annual interest rate of 8.5% compounded continuously?**

● **SOLUTION**

PROBLEM SOLVING

Use the formula $A = Pe^{rt}$ **with** $r = 0.085$.

$$A = Pe^{0.085t}$$
$$2 \cdot P = Pe^{0.085t} \qquad \textit{When the investment doubles, } A = 2 \cdot P.$$
$$2 = e^{0.085t}$$
$$\ln 2 = \ln e^{0.085t} \qquad \textit{Take the natural logarithm of both sides.}$$
$$\ln 2 = 0.085t \qquad \textit{Use the Exponential-Logarithmic Inverse Property.}$$
$$t = \frac{\ln 2}{0.085}$$
$$t \approx 8.15$$

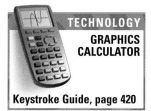
TECHNOLOGY
GRAPHICS CALCULATOR
Keystroke Guide, page 420

CHECK
Graph $y = e^{0.085x}$ and $y = 2$, and find the point of intersection.

Notice that the graph of $y = e^{0.085x}$ is a horizontal stretch of the function $y = e^x$ by a factor of $\frac{1}{0.085}$, or almost 12.

Thus, it takes about 8 years and 2 months to double an investment at an annual interest rate of 8.5% compounded continuously.

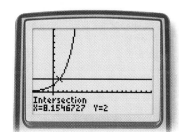
Intersection
X=8.1546727 Y=2

TRY THIS

How long does it take for an investment to triple at an annual interest rate of 7.2% compounded continuously?

CRITICAL THINKING

Explain why the time required for the value of an investment to double or triple does not depend on the amount of principal.

Radioactive Decay

Most of the carbon found in the Earth's atmosphere is the isotope carbon-12, but a small amount is the radioactive isotope carbon-14. Plants absorb carbon dioxide from the atmosphere, and animals obtain carbon from the plants they consume. When a plant or animal dies, the amount of carbon-14 it contains decays in such a way that exactly half of its initial amount is present after 5730 years. The function below models the decay of carbon-14, where N_0 is the initial amount of carbon-14 and $N(t)$ is the amount present t years after the plant or animal dies.

$$N(t) = N_0 e^{-0.00012t}$$

Example 5 shows how *radiocarbon dating* is used to estimate the age of an archaeological artifact.

EXAMPLE **5** Suppose that archaeologists find scrolls and claim that they are 2000 years old. Tests indicate that the scrolls contain 78% of their original carbon-14.

APPLICATION
ARCHAEOLOGY

Could the scrolls be 2000 years old?

SOLUTION

Since the scrolls contain 78% of their original carbon-14, substitute $0.78N_0$ for $N(t)$.

$$N(t) = N_0 e^{-0.00012t}$$
$$0.78N_0 = N_0 e^{-0.00012t} \quad \text{Substitute } 0.78N_0 \text{ for } N(t).$$
$$0.78 = e^{-0.00012t}$$
$$\ln 0.78 = -0.00012t \quad \text{Take the natural logarithm of each side.}$$
$$-0.00012t = \ln 0.78$$
$$t = \frac{\ln 0.78}{-0.00012}$$
$$t \approx 2070.5$$

Thus, it appears that the scrolls are about 2000 years old.

Exercises

Communicate

1. Compare the natural and exponential logarithmic functions with the base-10 exponential and logarithmic functions.

2. Give a real-world example of an exponential growth function and of an exponential decay function that each have the base *e*.

3. State the continuous compounding formula, and describe what each variable represents.

4. Describe how the continuous compounding formula can represent continuous growth as well as continuous decay.

Guided Skills Practice

APPLICATION

Evaluate $f(x) = e^x$ to the nearest thousandth for each value of x.
(EXAMPLE 1)

5. $x = 3$ **6.** $x = 3.5$

7. INVESTMENTS An investment of $1500 earns an annual interest rate of 8.2%. Compare the final amounts after 5 years for interest compounded quarterly and for interest compounded continuously. *(EXAMPLE 2)*

Evaluate *f(x) = ln x* to the nearest thousandth for each value of *x*.
(EXAMPLE 3)

8. $x = 5$ **9.** $x = 2.5$

APPLICATIONS

10. INVESTMENTS How long does it take an investment to double at an annual interest rate of 7.5% compounded continuously? *(EXAMPLE 4)*

11. ARCHAEOLOGY A piece of charcoal from an ancient campsite is found in an archaeological dig. It contains 9% of its original amount of carbon-14. Estimate the age of the charcoal. *(EXAMPLE 5)*

Practice and Apply

Evaluate each expression to the nearest thousandth. If the expression is undefined, write *undefined*.

12. e^6 **13.** e^9 **14.** $e^{1.2}$ **15.** $e^{3.4}$

16. $2e^{0.3}$ **17.** $3e^{0.05}$ **18.** $2e^{-0.5}$ **19.** $3e^{-0.257}$

20. $e^{\sqrt{2}}$ **21.** $e^{\frac{1}{4}}$ **22.** $\ln 3$ **23.** $\ln 7$

24. $\ln 10{,}002$ **25.** $\ln 99{,}999$ **26.** $\ln 0.004$ **27.** $\ln 0.994$

28. $\ln \frac{1}{5}$ **29.** $\ln \sqrt{5}$ **30.** $\ln(-2)$ **31.** $\ln(-3)$

For Exercises 32–35, write the expressions in ascending order.

32. $e^2,\ e^5,\ \ln 2,\ \ln 5$ **33.** $e,\ e^0,\ \ln 1,\ \ln \frac{1}{2}$

34. $e^{2.5},\ \ln 2.5,\ 10^{2.5},\ \log 2.5$ **35.** $e^{1.3},\ \ln 1.3,\ 10^{1.3},\ \log 1.3$

State whether each equation is always true, sometimes true, or never true.

36. $e^{5x} \cdot e^3 = e^{15x}$ **37.** $\left(e^{4x}\right)^3 = e^{12x}$ **38.** $e^{6x-4} = e^{6x} \cdot e^{-4}$ **39.** $\dfrac{e^{8x}}{e^4} = e^{2x}$

Simplify each expression.

40. $e^{\ln 2}$ **41.** $e^{\ln 5}$ **42.** $e^{3\ln 2}$ **43.** $e^{2\ln 5}$

44. $\ln e^3$ **45.** $\ln e^4$ **46.** $3 \ln e^2$ **47.** $2 \ln e^4$

Write an equivalent exponential or logarithmic equation.

48. $e^x = 30$ **49.** $e^x = 1$ **50.** $\ln 2 \approx 0.69$

51. $\ln 5 \approx 1.61$ **52.** $e^{\frac{1}{3}} \approx 1.40$ **53.** $e^{0.69} \approx 1.99$

Solve each equation for *x* by using the natural logarithm function. Round your answers to the nearest hundredth.

54. $35^x = 30$ **55.** $1.3^x = 8$ **56.** $3^{-3x} = 17$

57. $36^{2x} = 20$ **58.** $0.42^{-x} = 7$ **59.** $2^{-\frac{1}{3}x} = 10$

CHALLENGE

60. Sketch $f(x) = e^x$ for $-1 \le x \le 2$. A line that intersects a curve at only one point is called a *tangent line* of the curve.
  a. Sketch lines that are tangent to the graph of $f(x) = e^x$ at $x = 0.5$, $x = 0$, $x = 1$, and $x = 2$.
  b. Find the approximate slope of each tangent line. Compare the slope of each tangent line with the corresponding *y*-coordinate of the point where the tangent line intersects the graph.
  c. Make a conjecture about the slope of $f(x) = e^x$ as *x* increases.

TRANSFORMATIONS Let $f(x) = e^x$. For each function, describe the transformations from f to g.

61. $g(x) = 6e^x + 1$

62. $g(x) = 0.75e^x - 4$

63. $g(x) = 0.25e^{(4x+4)}$

64. $g(x) = 3e^{(2x-4)}$

TRANSFORMATIONS Let $f(x) = \ln x$. For each function, describe the transformations from f to g.

65. $g(x) = 3\ln(x+1)$

66. $g(x) = -2\ln(x-1)$

67. $g(x) = 0.5\ln(5x) - 2$

68. $g(x) = 5\ln(0.25x) - 1$

$f(x) = e^{-2x}$ $i(x) = e^{2x}$
$g(x) = e^{-x}$ $h(x) = e^x$

69. TRANSFORMATIONS The graphs of $f(x) = e^{-2x}$, $g(x) = e^{-x}$, $h(x) = e^x$, and $i(x) = e^{2x}$ are shown on the same coordinate plane at left. What transformations relate each function, f, g, and i, to h?

70. TRANSFORMATIONS For $f(x) = e^x$, describe how each transformation affects the domain, range, asymptotes, and y-intercept.
   a. a vertical stretch
   b. a horizontal stretch
   c. a vertical translation
   d. a horizontal translation

71. TRANSFORMATIONS For $f(x) = \ln x$, describe how each transformation affects the domain, range, asymptotes, and x-intercept.
   a. a vertical stretch
   b. a horizontal stretch
   c. a vertical translation
   d. a horizontal translation

APPLICATIONS

72. PHYSICS The amount of radioactive strontium-90 remaining after t years decreases according to the function $N(t) = N_0 e^{-0.0238t}$. How much of a 40-gram sample will remain after 25 years?

73. ECONOMICS The factory sales of pagers from 1990 through 1995 can be modeled by the function $S = 116e^{0.18t}$, where $t = 0$ in 1990 and S represents the sales in millions of dollars. [*Source: Electronic Market Data Book*]
   a. According to this function, find the factory sales of pagers in 1995 to the nearest million.
   b. If the sales of pagers continued to increase at the same rate, when would the sales be double the 1995 amount?

74. INVESTMENTS Compare the growth of an investment of $2000 in two different accounts. One account earns 3% annual interest, the other earns 5% annual interest, and both are compounded continuously over 20 years.

75. ARCHAEOLOGY A wooden chest is found and is said to be from the second century B.C.E. Tests on a sample of wood from the chest reveal that it contains 92% of its original carbon-14. Could the chest be from the second century B.C.E.?

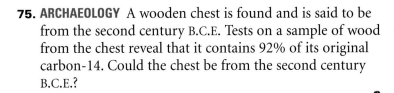

Basketball Backboard Sales

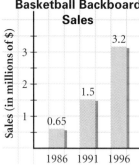

Sales (in millions of $)

3.2

1.5

0.65

1986 1991 1996

76. BUSINESS Sales of home basketball backboards from 1986 to 1996 can be modeled by $S = 0.65e^{0.157t}$, where S is the sales in millions of dollars, t is time in years, and $t = 0$ in 1986. [*Source: Huffy Sports*]
  a. Use this model to estimate the sales of backboards in 1997 to the nearest thousand.
  b. If the sales of basketball backboards continued to increase at the same rate, when would the sales of basketball backboards be double the amount of 1996?

INVESTMENTS **For Exercises 77–79, assume that all interest rates are compounded continuously.**

77. How long will it take an investment of $5000 to double if the annual interest rate is 6%?

78. How long will it take an investment to double at 10% annual interest?

79. If it takes a certain amount of money 3.7 years to double, at what annual interest rate was the money invested?

80. AGRICULTURE The percentage of farmers in the United States workforce has declined since the turn of the century. The percent of farmers in the workforce, f, can be modeled by the function $f(t) = 29e^{-0.036t}$, where t is time in years and $t = 0$ in 1920. Find the percent of farmers in the workforce in 1995. [*Source: Bureau of Labor Statistics*]

Look Back

Solve each inequality, and graph the solution on a number line. *(LESSON 1.8)*

81. $|-3x| \geq 15$

82. $|3x - 4| \geq 12$

83. $\left| \dfrac{3x + 2}{-4} \right| \geq 5$

Graph each function. *(LESSON 2.7)*

84. $f(x) = \frac{1}{2}|x|$

85. $g(x) = -\lceil x \rceil$

86. $h(x) = [x - 3]$

Graph each system. *(LESSON 3.4)*

87. $\begin{cases} y > 2x - 1 \\ 4 - 3x \geq y \end{cases}$

88. $\begin{cases} 1 - 3x > y + 4 \\ 2x + 3y \leq 8 \end{cases}$

89. $\begin{cases} y + 2x \geq 0 \\ 4 - 2x > y \\ x \leq 3 \end{cases}$

Factor each expression. *(LESSON 5.3)*

90. $x^2 - 3x - 10$

91. $3x^2 - 6x + 3$

92. $x^2 - 49$

Look Beyond

93 Solve $\ln x + \ln(x + 2) = 5$ by graphing $y = \ln x + \ln(x + 2)$ and $y = 5$ and finding the x-coordinate of the point of intersection.

Meet "e" in St. Louis

How does a 630-foot-high arch stand up to the forces of nature? Will it last for its projected life of 1000 years? How does it withstand winds up to 150 miles per hour?

The secret is in the shape of the arch, which transfers forces downward through its legs into huge underground foundations. You can learn more about this remarkable shape, called a **catenary curve,** by looking at some of its simpler forms.

The general equation for a catenary curve is $y = \frac{a}{2}\left(e^{\frac{x}{a}} + e^{-\frac{x}{a}}\right)$, where a is a real nonzero constant.

ARCH COMPLETED

St. Louis Can Now Boast of the Nation's Highest Memorial

With the joining of the stainless steel legs of the Gateway Arch Thursday, St. Louis became the location of the tallest—630 feet—national memorial in the United States. More than 10,000 persons—including hundreds of school children who attended the "topping out" as a field trip—look upward as the leg-locking segment is hoisted off the ground and begins the long trip to the Arch.

[*Source*: St. Louis Globe-Democrat, *October 29, 1965*]

The shape of the St. Louis arch is approximately that of an inverted, weighted catenary curve—inverted because it is upside down and weighted because the lower sections of the legs are wider than the upper sections.

Cooperative Learning

1. Begin exploring the catenary by letting $a = 2$.
   a. Write the equation for a catenary curve with $a = 2$.
   b. Copy and complete the table below.

x	0	1	2	3	4	5
y						

   c. What is y when $x = -1$? Compare this value for y with the value of y when $x = 1$.
   d. Why will the y-values for $-x$ and x always be equal for this equation?

2. Now explore the graph of the equation for the curve with $a = 2$.
   a. Graph the equation for a catenary curve with $a = 2$. Describe the graph.
   b. Your graph should look like an upside-down arch. What can you do to the equation to invert the graph? (Hint: Think about how to invert, or reflect, a parabola.) Check your new equation by graphing it.

3. Your catenary curve may look similar to a parabola. To see how it is different, follow the steps below.
   a. Write an equation and draw the graph for a parabola that resembles your graph from part **a** of Step 2. (Hint: How do the values of a, h, and k in a quadratic equation of the form $y = a(x - h)^2 + k$ affect the location and shape of the parabola?)
   b. Compare the graph of your parabola with that of the catenary curve.

Solving Equations and Modeling

Objectives

- Solve logarithmic and exponential equations by using algebra and graphs.

- Model and solve real-world problems involving exponential and logarithmic relationships.

Why *Physicists, chemists, and geologists use exponential and logarithmic equations to model various phenomena, such as the magnitude of earthquakes.*

RICHTER SCALE RATINGS		
Magnitude	Result near the epicenter	Approximate number of occurrences per year
8–9	near total damage	0.2
7.0–7.9	serious damage to buildings	14
6.0–6.9	moderate damage to buildings	185
5.0–5.9	slight damage to buildings	1000
4.0–4.9	felt by most people	2800
3.0–3.9	felt by some people	26,000
2.0–2.9	not felt but recorded	800,000

APPLICATION

GEOLOGY

On the Richter scale, the magnitude, M, of an earthquake depends on the amount of energy, E, released by the earthquake as follows:

$$M = \frac{2}{3} \log \frac{E}{10^{11.8}}$$

The amount of energy, measured in ergs, is based on the amount of ground motion recorded by a seismograph at a known distance from the epicenter of the quake.

The logarithmic function for the Richter scale assigns very large numbers for the amount of energy, E, to numbers that range from 1 to 9. A rating of 2 on the Richter scale indicates the smallest tremor that can be detected. Destructive earthquakes are those rated greater than 6 on the Richter scale.

EXAMPLE ❶ One of the strongest earthquakes in recent history occurred in Mexico City in 1985 and measured 8.1 on the Richter scale.

APPLICATION
GEOLOGY

Find the amount of energy, E, released by this earthquake.

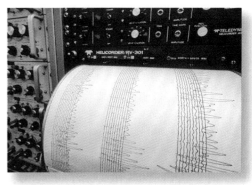

● **SOLUTION**

PROBLEM SOLVING   **Use a formula.**

$$M = \frac{2}{3} \log \frac{E}{10^{11.8}}$$

$$8.1 = \frac{2}{3} \log \frac{E}{10^{11.8}}$$ *Substitute 8.1 for the magnitude, M.*

$$12.15 = \log \frac{E}{10^{11.8}}$$

$$10^{12.15} = \frac{E}{10^{11.8}}$$ *Use the definition of logarithm.*

$$10^{11.8} \cdot 10^{12.15} = E$$

$$8.91 \times 10^{23} \approx E$$ *Write the answer in scientific notation.*

A seismogram produced by a seismograph

The amount of energy, E, released by this earthquake was approximately 8.91×10^{23} ergs. *In physics, an erg is a unit of work or energy.*

To solve the logarithmic equation in Example 1, you must use the definition of a logarithm. However, solving exponential and logarithmic equations often requires a variety of the definitions and properties from this chapter. A summary of the definitions and properties that you have learned is given below.

Copy these properties and definitions into your notebook for reference.

SUMMARY	
Exponential and Logarithmic Definitions and Properties	
Definition of logarithm	$y = \log_b x$ if and only if $b^y = x$
Product Property	$\log_b mn = \log_b m + \log_b n$
Quotient Property	$\log_b\left(\dfrac{m}{n}\right) = \log_b m - \log_b n$
Power Property	$\log_b m^p = p \log_b m$
Exponential-Logarithmic Inverse Properties	$b^{\log_b x} = x$ for $x > 0$ $\log_b b^x = x$ for all x
One-to-One Property of Exponents	If $b^x = b^y$, then $x = y$.
One-to-One Property of Logarithms	If $\log_b x = \log_b y$, then $x = y$.
Change-of-base formula	$\log_c a = \dfrac{\log_b a}{\log_b c}$

CHECKPOINT ✔ Show how to solve $M = \frac{2}{3} \log \frac{E}{10^{11.8}}$ for E.

CRITICAL THINKING   Use the properties of exponents and logarithms to show that $\log_a\left(\frac{1}{x}\right) = \log_{\frac{1}{a}} x$.

E X A M P L E ❷ Solve $\log x + \log(x - 3) = 1$ for x.

● SOLUTION

Method 1 Use algebra.

$$\log x + \log(x - 3) = 1$$
$$\log[x(x - 3)] = 1 \qquad \textit{Apply the Product Property of Logarithms.}$$
$$x(x - 3) = 10^1 \qquad \textit{Write the equivalent exponential equation.}$$
$$x^2 - 3x - 10 = 0$$
$$(x - 5)(x + 2) = 0$$
$$x = 5 \quad or \quad x = -2$$

CHECK

Let $x = 5$.

$$\log x + \log(x - 3) = 1$$
$$\log 5 + \log 2 \overset{?}{=} 1$$
$$1 = 1 \quad \textbf{True}$$

Let $x = -2$.

$$\log x + \log(x - 3) = 1$$
$$\log(-2) + \log(-5) = 1 \quad \textbf{Undefined}$$

Since the domain of a logarithmic function excludes negative numbers, the only solution is 5.

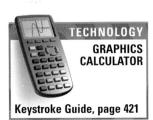

TECHNOLOGY
GRAPHICS CALCULATOR

Keystroke Guide, page 421

Method 2 Use a graph.
Graph $y = \log x + \log(x - 3)$ and $y = 1$, and find the point of intersection.

The coordinates of the point of intersection are $(5, 1)$, so the solution is 5.

TRY THIS Solve $\log(x + 48) + \log x = 2$ by using algebra and a graph.

E X A M P L E ❸ Solve $4e^{3x-5} = 72$ for x.

● SOLUTION

Method 1 Use algebra.

$$4e^{3x-5} = 72$$
$$e^{3x-5} = 18$$
$$\ln e^{3x-5} = \ln 18 \qquad \textit{Take the natural logarithm of each side.}$$
$$3x - 5 = \ln 18 \qquad \textit{Use Exponential-Logarithmic Inverse Properties.}$$
$$x = \frac{\ln 18 + 5}{3} \qquad \textit{Exact solution}$$
$$x \approx 2.63 \qquad \textit{Approximate solution}$$

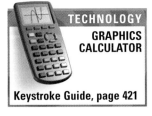

TECHNOLOGY
GRAPHICS CALCULATOR

Keystroke Guide, page 421

Method 2 Use a graph.
Graph $y = 4e^{3x-5}$ and $y = 72$, and find the point of intersection.

The coordinates of the point of intersection are approximately $(2.63, 72)$, so the solution is approximately 2.63.

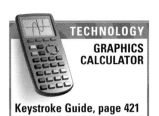

TECHNOLOGY
GRAPHICS
CALCULATOR

Keystroke Guide, page 421

Activity
Solving Exponential Inequalities

You will need: a graphics calculator

1. Graph $y_1 = \log x + \log(x + 21)$ and $y_2 = 2$ on the same screen.
2. For what value(s) of x is $y_1 = y_2$? $y_1 < y_2$? $y_1 > y_2$?

CHECKPOINT ✔ 3. Explain how you can use a graph to solve $\log x + \log(x + 21) > 2$.

4. Graph $y_1 = 2e^{4x-1}$ and $y_2 = 38$ on the same screen.
5. For what approximate value(s) of x is $y_1 = y_2$? $y_1 < y_2$? $y_1 > y_2$?

CHECKPOINT ✔ 6. Explain how you can use a graph to solve $2e^{4x-1} < 38$.

Newton's Law of Cooling

An object that is hotter than its surroundings will cool off, and an object that is cooler than its surroundings will warm up. **Newton's law of cooling** states that the temperature difference between an object and its surroundings decreases exponentially as a function of time according to the following:

$$T(t) = T_s + (T_0 - T_s)e^{-kt}$$

T_0 is the initial temperature of the object, T_s is the temperature of the object's surroundings (assumed to be constant), t is the time, and $-k$ represents the constant rate of decrease in the temperature difference $(T_0 - T_s)$.

E X A M P L E ④ When a container of milk is taken out of the refrigerator, its temperature is 40°F. An hour later, its temperature is 50°F. Assume that the temperature of the air is a constant 70°F.

APPLICATION
PHYSICS

a. Write the function for the temperature of this container of milk as a function of time, t.
b. What is the temperature of the milk after 2 hours?
c. After how many hours is the temperature of the milk 65°F?

● **SOLUTION**

a. First substitute 40 for T_0 and 70 for T_s, and simplify.

$$T(t) = T_s + (T_0 - T_s)e^{-kt}$$
$$T(t) = 70 + (40 - 70)e^{-kt}$$
$$T(t) = 70 + (-30)e^{-kt}$$

Since $T(1) = 50$, substitute 1 for t and 50 for $T(t)$, and solve for $-k$.

$$50 = 70 - 30e^{-k}$$
$$30e^{-k} = 20$$
$$e^{-k} = \frac{2}{3}$$
$$\ln e^{-k} = \ln \frac{2}{3}$$
$$-k = \ln \frac{2}{3}$$

Substitute $\ln \frac{2}{3}$ for $-k$ and simplify to get the function for the temperature of this container of milk.

$$T(t) = 70 - 30e^{-kt}$$
$$T(t) = 70 - 30e^{(\ln \frac{2}{3})t}$$
$$T(t) = 70 - 30\left(\frac{2}{3}\right)^t \quad \textit{Apply the Exponential-Logarithmic Inverse Property.}$$

The function for the temperature of this container of milk is
$$T(t) = 70 - 30\left(\frac{2}{3}\right)^t.$$

TECHNOLOGY
GRAPHICS CALCULATOR

Keystroke Guide, page 421

b. Find $T(2)$.
$$T(t) = 70 - 30\left(\frac{2}{3}\right)^t$$
$$T(2) = 70 - 30\left(\frac{2}{3}\right)^2 \approx 56.7$$

The temperature of the milk after 2 hours is approximately 56.7°F.

c. Substitute 65 for $T(t)$, and solve for t.
$$T(t) = 70 - 30\left(\frac{2}{3}\right)^t$$
$$65 = 70 - 30\left(\frac{2}{3}\right)^t$$
$$30\left(\frac{2}{3}\right)^t = 5$$
$$\left(\frac{2}{3}\right)^t = \frac{1}{6}$$
$$t \ln \frac{2}{3} = \ln \frac{1}{6}$$
$$t = \frac{\ln \frac{1}{6}}{\ln \frac{2}{3}} \approx 4.42$$

It will take approximately 4.42 hours, or about 4 hours and 25 minutes, for the milk to warm up to 65°F.

Exercises

Communicate

1. Explain how to solve the exponential equation $e^{x+7} = 98$ by algebraic methods.

2. How can you solve the logarithmic equation $\log_2 x + \log_2 (x + 3) = 2$ by algebraic methods?

3. Explain how to solve exponential and logarithmic equations by graphing.

APPLICATIONS

4. GEOLOGY In 1989, an earthquake that measured 7.1 on the Richter scale occurred in San Francisco, California. Find the amount of energy, E, released by this earthquake. **(EXAMPLE 1)**

5. Solve $\log(x - 90) + \log x = 3$ for x. **(EXAMPLE 2)**

6. Solve $0.5e^{0.08t} = 40$ for x. **(EXAMPLE 3)**

7. PHYSICS When the air temperature is a constant 70°F, an object cools from 170°F to 140°F in one-half hour. **(EXAMPLE 4)**
 a. Write the function for the temperature of this object, T, as a function of time, t.
 b. What is the temperature of this object after 1 hour?
 c. After how many hours is the temperature of this object 90°F?

● *Practice and Apply*

Solve each equation for x. Write the exact solution and the approximate solution to the nearest hundredth, when appropriate.

8. $3^x = 3^4$ **9.** $3^{2x} = 81$ **10.** $5^{x-2} = 25$

11. $x = \log_3 \frac{1}{27}$ **12.** $x = \log_4 \frac{1}{64}$ **13.** $\log_x \frac{1}{16} = -2$

14. $4 = \log_x \frac{1}{16}$ **15.** $e^{2x} = 20$ **16.** $e^{-2(x+1)} = 2$

17. $\ln(2x - 3) = \ln 21$ **18.** $\ln(x + 3) = 2 \ln 4$ **19.** $10^{2x} + 75 = 150$

20. $e^{-4x} - 22 = 56$ **21.** $3 \ln x = \ln 4 + \ln 2$ **22.** $\ln x + \ln(x + 1) = \ln 2$

23. $2 \ln x + 2 = 1$ **24.** $3 \ln x + 3 = 1$ **25.** $3 \log x + 7 = 5$

CHALLENGE

Solve each equation for x. Write the exact solution and the approximate solution to the nearest hundredth, when appropriate.

26. $\ln(3\sqrt{x}) = \sqrt{\ln x}$ **27.** $\log x^3 = (\log x)^3$

APPLICATIONS

28. GEOLOGY On May 10, 1997, a light earthquake with a magnitude of 4.7 struck the Calaveras Fault 10 miles east of San Jose, California. Find the amount of energy, E, released by this earthquake.

29. GEOLOGY In 1976, an earthquake that released about 8×10^{19} ergs of energy occurred in San Salvador, El Salvador. Find the magnitude, M, of this earthquake to the nearest tenth.

30. PHYSICS A hot coal (at a temperature of 160°C) is immersed in ice water (at a temperature of 0°C). After 30 seconds, the temperature of the coal is 60°C. Assume that the ice water is kept at a constant temperature of 0°C.
 a. Write the function for the temperature, T, of this object as a function of time, t, in seconds.
 b. What will be the temperature of this coal after 2 minutes (120 seconds)?
 c. After how many minutes will the temperature of the coal be 1°C?

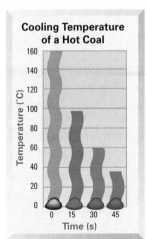

Cooling Temperature of a Hot Coal

31. GEOLOGY Compare the amounts of energy released by earthquakes that differ by 1 in magnitude. In other words, how much more energy is released by an earthquake of magnitude 6.8 than an earthquake of magnitude 5.8?

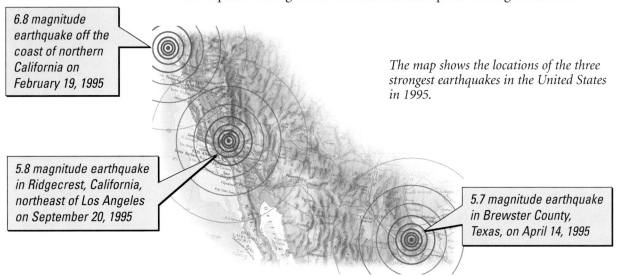

6.8 magnitude earthquake off the coast of northern California on February 19, 1995

The map shows the locations of the three strongest earthquakes in the United States in 1995.

5.8 magnitude earthquake in Ridgecrest, California, northeast of Los Angeles on September 20, 1995

5.7 magnitude earthquake in Brewster County, Texas, on April 14, 1995

32. PSYCHOLOGY Educational psychologists sometimes use mathematical models of memory. Suppose that some students take a chemistry test. After a time, t (in months), without a review of the material, they take an equivalent form of the same test. The mathematical model $a(t) = 82 - 12 \log(t + 1)$, where a is the average score at time t, is a function that describes the students' retention of the material.
   a. What is the average score when the students first took the test ($t = 0$)?
   b. What is the average score after 6 months?
   c. After how many months is the average score 60?

33. BIOLOGY A population of bacteria grows exponentially. A population that initially consists of 10,000 bacteria grows to 25,000 bacteria after 2 hours.
   a. Use the exponential growth function, $P(t) = P_0 e^{kt}$, to find the value of k. Then write a function for this population of bacteria in terms of time, t. Round the value of k to the nearest hundredth.
   b. How many bacteria will the population consist of after 12 hours, rounded to the nearest hundred thousand?
   c. How many bacteria will the population consist of after 24 hours?

34. DEMOGRAPHICS The population of India was estimated to be 574,220,000 in 1974 and 746,388,000 in 1984. Assume that this population growth is exponential. Let $t = 0$ represent 1974 and $t = 10$ represent 1984.
   a. Use the exponential growth function, $P(t) = P_0 e^{kt}$, to find the value of k. Then write the function for this population as a function of time, t.
   b. Estimate the population in 2004, rounded to the nearest hundred thousand.
   c. Use the function you wrote in part **a** to estimate the year in which the population will reach 1.5 billion.

35. ARCHEOLOGY Refer to the discussion of radioactive decay on page 395. Suppose that an animal bone is unearthed and it is determined that the amount of carbon-14 it contains is 40% of the original amount.
   a. Use the decay function for carbon-14, $N(t) = N_0 e^{-0.00012t}$, to write an equation using the percentage of carbon-14 given above.
   b. Use the equation you wrote in part **a** to find the approximate age, t, of the bone.

 **Look Back**

Graph each system of linear inequalities. *(LESSON 4.8)*

36. $\begin{cases} 2x - 5y < 4 \\ -3x \geq 2y \end{cases}$ **37.** $\begin{cases} -x \leq -3 \\ y - 5 > -3 \end{cases}$ **38.** $\begin{cases} -y + 3 \leq 12 \\ -x < y + 8 \end{cases}$

Solve each equation for x. *(LESSON 5.2)*

39. $x^2 - 3 = 46$ **40.** $7 - x^2 = 4$

Solve for x, and check your answers. *(LESSON 6.4)*

41. $\log_b(x^2 - 11) = \log_b(2x + 4)$ **42.** $\log_{10}(8x + 1) = \log_{10}(x^2 - 8)$

43. $\log_a(x^2 + 1) + 2\log_a 4 = \log_a 40x$ **44.** $2\log_b x - \log_b 3 = \log_b(2x - 3)$

APPLICATION

INVESTMENTS Assume that all interest rates are compounded continuously in Exercises 45–47. *(LESSON 6.6)*

45. How long will it take an investment of $5000 to double if the annual interest rate is 5%?

46. How long will it take an investment to double at 8% annual interest?

47. If it takes a certain amount of money 3.2 years to double, at what annual interest rate was the money invested?

 **Look Beyond**

48. Graph each function and compare the shapes of the graphs.
   a. $y = x^2$ **b.** $y = x^3 - 2x$ **c.** $y = x^4 - 2x^2$

This activity requires the data collected for the Portfolio Activities on pages 361, 369, and 384.

1. Refer to your data from the Portfolio Activity on page 361.
   a. Use Newton's law of cooling, found in Example 4 on page 405, to write a function that models the temperature of the probe as it cooled to the temperature of ice water.
   b. Compare the graph of this function with the graph of the exponential function that you generated for the same data in the Portfolio Activity on page 369. (Hint: You can use the table function on your graphics calculator to compare the y-values of these functions with the original values.)

2. a. Repeat part **a** of Step 1, using the data collected in the Portfolio Activity on page 384.

   b. Repeat part **b** from Step 1, comparing your new graph with the graphs of both the exponential function and the approximating function from the Portfolio Activity on page 384.

WORKING ON THE PROJECT

You should now be able to complete the Chapter Project.

PROJECT WARM UPS

You will need a CBL with a temperature probe, a glass of ice water, and a graphics calculator. Refer to the discussion of the Chapter Project on page 358.

Step 1: First use the CBL to measure the air temperature. Record this temperature.

Step 2: Cool the temperature probe in the ice water to near 0°C.

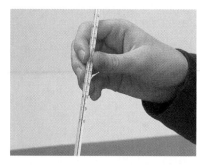

Step 3: Remove the probe from the water. Record 30 CBL readings taken at 2-second intervals. These readings will be your data set.

Step 4: Take and record a final reading at 2 minutes.

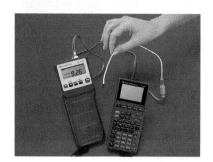

Activity 1

1. Find the function that models the linear regression of your data set. Use the variable *t* for time in seconds.

2. Use the linear model to predict the temperature of the probe after 2 minutes. Compare the prediction to your actual 2-minute reading. Discuss the usefulness of a linear function for modeling the warming process.

Activity 2

1. Use the regression feature on your calculator to find a quadratic function and an exponential function that model your data set.

2. Predict the temperature of the probe after 2 minutes by using the quadratic and exponential models. Compare the predictions with your actual 2-minute reading. Discuss the usefulness of each function for modeling the warming process.

Activity 3

1. Transform your data by taking the opposite of each temperature in the data set and add the air temperature to it. Store this data in a new list.

2. Use the exponential regression feature on your calculator to find an exponential function to model this transformed data. Discuss the usefulness of this function for modeling the warming process.

3. Add the air temperature to the exponential function in Step 2. This new function will be called the "approximating function."

4. Use the approximating function to predict the temperature of the probe after 2 minutes. Discuss the usefulness of this function for modeling the warming process.

Activity 4

1. Use your data and Newton's law of cooling (from page 405) to write a function for the temperature of the probe as it warms to room temperature. Use this function to predict the temperature of the probe after 2 minutes.

2. Compare the accuracy of the prediction from Step 1 with the accuracy of the prediction obtained with the approximating function in Step 4 of Activity 3.

Chapter Review and Assessment

VOCABULARY

asymptote	362	exponential function	362	Newton's law of cooling	405
base	362	exponential growth	363	One-to-One Property of	
change-of-base formula	388	Exponential-Logarithmic		Exponents	372
common logarithm	385	Inverse Properties	380	One-to-One Property of	
compound interest formula	365	logarithmic function	372	Logarithms	380
continuous compounding		multiplier	355	Power Property of	
formula	393	natural base	393	Logarithms	379
effective yield	365	natural exponential		Product Property	
exponential decay	363	function	393	of Logarithms	378
exponential expression	355	natural logarithmic		Quotient Property	
		function	394	of Logarithms	378

Key Skills & Exercises

LESSON 6.1

Key Skills

Write and evaluate exponential expressions.

The world population rose to about 5,734,000,000 in 1995. The world population was increasing at an annual rate of 1.6%. Write and evaluate an expression to predict the world population in 2020. [*Source: Worldbook Encyclopedia*]

$$5{,}734{,}000{,}000(1.016)^x$$
$$5{,}734{,}000{,}000(1.016)^{25} \approx 8{,}527{,}000{,}000$$

The projected world population for 2020 is about 8.5 billion people.

Exercises

1. **INVESTMENTS** The value of a painting is $12,000 in 1990 and increases by 8% of its value each year. Write and evaluate an expression to estimate the painting's value in 2005.

2. **DEPRECIATION** The value of a new car is $23,000 in 1998; it loses 15% of its value each year. Write and evaluate an expression to estimate the car's value in 2005.

LESSON 6.2

Key Skills

Classify an exponential function as exponential growth or exponential decay.

When $b > 1$, the function $f(x) = b^x$ represents exponential growth.

When $0 < b < 1$, the function $f(x) = b^x$ represents exponential decay.

Calculate the growth of investments.

The total amount of an investment, A, earning compound interest is $A(t) = P\left(1 + \frac{r}{n}\right)^{nt}$, where P is the principal, r is the annual interest rate, n is the number of times interest is compounded per year, and t is the time in years.

Exercises

Identify each function as representing exponential growth or decay.

3. $f(x) = 4(0.89)^x$

4. $g(x) = \frac{1}{3}(1.06)^x$

5. $h(x) = 5(1.06)^x$

6. $j(x) = 25\left(\frac{2}{5}\right)^x$

INVESTMENTS For each compounding period below, find the final amount of a $2400 investment after 12 years at an annual interest rate of 4.5%.

7. annually

8. quarterly

9. daily

Key Skills

Write equivalent forms of exponential and logarithmic equations.

$3^4 = 81$ is $\log_3 81 = 4$ in logarithmic form.

$\log_2 64 = 6$ is $2^6 = 64$ in exponential form.

Use the definitions of exponential and logarithmic functions to solve equations.

$$v = \log_6 36 \qquad 3 = \log_4 v \qquad 4 = \log_v 81$$
$$6^v = 36 \qquad\quad 4^3 = v \qquad\quad v^4 = 81$$
$$6^v = 6^2 \qquad\quad 64 = v \qquad\quad v^4 = 3^4$$
$$v = 2 \qquad\qquad\qquad\qquad\qquad v = 3$$

Exercises

10. Write $5^2 = 25$ in logarithmic form.

11. Write $\log_3 27 = 3$ in exponential form.

12. Write $\log_3 \frac{1}{9} = -2$ in exponential form.

Find the value of *v* in each equation.

13. $v = \log_8 64$ **14.** $\log_v 4 = 2$

15. $2 = \log_{12} v$ **16.** $3 = \log_v 1000$

17. $\log_2 v = -3$ **18.** $\log_{27} 3 = v$

19. $\log_v 49 = 2$ **20.** $\log_4 \frac{1}{16} = v$

Key Skills

Use the Product, Quotient, and Power Properties of Logarithms to simplify and evaluate expressions involving logarithms.

Given $\log_3 7 \approx 1.7712$, $\log_3 66$ can be approximated as shown below.

$$\log_3 63 = \log_3 9 + \log_3 7$$
$$= 2 + 2.1827 \approx 4.1827$$

$$\log_5 25^7 = 7 \log_5 25 = 7 \cdot 2 = 14$$

Exercises

Given $\log_7 5 \approx 0.8271$ and $\log_7 9 \approx 1.1292$, approximate the value of each logarithm.

21. $\log_7 45$ **22.** $\log_7 \frac{5}{9}$ **23.** $\log_7 35$

Write each expression as a single logarithm. Then simplify, if possible.

24. $\log_5 3 + \log_5 6 + \log_5 9$

25. $\log 6 - \log 3 + 2 \log 7$

Evaluate each expression.

26. $2^{\log_2 12}$ **27.** $\log_7 7^3$ **28.** $\log_6 36^7$

Key Skills

Use the common logarithmic function to solve exponential and logarithmic equations.

$$4 = \log x \qquad\qquad 2^x = 34$$
$$10^4 = x \qquad\qquad \log 2^x = \log 34$$
$$10{,}000 = x \qquad\qquad x \log 2 = \log 34$$
$$x = \frac{\log 34}{\log 2}$$
$$x \approx 5.09$$

Apply the change-of-base formula to evaluate logarithmic expressions.

The change-of-base formula is $\log_a x = \dfrac{\log_b x}{\log_b a}$, where $a \neq 1$, $b \neq 1$, and $x > 0$.

$$\log_2 5 = \frac{\log 5}{\log 2} \approx 2.32$$

Exercises

Solve each equation. Give your answers to the nearest hundredth.

29. $\log x = 8$ **30.** $\log 0.01 = x - 5$

31. $5^x + 100 = 98$ **32.** $5 - 2^x = 40$

33. $7 + 3^{2x-1} = 154$ **34.** $3 + 7^{3x+1} = 346$

Evaluate each logarithmic expression to the nearest hundredth.

35. $\log_3 14$ **36.** $\log_{16} 3$

37. $\log_{0.5} 6$ **38.** $\log_{1.5} 10$

39. CHEMISTRY What is $[H^+]$ of a carbonated soda if its pH is 2.5?

Key Skills

Evaluate exponential functions of base e and natural logarithms.

Using a calculator and rounding to the nearest thousandth, $e^{2.5} \approx 12.182$ and $\ln 3.5 \approx 1.253$.

Model exponential growth and decay processes by using base e.

The continuous compounding formula is $A = Pe^{rt}$, where A is the final amount when the principal P is invested at an annual interest rate of r for t years.

Exercises

Evaluate each expression to the nearest thousandth.

40. $e^{0.5}$

41. e^{-5}

42. $\ln 5$

43. $\ln 0.05$

44. INVESTMENTS Sharon invests $2500 at an annual interest rate of 9%. How much is the investment worth after 10 years if the interest is compounded continuously?

Key Skills

Solve logarithmic and exponential equations.

$$\log_x \frac{1}{32} = -5$$
$$x^{-5} = \frac{1}{32}$$
$$x^{-5} = 2^{-5}$$
$$x = 2$$

$$\ln x^3 + 5 = 1$$
$$3 \ln x = -4$$
$$\ln x = -\frac{4}{3}$$
$$x = e^{-\frac{4}{3}}$$
$$x \approx 0.264$$

$$\ln(x+6) = 2 \ln 3$$
$$\ln(x+6) = \ln 9$$
$$x + 6 = 9$$
$$x = 3$$

Exercises

Solve each equation for x. Write the exact solution and the approximate solution to the nearest hundredth, when appropriate.

45. $\log_x \frac{1}{128} = -7$

46. $\ln(2x) = 4 \ln 2$

47. $x \log \frac{1}{6} = \log 6$

48. $\ln \sqrt{x} - 3 = 1$

49. HEALTH The normal healing of a wound can be modeled by $A = A_0 e^{-0.35n}$, where A is the area of the wound in square centimeters after n days. After how many days is the area of the wound half of its original size, A_0?

Applications

50. BIOLOGY Given favorable living conditions, fruit fly populations can grow at the astounding rate of 28% per day. If a laboratory selects a population of 25 fruit flies to reproduce, about how big will the population be after 3 days? after 5 days? after 1 week?

51. PHYSICS Suppose that the sound of busy traffic on a four-lane street is about $10^{8.5}$ times the intensity of the threshold of hearing, I_0. Find the relative intensity, R, in decibels of thetraffic on this street.

52. PHYSICS Radon is a radioactive gas that has a half-life of about 3.8 days. This means that only half of the original amount of radon gas will be present after about 3.8 days. Using the exponential decay function $A = Pe^{-kt}$, find the value of k to the nearest hundredth, and write the function for the amount of radon remaining after t days.

Fruit fly

6 Alternative Assessment

Performance Assessment

1. **EARTH SCIENCE** Research the Richter magnitudes of two recent earthquakes. Use the magnitude equation $M = \frac{2}{3} \log\left(\frac{E}{10^{11.8}}\right)$ to compare the amounts of energy released by each earthquake.

2. **DEMOGRAPHICS** In 1972, figures provided by the United Nations showed the population of the Republic of Korea (R.O.K.) as 32,530,000 with a growth rate of 2.2% per year.
   a. At that rate, what would be the expected population of the R.O.K. in 1994?
   b. The *1995 World Almanac* lists the 1994 R.O.K. population as 45,083,000. What is the difference between the actual population and the expected population?
   c. Determine the average growth rate per year for the R.O.K. from 1972 to 1994 by using the actual populations from these two years. How does it compare with the 1972 growth rate?

3. **INVESTMENTS** Go to a local bank and find out about different investment options. Use the compounding interest formula to compare the returns of each option for a given time period.

4. **GEOMETRY** Fold a large piece of paper in half. Fold the paper again several times. Record the following information:
   • the number of times the paper is folded and the number of layers in the folded "booklet"
   • the number of times the paper is folded and the area of the cover page in the "booklet"
   Find exponential models for your data.

Portfolio Projects

BOUNCING BALL EXPERIMENT The object of this activity is to demonstrate that the height of successive bounces of a ball decreases exponentially as the number of bounces increases.

1. Find the average rebound heights of successive bounces of a ball dropped from three different initial heights. Use a table to organize your data.

2. Graph the data for each initial height. Let the bounce number be the x-coordinate and the rebound height be the y-coordinate.

3. Find an exponential regression equation for the data. What is the base of the exponential regression model?

   It can be demonstrated that there is a constant ratio of the height after the first bounce to the initial height. That is,

   $$\frac{\text{Height after first bounce}}{\text{Initial height}} = k$$

   Then the heights of successive bounces should correspond to the following sequence:

   $$h_0 k, \; h_0 k^2, \; h_0 k^3, \; \ldots, \; h_0 k^n$$

   This corresponds to the exponential function $f(x) = h_0 k^x$ for integer values of x from 0 to n.

4. For each initial height, find the value of k from your data. Compare your value of k with the base for the exponential regression equation from Step 3.

5. Do your data and calculations support the conclusion that the height of successive bounces of a ball decreases exponentially? Explain your reasoning.

---

internetconnect

HRW The HRW Web site contains many resources to reinforce and expand your knowledge of exponential and logarithmic functions. This Web site also provides Internet links to other sites where you can find information and real-world data for use in research projects, reports, and activities that involve exponential and logarithmic functions. Visit the HRW Web site at **go.hrw.com,** and enter the keyword **MB1 CH6** to access the resources for this chapter.

QUANTITATIVE COMPARISON For Items 1–5, write
A if the quantity in Column A is greater that the quantity in Column B;
B if the quantity in Column B is greater that the quantity in Column A;
C if the quantities are equal; or
D if the relationship cannot be determined from the given information.

	Column A	Column B	Answers
1.	The minimum value in the range of the function $f(x) = |x - 2|$	The minimum value in the range of the function $f(x) = |x| - 2$	Ⓐ Ⓑ Ⓒ Ⓓ [Lesson 2.6]
2.	$(5 - 2i)(5 + 2i)$ where $i = \sqrt{-1}$	$6i^2 \cdot 7i^2$ where $i = \sqrt{-1}$	Ⓐ Ⓑ Ⓒ Ⓓ [Lesson 5.6]
3.	$\frac{1}{5}(x - 2)^2 = 1$		
	The absolute value of the difference of the solutions	The absolute value of the sum of the solutions	Ⓐ Ⓑ Ⓒ Ⓓ [Lesson 5.2]
4.	Let $f(x) = 3x$ and $g(x) = x^2 + 2$		
	$(f \circ g)(-2)$	$(g \circ f)(-2)$	Ⓐ Ⓑ Ⓒ Ⓓ [Lesson 2.4]
5.	The number of real solutions		
	$2x^2 - 3x = 3$	$4x^2 - 4x = -1$	Ⓐ Ⓑ Ⓒ Ⓓ [Lesson 5.6]

6. What is the slope of the line that contains the points $(6, -8)$ and $(-2, -4)$? **(LESSON 1.2)**
  a. 2
  b. −2
  c. $-\frac{1}{2}$
  d. $\frac{1}{2}$

7. Which term describes the system of equations below? **(LESSON 3.1)**
$$\begin{cases} 2x - y = 7 \\ 2y - 4x = -14 \end{cases}$$
  a. inconsistent
  b. dependent
  c. independent
  d. incompatible

8. What are the coordinates of the vertex for the graph of $y = (x - 2)(x + 1)$? **(LESSON 5.5)**
  a. $(-0.5, -2.25)$
  b. $(-1, 0)$
  c. $(0.5, -2.25)$
  d. $(-0.5, 3.75)$

9. In triangle ABC below, what is the value of a? **(LESSON 5.2)**
  a. 28
  b. $2\sqrt{7}$
  c. 2
  d. 4

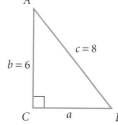

10. Which is a solution for the system below? *(LESSON 3.1)*

$$\begin{cases} y = x + 3 \\ y - x = 4 \end{cases}$$

   a. $(3, 7)$ **b.** $(2, 5)$
   c. both **a** and **b**   **d.** neither **a** nor **b**

11. Simplify $\left(\dfrac{-x^{-3}y^5}{2xy^{-2}} \right)^4$. *(LESSON 2.2)*

   a. $\dfrac{y^{28}}{8x^{16}}$ **b.** $-\dfrac{y^{28}}{8x^{16}}$

   c. $\dfrac{y^{28}}{16x^{16}}$ **d.** $\dfrac{1}{16}x^{11}y^{22}$

12. Determine which set of ordered pairs represents a function. *(LESSON 2.3)*
   a. $\{(1, -1), (-1, 1), (1, 1)\}$
   b. $\{(0, 1), (1, 0), (0, 0)\}$
   c. $\{(-1, 1), (1, -1), (1, 0), (0, -1)\}$
   d. $\{(0, 1), (1, 2), (2, 1), (-1, 0)\}$

13. Solve $\begin{cases} 2x + 8y = -10 \\ -3x + 12y = 3 \end{cases}$.

   (LESSONS 3.1 AND 3.2)

14. Solve $2x^2 - 7 = 121$ for x. *(LESSON 5.2)*

15. Write the equation in vertex form for the parabola described by $f(x) = 2x^2 - 3x + 7$. *(LESSON 5.4)*

16. If $f(x) = x^2 - 2x$, find the inverse of f. *(LESSON 2.5)*

17. Find the matrix product below. *(LESSON 4.2)*
$$\begin{bmatrix} 3 & -6 \\ 5 & 4 \end{bmatrix} \begin{bmatrix} 1 & 0 \\ 0 & 1 \end{bmatrix}$$

18. Factor to find the zeros of $f(x) = x^2 - x - 6$. *(LESSON 5.3)*

19. Let $f(x) = 2x - 3$ and $g(x) = -3x$. Find $(f \cdot g)(x)$. *(LESSON 2.4)*

20. Let $A = \begin{bmatrix} 2 & 3 & 8 \\ -4 & 5 & -8 \\ 0 & 6 & -5 \end{bmatrix}$ and let

$B = \begin{bmatrix} 0 & 3 & -1 \\ -1 & 4 & 3 \\ 2 & -7 & 2 \end{bmatrix}$. Find $A - B$.

   (LESSON 4.1)

FREE-RESPONSE GRID The following questions may be answered by using a free-response grid such as that commonly used by standardized-test services.

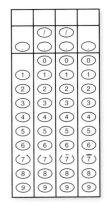

21. In the formula $F = \dfrac{9}{5}C + 32$, find the value of C if $F = 95$. *(LESSON 1.6)*

22. What is the value of $\log_2 \dfrac{1}{8}$? *(LESSON 6.3)*

23. What is the minimum value of $f(x) = x^2 - 5x + 8$? *(LESSON 5.1)*

24. Solve the equation $5e^{3-x} = 2$ for x. *(LESSON 6.6)*

25. **INVESTMENTS** If $2500 is invested at 6.9% compounded daily, determine the value of the investment after 12 years. *(LESSON 6.2)*

26. Simplify $\dfrac{(9 - 3)^2}{2(3 - 1)}$. *(LESSON 2.1)*

27. Evaluate $[3.2] - [4.99]$. *(LESSON 2.6)*

28. Find the determinant of $\begin{bmatrix} 3 & 6 \\ -1 & 4 \end{bmatrix}$. *(LESSON 4.3)*

BUSINESS A skate store makes two kinds of in-line skates: regular skates and those with custom boots. The store can make 90 pairs of skates per month and can spend, at most, no more than $11,400 per month to produce them. Each pair of regular skates costs $80 to make and brings a profit of $60. Each pair of skates with custom boots costs $150 to make and brings a profit of $70. *(LESSON 3.5)*

29. Find the number of regular in-line skates that the skate store needs to sell in order to maximize its profit.

30. Find the number of in-line skates with custom boots that the skate store needs to sell in order to maximize its profit.

Keystroke Guide for Chapter 6

Essential keystroke sequences (using the model TI-82 or TI-83 graphics calculator) are presented below for all Activities and Examples found in this chapter that require or recommend the use of a graphics calculator.

 internet**connect**

Keystrokes for other models of graphics calculators are found on the HRW Web site.

LESSON 6.1

Page 354

Use a calculator to model the population growth of 25 bacteria that double every hour for 6 hours.

25 `ENTER` `×` 2 `ENTER` `ENTER` `ENTER` `ENTER` `ENTER` `ENTER`

LESSON 6.2

Page 363

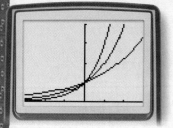

For Step 1, graph $y_1 = 3^x$, $y_2 = 2^x$, and $y_3 = (1.5)^x$ on the same screen.

Use viewing window $[-3, 3]$ by $[0, 4]$.

`Y=` 3 `^` `X,T,θ,n` `ENTER` (Y2 =) 2 `^` `X,T,θ,n` `ENTER`
(Y3 =) 1.5 `^` `X,T,θ,n` `ENTER`

For Step 3, graph $y_4 = \left(\frac{1}{3}\right)^x$, $y_5 = \left(\frac{1}{2}\right)^x$, and $y_6 = \left(\frac{1}{1.5}\right)^x$ on the same screen as the graphs above.

`Y=` (Y4=) `(` 1 `÷` 3 `)` `^` `X,T,θ,n` `ENTER`
(Y5=) `(` 1 `÷` 2 `)` `^` `X,T,θ,n` `ENTER`
(Y6=) `(` 1 `÷` 1.5 `)` `^` `X,T,θ,n` `ENTER`

E X A M P L E ❶

Page 364

For part a, graph $y_1 = 2^x$ and $y_2 = 3 \cdot 2^x$ together, and find the y-intercepts.

Use viewing window $[-5, 5]$ by $[-2, 12]$.

To graph the functions, use a keystroke sequence similar to that in the Activity for this lesson.

Find the y-intercepts:

`2nd` `TRACE` **1: value** `ENTER` `ENTER` (X=) 0 `ENTER` `▼`
(CALC)

For part **b**, use a similar keystroke sequence.

EXAMPLE ③

Page 366

Find the exponential regression equation that best fits the points **(0, 100,000)** and **(5, 150,000)**.

Use viewing window [−2, 7] by [−20,000, 200,000] and Yscl: 20,000.

Enter the data:

STAT EDIT 1: edit ENTER L1 0 ENTER 5 ENTER ▶ L2 100000 ENTER

150000 ENTER

Create the scatter plot:

STATPLOT
2nd Y= 1:Plot 1 ENTER On ENTER ▼ (Type:) ⬚ ENTER ▼ (Xlist:)

L1
2nd 1 ▼ (Ylist:) 2nd L2 2 ▼ (Mark:) ◻ ENTER 2nd QUIT MODE

Graph an exponential model for the data:

STAT CALC 0:ExpReg ENTER ENTER Y= VARS 5:Statistics ENTER EQ 1:RegEQ

ENTER GRAPH

TI-82:

STAT CALC A:ExpReg ENTER ENTER Y= VARS 5:Statistics ENTER EQ 7:RegEQ ENTER GRAPH

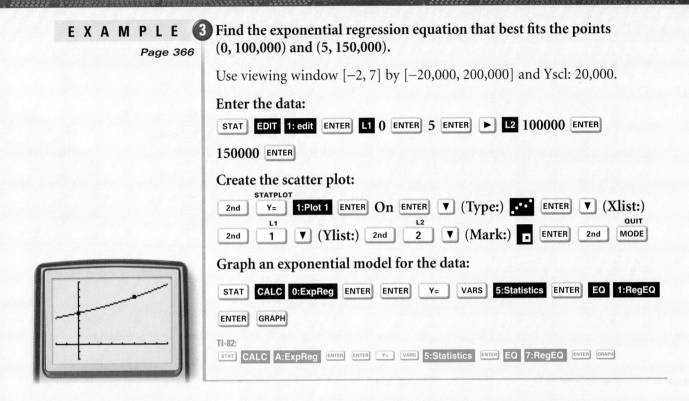

LESSON 6.3

Activity

Page 370

Make a table of values for $y = 10^x$, and use the table to approximate the solution to $10^x = 7$ to the nearest hundredth.

Y= 10 ∧ X,T,θ,n 2nd TBLSET WINDOW

(TblStart=) **0.83** ENTER (△Tbl=) **0.01** ENTER

(Indpnt:) Auto ENTER ▼

(Depend:) Auto ENTER 2nd TABLE GRAPH

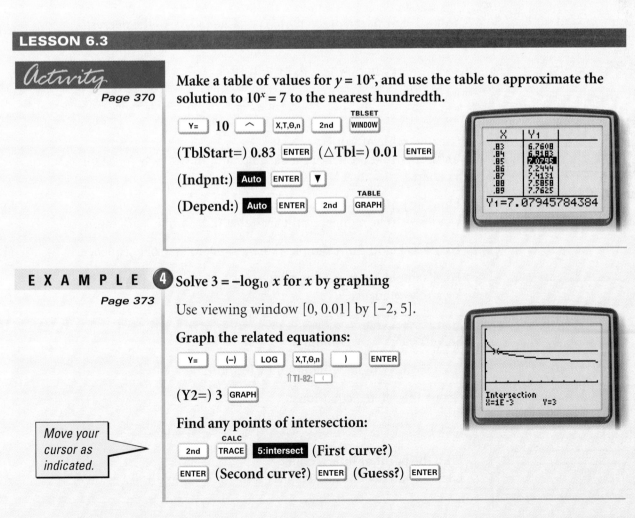

EXAMPLE ④

Page 373

Solve $3 = -\log_{10} x$ for x by graphing

Use viewing window [0, 0.01] by [−2, 5].

Graph the related equations:

Y= (−) LOG X,T,θ,n) ENTER

⇑TI-82: (

(Y2=) **3** GRAPH

Find any points of intersection:

Move your cursor as indicated.

2nd CALC TRACE 5:intersect (First curve?)

ENTER (Second curve?) ENTER (Guess?) ENTER

E X A M P L E **①** Graph $y = 10 \log x$, and evaluate y for $x = 300$.

Page 387

Use viewing window $[-50, 350]$ by $[-10, 50]$.

Graph the function:

⇑ TI-82: ( )

Find the point on the graph where $x = 300$:

CALC
2nd   TRACE   **1: value**   ENTER   (X=) 300   ENTER

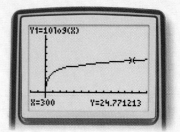

E X A M P L E **③** Solve $5^x = 62$ by graphing.

Page 387

Use viewing window $[-1, 5]$ by $[-40, 100]$.

Graph the related equations, and use a keystroke sequence similar to that in Example 4 of Lesson 6.3 to find any points of intersection.

E X A M P L E S **①** and **③** For part a of Example 1, evaluate $y = e^x$ to the nearest thousandth for $x = 2$.

Pages 393 and 394

Use viewing window $[-2, 3]$ by $[-1, 10]$.

Enter the equation: Y=   2nd   LN $\overset{e^x}{}$ X,T,θ,n   )   ENTER

⇑ TI-82: ( )

Create a table of values:
Use a keystroke sequence similar to that in the Activity in Lesson 6.3. Use TblStart $= -1$ and $\triangle$Tbl $= 0.5$.

Find the point on the graph where $x = 2$:
Use a keystroke sequence similar to that in Example 1 of Lesson 6.5.

For parts **b** and **c** of Example 1, use a similar keystroke sequence.

For Example 3, use viewing window $[-2, 10]$ by $[-2, 4]$ and a similar keystroke sequence.

E X A M P L E **④** Solve $2 = e^{0.085x}$ by graphing.

Page 395

Use viewing window $[-20, 100]$ by $[-3, 10]$.

Graph the related equations:

Y=   2   ENTER   (Y2=)   2nd   LN $\overset{e^x}{}$ .085   X,T,θ,n   )   ENTER

⇑ TI-82: ( )

Find the point of intersection:
Use a keystroke sequence similar to that in Example 4 of Lesson 6.3.

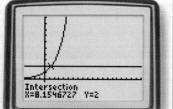

E X A M P L E ❷ Solve $\log x + \log(x - 3) = 1$ by graphing.

Page 404

Use viewing window $[-2, 8]$ by $[-1, 5]$.

Graph the related equations:

⇑TI-82: ⎍

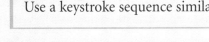

⇑TI-82: ⎍

(Y2=) 1 GRAPH

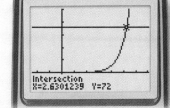

Find the point of intersection:
Use a keystroke sequence similar to that in Example 4 of Lesson 6.3.

E X A M P L E ❸ Solve $4e^{3x-5} = 72$ by graphing.

Page 404

Use viewing window $[-1, 4]$ by $[-30, 100]$.

Graph the related equations:

Y= 4 2nd [e^x] LN 3 X,T,θ,n — 5)

ENTER (Y2=) 72 GRAPH

Find the point of intersection:
Use a keystroke sequence similar to that in Example 4 of Lesson 6.3.

 Activity

Page 405

For Step 1, graph $y_1 = \log x + \log(x + 21)$ and $y_2 = 2$ together, and find any points of intersection.

Use viewing window $[-1, 6]$ by $[-1, 3]$.

Use a keystroke sequence similar to that in Example 2 of Lesson 6.7.

For Step 4, use viewing window $[-1, 4]$ by $[-30, 100]$ and a keystroke sequence similar to that in Example 3 of Lesson 6.7.

E X A M P L E ❹ For part b, evaluate $y = 70 - 30\left(\frac{2}{3}\right)^x$ for $x = 2$.

Page 406

Use viewing window $[-1, 10]$ by $[-20, 100]$.

Graph the function:

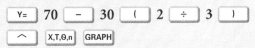

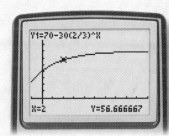

Find the y-value for $x = 2$:
Use a keystroke sequence similar to that in Example 1 of Lesson 6.2.

For part c, use a keystroke sequence similar to that in Example 4 of Lesson 6.3.

7

Polynomial Functions

POLYNOMIAL FUNCTIONS CAN BE USED TO model many real-world situations, including annuities and volumes. For example, the volumes of the irregularly shaped buildings shown here can be modeled by polynomial functions.

Polynomial functions are important in algebra. In this chapter, you will learn how to combine polynomial functions, how to graph them, and how to find their roots.

*Atomium in
Brussels, Belgium*

*Montreal Expo Habitat in
Montreal, Canada*

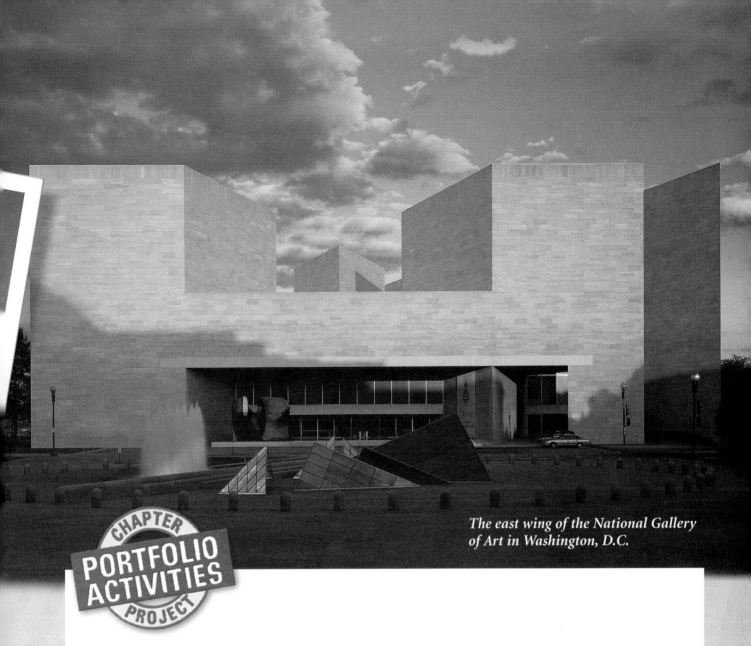

The east wing of the National Gallery of Art in Washington, D.C.

PORTFOLIO ACTIVITIES — CHAPTER PROJECT

About the Chapter Project

In this chapter, you will use polynomial functions to model real-world data. A good model must consistently provide answers to the question or problem it was created to solve. In the Chapter Project, *Fill It Up!*, you will predict the shape of containers by using polynomial models that are created from the relationship between the volume of water contained and the height of water in the container.

After completing the Chapter Project, you will be able to do the following:

- Collect and organize data.
- Determine a polynomial model that best fits a data set.
- Test your polynomial model.

About the Portfolio Activities

Throughout the chapter, you will be given opportunities to complete Portfolio Activities that are designed to support your work on the Chapter Project.

- Creating a polynomial model for the volume of an irregularly shaped container is included in the Portfolio Activity on page 431.

- Analyzing the behavior of the polynomial model is included in the Portfolio Activity on page 439.

- Creating a polynomial model and using it to solve problems is included in the Portfolio Activity on page 455.

An Introduction to Polynomials

Objectives

- Identify, evaluate, add, and subtract polynomials.

- Classify polynomials, and describe the shapes of their graphs.

Why *Polynomial functions can be used to describe real-world events such as the growing value of an annuity investment.*

Periodically adding a fixed amount of money to an account that pays compound interest is an investment that people often use to prepare for the future. Such an investment option is called an *annuity*.

Consider an annuity of $1000 invested at the beginning of each year in an account that pays 5% interest compounded annually. The diagram below illustrates the growth of this investment over 4 years.

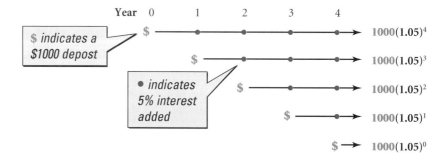

The total value of this investment after 4 years can be written as the sum below.

$$1000(1.05)^4 + 1000(1.05)^3 + 1000(1.05)^2 + 1000(1.05)^1 + 1000(1.05)^0$$

To consider different interest rates, replace 1.05 with 1.06 for 6%, 1.07 for 7%, and so on. In general, the value of this investment after 4 years can be represented by the *polynomial* expression $1000x^4 + 1000x^3 + 1000x^2 + 1000x + 1000$, where x is the multiplier determined by the annual interest rate.

How much will the investment be worth at the time the last payment is made if the interest rate is 6%? *You will answer this question in Example 2.*

A **monomial** is a numeral, a variable, or the product of a numeral and one or more variables. A monomial with no variables, such as -1 or $\frac{2}{3}$, is called a **constant**.

A **coefficient** is the numerical factor in a monomial. For example:

- x has a coefficient of 1.
- $-2t$ has a coefficient of -2.
- $\frac{-x^3 y^2}{3}$ has a coefficient of $-\frac{1}{3}$ because it can be written as $-\frac{1}{3}x^3 y^2$.
- $-ab$ has a coefficient of -1.

The **degree of a monomial** is the sum of the exponents of its variables. For example, $x^2 yz$ is of degree 4 because $x^2 yz = x^2 y^1 z^1$ and $2 + 1 + 1 = 4$. A nonzero constant such as 3 is of degree 0 because it can be written as $3x^0$.

A **polynomial** is a monomial or a sum of terms that are monomials. In this chapter, you will study polynomials in one variable. Polynomials can be classified by the number of terms they contain. A polynomial with two terms is a **binomial**. A polynomial with three terms is a **trinomial**.

The **degree of a polynomial** is the same as that of its term with the greatest degree. Polynomials can also be classified by degree, as shown below.

CLASSIFICATION OF A POLYNOMIAL BY DEGREE		
Degree	Name	Example
$n = 0$	constant	3
$n = 1$	linear	$5x + 4$
$n = 2$	quadratic	$-x^2 + 11x - 5$
$n = 3$	cubic	$4x^3 - x^2 + 2x - 3$
$n = 4$	quartic	$9x^4 + 3x^3 + 4x^2 - x + 1$
$n = 5$	quintic	$-2x^5 + 3x^4 - x^3 + 3x^2 - 2x + 6$

E X A M P L E 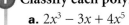 Classify each polynomial by degree and by number of terms.

    a. $2x^3 - 3x + 4x^5$ **b.** $-2x^3 + 3x^4 + 2x^3 + 5$

SOLUTION

a. The greatest exponent of x is 5, so the degree is 5.

The polynomial has three terms, so it is a trinomial.

The polynomial is a quintic trinomial.

b. When simplified to $3x^4 + 5$, the greatest exponent of x is 4, so the degree is 4.

The simplified polynomial has two terms, so it is a binomial.

The polynomial is a quartic binomial.

TRY THIS   Classify each polynomial by degree and by number of terms.

    a. $x^2 + 4 - 8x - 2x^3$ **b.** $3x^3 + 2 - x^3 - 6x^5$

Evaluating Polynomials

Example 2 shows you how polynomials can be used for calculations in real-world situations.

E X A M P L E ② Refer to the annuity described at the beginning of the lesson.

How much will the investment be worth at the time the last payment is made if the annual interest rate is 6%?

● **SOLUTION**

Method 1 Use substitution.
$$1000x^4 + 1000x^3 + 1000x^2 + 1000x + 1000$$
$$= 1000(1.06)^4 + 1000(1.06)^3 + 1000(1.06)^2 + 1000(1.06) + 1000$$
$$= 5637.09$$

Method 2 Use a table or a graph.
Enter $y = 1000x^4 + 1000x^3 + 1000x^2 + 1000x + 1000$ into a graphics calculator. **Use a table of values or a graph** to find the y-value for $x = 1.06$.

PROBLEM SOLVING

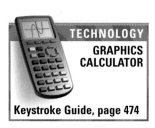

TECHNOLOGY
GRAPHICS CALCULATOR

Keystroke Guide, page 474

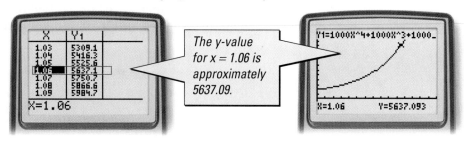

The y-value for x = 1.06 is approximately 5637.09.

The investment will be worth $5637.09.

TRY THIS Evaluate the polynomial $3x^4 + 2x^2 + 2x - 5$ for $x = 1.5$.

Adding and Subtracting Polynomials

To add and subtract polynomials, combine like terms. Recall that *like terms* have the same degree, or exponent, of the variable. When you write your answer, use *standard form*. The **standard form** of a polynomial expression is written with the exponents in *descending order* of degree.

E X A M P L E ③ Find the sum. $(-2x^2 - 3x^3 + 5x + 4) + (-2x^3 + 7x - 6)$

● **SOLUTION**

$$(-2x^2 - 3x^3 + 5x + 4) + (-2x^3 + 7x - 6)$$
$$= (-3x^3 - 2x^3) + (-2x^2) + (5x + 7x) + (4 - 6) \quad \textit{Combine like terms.}$$
$$= -5x^3 - 2x^2 + 12x - 2 \quad \textit{Write in standard form.}$$

TRY THIS Find the sum. $(2x^4 + 4x^3 + 5x - 2) + (-2x^4 - 7x^2 + 8x - 10)$

CRITICAL THINKING Find a polynomial expression P such that $(2x^2 - 3x + 5) + P = 0$.

E X A M P L E **4** Find the difference. $(-6x^3 - 6x^2 + 7x - 1) - (3x^3 - 5x^2 - 2x + 8)$

SOLUTION

$(-6x^3 - 6x^2 + 7x - 1) - (3x^3 - 5x^2 - 2x + 8)$
$= (-6x^3 - 3x^3) + (-6x^2 + 5x^2) + (7x + 2x) + (-1 - 8)$ *Combine like terms.*
$= -9x^3 - x^2 + 9x - 9$ *Write in standard form.*

TRY THIS Find the difference. $(3x^3 - 12x^2 - 5x + 1) - (-x^2 + 5x + 8)$

Graphing Polynomial Functions

A **polynomial function** is a function that is defined by a polynomial expression. In the Activity below, you will explore the characteristic shapes of the graphs of some polynomial functions.

Exploring Graphs of Polynomial Functions

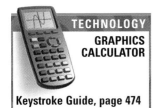

TECHNOLOGY
GRAPHICS CALCULATOR

Keystroke Guide, page 474

You will need: a graphics calculator

Graph each function below in a viewing window that shows all of the "U-turns" in the graph. Copy the table and record the degree and number of U-turns.

	Function	Degree	Number of U-turns in the graph
1.	$y = x^2 + x - 2$	2	1
2.	$y = 3x^3 - 12x + 4$		
3.	$y = -2x^3 + 4x^2 + x - 2$		
4.	$y = x^4 + 5x^3 + 5x^2 - x - 6$		
5.	$y = x^4 + 2x^3 - 5x^2 - 6x$		

PROBLEM SOLVING

6. **Look for a pattern.** Make a conjecture about the degree of a function and the number of U-turns in its graph.

Graph each function below in a viewing window that shows all of the U-turns in the graph. Copy the table and record the degree and number of U-turns.

	Function	Degree	Number of U-turns in the graph
7.	$y = x^3$		
8.	$y = x^3 - 3x^2 + 3x - 1$		
9.	$y = x^4$		

CHECKPOINT ✔ 10. Now make another conjecture about the degree of a function and the number of U-turns in its graph. Is this conjecture different from the conjecture you made in Step 6? Explain.

EXAMPLE **5** Graph each function. Describe its general shape.

a. $P(x) = 3x^3 - 5x^2 - 2x + 1$ **b.** $Q(x) = x^4 - 8x^2$

SOLUTION

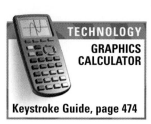

TECHNOLOGY
GRAPHICS CALCULATOR

Keystroke Guide, page 474

a.

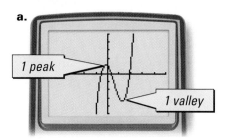

1 peak

1 valley

The graph of this cubic function has an S-shape with 2 U-turns.

b.

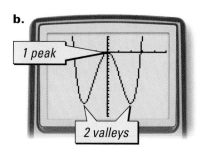

1 peak

2 valleys

The graph of this quartic function has a W-shape with 3 U-turns.

TRY THIS Graph each function. Describe its general shape.

a. $P(x) = -3x^3 - 2x^2 + 2x - 1$ **b.** $Q(x) = 2x^4 - 3x^2 - x + 2$

Examine the shapes of the linear, quadratic, cubic, and quartic functions shown below.

Linear

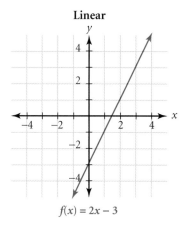

$f(x) = 2x - 3$

Quadratic

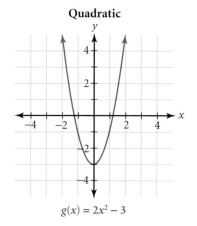

$g(x) = 2x^2 - 3$

Cubic

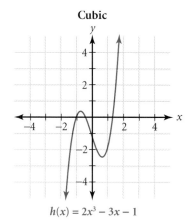

$h(x) = 2x^3 - 3x - 1$

Quartic

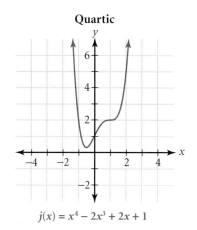

$j(x) = x^4 - 2x^3 + 2x + 1$

CHECKPOINT ✔ What is the range of the polynomial functions above that are of an odd degree? What can you say about the ranges of the polynomial functions above that are of an even degree?

In Lesson 7.2, you will learn more about the graphs of polynomial functions.

Exercises

Communicate

1. In your own words, define a *polynomial*.

2. Describe how to determine the degree of a polynomial function.

3. Use the definition of a polynomial function to explain how you know that a quadratic function is a polynomial function.

Guided Skills Practice

Classify each polynomial by degree and by number of terms. *(EXAMPLE 1)*

4. $x^4 + 3x^3 - x^2$ **5.** $x^5 + 3x^4 - 4x^2 + x - 1$

6. Evaluate the polynomial $x^3 + 2x^2 - x + 1$ for $x = 2$. *(EXAMPLE 2)*

7. Find the sum. $(2x^3 + 3x^2 - x + 2) + (-3x^2 + 4x + 5)$ *(EXAMPLE 3)*

8. Find the difference. $(6x^3 - 5x^2 + 14x + 3) - (3x^3 - 2x^2 + 7x - 2)$ *(EXAMPLE 4)*

Graph each function and describe the general shape. *(EXAMPLE 5)*

9. $f(x) = x^3 - x$ **10.** $f(x) = x^4 - x^2 + 1$

Practice and Apply

Write each polynomial in standard form.

11. $5x^3 + 4x + 2x^2 + 1$ **12.** $4x^4 + x^2 + x^3 + x + 1$

13. $2.7x^3 + 3.3x^8 + 4.1x^2$ **14.** $9.1x^2 + 5.4x^5 + 3.3x^2 + 2.1$

15. $\dfrac{x^7}{13} + \dfrac{x^9}{7} - \dfrac{2}{3}$ **16.** $\dfrac{13}{15}x^4 + \dfrac{5}{7}x^3 + \dfrac{3}{5}x^5 + \dfrac{1}{2}$

Determine whether each expression is a polynomial. If so, classify the polynomial by degree and by number of terms.

17. $7x^5 + 3x^3 - 2x + 4$ **18.** $-4x^2 + 3x^3 - 5x^6 + 4$

19. $3^x + 2^x - x - 7$ **20.** $4^{2x} + 5^x - x + 1$

21. $0.35x^4 + 2x^2 + 3.8x$ **22.** $7.81x^4 + 8.9x^3 + 2.5x^2$

23. $\dfrac{3}{x^2} + \dfrac{5}{x} + 6$ **24.** $\dfrac{8}{x^3} - \dfrac{7}{x^2} + x$ **25.** $\dfrac{5}{7}x^6 + \dfrac{2}{3}x^4 + 5$

26. $\dfrac{x^5}{5} - \dfrac{x^3}{3}$ **27.** $\sqrt{x} - 1$ **28.** $7\sqrt{x} + 4$

Evaluate each polynomial expression for the indicated value of *x*.

29. $x^3 + x^2 + 1$ for $x = -3$ **30.** $x^4 + 2x^3 + 2$ for $x = -2$

31. $-2x^3 - 3x + 2$ for $x = 4$ **32.** $-4x^3 + 1 + x$ for $x = 3$

33. $3x^3 + x^2 + 2x + 4$ for $x = 5$ **34.** $5x^3 + 2x^2 - 5x + 2$ for $x = 6$

35. $\dfrac{1}{4}x^4 + \dfrac{1}{8}x^3 + \dfrac{3}{8}x^2 + \dfrac{5}{8}x + \dfrac{7}{8}$ for $x = 2$ **36.** $\dfrac{3}{10}x^3 + \dfrac{7}{10}x^2 + \dfrac{1}{10}x + \dfrac{9}{10}$ for $x = 10$

37. $1 + x^2 - 3x^3$ for $x = 2.5$ **38.** $5x^3 + 4x + 2x^2 + 1$ for $x = 3.8$

Write each sum or difference as a polynomial in standard form. Then classify the polynomial by degree and by number of terms.

39. $(x^3 + x^2 + x + 1) + (2x^3 + 3x^2 + x + 3)$

40. $(x^5 + x^3 + x) + (x^4 + x^2 + 1)$

41. $(1 - 5x + x^3) - (2x^4 + 5x^3 - 10x^2)$

42. $(5x^3 + 3x^2 + 8x + 2) - (2x^2 + 4x + 7)$

43. $(2x^2 - 5x + 3) + (4x^3 + 6x^2 - 2x + 5)$

44. $(x^2 - 5x^3 + 7) + (6x + x^3 + 3x^2)$

45. $(x^4 + 5x^2 + x) - (x^4 + 2x^3 + x - 4)$

46. $(8x^2 + x^3 + 1 - 3x) + (2x^3 + 11x^4)$

47. $\left(\frac{2}{3}x + \frac{2}{3}x^3 + 1\right) + \left(\frac{2}{3} + \frac{1}{3}x^2 + \frac{1}{3}x\right)$

48. $\left(\frac{2}{7}x^2 + \frac{1}{7}x + \frac{3}{7}\right) - \left(\frac{4}{7}x^3 + \frac{6}{7}x^2 + \frac{2}{7}\right)$

49. $(-3.2x^2 + 2.7x^3 + 7.8x) + (4.9x^3 + 2.5x^4)$

50. $(4.1x^2 + 5.6x + 7.8) - (x^4 + 7.6x^2 + 9.8x)$

Graph each function. Describe its general shape.

51 $f(x) = x^3 - 3x^2 - 3x + 9$

52 $b(x) = x^3 - 4x^2 - 2x + 8$

53 $k(x) = x^4 - x^3 - x^2$

54 $m(x) = x^4 - 10x^2 + 9$

55 $r(x) = -4x^3 + 4x^2 + 19x - 10$

56 $s(x) = -2x^3 + x^2 + 10x - 5$

57 $j(x) = -x^4 + 7x^2 - 6$

58 $k(x) = -x^4 + 2x^3 + 13x^2 - 14x - 24$

CHALLENGES

59. When $4x^3 - 3ax + 5$ is subtracted from $11x^3 + ax^2 - x + b$, the result is $cx^3 - 2x^2 + dx - 1$. Find a, b, c, and d.

60. The expression $ax^3 + 2x^2 + cx + 1$ is $5x^3 - 3$ greater than $3x^3 + bx^2 + d - 7x$. Find a, b, c, and d.

CONNECTION

61. GEOMETRY Find the total area of the faces of the rectangular prism at right.

APPLICATIONS

CDs on a conveyor belt

62. BUSINESS Polynomials are used in business to express the cost of manufacturing products. If the cubic function $C(x) = x^3 - 15x + 15$ gives the cost of manufacturing x units (in thousands) of a product, what is the cost to manufacture 10,000 units of the product?

63. BUSINESS The cost of manufacturing a certain product can be represented by $C(x) = 3x^3 - 18x + 45$, where x is the number of units of the product in hundreds. What is the cost to manufacture 20,000 units of the product?

Look Back

Let $A = \begin{bmatrix} 1 & -1 \\ 0 & 2 \end{bmatrix}$ and $B = \begin{bmatrix} -1 & 4 \\ 5 & 3 \end{bmatrix}$. **Perform each operation below.**
(LESSONS 4.1 AND 4.2)

64. $A - B$ **65.** $B - A$ **66.** $2A$ **67.** $2B$

68. AB **69.** BA **70.** $A - 4B$ **71.** $B - 3A$

Solve each equation by factoring. *(LESSON 5.2)*

72. $x^2 + 12x + 11 = 0$

73. $x^2 - 2x - 15 = 0$

74. $x^2 + 14x + 48 = 0$

75. $x^2 + 17x + 72 = 0$

76. Give an example of a perfect-square trinomial and then write it as a binomial squared. *(LESSON 5.3)*

Use the quadratic formula to solve each equation. *(LESSONS 5.5 AND 5.6)*

77. $3x^2 + 7x + 2 = 0$

78. $-2x^2 + 4x + 5 = 0$

79. $5x^2 + 2x + 4 = 0$

80. $-6x^2 + 5x - 4 = 0$

 Look Beyond

81. Sketch the graph of a cubic polynomial that intersects the *x*-axis at exactly the number of points indicated. Write *impossible* if appropriate.
   a. 3 points   **b.** 2 points   **c.** 1 point   **d.** 0 points

The bottle below has a circular base, a flat bottom, and curved sides. There is no geometric formula for the volume of a solid with this shape. In this activity, you will find a polynomial function that models the volume of a solid with this shape.

1. Obtain a bottle with a circular base, a flat bottom, and curved sides. Measure the diameter of the circular base in centimeters. Calculate the radius and the area of the circular base ($A = \pi r^2$).

2. Pour water into the bottle until the bottle is approximately half full. Place a cap on the bottle, and measure the height, h_1, in centimeters of the water. The volume in milliliters of the part of the bottle containing water, W, can be approximated by $W(r) = \pi r^2 h_1$. Calculate the approximate volume of this part of the bottle.

3. Turn the bottle upside-down, and measure the height, h_2, in centimeters of the air space above the water. The volume of the air space, A, in milliliters can be approximated by $A(r) = \pi r^2 h_2$. Calculate the approximate volume of the air space.

4. The total volume in milliliters of the bottle, V, can be modeled by the function below. Find the total volume of the bottle.

$$V(r) = W(r) + A(r)$$
$$= \pi r^2 h_1 + \pi r^2 h_2$$

WORKING ON THE CHAPTER PROJECT

You should now be able to complete Activity 1 of the Chapter Project.

Polynomial Functions and Their Graphs

Objectives

- Identify and describe the important features of the graph of a polynomial function.

- Use a polynomial function to model real-world data.

Why *You can use a polynomial function to model real-world data such as the number of high school graduates in the United States.*

APPLICATION

EDUCATION

The table below gives the number of students who graduated from high school in the United States from 1960 to 1994. The scatter plot of the data indicates an increase and then a decrease in the number of graduates since 1960. Find a quartic regression model for the data in this table. *You will solve this problem in Example 3.*

Year	Graduates	Year	Graduates
1960	1679	1978	3161
1961	1763	1979	3160
1962	1838	1980	3089
1963	1741	1981	3053
1964	2145	1982	3100
1965	2659	1983	2964
1966	2612	1984	3012
1967	2525	1985	2666
1968	2606	1986	2786
1969	2842	1987	2647
1970	2757	1988	2673
1971	2872	1989	2454
1972	2961	1990	2355
1973	3059	1991	2276
1974	3101	1992	2398
1975	3186	1993	2338
1976	2987	1994	2517
1977	3140		

Number of High School Graduates in the United States

[*Source: Statistical Abstract of the United States, 1996*]

CHECKPOINT ✔ Explain why a quadratic model with a vertex near point C in the scatter plot would not be suitable for predicting the number of graduates after 1994.

Graphs of Polynomial Functions

When a function rises and then falls over an interval from left to right, the function has a *local maximum*. If the function falls and then rises over an interval from left to right, it has a *local minimum*.

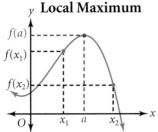

For $x \neq a$ in the interval, $f(a) > f(x)$.

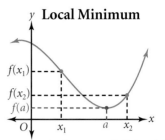

For $x \neq a$ in the interval, $f(a) < f(x)$.

Local Maximum and Minimum

$f(a)$ is a **local maximum** (plural, *local maxima*) if there is an interval around a such that $f(a) > f(x)$ for all values of x in the interval, where $x \neq a$.

$f(a)$ is a **local minimum** (plural, *local minima*) if there is an interval around a such that $f(a) < f(x)$ for all values of x in the interval, where $x \neq a$.

The points on the graph of a polynomial function that correspond to local maxima and local minima are called **turning points**. Functions change from *increasing* to *decreasing* or from *decreasing* to *increasing* at turning points. A cubic function has at most 2 turning points, and a quartic function has at most 3 turning points. In general, a polynomial function of degree n has at most $n - 1$ turning points.

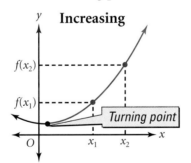

For every $x_1 < x_2$ in the interval, $f(x_1) < f(x_2)$.

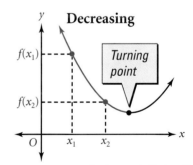

For every $x_1 < x_2$ in the interval, $f(x_1) > f(x_2)$.

Increasing and Decreasing Functions

Let x_1 and x_2 be numbers in the domain of a function, f.

The function f is **increasing** over an open interval if for every $x_1 < x_2$ in the interval, $f(x_1) < f(x_2)$.

The function f is **decreasing** over an open interval if for every $x_1 < x_2$ in the interval, $f(x_1) > f(x_2)$.

EXAMPLE ① Graph $P(x) = x^3 + 3x^2 - x - 3$.

a. Approximate any local maxima or minima to the nearest tenth.
b. Find the intervals over which the function is increasing and decreasing.

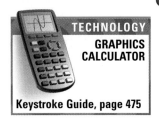

TECHNOLOGY
GRAPHICS CALCULATOR
Keystroke Guide, page 475

SOLUTION

a. The graph of P has 2 turning points, a local maximum of about 3.1, and a local minimum of about −3.1.

b. The function increases for all values of x except over the interval of approximately $-2.2 < x < 0.2$, where it decreases.

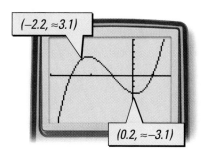
$(-2.2, \approx 3.1)$
$(0.2, \approx -3.1)$

CHECK

You can use the table feature to verify the approximate coordinates of the turning points.

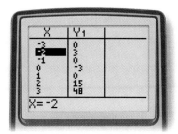

In the table above, when $x = -2$, the y-value, 3, is greater than the neighboring y-values. This indicates that the maximum point has an x-value between −3 and −1.

In the table above, the local maximum can be approximated more closely as 3.1, to the nearest tenth.

A similar procedure can be used to check the local minimum.

TRY THIS Graph $Q(x) = -x^3 + 2x^2 + x + 4$.

a. Approximate any local maxima or minima to the nearest tenth.
b. Find the intervals over which the function is increasing and decreasing.

Recall from Lesson 5.3 that a zero of a function $P(x)$ is any number r such that $P(r) = 0$. The real zeros of a polynomial function correspond to the x-intercepts of the graph of the function. For example, the graph of $P(x) = x^3 + 3x^2 - x - 3$ in Example 1 above shows zeros of P at x-values of $-3, -1,$ and 1.

Polynomial functions are one type of *continuous functions*. The graph of a **continuous function** is unbroken. The graph of a **discontinuous function** has breaks or holes in it.

Continuous Functions   **Discontinuous Functions**

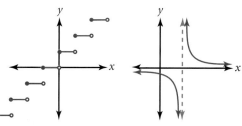

Continuity of a Polynomial Function

Every polynomial function $y = P(x)$ is continuous for all values of x.

The domain of every polynomial function is the set of all real numbers. As a result, the graph of a polynomial function extends infinitely. What happens to a polynomial function as its domain values get very small and very large is called the **end behavior** of a polynomial function.

Exploring the End Behavior of $f(x) = ax^n$

TECHNOLOGY
GRAPHICS CALCULATOR

Keystroke Guide, page 475

You will need: a graphics calculator

Graph each function separately. For each function, answer parts a–c.

1. $y = x^2$	**2.** $y = x^4$	**3.** $y = 2x^2$	**4.** $y = 2x^4$
5. $y = x^3$	**6.** $y = x^5$	**7.** $y = 2x^3$	**8.** $y = 2x^5$
9. $y = -x^2$	**10.** $y = -x^4$	**11.** $y = -2x^2$	**12.** $y = -2x^4$
13. $y = -x^3$	**14.** $y = -x^5$	**15.** $y = -2x^3$	**16.** $y = -2x^5$

  a. Is the degree of the function even or odd?
  b. Is the leading coefficient positive or negative?
  c. Does the graph rise or fall on the left? on the right?

CHECKPOINT ✔

17. Write a conjecture about the end behavior of a function of the form $f(x) = ax^n$ for each pair of conditions below. Then test each conjecture.
  a. when $a > 0$ and n is even
  b. when $a < 0$ and n is even
  c. when $a > 0$ and n is odd
  d. when $a < 0$ and n is odd

If a polynomial function is written in standard form,
$$f(x) = a_n x^n + a_{n-1} x^{n-1} + \cdots + a_1 x + a_0,$$
the **leading coefficient** is a_n. That is, the leading coefficient is the coefficient of the term of greatest degree in the polynomial.

The end behavior of a polynomial function depends on the sign of its leading coefficient and whether the degree of the polynomial is odd or even. Let P be a polynomial function of degree n and with a leading coefficient of a. There are four possible end behaviors for P. The end behavior of P can rise on the left and rise on the right (↖ ↗), fall on the left and fall on the right (↙ ↘), fall on the left and rise on the right (↙ ↗), or rise on the left and fall on the right (↖ ↘). These four possible end behaviors are summarized below.

END BEHAVIOR OF A POLYNOMIAL FUNCTION, $f(x) = ax^n + \cdots$				
	$a > 0$		$a < 0$	
	left	right	left	right
n is even.	↖ rise	rise ↗	↗ fall	fall ↘
n is odd.	↙ fall	rise ↗	↖ rise	fall ↘

EXAMPLE ② Describe the end behavior of each function.

a. $P(x) = -x^3 + x^2 + 3x - 1$ b. $Q(x) = -x + 3 - x^4 + 3x^2 + x^3$

● **SOLUTION**

a. $P(x)$ is written in standard form.

$$P(x) = -x^3 + x^2 + 3x - 1$$

The degree of P is 3, which is odd, so the graph will rise at one end and fall at the other end. The leading coefficient is negative, so the graph rises on the left and falls on the right.

b. Write $Q(x)$ in standard form.

$$Q(x) = -x^4 + x^3 + 3x^2 - x + 3$$

The degree of Q is 4, which is even, so its graph will either rise at both ends or fall at both ends. The leading coefficient is negative, so the graph falls on the left and the right.

CHECK
Graph $y = -x^3 + x^2 + 3x - 1$.

CHECK
Graph $y = -x^4 + x^3 + 3x^2 - x + 3$.

TECHNOLOGY
GRAPHICS CALCULATOR

Keystroke Guide, page 475

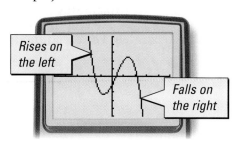

Rises on the left

Falls on the right

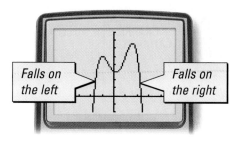

Falls on the left

Falls on the right

TRY THIS Describe the end behavior of each function.

a. $P(x) = -6x^2 + x^3 + 32$ b. $Q(x) = x^4 + x^3 - 2x^2 + 1$

Modeling With Polynomial Functions

You can use a polynomial of degree 3 or higher to fit a data set that has more than one local maximum and minimum.

EXAMPLE ③ Selected data from the table at the beginning of the lesson are given at right.

CONNECTION
STATISTICS

	A	B	C	D	E
x	10	18	30	41	44
y	1679	2606	3089	2276	2517

a. Find a quartic regression model for the number of high school graduates in the United States from 1960 to 1994.

b. Use your quartic regression model to estimate the number of high school graduates in 1970. Compare the value given by the regression model with the actual data value given for 1970.

TECHNOLOGY
GRAPHICS CALCULATOR

Keystroke Guide, page 475

● **SOLUTION**

a. Make a scatter plot of the selected data points, and find the quartic regression model. The calculator gives the following quartic regression model:

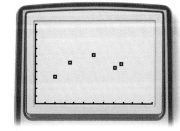

$$P(x) \approx 0.02x^4 - 1.94x^3 + 63.67x^2 - 723.74x + 4296.30$$

b. Because x represents the number of years since 1950, $x = 20$ represents the year 1970. Find $P(20)$.

The quartic model gives the number of high school graduates (in thousandths) in 1970 as 2850. The actual value given in the table is 2757, which differs by only 93 students.

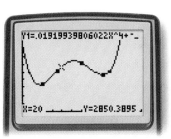

TRY THIS   Find a quartic regression model for the data in the table below.

x	2	5	6	9	11
y	4	16	11	14	9

CRITICAL THINKING   The function in Example 3 models the number of high school graduates for the period from 1960 to 1994. Explain why this function may not be a good model for estimating the number of high school graduates after 1994.

Exercises

● *Communicate*

1. Describe the graph of $f(x) = 2x^2 + x^3 + 3x + 1$. Include any turning points, its continuity, and its end behavior.

2. Using your own words, define a local maximum and a local minimum.

3. Describe the four possibilities for the end behavior of the graph of a polynomial function.

4. Using your own words, define increasing and decreasing functions.

● *Guided Skills Practice*

5 Graph $P(x) = x^3 + x^2 - 2x$. Approximate any local maxima or minima to the nearest tenth. Find the intervals over which the function is increasing and decreasing. *(EXAMPLE 1)*

Describe the end behavior of each function. *(EXAMPLE 2)*

6. $P(x) = x^6 + x^4 + x + 1$ **7.** $P(x) = x^4 + 1 + x^3 - x^5$

8 Find a quartic regression model for the data in the table below. *(EXAMPLE 3)*

x	1	2	3	4	5
y	2	3	2	1	5

Practice and Apply

Graph each function and approximate any local maxima or minima to the nearest tenth.

9 $P(x) = x^3 - 3x + 3$

10 $P(x) = -x^3 + 4x - 2$

11 $P(x) = 2x^3 - 4x + 1$

12 $P(x) = 3x - 3 - 3x^3$

13 $P(x) = -2x + 3 + x^2$

14 $P(x) = -x^2 + 6x - 11$

15 $P(x) = x^4 - 5x^2 + 2$

16 $P(x) = -x^4 + x^3 + 4x^2 - 3$

17 $P(x) = -3x^3 + 3x + x^4 + 3$

18 $P(x) = 3x^3 - x^4 - 3x - 3$

Graph each function. Find any local maxima or minima to the nearest tenth. Find the intervals over which the function is increasing and decreasing.

19 $P(x) = x^3 - 4x; -8 \leq x \leq 8$

20 $P(x) = -2x^3 + 3x; -5 \leq x \leq 5$

21 $P(x) = x^4 - 2x^2 + 2; -5 \leq x \leq 5$

22 $P(x) = -x^4 + 3x^2 + 3; -5 \leq x \leq 5$

23 $P(x) = -x^2 + 4x - 1; -5 \leq x \leq 10$

24 $P(x) = x^2 - 6x + 7; -5 \leq x \leq 10$

25 $P(x) = x^4 - 3x^3 + 3x + 3; -2 \leq x \leq 5$

26 $P(x) = -x^4 + 3x^3 - 3x - 3; -2 \leq x \leq 5$

27 $P(x) = x^3 - 3x + 3; -3 \leq x \leq 4$

28 $P(x) = -x^3 + 4x - 2; -3 \leq x \leq 3$

Describe the end behavior of each function.

29. $P(x) = 2x^3 + x^2 + 3x + 2$

30. $P(x) = -3x^3 + 5x^2 + x + 2$

31. $P(x) = 6x + 1 - x^2$

32. $P(x) = x^2 - 8x + 3$

33. $P(x) = 4x^4 + x^5 + 1 + 3x^3$

34. $P(x) = x^6 + x^4 + 3x^2 + 2$

35. $P(x) = 7x^3 + 2 - 8x^5$

36. $P(x) = 5x^4 - 6x^6 + 3x + 2$

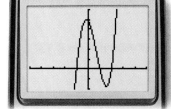

37 The function $y = 10x^3 - 25x^2 + x^4 - 10x + 24$ is graphed at left. Explain how you can tell that the viewing window chosen here does not show all of the important characteristics of the graph. Find a viewing window that does show all of the important characteristics of the graph.

CHALLENGE

38 Solve a system of equations by using a matrix equation to find the coefficients a_3, a_2, a_1, and a_0 such that the polynomial function $P(x) = a_3x^3 + a_2x^2 + a_1x + a_0$ passes through the points $(0, 0)$, $(1, 1)$, $(2, 0)$, and $(3, 2)$.

CONNECTION

STATISTICS Find a quartic regression model for each data set.

39

x	1	2	3	4	5
y	1	−2	3	0	1

40

x	1	2	3	4	5
y	0	4	3	1	4

41

x	2	4	6	8	10
y	3	−1	4	−3	4

42

x	−1	0	2	4	5
y	2	1	1	6	3

APPLICATION

43 REAL ESTATE The median monthly rent (in dollars) in the United States for 1988 through 1996 is given in the table below. Find a quartic regression model for the data by using $x = 0$ for 1980. [*Source: U.S. Bureau of Census*]

1988	1989	1990	1991	1992	1993	1994	1995	1996
343	346	371	398	411	430	429	438	444

APPLICATION

44 TRAVEL The number of business and pleasure travelers (in thousands) to the United States from Canada is given in the table below for certain years. Find a quartic regression model for the data by using $x = 0$ for 1980. [*Source: U.S. Travel and Tourism Administration*]

1985	1989	1990	1991	1992	1993	1994	1995
10,721	15,325	17,263	19,113	18,596	17,293	14,970	13,668

Look Back

Find the inverse of each matrix, if it exists. If the inverse does not exist, write *no inverse*. (LESSON 4.3)

45 $\begin{bmatrix} 1 & 1 \\ 1 & 1 \end{bmatrix}$ **46** $\begin{bmatrix} 1 & 3 \\ 1 & 2 \end{bmatrix}$ **47** $\begin{bmatrix} 2 & 5 \\ 4 & 11 \end{bmatrix}$ **48** $\begin{bmatrix} 2 & 2 \\ 4 & 4 \end{bmatrix}$

Solve each quadratic equation. Give exact solutions. (LESSON 5.2)

49. $x^2 - 50 = 0$ **50.** $(x + 3)^2 - 36 = 0$ **51.** $3(x - 1)^2 = 12$

Solve each logarithmic equation. (LESSON 6.3)

52. $\log 1000 = x$ **53.** $\log_x 8 = 3$ **54.** $\log_3 x = 2$ **55.** $\log_x 1 = 0$

Look Beyond

56. Find $(x + y)(x^2 - xy + y^2)$.   **57.** Find $(x - y)(x^2 + xy + y^2)$.

Examining the behavior of a polynomial function can often provide insight into the real-world situation that the function models.

1. Graph each function in a viewing window that includes all of the x- and y-intercepts. For each function, answer questions **a** and **b** below.
   $f(x) = x^2 - 2x + 1$ $g(x) = x^3 - 3x + 2$
   $h(x) = x^4 - 4x + 3$ $j(x) = x^5 - 5x + 4$

   a. Describe the shape of the graph, and state the number of local maxima and minima.
   b. Does the function have any zeros that are local maxima or minima?

2. Compare the graphs of the functions from Step 1. How are they alike? How are they different?

3. Refer to the bottle from the Portfolio Activity on page 431. If height h_1 is 1 unit less than the radius, r, and height h_2 is 2 units less than the radius, r, write a function for the total volume, V, in terms of r.

4. Graph the function you wrote in Step 3, and describe the graph. Explain how the graph relates to the real-world situation that it models.

WORKING ON THE CHAPTER PROJECT

You should now be able to complete Activity 2 of the Chapter Project.

Products and Factors of Polynomials

Why
You can use the factored form of a polynomial function to create a model for the volume of an open-top box.

Objectives

- Multiply polynomials, and divide one polynomial by another by using long division and synthetic division.

- Use the Remainder and Factor Theorems to solve problems.

Making an open-top box out of a single rectangular sheet involves cutting and folding square flaps at each of the corners. These flaps are then pasted to the adjacent side to provide reinforcement for the corners.

The dimensions of the rectangular sheet and the square flaps determine the volume of the resulting box. For the 12-inch-by-16-inch sheet shown, the volume function is $V(x) = x(16 - 2x)(12 - 2x)$, where x is the side length in inches of the square flap.

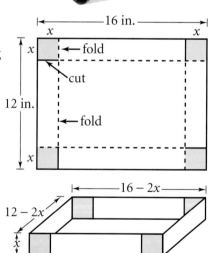

Multiplying Polynomials

E X A M P L E   **1** Write the volume function for the open-top box, $V(x) = x(16 - 2x)(12 - 2x)$, as a polynomial function in standard form.

SOLUTION

$$
\begin{aligned}
x(16 - 2x)(12 - 2x) &= x[(16 - 2x)(12 - 2x)] \\
&= x[16(12 - 2x) - 2x(12 - 2x)] \\
&= x(192 - 32x - 24x + 4x^2) \\
&= x(192 - 56x + 4x^2) \\
&= 192x - 56x^2 + 4x^3 \\
&= 4x^3 - 56x^2 + 192x
\end{aligned}
$$

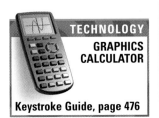

TECHNOLOGY

GRAPHICS CALCULATOR

Keystroke Guide, page 476

CHECK

You can check your multiplication by graphing the polynomial function in factored form and in standard form. If the graphs coincide, then the functions are equivalent.

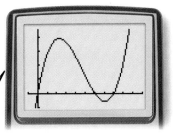

The graphs of Y1 = x(16 − 2x)(12 − 2x) and Y2 = 4x³ − 56x² + 192x appear to coincide.

TRY THIS   Write $f(x) = 2x^2(x^2 + 2)(x - 3)$ as a polynomial in standard form.

Factoring Polynomials

Just as a quadratic expression is factored by writing it as a product of two factors, a polynomial expression of a degree greater than 2 is factored by writing it as a product of more than two factors.

E X A M P L E **2** Factor each polynomial.

     a. $x^3 - 5x^2 - 6x$ **b.** $x^3 + 4x^2 + 2x + 8$

● **SOLUTION**

     a. $x^3 - 5x^2 - 6x = x(x^2 - 5x - 6)$ *Factor out the GCF, x.*

                         $= x(x - 6)(x + 1)$ *Factor the trinomial into binomials.*

     b. The polynomial $x^3 + 4x^2 + 2x + 8$ can be factored in pairs.

       $x^3 + 4x^2 + 2x + 8 = (x^3 + 4x^2) + (2x + 8)$ *Group the terms in pairs.*

                        $= x^2(x + 4) + 2(x + 4)$ *Factor each pair of terms.*

                        $= (x^2 + 2)(x + 4)$ *Factor (x + 4) from each term.*

TRY THIS   Factor the polynomials $x^3 - 9x$ and $x^3 - x^2 + 2x - 2$.

Factoring the Sum and Difference of Two Cubes

$a^3 + b^3 = (a + b)(a^2 - ab + b^2)$ $a^3 - b^3 = (a - b)(a^2 + ab + b^2)$

E X A M P L E **3** Factor each polynomial.

     a. $x^3 + 27$ **b.** $x^3 - 1$

● **SOLUTION**

     a. $x^3 + 27 = x^3 + 3^3$ **b.** $x^3 - 1 = x^3 - 1^3$

                $= (x + 3)(x^3 - 3x + 9)$ $= (x - 1)(x^2 + x + 1)$

TRY THIS   Factor the polynomials $x^3 + 1000$ and $x^3 - 125$.

The *Factor Theorem*, given below, states the relationship between the linear factors of a polynomial expression and the zeros of the related polynomial function.

Factor Theorem

$x - r$ is a factor of the polynomial expression that defines the function P if and only if r is a solution of $P(x) = 0$, that is, if and only if $P(r) = 0$.

With the Factor Theorem, you can test for linear factors involving integers by using substitution.

E X A M P L E **4** **Use substitution to determine whether $x + 2$ is a factor of $x^3 - 2x^2 - 5x + 6$.**

TECHNOLOGY
GRAPHICS CALCULATOR

Keystroke Guide, page 476

SOLUTION

Write the related function, $f(x) = x^3 - 2x^2 - 5x + 6$.

Write $x + 2$ as $x - (-2)$.

Find $f(-2)$.

$f(-2) = (-2)^3 - 2(-2)^2 - 5(-2) + 6$
$\quad\quad = 0$

Because $f(-2) = 0$, the Factor Theorem states that $x + 2$ is a factor of $x^3 - 2x^2 - 5x + 6$.

CHECK

Graph $y = x^3 - 2x^2 - 5x + 6$.

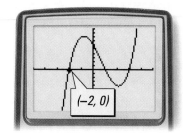

The graph confirms that -2 is a zero of the related function.

TRY THIS Use substitution to determine whether $x + 3$ is a factor of $x^3 - 3x^2 - 6x + 8$.

Dividing Polynomials

A multiplication equation can be rewritten as two or more division equations.

$$x^3 + 3x^2 - 4x - 12 = (x^2 + 5x + 6)(x - 2)$$

$$\frac{x^3 + 3x^2 - 4x - 12}{x^2 + 5x + 6} = x - 2 \qquad \frac{x^3 + 3x^2 - 4x - 12}{x - 2} = x^2 + 5x + 6$$

A polynomial can be divided by a divisor of the form $x - r$ by using **long division** or a shortened form of long division called **synthetic division**.

Long division of polynomials is similar to long division of real numbers. Examine the division of $\frac{x^3 + 3x^2 - 4x - 12}{x - 2}$ shown at right.

Long Division

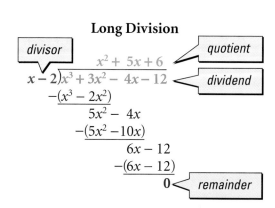

In synthetic division, you do not write the variables.

Synthetic Division

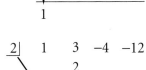

Step 1: Write the coefficients of the polynomial $x^3 + 3x^2 - 4x - 12$, and then write the r-value, 2, of the divisor, $x - 2$, on the left. Write the first coefficient, 1, below the line.

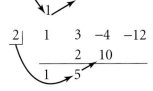

Step 2: Multiply the r-value, 2, by the number below the line, and write the product below the next coefficient.

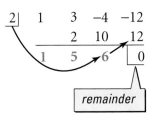

Step 3: Write the *sum* (not the difference) of 3 and 2 below the line. Multiply 2 by the number below the line, and write the product below the next coefficient.

Step 4: Write the sum of -4 and 10 below the line. Multiply 2 by the number below the line, and write the product below the next coefficient.

The remainder is 0, and the resulting numbers, 1, 5, and 6, are the coefficients of the quotient, $x^2 + 5x + 6$.

Synthetic division can be used to divide a polynomial only by a linear binomial of the form $x - r$. When dividing by nonlinear divisors, long division must be used. This is shown in Example 5.

E X A M P L E 5 Find the quotient. $(x^3 + 3x^2 + 3x + 2) \div (x^2 + x + 1)$

SOLUTION

Step 1: Divide the first term of the **dividend** by the first term of the **divisor**:
$x^3 \div x^2 = x$.

Step 2: Write x in the **quotient** and use it to multiply the **divisor**:
$x(x^2 + x + 1)$.

Step 3: Subtract the product, $x^3 + x^2 + x$, from the **dividend**.

Step 4: Repeat Steps 1–3, using the difference from Step 3 as the new dividend.

$$
\begin{array}{r}
x + 2 \\
x^2 + x + 1\overline{)x^3 + 3x^2 + 3x + 2} \\
-(x^3 + x^2 + x) \\
\hline
2x^2 + 2x + 2 \\
-(2x^2 + 2x + 2) \\
\hline
0
\end{array}
$$

quotient

dividend

divisor

remainder

$$(x^3 + 3x^2 + 3x + 2) \div (x^2 + x + 1) = x + 2$$

TRY THIS Find the quotient. $(x^3 + 3x^2 - 13x - 15) \div (x^2 - 2x - 3)$

If there is a nonzero remainder after dividing with either method, it is usually written as the numerator of a fraction, with the divisor as the denominator.

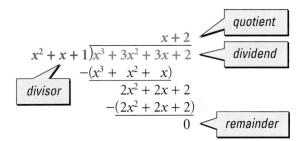

$$(x^3 + 48) \div (x + 3) = x^2 - 3x + 9 + \frac{21}{x + 3}$$

EXAMPLE ⑥ Given that 2 is a zero of $P(x) = x^3 + x - 10$, use division to factor $x^3 + x - 10$.

● **SOLUTION**

Method 1 Use long division.

$$
\begin{array}{r}
x^2 + 2x + 5 \\
x - 2{\overline{\smash{\big)}\,x^3 + 0x^2 + x - 10}} \\
\underline{-(x^3 - 2x^2)} \\
2x^2 + x \\
\underline{-(2x^2 - 4x)} \\
5x - 10 \\
\underline{-(5x - 10)} \\
0
\end{array}
$$

Method 2 Use synthetic division.

$$
\begin{array}{r|rrrr}
2 & 1 & 0 & 1 & -10 \\
  &   & 2 & 4 & 10 \\
\hline
  & 1 & 2 & 5 & \boxed{0}
\end{array}
$$

Notice that zeros are used for the coefficients of terms that do not exist.

Quotient: $x^2 + 2x + 5$

Thus, $x^3 + x - 10 = (x - 2)(x^2 + 2x + 5)$.   *$x^2 + 2x + 5$ cannot be factored.*

TRY THIS Given that −3 is a zero of $P(x) = x^3 - 13x - 12$, use division to factor $x^3 - 13x - 12$.

CRITICAL THINKING Explain why you add the products in synthetic division instead of subtracting them as in long division.

Given $P(x) = 2x^3 + 7x^2 + 2x + 1$, the *Remainder Theorem* states that $P(-3)$ is the value of the remainder when $2x^3 + 7x^2 + 2x + 1$ is divided by $x + 3$.

synthetic division:

$$
\begin{array}{r|rrrr}
-3 & 2 & 7 & 2 & 1 \\
   &   & -6 & -3 & 3 \\
\hline
   & 2 & 1 & -1 & \boxed{4}
\end{array}
$$

The remainder is 4.

substitution:

$$P(x) = 2x^3 + 7x^2 + 2x + 1$$
$$P(-3) = 2(-3)^3 + 7(-3)^2 + 2(-3) + 1 = 4$$

Remainder Theorem

If the polynomial expression that defines the function of P is divided by $x - a$, then the remainder is the number $P(a)$.

EXAMPLE ⑦ Given $P(x) = 2x^3 + 7x^2 + 2x + 1$, find $P(5)$.

● **SOLUTION**

Method 1 Use synthetic division.

$$
\begin{array}{r|rrrr}
5 & 2 & 7 & 2 & 1 \\
  &   & 10 & 85 & 435 \\
\hline
  & 2 & 17 & 87 & \boxed{436}
\end{array}
$$

Thus, $P(5) = 436$.

Method 2 Use substitution.

$$P(x) = 2x^3 + 7x^2 + 2x + 1$$
$$P(5) = 2(5)^3 + 7(5)^2 + 2(5) + 1$$
$$= 250 + 175 + 10 + 1$$
$$= 436$$

TRY THIS Given $P(x) = 3x^3 + 2x^2 - 3x + 4$, find $P(3)$.

CHAPTER 7

Exercises

Communicate

1. Describe how the Factor Theorem can be used to determine whether $x + 1$ is a factor of $x^3 - 2x^2 - 8x - 5$.

2. Describe the condition necessary to use synthetic division to divide polynomials.

3. Explain how to use the Remainder Theorem to evaluate $P(5)$ if P is a polynomial function.

Guided Skills Practice

4. Write $P(x) = x(10 - x)(2 + x)$ as a polynomial function in standard form. *(EXAMPLE 1)*

Factor each polynomial. *(EXAMPLES 2 AND 3)*

5. $x^3 - 5x^2 + 6x$ 6. $x^3 + 5x^2 + 3x + 15$ 7. $x^3 - 216$

8. Use substitution to determine whether $x + 2$ is a factor of $x^3 + 4x^2 + 5x + 2$. *(EXAMPLE 4)*

9. Find the quotient. $(x^3 + 4x^2 + 4x + 3) \div (x^2 + x + 1)$ *(EXAMPLE 5)*

Given that –3 is a zero of $P(x) = x^3 - 14x - 15$, use each method below to factor $x^3 - 14x - 15$. *(EXAMPLE 6)*

10. long division   11. synthetic division

Given $P(x) = 2x^3 + 3x^2 + 4x + 1$, find $P(2)$ by using each method below. *(EXAMPLE 7)*

12. synthetic division   13. substitution

Practice and Apply

Write each product as a polynomial in standard form.

14. $3x^2(4x^3 - 2x^2 + 5x + 2)$ 15. $2x^3(4x^3 - 2x^2 + x + 3)$

16. $(2x - 3)(x + 4)$ 17. $(x + 7)(5x - 3)$

18. $(x + 2)(x^2 + 4x + 1)$ 19. $(x + 3)(2x^3 + 3x^2 + 1)$

20. $(2x + 3)(x^3 - 5x^2 + 4)$ 21. $(2x + 1)(x^2 - 4x - 3)$

22. $(x - 4)(2x^3 - 3x^2 + 2)$ 23. $(x - 5)(-3x^3 - 4x - 1)$

24. $(x - 3)(2 - x)(x - 1)$ 25. $(x - 2)(2x + 3)(3 - x)$

26. $(x + 1)^2(x - 2)$ 27. $(2x - 4)(x + 1)^2$

28. $(2x + 1)^3$ 29. $(3x + 2)^3$

30. $(x - 1)^2(x^2 - 3x + 2)$ 31. $(-3x^2 - x + 2)(x + 1)^2$

32. $\left(x - \frac{5}{7}\right)\left(\frac{2}{5}x^2 - \frac{1}{5}x + \frac{3}{5}\right)$ 33. $\left(x - \frac{1}{4}\right)\left(\frac{2}{3}x^2 + \frac{1}{3}x + \frac{2}{3}\right)$

Factor each polynomial.

34. $x^3 + 8x^2 + 15x$ **35.** $x^3 + 6x^2 + 8x$ **36.** $x^3 - 10x^2 + 24x$

37. $x^3 + 2x^2 - 3x$ **38.** $x^3 - x^2 - 30x$ **39.** $x^3 - 2x^2 - 3x$

40. $3x^3 - 300x$ **41.** $18x^3 - 60x^2 + 50x$ **42.** $x^3 + 3x^2 - 2x - 6$

43. $x^3 - 3x^2 + 4x - 12$ **44.** $x^3 + 3x^2 - x - 3$ **45.** $x^3 - 2x^2 - 5x + 10$

46. $x^3 + x^2 + x + 1$ **47.** $1 - x + x^2 - x^3$ **48.** $x^3 + 2x^2 + 14x + 7x^2$

49. $x^3 + x^2 + 2 + 2x$ **50.** $x^3 - 64$ **51.** $x^3 + 1000$

52. $x^6 + 125$ **53.** $x^6 + 27$ **54.** $x^3 - 8$

55. $x^3 - 216$ **56.** $8x^3 - 1$ **57.** $27x^3 - 125$

58. $x^6 - 1$ **59.** $64 - x^3$ **60.** $27 + 8x^3$

Use substitution to determine whether the given linear expression is a factor of the polynomial.

61. $x^2 + x + 1;\ x - 1$ **62.** $x^2 + 2x + 1;\ x + 2$

63. $x^3 + 3x^2 - 33x - 35;\ x + 1$ **64.** $x^3 + 5x^2 - 18x - 48;\ x + 6$

65. $x^3 + 3x^2 - 18x - 40;\ x - 4$ **66.** $x^3 - 8x^2 + 9x + 18;\ x - 6$

67. $x^3 + 6x^2 - x - 30;\ x - 2$ **68.** $x^3 - x^2 - 17x - 15;\ x + 3$

69. $2x^3 + 9x^2 + 6x + 8;\ x + 4$ **70.** $2x^3 - x^2 - 12x - 9;\ x - 3$

Divide by using long division.

71. $(x^2 + 4x + 4) \div (x + 2)$ **72.** $(x^2 - 3x + 2) \div (x - 1)$

73. $(x^3 - 7x - 6) \div (x + 1)$ **74.** $(x^3 + 11x^2 + 39x + 45) \div (x + 5)$

75. $(3x^2 - x + x^3 - 3) \div (x^2 + 4x + 3)$ **76.** $(x^3 + 6x^2 - x - 30) \div (x^2 + 8x + 15)$

77. $(x^3 - 43x + 42) \div (x^2 + 6x - 7)$ **78.** $(10x - 5x^2 + x^3 - 24) \div (x^2 - x + 6)$

79. $\left(x^2 - \frac{1}{6}x - \frac{1}{6}\right) \div \left(x - \frac{1}{2}\right)$ **80.** $\left(x^2 + \frac{1}{2}x - \frac{3}{16}\right) \div \left(x + \frac{3}{4}\right)$

Divide by using synthetic division.

81. $(x^2 - 4x - 12) \div (x - 4)$ **82.** $(x^2 - 3x + 2) \div (x - 1)$

83. $(x^3 + x^2 - 9x - 9) \div (x + 1)$ **84.** $(x^3 - 2x^2 - 22x + 40) \div (x - 4)$

85. $(x^3 + 5x^2 - 18) \div (x + 3)$ **86.** $(x^3 - 27) \div (x - 3)$

87. $(x^3 + 3) \div (x - 1)$ **88.** $(x^2 - 6) \div (x + 4)$

89. $(x^4 - 3x + 2x^3 - 6) \div (x - 2)$ **90.** $(x^5 + 6x^3 - 5x^4 + 5x - 15) \div (x - 3)$

For each function below, use synthetic division and substitution to find the indicated value.

91. $P(x) = x^2 + 1;\ P(1)$ **92.** $P(x) = x^2 + 1;\ P(2)$

93. $P(x) = x^2 + x;\ P(2)$ **94.** $P(x) = x^2 + x;\ P(1)$

95. $P(x) = 4x^2 - 2x + 3;\ P(3)$ **96.** $P(x) = 3x^3 + 2x^2 + 3x + 1;\ P(-2)$

97. $P(x) = 2x^4 + x^3 - 3x^2 + 2x;\ P(-4)$ **98.** $P(x) = 2x^3 - 3x^2 + 2x - 2;\ P(3)$

CHALLENGE

Find the value of k that makes the linear expression a factor of the cubic expression.

99. $x^3 + 3x^2 - x + k;\ x - 2$ **100.** $kx^3 - 2x^2 + x - 6;\ x + 3$

101. MANUFACTURING An open-top box is made from a 14-inch-by-32-inch piece of cardboard, as shown at right. The volume of the box is represented by $V(x) = x(14 - 2x)(32 - 2x)$, where x is the height of the box.

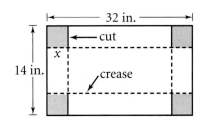
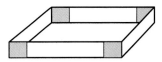

a. Write the volume of the box as a polynomial function in standard form.

b. Find the volume of the box if the height is 2 inches.

102. PACKAGING A pizza box with a lid is made from a 19-inch-by-40-inch piece of cardboard, as shown below. The volume of the pizza box is represented by $V(x) = \frac{1}{2}x(19 - 2x)(40 - 5x)$, where x is the height of the box.

a. Write the volume of the box as a polynomial function in standard form.

b. Find the volume of the box if its height is 2 inches.

c. Find the volume of the box if its height is 2.5 inches.

 Look Back

103. Solve $x + 3 \le 3(x - 1)$ for x. Graph the solution on a number line. *(LESSON 1.7)*

104. Does the set of ordered pairs $\{(2, 3), (3, 5), (4, 3)\}$ represent a function? Explain. *(LESSON 2.3)*

Factor each expression. *(LESSON 5.3)*

105. $5a^2 - 5b^2$ **106.** $2x^2 - 32y^2$ **107.** $n^2 + n - 12$

108. $5 - 6s + s^2$ **109.** $4x^2 + 4x + 1$ **110.** $2x^2 + 11x + 15$

Solve for x. Round your answers to the nearest hundredth.
(LESSONS 6.3 AND 6.6)

111. $10^x = 32$ **112.** $3^x = 7$ **113.** $e^x = 5$ **114.** $e^{2x} = 7$

Look Beyond

115. If $f(x) = x^3 + 4x^2 - 3x - 18$ and $f(2) = 0$, how many other values of x are zeros of f? How many times does the graph of f cross the x-axis?

Solving Polynomial Equations

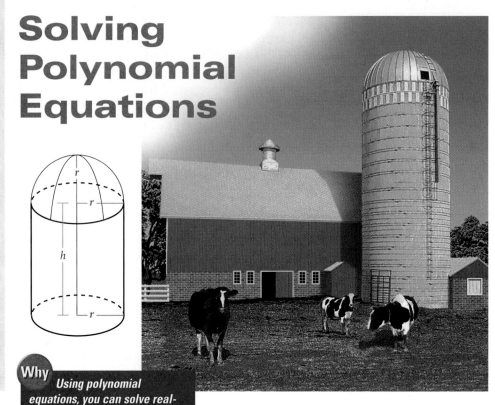

Objectives

- Solve polynomial equations.

- Find the real zeros of polynomial functions and state the multiplicity of each.

Why *Using polynomial equations, you can solve real-world problems such as finding the radius needed for the base of a grain silo in order to have a desired volume.*

CONNECTION
GEOMETRY

A silo that stores grain is often shaped as a cylinder with a hemispherical top (dome), as shown above. From geometry, you know that the volume of the cylinder, C, is represented by $C(r) = \pi r^2 h$ and that the volume of the hemispherical top, H, is represented by $H(r) = \left(\frac{1}{2}\right)\left(\frac{4}{3}\pi r^3\right)$, or $\frac{2}{3}\pi r^3$. Therefore, the total volume of the silo is given by the function T below.

$$T(r) = H(r) + C(r)$$
$$= \frac{2}{3}\pi r^3 + \pi r^2 h$$

A farmer wants to design a silo whose cylindrical part has a height of 20 feet. Approximately what radius of the cylinder and hemispherical top will give a total volume of 1830 cubic feet? To answer this question, you will solve a polynomial equation. *You will answer this question in Example 4.*

EXAMPLE ① Use factoring to solve $2x^3 - 7x^2 + 3x = 0$.

● **SOLUTION**

$$2x^3 - 7x^2 + 3x = 0$$
$$x(2x^2 - 7x + 3) = 0 \qquad \textit{Factor out the GCF.}$$
$$x(2x - 1)(x - 3) = 0 \qquad \textit{Factor the remaining trinomial.}$$
$$x = 0 \quad or \quad 2x - 1 = 0 \quad or \quad x - 3 = 0 \qquad \textit{Use the Zero-Product Property.}$$
$$x = \frac{1}{2} \qquad\qquad x = 3$$

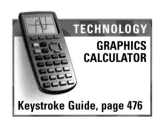

CHECK

Graph $y = 2x^3 - 7x^2 + 3x$, and look for any zeros of the function.

The graph of $y = 2x^3 - 7x^2 + 3x$ confirms that the solutions of $2x^3 - 7x^2 + 3x = 0$ are $x = 0$, $x = \frac{1}{2}$, and $x = 3$.

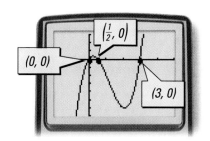

TRY THIS Use factoring to solve $2x^3 + x^2 - 6x = 0$.

The polynomial equation in Example 1 has three linear factors and three distinct solutions, or **roots.** Some polynomial equations have factors (and roots) that occur more than once, as shown in Example 2.

E X A M P L E ❷ **Use a graph, synthetic division, and factoring to find all of the roots of $x^3 - 7x^2 + 15x - 9 = 0$.**

● **SOLUTION**

PROBLEM SOLVING

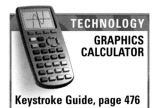

Use a graph of the related function to approximate the roots. Then use synthetic division to test your choices.

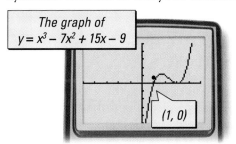

The graph of $y = x^3 - 7x^2 + 15x - 9$

(1, 0)

$$\begin{array}{r|rrrr} 1 & 1 & -7 & 15 & -9 \\ & & 1 & -6 & 9 \\ \hline & 1 & -6 & 9 & \boxed{0} \end{array}$$

The remainder is 0.

The quotient is $x^2 - 6x + 9$.

Since the remainder is 0, $x - 1$ is a factor of $x^3 - 7x^2 + 15x - 9$.

$$x^3 - 7x^2 + 15x - 9 = 0$$
$$(x - 1)(x^2 - 6x + 9) = 0 \qquad \textit{Factor out x - 1.}$$
$$(x - 1)(x - 3)^2 = 0 \qquad \textit{Factor the remaining trinomial.}$$
$$x - 1 = 0 \quad or \quad x - 3 = 0 \quad or \quad x - 3 = 0 \quad \textit{Use the Zero-Product Property.}$$
$$x = 1 \qquad\qquad x = 3 \qquad\qquad x = 3$$

The roots of $x^3 - 7x^2 + 15x - 9 = 0$ are 1 and 3, with the root 3 occurring twice.

TRY THIS Use a graph, synthetic division, and factoring to find all of the roots of $x^3 + 2x^2 - 4x - 8 = 0$.

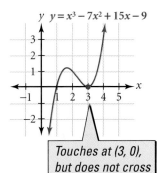

Touches at (3, 0), but does not cross

If $x - r$ is a factor that occurs m times in the factorization of a polynomial expression, P, then r is a root with **multiplicity** m of the related polynomial equation, $P = 0$. In Example 2 above, 3 is a root with multiplicity 2 of the equation $x^3 - 7x^2 + 15x - 9 = 0$.

When r is a root with *even multiplicity*, then the graph of the related function *will touch but not cross* the x-axis at $(r, 0)$. This is shown at left for the related function from Example 2 above.

In general, you cannot tell the multiplicity of a root by a graph of the related function alone. The graph may appear to touch but actually cross the x-axis.

Sometimes polynomials can be factored by using *variable substitution*. This is shown in Example 3.

E X A M P L E ③ Use variable substitution and factoring to find all of the roots of
$x^4 - 4x^2 + 3 = 0$.

● **SOLUTION**

PROBLEM SOLVING

1. Solve a simpler problem. The expression $x^4 - 4x^2 + 3$ can be put in the form of a factorable quadratic expression by substituting u for x^2. Solve the resulting equation for u.

$$x^4 - 4x^2 + 3 = 0$$
$$(x^2)^2 - 4(x^2) + 3 = 0$$
$$u^2 - 4u + 3 = 0$$
$$(u - 1)(u - 3) = 0$$
$$u = 1 \ or \ u = 3$$

2. Replace u with x^2, and solve for x by using the Zero-Product Property.

$$x^2 = 1 \quad or \quad x^2 = 3$$
$$x = \pm\sqrt{1} \qquad x = \pm\sqrt{3}$$

The roots of $x^4 - 4x^2 + 3 = 0$ are $\sqrt{1}, -\sqrt{1}, \sqrt{3},$ and $-\sqrt{3}$.

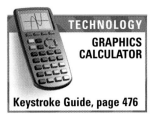

TECHNOLOGY

GRAPHICS CALCULATOR

Keystroke Guide, page 476

CHECK

Graph $y = x^4 - 4x^2 + 3$, and look for any zeros of the function.

Because $\sqrt{3} \approx 1.73$ and $\sqrt{1} = 1$, the graph of $y = x^4 - 4x^2 + 3$ confirms that the roots of the related equation are $-\sqrt{3}, -\sqrt{1}, \sqrt{1},$ and $\sqrt{3}$.

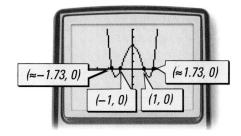

$(\approx -1.73, 0)$ $(\approx 1.73, 0)$
$(-1, 0)$ $(1, 0)$

TRY THIS

Use variable substitution and factoring to find all of the roots of $x^4 - 9x^2 + 14 = 0$.

CRITICAL THINKING

Let a, b, and c be real numbers. Find all roots of $ax^3 + bx^2 + cx = 0$, where $a \neq 0$. Classify the roots as real or complex.

Finding Real Zeros

The *Location Principle*, given below, can be used to find real zeros.

Location Principle

If P is a polynomial function and $P(x_1)$ and $P(x_2)$ have opposite signs, then there is a real number r between x_1 and x_2 that is a zero of P, that is, $P(r) = 0$.

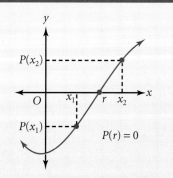

The graph of $P(x) = x^3 - 4x + 2$ at right shows that when x is 1, $P(x) < 0$, and when x is 2, $P(x) > 0$.

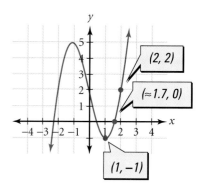

(2, 2)

(≈1.7, 0)

(1, −1)

According to the Location Principle, there is a zero of $P(x) = x^3 - 4x + 2$ somewhere between 1 and 2. It is about 1.7.

When you use a graph to find a zero of a continuous function, you are actually using the Location Principle.

CHECKPOINT ✔ Graph $y = x^2 + 2$. Use the graph and the Location Principle to explain why $y = x^2 + 2$ has no real zeros.

E X A M P L E ④ Refer to the silo described at the beginning of the lesson.

What radius of the cylinder and hemispherical top gives a total volume of 1830 cubic feet if the cylinder's height is 20 feet?

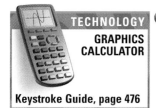

TECHNOLOGY
GRAPHICS
CALCULATOR

Keystroke Guide, page 476

SOLUTION

The total volume is represented by $T(r) = \frac{2}{3}\pi r^3 + \pi r^2 h$. Substituting 20 for the height and 1830 for the total volume gives $1830 = \frac{2}{3}\pi r^3 + 20\pi r^2$.

Solve for r by graphing the related function, $y = \frac{2}{3}\pi x^3 + 20\pi x^2 - 1830$, and approximating the real zeros.

The only reasonable radius is a positive x-value.

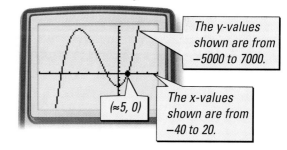

The y-values shown are from −5000 to 7000.

(≈5, 0)

The x-values shown are from −40 to 20.

Thus, a radius of about 5 feet gives a volume of approximately 1830 cubic feet.

The Activity below involves using a table of values and the Location Principle to find the zeros of a function.

Activity
Exploring With Tables

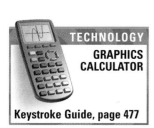

TECHNOLOGY
GRAPHICS
CALCULATOR

Keystroke Guide, page 477

You will need: a graphics calculator

Let $P(x) = x^4 - 3x^3 - 5x^2 + 13x + 6$.

1. Use the table feature of a calculator to find $P(x)$ for each x-value listed in the table at right.

2. From the table, what integer zeros of P can you find?

3. Use the table feature of a graphics calculator and the Location Principle to locate another zero of P to the nearest hundredth.

x	P(x)
−3	
−2	
−1	
0	
1	
2	
3	

4. Now graph $P(x) = x^4 - 3x^3 - 5x^2 + 13x + 6$ in a viewing window that shows x-values from -5 to 5 and y-values from -15 to 15. Use the graph to locate a fourth zero.

CHECKPOINT ✔ **5.** Explain how to use a graph and a table to find the real zeros of a polynomial function. Explain how to use a graph and a table to find the real roots of a polynomial equation.

Below is a summary of what you have learned about real roots and zeros.

SUMMARY
Roots and Zeros

The real number r is a zero of $f(x)$ if and only if all of the following are true:

- r is a solution, or root, of $f(x) = 0$.
- $x - r$ is a factor of the expression that defines f (that is, $f(r) = 0$).
- When the expression that defines f is divided by $x - r$, the remainder is 0.
- r is an x-intercept of the graph of f.

Exercises

● Communicate

1. If a polynomial has an even number of repeated factors, what do you know about its graph?

2. Describe how the Location Principle can help you to find the zeros of a polynomial function.

3. Explain how these terms are related: zeros, solutions, roots, factors, and x-intercepts.

● Guided Skills Practice

Use factoring to solve each equation. *(EXAMPLE 1)*

4. $x^3 - x^2 - 12x = 0$

5. $y^3 + 15y^2 + 54y = 0$

Use a graph, synthetic division, and factoring to find all of the roots of each equation. *(EXAMPLE 2)*

6 $x^3 - 5x^2 + 3x = 0$

7 $x^3 - 3x - 2 = 0$

Use variable substitution and factoring to find all of the roots of each equation. *(EXAMPLE 3)*

8. $x^4 - 8x^2 + 16 = 0$

9. $x^4 - 2x^2 + 1 = 0$

10 **AGRICULTURE** The volume of a cylindrical silo with a cone-shaped top is represented by $V(x) = \frac{1}{3}\pi r^3 + 25\pi r^2$, where r is the radius of the silo in feet. Find the radius to the nearest tenth of a foot that gives a volume of 2042 cubic feet. *(EXAMPLE 4)*

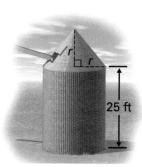

25 ft

Practice and Apply

Use factoring to solve each equation.

11. $x^3 + 2x^2 - 35x = 0$

12. $x^3 + 2x^2 - 48x = 0$

13. $y^3 - 6y^2 - 27y = 0$

14. $a^3 - 8a^2 - 48a = 0$

15. $x^3 - 13x^2 + 40x = 0$

16. $x^3 - 7x^2 + 10x = 0$

17. $x^3 = 25x$

18. $y^3 = 49y$

19. $2x^3 - 10x^2 - 100x = 0$

20. $16x - 6x^2 - x^3 = 0$

21. $3y^3 + 9y^2 - 162y = 0$

22. $20a^2 + 5a^3 - 60a = 0$

23. $110x - 2x^3 = 12x^2$

24. $3y^3 + 36y^2 = 3y^4$

25. $28a - 5a^2 - 3a^3 = 0$

26. $15y - 4y^2 - 3y^3 = 0$

Use a graph, synthetic division, and factoring to find all of the roots of each equation.

27 $a^3 - a^2 - 5a - 3 = 0$

28 $x^3 + 5x^2 + 7x + 3 = 0$

29 $x^3 + 5x^2 + 3x - 9 = 0$

30 $x^3 - 4x^2 - 3x + 18 = 0$

31 $2b^3 + 16b^2 + 32b = 0$

32 $5h^3 - 60h^2 + 180h = 0$

33 $x^3 - 3x - 2 = 0$

34 $x^3 - 3x + 2 = 0$

35 $x^3 - 2x^2 - 9x + 18 = 0$

36 $x^3 + 3x^2 - 4x - 12 = 0$

37 $n^3 + 8 = 2n^2 + 4n$

38 $x^3 + 3x^2 = 27 + 9x$

Use variable substitution and factoring to find all of the roots of each equation.

39. $x^4 - 4x^2 + 4 = 0$

40. $x^4 - 6x^2 + 9 = 0$

41. $y^4 - 18y^2 + 81 = 0$

42. $a^4 - 24a^2 + 144 = 0$

43. $x^4 - 13x^2 + 36 = 0$

44. $x^4 - 9x^2 + 18 = 0$

45. $x^5 - 9x^3 + 8x = 0$

46. $z^5 - 28z^3 + 27z = 0$

47. $x^4 - 12x^2 = -36$

48. $x^4 - 14x^2 = -49$

49. $h^4 + 12 = 7h^2$

50. $t^4 + 14 = 9t^2$

Use a graph and the Location Principle to find the real zeros of each function. Give approximate values to the nearest hundredth, if necessary.

51 $f(x) = 9x^3 - x^4 - 23$

52 $g(x) = x^3 - 3x - 2$

53 $f(a) = a^3 - a^2 - 8a + 12$

54 $h(x) = x^3 - 36x^2 + 18x - 27$

55 $m(n) = n^3 - 6n^2 + 12n - 8$

56 $f(t) = 64t^2 - 80t + 25$

57 $g(x) = 2x^4 - 2x^2 + 3x - 1$

58 $h(x) = 13x^4 - 21x + 7$

59 $f(x) = x^2 - 5x^3 + 3x$

60 $a(x) = x^2 + 12x^3 - 3x$

61. Find the range of values of c such that the function $f(x) = 2x^3 - x^2 - 6x + c$ has a zero between $x = 0$ and $x = 1$.

62 **CULTURAL CONNECTION: ASIA** Omar Khayyam, 1050–1122 C.E., of Persia (modern-day Iran) is usually remembered as a poet and the author of *The Rubaiyat*, although he was also a scientist and mathematician. Khayyam developed a method for finding the zeros of a cubic polynomial function of the form $f(x) = x^3 - bx - a$, where $a > 0$ and $b > 0$, by finding the x-coordinates of the intersection points of the graphs of familiar curves.

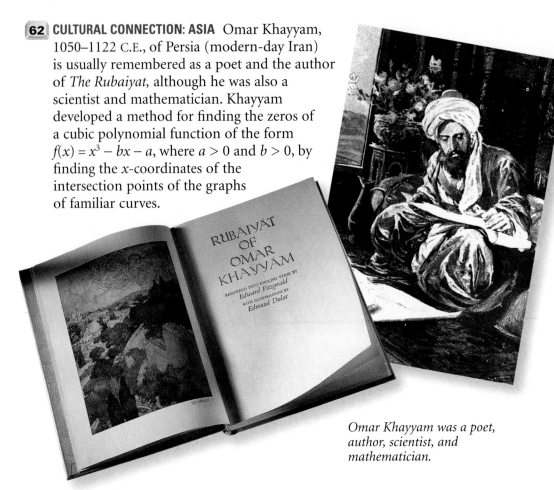

Omar Khayyam was a poet, author, scientist, and mathematician.

a. Given $f(x) = x^3 - 7x - 6$, identify the values of a and b.

b. Graph $y = -\frac{1}{\sqrt{b}}x^2$, $y = \sqrt{x^2 + \frac{a}{b}x}$, and $y = -\sqrt{x^2 + \frac{a}{b}x}$, using the values of a and b from part **a**.

c. Find all nonzero x-coordinates of the intersection points of these graphs. The x-coordinates represent the zeros of the original function, f.

d. Graph $f(x) = x^3 - 7x - 6$ and find all of its zeros to verify that the x-coordinates from part **c** are the zeros.

63. **MANUFACTURING** The volume of a cedar chest whose length is 3 times its width and whose height is 1 foot greater than its width is represented by $V(x) = 3x^3 + 3x^2$, where V is the volume in cubic feet and x is the width in feet. If the volume of the chest is 36 cubic feet, what are its dimensions?

64. **MEDICINE** The volume of a cylindrical vitamin with a hemispherical top and bottom can be represented by the function $V(x) = 10\pi r^2 + \frac{4}{3}\pi r^3$, where V is the volume in cubic millimeters and r is the radius in millimeters. What should be the radius of the cylinder and hemispherical ends (to the nearest thousandth) so that the total volume is 160 cubic millimeters?

 **Look Back**

Solve each equation by factoring and applying the Zero-Product Property. *(LESSON 5.3)*

65. $x^2 - 2x = 63$ **66.** $2x^2 - 5 = -9x$ **67.** $3x^2 + 60 = 27x$

Simplify. *(LESSON 5.6)*

68. $\sqrt{-49}$ **69.** $\sqrt{-81}$ **70.** $\sqrt{-11}$

Write the conjugate of each complex number. *(LESSON 5.6)*

71. $6 - 2i$ **72.** $4i - 2$ **73.** 5

Plot each number and its conjugate in the complex plane. *(LESSON 5.6)*

74. $-4 - 3i$ **75.** $-1 - 3i$ **76.** $2i - 4$

Use the quadratic formula to find the solutions to each equation. Write your answers in the form $a + bi$. *(LESSON 5.6)*

77. $x^2 + 2x + 7 = 0$ **78.** $4x^2 - 3x + 5 = 0$ **79.** $x^2 - 3x = -9$

Look Beyond

80. Let $P(x) = x^3 - 2x^2 + 5x + 26$.
    a. Verify that $x - (2 + 3i)$ and $x - (2 - 3i)$ are factors of P.
    b. Find the third factor and write P in factored form.

In the Portfolio Activity on page 431, you took measurements and made calculations to find a polynomial model for a cylindrical container with a flat circular base. In this activity, you will find a model for the volume of a bottle with a different shape.

1. Obtain a bottle with a flat square base. Fill the bottle about halfway with water.

2. Write a function that approximates the volume, in milliliters, of the part of the bottle containing water, W.

3. Turn the bottle upside-down, and write a function that approximates the volume, in milliliters, of the air space in the bottle, A.

4. Write a function that models the total volume, in milliliters, of the bottle, V.

5. Suppose that the height of the water is equal to the length of each side of the square base. If the height of the air space above the water is 2 centimeters, what side length of the base will give a total volume of 96 milliliters?

WORKING ON THE CHAPTER PROJECT

You should now be able to complete Activity 3 of the Chapter Project.

SCREAM MACHINE!

'Highest, fastest, steepest' in the world

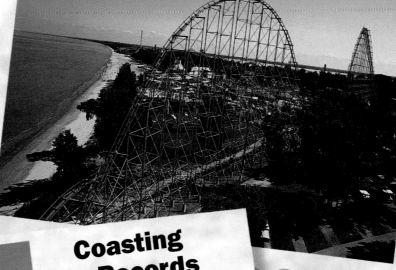

[Source: Sandusky Register, January 31, 1989]

Coasting to Records

On June 9, 1988, *Cedar Point's Magnum XL-200* roller coaster was certified as the fastest roller coaster in the world, with the longest vertical drop. As a result, it was listed in the 1990 edition of the *Guinness Book of World Records*. To enter the record books, the coaster needed two witnesses: one was Lt. Gov. Paul Leonard, who observed the ride's 72 miles per hour top speed and vertical drop of 194 feet, 8 inches.

[Source: Sandusky Register, July 27, 1989]

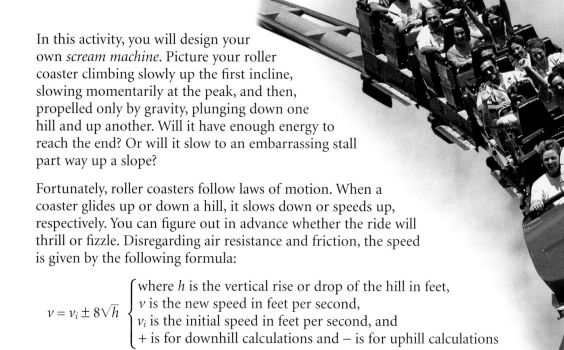

In this activity, you will design your own *scream machine*. Picture your roller coaster climbing slowly up the first incline, slowing momentarily at the peak, and then, propelled only by gravity, plunging down one hill and up another. Will it have enough energy to reach the end? Or will it slow to an embarrassing stall part way up a slope?

Fortunately, roller coasters follow laws of motion. When a coaster glides up or down a hill, it slows down or speeds up, respectively. You can figure out in advance whether the ride will thrill or fizzle. Disregarding air resistance and friction, the speed is given by the following formula:

$$v = v_i \pm 8\sqrt{h} \quad \begin{cases} \text{where } h \text{ is the vertical rise or drop of the hill in feet,} \\ v \text{ is the new speed in feet per second,} \\ v_i \text{ is the initial speed in feet per second, and} \\ + \text{ is for downhill calculations and } - \text{ is for uphill calculations} \end{cases}$$

In real life, however, there is air resistance and friction. Take the Magnum XL-200, for example. Its first drop, *h,* is 195 feet. Assume that the initial speed, v_i, at the top of the hill is 0.

$$v = v_i \pm 8\sqrt{h}$$

$$v = 0 + 8\sqrt{195} \approx 112 \quad \textit{Use + for downhill calculations.}$$

According to the formula, the Magnum XL-200 will be traveling at a speed of about 112 feet per second, or about 76 miles per hour. Actually, the Magnum reaches a speed of only 72 miles per hour. Friction and air resistance on the first descent cause the coaster to lose about 4 miles per hour, or about 5%, of its *theoretical* speed.

Cooperative Learning

Design your own roller-coaster track. Include at least three hills. Assume that the coaster loses 5% of its theoretical speed each time it goes up or down a hill. Make sure your roller coaster doesn't stall going up a hill.

1. Determine the vertical rise of each hill.

2. Assuming that the speed at the top of the first hill is 0 feet per second, determine the actual speeds at the top and the bottom of each hill.

3. What would it mean if the speed at the top of a hill was negative? How would you change the design to fix this situation?

Zeros of Polynomial Functions

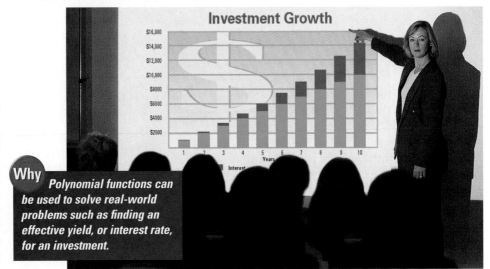

Investment Growth

Objectives

- Use the Rational Root Theorem and the Complex Conjugate Root Theorem to find the zeros of a polynomial function.

- Use the Fundamental Theorem to write a polynomial function given sufficient information about its zeros.

Why *Polynomial functions can be used to solve real-world problems such as finding an effective yield, or interest rate, for an investment.*

APPLICATION

INVESTMENTS

Polynomial functions can be used to solve problems in a variety of fields. Consider the following example from the field of finance:

> $1000 is invested at the beginning of each year in a fund that earns a variable interest rate. At the end of 10 years, the account is worth $14,371.56. To find the *effective interest rate* of this investment over these 10 years, you can solve the polynomial equation
> $$1000x^{10} + 1000x^9 + \cdots + 1000x^2 + 1000x = 14{,}371.56,$$
> or find the roots of
> $$1000x^{10} + 1000x^9 + \cdots + 1000x^2 + 1000x - 14{,}371.56 = 0.$$

The *Rational Root Theorem* can be used to identify possible roots of polynomial equations with integer coefficients. To see how this theorem can be used, examine the solution to the equation $3x^2 + 10x - 8 = 0$ below.

$$3x^2 + 10x - 8 = 0$$
$$(3x - 2)(x + 4) = 0$$
$$3x - 2 = 0 \quad or \quad x + 4 = 0$$
$$x = \frac{2}{3} \qquad\qquad x = -4, \text{ or } \frac{-4}{1}$$

Notice that the numerators, 2 and −4, are factors of the constant term, −8, in the polynomial. Also notice that the denominators, 3 and 1, are the factors of the leading coefficient, 3, in the polynomial.

Rational Root Theorem

Let P be a polynomial function with integer coefficients in standard form. If $\frac{p}{q}$ (in lowest terms) is a root of $P(x) = 0$, then

- p is a factor of the constant term of P and

- q is a factor of the leading coefficient of P.

E X A M P L E ❶ Find all of the rational roots of $10x^3 + 9x^2 - 19x + 6 = 0$.

● **SOLUTION**

Write the related function, $P(x) = 10x^3 + 9x^2 - 19x + 6$. According to the Rational Root Theorem, $\frac{p}{q}$ is a root of $10x^3 + 9x^2 - 19x + 6 = 0$ if p is a factor of the constant term, 6, and q is a factor of the leading coefficient, 10.

PROBLEM SOLVING

Make an organized list. Form all quotients that have factors of 6 in the numerator and factors of 10 in the denominator.

factors of 6: $\pm1, \pm2, \pm3, \pm6$
factors of 10: $\pm1, \pm2, \pm5, \pm10$

| $\pm\frac{1}{1}, \pm\frac{1}{2}, \pm\frac{1}{5}, \pm\frac{1}{10}$ | $\pm\frac{2}{1}, \pm\frac{2}{2}, \pm\frac{2}{5}, \pm\frac{2}{10}$ | $\pm\frac{3}{1}, \pm\frac{3}{2}, \pm\frac{3}{5}, \pm\frac{3}{10}$ | $\pm\frac{6}{1}, \pm\frac{6}{2}, \pm\frac{6}{5}, \pm\frac{6}{10}$ |

Notice that some rational numbers are repeated, such as $\frac{3}{1}$ and $\frac{6}{2}$.

PROBLEM SOLVING

Use a graph. Rather than testing each quotient to see which ones satisfy $10x^3 + 9x^2 - 19x + 6 = 0$, you can examine the graph of the related function, $P(x) = 10x^3 + 9x^2 - 19x + 6$, and use the process of elimination.

TECHNOLOGY
GRAPHICS CALCULATOR

Keystroke Guide, page 477

One root of $P(x) = 0$ appears to be -2. Test whether $P(-2) = 0$ is true.

$$\begin{array}{r|rrrr} -2 & 10 & 9 & -19 & 6 \\ & & -20 & 22 & -6 \\ \hline & 10 & -11 & 3 & \boxed{0} \end{array}$$ ← remainder

Since the remainder is 0, $P(-2) = 0$ is true and -2 is a root of $P(x) = 0$.

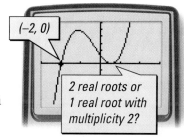
(–2, 0)

2 real roots or 1 real root with multiplicity 2?

From the graph of the related function, there appears to be two real zeros or one real zero with a multiplicity of 2 between 0 and 1.

A closer look between 0 and 1 on the graph of the related function shows two zeros at $\frac{1}{2}$ and $\frac{3}{5}$, which are possible roots of $P(x) = 0$ according to the Rational Root Theorem.

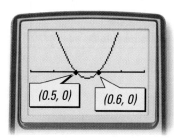
(0.5, 0)   (0.6, 0)

Test whether $P\left(\frac{1}{2}\right) = 0$ and $P\left(\frac{3}{5}\right) = 0$ are true.

$$\begin{array}{r|rrrr} \frac{1}{2} & 10 & 9 & -19 & 6 \\ & & 5 & 7 & -6 \\ \hline & 10 & 14 & -12 & \boxed{0} \end{array}$$ ← remainder

$$\begin{array}{r|rrrr} \frac{3}{5} & 10 & 9 & -19 & 6 \\ & & 6 & 9 & -6 \\ \hline & 10 & 15 & -10 & \boxed{0} \end{array}$$ ← remainder

Thus, there are three rational roots: $-2, \frac{1}{2}$, and $\frac{3}{5}$.

TRY THIS Find all of the rational roots of $3x^3 - 17x^2 + 59x - 65 = 0$.

You can often use the quadratic formula to solve a polynomial equation.

EXAMPLE **2** Find all of the zeros of $Q(x) = x^3 - 2x^2 - 2x + 1$.

● **SOLUTION**

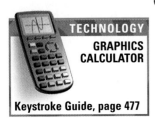

From the Rational Root Theorem and the graph of $Q(x) = x^3 - 2x^2 - 2x + 1$, you know that a zero may occur at -1. Test whether $Q(-1) = 0$ is true.

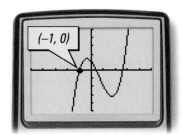
(−1, 0)

$$\begin{array}{r|rrrr} -1 & 1 & -2 & -2 & 1 \\ & & -1 & 3 & -1 \\ \hline & 1 & -3 & 1 & \boxed{0} \end{array}$$

Because $Q(-1) = 0$, $x + 1$ is a factor of $x^3 - 2x^2 - 2x + 1$.

$x^3 - 2x^2 - 2x + 1 = 0$

$(x + 1)(x^2 - 3x + 1) = 0$ *Factor out x + 1.*

$x + 1 = 0$ *or* $x^2 - 3x + 1 = 0$ *Apply the Zero-Product Property.*

$x = -1$ $x = \dfrac{3 \pm \sqrt{9 - 4}}{2}$ *Use the quadratic formula.*

Notice that $\dfrac{3 + \sqrt{5}}{2}$ and $\dfrac{3 - \sqrt{5}}{2}$ are conjugates. $\longrightarrow$ $x = \dfrac{3 \pm \sqrt{5}}{2}$

The zeros of $Q(x) = x^3 - 2x^2 - 2x + 1$ are -1, $\dfrac{3 + \sqrt{5}}{2}$, and $\dfrac{3 - \sqrt{5}}{2}$.

TRY THIS   Find all of the zeros of $P(x) = x^3 - 6x^2 + 7x + 2$.

EXAMPLE **3** Find all of the zeros of $P(x) = 3x^3 - 10x^2 + 10x - 4$.

● **SOLUTION**

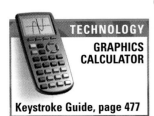

From the Rational Root Theorem and the graph of $P(x) = 3x^3 - 10x^2 + 10x - 4$, you know that a zero may occur at 2. Test whether $P(2) = 0$ is true.

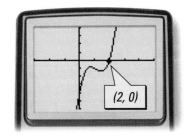
(2, 0)

$$\begin{array}{r|rrrr} 2 & 3 & -10 & 10 & -4 \\ & & 6 & -8 & 4 \\ \hline & 3 & -4 & 2 & \boxed{0} \end{array}$$

Because $P(2) = 0$, $x - 2$ is a factor of $3x^3 - 10x^2 + 10x - 4$.

$3x^3 - 10x^2 + 10x - 4 = 0$

$(x - 2)(3x^2 - 4x + 2) = 0$ *Factor out x – 2.*

$x - 2 = 0$ *or* $3x^2 - 4x + 2 = 0$ *Apply the Zero-Product Property.*

$x = 2$ $x = \dfrac{4 \pm \sqrt{16 - 24}}{6}$ *Use the quadratic formula.*

Notice that $\dfrac{2 + i\sqrt{2}}{3}$ and $\dfrac{2 - i\sqrt{2}}{3}$ are conjugates. $\longrightarrow$ $x = \dfrac{2 \pm i\sqrt{2}}{3}$

The zeros of $P(x) = 3x^3 - 10x^2 + 10x - 4$ are 2, $\dfrac{2 + i\sqrt{2}}{3}$, and $\dfrac{2 - i\sqrt{2}}{3}$.

TRY THIS   Find all of the zeros of $P(x) = x^3 - 9x^2 + 49x - 145$.

Complex Conjugate Root Theorem

If P is a polynomial function with real-number coefficients and $a + bi$ (where $b \neq 0$) is a root of $P(x) = 0$, then $a - bi$ is also a root of $P(x) = 0$.

Exploring Zeros of Cubic Functions

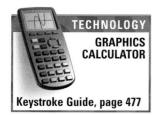

TECHNOLOGY

GRAPHICS CALCULATOR

Keystroke Guide, page 477

You will need: a graphics calculator

1. How many real zeros does the function in Example 2 have? How many real zeros does the function in Example 3 have?

2. Graph $R(x) = 2x^3 - x^2 - 4x$. How many real zeros does R have?

3. Graph $S(x) = 2x^3 - x^2 - 4x + 3$. How many real zeros does S have?

4. Graph $T(x) = 2x^3 - x^2 - 4x + 6$. How many real zeros does T have?

CHECKPOINT ✔   5. Write a conjecture about the number of real zeros that a cubic function can have. How does the Complex Conjugate Root Theorem help you to determine whether your conjecture is true?

E X A M P L E ④ Jasmine is a manufacturing engineer who is trying to find out if she can use a 12-inch-by-20-inch sheet of cardboard and a 15-inch-by-16-inch sheet of cardboard to make boxes with the same height and volume.

APPLICATION

MANUFACTURING

Is such a pair of boxes possible?

● **SOLUTION**

Box 1: 12 inches by 20 inches
$$V_1(x) = x(12 - 2x)(20 - 2x)$$

Box 2: 15 inches by 16 inches
$$V_2(x) = x(15 - 2x)(16 - 2x)$$

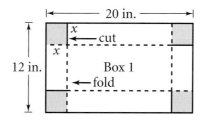

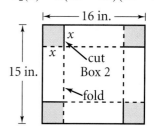

Find x such that $V_1(x) = V_2(x)$. Because x represents height, find $x > 0$ such that $x(20 - 2x)(12 - 2x) = x(16 - 2x)(15 - 2x)$.

Graph $y = x(20 - 2x)(12 - 2x)$ and $y = x(16 - 2x)(15 - 2x)$ on the same screen.

TECHNOLOGY

GRAPHICS CALCULATOR

Keystroke Guide, page 477

When you look for the intersection, you will find that the only solution is $x = 0$.

Since it is not possible to have a height of 0, it is not possible to make boxes with the same height and volume from the given materials.

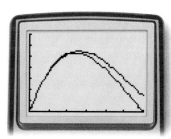

In this chapter, you have learned several different methods of finding the zeros of polynomial functions. The following theorem, along with its important corollary, tells you how many zeros a function has.

Fundamental Theorem of Algebra

Every polynomial function of degree $n \geq 1$ has at least one complex zero.

Corollary: Every polynomial function of degree $n \geq 1$ has exactly n complex zeros, counting multiplicities.

CULTURAL CONNECTION: EUROPE At the age of 20, German mathematician Karl Frederick Gauss, 1777–1855, earned his Ph.D. by proving that every polynomial equation has at least one complex root. The proof is beyond the scope of this book, but it remains one of the outstanding accomplishments of modern mathematics.

Karl Frederick Gauss
1777–1855

When given enough information about a polynomial function, you can find and write the function. One possibility is shown in Example 5.

EXAMPLE 5 The zeros of a fourth-degree polynomial function, P, include 3, with a multiplicity of 2, and $5 + 3i$. Also, $P(0) = 1224$.

Write the function in factored form and in standard form.

● **SOLUTION**

The four factors of the polynomial are as follows:
$$(x - 3) \quad (x - 3) \quad [x - (5 + 3i)] \quad [x - (5 - 3i)]$$
The simplest possible polynomial is $(x - 3)^2[x - (5 + 3i)][x - (5 - 3i)]$.

Because the graph of P can be stretched vertically by any nonzero constant factor and retain the same zeros, let a represent the stretch factor for this polynomial.
$$P(x) = a(x - 3)^2[x - (5 + 3i)][x - (5 - 3i)], \text{ where } a \neq 0$$
$$P(x) = a(x - 3)^2(x^2 - 10x + 34)$$

CONNECTION
TRANSFORMATIONS

Since $P(0) = 1224$, substitute 0 for x and 1224 for $P(x)$. Solve for a.
$$P(x) = a(x - 3)^2(x^2 - 10x + 34)$$
$$1224 = a(0 - 3)^2[0^2 - 10(0) + 34]$$
$$1224 = a(-3)^2(34)$$
$$1224 = 306a$$
$$4 = a$$
The function in factored form is $P(x) = 4(x - 3)^2(x^2 - 10x + 34)$.

Multiplying $4(x - 3)^2(x^2 - 10x + 34)$ gives the standard form,
$P(x) = 4x^4 - 64x^3 + 412x^2 - 1176x + 1224$.

TRY THIS   The zeros of a third-degree polynomial function, P, include 1 and $3 + 4i$. Also, $P(0) = 50$. Write the function in factored form and standard form.

Exercises

Communicate

1. What are the possible rational roots for the polynomial equation $2x^3 + a_2x^2 + a_1x + 3 = 0$, where a_2 and a_1 are integers?

2. If 0 and $3 - 2i$ are roots of a polynomial equation with rational coefficients, what other numbers must also be roots of the equation?

3. How many zeros does $P(x) = x^5 + x - 3$ have? Are all of the zeros distinct? Why or why not? How many are real zeros?

4. Let $P(x) = x(x - 1)(x - 2i)$ and $Q(x) = x(x - 1)(x - 2i)(x + 2i)$. Does P have real-number coefficients? Does Q have real-number coefficients? Multiply to verify your responses. How do your answers support the Complex Conjugate Root Theorem?

Guided Skills Practice

5. Find all of the rational roots of $12x^3 - 32x^2 - 145x + 250 = 0$. *(EXAMPLE 1)*

6. Find all of the zeros of $Q(x) = x^3 + 3x^2 - 8x - 4$. *(EXAMPLE 2)*

7. Find all of the zeros of $Q(x) = 2x^3 - 4x^2 - 5x - 3$. *(EXAMPLE 3)*

8. Let $P(x) = (x - 1)^3$ and $Q(x) = (x - 3)^2$. Find all real values of x such that $P(x) = Q(x)$. *(EXAMPLE 4)*

9. The zeros of a fourth-degree polynomial function P include 3, with a multiplicity of 2, and $3 + 4i$. Also, $P(0) = -6$. Write the function in factored form and in standard form. *(EXAMPLE 5)*

Practice and Apply

Find all of the rational roots of each polynomial equation.

10. $2x^2 + 3x + 1 = 0$

11. $6x^3 - 29x^2 - 45x + 18 = 0$

12. $4x^3 - 13x^2 + 11x - 2 = 0$

13. $3x^3 - 2x^2 - 12x + 8 = 0$

14. $3x^3 + 3x^2 - 4x + 4 = 0$

15. $4x^3 + 3x^2 + x + 2 = 0$

16. $15a^3 + 38a^2 + 17a + 2 = 0$

17. $10x^3 + 69x^2 - 9x - 14 = 0$

18. $18c^3 - 23c + 6 + 9c^2 = 0$

19. $50x^3 - 7x + 35x^2 - 6 = 0$

20. $18x^4 + 15x + 15x^3 - 34x^2 - 2 = 0$

21. $10x^4 - 103x^3 - 207x + 294x^2 - 54 = 0$

Find all zeros of each polynomial function.

22 $B(x) = x^3 - 4x^2 - 3x + 12$

23 $P(x) = 3x^3 - x^2 - 24x + 8$

24 $f(x) = 4x^3 - 20x^2 - 3x + 15$

25 $f(x) = 9x^3 + 72x^2 - 5x - 40$

26 $t(x) = x^3 - 2x^2 + 78 - 35x$

27 $g(x) = x^3 - 5x^2 + 144x - 720$

28 $N(x) = x^3 - 3x^2 + 4x - 12$

29 $f(b) = b^3 - 5b^2 + 9b - 45$

30 $G(x) = x^3 + 5x^2 + 10 + 2x$

31 $a(x) = x^3 - 3x^2 + 12x - 36$

32 $W(x) = x^3 + 2x^4 - 5x + 5 - 11x^2$

33 $H(x) = x^4 + 16x - x^2 + 4x^3 - 20$

Find all real values of *x* for which the functions are equal. Give your answers to the nearest hundredth.

34 $P(x) = x^2$, $Q(x) = x^3 + 3x^2 + 3x + 1$

35 $P(x) = x^2 - 2x + 1$, $Q(x) = -x^3 + 3x^2 - 3x + 3$

36 $P(x) = x^4 - 6x + 3$, $Q(x) = -0.2x^4$

37 $P(x) = x^3 - 5x$, $Q(x) = 0.5x^4$

38 $P(x) = x^4 - 4x^2 + 3$, $Q(x) = x^2$

39 $P(x) = x^4 - 5x^2 + 4$, $Q(x) = 2$

40 $P(x) = 0.25x^4$, $Q(x) = -x^2 + 2$

Write a polynomial function, *P*, in factored form and in standard form by using the given information.

41. *P* is of degree 2; $P(0) = 12$; zeros: 2, 3

42. *P* is of degree 2; $P(0) = 4$; zeros: −1, 4

43. *P* is of degree 3; $P(0) = 20$; zeros: −2, 1, 2

44. *P* is of degree 3; $P(0) = 24$; zeros: −1, 2, 4

45. *P* is of degree 4; $P(0) = 1$; zeros: 1 (multiplicity 2), 2 (multiplicity 2)

46. *P* is of degree 5; $P(0) = 2$; zeros: 1 (multiplicity 3), 2 (multiplicity 2)

47. *P* is of degree 3; $P(0) = -1$; zeros: 1, i

48. *P* is of degree 3; $P(0) = 4$; zeros: −1, $2i$

49. *P* is of degree 4; $P(0) = 3$; zeros: 1, 2, $5i$

50. *P* is of degree 4; $P(0) = -3$; zeros: 2, 5, $3i$

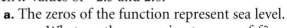

CHALLENGE

51. Use the Rational Root Theorem and the polynomial $P(x) = x^2 - 3$ to show that $\sqrt{3}$ is irrational.

APPLICATION

52 GEOGRAPHY A mountain ridge is drawn to scale on the wall of a visitors' center in West Virginia. The ridge has approximately the same shape as the graph of the function $f(x) = -x^4 + 3x^2 - 3x + 6$ between *x*-values of −2.5 and 2.0.

y

a. The zeros of the function represent sea level. What are the approximate zeros of *f*?

b. Find the approximate maximum value of *f*.

c. Find the vertical scale factor that would place the maximum height of the ridge at 3200 feet above sea level.

x

53. THERMODYNAMICS A hot-air balloon rises at an increasing rate as its altitude increases. Its altitude, in feet, can be modeled by the function $y = 0.025t^2 + 2t$, where t is time in seconds. How long will it take for the balloon to reach an altitude of 800 feet?

Look Back

Let $f(x) = 5x + 4$ and $g(x) = 2 - x$. Find or evaluate each composite function. *(LESSON 2.4)*

54. $f \circ g$ **55.** $g \circ f$ **56.** $f \circ f$

57. $(f \circ g)(-2)$ **58.** $(g \circ f)(5)$ **59.** $(f \circ f)(0.2)$

Write the equation for the axis of symmetry and find the coordinates of the vertex. *(LESSON 5.5)*

60. $y = 6x^2 - x - 12$ **61.** $y = 2x^2 + 5x + 2$ **62.** $y = x^2 + 3x - 2$

63 Graph $f(x) = x^3 - 3x^2 + 4x - 5$, and describe its end behavior. *(LESSON 7.2)*

64. Describe the end behavior of the function $f(x) = -3(x + 1)^2(x - 1)^3(x - 2)^4$. *(LESSON 7.2)*

In Exercises 65 and 66, divide by using synthetic division. *(LESSON 7.3)*

65. $\dfrac{3x^4 - 4x^2 + 2x - 1}{x - 1}$ **66.** $\dfrac{x^4 + 4x^3 + 5x^2 - 5x - 14}{x + 2}$

Look Beyond

67. Use factoring to simplify the expression $\dfrac{x^2 + 5x + 6}{x^2 + 7x} \cdot \dfrac{x^2 - 2x}{x^2 - 4}$.

68. Solve the equation $\sqrt{x + 1} = \sqrt{2x}$. Begin by squaring both sides. Check by substituting your solution(s) into the original equation.

FILL IT UP!

In this project you will find polynomial models to represent the shapes of various containers. You will perform experiments that involve adding water to a container in equal increments until the container is full. After each addition of water, the height of the water in the container is measured. The volume of water in the container and the height of the water are both recorded. Ordered pairs are formed from the data and displayed in a scatter plot. A polynomial regression model is selected to represent the data.

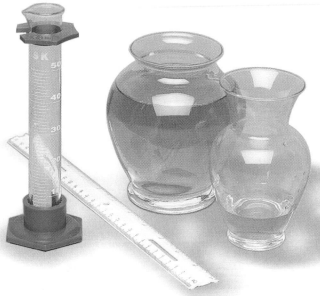

Materials:
- flat-bottomed, medium-size, clear container of irregular shape
- plastic beaker with measurements labeled in milliliters
- centimeter ruler
- water

Activity 1

1. Each student should have a flat-bottomed, clear container of irregular shape. First determine the total volume of the container. Divide the total volume by 10, and round to the nearest whole number. (For example, if the total volume is 347 milliliters, divide by 10 and round 34.7 to 35.)

2. Add water to the container in 10 equal increments based on your answer from Step 1. After each increment is added, measure the height of the water in the container. Record your data in a table like the one below. Continue this procedure until the container is full.

[Note: $1 \text{ cm}^3 = 1 \text{ mL}$]

	Volume (mL)	Height (cm)
1.		
2.		
3.		
4.		
5.		
6.		
7.		
8.		
9.		
10.		

Activity 2

1. Using the data in your table from Activity 1, let x represent the volume in milliliters, and let y represent the height in centimeters. Make a scatter plot of the data in the table.

2. Use the regression feature on your graphics calculator to find a cubic polynomial model and a quadratic polynomial model for the data you collected.

3. Compare the two models. Choose the model that appears to best fit the data.

4. Can you use this model to predict data points not plotted? Explain.

Activity 3

In this activity, you will test the validity of the polynomial model that you chose as the best fit in Activity 2.

1. In small groups, mix up the containers and graphs so that the graphs are not matched with the containers.

2. Trade containers and graphs with another group. Each group must match the containers they receive with the corresponding graphs.

3. Discuss how each group's matching choices were made.

7 Chapter Review and Assessment

Key Skills & Exercises

LESSON 7.1

Key Skills

Classify polynomials.

$5x - 4x^4 + -5x^3 - 9x + 4x + 1$

$= 4x^4 + 5x^3 + 1$ *Combine like terms.*

The polynomial is a quartic trinomial.

Evaluate, add, and subtract polynomial functions.

Evaluate $g(x) = x^3 - 2x^2 + 4x$ for $x = -5$.

$g(-5) = (-5)^3 - 2(-5)^2 + 4(-5)$

$= -125 - 50 - 20 = -195$

Simplify $(-2x^3 + 4x^2 - 9x + 5) - (5x^3 - x + 7)$.

$(-2x^3 + 4x^2 - 9x + 5) - (5x^3 - x + 7)$

$= -2x^3 - 5x^3 + 4x^2 - 9x + x + 5 - 7$

$= -7x^3 + 4x^2 - 8x - 2$

Exercises

Classify each polynomial by degree and by number of terms.

1. $3a^3 + 11a^2 - 2a + 1$ **2.** $8x^5 - 6x^2 + 10x^3$

3. $-b^2 + 8b - 5b^4 - 3$ **4.** $-2x^2 - x^3 + 7x^4$

Evaluate each polynomial for $x = 2$ and $x = -1$.

5. $-x^3 + 4x^2 - 2$ **6.** $x^3 + 2x^2 - 1$

7. $x^4 - 22$ **8.** $19 - x^2 - x^3$

Write each sum or difference as a polynomial in standard form. Then classify the polynomial by degree and by number of terms.

9. $(3x^3 - 5x^2 + 8x + 1) + (11x^3 - x^2 + 2x - 3)$

10. $(7x^3 - 8x^2 + 2x - 3) - (2x^3 + x^2 - 6)$

LESSON 7.2

Key Skills

Identify and describe the important features of the graph of a polynomial function.

Let $f(x) = -x^3 - 3x^2 + 10$. Because the leading coefficient of f is negative and the degree of f is odd, its graph rises on the left and falls on the right.

Exercises

Describe the end behavior of each function.

11. $c(a) = -a^2 - 2a + 22$

12. $d(x) = -2x^3 + 3x^2 - 7$

13. $f(x) = x^4 + 7x + 1$

14. $f(x) = 4x + x^3 - 6$

The graph of $f(x) = -x^3 - 3x^2 + 10$ below shows that f increases for $-2 < x < 0$ and f decreases for $x < -2$ and for $x > 0$.

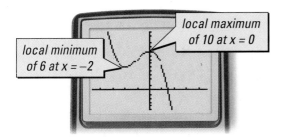

local minimum of 6 at $x = -2$

local maximum of 10 at $x = 0$

Graph each function. Find any local maxima and minima to the nearest tenth and the intervals over which the function is increasing and decreasing.

15 $f(x) = x^2 - 2x + 9$

16 $g(x) = -x^2 + 5x - 4$

17 $f(a) = 2a^3 + 5a^2 - 1$

18 $m(x) = -2x^3 + x^2 - 9$

LESSON 7.3

Key Skills

Use long division and synthetic division to find factors and remainders of polynomials.

Use long division to find whether $x - 5$ is a factor of $x^3 - 2x^2 - 13x - 10$.

$$\begin{array}{r}
x^2 + 3x + 2 \\
x - 5 \overline{)x^3 - 2x^2 - 13x - 10} \\
\underline{-(x^3 - 5x^2)} \\
3x^2 - 13x \\
\underline{-(3x^2 - 15x)} \\
2x - 10 \\
\underline{-(2x - 10)} \\
0
\end{array}$$

The remainder is 0, so $x - 5$ is a factor and $x^3 - 2x^2 - 13x - 10 = (x - 5)(x^2 + 3x + 2)$.

Because $P(5) = 0$, $x - 5$ is a factor.

Use synthetic division to find whether $x - 2$ is a factor of $x^3 + 2x - 3$.

$$\begin{array}{r|rrrr}
2 & 1 & 0 & 2 & -3 \\
& & 2 & 4 & 12 \\
\hline
& 1 & 2 & 6 & \boxed{9}
\end{array}$$

The remainder is 9, so $x - 2$ is not a factor of $x^3 + 2x - 3$.

The Remainder Theorem states that if the expression that defines $P(x) = x^3 + 2x - 3$ is divided by $x - 2$, the remainder is the value of $P(2)$.

$P(2) = 2^3 + 2(2) - 3 = 9$

Exercises

Write each product as a polynomial in standard form.

19. $-2x^3(5x^4 - 3x + x^2 - 6 - x^3)$

20. $(x + 4)(x^3 - 7)(x + 1)$

Factor each polynomial.

21. $x^3 + 4x^2 - 5x$ **22.** $x^3 - 3x^2 - 10x$

23. $x^3 - 125$ **24.** $27x^3 + 1$

Use substitution to tell whether the given binomial is a factor of the polynomial.

25. $(x^3 - 7x^2 + 4x + 12)$; $(x - 2)$

26. $(x^3 - 5x^2 - 2x + 24)$; $(x + 2)$

Divide by using long division.

27. $(x^3 + 6x^2 - x - 30) \div (x - 2)$

28. $(x^3 - 2x^2 - 11x + 12) \div (x^2 - x - 12)$

Divide by using synthetic division.

29. $(x^3 + 3x^2 - 34x + 48) \div (x - 3)$

30. $(x^3 + x^2 - 22x - 40) \div (x + 4)$

LESSON 7.4

Key Skills

Find all of the roots of a polynomial equation.

Use variable substitution to find all of the roots of $x^4 - 7x^2 + 12 = 0$.

Substitute u for x^2: $(u)^2 - 7(u) + 12 = 0$
Factor and solve for u: $u = 3$ or $u = 4$
Substitute x^2 for u: $x^2 = 3$ or $x^2 = 4$

Thus, the roots are $\sqrt{3}$, $-\sqrt{3}$, 2, and -2.

Exercises

Find all of the real roots of each polynomial equation.

31. $x^4 - 8x^2 + 16 = 0$

32. $x^4 - 10x^2 + 24 = 0$

33. $x^4 - 10x^2 + 9 = 0$

34. $x^4 - 13x^2 + 12 = 0$

35. $x^3 - x^2 - 6x + 6 = 0$

Use factoring to find all of the roots of
$x^3 - 4x^2 - 3x + 12 = 0$.

Factor by grouping:

$$(x^3 - 12x^2) - (3x - 12) = 0$$
$$x^2(x - 4) - 3(x - 4) = 0$$
$$(x^2 - 3)(x - 4) = 0$$

Thus, the roots are $\sqrt{3}$, $-\sqrt{3}$, and 4.

Given that one root of $x^3 - 3x - 2 = 0$ is 2, use
synthetic division to find all of the other roots.

$$
\begin{array}{r|rrrr}
2 & 1 & 0 & -3 & -2 \\
  &   & 2 & 4 & 2 \\
\hline
  & 1 & 2 & 1 & 0
\end{array}
$$

$x^3 - 3x - 2 = 0$
$\rightarrow (x - 2)(x^2 + 2x + 1) = 0$
$(x - 2)(x + 1)^2 = 0$

Thus, the remaining root is -1 (multiplicity 2).

36. $x^5 - x^3 - 8x^2 + 8 = 0$

37. $x^4 + 2x^3 - x - 2 = 0$

38. $x^5 - 9x^3 - x^2 + 9 = 0$

Given the indicated root, find all of the other roots of the polynomial equation.

39. -3; $x^3 + 7x^2 + 16x + 12 = 0$

40. -3; $x^3 + 3x^2 - 16x - 48 = 0$

41. 4; $x^3 - 11x^2 + 38x - 40 = 0$

42. 6; $x^3 - 6x^2 - x + 6 = 0$

LESSON 7.5

Key Skills

Find all rational roots of a polynomial equation.

Find all rational roots of $9x^2 - 9x + 2 = 0$. The
possible values are $\pm\frac{1}{1}$, $\pm\frac{1}{3}$, $\pm\frac{1}{9}$, $\pm\frac{2}{1}$, $\pm\frac{2}{3}$, and $\pm\frac{2}{9}$.
Checking each possibility reveals that the rational
roots are $\frac{1}{3}$ and $\frac{2}{3}$.

Write a polynomial function given sufficient information.

The zeros of a fourth degree polynomial include
1 (multiplicity 2) and i. Also, $P(0) = 4$. Write the
function in factored form and in standard form.

$$P(x) = a(x - 1)^2(x - i)(x + i)$$
$$4 = a(0 - 1)^2(0 - i)(0 + i)$$
$$4 = a$$

$$P(x) = 4(x - 1)^2(x - i)(x + i)$$
$$= 4x^4 - 8x^3 + 8x^2 - 8x + 4$$

Exercises

Find all of the rational roots of each polynomial equation.

43. $15x^2 + x - 2 = 0$

44. $9x^3 - 27x^2 - 34x - 8 = 0$

45. $9x^3 - 18x^2 + 2x - 4 = 0$

46. $x^3 - 3x^2 + 4x - 12 = 0$

Write a polynomial function of degree 4 in factored form and in standard form by using the given information.

47. $P(0) = 6$; zeros: 2, -1(multiplicity 2), and 3

48. $P(0) = -16$; zeros: -2 (multiplicity 3) and 1

49. $P(0) = -45$; zeros: 3 (multiplicity 2) and $2 + i$

50. $P(0) = -140$; zeros: 5, -7, and $-\frac{2}{3}i$

Applications

51. **INVESTMENTS** Suppose that $500 is invested at the end of every year for 5
years. One year after the last payment, the investment is worth $3200. Use
the polynomial equation $500x^5 + 500x^4 + 500x^3 + 500x^2 + 500x = 3200$ to
find the effective interest rate of this investment.

52. **MANUFACTURING** Using standard form, write the polynomial function that
represents the volume of a crate with a length of x feet, a width of $8 - x$
feet, and a height of $x - 3$ feet. Then find the maximum volume of the
crate and the dimensions for this volume.

Alternative Assessment

Performance Assessment

1. **END BEHAVIOR** Describe each possibility for the end behavior of a polynomial function of positive degree. Give an example for each possibility, and sketch the graph.

2. **PACKAGING** The U.S. Postal Service requires that the sum of the height and the girth of a parcel is no greater than 108 inches. The girth is the distance around the package, $2l + 2w$. Suppose that a box has the same length and width. The volume of the box is given by $V(x) = x(x)(108 - 4x)$, where x is the length.
   a. Write the volume of the box as a polynomial function in standard form.
   b. Find the maximum possible volume for such a box.
   c. Find the volume of the box if its length is 24 inches.
   d. Write the volume function for an acceptable box whose length is twice its width.

3. **TESTING LINEAR FACTORS** Use as many ways as possible to determine whether $x - 2$ is a factor of $x^3 + x^2 - 8x - 15$. Show your work.

4. **COMPLEX ZEROS** Two zeros of a polynomial function are -5 and $3 - 2i$. What other zero must the function have? Write in standard form the polynomial function of least degree that has these zeros.

5. **RATIONAL ZEROS** Let $f(x) = 9x^3 + 6x^2 - 5x - 2$. Find all possible rational zeros of $f(x)$. Then determine which of these are actual zeros.

Portfolio Projects

1. **STACKING BALLS** A pyramid can be formed with equal-size balls. For example, 3 balls can be arranged in a triangle with a fourth ball in the middle and on top of the other 3 balls. The function $p(n) = \frac{n}{6}(n + 1)(n + 2)$ gives the number of balls in a pyramid, where n is the number of balls on a side of the bottom layer.
   a. What restriction for n is necessary in order for p to be meaningful? Explain.
   b. Make a table and graph the function.
   c. Find a pattern in the number of balls added to the pyramid for each increase on one side of the bottom layer. (Hint: Examine first and second differences.)

2. **PACKAGING** Yogurt is packaged in containers that are shaped like truncated cones. The formula for the volume of these containers is given below.

$$V = \frac{1}{3}\pi h(R^2 + r^2 + Rr)$$

   a. Measure a yogurt container and verify that its volume is modeled by the formula above.
   b. How many variables are in this formula? How can the formula be defined by a polynomial function in one variable?
   c. How could you alter the dimensions of the container but maintain the same volume?

🔲 internet**connect**

(HRW) The HRW Web site contains many resources to reinforce and expand your knowledge of polynomial functions. This Web site also provides Internet links to other sites where you can find information and real-world data for use in research projects, reports, and activities that involve polynomial functions. Visit the HRW Web site at **go.hrw.com,** and enter the keyword **MB1 CH7** to access the resources for this chapter.

QUANTITATIVE COMPARISON For Items 1–5, write
A if the quantity in Column A is greater than the quantity in Column B;
B if the quantity in Column B is greater than the quantity in Column A;
C if the two quantities are equal; or
D if the relationship cannot be determined from the given information.

	Column A	Column B	Answers
1.	The degree of $x^4 + 2x^3 + x + 1$	$3x^2 + 2x + 1$	Ⓐ Ⓑ Ⓒ Ⓓ [Lesson 7.1]
2.	$\ln \frac{1}{2}$	$\ln 2$	Ⓐ Ⓑ Ⓒ Ⓓ [Lesson 6.6]
3.	$e^{\ln 2}$	2	Ⓐ Ⓑ Ⓒ Ⓓ [Lessons 6.4 and 6.6]
4.	The number of factors of $x^3 - 4x$	$x^3 - 5x^2 + 6x$	Ⓐ Ⓑ Ⓒ Ⓓ [Lesson 7.5]
5.	The minimum value of $f(x) = x^2 + 1$	$f(x) = (x-1)^2 + 1$	Ⓐ Ⓑ Ⓒ Ⓓ [Lesson 5.1]

6. Which is a solution of the system below?
$$\begin{cases} y \geq -x \\ y \geq 3x + 2 \end{cases}$$ *(LESSON 3.4)*

    a. $(1, -5)$ **b.** $(0, 5)$
    c. both **a** and **b**   **d.** neither **a** nor **b**

7. Find the slope of the line $3x + 4y = 2$.
    (LESSON 1.2)

    a. 3   **b.** $\frac{2}{3}$
    c. $-\frac{3}{4}$ **d.** 4

8. Which equation contains the point $(1, -3)$ and is perpendicular to $y = 2x - 2$?
    (LESSON 1.3)

    a. $2y = -x + 5$ **b.** $2y = -x - 5$
    c. $y = -\frac{1}{2}x + 6$ **d.** $y = -\frac{1}{2}x + \frac{3}{2}$

9. Which is the solution of the system below?
$$\begin{cases} x + 2y = 4 \\ 2x + y = 5 \end{cases}$$ *(LESSON 3.1)*

    a. $(2, 3)$ **b.** $(2, 1)$
    c. $(-3, 2)$ **d.** $(0, 1)$

10. Which set of ordered pairs represents a function? *(LESSON 2.3)*

    a. $\{(0, 3), (1, 4), (1, 3)\}$
    b. $\{(2, 1), (4, -1), (6, 2)\}$
    c. $\{(3, 5), (2, 10), (3, 15)\}$
    d. $\{(10, 4), (10, 5), (20, 6)\}$

11. For which function does the vertex give a maximum value? *(LESSON 5.1)*

    a. $a(x) = 3x^2 + 5x$ **b.** $b(x) = 7x + 5x - 3x^2$
    c. $c(x) = 3 + 5x + \frac{1}{3}x^2$ **d.** $d(x) = \frac{1}{3}x^2$

12. How many solutions does a consistent system of linear equations have? *(LESSON 3.1)*
  a. 0 **b.** 1
  c. at least 1 **d.** infinitely many

13. What is the y-intercept for the graph of the equation $x - 5y = 15$? *(LESSON 1.2)*
  a. 15 **b.** -1
  c. 3 **d.** -3

14. Which is the solution of the inequality $4x + 2 < 2x + 1$? *(LESSON 1.7)*
  a. $x \geq 1$ **b.** $x > 2$
  c. $x < \frac{1}{3}$ **d.** $x < -\frac{1}{2}$

15. Which is the solution to the inequality $|x| \leq 5$? *(LESSON 1.8)*
  a. $-5 \leq x \leq 5$ **b.** $-2 \leq x \leq 2$
  c. $-5 \geq x \geq 5$ **d.** $-3 \leq x \leq 3$

16. Which is the factorization of $x^2 - 5x + 6$? *(LESSON 5.3)*
  a. $(x - 2)(x - 3)$ **b.** $(x + 2)(x - 3)$
  c. $(x + 1)(x + 6)$ **d.** $(x - 1)(x - 6)$

17. Write $(x + 1)(x + 2)(x - 4)$ in standard form. *(LESSON 7.3)*

18. Find the product. $\begin{bmatrix} 2 & 3 \\ 4 & 3 \end{bmatrix}\begin{bmatrix} 1 & 1 \\ 2 & 3 \end{bmatrix}$
  (LESSON 4.2)

19. Let $f(x) = 3x + 5$ and $g(x) = x^2 + x + 5$. Find $f + g$. *(LESSON 2.4)*

20. Solve $\ln x = 5$ for x. *(LESSONS 6.3 AND 6.6)*

21. Write the equation in vertex form for the parabola described by $f(x) = 2x^2 - 8x + 9$. *(LESSON 5.4)*

22. Find the sum. $(2x^3 + 3x^2 + 1) + (5x^2 - 2x + 2)$ *(LESSON 7.1)*

23. Find the difference below. *(LESSON 7.1)*
  $(5x^3 + 4x^2 - x) - (x^3 + 2x^2 - 1)$

24. Let $f(x) = 3x + 2$. Find the inverse of f. *(LESSON 2.5)*

25. Find all rational roots of $3x^2 + 5x - 2 = 0$. *(LESSON 7.5)*

26. Multiply. $(4 - 2i)(4 + 2i)$ *(LESSON 5.6)*

Factor each quadratic expression, if possible. *(LESSON 5.3)*

27. $-3y^2 - 5y$ **28.** $x^2 - 5x - 36$
29. $24x^2 + 5x - 36$ **30.** $36x^2 - 46x - 12$

FREE-RESPONSE GRID The following questions may be answered by using a free-response grid such as that commonly used by standardized-test services.

31. Evaluate $\lceil 3.1 \rceil + \lfloor 2.5 \rfloor$. *(LESSON 2.6)*

32. Find the value of $\log_5 25$. *(LESSON 6.3)*

33. Solve the equation $\ln x + \ln(2 - x) = 0$ for x. *(LESSON 6.7)*

34. Simplify $5[3 - (3 - 2)]^2$. *(LESSON 2.1)*

35. Find the rational zeros of the polynomial function $f(x) = 2x^3 - x^2 - 4x + 2$. *(LESSON 7.5)*

36. Solve the proportion $\frac{x + 2}{2} = \frac{2x}{3}$ for x. *(LESSON 1.4)*

37. Evaluate $|-2.5| - |3.2|$. *(LESSON 2.6)*

38. Solve $-3x + 4 = 5 - x$ for x. *(LESSON 1.6)*

39. **INVESTMENTS** Find the final amount in dollars of a $1000 investment after 5 years at an interest rate of 8% compounded annually. *(LESSON 6.2)*

40. **ARCHAEOLOGY** A sample of wood found at an archaeological site contains 60% of its original carbon-14. Use the function $N(t) = N_0 e^{-0.00012t}$, which gives the amount of remaining carbon-14, to estimate the age of the sample of wood. *(LESSON 6.6)*

41. **INVESTMENTS** If $1000 is invested at 8% annual interest, compounded continuously, find the dollar amount of the investment after 5 years. *(LESSON 6.6)*

Keystroke Guide for Chapter 7

Essential keystroke sequences (using the model TI-82 or TI-83 graphics calculator) are presented below for all Activities and Examples found in this chapter that require or recommend the use of a graphics calculator.

☑ internet connect

HRW Keystrokes for other models of graphics calculators are found on the HRW Web site.

LESSON 7.1

EXAMPLE Graph $y = 1000x^4 + 1000x^3 + 1000x^2 + 1000x + 1000$, and evaluate for
Page 426 $x = 1.06$.

Use viewing window [0, 1.5] by [−1000, 7000].

Graph the function:

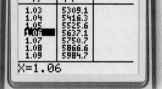

[Y=] 1000 [X,T,θ,n] [^] 4 [+] 1000 [X,T,θ,n] [^] 3 [+] 1000 [X,T,θ,n]

[x²] [+] 1000 [X,T,θ,n] [+] 1000 [GRAPH]

Use the graph:

      CALC
[2nd] [TRACE] [1:value] [ENTER] (X=) 1.06 [ENTER]

Use a table:

      TBLSET
[2nd] [WINDOW] (TblStart=) 1.03 [▼] (△Tbl=) .01 [▼] (Indpt:) [Auto] [ENTER] [▼]

      ⇑ TI-82: (TblMin=)   **TABLE**
(Depend:) [Auto] [ENTER] [▼] [2nd] [GRAPH]

Activity
Page 427

For Step 1, graph $y = x^2 + x - 2$.

Use viewing window [−15, 15] by [−15, 15].

[Y=] [X,T,θ,n] [x²] [+] [X,T,θ,n] [−] 2 [GRAPH]

Use a similar keystroke sequence for Steps 2–9. For Steps 7–9, use viewing window [−4, 4] by [−4, 4].

EXAMPLE 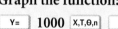 **5** For part a, graph $y = 3x^3 - 5x^2 - 2x + 1$.
Page 428

Use viewing window [−5, 5] by [−5, 5].

[Y=] 3 [X,T,θ,n] [^] 3 [−] 5 [X,T,θ,n] [x²]

[−] 2 [X,T,θ,n] [+] 1 [GRAPH]

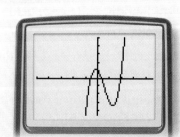

For part **b**, use a similar keystroke sequence.
Use viewing window [−5, 5] by [−20, 5].

E X A M P L E ❶

Page 434

Graph $y = x^3 + 3x^2 - x - 3$, and approximate the coordinates of any local maxima or minima.

Use friendly viewing window $[-4.7, 4.7]$ by $[-10, 10]$.

Graph the function:

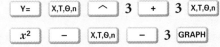

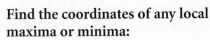

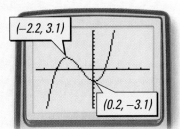

Find the coordinates of any local maxima or minima:

Press ⟨TRACE⟩, and move the cursor.

Make a table of values:

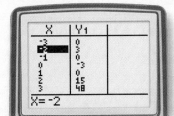

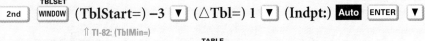

⟨2nd⟩ ⟨WINDOW⟩ **TBLSET** (TblStart=) −3 ⟨▼⟩ (△Tbl=) 1 ⟨▼⟩ (Indpt:) **Auto** ⟨ENTER⟩ ⟨▼⟩

⇑ TI-82: (TblMin=)

(Depend:) **Auto** ⟨ENTER⟩ ⟨▼⟩ ⟨2nd⟩ ⟨GRAPH⟩ **TABLE**

To approximate more closely, change to TblStart= −2.5 and △Tbl= 0.1.

Activity

Page 435

For Steps 1–16, graph each function by using a keystroke sequence similar to that in Example 2 of Lesson 7.1.

Use viewing window $[-5, 5]$ by $[-5, 5]$.

E X A M P L E ❷

Page 436

For part a, graph $y = -x^3 + x^2 + 3x - 1$.

Use viewing window $[-5, 5]$ by $[-5, 5]$.

⟨Y=⟩ ⟨(-)⟩ ⟨X,T,θ,n⟩ ⟨^⟩ 3 ⟨+⟩ ⟨X,T,θ,n⟩ ⟨x²⟩ ⟨+⟩ 3 ⟨X,T,θ,n⟩ ⟨−⟩ 1 ⟨GRAPH⟩

For part **b**, use a similar keystroke sequence to graph $y = -x^4 + x^3 + 3x^2 - x + 3$. Use viewing window $[-5, 5]$ by $[-2, 8]$.

E X A M P L E ❸

Page 436

Enter the given data, and find a quartic regression model for the data. Then estimate y when x is 20.

Use viewing window $[0, 60]$ by $[0, 5000]$.

Enter the data:

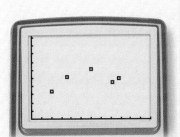

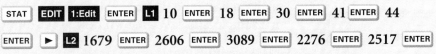

⟨STAT⟩ **EDIT 1:Edit** ⟨ENTER⟩ **L1** 10 ⟨ENTER⟩ 18 ⟨ENTER⟩ 30 ⟨ENTER⟩ 41 ⟨ENTER⟩ 44

⟨ENTER⟩ ⟨▶⟩ **L2** 1679 ⟨ENTER⟩ 2606 ⟨ENTER⟩ 3089 ⟨ENTER⟩ 2276 ⟨ENTER⟩ 2517 ⟨ENTER⟩

Graph the scatter plot:

⟨2nd⟩ ⟨Y=⟩ **STATPLOT** **STATPLOT 1:Plot 1** ⟨ENTER⟩ **On** ⟨ENTER⟩ ⟨▼⟩ (Type:) ⬝⬝⬝ ⟨ENTER⟩ ⟨▼⟩

(Xlist:) ⟨2nd⟩ **L1** 1 ⟨▼⟩ (Ylist:) ⟨2nd⟩ **L2** 2 ⟨▼⟩ (Mark:) ■ ⟨ENTER⟩ ⟨GRAPH⟩

⇑ TI-82: **L1** ⟨ENTER⟩   ⇑ TI-82: **L2** ⟨ENTER⟩

Find and graph the quartic regression model:

STAT CALC 7:QuartReg ENTER ENTER Y=

⇑ TI-82: 8:QuartReg

VARS 5:Statistics EQ 1:RegEQ ENTER GRAPH

⇑ TI-82: 7:RegEQ

Evaluate _y_ for _x_ = 20:

2nd TRACE [CALC] 1:value ENTER (X=) 20 ENTER

LESSON 7.3

E X A M P L E S ① and ④   Graph $y = x(16 - 2x)(12 - 2x)$ and $y = 4x^3 - 56x^2 + 192x$ on the same screen.

Pages 441 and 442

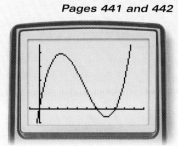

Use viewing window $[-1, 10]$ by $[-30, 200]$.

Y= X,T,θ,n (16 − 2 X,T,θ,n) (12 − 2 X,T,θ,n)

ENTER (Y2=) 4 X,T,θ,n ^ 3 − 56 X,T,θ,n x^2 + 192

X,T,θ,n GRAPH

For Example 4, use a similar keystroke sequence.

LESSON 7.4

E X A M P L E ①   Graph $y = 2x^3 - 7x^2 + 3x$, and look for any zeros of the function.

Page 449

Use viewing window $[-2, 5]$ by $[-8, 4]$.

Graph the function:

Y= 2 X,T,θ,n ^ 3 − 7 X,T,θ,n x^2 + 3 X,T,θ,n GRAPH

Move your cursor as indicated.

Find any zeros:

2nd TRACE [CALC] 2:zero ENTER (Left Bound?)

⇑ TI-82: 2:root

ENTER (Right Bound?) ENTER (Guess?)

ENTER

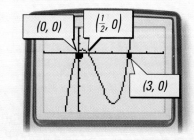

(0, 0) $\left(\frac{1}{2}, 0\right)$ (3, 0)

E X A M P L E S ②, ③, and ④   Graph each function, and find any zeros.

Pages 449–451

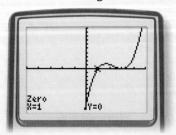

For Examples 2 and 3, use viewing window $[-5, 5]$ by $[-5, 5]$.
For Example 4, use viewing window $[-40, 20]$ by $[-5000, 7000]$.

Graph the function:

Use a keystroke sequence similar to that in Example 2 of Lesson 7.1.

Find any zeros:

Use a keystroke sequence similar to that in Example 1 of Lesson 7.4.

For Step 1, enter $y = x^4 - 3x^3 - 5x^2 + 13x + 6$, and use a table of values to find the corresponding y-value for each x-value in the table.

Use viewing window $[-5, 5]$ by $[-15, 15]$.

Enter and graph the function:
Use a keystroke sequence similar to that in Example 2 of Lesson 7.1.

Make a table of values:
Use a keystroke sequence similar to that in Example 1 of Lesson 7.2.

LESSON 7.5

E X A M P L E S ❶, ❷, and ❸ For Example 1, graph $y = 10x^3 + 9x^2 - 19x + 6$, and verify

Pages 459 and 460

that -2, $\frac{1}{2}$, and $\frac{3}{5}$ are zeros.

Use viewing window $[-3, 3]$ by $[-30, 30]$.

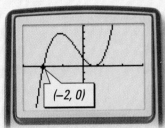

Graph the function:
Use a keystroke sequence similar to that in Example 1 of Lesson 7.1.

Evaluate y for x-values of -2, $\frac{1}{2}$, and $\frac{3}{5}$:
Use a keystroke similar to that used in Example 2 of Lesson 7.2. For a closer look around $x = \frac{1}{2}$ and $x = \frac{3}{5}$, use viewing window $[0.3, 0.8]$ by $[-1, 1]$.

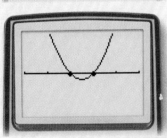

For Example 2, graph $y = x^3 - 2x^2 - 2x + 1$, and evaluate for $x = -1$. Use viewing window $[-5, 5]$ by $[-5, 5]$.

For Example 3, graph $y = 3x^3 - 10x^2 + 10x - 4$, and evaluate for $x = 2$. Use viewing window $[-3, 5]$ by $[-6, 4]$.

For Step 2, graph $y = 2x^3 - x^2 - 4x$.

Use viewing window $[-5, 5]$ by $[-3, 8]$.

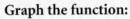

Y= | 2 | X,T,θ,n | ^ | 3 | – | X,T,θ,n | x² | – | 4 | X,T,θ,n | GRAPH

For Steps 3 and 4, use a similar keystroke sequence.

E X A M P L E ❹ Graph $y = x(20 - 2x)(12 - 2x)$ and $y = x(16 - 2x)(15 - 2x)$ on the same

Page 461

screen, and look for any points of intersection.

Use viewing window $[0, 6]$ by $[0, 350]$.

Graph the functions:
Use a keystroke sequence similar to that in Example 1 of Lesson 7.3.

Look for any points of intersection:

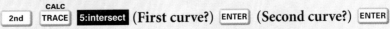

2nd | TRACE (CALC) | 5:intersect **(First curve?)** ENTER **(Second curve?)** ENTER

(Guess?) ENTER

8

Rational Functions and Radical Functions

IN THIS CHAPTER, YOU WILL STUDY RATIONAL functions and radical functions. Rational functions are ratios of polynomials. Radical functions are formed from the *n*th roots of numbers. The square-root function studied in Chapter 5 is an example of a radical function. Rational functions and radical functions have applications in physics, chemistry, engineering, business, economics, and many other fields.

Lessons

The size of the pupil determines the amount of light that enters the eye. In the same way, a camera's aperture, or opening, determines the amount of light that enters the camera.

Galileo is credited as the first person to notice that the motion of a pendulum depends only upon its length.

CHAPTER PORTFOLIO ACTIVITIES PROJECT

About the Chapter Project

Finding an average is something that most people can do almost instinctively. Currency exchange, hourly wage, car mileage, and average speed are common daily topics of discussion. You can measure an average in various ways. Two common averages are the arithmetic mean and the harmonic mean. In the Chapter Project, *Means to an End*, you will use the data provided to determine the most appropriate average.

After completing the Chapter Project, you will be able to do the following:

- Find the arithmetic mean and the harmonic mean of a set of data.

- Determine the relationship between the arithmetic and harmonic mean.

- Determine which of the averages—arithmetic mean, harmonic mean, or weighted harmonic mean—best represents a data set.

About the Portfolio Activities

Throughout the chapter, you will be given opportunities to complete Portfolio Activities that are designed to support your work on the Chapter Project.

- Exploring a historical representation of harmonic means is included in the Portfolio Activity on page 488.

- Exploring a geometric representation of harmonic means is included in the Portfolio Activity on page 497.

- Extending the definition of harmonic mean to n numbers is included in the Portfolio Activity on page 511.

- Using harmonic means to find average speeds is included in the Portfolio Activity on page 519.

Inverse, Joint, and Combined Variation

Why Inverse, joint, and combined variation relationships occur frequently in the real world. For example, the per-person cost of renting property decreases as the number of people paying increases.

Objectives

- Identify inverse, joint, and combined variations, find the constant of variation, and write an equation for the variation.

- Solve real-world problems involving inverse, joint, or combined variation.

APPLICATION

BUSINESS

A ranch can be rented for rodeos for a flat fee of $6000 per day. Janet Flores, a promoter, wants to rent the ranch for a 1-day rodeo. She knows that an admission price of $20 or less will be acceptable to the general public.

The table at right indicates what the per-person charge, c, would be if n people attend the rodeo. From the table, any number of attendees greater than 300 people will enable the promoter to cover the ranch's rental fee.

Notice that as the number of attendees increases, the per-person charge decreases. That is, as n increases, c decreases, which is characteristic of an *inverse-variation relationship*.

n	$c = \dfrac{6000}{n}$
300	20.00
320	18.75
340	≈17.65
360	≈16.67
380	≈15.79
400	15.00
420	≈14.29
440	≈13.64
460	≈13.04
480	12.50
500	12.00
520	≈11.54
540	≈11.11

Inverse Variation

Two variables, x and y, have an **inverse-variation** relationship if there is a nonzero number k such that $xy = k$, or $y = \dfrac{k}{x}$. The **constant of variation** is k.

Activity
Exploring Inverse Variation

You will need: no special materials

1. Copy and complete the table below for $y = \frac{1}{x}$.

x	$\frac{1}{10}$	$\frac{1}{4}$	$\frac{1}{2}$	1	2	3	4	5	6
y									
xy									

PROBLEM SOLVING

2. **Look for a pattern.** What can you say about the values of y as the values of x increase? What can you say about the values of y as the values of x decrease?

3. Repeat Step 1 for $y = \frac{2}{x}$ and $y = \frac{4}{x}$. Do you think that the pattern you identified in Step 2 will also be true for $y = \frac{3}{x}$? Repeat Step 1 for $y = \frac{3}{x}$.

CHECKPOINT ✔ 4. Describe the behavior of $y = \frac{k}{x}$, where $k > 0$, as x increases and as x decreases.

5. Let $y = \frac{k}{x}$, where $k > 0$. What happens when $x = 0$?

CONNECTION
TRANSFORMATIONS

The functions $y = \frac{1}{x}$, $y = \frac{2}{x}$, and $y = \frac{4}{x}$ all represent inverse-variation relationships. The typical graphical behavior of such a relationship can be observed at right.

Notice that the graphs of $y = \frac{2}{x}$ and $y = \frac{4}{x}$ are vertical stretches of the graph of the parent function $y = \frac{1}{x}$. That is, if $f(x) = \frac{1}{x}$, $g(x) = \frac{2}{x}$, and $h(x) = \frac{4}{x}$, then $g(x) = 2 \cdot f(x)$ and $h(x) = 4 \cdot f(x)$.

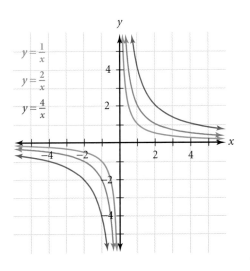

CHECKPOINT ✔ Describe where the graph of $y = \frac{3}{x}$ would lie in relation to the graphs shown above.

If you know one ordered pair (x, y) in a given inverse-variation relationship, you can find the constant of variation, k, and write the inverse-variation equation, $y = \frac{k}{x}$. In real-world situations, the x- and y-values are usually positive, and as the x-values increase, the y-values decrease. This is shown in Example 1 on the next page.

EXAMPLE ❶ The variable *y* varies inversely as *x*, and *y* = 13.5 when *x* = 4.5.

a. Find the constant of variation, and write an equation for the relationship.

b. Find *y* when *x* is 0.5, 1, 1.5, 2, and 2.5.

● **SOLUTION**

a.
$$xy = k$$
$$(4.5)(13.5) = k$$
$$k = 60.75$$

Thus, an equation for the relationship is $y = \frac{60.75}{x}$.

b. Enter $y = \frac{60.75}{x}$, and use the table feature with an *x*-increment of 0.5.

From the table, you can see that the *x*-values of 0.5, 1, 1.5, 2, and 2.5 have corresponding *y*-values of 121.5, 60.75, 40.5, 30.375, and 24.3, respectively.

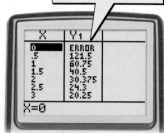

> Notice that when *x* is 0, the function is undefined.

TECHNOLOGY

GRAPHICS CALCULATOR

Keystroke Guide, page 554

TRY THIS   The variable *y* varies inversely as *x*, and *y* = 120 when *x* = 6.5. Find the constant of variation, and write an equation for the relationship. Then find *y* when *x* is 1.5, 4.5, 8, 12.5, and 14.

Recall from Lesson 1.4 that in a direct-variation relationship, *y* varies directly as *x* for any nonzero value of *k* such that *y* = *kx*. In *joint variation*, one quantity varies directly as two quantities.

Joint Variation

If *y* = *kxz*, then *y* **varies jointly** as *x* and *z*, and the constant of variation is *k*.

EXAMPLE ❷ **Refer to the rectangular prism shown at right.**

a. Write an equation for the volume of the prism, and identify the type of variation and the constant of variation.

b. Find the volume of the prism if the length of the base is 4 inches and the width of the base is 2 inches.

CONNECTION

GEOMETRY

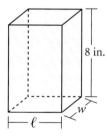

8 in.

ℓ   *w*

● **SOLUTION**

a. The volume of a rectangular prism is $V = \ell w h$.
$$V = \ell w h$$
$$V = \ell w(8), \text{ or } 8\ell w$$

Volume varies jointly as the length, *ℓ*, and width, *w*. The constant of variation is 8.

b. $V = 8\ell w = 8(4)(2) = 64$ The volume is 64 cubic inches.

TRY THIS

a. Write an equation for the volume of a rectangular prism whose base has a length of 12 inches. Identify the type of variation and the constant of variation.
b. Find the volume of the prism if the width of the base is 2 inches and the height of the prism is 4 inches.

If $y = kx^2$, where k is a nonzero constant, then y varies directly as the square of x. Many geometric relationships involve this type of joint variation, as shown in Example 3.

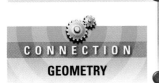

EXAMPLE 3

CONNECTION
GEOMETRY

a. Write an equation to represent the area, A, of the isosceles right triangle shown at right. Identify the type of variation and the constant of variation.
b. Find the area of the triangle when x is 1.5, 2.5, 3.5, and 4.5.

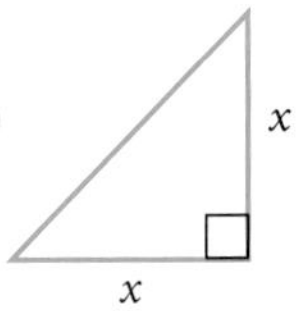

SOLUTION

a. The equation for the area is $A = \frac{1}{2}bh$, where b is the base and h is the height. Since the base is x and the height is x, A varies directly as the square of x. The constant of variation is $\frac{1}{2}$.

$$A = \frac{1}{2}bh$$
$$A = \frac{1}{2}(x)(x)$$
$$A = \frac{1}{2}x^2$$

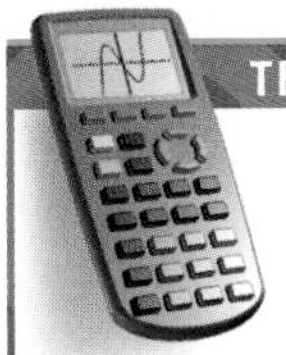

TECHNOLOGY
GRAPHICS CALCULATOR

Keystroke Guide, page 554

b. Enter $y = \frac{1}{2}x^2$ into a graphics calculator, and use the table feature. Begin with $x = 1.5$, and use an x-increment of 1.

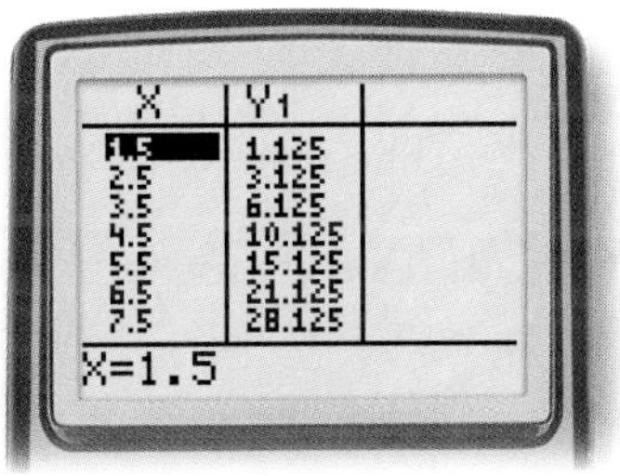

From the table, you can read the areas.

x	Area
1.5	1.125 square units
2.5	3.125 square units
3.5	6.125 square units
4.5	10.125 square units

TRY THIS

a. Write the formula for the area, A, of a circle whose radius is r. Identify the type of variation and the constant of variation.
b. Find the area of the circle when r is 1.5, 2.5, 3.5, and 4.5.

CRITICAL THINKING

Let y vary as the square of x. How does y change when x is doubled, tripled, and quadrupled? Justify your response.

When more than one type of variation occurs in the same equation, the equation represents a **combined variation**.

The rotational speeds, s_A and s_B, of gear A with t_A teeth and gear B with t_B teeth are related as indicated below.

$$t_A s_A = t_B s_B$$

The combined-variation equation for the rotational speed of gear B in terms of t_A, s_A, and t_B is as follows:

$$s_B = \frac{t_A s_A}{t_B}$$

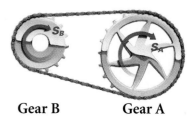

Gear B   Gear A

EXAMPLE ④ A bicycle's pedal gear has 52 teeth and is rotating at 65 revolutions per minute. A chain links the pedal gear to a rear-wheel gear that has 18 teeth and is attached to a 26-inch wheel.

At what speed, in miles per hour, is the bicycle traveling?

● **SOLUTION**

Let the pedal gear be gear A and the rear-wheel gear be gear B.

1. Find the rotational speed in revolutions per minute for gear B.

$$s_B = \frac{t_A s_A}{t_B}$$

$$s_B = \frac{(52)(65)}{18}$$

$$s_B \approx 188$$

The rear-wheel gear is rotating at about 188 revolutions per minute.

2. Convert revolutions per minute to miles per hour to find the speed of the bicycle.

A 26-inch wheel (including tire) has a circumference of 26π inches. Therefore, the bicycle is traveling at about $26\pi \times 188$ inches per minute. To convert to miles per hour, multiply by fractions equal to 1.

$$\frac{(26\pi)(188) \text{ in.}}{1 \text{ min}} \times \frac{1 \text{ ft}}{12 \text{ in.}} \times \frac{1 \text{ mi}}{5280 \text{ ft}} \times \frac{60 \text{ min}}{1 \text{ hr}} \approx 14.5 \text{ miles per hour}$$

TRY THIS   A bicycle's pedal gear has 46 teeth and is rotating at 55 revolutions per minute. If the pedal gear is linked to a rear-wheel gear that has 24 teeth and is attached to a 27-inch wheel, at what speed, in miles per hour, is the bicycle traveling?

CHECKPOINT ✔ Predict the effect of a rear-wheel gear with more teeth than the pedal gear. Verify your prediction by reworking Example 4 for a rear-wheel gear that has 60 teeth, 80 teeth, and 100 teeth.

CRITICAL THINKING   Suppose that the pedal gear in Example 4 has n teeth, the rear-wheel gear has m teeth, and $n > m$. What is the rotational speed of the rear-wheel gear relative to the speed of the pedal gear?

Exercises

● Communicate

1. Explain how direct variation and joint variation are related.

2. Let $xy = k$, where k is a constant greater than zero. Explain how you know that y must decrease when x increases.

CONNECTION

GEOMETRY Two formulas from geometry are shown below. Explain how to identify the type of variation found in each formula.

3. area, A, of a rhombus with diagonals of lengths p and q
$$A = \tfrac{1}{2}pq$$

4. area, A, of an equilateral triangle with sides of length s
$$A = \frac{\sqrt{3}}{4}s^2$$

5. Identify and explain how z varies as x, y, and d in the equation $z = \dfrac{2xy}{d^2}$.

6. Given the proportion $\dfrac{a}{b} = \dfrac{c}{d}$, write a related combined-variation equation. Explain how to form a different proportion from the combined-variation equation you wrote.

● Guided Skills Practice

7. The variable y varies inversely as x, and $y = 132$ when $x = 15$. Find the constant of variation, and write an equation for the relationship. Then find y when x is 1.5, 2.0, 2.5, 3.0, and 3.5. *(EXAMPLE 1)*

CONNECTIONS

GEOMETRY Refer to the rectangular prism at right. *(EXAMPLE 2)*

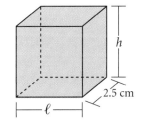

8. Write an equation for the volume of the prism, and identify the type of variation and the constant of variation.

9. Find the volume of the prism if the length of the base is 2 centimeters and the height is 8 centimeters.

GEOMETRY Refer to the figure at right, which consists of one square inside a larger square. *(EXAMPLE 3)*

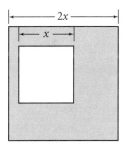

10. Write an equation to represent the area, A, of the shaded region. Identify the type of variation and the constant of variation.

11. Find the area of the shaded region for x-values of 1.5, 2.5, 3.5, 4.5, 5.5, and 6.5.

APPLICATION

12. **RECREATION** A bicycle's pedal gear has 52 teeth and is rotating at 145 revolutions per minute. At what speed, in miles per hour, is the bicycle traveling if the rear-wheel gear has 28 teeth and the wheels are 26 inches in diameter? *(EXAMPLE 4)*

For Exercises 13–20, *y* varies inversely as *x*. Write the appropriate inverse-variation equation, and find *y* for the given values of *x*.

13. $y = 36$ when $x = 9$; *x*-values: 3, 4, 5, 6, and 7

14. $y = 10$ when $x = 5$; *x*-values: 2.5, 3, and 3.5

15. $y = 0.5$ when $x = 8$; *x*-values: 5, 4, 3, 2, and 1

16. $y = 0.25$ when $x = 0.3$; *x*-values: 0.1, 0.2, 0.3, and 0.4

17. $y = 14$ when $x = 8$; *x*-values: 10, 15, and 20

18. $y = 2.25$ when $x = 1.5$; *x*-values: 0.1, 0.2, 0.3, and 0.4

19. $y = 1000$ when $x = 0.2$; *x*-values: 10^2, 10^3, and 10^4

20. $y = 10^{-2}$ when $x = 50$; *x*-values: 10^2, 10^3, and 10^4

For Exercises 21–28, *y* varies jointly as *x* and *z*. Write the appropriate joint-variation equation, and find *y* for the given values of *x* and *z*.

21. $y = -108$ when $x = -4$ and $z = 3$; $x = 6$ and $z = -2$

22. $y = -315$ when $x = 5$ and $z = 9$; $x = -7$ and $z = 8$

23. $y = 15$ when $x = 9$ and $z = 1.5$; $x = 18$ and $z = 3$

24. $y = 0.5$ when $x = 10$ and $z = 3$; $x = 1.8$ and $z = 6$

25. $y = 120$ when $x = 8$ and $z = 20$; $x = 54$ and $z = 7$

26. $y = 0.1$ when $x = 0.1$ and $z = 5$; $x = 0.2$ and $z = 0.4$

27. $y = 10^4$ when $x = 10^2$ and $z = 10^1$; $x = 10^5$ and $z = 10^2$

28. $y = 2 \times 10^5$ when $x = 10^1$ and $z = 10^3$; $x = 3 \times 10^4$ and $z = 1.5 \times 10^3$

For Exercises 29–34, *z* varies jointly as *x* and *y* and inversely as *w*. Write the appropriate combined-variation equation, and find *z* for the given values of *x*, *y*, and *w*.

29. $z = 3$ when $x = 3$, $y = -2$, and $w = -4$; $x = 6$, $y = 7$, and $w = -4$

30. $z = 10$ when $x = 5$, $y = -2$, and $w = 3$; $x = 8$, $y = 6$, and $w = -12$

31. $z = 36$ when $x = 9$, $y = 10$, and $w = 15$; $x = 10$, $y = 18$, and $w = 5$

32. $z = 15$ when $x = 3$, $y = 4$, and $w = 9$; $x = 1.5$, $y = 20.5$, and $w = 5.4$

33. $z = 100$ when $x = 100$, $y = 7$, and $w = 2$; $x = 3.5$, $y = 24$, and $w = 27$

34. $z = 54$ when $x = 8$, $y = 10$, and $w = 1.5$; $x = 1.5$, $y = 2.4$, and $w = 3$

If (x_1, y_1) and (x_2, y_2) satisfy $xy = k$, then $x_1 y_1 = x_2 y_2$. Find *x* or *y* as indicated.

35. $(x, 2.5)$ and $(6, 4)$ **36.** $(4.5, y)$ and $(12, 6)$

37. $(3.6, 5)$ and $(7.2, y)$ **38.** $(3, y)$ and $(18, 6)$

39. $(18, 2)$ and (y, y) **40.** (x, x) and $(5, 125)$

CHALLENGE

41. Show that if (x_1, y_1) and (x_2, y_2) satisfy the inverse-variation equation $xy = k$ and if $x_1, y_1, x_2,$ and y_2 are nonzero, then $\frac{x_1}{x_2} = \frac{y_2}{y_1}$ and $y_2 = y_1\left(\frac{x_1}{x_2}\right)$.

42 **STATISTICS** Refer to the table and scatter plot below.

x	0	1	2	3	4	5	6
y	0.00	0.25	1.00	2.25	4.00	6.25	9.00

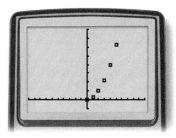

a. Use a graphics calculator to find an equation of the form $y = kx^2$ to represent the data.

b. Find y for x-values of 24, 25, 26, 27, 28, 29, and 30.

43. PHOTOGRAPHY Under certain conditions of artificial light, the exposure time required to photograph an object varies directly as the candlepower of the light and varies inversely as the square of the object's distance from the light source. If the exposure time is 0.01 second when the light source is 6.00 feet from the object, how far from the object should the light source be when both the candlepower and the exposure time are doubled?

44. AVIATION The lifting force exerted by the atmosphere on the wings of an airplane in flight varies directly as the surface area of the wings and the square of the plane's airspeed. A small private plane has a cruising airspeed of 250 miles per hour. In order to obtain 3 times the lifting force, a new plane is designed with a wing surface area twice that of the older model. What cruising speed, to the nearest mile per hour, is planned for the new model?

45. PHYSICS Heat loss, h, in calories per hour through a glass window varies jointly as the difference, d, between the inside and outside temperatures and as the area, A, of the window and inversely as the thickness, t, of the pane of glass. If the temperature difference is 30°F, there is a heat loss of 9000 calories per hour through a window with an area of 1500 cubic centimeters and thickness of 0.25 centimeter. Find the heat loss through a window with the same area and a thickness of 0.2 centimeter when the temperature difference is 15°F.

46. ORNITHOLOGY There are many forces that work together to make both airplanes and birds fly. Although wingshape varies greatly among birds, the number of wing beats per second (one wing beat is considered to be one upward and downward motion) for any bird in flight is approximately inversely related to the length of its wing.

a. Find the approximate constant of variation, k, to the nearest tenth, if a herring gull flaps its wings at a rate of about 2.8 wing beats per second and has a wing length of about 24.1 centimeters.

b. Use the approximate value of k from part **a** to find the approximate number of wing beats per second for a starling that has a wing length of about 13.2 centimeters.

c. Use the approximate value of k from part **a** to find the approximate wing length of a cormorant who flaps its wings at a rate of about 1.9 wing beats per second.

Double-crested cormorant

Starling

 *Look Back*

Rewrite each expression with positive exponents only. *(LESSON 2.2)*

47. x^{-1} **48.** ab^{-3} **49.** $\left(\dfrac{x}{y}\right)^{-2}$ **50.** $a^{-2}b^3c^{-5}d$ **51.** $[(x^{-3})^{-2}]^{-3}$

Identify the vertex and the axis of symmetry in the graph of each function. *(LESSON 5.4)*

52. $f(x) = -3x^2 + 5$ **53.** $h(x) = x^2 + 2x - 3$ **54.** $b(t) = -t^2 - 5t + 6$

55. $g(x) = x^2 + 2$ **56.** $d(t) = t^2 + t + 1$ **57.** $r(t) = 2t^2 - 3t + 2$

Give the degree of each polynomial. *(LESSON 7.1)*

58. $3x^5 - 2x^4 + x^2 - 1$ **59.** $2 - 5x + 7x^2 - x^3$ **60.** $-5x^3 - x^4 + 1$

Describe the end behavior of each function. *(LESSON 7.2)*

61. $f(x) = x^4 + 2x^3 - x^2 + 2$ **62.** $g(x) = -3x^3 - 2x^2 + x - 4$

 Look Beyond

63. Make a table of values for $f(x) = \dfrac{1}{x+2}$ for values of x near -2. Use this table to describe the values of f near $x = -2$.

As early as 300 C.E., Pappus of Alexandria represented the arithmetic mean and the harmonic mean geometrically by constructing the figure shown below. In the figure, arc *ADC* is a semicircle of circle *O*.

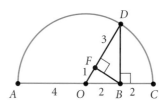

For any two numbers a and b, the arithmetic mean is $\dfrac{a+b}{2}$.

For any two nonzero numbers a and b, the harmonic mean is $\dfrac{2}{\dfrac{1}{a}+\dfrac{1}{b}}$.

1. Find the arithmetic mean and the harmonic mean of *AB* and *BC*.

2. Identify the side of a triangle in the figure whose length equals the arithmetic mean that you found in Step 1.

3. Identify the side of a triangle in the figure whose length equals the harmonic mean that you found in Step 1.

WORKING ON THE CHAPTER PROJECT

You should now be able to complete Activity 1 of the Chapter Project.

Rational Functions and Their Graphs

Objectives

- Identify and evaluate rational functions.

- Graph a rational function, find its domain, write equations for its asymptotes, and identify any holes in its graph.

Why *Rational functions are used to describe many real-world relationships. For example, rational functions are often used to solve mixture problems.*

Dane is a chemist who is varying the salt concentration of a solution. He can use a *rational function* to represent the salt concentration of the solution.

E X A M P L E **1** Dane begins with 65 milliliters of a 10% saline solution. He adds x milliliters of distilled water to the container holding the saline solution.

a. Write a function, C, that represents the salt concentration of the solution.

APPLICATION
CHEMISTRY

b. What is the salt concentration of the solution if 100 millimeters of distilled water is added?

● **SOLUTION**

a. Original concentration of salt solution:

$$10\% \text{ of } 65 = 6.5 \qquad \frac{6.5}{65} \quad \begin{matrix} \leftarrow salt \\ \leftarrow solution \end{matrix}$$

New concentration of salt solution:

Add x millimeters of distilled water. $\quad \dfrac{6.5}{65 + x} \quad \begin{matrix} \leftarrow salt \\ \leftarrow solution \end{matrix}$

Function for the salt concentration in this solution:

$$C(x) = \frac{6.5}{65 + x}$$

b. Salt concentration when 100 milliliters of distilled water is added:

$$C(100) = \frac{6.5}{65 + 100} \approx 0.039, \text{ or } 3.9\%$$

A **rational expression** is the quotient of two polynomials. A **rational function** is a function defined by a rational expression. The function $C(x) = \dfrac{6.5}{65 + x}$ from Example 1 is a rational function.

CHECKPOINT ✔ Explain why $y = \dfrac{e^x}{x - 1}$ and $y = \dfrac{x^2 + 2}{|x|}$ are not rational functions.

The rational function $f(x) = \frac{1}{x}$ is undefined when $x = 0$. In general, the domain of a rational function is the set of all real numbers except those real numbers that make the denominator equal to zero.

E X A M P L E **2** Find the domain of $g(x) = \frac{x^2 - 7x + 12}{x^2 + 9x + 20}$.

SOLUTION

Find the values of x for which the denominator, $x^2 + 9x + 20$, equals 0.

$$x^2 + 9x + 20 = 0$$
$$(x + 4)(x + 5) = 0$$
$$x = -4 \ \ or \ \ x = -5$$

The domain is all real numbers except -4 and -5.

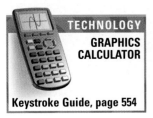
TECHNOLOGY
GRAPHICS CALCULATOR

Keystroke Guide, page 554

CHECK

Enter $y = \frac{x^2 - 7x + 12}{x^2 + 9x + 20}$ into a graphics calculator. Use the table feature to verify that -4 and -5 are not included in the domain.

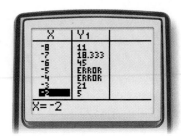

TRY THIS Find the domain of $j(x) = \frac{3x^2 + x - 2}{x^2 + 2x - 3}$.

Vertical Asymptotes

Recall from Lesson 6.2 that exponential functions, such as $y = 2^x$, have a horizontal asymptote. Rational functions can have horizontal *and* vertical asymptotes. In the Activity below, you will explore the vertical asymptotes of some rational functions.

Exploring Vertical Asymptotes

TECHNOLOGY
GRAPHICS CALCULATOR

Keystroke Guide, page 555

You will need: a graphics calculator

1. Enter the function $y = \frac{1}{x - 2}$ into a graphics calculator.

a. Copy the table below. Use the table feature to complete it.

x	1.0	1.1	1.2	1.3	1.4	1.5	1.6	1.7	1.8	1.9
y										

b. Copy the table below. Use the table feature to complete it.

x	3.0	2.9	2.8	2.7	2.6	2.5	2.4	2.3	2.2	2.1
y										

CHECKPOINT ✔ **2.** What can you say about y as x approaches 2 from values of x less than 2? What can you say about y as x approaches 2 from values of x greater than 2? What do you think is the value of y when $x = 2$?

CHECKPOINT ✔ **3.** Let $y = \dfrac{1}{x+3}$. Use the table feature of a graphics calculator to evaluate y for values of x a little less than -3 and for values of x a little greater than -3. What can you say about y as x approaches -3 from values of x less than -3? What can you say about y as x approaches -3 from values of x greater than -3? What do you think is the value of y when $x = -3$?

Real numbers for which a rational function is not defined are called **excluded values**.

CHECKPOINT ✔ Find the excluded values for the function $y = \dfrac{x+3}{x^2-x-6}$.

At an excluded value, a rational function *may* have a vertical asymptote. The necessary conditions for a vertical asymptote are given below.

Vertical Asymptote

If $x - a$ is a factor of the denominator of a rational function but not a factor of its numerator, then $x = a$ is a vertical asymptote of the graph of the function.

E X A M P L E ③ Identify all vertical asymptotes of the graph of $r(x) = \dfrac{2x}{x^2-1}$.

● **SOLUTION**

Factor the denominator: $\qquad r(x) = \dfrac{2x}{x^2-1} = \dfrac{2x}{(x-1)(x+1)}$

Since neither factor of the denominator is a factor of the numerator, equations for the vertical asymptotes are $x = -1$ and $x = 1$.

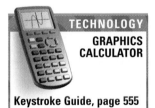
TECHNOLOGY
GRAPHICS CALCULATOR

Keystroke Guide, page 555

CHECK

Graph $y = \dfrac{2x}{x^2-1}$, and look for the vertical asymptotes, $x = -1$ and $x = 1$.

Note: Depending on the viewing window used, the calculator may display lines that look like vertical asymptotes but are actually lines that connect consecutive points on each side of the asymptotes.

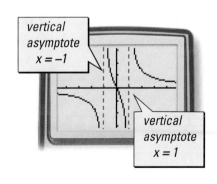

vertical asymptote $x = -1$

vertical asymptote $x = 1$

TRY THIS Identify all vertical asymptotes of the graph of $r(x) = \dfrac{x}{x^2+5x+6}$.

CRITICAL THINKING Let P be a polynomial expression. Write a rational function of the form $R(x) = \dfrac{1}{P}$ that has vertical asymptotes at $x = -2$, $x = 0$, and $x = 2$.

Horizontal Asymptotes

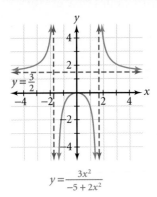

$$y = \frac{3x^2}{-5 + 2x^2}$$

To examine the *horizontal asymptotes* of rational functions, consider the graph of $y = \frac{3x^2}{-5 + 2x^2}$ shown at left. The graph shows a horizontal asymptote at $y = \frac{3}{2}$, or $y = 1.5$. The tables below confirm that as the x-values get farther away from 0, the y-values approach 1.5.

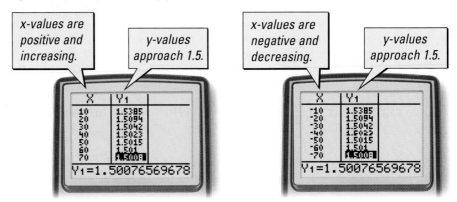

Because both the numerator and the denominator of the function $y = \frac{3x^2}{-5 + 2x^2}$ have the same degree, you can use the leading coefficients, 3 and 2, of the numerator and denominator to write the equation for the horizontal asymptote of its graph, $y = \frac{3}{2}$.

Horizontal Asymptote

Let $R(x) = \frac{P}{Q}$ be a rational function, where P and Q are polynomials.

- If the degree of P is less than the degree of Q, then $y = 0$ is the equation of the horizontal asymptote of the graph of R.

- If the degree of P equals the degree of Q and a and b are the leading coefficients of P and Q, respectively, then $y = \frac{a}{b}$ is the equation of the horizontal asymptote of the graph of R.

- If the degree of P is greater than the degree of Q, then the graph of R has no horizontal asymptote.

E X A M P L E ④ Let $R(x) = \frac{x}{x^2 - 2x - 3}$. Identify all vertical asymptotes and all horizontal asymptotes of the graph of R.

SOLUTION

1. To find the equations of all vertical asymptotes, factor the denominator, and look for excluded values of the domain.

$$R(x) = \frac{x}{(x - 3)(x + 1)}$$

Since neither factor of the denominator is a factor of the numerator, the equations for the vertical asymptotes are $x = 3$ and $x = -1$.

2. Because the degree of the numerator is less than the degree of the denominator, the equation for the horizontal asymptote is $y = 0$.

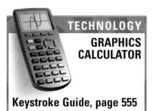

TECHNOLOGY
GRAPHICS CALCULATOR

Keystroke Guide, page 555

CHECK
Graph $y = \dfrac{x}{x^2 - 2x - 3}$, and look for the vertical and horizontal asymptotes.

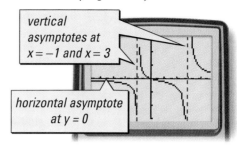

vertical asymptotes at $x = -1$ and $x = 3$

horizontal asymptote at $y = 0$

TRY THIS   Let $R(x) = \dfrac{2x^2 - 2x + 1}{x^2 - x - 12}$. Find the equations of all vertical asymptotes and all horizontal asymptotes of the graph of R.

Using Asymptotes to Graph

You can graph a rational function by using the asymptotes, as shown in Example 5.

E X A M P L E ⑤ Graph $y = \dfrac{x + 2}{x - 2}$, showing all asymptotes.

● **SOLUTION**

Write equations for the asymptotes, and graph them as dashed lines.

vertical asymptote: $x = 2$

horizontal asymptote: $y = 1$

PROBLEM SOLVING **Use a table.** To help obtain an accurate graph, plot some points on each branch of the graph, and sketch the curves through these points.

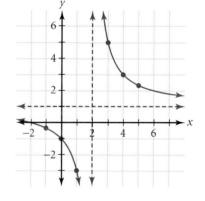

x	-1	0	1	3	4	5
y	$-\frac{1}{3}$	-1	-3	5	3	$2\frac{1}{3}$

C O N N E C T I O N
TRANSFORMATIONS

By dividing, you can rewrite $y = \dfrac{x + 2}{x - 2}$ from Example 5 as $y = 1 + \dfrac{4}{x - 2}$.

From this form, you can see the transformations of the graph of $y = \dfrac{1}{x}$.

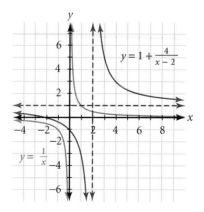

$$y = 1 + \frac{4}{x - 2}$$

vertical stretch by a factor of 4

translation of 1 unit up

translation of 2 units to the right

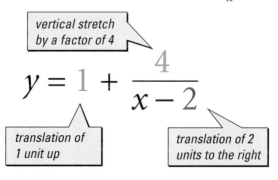

Holes in Graphs

The graph of a rational function may have a *hole* in it. For example, $f(x) = \dfrac{x^2 - 9}{x - 3}$ can be written as $f(x) = \dfrac{(x - 3)(x + 3)}{x - 3}$. Because $x - 3$ is a factor of *both* the numerator *and* the denominator, the graph of f has a hole when $x = 3$.

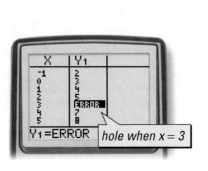

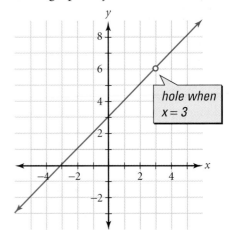

Hole in the Graph

If $x - b$ is a factor of the numerator and the denominator of a rational function, then there is a **hole in the graph** of the function when $x = b$ unless $x = b$ is a vertical asymptote.

EXAMPLE ⑥ Let $y = \dfrac{3 - 2x - x^2}{x^2 + x - 2}$. **Identify all asymptotes and holes in the graph.**

● **SOLUTION**

Factor the numerator and denominator.

$$y = \frac{3 - 2x - x^2}{x^2 + x - 2} = \frac{-(x^2 + 2x - 3)}{(x - 1)(x + 2)} = \frac{-(x + 3)(x - 1)}{(x - 1)(x + 2)}$$

Because $x - 1$ is a factor of *both* the numerator and the denominator, the graph has a hole when $x = 1$.

Because $x + 2$ is a factor of *only* the denominator, there is a vertical asymptote at $x = -2$.

Because the degree of the numerator equals the degree of the denominator, there is a horizontal asymptote at $y = \dfrac{-1}{1} = -1$.

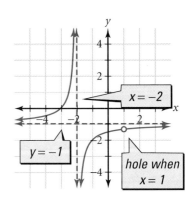

TRY THIS   Let $y = \dfrac{3x^2 + x^3}{x^2 + 2x - 3}$. Identify all asymptotes and holes in the graph.

Exercises

Communicate

1. Why is the quotient of two polynomials described as "rational"?

2. Describe how to find the excluded values of a rational function.

3. Explain how to decide whether a linear factor of the denominator of a rational function is related to a vertical asymptote of the graph of the function or to a hole in the graph of the function.

4. Explain how to use the asymptotes of the graph of $g(x) = \frac{x-5}{x-3}$ to sketch the graph of the function.

Guided Skills Practice

APPLICATION

5. **CHEMISTRY** Refer to the salt-concentration problem at the beginning of the lesson. If Dane begins with 90 milliliters of a 15% saline solution and adds x milliliters of distilled water, what function represents the salt concentration of the new solution? What is the concentration of the solution if 150 milliliters of distilled water is added? *(EXAMPLE 1)*

6. Find the domain of $h(x) = \frac{2x^2 - 5}{x^2 - 7x + 12}$. *(EXAMPLE 2)*

Identify all asymptotes and holes in the graph of each rational function. *(EXAMPLES 3, 4, AND 6)*

7. $r(x) = \frac{3x - 1}{4x^2 - 9}$

8. $R(x) = \frac{2x^2 - 1}{x^2 - 9}$

9. $f(x) = \frac{(x-3)^2}{x^2 - 5x + 6}$

10. Graph $f(x) = \frac{2x+1}{x-3}$, showing all asymptotes. *(EXAMPLE 5)*

Practice and Apply

Determine whether each function is a rational function. If so, find the domain. If the function is not rational, state why not.

11. $f(x) = \frac{x}{2x - 7}$

12. $g(x) = \frac{x+2}{2x}$

13. $h(x) = \frac{x^{-\frac{1}{2}}}{x^2}$

14. $f(x) = \frac{x}{(2x-7)(x+3)}$

15. $g(x) = \frac{5^x}{x^5}$

16. $h(x) = \frac{|x^2 - 4|}{|x + 2|}$

Identify all asymptotes and holes in the graph of each rational function.

17. $f(x) = \frac{3x + 5}{x - 2}$

18. $g(x) = \frac{x+2}{2x^2}$

19. $d(x) = \frac{x^2 - 4}{x^2 - 4x + 4}$

20. $g(x) = \frac{(x+2)^2}{x^2 + 5x + 6}$

21. $r(x) = \frac{x^2 - 16}{4 - 5x + x^2}$

22. $b(x) = \frac{x^2 - 2x + 1}{x^2 + x - 2}$

Find the domain of each rational function. Identify all asymptotes and holes in the graph of each rational function. Then graph.

23. $h(x) = \dfrac{2x - 2}{2x + 2}$

24. $r(x) = \dfrac{2x}{2x(x - 5)}$

25. $w(x) = \dfrac{(3x - 1)(x + 2)}{x + 2}$

26. $a(x) = \dfrac{x + 1}{x^2 + 4x - 21}$

27. $d(x) = \dfrac{3x - 1}{9x^2 - 36}$

28. $d(x) = \dfrac{7x + 8}{x^2 - 10x + 25}$

29. $f(x) = \dfrac{7x + 1}{5x^2 + 3}$

30. $r(x) = \dfrac{x^2 - 4}{x^2 + 4}$

31. $m(x) = \dfrac{x(x^2 - 4)}{x^2 - 7x + 6}$

32. $t(x) = \dfrac{x^2 - 4x}{x^3 - x^2 - 20x}$

33. $g(x) = \dfrac{5x^2 - 3x}{x^3 - 8x^2 + 16x}$

34. $t(x) = \dfrac{2x + 1}{x^3 - 27}$

Write a rational function with the given asymptotes and holes.

35. $x = 2$ and $y = 3$

36. $x = -2$ and $y = 0$

37. $x = \pm 1$, $y = 1.5$, hole when $x = 0$

38. $x = 1$, $y = 3$, hole when $x = 2$

39. holes when $x = 0$ and $x = 2$

40. holes when $x = 0$, $x = 2$, and $x = 3$

41. Let $f(x) = \dfrac{1}{x^2 - 3x + c}$. Find c such that the graph of f has the given number of vertical asymptotes. Justify your responses.

a. none

b. one

c. two

42. GEOMETRY Refer to the rectangle at right.
a. Write a rational function, R, to represent the ratio of the perimeter, P, to the area, A.
b. For what values of x is P defined? is A defined? is R defined?

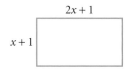

43. GEOMETRY Refer to the circle at right.
a. Write a rational function, R, to represent the ratio of the circumference, C, to the area, A.
b. For what values of x is C defined? is A defined? is R defined?

44. CHEMISTRY Leon begins with 72 milliliters of an 8% saline solution. He adds x milliliters of distilled water to the saline solution.
a. What function represents salt concentration, C, of the new solution?
b. What is the approximate concentration if 720 milliliters of distilled water is added?

45. ECONOMICS Max owns a small florist shop. His fixed costs are $250 per week, and his average variable costs are $11.45 per arrangement.
a. Write a function, T, that represents Max's total costs for one week if he makes x floral arrangements that week.
b. Write a function in terms of T and x for the cost, C, per floral arrangement during that week.

46. PHYSICS An object weighing w_0 kilograms on Earth is h kilometers above the surface of the Earth. Then the function for the object's weight at that altitude is $w(h) = w_0\left(\dfrac{6400}{6400 + h}\right)^2$.

    a. Explain why w is a rational function of h.

    b. Use a table to find w for h-values of 10, 20, and 100.

    c. At about what altitude will an object weigh half of what it weighs on Earth?

Look Back

Solve. *(LESSON 1.8)*

47. $|5x - 6| > 2$ **48.** $|x + 5| \geq 7$ **49.** $\left|\dfrac{3}{2} - \dfrac{5}{2}x\right| \leq \dfrac{7}{2}$ **50.** $\left|\dfrac{3}{2} - \dfrac{5}{2}x\right| \leq -\dfrac{7}{2}$

Write each expression in standard form, $ax^2 + bx + c$. *(LESSON 5.1)*

51. $-12x(3x - 2)$ **52.** $(3x - 1)(6x - 7)$ **53.** $(4 - 5x)(x - 9)$

54. $(x - 5)(2x + 3)$ **55.** $(3x - 4)(3x + 4)$ **56.** $-4(x - 3)^2$

Factor each expression. *(LESSON 5.3)*

57. $3x^2 - 6x$ **58.** $1 - 25y^2$ **59.** $9x^2 - 49$

60. $t^2 - 5t - 24$ **61.** $x^2 + 12x + 36$ **62.** $x^2 - 16x + 64$

Look Beyond

Simplify.

63. $\dfrac{9}{3}$ **64.** $\dfrac{x^2}{x}$ **65.** $\dfrac{x^2 + 4x + 4}{x + 2}$

In this activity you will use rational functions to show that if a rectangle and a square have the same ratio of area to perimeter, then the side length of the square is the harmonic mean of the width and length of the rectangle.

Refer to the rectangle and square shown at left.

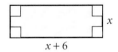
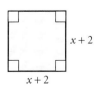

    1. Write a rational function, R, to represent the ratio of the area, A, of the rectangle to its perimeter, P.

    2. Find a value of x such that the ratio of the area to the perimeter is 2.

    3. Use this value to find the length and width of the rectangle.

    4. Write a rational function, S, to represent the ratio of the area, A, of the square to its perimeter, P.

    5. Find a value of x such that the ratio of the area to the perimeter is 2.

    6. Use this value to find the side length of the square.

    7. Show that the side length of the square is the harmonic mean of the length and width of the rectangle.

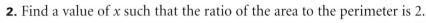
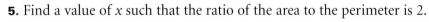

Multiplying and Dividing Rational Expressions

Why Multiplying and dividing rational expressions are sometimes used to solve real-world problems, such as analyzing the revenue and cost for a fund-raising activity.

Objectives

● Multiply and divide rational expressions.

● Simplify rational expressions, including complex fractions.

APPLICATION
FUND-RAISING

To analyze the revenue and costs from the sale of school-spirit ribbons, members of the Jamesville High School Home Economics Club used the revenue-to-cost ratio below.

$$\frac{\text{revenue from the sale of each ribbon}}{\text{cost of making each ribbon}}$$

They represented the number of ribbons produced and sold by x and the total production cost in dollars by $0.8x + 25$. If the revenue for each ribbon was \$3, for how many ribbons was the revenue-to-cost ratio 1.5 or greater? Finding the answer to this question involves writing and simplifying a rational expression. *You will answer this question in Example 6.*

Simplifying Rational Expressions

To *simplify* a rational expression, divide the numerator and the denominator by a common factor. The expression is simplified when you can no longer divide the numerator and denominator by a common factor other than 1.

EXAMPLE ❶ Simplify $\frac{x^2 + 5x - 6}{x^2 - 36}$.

● **SOLUTION**

$$\frac{x^2 + 5x - 6}{x^2 - 36} = \frac{(x + 6)(x - 1)}{(x - 6)(x + 6)} \qquad \textit{Factor the numerator and denominator.}$$

$$= \frac{(x + 6)(x - 1)}{(x - 6)(x + 6)} \qquad \textit{Divide out the common factor.}$$

$$= \frac{x - 1}{x - 6}$$

Note that 6 and −6 are excluded values of x in the original expression.

TRY THIS Simplify $\frac{b^2 - 49}{b^2 - 8b + 7}$.

Multiplying Rational Expressions

Multiplying rational expressions is similar to multiplying rational numbers.

Rational Numbers	**Rational Expressions**

$$\frac{15}{4} \cdot \frac{14}{9} = \frac{\overset{1}{\cancel{3}} \cdot 5}{\cancel{4}_2} \cdot \frac{\overset{1}{\cancel{2}} \cdot 7}{\cancel{9}_3} = \frac{35}{6} \qquad\qquad \frac{15}{x^2} \cdot \frac{4x^4}{21} = \frac{\overset{1}{\cancel{3}} \cdot 5}{x_1^2} \cdot \frac{4 \cdot \overset{x^2}{\cancel{x^4}}}{\cancel{3}_1 \cdot 7} = \frac{20x^2}{7}$$

E X A M P L E ❷ Simplify $\dfrac{3}{4x^2} \cdot \dfrac{4x^3}{21} \cdot \dfrac{14}{4x^5}$.

SOLUTION

$$\frac{3}{4x^2} \cdot \frac{4x^3}{21} \cdot \frac{14}{4x^5} = \frac{\overset{1}{\cancel{3}} \cdot \overset{1}{\cancel{4}} \cdot \overset{1}{\cancel{2}} \cdot \overset{1}{\cancel{7}}}{\cancel{4}_1 \cdot \cancel{3}_1 \cdot \cancel{7}_1 \cdot \cancel{2}_1 \cdot 2} \cdot \frac{\overset{1}{\cancel{x^3}}}{\underset{x^4}{\cancel{x^7}}} = \frac{1}{2x^4}$$

TRY THIS   Simplify $\dfrac{28}{4a^3} \cdot \dfrac{4a^5}{21} \cdot \dfrac{3}{49a^4}$.

To multiply one rational expression by another, multiply as with fractions.

$$\frac{a}{b} \cdot \frac{c}{d} = \frac{ac}{bd}, \text{ where } b \neq 0 \text{ and } d \neq 0$$

You can simplify the product by dividing out the common factors in the numerator and denominator before or after multiplying.

E X A M P L E ❸ Simplify $\dfrac{x+1}{x^2+2x-3} \cdot \dfrac{x^2+x-6}{x^2-2x-3}$.

SOLUTION

$$\frac{x+1}{x^2+2x-3} \cdot \frac{x^2+x-6}{x^2-2x-3} = \frac{\overset{1}{\cancel{x+1}}}{(x+3)(x-1)} \cdot \frac{\overset{1}{\cancel{(x+3)}}(x-2)}{(x-3)\cancel{(x+1)}_1}$$

$$= \frac{x-2}{(x-1)(x-3)}, \quad \text{or} \quad \frac{x-2}{x^2-4x+3}$$

TRY THIS   Simplify $\dfrac{x^2-25}{x^2-5x+6} \cdot \dfrac{x^2-4}{x^2+2x-15}$.

Dividing Rational Expressions

Dividing one rational expression by another is similar to dividing one rational number by another.

Rational Numbers	**Rational Expressions**

$$\frac{6}{8} \div \frac{12}{32} = \frac{6}{8} \cdot \frac{32}{12} \quad \boxed{\textit{Multiply by the reciprocal of }\frac{12}{32}.} \qquad \frac{6}{x^3} \div \frac{12}{x^5} = \frac{6}{x^3} \cdot \frac{x^5}{12} \quad \boxed{\textit{Multiply by the reciprocal of }\frac{12}{x^5}.}$$

$$= \frac{\overset{1}{\cancel{6}}}{\cancel{8}_1} \cdot \frac{\overset{4}{\cancel{32}}}{\cancel{12}_2} \qquad\qquad\qquad = \frac{\overset{1}{\cancel{6}}}{x_1^3} \cdot \frac{\overset{x^2}{\cancel{x^5}}}{\cancel{12}_2}$$

$$= \frac{4}{2}, \text{ or } 2 \qquad\qquad\qquad\qquad = \frac{x^2}{2}, \text{ or } \frac{1}{2}x^2$$

To divide one rational expression by another, multiply by the reciprocal of the divisor.

$$\frac{a}{b} \div \frac{c}{d} = \frac{a}{b} \cdot \frac{d}{c} = \frac{ad}{bc}, \text{ where } b \neq 0, c \neq 0, \text{ and } d \neq 0$$

Simplify by dividing out common factors in the numerator and denominator.

EXAMPLE ④ Simplify $\frac{x-4}{(x-2)^2} \div \frac{x^2-3x-4}{x^2-4}$.

● **SOLUTION**

$$\frac{x-4}{(x-2)^2} \div \frac{x^2-3x-4}{x^2-4} = \frac{x-4}{(x-2)^2} \cdot \frac{x^2-4}{x^2-3x-4}$$ *Multiply by the reciprocal.*

$$= \frac{\overset{1}{\cancel{x-4}}}{(x-2)\cancel{(x-2)}} \cdot \frac{\cancel{(x-2)}(x+2)}{\cancel{(x-4)}(x+1)}$$ *Divide out common factors.*

$$= \frac{x+2}{(x-2)(x+1)}, \quad \text{or} \quad \frac{x+2}{x^2-x-2}$$

TRY THIS Simplify $\frac{(x+3)^2}{x-5} \div \frac{x^2-9}{x^2-8x+15}$.

PROBLEM SOLVING You can **use a graph** to identify polynomials in a rational expression that cannot be factored with real numbers. For example, to determine whether $x^2 - x + 1$ in the rational expression $\frac{x-4}{x-1} \cdot \frac{x^2-x+1}{x^2}$ can be factored with real numbers, look for x-intercepts in the graph of $y = x^2 - x + 1$.

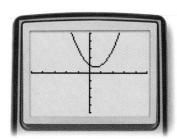

The graph of $y = x^2 - x + 1$ has no x-intercepts, so $y = x^2 - x + 1$ has no real zeros and $x^2 - x + 1$ cannot be factored with real numbers. Thus, the rational expression $\frac{x-4}{x-1} \cdot \frac{x^2-x+1}{x^2}$ cannot be simplified further.

Complex Fractions

A **complex fraction** is a quotient that contains one or more fractions in the numerator, the denominator, or both.

EXAMPLE ⑤ Simplify the complex fraction $\dfrac{\dfrac{4a^2-1}{a^2-4}}{\dfrac{2a-1}{a+2}}$.

● **SOLUTION**

$$\frac{\dfrac{4a^2-1}{a^2-4}}{\dfrac{2a-1}{a+2}} = \frac{4a^2-1}{a^2-4} \cdot \frac{a+2}{2a-1}$$ *Multiply by the reciprocal.*

$$= \frac{(2a-1)(2a+1)}{(a-2)(a+2)} \cdot \frac{a+2}{2a-1}$$ *Factor.*

$$= \frac{\overset{1}{\cancel{(2a-1)}}(2a+1)\overset{1}{\cancel{(a+2)}}}{(a-2)\underset{1}{\cancel{(a+2)}}\underset{1}{\cancel{(2a-1)}}}$$ *Divide out common factors.*

$$= \frac{2a+1}{a-2}$$

TRY THIS

Simplify $\dfrac{\frac{(x+2)^2}{x-3}}{\frac{x^2-4}{(x-3)^2}}$.

CRITICAL THINKING

Use mental math to simplify $\dfrac{\frac{x+y}{x-y}}{\frac{y+x}{y-x}}$.

E X A M P L E **6**

APPLICATION
ECONOMICS

Refer to the revenue-to-cost ratio given at the beginning of the lesson.

For how many ribbons was the revenue-to-cost ratio 1.5 or greater?

SOLUTION

$\dfrac{\text{revenue from the sale of each ribbon}}{\text{cost of making each ribbon}} = \dfrac{3}{\frac{0.8x+25}{x}}$

Simplify the complex fraction.

$\dfrac{3}{\frac{0.8x+25}{x}} = 3 \cdot \dfrac{x}{0.8x+25} = \dfrac{3x}{0.8x+25}$

TECHNOLOGY
GRAPHICS CALCULATOR

Keystroke Guide, page 555

Enter $y = \dfrac{3x}{0.8x+25}$ into a graphics calculator, and examine a table of values.

> *Since x represents the number of ribbons, use an increment of 1.*

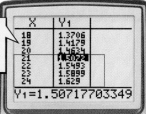

From the table, you can see that the revenue-to-cost ratio, *y*, is greater than 1.5 when 21 or more ribbons, *x*, were produced and sold.

Activity
Exploring Excluded Values in Quotients

TECHNOLOGY
GRAPHICS CALCULATOR

Keystroke Guide, page 555

You will need: a graphics calculator

1. Let $f(x) = \dfrac{\frac{x-3}{x+2}}{\frac{x-2}{x+2}}$. When the complex fraction that defines *f* is simplified,

it becomes $\dfrac{x-3}{x-2}$. Let $g(x) = \dfrac{x-3}{x-2}$. Graph *f* and *g* on the same screen. What observations can you make about these graphs?

PROBLEM SOLVING

2. Make a table to evaluate *f* and *g* for *x*-values of $-3, -2, -1, 0, 1, 2,$ and 3. How do the entries in the table compare?

3. Repeat Steps 1 and 2 for the functions $f(x) = \dfrac{\frac{x^2-4}{x-1}}{\frac{x^2-9}{x-1}}$ and $g(x) = \dfrac{x^2-4}{x^2-9}$.

CHECKPOINT ✔

4. Let $f(x) = \dfrac{\frac{P}{Q}}{\frac{R}{Q}}$ and $g(x) = \dfrac{P}{R}$, where *P*, *Q*, and *R* are polynomials. Explain

how to find the excluded values of *f* and why you should not try to find those values by examining *g*.

Exercises

Communicate

1. In what ways is the multiplication of two rational expressions similar to the multiplication of two rational numbers?

2. In what ways is the division of two rational expressions similar to the division of two rational numbers?

3. Explain how to simplify a complex fraction such as $\dfrac{\dfrac{x^2}{x^2-1}}{\dfrac{x}{x^2+2x-3}}$. Compare the excluded values of x in the complex fraction and in its simplified form.

Guided Skills Practice

Simplify each rational expression. *(EXAMPLES 1 AND 2)*

4. $\dfrac{x^2-25}{x^2-10x+25}$

5. $\dfrac{4x^2}{5} \cdot \dfrac{30}{x^4} \cdot \dfrac{20x^3}{60}$

Simplify each rational expression. *(EXAMPLES 3 AND 4)*

6. $\dfrac{x^2+8x+12}{x^2+2x-15} \cdot \dfrac{x^2+8x+15}{x^2+9x+18}$

7. $\dfrac{x^2-2x+1}{x^2+6x+8} \div \dfrac{x^2-1}{x^2+3x+2}$

8. Simplify the complex fraction $\dfrac{\dfrac{2x-6}{x^2+9x+20}}{\dfrac{x^2-9}{x^2+5x+4}}$. *(EXAMPLES 5 AND 6)*

Practice and Apply

Simplify each rational expression.

9. $\dfrac{4x^2+8x+4}{x+1}$

10. $\dfrac{x^2-6x+9}{x^2-9}$

11. $\dfrac{15}{x^2} \cdot \dfrac{x^5}{12} \cdot \dfrac{4}{x}$

12. $\dfrac{36x}{9x^2} \cdot \dfrac{12x^7}{2x} \cdot \dfrac{5}{x^2}$

13. $\dfrac{x^2-10x+9}{x^2+2x-3}$

14. $\dfrac{-x^2-x+6}{x^2-5x+6}$

15. $\dfrac{x}{9x^8} \cdot \dfrac{x^7}{2x} \cdot \dfrac{45}{x^4}$

16. $\dfrac{-5}{x^3} \cdot \dfrac{-x^5}{3} \cdot \dfrac{-4}{x} \cdot \dfrac{20}{x^3}$

17. $\dfrac{x^2-4x-5}{x^2-3x+2} \cdot \dfrac{x^2-4}{x^2-3x-10}$

18. $\dfrac{x^2-9}{x^2-4x+4} \cdot \dfrac{x^2-4}{x^2-x-6}$

19. $\dfrac{2x^2-2x}{x^2-9} \div \dfrac{x^2+x-2}{x^2+2x-3}$

20. $\dfrac{4x^2+20x}{9+6x+x^2} \div \dfrac{x+5}{x^2-9}$

21. $\dfrac{x^4+2x^3+x^2}{x^2+x-6} \cdot \dfrac{x^2-x-2}{x^4-x^2}$

22. $\dfrac{x^5-4x^3}{x^2-x-2} \cdot \dfrac{x^2-1}{x^5-x^4-2x^3}$

23. $\dfrac{4x^3-9x}{2x-7} \div \dfrac{3x^3+2x^2}{4x^2-14x}$

24. $\dfrac{x^4-4x^2}{x^2-9} \div \dfrac{4x^2-4x^3+x^4}{x^2-6x+9}$

25. $\dfrac{ax-bx+ay-by}{ax+bx+ay+by}$

26. $\dfrac{x^2-y^2-4x+4y}{x^2-y^2+4x-4y}$

27. $\dfrac{x^2}{4} \cdot \left(\dfrac{xy}{6}\right)^{-1} \cdot \dfrac{2y^2}{x}$

28. $2rs \div \dfrac{2r^2}{s} \div \dfrac{2s^2}{r}$

Simplify each expression.

29. $\dfrac{\dfrac{(x+2)^2}{(x+3)^2}}{\dfrac{x+3}{x+2}}$

30. $\dfrac{\dfrac{x^2-4}{x^2-9}}{\dfrac{(x-2)^2}{(x-3)^2}}$

31. $\dfrac{\dfrac{x^2-9x+14}{x^2-6x+5}}{\dfrac{x^2-8x+7}{x^2-7x+10}}$

32. $\dfrac{\dfrac{x^2+4x+3}{x^2+6x+8}}{\dfrac{x^2+9x+18}{x^2+7x+10}}$

33. $\dfrac{x+2}{x+5} \cdot \dfrac{\dfrac{x^2}{x+2}}{\dfrac{x+1}{x+5}}$

34. $\dfrac{\dfrac{1}{x+3}}{\dfrac{x^2}{x-7}} \cdot \dfrac{x}{x-7}$

35. $\dfrac{2x+3}{x-1} \div \dfrac{\dfrac{x}{x-1}}{\dfrac{3x}{2x+3}}$

36. $\dfrac{x}{x^2-1} \div \dfrac{\dfrac{x+1}{x-1}}{\dfrac{x}{x+1}}$

37. $\dfrac{\dfrac{x+3}{x-1}}{x(x-1)^{-1}}$

38. $\dfrac{\dfrac{2y+6}{y-7}}{(y+2)(y+3)^{-1}}$

39. $\dfrac{\dfrac{(x+y)^2}{(x+y)^3}}{\dfrac{x+y}{x^2+2xy+y^2}}$

40. $\dfrac{\dfrac{x+2y}{2x^2+3xy+y^2}}{\dfrac{2x^2+5xy+2y^2}{x+y}}$

41. $\dfrac{1-7x^{-1}-18x^{-2}}{1-4x^{-2}}$

42. $\dfrac{1+12x^{-1}+27x^{-2}}{x^{-1}+9x^{-2}}$

43. $\dfrac{(x+y)y^{-1}-2x(x+y)^{-1}}{(x-y)y^{-1}+2x(x-y)^{-1}}$

CHALLENGE

44. Find the rational expression R whose numerator and denominator have degree 2 and leading coefficients of 1 such that $\dfrac{x^2+3x-10}{x^2-8x+15} \cdot R = \dfrac{x-2}{x-3}$.

CONNECTION

45. **GEOMETRY** An open-top box is to be made from a sheet of cardboard that is 20 inches by 16 inches. Squares with sides of x inches are to be cut on one side and creased on another to form tabs. When the sides are folded up, these tabs are glued to the adjacent sides to provide reinforcement.

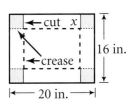

a. Show that $x(20-2x)(16-2x)$ represents the volume of the box.

b. Show that $320-4x^2$ represents the surface area of the bottom and sides of the inside of the box.

c. Write and simplify an expression for the ratio of the volume of the box to the inside surface area of the box.

d. How does the ratio from part **c** change as x increases?

APPLICATION

46. **ECONOMICS** It costs Emilio and Maria Vianco $1200 to operate their sandwich shop for one month. The average cost of preparing one sandwich is $1.69.

a. Using the menu shown, find the average revenue per sandwich.

b. Let x represent the number of sandwiches sold in one month. Write a function for the total cost, C, of operating the business for one month by using the average cost of preparing one sandwich.

c. Write a function for the ratio, R, of average revenue per sandwich to the average cost per sandwich.

47. PHYSICS The diagram below illustrates an ambulance traveling a definite distance in a specific period of time. The average acceleration, a, is defined as the change in velocity over the corresponding change in time.

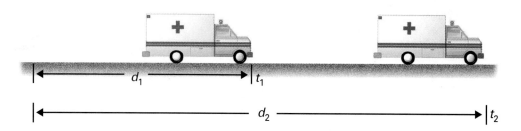

a. Simplify the expression at right that defines a.

b. If the distance, d, is measured in feet and the time, t, is measured in seconds, in what units is acceleration measured?

$$a = \frac{\dfrac{d_2}{t_2} - \dfrac{d_1}{t_1}}{t_2 - t_1}$$

 Look Back

Write an equation in slope-intercept form for the line that contains the given point and is perpendicular to the given line. *(LESSON 1.3)*

48. $(8, -4)$, $y = -6x - 1$

49. $(3, 5)$, $y = \frac{1}{5}x - 11$

Graph each piecewise function. *(LESSON 2.6)*

50. $f(x) = \begin{cases} x - 5 & \text{if } -1 < x \le 4 \\ 9 - 2x & \text{if } 4 < x \le 5 \end{cases}$

51. $g(x) = \begin{cases} -4 & \text{if } x < 0 \\ 2x - 4 & \text{if } 0 \le x \le 5 \\ -\frac{2}{5}x + 8 & \text{if } x > 5 \end{cases}$

Factor each expression. *(LESSON 5.3)*

52. $8x^2 - 4x$

53. $12x^2 - 3x + 6$

54. $12 - 4a - 22a^2$

Simplify each expression. Write your answer in the standard form for a complex number. *(LESSON 5.6)*

55. $\frac{2 + i}{3 + 2i}$

56. $\frac{4 - i}{6 - 3i}$

57. $\frac{3 - 2i}{5 + i}$

Write each product as a polynomial expression in standard form. *(LESSON 7.3)*

58. $x^2(x^3 - x^2 - 6x + 2)$

59. $(x - 2)(3x^3 - 6x - x^2)$

60. $(x^2 + 1)(2x^3 - 9)$

Factor each polynomial expression. *(LESSON 7.3)*

61. $x^3 - 1$

62. $125x^3 + 27$

63. $x^3 - 6x^2 - 8x$

 Look Beyond

Simplify.

64. $\frac{5}{8} + \frac{1}{8}$

65. $\frac{3}{x} + \frac{1}{x}$

66. $\frac{3}{2x} + \frac{1}{x}$

67. $\frac{3}{2x} + \frac{1}{3x}$

Adding and Subtracting Rational Expressions

Why Adding and subtracting rational expression can be used to solve real-world problems, such as calculating the average rate of speed for an entire trip.

Objective

● Add and subtract rational expressions.

A cab driver drove from the airport to a passenger's home at an average speed of 55 miles per hour. He returned to the airport along the same highway at an average speed of 45 miles per hour. What was the cab driver's average speed over the entire trip? The answer is not the average of 45 and 55. To answer this question, you need to add two rational expressions. *You will answer this question in Example 5.*

Adding two rational expressions with the same denominator is similar to adding two rational numbers with the same denominator.

Rational Numbers

$$\frac{1}{7} + \frac{3}{7} = \frac{1+3}{7} = \frac{4}{7}$$

Common denominator

Rational Expressions

$$\frac{3}{x^2} + \frac{5}{x^2} = \frac{3+5}{x^2} = \frac{8}{x^2}$$

Common denominator

EXAMPLE ① **Simplify.**

a. $\dfrac{2x}{x+3} + \dfrac{5}{x+3}$

b. $\dfrac{x^2}{x-3} - \dfrac{9}{x-3}$

● **SOLUTION**

a. $\dfrac{2x}{x+3} + \dfrac{5}{x+3} = \dfrac{2x+5}{x+3}$

b. $\dfrac{x^2}{x-3} - \dfrac{9}{x-3} = \dfrac{x^2-9}{x-3}$

$= \dfrac{(x+3)(x-3)^{1}}{x-3_{1}}$

$= x+3$

Note that 3 is an excluded value of x in the original expression.

TRY THIS Simplify.

a. $\dfrac{3x-1}{2x-1} + \dfrac{5+2x}{2x-1}$

b. $\dfrac{2x}{x-5} - \dfrac{10}{x-5}$

To add two rational expressions with unlike denominators, you first need to find common denominators. The **least common denominator (LCD)** of two rational expressions is the *least common multiple* of the denominators. The **least common multiple (LCM)** of two polynomials is the polynomial of lowest degree that is divisible by each polynomial.

Finding the LCM for two rational expressions is similar to finding the LCM for two rational numbers. Compare the procedures for rational numbers and for rational expressions shown below.

<table>
<tr><td style="text-align:center">Rational Numbers</td><td style="text-align:center">Rational Expressions</td></tr>
</table>

$$\frac{7}{300} + \frac{1}{90} = \frac{7}{300}\left(\frac{3}{3}\right) + \frac{1}{90}\left(\frac{10}{10}\right)$$

$$\frac{7}{3x^2} + \frac{1}{9x} = \frac{7}{3x^2}\left(\frac{3}{3}\right) + \frac{1}{9x}\left(\frac{x}{x}\right)$$

$$= \frac{21 + 10}{900}$$

$$= \frac{21 + x}{9x^2}$$

Least common denominator

$$= \frac{31}{900}$$

Least common denominator

Adding and Subtracting Rational Expressions

To add or subtract two rational expressions, find a common denominator, rewrite each expression by using the common denominator, and then add or subtract. Simplify the resulting rational expression.

E X A M P L E ❷ Simplify $\dfrac{x}{x-2} + \dfrac{-8}{x^2-4}$.

● **SOLUTION**

$$\frac{x}{x-2} + \frac{-8}{x^2-4} = \frac{x}{x-2} + \frac{-8}{(x-2)(x+2)}$$

$$= \frac{x}{x-2}\left(\frac{x+2}{x+2}\right) + \frac{-8}{(x-2)(x+2)} \qquad \text{\textit{The LCD is } } (x-2)(x+2).$$

$$= \frac{x(x+2) - 8}{(x-2)(x+2)} \qquad \text{\textit{Add the fractions.}}$$

$$= \frac{x^2 + 2x - 8}{(x-2)(x+2)} \qquad \text{\textit{Write the numerator in standard form.}}$$

$$= \frac{(x+4)(x-2)}{(x-2)(x+2)} \qquad \text{\textit{Factor the numerator.}}$$

$$= \frac{(x+4)(x-2)^1}{(x-2)(x+2)_1} \qquad \text{\textit{Divide out the common factors.}}$$

$$= \frac{x+4}{x+2} \qquad \boxed{\textit{Note that 2 and } -2 \textit{ are excluded values of } x \textit{ in the original expression.}}$$

TRY THIS Simplify $\dfrac{x}{x+5} + \dfrac{-50}{x^2-25}$.

CHECKPOINT ✔ Explain how factoring a polynomial can help you to add two rational expressions. Illustrate your response by simplifying $\dfrac{x}{x-3} + \dfrac{5}{x^2-6x+9}$.

❸ Simplify $\dfrac{6x}{3x-1} - \dfrac{4x}{2x+5}$.

SOLUTION

$$\dfrac{6x}{3x-1} - \dfrac{4x}{2x+5} = \dfrac{6x}{3x-1}\left(\dfrac{2x+5}{2x+5}\right) - \dfrac{4x}{2x+5}\left(\dfrac{3x-1}{3x-1}\right)$$ *The LCD is $(3x-1)(2x+5)$.*

$$= \dfrac{6x(2x+5) - 4x(3x-1)}{(3x-1)(2x+5)}$$ *Subtract.*

$$= \dfrac{12x^2 + 30x - 12x^2 + 4x}{(3x-1)(2x+5)}$$

$$= \dfrac{34x}{(3x-1)(2x+5)}, \quad \text{or} \quad \dfrac{34x}{6x^2 + 13x - 5}$$

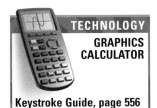

TECHNOLOGY

GRAPHICS CALCULATOR

Keystroke Guide, page 556

CHECK

Graph $y = \dfrac{6x}{3x-1} - \dfrac{4x}{2x+5}$ and $y = \dfrac{34x}{6x^2 + 13x - 5}$

together on the same screen to see if the graphs are the same.

You can also use a table of values to verify that the corresponding y-values are the same.

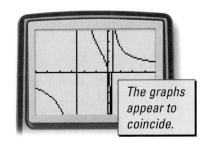

The graphs appear to coincide.

CHECKPOINT ✔ Identify the excluded values of x for the original expression and for the simplified expression in Example 3. Are they the same or different? Explain.

TRY THIS   Simplify $\dfrac{6}{x^2 - 2x} - \dfrac{1}{x^2 - 4}$.

Sometimes you need to rewrite complex fractions as rational expressions in order to add or subtract them, as shown in Example 4.

E X A M P L E ❹ Simplify $\dfrac{1}{1+\dfrac{1}{a}} + \dfrac{1}{1-\dfrac{1}{a}}$.

SOLUTION

$$\dfrac{1}{1+\dfrac{1}{a}} + \dfrac{1}{1-\dfrac{1}{a}} = \dfrac{1}{\dfrac{a+1}{a}} + \dfrac{1}{\dfrac{a-1}{a}}$$ *Add or subtract within the denominators.*

$$= 1 \cdot \dfrac{a}{a+1} + 1 \cdot \dfrac{a}{a-1}$$ *Multiply by the reciprocals.*

$$= \dfrac{a}{a+1} + \dfrac{a}{a-1}$$

$$= \dfrac{a}{a+1}\left(\dfrac{a-1}{a-1}\right) + \dfrac{a}{a-1}\left(\dfrac{a+1}{a+1}\right)$$ *The LCD is $(a+1)(a-1)$.*

$$= \dfrac{a^2 - a + a^2 + a}{(a+1)(a-1)}$$ *Multiply, and then add.*

$$= \dfrac{2a^2}{a^2 - 1}$$

TRY THIS   Simplify $\dfrac{a}{a-\dfrac{1}{a}} - \dfrac{a}{a+\dfrac{1}{a}}$.

EXAMPLE **5**

Refer to the cab driver's round trip described at the beginning of the lesson.

What is the cab driver's average speed for the entire trip?

SOLUTION

Let d represent the length of the trip one way, let t_1 represent the cab driver's travel time to the passenger's home, and let t_2 represent his travel time back to the airport.

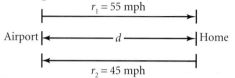

$r_1 = 55$ mph

Airport $\longleftarrow d \longrightarrow$ Home

$r_2 = 45$ mph

$d = r_1 t_1$ and $d = r_2 t_2$

$t_1 = \dfrac{d}{r_1} = \dfrac{d}{55}$ $t_2 = \dfrac{d}{r_2} = \dfrac{d}{45}$

$$\text{average speed} = \frac{\text{total distance}}{\text{total time}}$$

$$= \frac{d + d}{t_1 + t_2}$$

$$= \frac{d + d}{\dfrac{d}{55} + \dfrac{d}{45}} \qquad \textit{Substitute } \tfrac{d}{55} \textit{ for } t_1 \textit{ and } \tfrac{d}{45} \textit{ for } t_2.$$

$$= \frac{2d}{\dfrac{9d + 11d}{495}} \qquad \textit{The LCD for } \tfrac{d}{55} \textit{ and } \tfrac{d}{45} \textit{ is 495.}$$

$$= \frac{2d}{\dfrac{20d}{495}}$$

$$= 2d \times \frac{495}{20d} \qquad \textit{Multiply by the reciprocal.}$$

$$= 49.5$$

Thus, the cab driver's average speed was 49.5 miles per hour. The average speed was less than the average of 45 and 55 because he spent more time driving at 45 miles per hour than at 55 miles per hour.

CRITICAL THINKING

Suppose that the cab driver travels to the passenger's home at a miles per hour and returns along the same route at b miles per hour. Show that his average speed for the entire trip is not simply $\dfrac{a + b}{2}$.

Exercises

● Communicate

1. Explain how to find the least common denominator in order to add $\dfrac{x + 5}{x^2 - 7x + 6} + \dfrac{x - 1}{x^2 - 36}$.

2. Explain how to use a graph to check your answer when you add two rational expressions.

3. Choose the two expressions below that are equivalent and explain why they are equivalent.

   a. $\dfrac{3 + 7}{x^2 + 4}$ **b.** $\dfrac{10}{x^2} + \dfrac{10}{4}$ **c.** $\dfrac{3}{x^2} + \dfrac{7}{4}$ **d.** $\dfrac{3}{x^2 + 4} + \dfrac{7}{x^2 + 4}$

Guided Skills Practice

Simplify. *(EXAMPLES 1 AND 2)*

4. $\dfrac{3x}{x-1} + \dfrac{2}{x-1}$

5. $\dfrac{3x+5}{x+2} - \dfrac{x+1}{x+2}$

6. $\dfrac{12}{x^2-1} + \dfrac{4}{x+1}$

Simplify. *(EXAMPLES 3 AND 4)*

7. $\dfrac{x+1}{2x-1} - \dfrac{2x+1}{x-1}$

8. $\dfrac{1}{1-\dfrac{1}{t}}$

APPLICATION

9. TRAVEL Refer to the cab driver's round trip described at the beginning of the lesson. What is the average speed for the entire trip if he drives to the passenger's home at 52 miles per hour and returns to the airport along the same route at 38 miles per hour? *(EXAMPLE 5)*

Practice and Apply

Simplify.

10. $\dfrac{2x-3}{x+1} + \dfrac{6x+5}{x+1}$

11. $\dfrac{7x-13}{2x-1} + \dfrac{x+9}{2x-1}$

12. $\dfrac{r+9}{4} + \dfrac{r-3}{2}$

13. $\dfrac{x+7}{3} - \dfrac{4x+1}{9}$

14. $\dfrac{x}{x^2-4} - \dfrac{2}{x-2}$

15. $\dfrac{2x}{x+3} - \dfrac{x-3}{x^2+6x+9}$

16. $\dfrac{-4}{x-5} + \dfrac{5}{x+3}$

17. $\dfrac{2}{x+2} - \dfrac{6}{x-2}$

18. $\dfrac{3}{x-1} - \dfrac{2}{x+1}$

19. $\dfrac{8}{3x-5} + \dfrac{7}{2x+3}$

20. $\dfrac{2x+3}{x+3} + \dfrac{x}{x-2}$

21. $\dfrac{x+2}{2x-1} - \dfrac{2x}{x-1}$

22. $x^2 + \dfrac{2x}{3x-5}$

23. $\dfrac{x+1}{(x-1)^2} + \dfrac{x-2}{x-1}$

24. $2x^2 - 1 - \dfrac{x-1}{x+2}$

25. $\dfrac{3}{\dfrac{2x-1}{x}}$

26. $\dfrac{\dfrac{1}{3x+1}}{2}$

27. $\dfrac{\dfrac{4}{x-1}}{\dfrac{2}{x-1}} + \dfrac{3}{x-1}$

28. $\dfrac{\dfrac{4}{x+2}}{\dfrac{x+2}{3}} - \dfrac{3}{x+2}$

29. $\dfrac{\dfrac{x+2}{x+5}}{\dfrac{x-1}{x+5}} + \dfrac{1}{x+1}$

30. $\dfrac{\dfrac{2x+10}{x-1}}{\dfrac{x+5}{x^2-1}} - \dfrac{4}{x+1}$

31. $\dfrac{1-xy^{-1}}{x^{-1}-y^{-1}}$

32. $\dfrac{x-y}{x^{-1}-y^{-1}}$

33. $\dfrac{\dfrac{1}{a^2}-\dfrac{1}{b^2}}{a^{-2}+2(ab)^{-1}+b^{-2}}$

Write each expression as a single rational expression in simplest form.

34. $\dfrac{3x}{x-1} + \dfrac{5x+2}{x-1} - \dfrac{10}{x-1}$

35. $\dfrac{7x}{x^2-1} - \dfrac{x}{x^2-1} + \dfrac{6}{x^2-1}$

36. $\dfrac{7}{x+7} + \dfrac{-x}{x-7} + \dfrac{2x}{x^2-49}$

37. $\dfrac{x}{x-3} - \dfrac{3}{x+4} + \dfrac{7}{x^2+x-12}$

38. $(a-b)^{-1} - (a+b)^{-1}$

39. $(a-b)^{-2} - (a+b)^{-2}$

40. $\dfrac{x}{x-y} - \dfrac{x^2+y^2}{x^2-y^2} + \dfrac{y}{x+y}$

41. $\dfrac{3r}{2r-s} - \dfrac{2r}{2r+s} + \dfrac{2s^2}{4r^2-s^2}$

CHALLENGE

Find numbers *A*, *B*, *C*, and *D* such that the given rational expression equals the sum of the two simpler rational expressions, as indicated.

42. $\dfrac{3x+2}{x-5} = \dfrac{Ax}{x-5} + \dfrac{D}{x-5}$

43. $\dfrac{-x+1}{(x-2)(x-3)} = \dfrac{B}{x-2} + \dfrac{D}{x-3}$

44. $\dfrac{2x^2+5}{x^2+11x+30} = \dfrac{Ax}{x+5} + \dfrac{Cx+D}{x+6}$

45. $\dfrac{x^2-7}{x^2+2x-3} = \dfrac{Ax}{x+3} + \dfrac{Cx+D}{x-1}$

CONNECTION

46. GEOMETRY In the diagram at right, square A is 1 unit on a side, square B is $\frac{1}{2}$ of a unit on a side, square C is $\frac{1}{4}$ of a unit on a side, and so on.

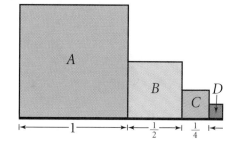

a. Write a sum for the total area of squares A, B, C, and D, using only powers of 2.

b. Rewrite the sum you wrote in part **a** as a single rational number.

c. Suppose that two more squares, E and F, are added to the set of squares, continuing the pattern. Write a single rational number for the total area of squares A through F.

d. Convert your answers from parts **b** and **c** to decimals rounded to the nearest ten-thousandth. What common fraction do the answers appear to be getting closer and closer to?

APPLICATIONS

47. ELECTRICITY The effective resistance, R_T, of parallel resistors in an electric circuit equals the reciprocal of the sum of the reciprocals of the individual resistances.

$$R_T = \frac{1}{\dfrac{1}{R_A} + \dfrac{1}{R_B} + \dfrac{1}{R_C}}$$

Resistance in an electric circuit is measured in ohms.

a. A circuit has three parallel resistors, R_A, R_B, and R_C. Find R_T to the nearest hundredth, given $R_A = 5$ ohms, $R_B = 8$ ohms, and $R_C = 12$ ohms.

b. Write R_T as a rational expression with no fractions in the denominator.

TRAVEL The diagram below shows the parts of a trip that Justine recently took. The distances between A and B, B and C, and C and D are all equal. The speed in each direction is shown in the diagram. Find each average speed listed below to the nearest tenth of a mile per hour.

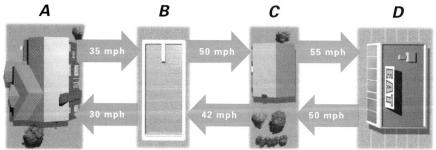

48. Justine's average speed for a trip from A to C and back to A

49. Justine's average speed for a trip from B to D and back to B

50. Justine's average speed for a trip from A to D and back to A

 **Look Back**

State the property that is illustrated in each statement. All variables represent real numbers. *(LESSON 2.1)*

51. $-8x(5x + 2) = -40x^2 - 16x$ **52.** $(3 - x)12x = 12x(3 - x)$

Find the discriminant, and determine the number of real solutions. Then solve. *(LESSON 5.6)*

53. $0 = x^2 - 3x + 4$ **54.** $x^2 - 2x + 1 = 0$ **55.** $-2x^2 - 5x + 12 = 0$

APPLICATION

56. PHYSICAL SCIENCE When sunlight strikes the surface of the ocean, the intensity of the light beneath the surface decreases exponentially with the depth of the water. If the intensity of the light is *reduced* by 75% for each meter of depth, what expression represents the intensity of light beneath the surface? *(LESSON 6.2)*

Write each expression as a single logarithm. Then evaluate. *(LESSON 6.4)*

57. $\log_2 32 - \log_2 8$ **58.** $\log_2 4^3 + \log_2 16$

Use a graph and the Location Principle to find the real zeros of each function. *(LESSON 7.4)*

59 $d(x) = x^3 - 6x^2 + 5x + 12$ **60** $f(x) = x^3 - 2x^2 - 11x + 12$

61 $f(x) = x^3 + 2x^2 - 5x - 6$ **62** $g(x) = x^3 + 8x^2 + 4x - 48$

 **Look Beyond**

63 Find all real solutions of the rational equation $1.4 = \dfrac{(x + 3)(x - 1)}{x^2 - 1}$. Be sure to check for excluded values.

The definition of a harmonic mean may be extended for 3, 4, or n numbers. For any three numbers a, b, and c, the harmonic mean is $\dfrac{3}{\frac{1}{a} + \frac{1}{b} + \frac{1}{c}}$.

1. Simplify this complex fraction.

2. Find the harmonic mean of the numbers 3, 4, and 5.

For any four numbers a, b, c, and d, the harmonic mean is $\dfrac{4}{\frac{1}{a} + \frac{1}{b} + \frac{1}{c} + \frac{1}{d}}$.

3. Simplify this complex fraction.

4. Find the harmonic mean of the numbers 2, 4, 6, and 8.

WORKING ON THE CHAPTER PROJECT

You should now be able to complete Activity 2 of the Chapter Project.

Solving Rational Equations and Inequalities

Objectives

- Solve a rational equation or inequality by using algebra, a table, or a graph.

- Solve problems by using a rational equation or inequality.

Why *There are many events in the real world that can be represented by a rational equation or inequality. For example, you can write a rational equation to represent speed and distance information for a triathlon.*

Rachel finished a triathlon involving swimming, bicycling, and running in 2.5 hours. Rachel's bicycling speed was about 6 times her swimming speed, and her running speed was about 5 miles per hour greater than her swimming speed. To find the speeds at which Rachel competed, you can solve a *rational equation*. A **rational equation** is an equation that contains at least one rational expression.

	Distance (mi)	Speed (mph)
Swimming	$d_s = 0.5$	s
Bicycling	$d_b = 25$	$6s$
Running	$d_r = 6$	$s + 5$

E X A M P L E ❶ Find the speeds at which Rachel competed if she finished the triathlon in 2.5 hours.

● **SOLUTION**

1. Find the time for each part of the triathlon.

Swimming time	Bicycling time	Running time
$d_s = rt_s$	$d_b = rt_b$	$d_r = rt_r$
$0.5 = st_s$	$25 = (6s)t_b$	$6 = (s + 5)t_r$
$\dfrac{0.5}{s} = t_s$	$\dfrac{25}{6s} = t_b$	$\dfrac{6}{s + 5} = t_r$

GRAPHICS CALCULATOR

Keystroke Guide, page 556

2. Write a rational function to represent the total time, T, in hours for the triathlon in terms of the swimming speed, s, in miles per hour.

$$T(s) = t_s + t_b + t_r$$

$$T(s) = \frac{0.5}{s} + \frac{25}{6s} + \frac{6}{s+5}$$

$$T(s) = \frac{0.5}{s}\left[\frac{6(s+5)}{6(s+5)}\right] + \frac{25}{6s}\left(\frac{s+5}{s+5}\right) + \frac{6}{s+5}\left(\frac{6s}{6s}\right) \quad \textit{The LCD is } 6s(s+5).$$

$$T(s) = \frac{3s + 15 + 25s + 125 + 36s}{6s(s+5)}$$

$$T(s) = \frac{64s + 140}{6s(s+5)}$$

3. Solve the rational equation $2.5 = \frac{64s + 140}{6s(s+5)}$.
Graph $y = \frac{64x + 140}{6x(x+5)}$ and $y = 2.5$, and find the x-coordinate of the point of intersection.

Thus, Rachel swam at about 2.7 miles per hour, bicycled at about $6 \cdot 2.7$, or 16.2, miles per hour, and ran at about $5 + 2.7$, or 7.7, miles per hour.

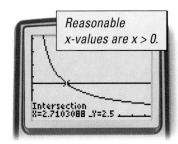

Reasonable x-values are $x > 0$.

Intersection
X=2.7103088 Y=2.5

CHECKPOINT ✔ Examine the table of values at right for $y = \frac{64x + 140}{6x(x+5)}$. Describe Rachel's triathlon times if her swimming speed (x-value) were less than 2.7 miles per hour and if her swimming speed were greater than 2.7 miles per hour.

CRITICAL THINKING How can you solve $2.5 = \frac{64x + 140}{6x(x+5)}$ by using the quadratic formula?

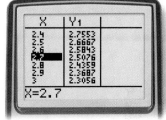

X	Y1
2.4	2.7553
2.5	2.6667
2.6	2.5843
2.7	2.5076
2.8	2.4359
2.9	2.3687
3	2.3056

X=2.7

E X A M P L E ❷ Solve $\frac{x}{x-6} = \frac{1}{x-4}$.

● **SOLUTION**

TECHNOLOGY
GRAPHICS CALCULATOR

Keystroke Guide, page 556

Method 1 Use algebra.

$$\frac{x}{x-6} = \frac{1}{x-4} \quad x \neq 6, x \neq 4$$
$$x(x-4) = 1(x-6)$$
$$x^2 - 4x = x - 6$$
$$x^2 - 5x + 6 = 0$$
$$(x-2)(x-3) = 0$$
$$x = 2 \quad or \quad x = 3$$

CHECK

Let $x = 2$.
$$\frac{x}{x-6} = \frac{1}{x-4}$$
$$\frac{2}{2-6} \stackrel{?}{=} \frac{1}{2-4}$$
$$-\frac{1}{2} = -\frac{1}{2} \text{ True}$$

Let $x = 3$.
$$\frac{x}{x-6} = \frac{1}{x-4}$$
$$\frac{3}{3-6} \stackrel{?}{=} \frac{1}{3-4}$$
$$-1 = -1 \text{ True}$$

The solutions are 2 and 3.

Method 2 Use a graph.

Because it is not easy to see the intersection of $y = \frac{x}{x-6}$ and $y = \frac{1}{x-4}$, use another graphing method.

Write $\frac{x}{x-6} = \frac{1}{x-4}$ as $\frac{x}{x-6} - \frac{1}{x-4} = 0$. Then graph $y = \frac{x}{x-6} - \frac{1}{x-4}$, and find the zeros of the function.

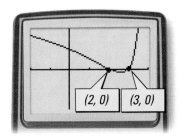

(2, 0)   (3, 0)

TRY THIS Solve $\frac{x}{3} = \frac{1}{x-2}$.

LESSON 8.5 SOLVING RATIONAL EQUATIONS AND INEQUALITIES **513**

Sometimes solving a rational equation introduces *extraneous solutions*. An **extraneous solution** is a solution to a resulting equation that is not a solution to the original equation. Therefore, it is important to check your answers, as shown in Example 3.

E X A M P L E ③ Solve $\dfrac{x}{x-3} + \dfrac{2x}{x+3} = \dfrac{18}{x^2-9}$.

● SOLUTION

Method 1 Use algebra.
Multiply each side of the equation by the LCD, $(x-3)(x+3)$, or x^2-9.

$$\frac{x}{x-3} + \frac{2x}{x+3} = \frac{18}{x^2-9}, \text{ where } x \neq 3 \text{ and } x \neq -3$$

$$\frac{x}{x-3}(x+3)(x-3) + \frac{2x}{x+3}(x+3)(x-3) = \frac{18}{x^2-9}(x+3)(x-3)$$

$$x(x+3) + 2x(x-3) = 18$$

$$x^2 + 3x + 2x^2 - 6x = 18$$

$$3x^2 - 3x - 18 = 0$$

$$3(x^2 - x - 6) = 0$$

$$3(x-3)(x+2) = 0$$

$$x = 3 \quad or \quad x = -2$$

CHECK

Since $x = 3$ is an excluded value of x in the original equation, it is an extraneous solution. Check $x = -2$.

$$\frac{x}{x-3} + \frac{2x}{x+3} = \frac{18}{x^2-9}$$

$$\frac{-2}{-2-3} + \frac{2(-2)}{-2} + 3 \overset{?}{=} \frac{18}{(-2)^2-9}$$

$$-3\frac{3}{5} = \frac{-18}{5} \quad \textbf{True}$$

Thus, the only solution is $x = -2$.

Method 2 Use a graph.
Because it is not easy to see the intersection of $y = \dfrac{x}{x-3} + \dfrac{2x}{x+3}$ and $y = \dfrac{18}{x^2-9}$, use another graphing method.

Write $\dfrac{x}{x-3} + \dfrac{2x}{x+3} = \dfrac{18}{x^2-9}$ as $\dfrac{x}{x-3} + \dfrac{2x}{x+3} - \dfrac{18}{x^2-9} = 0$. Then graph $y = \dfrac{x}{x-3} + \dfrac{2x}{x+3} - \dfrac{18}{x^2-9}$, and find any zeros of the function.

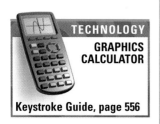

TECHNOLOGY
GRAPHICS
CALCULATOR

Keystroke Guide, page 556

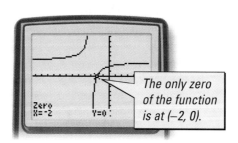

The only zero of the function is at (−2, 0).

The solution is −2.

TRY THIS Solve $\dfrac{x}{x-2} + \dfrac{x}{x-3} = \dfrac{3}{x^2-5x+6}$.

CRITICAL THINKING Explain why an extraneous solution is obtained in Example 3 above.

A **rational inequality** is an inequality that contains at least one rational expression.

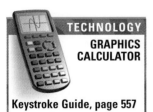

TECHNOLOGY
GRAPHICS CALCULATOR

Keystroke Guide, page 556

Solving Rational Inequalities

You will need: a graphics calculator

1. Graph $y_1 = \dfrac{x+2}{x-4}$.

2. Use the table feature and the graph to identify the values of x for which y_1 is 0, y_1 is undefined, y_1 is positive, and y_1 is negative.

3. On the same screen, graph $y_2 = 2x - 11$.

4. For what values of x is $y_1 = y_2$? $y_1 < y_2$? $y_1 > y_2$?

CHECKPOINT ✔ 5. Explain how to use a graph and a table of values to solve $\dfrac{x+2}{x-4} < 2x - 11$ and $\dfrac{x+2}{x-4} > 2x - 11$.

E X A M P L E ④ Solve $\dfrac{x}{2x-1} \le 1$.

● **SOLUTION**

Method 1 Use algebra.
To clear the inequality of fractions, multiply each side by $2x - 1$. You must consider both cases: $2x - 1$ is positive *or* $2x - 1$ is negative.

$$\frac{x}{2x-1} \le 1, \text{ where } 2x - 1 > 0 \qquad or \qquad \frac{x}{2x-1} \le 1, \text{ where } 2x - 1 < 0$$

$$\frac{x}{2x-1} \le 1 \qquad\qquad\qquad\qquad \frac{x}{2x-1} \le 1$$

$$x \le 2x - 1 \qquad\qquad\qquad\qquad x \ge 2x - 1 \quad \textit{Change} \le \textit{to} \ge.$$

$$-x \le -1 \qquad\qquad\qquad\qquad -x \ge -1$$

$$x \ge 1 \quad \textit{Change} \le \textit{to} \ge. \qquad\qquad x \le 1 \quad \textit{Change} \ge \textit{to} \le.$$

For this case, $x > \tfrac{1}{2}$ because $2x - 1 > 0$. | For this case, $x < \tfrac{1}{2}$ because $2x - 1 < 0$.
Therefore, the solution must satisfy $x \ge 1$ *and* $x > \tfrac{1}{2}$. | Therefore, the solution must satisfy $x \le 1$ *and* $x < \tfrac{1}{2}$.

For this case, $x \ge 1$. | For this case, $x < \tfrac{1}{2}$.

Thus, the solution is $x \ge 1$ *or* $x < \tfrac{1}{2}$.

TECHNOLOGY
GRAPHICS CALCULATOR

Keystroke Guide, page 557

Method 2 Use a graph.
Graph $y = \dfrac{x}{2x-1}$ and $y = 1$, and find the values of x for which the graph of $y = \dfrac{x}{2x-1}$ is below the graph of $y = 1$.

Thus, the solution is $x \ge 1$ *or* $x < \tfrac{1}{2}$.

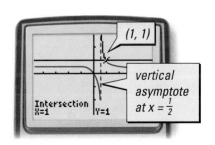

TRY THIS Solve $\dfrac{x-1}{x+2} < 3$.

EXAMPLE **5** Solve $\dfrac{x-2}{2(x-3)} > \dfrac{x}{x+3}$.

● **SOLUTION**

In order to clear the inequality of fractions, you can multiply each side by the LCD, $2(x-3)(x+3)$. You must consider four possible cases:

Case 1: $x-3$ is positive *and* $x+3$ is positive,
or
Case 2: $x-3$ is positive *and* $x+3$ is negative,
or
Case 3: $x-3$ is negative *and* $x+3$ is positive,
or
Case 4: $x-3$ is negative *and* $x+3$ is negative.

The algebraic method of solution is beyond the scope of this textbook, but with a graphics calculator, the solution is much easier to find.

Rewrite $\dfrac{x-2}{2(x-3)} > \dfrac{x}{x+3}$ as $\dfrac{x-2}{2(x-3)} - \dfrac{x}{x+3} > 0$.

Graph $y = \dfrac{x-2}{2(x-3)} - \dfrac{x}{x+3}$, and find the values of x for which $y > 0$.

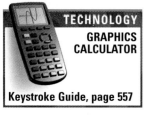

TECHNOLOGY
GRAPHICS CALCULATOR

Keystroke Guide, page 557

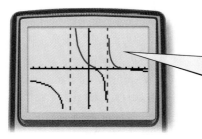

Any part of the graph that is above the x-axis indicates solutions to the inequality.

The graph shows that there are two intervals of x for which $y > 0$. These two intervals can be found by using a table of values.

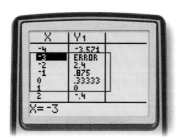
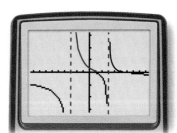

One interval for which $y > 0$ is $-3 < x < 1$, as shown above. The other interval for which $y > 0$ is $3 < x < 6$, as shown below.

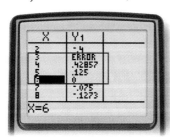
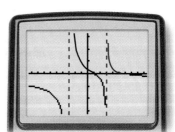

Thus, the solution is $-3 < x < 1$ *or* $3 < x < 6$.

TRY THIS Solve $\dfrac{x+1}{x-1} < \dfrac{x}{x-1}$.

Exercises

Communicate

1. Explain what an extraneous solution is and how you can tell whether a solution to a rational equation is extraneous.

2. Explain how to use a graph to check the solutions to a rational equation that are obtained by using algebra.

3. Explain how to use the graphs of $y = \dfrac{x-1}{x+2}$ and $y = 3$, shown at right, to solve $\dfrac{x-1}{x+2} < 3$ and $\dfrac{x-1}{x+2} > 3$.

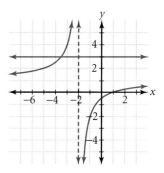

Guided Skills Practice

APPLICATION

4 SPORTS Refer to Rachel's triathlon information given at the beginning of the lesson. At what swimming, bicycling, and running speeds must Rachel compete in order to finish the triathlon in 2 hours? *(EXAMPLE 1)*

Solve each equation.

5. $\dfrac{2x-1}{x} = \dfrac{3}{x+2}$ *(EXAMPLE 2)*

6. $\dfrac{2}{x-1} + \dfrac{2}{x+1} = \dfrac{-4}{x^2-1}$ *(EXAMPLE 3)*

Solve each inequality.

7. $\dfrac{2x-3}{x} \geq 2$ *(EXAMPLE 4)*

 8 $\dfrac{1}{x+2} < \dfrac{1}{x+3}$ *(EXAMPLE 5)*

Practice and Apply

Solve each equation. Check your solution.

9. $\dfrac{x+3}{2x} = \dfrac{5}{8}$

10. $\dfrac{2y-1}{4y} = \dfrac{4}{6}$

11. $\dfrac{4}{n+4} = 1$

12. $\dfrac{-6}{m-3} = 1$

13. $\dfrac{1}{3z} + \dfrac{1}{8} = \dfrac{4}{3z}$

14. $\dfrac{1}{t} + \dfrac{1}{3} = \dfrac{8}{3t}$

15. $\dfrac{y+3}{y-1} = \dfrac{y+2}{y-3}$

16. $\dfrac{2n+1}{3n+4} = \dfrac{2n-8}{3n+8}$

17. $\dfrac{x+3}{x} + 1 = \dfrac{x+5}{x}$

18. $\dfrac{2x}{x+3} - 1 = \dfrac{x}{x+3}$

19. $\dfrac{x+1}{x-1} + \dfrac{2}{x} = \dfrac{x}{x+1}$

20. $\dfrac{3}{x+2} - \dfrac{x}{1} = \dfrac{4}{3}$

21. $\dfrac{1}{6} - \dfrac{1}{x} = \dfrac{4}{3x^2}$

22. $\dfrac{1}{1+c} - \dfrac{1}{2+c} = \dfrac{1}{4}$

23. $\dfrac{2x+3}{x-1} - \dfrac{2x-3}{x+1} = \dfrac{10}{x^2-1}$

24. $\dfrac{x-4}{x+2} + \dfrac{2}{x-2} = \dfrac{17}{x^2-4}$

25. $\dfrac{b}{b+3} - \dfrac{b}{b-2} = \dfrac{10}{b^2+b-6}$

26. $\dfrac{3z}{z-1} + \dfrac{2z}{z-6} = \dfrac{5z^2-15z+20}{z^2-7z+6}$

27. $\dfrac{3}{x+2} + \dfrac{12}{x^2-4} = \dfrac{-1}{x-2}$

28. $\dfrac{x+2}{2x-3} - \dfrac{x-2}{2x+3} = \dfrac{21}{4x^2-9}$

Solve each inequality. Check your solution.

29. $\dfrac{x+3}{3x} > 2$

30. $\dfrac{x+5}{4x} > 3$

31. $\dfrac{x-5}{3x} < -3$

32. $\dfrac{x-5}{3x} < 3$

33. $\dfrac{2x+1}{x-2} > 4$

34. $3 < \dfrac{3x+4}{2+1}$

35. $\dfrac{x+1}{x} \le \dfrac{1}{2}$

36. $-\dfrac{1}{2} \ge \dfrac{1}{x-4}$

37. $\dfrac{7x}{3x+2} < 2$

Use a graphics calculator to solve each rational inequality. Round answers to the nearest tenth.

38. $\dfrac{1}{2} > x^2$

39. $\dfrac{1}{x} \le x^2 - 1$

40. $\dfrac{x-2}{x-1} \ge 2x$

41. $x^2 - 4 \le \dfrac{1}{x^2}$

42. $2x + 1 \ge \dfrac{1}{2x+1}$

43. $\dfrac{t}{t-1} - \dfrac{2}{t+1} \le \dfrac{5}{t^2-1}$

44. $\dfrac{x+1}{x-1} + \dfrac{2}{x} \ge 1$

45. $\dfrac{a-3}{3a} \ge \dfrac{1}{3a^2+9a} + \dfrac{1}{a+3}$

46. $\dfrac{x^2+1}{(x-1)^2} > \dfrac{1}{x}$

State whether each equation is always true, sometimes true, or never true.

47. $\dfrac{2x+8}{x^2-16} = \dfrac{2}{x-4}, x \ne \pm 4$

48. $\dfrac{1-5x^{-1}+4x^{-2}}{1-16x^{-2}} = \dfrac{x-1}{x+4}, x \ne 0 \text{ or } \pm 4$

49. $\dfrac{3}{x+2} + \dfrac{12}{x^2-4} = \dfrac{-1}{x-2}$

50. $\dfrac{2x+3}{x-1} - \dfrac{2x-3}{x+1} = \dfrac{10}{x^2-1}$

51. $\dfrac{x}{x+4} > 2x + 6$

52. $\dfrac{x-6}{x^2-2x-8} + \dfrac{3}{x-4} \le \dfrac{2}{x+2}$

CHALLENGE

53. Solve $\dfrac{3}{(x-1)^2} > 0$ by using mental math.

54. CULTURAL CONNECTION: ASIA A ninth-century Indian mathematician, Mahavira, posed the following problem:

There are four pipes leading into a well. Individually, the four pipes can fill the well in $\frac{1}{2}$, $\frac{1}{3}$, $\frac{1}{4}$, and $\frac{1}{5}$ of a day. How long would it take for the pipes to fill the well if they were all working simultaneously, and what fraction of the well would be filled by each pipe?

CONNECTION

55. GEOMETRY The length of a rectangle is 5 more than its width. Find the length and the width of the rectangle if the ratio of the length to the width is at least 1.5 and no more than 3.

APPLICATIONS

Satellite in orbit over Earth.

56. SPORTS Michael is training for a triathlon. He swims 0.6 miles, bicycles 15 miles, and runs 8 miles. Michael bicycles about 9 times as fast as he swims, and he runs about 6 miles per hour faster than he swims.
  a. Write a rational function, in terms of swimming speed, for the total time it takes Michael to complete his workout.
  b. Find the speeds at which Michael must swim, run, and bike to complete his workout in 1.5 hours.

57. PHYSICS An object weighing w_0 kilograms on Earth is h kilometers above Earth. The function that represents the object's weight at that altitude is $w(h) = w_0 \left(\dfrac{6400}{6400+h} \right)^2$. Find the approximate altitude of a satellite that weighs 3500 kilograms on Earth and 1200 kilograms in space.

Evaluate each expression. *(LESSON 2.2)*

58. $81^{\frac{1}{2}}$ **59.** 13^0 **60.** $9^{\frac{3}{2}}$ **61.** $27^{\frac{1}{3}}$

Find the inverse of each function. State whether the inverse is a function. *(LESSON 2.5)*

62. $\{(3, 5), (2, 8), (1, 5), (0, 3)\}$ **63.** $\{(-1, -4), (-2, -3), (-3, -2), (0, -1)\}$

64. $g(x) = \frac{1}{4}x - 5$ **65.** $h(x) = \frac{5 - x}{2}$

Identify each transformation from the parent function $f(x) = x^2$ to g. *(LESSON 2.7)*

66. $g(x) = -2x^2$ **67.** $g(x) = (x - 2)^2$ **68.** $g(x) = \frac{1}{2}(x + 3)^2$

69. $g(x) = 3x^2 - 5$ **70.** $g(x) = (-2x)^2 + 1$ **71.** $g(x) = 2(4 - x)^2 - 6$

 *Look Beyond*

72 Graph the functions $f(x) = \sqrt{x}$, $g(x) = \sqrt[3]{x}$, $h(x) = \sqrt[4]{x}$, and $k(x) = \sqrt[5]{x}$. How are they alike? How are they different? (Hint: Use the fact that $\sqrt[n]{x} = x^{\frac{1}{n}}$.)

PORTFOLIO ACTIVITY

Refer to Example 5 on page 508. Notice that the cab driver's average speed is the total distance divided by the total time. The harmonic mean of the two speeds, 45 miles per hour and 55 miles per hour, gives the average speed for the entire trip.

1. Find the harmonic mean of 45 and 55.

2. How does your answer to Step 1 compare with the average speed found in Example 5?

Justin cycles for $4\frac{1}{2}$ hours. He cycles along a level road for 24 miles, and then he cycles up an incline for 24 miles more. Justin immediately turns around and cycles back to his starting point along the same route. Justin cycles on level ground at a rate of 24 miles per hour, uphill at a rate of 12 miles per hour, and downhill at a rate of 48 miles per hour.

3. Explain why Justin's average speed over the entire trip is the harmonic mean of 24, 12, 48, and 24.

4. Find Justin's average speed over the entire trip.

WORKING ON THE CHAPTER PROJECT

You should now be able to complete the Chapter Project.

Radical Expressions and Radical Functions

Objectives

- Analyze the graphs of radical functions, and evaluate radical expressions.

- Find the inverse of a quadratic function.

APPLICATION

PHYSICS

Nancy noticed that a long pendulum swings more slowly than a short pendulum. The time it takes for a pendulum to complete one full swing, or cycle, is called the *period*. The relationship between the period, T, (in seconds) of the pendulum and its length, x, (in meters) is given below.

$$T(x) = 2\pi\sqrt{\frac{x}{9.8}}$$

Find the period for pendulums whose lengths are 0.1 meter, 0.2 meter, and 0.3 meter. *You will do this in Example 4.*

Square-Root Functions

The **square root** of a number, $\sqrt{x}$, is a number that when multiplied by itself produces the given number, x. Recall from Lesson 5.6 that the expression $\sqrt{-4}$ is not a real number.

Since the domain of a function is the set of all real-number values of x for which a function, f, is defined, the domain of the square-root function, $f(x) = \sqrt{x}$, does not include negative numbers.

The domain of $f(x) = \sqrt{x}$ is all nonnegative real numbers, and the range of $f(x) = \sqrt{x}$ is all nonnegative real numbers.

The graph of $f(x) = \sqrt{x}$ is shown at right.

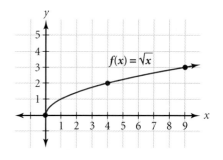

Example 1 shows you how to determine the domain of a square-root function.

Find the domain of $f(x) = \sqrt{2x - 5}$.

● **SOLUTION**

The domain is all real numbers x that do not make $2x - 5$ negative. Solve $2x - 5 \geq 0$ to find the domain of $f(x) = \sqrt{2x - 5}$.

$$2x - 5 \geq 0$$
$$x \geq \frac{5}{2}, \text{ or } 2.5$$

CHECK

Graph $y = \sqrt{2x - 5}$.

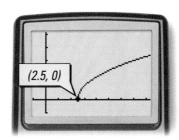

(2.5, 0)

The domain of $f(x) = \sqrt{2x - 5}$ is $x \geq \frac{5}{2}$.

TECHNOLOGY
GRAPHICS CALCULATOR

Keystroke Guide, page 557

TRY THIS   Find the domain of $g(x) = \sqrt{5x + 18}$.

CONNECTION
TRANSFORMATIONS

The transformations given in Lesson 2.7 are summarized below for the square-root parent function, $y = \sqrt{x}$.

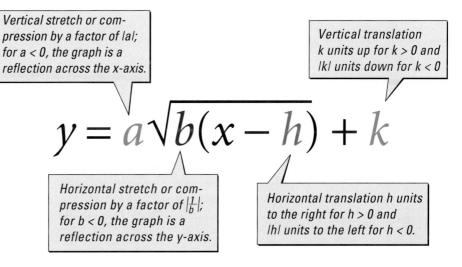

Vertical stretch or compression by a factor of |a|; for a < 0, the graph is a reflection across the x-axis.

Vertical translation k units up for k > 0 and |k| units down for k < 0

$$y = a\sqrt{b(x - h)} + k$$

Horizontal stretch or compression by a factor of $\left|\frac{1}{b}\right|$; for b < 0, the graph is a reflection across the y-axis.

Horizontal translation h units to the right for h > 0 and |h| units to the left for h < 0.

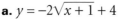 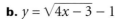

E X A M P L E **2** For each function, describe the transformations applied to $y = \sqrt{x}$.

 a. $y = -2\sqrt{x+1} + 4$ **b.** $y = \sqrt{4x - 3} - 1$

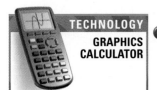

TECHNOLOGY

GRAPHICS CALCULATOR

Keystroke Guide, page 557

● **SOLUTION**

 a. Use the form $y = a\sqrt{b(x - h)} + k$.   **b.** Use the form $y = a\sqrt{b(x - h)} + k$.

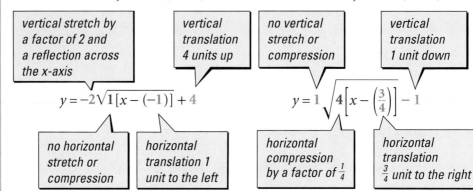

vertical stretch by a factor of 2 and a reflection across the x-axis

vertical translation 4 units up

no vertical stretch or compression

vertical translation 1 unit down

$$y = -2\sqrt{1[x - (-1)]} + 4$$

$$y = 1\sqrt{4\left[x - \left(\tfrac{3}{4}\right)\right]} - 1$$

no horizontal stretch or compression

horizontal translation 1 unit to the left

horizontal compression by a factor of $\tfrac{1}{4}$

horizontal translation $\tfrac{3}{4}$ unit to the right

CHECK

Graph $y = -2\sqrt{x+1} + 4$ and $y = \sqrt{x}$ on the same screen, and compare the graphs.

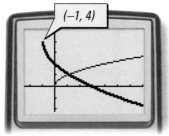

$(-1, 4)$

CHECK

Graph $y = \sqrt{4x - 3} - 1$ and $y = \sqrt{x}$ on the same screen, and compare the graphs.

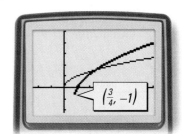

$\left(\tfrac{3}{4}, -1\right)$

TRY THIS   For each function, describe the transformations applied to $y = \sqrt{x}$.

 a. $y = 3\sqrt{x - 1} - 2$ **b.** $y = \sqrt{2x + 1} + 3$

Recall from Lesson 2.5 that you can find the inverse of a function by interchanging x and y and then solving for y. This is shown for a quadratic function in Example 3.

E X A M P L E **3** Find the inverse of $y = x^2 - 2x$. Then graph the function and its inverse together.

● **SOLUTION**

 1. Interchange x and y.

$$y = x^2 - 2x \quad \rightarrow \quad x = y^2 - 2y$$

 2. Solve $x = y^2 - 2y$ for y.

$$x = y^2 - 2y$$

$$y^2 - 2y - x = 0 \quad \text{\textit{Write as a quadratic equation in terms of y.}}$$

$$y = \frac{-(-2) \pm \sqrt{(-2)^2 - 4(1)(-x)}}{2(1)} \quad \begin{array}{l}\textit{Apply the quadratic formula for a = 1, b = -2,}\\ \textit{and c = -x.}\end{array}$$

$$y = \frac{2 \pm \sqrt{4 + 4x}}{2}$$

$$y = 1 \pm \sqrt{1 + x}$$

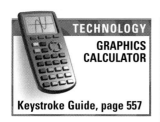

TECHNOLOGY
GRAPHICS
CALCULATOR

Keystroke Guide, page 557

3. Graph $y = x^2 - 2x$ and its inverse, $y = 1 + \sqrt{1 + x}$ and $y = 1 - \sqrt{1 + x}$, along with $y = x$.

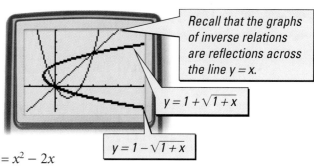

Recall that the graphs of inverse relations are reflections across the line $y = x$.

$y = 1 + \sqrt{1 + x}$

$y = 1 - \sqrt{1 + x}$

Thus, the inverse of $y = x^2 - 2x$ is $y = 1 \pm \sqrt{1 + x}$.

TRY THIS   Find the inverse of $y = x^2 + 3x - 4$. Then graph the function and its inverse together.

CRITICAL THINKING   Show that if $y = ax^2 + bx + c$, then $x = \dfrac{-b \pm \sqrt{b^2 - 4a(c - y)}}{2a}$.

E X A M P L E ④ Recall the pendulum problem described at the beginning of the lesson. The relationship between the period, T, (in seconds) of a pendulum and its length, x, (in meters) is $T(x) = 2\pi\sqrt{\dfrac{x}{9.8}}$.

APPLICATION
PHYSICS

Find the period for pendulums whose lengths are 0.1 meter, 0.2 meter, and 0.3 meter.

SOLUTION

Enter the function $y = 2\pi\sqrt{\dfrac{x}{9.8}}$ into a graphics calculator, and use the table feature with an x-increment of 0.1.

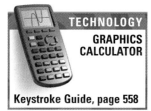

TECHNOLOGY
GRAPHICS
CALCULATOR

Keystroke Guide, page 558

For a 0.1-meter pendulum, the period is about 0.6 second.

For a 0.2-meter pendulum, the period is about 0.9 second.

For a 0.3-meter pendulum, the period is about 1.1 seconds.

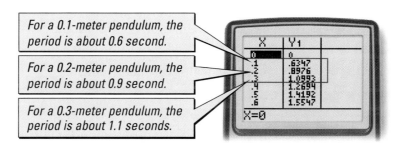

Cube-Root Functions

The **cube root** of a number, $\sqrt[3]{x}$, is a number that when multiplied by itself 3 times produces the given number, x. Recall from Lesson 2.2 that the expressions $\sqrt[3]{-8}$ and $\sqrt[3]{8}$ are both defined.

$$(-2)(-2)(-2) = -8 \text{ and } \sqrt[3]{-8} = -2$$

$$(2)(2)(2) = 8 \text{ and } \sqrt[3]{8} = 2$$

The domain of $f(x) = \sqrt[3]{x}$ is all real numbers, and the range of f is all real numbers, as shown in the graph at right.

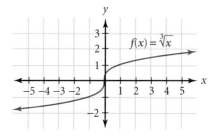

$f(x) = \sqrt[3]{x}$

Evaluate each expression.

a. $3\sqrt[3]{27} - 5$

b. $2\left(\sqrt[3]{-64}\right)^2 + 7$

● **SOLUTION**

a. $3\sqrt[3]{27} - 5$

$= 3(3) - 5$ *$3^3 = 27$*

$= 4$

b. $2\left(\sqrt[3]{-64}\right)^2 + 7$

$= 2(-4)^2 + 7$ *$(-4)^3 = -64$*

$= 39$

TRY THIS   Evaluate $-2\sqrt[3]{-125} - 10$ and $6\left(\sqrt[3]{8}\right)^2 + 2$.

A **radical function** is a function that is defined by a *radical expression*. A **radical expression** is an expression that contains at least one **radical symbol,** such as $2\pi\sqrt{\dfrac{x}{9.80}}$, $\sqrt[4]{x}$, $\sqrt[7]{x + 1}$, and $\sqrt[3]{2x + 5}$. In the radical expression $\sqrt[3]{2x + 5}$, $2x + 5$ is the **radicand** and the number 3 is the **index.** Read the expression $\sqrt[3]{2x + 5}$ as "the cube root of $2x + 5$."

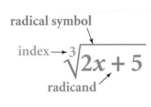

radical symbol

index → $3\sqrt{}$

$\sqrt[3]{2x + 5}$

radicand

Index	Root	Symbol
2	square	$\sqrt{}$
3	cube	$\sqrt[3]{}$
4	fourth	$\sqrt[4]{}$
n	nth	$\sqrt[n]{}$

> *The index of the square root is usually omitted.*

Recall from Lesson 2.2 that the definition of a rational exponent $\frac{1}{n}$, where n is a positive integer, is as follows: $a^{\frac{1}{n}} = \sqrt[n]{a}$. This definition is used when entering a radical expression into a calculator. For example, to evaluate $3\sqrt[3]{27} - 5$ with a calculator, enter 3 ⌑(27 ⌑^ ⌑(1 ⌑÷ 3 ⌑) ⌑) ⌑- 5.

The Activity below introduces two *families* of radical functions.

Activity

Comparing Radical Functions

You will need: a graphics calculator

1. Graph $y = \sqrt{x}$, $y = \sqrt[3]{x}$, $y = \sqrt[4]{x}$, $y = \sqrt[5]{x}$, $y = \sqrt[6]{x}$, and $y = \sqrt[7]{x}$ one at a time. Sketch the shape of each graph.

2. Which functions appear similar?

3. Which functions have a domain of $x \geq 0$?

4. Which functions have a domain of all real numbers?

CHECKPOINT ✔   5. Make a conjecture about the domain and range of $y = \sqrt[n]{x}$ when n is a positive even integer and when n is a positive odd integer.

Exercises

Communicate

1. Describe the transformations applied to the graph of $f(x) = \sqrt{x}$ in order to obtain the graph of $y = 3\sqrt{x-4}$.

2. How do you determine the domain of a radical function?

3. Describe the procedure for finding the inverse of $y = 4x^3 + 2$.

Guided Skills Practice

4. Find the domain of $f(x) = \sqrt{-2x + 3}$. **(EXAMPLE 1)**

For each function, describe the transformations applied to $y = \sqrt{x}$.
(EXAMPLE 2)

5. $y = 2\sqrt{x-1} - 2$

6. $y = \sqrt{2x+1} + 2$

7. Find the inverse of $y = 4x^2 - x$. Then graph the function and its inverse together. **(EXAMPLE 3)**

APPLICATION

8. **PHYSICS** The vibration period of a mass on a spring is the time required for the mass to make a complete cycle in its motion. The relationship between the vibration period, T, (in seconds) of a certain spring and its mass, m, (in kilograms) is represented by $T(m) = 2\pi\sqrt{\dfrac{m}{200}}$. Find the period for a spring with masses of 1.0, 1.5, and 2.0 kilograms. Give answers to the nearest tenth. **(EXAMPLE 4)**

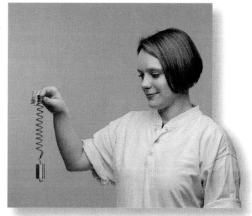

Evaluate each expression. (EXAMPLE 5)

9. $4\sqrt[3]{-8} + 3$

10. $-2\left(\sqrt[3]{64}\right)^2 - 3$

Practice and Apply

Find the domain of each radical function.

11. $f(x) = \sqrt{12x + 24}$

12. $f(x) = \sqrt{3x - 2}$

13. $f(x) = \sqrt{3(x-2)}$

14. $f(x) = \sqrt{3(x+2)} - 1$

15. $f(x) = \sqrt{2 - 3(x+1)}$

16. $f(x) = \sqrt{3 - 3(x-4)}$

17. $f(x) = \sqrt{x^2 - 25}$

18. $f(x) = \sqrt{9x^2 - 16}$

19. $f(x) = \sqrt{x^2 + 5x + 6}$

20. $f(x) = \sqrt{x^2 + 10x - 25}$

21. $f(x) = \sqrt{2x^2 + 5x - 12}$

22. $f(x) = \sqrt{3x^2 + 7x + 2}$

23. $f(x) = \sqrt{6x^2 - 13x + 5}$

24. $f(x) = \sqrt{8x^2 - 10x - 3}$

Find the inverse of each quadratic function. Then graph the function and its inverse in the same coordinate plane.

25. $y = x^2 - 1$

26. $y = x^2 + 3$

27. $y = 3x^2 + x$

28. $y = x^2 + 2x$

29. $y = x^2 + 4x + 4$

30. $y = x^2 + 6x + 9$

31. $y = x^2 - 2x + 1$

32. $y = x^2 - 7x + 12$

33. $y = 4 - x^2 + 3x$

34. $y = 2x + x^2 - 8$

35. $y = x + 2x^2 - 1$

36. $y = 3 + x - 2x^2$

Evaluate each expression.

37. $\frac{1}{2}\left(\sqrt[3]{8}\right)^6$

38. $2\left(\sqrt[4]{625}\right)^2$

39. $\frac{1}{2}\sqrt[3]{-8} + 3$

40. $-\frac{2}{5}\sqrt[3]{-125} - 3$

41. $\frac{1}{8}\left(\sqrt[3]{-8^3}\right)^2$

42. $2\left(\sqrt[3]{8}\right)^2 - 3$

43. $-2\sqrt[3]{216} - 3$

44. $3\sqrt[3]{343} + 1$

45. $10\left(\sqrt[3]{1000}\right)^3 - 1$

46. $\frac{1}{6}\left(\sqrt[3]{\frac{54}{4}}\right)^3 + 5$

47. $\frac{1}{2}\left(\sqrt[3]{-216}\right)^4$

48. $2\left(\sqrt[3]{-343}\right)^2$

49. $\frac{1}{2}\sqrt[3]{216}$

50. $\left(\sqrt[4]{81} - 1\right)^2$

51. $-\frac{1}{3}\left(\sqrt[4]{1296}\right)^2$

CHALLENGES

52. State the domain of $y = \sqrt{\dfrac{1}{x^2 + 1}}$. Graph the function to check.

53. Let $f(x) = ax^2 + bx + c$, where $a \neq 0$. Find an equation for the axis of symmetry for the graph of the inverse of f.

CONNECTIONS

TRANSFORMATIONS For each function, describe the transformations applied to $f(x) = \sqrt{x}$. Then graph each transformed function.

54. $g(x) = \sqrt{x} - 4$

55. $h(x) = \sqrt{x - 4}$

56. $p(x) = 3\sqrt{x - 4}$

57. $r(x) = -\frac{1}{5}\sqrt{x - 4}$

58. $s(x) = -2\sqrt{x - 4}$

59. $g(x) = \sqrt{x + 2} + 5$

60. $h(x) = 2\sqrt{x + 3} - 1$

61. $p(x) = 2(\sqrt{x + 3} - 1)$

62. $k(x) = \frac{1}{2}\sqrt{x - 1} + 4$

63. $m(x) = \frac{1}{3}\sqrt{x + 2} + 3$

64. GEOMETRY The volume, V, of a sphere with a radius of r is given by $V = \frac{4}{3}\pi r^3$.

  a. Solve this equation for r in terms of V.

  b. Show that if V increases, then r must increase.

  c. A spherical hot-air balloon has a volume of 12,000 cubic feet. Find the approximate radius of the balloon by using the equation you wrote in part **a** and a table. Give your answer to the nearest tenth of a foot.

65. PHYSICS If E represents the elevation in meters above sea level and T represents the boiling point of water in degrees Celsius at that elevation, then E and T are related by the equation below.

$$E \approx 1000(100 - T) + 580(100 - T)^2$$

a. Solve the equation above for T. (Hint: Begin by substituting x for $100 - T$. Then solve for x.)

b. What is the approximate boiling point of water at an elevation of 1600 meters?

66. PHYSICS In the 1840s, a French physiologist, Jean Marie Poiseuville, found a relationship between the flow rate, f, of a liquid flowing through a cylinder whose length is L and whose radius is r. The flow rate also depends on the pressure, p, exerted on the liquid and the coefficient of viscosity, N, of the liquid. (*Viscosity* is a measure of the resistance of a fluid to flow.)

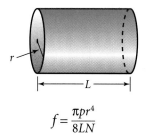

$$f = \frac{\pi p r^4}{8LN}$$

a. Solve the equation at right above for r in terms of the other variables. How does r vary as f, given that p, L, and N are constant?

b. Assume that r, L, and N are constant. How does f vary as p? How does f change if p is doubled?

c. Assume that p, L, and N are constant. How does f vary as r? How does f change if r is doubled?

Alaskan oil pipeline

 Look Back

Simplify each expression. Assume that no variable equals zero.
(LESSON 2.2)

67. $(-2y^3y^5)^2$

68. $2a^4(-3ab^2)^3$

69. $(5x^{-2}y^4)^{-1}$

70. $\left(\dfrac{-3xy^3}{x^{-4}y^5}\right)^3$

71. $\left(\dfrac{-4m^4n^3}{m^2n^3}\right)^{-1}$

72. $\left(\dfrac{3m^4n^{-2}}{2m^0n^3}\right)^{-2}$

Perform the indicated addition or subtraction. *(LESSON 5.6)*

73. $2i - (4 - 5i)$

74. $(-2 + 4i) + (-1 - i)$

75. $(-4 + i) - (3 - 2i)$

Write each expression as a sum or difference of logarithms.
(LESSON 6.4)

76. $\log(6 \cdot 3)$

77. $\log 2x$

78. $\log\left(\dfrac{17}{8}\right)$

79. $\log\left(\dfrac{xz}{y}\right)$

Look Beyond

80 COORDINATE GEOMETRY Let $x^2 + y^2 = 1$. Solve for y. Graph the two resulting equations together. Describe the shape that the pair of graphs creates.

Simplifying Radical Expressions

Objectives

- Add, subtract, multiply, divide, and simplify radical expressions.

- Rationalize a denominator.

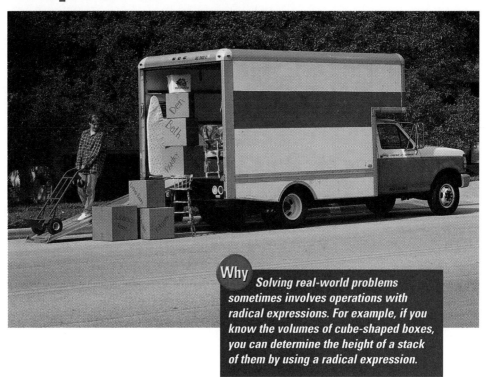

Why *Solving real-world problems sometimes involves operations with radical expressions. For example, if you know the volumes of cube-shaped boxes, you can determine the height of a stack of them by using a radical expression.*

APPLICATION

PACKAGING

Danielle is loading moving boxes onto a truck. She has three large cube-shaped boxes whose volumes are 54 cubic feet, 128 cubic feet, and 250 cubic feet. If she stacks them on top of one another, how tall will the stack be? Answering this question involves working with radical expressions. *You will answer this question in Example 3.*

In the Activity below, you will investigate some properties of radicals.

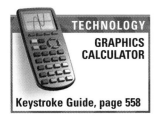

TECHNOLOGY

GRAPHICS CALCULATOR

Keystroke Guide, page 558

Activity

Exploring Properties of Radicals

You will need: a graphics calculator

Complete the following steps, using the fact that $\sqrt[n]{x} = x^{\frac{1}{n}}$:

PROBLEM SOLVING

1. Graph $y = \sqrt{x^2}$. What function does the graph represent?

2. Guess and check. Use your work from Step 1 to predict the appearance of the graph of $y = \sqrt[4]{x^4}$. Verify your response.

CHECKPOINT ✔ **3.** Predict the appearance of the graph of $y = \sqrt[n]{x^n}$, where n is a positive even integer. Then illustrate your prediction.

4. Graph $y = \sqrt[3]{x^3}$. What function does the graph represent?

5. Use your work from Step 4 to predict the appearance of the graph of $y = \sqrt[5]{x^5}$. Verify your response.

CHECKPOINT ✔ **6.** Predict the appearance of the graph of $y = \sqrt[n]{x^n}$, where n is a positive odd integer. Then illustrate your prediction, and explain your reasoning.

Just as there are Properties of Exponents that you can use to simplify exponential expressions, there are *Properties of Radicals* that are used to simplify radical expressions.

Properties of Radicals

For any real number a,
$$\sqrt[n]{a^n} = |a| \text{ if } n \text{ is a positive even integer, and}$$
$$\sqrt[n]{a^n} = a \text{ if } n \text{ is a positive odd integer.}$$

For example, $\sqrt{(-3)^2} = |-3| = 3$ and $\sqrt[3]{(-3)^3} = -3$.

E X A M P L E **Simplify each expression by using the Properties of Radicals.**

a. $\sqrt{49x^2y^5z^6}$ **b.** $\sqrt[3]{-27x^7y^3z^2}$

SOLUTION

a. $\sqrt{49x^2y^5z^6} = \sqrt{7^2x^2y^4yz^6}$ **b.** $\sqrt[3]{-27x^7y^3z^2} = \sqrt[3]{(-3)^3x^6xy^3z^2}$
$$= 7|x|y^2z^3\sqrt{y} \qquad\qquad = -3x^2y\sqrt[3]{xz^2}$$

TRY THIS Simplify each expression by using the Properties of Radicals.

a. $\sqrt{64a^4bc^3}$ **b.** $\sqrt[5]{-32f^6g^5h^2}$

Recall from Lesson 2.2 that $a^{\frac{m}{n}} = \left(a^{\frac{1}{n}}\right)^m = \left(\sqrt[n]{a}\right)^m$ and that $a^{\frac{m}{n}} = (a^m)^{\frac{1}{n}} = \sqrt[n]{a^m}$.

You can write an expression with a rational exponent in *radical form*.

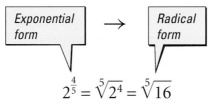

$$2^{\frac{4}{5}} = \sqrt[5]{2^4} = \sqrt[5]{16}$$

You can write an expression with a radical in *exponential form*.

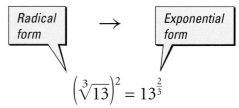

$$\left(\sqrt[3]{13}\right)^2 = 13^{\frac{2}{3}}$$

CHECKPOINT ✔ Write $2^{\frac{3}{5}}$ in radical form.

You can use the *Product and Quotient Properties of Radicals* to multiply, divide, and simplify radical expressions.

Product and Quotient Properties of Radicals

For $a \geq 0$, $b \geq 0$, and a positive integer n:
$$\sqrt[n]{ab} = \sqrt[n]{a} \cdot \sqrt[n]{b} \quad \text{and} \quad \sqrt[n]{\frac{a}{b}} = \frac{\sqrt[n]{a}}{\sqrt[n]{b}} \ (b \neq 0)$$

Simplify each expression. Assume that the value of each variable is positive.

a. $(27ab^3)^{\frac{1}{3}} \cdot \sqrt[3]{5a^4b}$

b. $\dfrac{8(54x^5)^{\frac{1}{2}}}{4\sqrt{3x^3}}$

SOLUTION

a. $(27ab^3)^{\frac{1}{3}} \cdot \sqrt[3]{5a^4b}$

$= \sqrt[3]{27ab^3} \cdot \sqrt[3]{5a^4b}$

$= \sqrt[3]{(27ab^3)(5a^4b)}$

$= \sqrt[3]{(3^3ab^3)(5a^4b)}$

$= \sqrt[3]{3^3a^3b^3 \cdot 5^1a^2b^1}$ *Associative Property*

$= \sqrt[3]{3^3} \cdot \sqrt[3]{a^3} \cdot \sqrt[3]{b^3} \cdot \sqrt[3]{5a^2b}$

$= 3ab\sqrt[3]{5a^2b}$

b. $\dfrac{8(54x^5)^{\frac{1}{2}}}{4\sqrt{3x^3}}$

$= \dfrac{8\sqrt{54x^5}}{4\sqrt{3x^3}}$

$= 2\sqrt{\dfrac{54x^5}{3x^3}}$

$= 2\sqrt{18x^2}$

$= 2\sqrt{3^2 \cdot x^2 \cdot 2}$ *Associative Property*

$= 2 \cdot 3 \cdot |x|\sqrt{2}$

$= 6x\sqrt{2}$ *Assume x is positive.*

TRY THIS   Simplify each expression. Assume that the value of each variable is positive.

a. $\sqrt[3]{3r^2s^3} \cdot (9r^3s^4)^{\frac{1}{3}}$

b. $\dfrac{\sqrt{54x^3y^3}}{(3xy^2)^{\frac{1}{2}}}$

Operations With Radical Expressions

When you add or subtract radical expressions, it is helpful to write your answers in *simplest radical form*. The expression $\sqrt{a}$ is in **simplest radical form** if no factor of a is a perfect square.

E X A M P L E ③

Refer to the cube-shaped boxes described at the beginning of the lesson. The volumes are 54 cubic feet, 128 cubic feet, and 250 cubic feet.

How tall will the stack of boxes be? Give both an exact answer and an answer rounded to the nearest hundredth of a foot.

SOLUTION

The formula for the volume, V, of a cube is $V = e^3$. The length of one edge is given by the radical expression $e = \sqrt[3]{V}$. The height of the stack is the sum of all three edge lengths.

$\sqrt[3]{54} + \sqrt[3]{128} + \sqrt[3]{250} = \sqrt[3]{3^3 \cdot 2} + \sqrt[3]{4^3 \cdot 2} + \sqrt[3]{5^3 \cdot 2}$

$= 3\sqrt[3]{2} + 4\sqrt[3]{2} + 5\sqrt[3]{2}$

$= 12\sqrt[3]{2}$

The stack of boxes will be $12\sqrt[3]{2}$, or about 15.12, feet tall.

EXAMPLE **4** Simplify each sum or difference.

a. $\left(6 + \sqrt{12}\right) + \left(-7 + \sqrt{75}\right)$ b. $\left(-5 - \sqrt{18}\right) - \left(6 + \sqrt{50}\right)$

SOLUTION

a. $\left(6 + \sqrt{12}\right) + \left(-7 + \sqrt{75}\right)$
$$= \left(6 + \sqrt{2^2 \cdot 3}\right) + \left(-7 + \sqrt{5^2 \cdot 3}\right)$$
$$= \left(6 + 2\sqrt{3}\right) + \left(-7 + 5\sqrt{3}\right)$$
$$= 6 - 7 + 2\sqrt{3} + 5\sqrt{3} \qquad \textit{Simplify.}$$
$$= -1 + 7\sqrt{3} \qquad \textit{Combine like terms.}$$

b. $\left(-5 - \sqrt{18}\right) - \left(6 + \sqrt{50}\right)$
$$= \left(-5 - \sqrt{3^2 \cdot 2}\right) - \left(6 + \sqrt{5^2 \cdot 2}\right)$$
$$= \left(-5 - 3\sqrt{2}\right) - \left(6 + 5\sqrt{2}\right)$$
$$= -5 - 6 - 3\sqrt{2} - 5\sqrt{2} \qquad \textit{Simplify.}$$
$$= -11 - 8\sqrt{2} \qquad \textit{Combine like terms.}$$

TRY THIS Simplify each sum or difference.

a. $\left(-3 + \sqrt{32}\right) + \left(6 + \sqrt{98}\right)$ b. $\left(8 - \sqrt{45}\right) - \left(-2 + \sqrt{20}\right)$

CHECKPOINT ✔ Since $\sqrt{3}$ is between $\sqrt{1} = 1$ and $\sqrt{4} = 2$, you can estimate that the value of $-1 + 7\sqrt{3}$ is between $-1 + 7\sqrt{1} = 6$ and $-1 + 7\sqrt{4} = 13$. Use this method of estimation to show that $-1 + 7\sqrt{3}$ is a reasonable answer for the sum $\left(6 + \sqrt{12}\right) + \left(-7 + \sqrt{75}\right)$ in part **a** of Example 4.

EXAMPLE **5** Simplify each product.

a. $\left(-3 + 5\sqrt{2}\right)\left(4 + 2\sqrt{2}\right)$ b. $\left(4 - \sqrt{3}\right)\left(2\sqrt{3} + 5\right)$

SOLUTION

a. $\left(-3 + 5\sqrt{2}\right)\left(4 + 2\sqrt{2}\right)$
$$= (-3)(4) + (-3)\left(2\sqrt{2}\right) + \left(5\sqrt{2}\right)(4) + \left(5\sqrt{2}\right)\left(2\sqrt{2}\right) \qquad \textit{Distributive Property}$$
$$= -12 - 6\sqrt{2} + 20\sqrt{2} + 20 \qquad \textit{Simplify.}$$
$$= 8 + 14\sqrt{2}$$

b. $\left(4 - \sqrt{3}\right)\left(2\sqrt{3} + 5\right)$
$$= (4)\left(2\sqrt{3}\right) + (4)(5) + \left(-\sqrt{3}\right)\left(2\sqrt{3}\right) + \left(-\sqrt{3}\right)(5) \qquad \textit{Distributive Property}$$
$$= 8\sqrt{3} + 20 - 6 - 5\sqrt{3} \qquad \textit{Simplify.}$$
$$= 14 + 3\sqrt{3}$$

TRY THIS Simplify each product.

a. $\left(3 - 5\sqrt{5}\right)\left(-4 + 6\sqrt{5}\right)$ b. $\left(-4\sqrt{6} + 1\right)\left(5 - 3\sqrt{6}\right)$

CRITICAL THINKING Show that $\left(a + b\sqrt{2}\right)\left(a - b\sqrt{2}\right) = a^2 - 2b^2$ is true.

Rationalizing a denominator is a procedure for transforming a quotient with a radical in the denominator into an expression with no radical in the denominator. Use this procedure so that your answers are in the same form as the answers in this textbook.

E X A M P L E ⑥ Write each expression with a rational denominator.

a. $\dfrac{1}{\sqrt{3}}$ **b.** $\dfrac{2}{1+\sqrt{3}}$

● **SOLUTION**

a. $\dfrac{1}{\sqrt{3}} = \dfrac{1}{\sqrt{3}}\left(\dfrac{\sqrt{3}}{\sqrt{3}}\right)$ *Multiply by 1.*

$\qquad = \dfrac{\sqrt{3}}{\sqrt{3}\cdot\sqrt{3}}$

$\qquad = \dfrac{\sqrt{3}}{3}$

b. $\dfrac{2}{1+\sqrt{3}} = \dfrac{2}{1+\sqrt{3}}\left(\dfrac{1-\sqrt{3}}{1-\sqrt{3}}\right)$ *Use the conjugate of $1+\sqrt{3}$ to multiply by 1.*

$\qquad = \dfrac{2-2\sqrt{3}}{1-\sqrt{3}+\sqrt{3}-3}$

$\qquad = \dfrac{2-2\sqrt{3}}{-2}$

$\qquad = -1+\sqrt{3}$

TRY THIS   Write each expression with a rational denominator.

a. $\dfrac{3}{\sqrt{5}}$ **b.** $\dfrac{-14}{3-\sqrt{2}}$

CRITICAL THINKING   Let a and b represent nonzero integers. Write $\dfrac{1}{a+b\sqrt{2}}$ as an expression with a rational denominator.

Exercises

● *Communicate*

1. Explain how to simplify $(1+2\sqrt{2})(2-3\sqrt{2})$. Include a description about how the Distributive Property is applied.

2. Explain how to simplify the radical expression $\sqrt{4x^3}$.

3. Explain how to rationalize the denominator of $\dfrac{5+3\sqrt{2}}{4+7\sqrt{2}}$.

● *Guided Skills Practice*

Simplify each expression by using the Properties of Radicals.
(EXAMPLE 1)

4. $\sqrt{128ab^2c^5}$ **5.** $\sqrt[3]{-54x^5y^9}$

Simplify each expression. Assume that the value of each variable is positive. *(EXAMPLE 2)*

6. $\sqrt[3]{27a^4b^3}(81a^2b)^{\frac{1}{3}}$

7. $\dfrac{12\sqrt{15x^3}}{6(3x)^{\frac{1}{2}}}$

APPLICATION

8. **BUSINESS** How tall is a stack of three cube-shaped boxes, one on top of the other, given that their volumes are 24 cubic inches, 81 cubic inches, and 375 cubic inches? Give both an exact answer and an answer rounded to the nearest hundredth of an inch. *(EXAMPLE 3)*

Simplify each sum or difference. *(EXAMPLE 4)*

9. $\left(-3 + \sqrt{32}\right) + \left(3 + 2\sqrt{98}\right)$

10. $\left(16 + \sqrt{75}\right) - \left(-4 + 10\sqrt{3}\right)$

11. Simplify the product $\left(-2 + 3\sqrt{5}\right)\left(3 - 6\sqrt{5}\right)$. *(EXAMPLE 5)*

Write each expression with a rational denominator. *(EXAMPLE 6)*

12. $\dfrac{2}{\sqrt{7}}$

13. $\dfrac{-3}{5 - \sqrt{3}}$

Practice and Apply

Simplify each radical expression by using the Properties of *n*th Roots.

14. $\sqrt{50}$

15. $\sqrt{128}$

16. $\sqrt[3]{-54}$

17. $-32\sqrt[3]{-48}$

18. $\sqrt{32x^3}$

19. $\sqrt{18x^3}$

20. $\sqrt[3]{-27x^5}$

21. $\sqrt[3]{-81x^7}$

22. $\sqrt{27b^3c^4}$

23. $\sqrt{50a^3b^4}$

24. $\sqrt[3]{24x^5y^3z^9}$

25. $\sqrt[3]{250r^7s^2t^3}$

26. $\sqrt{98x^8y^3z}$

27. $(16x^6)^{\frac{1}{4}}$

28. $(40a^7)^{\frac{1}{3}}$

Simplify each product or quotient. Assume that the value of each variable is positive.

29. $\sqrt{2x^3} \cdot \sqrt{4x^3}$

30. $\sqrt[3]{3y^3} \cdot \sqrt[3]{9y^2}$

31. $\sqrt[4]{25x^2} \cdot (25x^2)^{\frac{1}{4}}$

32. $(16x^2)^{\frac{1}{3}} \cdot \sqrt[3]{4x}$

33. $(24rs)^{\frac{1}{2}} \cdot \sqrt{6r^3s^4} \cdot \sqrt{rs^2}$

34. $\sqrt[3]{3a^2b^4} \cdot (a^3b^5)^{\frac{1}{3}} \cdot \sqrt[3]{ab}$

35. $\dfrac{(64y^7)^{\frac{1}{3}}}{\sqrt[3]{y^3}}$

36. $\dfrac{(42a^4)^{\frac{1}{2}}}{\sqrt{8a^5}}$

37. $\dfrac{\sqrt{24x^5}}{(6x^3)^{\frac{1}{2}}}$

38. $\dfrac{\sqrt[3]{32x^7}}{(4x^2)^{\frac{1}{3}}}$

39. $\dfrac{(64x^7)^{\frac{1}{4}}}{\sqrt[4]{x}}$

40. $\dfrac{(24x^5z^2)^{\frac{1}{2}}}{\sqrt{12x^2z^2}}$

41. $(21x^2y^3)^{\frac{1}{2}}\sqrt{3x^4y^8}$

42. $(81d^4f^4)^{\frac{1}{2}}\sqrt{5d^2f^8}\sqrt{d^2f^2}$

43. $\sqrt[3]{64y^7c^3t^5}(yct)^{-\frac{2}{3}}$

44. $\sqrt[3]{162a^7b^3c^5}(54abc)^{-\frac{1}{3}}$

Find each sum, difference, or product. Give your answer in simplest radical form.

45. $\left(3 + \sqrt{3}\right) + \left(3 + \sqrt{3}\right)$

46. $\left(4 + \sqrt{7}\right) - \left(-3 + 2\sqrt{7}\right)$

47. $\left(3 + \sqrt{18}\right) + \left(-1 - 4\sqrt{2}\right)$

48. $\left(-6 - \sqrt{6}\right) - \left(-1 - 3\sqrt{24}\right)$

49. $\left(3 + \sqrt{32}\right) - \left(4 + 2\sqrt{98}\right)$

50. $\left(5 + \sqrt{125}\right) + \left(-10 + 10\sqrt{5}\right)$

51. $\left(\sqrt{12} - 4\right) - \left(8 + \sqrt{27}\right)$

52. $\left(-3\sqrt{5} + 2\right) - \left(3 + 2\sqrt{20}\right)$

53. $\left(2 + \sqrt{3}\right)\left(-1 + \sqrt{3}\right)$

54. $\left(\sqrt{5} - 8\right)\left(-1 + 3\sqrt{5}\right)$

55. $\left(8 + \sqrt{12}\right)\left(3 - \sqrt{12}\right)$

56. $\left(-6 + \sqrt{5}\right)\left(-4 + 2\sqrt{5}\right)$

57. $\left(3 + \sqrt{2}\right)\left(3 + \sqrt{2}\right)$

58. $\left(2 + 3\sqrt{7}\right)\left(2 - 3\sqrt{7}\right)$

59. $\left(\sqrt{100} - 6\right)\left(-4 + \sqrt{12}\right)$

60. $\left(5 + \sqrt{18}\right)\left(-\sqrt{16} - 3\right)$

61. $\left(4 - 2\sqrt{27}\right)\left(1 + \sqrt{75}\right)$

62. $\left(-3 + 2\sqrt{8}\right)\left(\sqrt{20} - 5\right)$

63. $\left(13 + \sqrt{2}\right) - \left(-3 + 2\sqrt{2}\right) + 3\sqrt{2}$

64. $\left(1 + \sqrt{75}\right) + \left(-2 + \sqrt{125}\right) - 7\sqrt{3}$

65. $\left(3 - 5\sqrt{2}\right) - \left(-4 + \sqrt{2}\right)$

66. $\left(4 + 3\sqrt{7}\right) - \left(5 + 3\sqrt{7}\right)$

67. $2\sqrt{6}\left(\sqrt{24} - 7\right)$

68. $3\sqrt{5}\left(-\sqrt{20} + 2\right)$

69. $\left(\sqrt{75} - 8\right)\sqrt{12}$

70. $\left(3\sqrt{12} + 4\right)\sqrt{27}$

71. $4\sqrt{2}\left(\sqrt{12} - 3\sqrt{2} + 4\sqrt{8}\right)$

72. $2\sqrt{3}\left(7\sqrt{3} - \sqrt{8} + 2\sqrt{5}\right)$

Write each expression with a rational denominator and in simplest form.

73. $\dfrac{2}{\sqrt{5}}$

74. $\dfrac{1}{\sqrt{2}}$

75. $\dfrac{4}{\sqrt{6}}$

76. $\dfrac{5}{\sqrt{15}}$

77. $\dfrac{6}{\sqrt{12}}$

78. $\dfrac{15}{\sqrt{18}}$

79. $\dfrac{\sqrt{5}}{\sqrt{75}}$

80. $\dfrac{\sqrt{3}}{\sqrt{27}}$

81. $\dfrac{\sqrt{24}}{\sqrt{6}}$

82. $\dfrac{\sqrt{60}}{\sqrt{5}}$

83. $\dfrac{\sqrt{18}}{\sqrt{12}}$

84. $\dfrac{1}{\sqrt{3} + 3}$

85. $\dfrac{8}{\sqrt{2} + 4}$

86. $\dfrac{12}{\sqrt{5} - 1}$

87. $\dfrac{3}{2 + \sqrt{3}}$

88. $\dfrac{14}{\sqrt{5} + \sqrt{3}}$

89. $\dfrac{10}{\sqrt{7} + \sqrt{2}}$

90. $\dfrac{14}{\sqrt{3} - \sqrt{2}}$

CHALLENGE

Simplify.

91. $\dfrac{x}{3 - 5\sqrt{2}} - \left(2 + 3\sqrt{2}\right)$

92. $\dfrac{x}{4 + \sqrt{2}} - \left(-1 + 3\sqrt{2}\right)$

CONNECTIONS

93. GEOMETRY Refer to the figure at right. Find the length of the red path from point A to point B to point C. Give an exact answer and an answer rounded to the nearest hundredth.

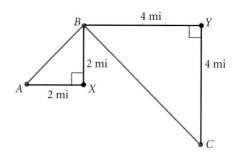

94. GEOMETRY Refer to the figure at right. Find the length of the red path from point A to point B to point C if $AX = BX = a$ and $BY = CY = 2a$, where $a > 0$. Give your answer in simplest radical form.

Coefficients of Friction

	concrete	tar
wet	$f = 0.4$	$f = 0.5$
dry	$f = 0.8$	$f = 1.0$

95. TRANSPORTATION Accident investigators can usually estimate a motorist's speed, s, in miles per hour by examining the length, d, in feet of the skid marks on the highway. The estimate of the speed also depends on the road surface and weather conditions. If f represents the coefficient of friction between rubber and concrete or tar, then $s = \sqrt{30fd}$ gives an estimate of the motorist's speed in miles per hour.

   a. Write a function for s in terms of d under wet conditions on a concrete road. Give an answer in simplest radical form, and give an approximation to the nearest tenth.

   b. Estimate a motorist's speed under wet conditions on a concrete road if the skid marks are estimated to be 200 feet long. Give your estimate to the nearest whole number of miles per hour.

   c. Compare the speed of a motorist whose skid marks are 200 feet long with that of a motorist whose skid marks are 400 feet long, both under wet conditions on a concrete road.

 *Look Back*

Solve each equation, giving both exact and approximate solutions.
(LESSON 5.2)

   96. $x^2 = 34$ **97.** $2x^2 - 6 = 26$ **98.** $(x - 3)^2 + 4 = 14$

Factor each expression. *(LESSON 5.3)*

   99. $x^2 + 6x + 5$ **100.** $x^2 - 2x - 15$ **101.** $x^2 - 3x - 40$

Solve each equation by factoring and applying the Zero Product Property. *(LESSON 5.3)*

   102. $x^2 + 3x = 28$ **103.** $x^2 - 11x = -30$ **104.** $-x^2 = 9x + 20$

Find the zeros of each quadratic function. *(LESSON 5.3)*

   105. $f(x) = x^2 + 9x + 18$ **106.** $f(x) = x^2 - 2x - 8$ **107.** $f(x) = x^2 - 3x - 18$

Find the domain of each radical function. *(LESSON 8.6)*

   108. $f(x) = \sqrt{3x - 1}$ **109.** $g(x) = 2\sqrt{5 - x}$ **110.** $h(x) = -\sqrt{2(3 - 5x)}$

Look Beyond

Rationalize each denominator. (Hint: $(1 + a)(1 - a + a^2) = 1 + a^3$)

   111. $\dfrac{1}{\sqrt[3]{5}}$ **112.** $\dfrac{\sqrt[3]{6}}{\sqrt[3]{3}}$ **113.** $\dfrac{2}{1 + \sqrt[3]{x}}$

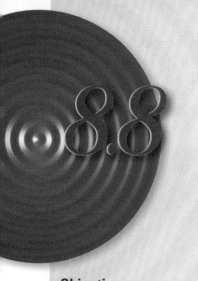

Solving Radical Equations and Inequalities

Why Sometimes solving a real-world problem involves solving a radical equation or inequality. For example, designing a bridge may involve solving a radical equation.

Objectives

● Solve radical equations.

● Solve radical inequalities.

APPLICATION

ENGINEERING

Engineers and town planners are proposing a new bridge to span a river. The diagram below shows a side view of the proposed bridge. The distance, d, across the river is 286 feet. Each vertical support, h, above the roadbed is 15 feet high, and there are 6 equally spaced piers below the roadbed.

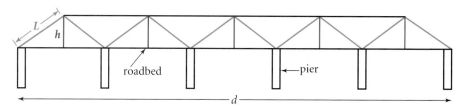

The function $n = \dfrac{d}{2\sqrt{L^2 - h^2}} + 1$ relates the number of piers, n, below the roadbed to d, L, and h. What is the length, L, of each slanted support? To answer this question you need to solve a *radical equation*. *You will answer this question in Example 4.*

A **radical equation** is an equation that contains at least one radical expression with a variable under the radical symbol. To solve a radical equation, you can raise each side of the equation to the same power.

Principle of Powers

If $a = b$ and n is a positive integer, then $a^n = b^n$.

To solve a radical equation with a square root on one side, square each side of the equation. Recall from Lesson 8.5 that an extraneous solution is a solution to a resulting equation that is not a solution to the original equation. Raising the expression on each side of an equation to an even power may introduce extraneous solutions, so it is important to check your solutions.

E X A M P L E ❶ Solve $2\sqrt{x+5} = 8$. Check your solution.

SOLUTION

$$2\sqrt{x+5} = 8$$
$$\sqrt{x+5} = 4$$
$$\left(\sqrt{x+5}\right)^2 = 4^2 \qquad \textit{Square each side of the equation.}$$
$$x+5 = 16$$
$$x = 11$$

CHECK

$$2\sqrt{x+5} = 8$$
$$2\sqrt{(11)+5} \overset{?}{=} 8$$
$$2 \cdot 4 = 8 \quad \textbf{True}$$

You can also check by graphing. Graph $y = 2\sqrt{x+5}$ and $y = 8$ on the same screen. The x-coordinate of the point of intersection is 11.

The solution to $2\sqrt{x+5} = 8$ is 11.

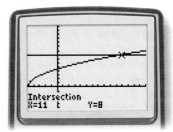

TECHNOLOGY
GRAPHICS CALCULATOR

Keystroke Guide, page 558

TRY THIS Solve $3\sqrt{2x-1} = 6$. Check your solution.

A radical equation may contain the variable on each side of the equation, as shown in Example 2 below and Example 3 on the next page.

E X A M P L E ❷ Solve $\sqrt[3]{x-5} = \sqrt[3]{7-x}$. Check your solution.

TECHNOLOGY
GRAPHICS CALCULATOR

Keystroke Guide, page 559

SOLUTION

Method 1 Use algebra.
$$\sqrt[3]{x-5} = \sqrt[3]{7-x}$$
$$\left(\sqrt[3]{x-5}\right)^3 = \left(\sqrt[3]{7-x}\right)^3$$
$$x-5 = 7-x$$
$$x = 6$$

CHECK

$$\sqrt[3]{x-5} = \sqrt[3]{7-x}$$
$$\sqrt[3]{(6)-5} \overset{?}{=} \sqrt[3]{7-(6)}$$
$$\sqrt[3]{1} = \sqrt[3]{1} \quad \textbf{True}$$

Method 2 Use a graph.
Graph $y = \sqrt[3]{x-5}$ and $y = \sqrt[3]{7-x}$ on the same screen, and find the x-coordinates of any points of intersection.

TRY THIS Solve $\sqrt{x+2} = \sqrt{5-2x}$. Check your solution.

③ Solve $\sqrt{x + 1} + 3 = 2x$. Check your solution.

● **SOLUTION**

$$\sqrt{x + 1} + 3 = 2x$$

$$\sqrt{x + 1} = 2x - 3 \qquad \textit{Isolate the radical before squaring.}$$

$$x + 1 = (2x - 3)^2 \qquad \textit{Square each side of the equation.}$$

$$x + 1 = 4x^2 - 12x + 9$$

$$4x^2 - 13x + 8 = 0 \qquad \textit{Write in standard form with a = 4, b = -13, c = 8.}$$

$$x = \frac{-(-13) \pm \sqrt{13^2 - 4(4)(8)}}{2(4)} \qquad \textit{Apply the quadratic formula.}$$

$$x = \frac{13 + \sqrt{41}}{8} \quad or \quad x = \frac{13 - \sqrt{41}}{8}$$

$$x \approx 2.43 \qquad\qquad x \approx 0.82$$

TECHNOLOGY
GRAPHICS
CALCULATOR

Keystroke Guide, page 558

CHECK

Graph $y = \sqrt{x + 1} + 3$ and $y = 2x$ on the same screen, and find the x-coordinates of any points of intersection. The graphs intersect at only one point, where $x \approx 2.43$.

Thus, $\frac{13 - \sqrt{41}}{8}$ is an extraneous solution; the only solution is $\frac{13 + \sqrt{41}}{8}$, or approximately 2.43.

TRY THIS Solve $\sqrt{x - 1} = -x + 2$. Check your solution.

---

④ Refer to the bridge described at the beginning of the lesson.

Find the length, L, of each slanted support.

APPLICATION
ENGINEERING

● **SOLUTION**

Substitute 6 for n, 286 for d, and 15 for h in the function $n = \dfrac{d}{2\sqrt{L^2 - h^2}} + 1$ to get $6 = \dfrac{286}{2\sqrt{L^2 - 15^2}} + 1$. Solve for L.

Method 1 Use a graph.
Graph $y = \dfrac{286}{2\sqrt{L^2 - 15^2}} + 1$ and $y = 6$, and find the x-coordinates of any points of intersection.

Method 2 Use a table.
Examine the table of values for the function $y = \dfrac{286}{2\sqrt{L^2 - 15^2}} + 1$.

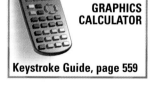
TECHNOLOGY
GRAPHICS
CALCULATOR

Keystroke Guide, page 559

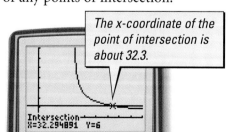

The x-coordinate of the point of intersection is about 32.3.

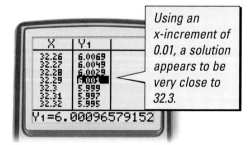

Using an x-increment of 0.01, a solution appears to be very close to 32.3.

Thus, the length of each slanted support is about 32.3 feet.

Some radical equations have no solutions, as shown in Example 5.

EXAMPLE ⑤ Solve $\sqrt{x} - 1 = \sqrt{2x + 1}$. **Check your solution.**

● **SOLUTION**

$$\sqrt{x} - 1 = \sqrt{2x + 1}$$

$$\left(\sqrt{x} - 1\right)^2 = \left(\sqrt{2x + 1}\right)^2 \quad \textit{Square each side of the equation.}$$

$$x - 2\sqrt{x} + 1 = 2x + 1$$

$$-2\sqrt{x} = x \quad \textit{Simplify.}$$

$$\left(-2\sqrt{x}\right)^2 = x^2 \quad \textit{Square each side of the equation again.}$$

$$4x = x^2$$

$$x^2 - 4x = 0$$

$$x(x - 4) = 0$$

$$x = 0 \quad or \quad x = 4$$

CHECK

$$\sqrt{0} - 1 \overset{?}{=} \sqrt{2(0) + 1} \qquad\qquad \sqrt{4} - 1 \overset{?}{=} \sqrt{2(4) + 1}$$

$$-1 = 1 \quad \textbf{False} \qquad\qquad\qquad\qquad 1 = 3 \quad \textbf{False}$$

The equation $\sqrt{x} - 1 = \sqrt{2x + 1}$ has no real solutions.

The graphs of $y = \sqrt{x} - 1$ and $y = \sqrt{2x + 1}$ are shown on the same screen at right.

Because the graphs do not intersect, the equation $\sqrt{x} - 1 = \sqrt{2x + 1}$ has no real solutions.

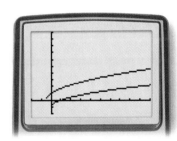

TRY THIS Solve $3\sqrt{x} + 2 = \sqrt{3x}$. Check your solution.

SUMMARY

Solving Radical Equations

To solve a radical equation, follow these steps:

1. If possible, write the equation with the radical expression isolated on one side.

2. Raise the expression on each side of the equation to the appropriate power.

3. Repeat Steps 1 and 2 as needed to obtain an equation with no radical expressions. Solve this equation.

4. Check your solutions and discard extraneous solutions.

CRITICAL THINKING Describe the algebraic strategy that you would use to solve the equation $\sqrt{x - 1} = \sqrt{x + 1} - 1$.

Solving Radical Inequalities

A **radical inequality** is an inequality that contains at least one radical expression. To explore solutions to radical inequalities, complete the Activity below.

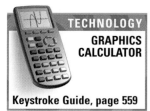

TECHNOLOGY

GRAPHICS CALCULATOR

Keystroke Guide, page 559

Exploring Radical Inequalities

You will need: a graphics calculator

1. **a.** Let $f(x) = \sqrt{x}$ and $g(x) = 1$. Graph f and g on the same screen.
   b. For what values of x is $f(x) \geq g(x)$?
   c. For what values of x is $f(x) \leq g(x)$?

2. Explain why the answer to part **b** of Step 1 is not $x \leq 1$.

CHECKPOINT ✔ 3. Do $\sqrt{x} \geq a$ and $\sqrt{x} \leq a$, where $a > 0$, always have solutions? Explain.

CHECKPOINT ✔ 4. Explain how to use a graph to solve $\sqrt{x} \geq x - 2$ and $\sqrt{x} \leq x - 2$. Then state the solutions.

The fact below is helpful for solving radical inequalities.

$$\text{If } a \geq 0, b \geq 0, \text{ and } a \geq b, \text{ then } a^n \geq b^n.$$

This fact allows you to square the expression on each side of an inequality, as shown in Example 6.

E X A M P L E ⑥ **Solve $\sqrt{x + 1} < 2$. Check your solution.**

● **SOLUTION**

Because the radicand of a radical expression cannot be negative, first solve $x + 1 \geq 0$.

$$x + 1 \geq 0$$
$$x \geq -1$$

Then solve the original inequality.

$$\sqrt{x + 1} < 2$$
$$\left(\sqrt{x + 1}\right)^2 < 2^2$$
$$x + 1 < 4$$
$$x < 3$$

It appears that the solution is $x \geq -1$ *and* $x < 3$, or $-1 \leq x < 3$.

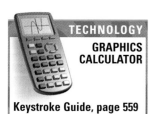

TECHNOLOGY

GRAPHICS CALCULATOR

Keystroke Guide, page 559

CHECK

Graph $y = \sqrt{x + 1}$ and $y = 2$ on the same screen.

The graph verifies that the solution is $-1 \leq x < 3$.

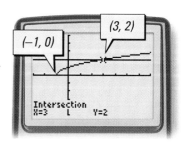

TRY THIS Solve $\sqrt{2x - 3} < 5$. Check your solution.

E X A M P L E **7** Solve $x < 3\sqrt[3]{x+1}$ by graphing. Give the solution to the nearest tenth.

SOLUTION

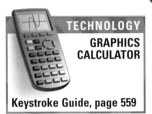

TECHNOLOGY

GRAPHICS CALCULATOR

Keystroke Guide, page 559

Graph $y = x$ and $y = 3\sqrt[3]{x+1}$ on the same screen.

The graph of $y = x$ is below that of $y = 3\sqrt[3]{x+1}$ for approximately $x < -4.6$ and for approximately $-1.0 < x < 5.6$.

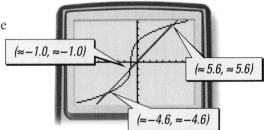

($\approx -1.0, \approx -1.0$)

($\approx 5.6, \approx 5.6$)

($\approx -4.6, \approx -4.6$)

Thus, the solution to $x < 3\sqrt[3]{x+1}$ is approximately $x < -4.6$ *or* $-1.0 < x < 5.6$.

TRY THIS Solve $x - 1 < 3\sqrt[3]{2x+1}$ by graphing. Give the solution to the nearest tenth.

Exercises

Communicate

1. Briefly describe two methods discussed in the lesson for solving a radical equation or inequality such as $\sqrt{x} = 3\sqrt{x-4}$ or $\sqrt{x} \le 3\sqrt{x-4}$.

2. Explain why it is necessary to check any solutions to a radical equation that you obtain algebraically.

3. Explain how to determine that $\sqrt{x} = \sqrt{x+1}$ has no solution. Use algebra and a graph in your explanation.

Guided Skills Practice

4. Solve $3\sqrt{2x-5} = 20$. Check your solution. *(EXAMPLE 1)*

5. Solve $\sqrt[3]{3x+1} = \sqrt[3]{2x+3}$. Check your solution. *(EXAMPLE 2)*

6. Solve $\sqrt{5x+7} - 2 = x$. Check your solution. *(EXAMPLE 3)*

APPLICATION

7. **ENGINEERING** Refer to the bridge described at the beginning of the lesson. Find the length of each slanted support given that there are 6 piers below the roadbed, the distance across the river is 560 feet, and the vertical supports above the roadbed are 17 feet tall. Give your answer to the nearest tenth of a foot. *(EXAMPLE 4)*

8. Solve $2\sqrt{x+1} = \sqrt{x} - 3$. Check your solution. *(EXAMPLE 5)*

9. Solve $\sqrt{3x-2} \le 8$. Check your solution. *(EXAMPLE 6)*

10. Solve $-0.5x + 1 \le 4\sqrt[3]{3x-2}$ by graphing. Give the solution to the nearest tenth. *(EXAMPLE 7)*

● *Practice and Apply*

Solve each radical equation by using algebra. If the equation has no real solution, write *no solution*. Check your solution.

11. $\sqrt{x} = 4$

12. $\sqrt{x-3} = 2$

13. $5 = \sqrt{x^2 + 16}$

14. $3 = \sqrt{x^2 - 16}$

15. $\sqrt{x+2} = 4\sqrt{x}$

16. $2\sqrt{x} = 3\sqrt{x-2}$

17. $\sqrt{3x-2} = x-2$

18. $x + 1 = \sqrt{6x-7} - 1$

19. $\sqrt[3]{x-2} = \sqrt[3]{2x+1}$

20. $\sqrt[3]{2x-3} = \sqrt[3]{2-x}$

21. $\sqrt[3]{x+2} = \sqrt[3]{x+3}$

22. $3\sqrt{2x+1} = 2\sqrt{2x} - 1$

23. $\sqrt{2x+1} = x+1$

24. $\sqrt{3x+2} = x-2$

Solve each radical inequality by using algebra. If the inequality has no real solution, write *no solution*. Check your solution.

25. $\sqrt{2x-1} \geq 1$

26. $\sqrt{3x+4} \geq 2$

27. $\sqrt{2x-1} \leq 1$

28. $\sqrt{3x+4} \leq 2$

29. $-\sqrt{x} \leq 2$

30. $-\sqrt{x} \geq 2$

31. $1 > 3\sqrt{3x-1}$

32. $\sqrt{2x+1} - 3 < 0$

33. $3\sqrt{3x-1} < -1$

34. $\sqrt{2x+1} + 3 < 0$

35. $\sqrt{2x+2} > \sqrt{3x}$

36. $\sqrt{9x+7} < \sqrt{14x}$

37. $x \leq \sqrt{x}$

38. $\frac{1}{8} \leq x \leq \sqrt{x}$

Solve each radical equation or inequality by using a graph. Round solutions to the nearest tenth. Check your solution by any method.

39 $\sqrt{2x-1} = x^2$

40 $(x+1)^2 = \sqrt{2x+1}$

41 $\sqrt[3]{2x+1} = x^2 + 2x$

42 $x^2 - x = \sqrt[3]{x-2}$

43 $\sqrt{x} = \sqrt[3]{x}$

44 $\sqrt[3]{x} = \sqrt[4]{x}$

45 $\sqrt{x} - 2x \geq 0$

46 $2x > \sqrt{3-x}$

47 $\sqrt[3]{x+2} > \sqrt[3]{x-2} + 2$

48 $\sqrt[3]{x} < \sqrt{x} + 3$

49 $\sqrt{x} \leq x^2 + \sqrt{x+1} - 2$

50 $0.5\sqrt[4]{x+2} > \sqrt[3]{x}$

51 $2\sqrt{x^2-1} \leq \sqrt{x+5}$

52 $2\sqrt{x^2-2} - \sqrt{3x+7} < 0$

Identify whether each statement is always true, sometimes true, or never true.

53. $\sqrt{x+3} = -12$

54. $\sqrt{x-6} = 3 + \sqrt{x}$

55. $\sqrt{3x-6} < 0$

56. $2\sqrt{2x-3} + 4 = 1$

57. $2\sqrt[4]{3x} = \sqrt[4]{3x+15}$

58. $\sqrt{x+4} + \sqrt{x-4} > 4$

59. $\sqrt{2x+5} - 7 \leq x - 2$

60. $\sqrt{x+5} - \sqrt{5x-21} \leq 4$

CHALLENGE

61. Find a value of a that makes each statement below true. Use a graph to confirm your response.

   a. The equation $\sqrt{x+a} = \sqrt{2x-a}$ has no solution.

   b. The equation $\sqrt{x+a} = \sqrt{2x-a}$ has one solution.

62. PHYSICS The function $h(t) = -16t^2 + 128t + 50$ models the height, h, in feet above the ground of a projectile after t seconds of flight.

  a. Write the inverse of h.
  b. Graph the equation you wrote in part **a.**
  c. After how many seconds will the height of the projectile above the ground be 270 feet?

63. SIGHTSEEING On a clear day, the approximate distance, d, in feet that a sightseer standing at the top of a building h feet tall can see is given by $d = 6397.2\sqrt{h}$.

  a. On a clear day, what distance in feet can a sightseer see from the top of a 900-foot building? Give your answer to the nearest foot.
  b. Convert your answer from part **a** to miles. (Note: 1 mile equals 5280 feet.)
  c. How tall is a building from which a sightseer can see 32 miles on a clear day? Give your answer to the nearest foot.

Look Back

Write each pair of parametric equations as a single equation in x and y. *(LESSON 3.6)*

64. $\begin{cases} x(t) = 3t \\ y(t) = t - 2 \end{cases}$
65. $\begin{cases} x(t) = t + 4 \\ y(t) = 2t + 1 \end{cases}$
66. $\begin{cases} x(t) = 3t + 1 \\ y(t) = -t \end{cases}$

Use the quadratic formula to solve each equation. Give your answers to the nearest tenth if necessary. *(LESSON 5.5)*

67. $2x^2 + 10x^2 + 12 = 0$
68. $2x^2 - 11x = 6$
69. $3x^2 + 4x = 5$

Divide by using synthetic division. *(LESSON 7.3)*

70. $(x^3 + 7x^2 - 10x - 16) \div (x - 2)$
71. $(x^3 - 63x - 162) \div (x + 6)$

Simplify each radical expression. Assume that the value of each variable is positive. *(LESSON 8.7)*

72. $\sqrt{28a^{16}}$
73. $4x^3y\sqrt{72x^7y^{10}}$
74. $\sqrt[3]{12s^2t} \cdot \sqrt[3]{36st^7}$

75. $\dfrac{\sqrt{30x^3}}{\sqrt{6x}}$
76. $\dfrac{\sqrt{4a^2}}{\sqrt{125b^3}}$
77. $\dfrac{\sqrt{80x^3}}{\sqrt{2x}}$

Look Beyond

78. Use the Pythagorean Theorem to find the distance between the two points graphed at right.

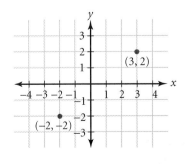

Means to an End

In problem-solving situations that are based on the calculation of an average, the choice of which average to use—arithmetic or harmonic—is critical. The results obtained from each average can be significantly different.

For any two numbers a and b, the *arithmetic mean* is $\frac{a+b}{2}$ and the *harmonic mean* is $\frac{2}{\frac{1}{a}+\frac{1}{b}}$.

To provide consumers with a standard to compare fuel economy for new cars, the Environmental Protection Agency (EPA) requires that estimates of fuel consumption be attached to the window of each new car.

For example, the EPA estimates that a certain car with a 1.9-liter engine and a 4-speed transmission can travel 24 miles per gallon (mpg) in the city and 34 miles per gallon on the highway.

The *Fuel Economy Guide,* published by the U.S. Department of Energy, is an aid to consumers who are considering the purchase of a new vehicle. The guide estimates the fuel consumption, in miles per gallon, for each vehicle available for the new model year. In the *Fuel Economy Guide,* the consumer is advised as follows:

Please be cautioned that simply averaging the mpg for city and highway driving and then looking up a single value in estimating may result in inaccurate estimates of the annual fuel cost.

Activity 1

1. For the car described above, find the arithmetic mean of the fuel consumption in miles per gallon for city driving and for highway driving.

2. Find the harmonic mean for the city driving rate and highway driving rate.

3. Examine each mean. Explain why there is a warning about "simply averaging" the city rate and the highway rate when finding the annual fuel cost.

The number of miles that a person drives in the city may not be the same as the number of miles that the person drives on the highway. Therefore, to find the average annual fuel consumption for a car, you need to use a *weighted harmonic mean*.

Let d_1 represent the number of miles driven in the city in one year.

Let d_2 represent the number of miles driven on the highway in one year.

Then the number of gallons of fuel used per year for each type of driving is as follows:

City: $(d_1 \text{ miles})\left(\dfrac{\text{gallon}}{24 \text{ miles}}\right) = \dfrac{d_1}{24}$ gallons

Highway: $(d_2 \text{ miles})\left(\dfrac{\text{gallon}}{34 \text{ miles}}\right) = \dfrac{d_2}{34}$ gallons

A rational function, a, for the average annual fuel consumption for the car described on the previous page can be expressed in terms of the total miles driven.

$$a(d) = \frac{\text{total distance}}{\text{total number of gallons}} = \frac{d_1 + d_2}{\dfrac{d_1}{24} + \dfrac{d_2}{34}}$$

1. Suppose that you purchased this car and drove it 12,000 miles in one year—8000 miles in the city and 4000 miles on the highway. Find the average annual fuel consumption for this car.

2. Determine the total fuel cost for the year if gasoline costs $1.099 per gallon.

Jennifer is considering a strategy for an upcoming 2-mile bicycle race. During practice she maintains a speed of 20 miles per hour for the first mile, but fatigue reduces her speed to 10 miles per hour for the second mile.

1. Explain why Jennifer's average speed over these 2 miles is not the same as the arithmetic mean of 20 miles per hour and 10 miles per hour. Find Jennifer's average speed for these 2 miles.

2. Determine the speed at which Jennifer must travel during the second mile if she rides 20 miles per hour during the first mile and she wants her average speed for the entire 2-mile trip to be 15 miles per hour.

Key Skills & Exercises

LESSON 8.1

Key Skills

Solve problems involving inverse, joint, or combined variation.

inverse variation: $y = \frac{k}{x}$ or $xy = k$

joint variation: $y = kxz$

combined variation: $y = \frac{kz}{x}$

A variable n varies jointly as x and y and varies inversely as the cube of z.

$$n = k\frac{xy}{z^3}$$

If $n = -14$ when $x = 3$, $y = 7$, and $z = -3$, what is n when $x = 4$, $y = 5$, and $z = 3$?

First find the constant, k, by solving $n = k\frac{xy}{z^3}$ for k and using substitution.

$$n = k\frac{xy}{z^3} \quad \rightarrow \quad k = \frac{nz^3}{xy}$$

$$k = \frac{nz^3}{xy} = \frac{(-14)(-3)^3}{(3)(7)} = 18$$

Now find n when $x = 4$, $y = 5$, and $z = 3$.

$$n = k\frac{xy}{z^3} = (18)\frac{(4)(5)}{(3)^3} = \frac{40}{3}$$

Exercises

1. A variable y varies jointly as x and z. If $y = 2$ when $x = 4$ and $z = 6$, what is y when $x = 3$ and $z = 8$?

2. A variable m varies directly as a and inversely as b. If $m = 6$ when $a = 7$ and $b = 4$, what is m when $a = 9$ and $b = 12$?

3. A variable a varies directly as b and inversely as the square of c. If $a = 3$ when $b = 18$ and $c = 2$, what is a when $b = 20$ and $c = 6$?

4. A variable f varies jointly as g and the square of h and inversely as j. If $f = -14$ when $g = 5$, $h = 8$, and $j = 20$, what is f when $g = 4$, $h = 6$, and $j = 9$?

Key Skills

Identify all excluded values, asymptotes, and holes in the graph of a rational function.

$$y = \frac{4x^2 + 12x}{x^2 + x - 6} = \frac{4x(x+3)}{(x-2)(x+3)}$$

The excluded values are $x = 2$ and $x = -3$.

$x + 3$ is a factor of the numerator and the denominator, so the graph has a hole when $x = -3$.

$x - 2$ is a factor of only the denominator, so the vertical asymptote is $x = 2$.

The degree of the numerator is equal to the degree of the denominator, so the horizontal asymptote is $y = \frac{4}{1} = 4$.

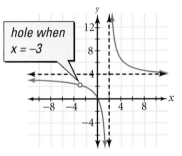

hole when $x = -3$

Exercises

Identify all excluded values, asymptotes, and holes in the graph of each rational function.

5. $R(x) = \dfrac{2x - 3}{x^2 - 8x + 12}$

6. $g(x) = \dfrac{3x - 5}{x^2 - 25}$

7. $f(x) = \dfrac{x^2 - x - 42}{x^2 + 5x - 14}$

8. $r(a) = \dfrac{a^2 + 4a - 12}{3a^2 - 12}$

9. $s(x) = \dfrac{x^2 - 9}{3x + 5}$

10. $M(x) = \dfrac{x^4 - 10x + 9}{3x^2 - 27}$

11. $h(y) = \dfrac{2y}{6y^4 - 18y^3}$

12. $r(t) = \dfrac{t^3 - t^2 - 4t + 4}{t^2 + t - 2}$

Key Skills

Multiply, divide, and simplify rational expressions, including complex fractions.

Simplify $\dfrac{x^2 + 2x - 3}{x^2 + 5x + 6} \div \dfrac{4x^2 - 4x}{x^2 + 3x + 2}$.

$$\frac{x^2 + 2x - 3}{x^2 + 5x + 6} \div \frac{4x^2 - 4x}{x^2 + 3x + 2}$$

$$= \frac{x^2 + 2x - 3}{x^2 + 5x + 6} \cdot \frac{x^2 + 3x + 2}{4x^2 - 4x}$$

$$= \frac{(x+3)(x-1)}{(x+2)(x+3)} \cdot \frac{(x+1)(x+2)}{4x(x-1)}$$

$$= \frac{x+1}{4x}$$

Simplify complex fractions.

$$\frac{\dfrac{x^2 - 1}{2x^2 - x - 15}}{\dfrac{4x + 4}{x^2 - 3x}} = \frac{x^2 - 1}{2x^2 - x - 15} \div \frac{4x + 4}{x^2 - 3x}$$

$$= \frac{(x+1)(x-1)}{(x-3)(2x+5)} \cdot \frac{x(x-3)}{4(x+1)}$$

$$= \frac{x(x-1)}{4(2x+5)}, \text{ or } \frac{x^2 - x}{8x + 20}$$

Exercises

Simplify each expression.

13. $\dfrac{x^2 + 6x}{10} \cdot \dfrac{4}{x^2 - 36}$

14. $\dfrac{3x^2 + 10x - 8}{3x^2 - 17x + 10} \cdot \dfrac{2x^2 + 9x - 5}{x^2 + 3x - 4}$

15. $\dfrac{4a + 8}{5a - 20} \div \dfrac{a^2 + 3a - 10}{a^2 - 4a}$

16. $\dfrac{x^2 - 9}{6} \div \dfrac{4x - 12}{x}$

17. $\dfrac{\dfrac{z}{z+1}}{\dfrac{z+2}{z}}$

18. $\dfrac{\dfrac{a+1}{a^2}}{\dfrac{(a-1)^2}{a}}$

19. $\dfrac{\dfrac{x+1}{x}}{\dfrac{(x+1)^2}{x+2}}$

20. $\dfrac{\dfrac{4x^2}{6x - 3}}{\dfrac{15x}{2x - 1}}$

Key Skills

Add and subtract rational expressions.

Simplify $\dfrac{2a}{a-5} - \dfrac{5a}{3a+2}$.

$$\dfrac{2a}{a-5} - \dfrac{5a}{3a+2} = \dfrac{2a}{a-5}\left(\dfrac{3a+2}{3a+2}\right) - \dfrac{5a}{3a+2}\left(\dfrac{a-5}{a-5}\right)$$

$$= \dfrac{2a(3a+2) - 5a(a-5)}{(a-5)(3a+2)}$$

$$= \dfrac{a^2 + 29a}{3a^2 - 13a - 10}$$

Exercises

Simplify each expression.

21. $\dfrac{3y-5}{2y-6} + \dfrac{4y-2}{5y-15}$

22. $\dfrac{9y+3}{y^2-11y+18} + \dfrac{y+3}{y-9}$

23. $\dfrac{2x-3}{x^2-3x} - \dfrac{3x+1}{x-3}$

24. $\dfrac{3b-39}{b^2-7b+10} - \dfrac{3}{b-2}$

25. $\dfrac{\frac{2}{x}}{4} + \dfrac{\frac{5}{x}}{3}$

26. $\dfrac{x}{3+\frac{5}{x}} - \dfrac{4}{1+\frac{2}{x}}$

Key Skills

Solve rational equations.

Solve $\dfrac{1}{x^2} = x$.

$$\dfrac{1}{x^2} = x$$
$$1 = x^3$$
$$x^3 - 1 = 0$$
$$(x-1)(x^2+x+1) = 0$$
$$x = 1 \;\; or \;\; x = -\dfrac{1}{2} + \dfrac{\sqrt{3}}{2}i \;\; or \;\; x = -\dfrac{1}{2} - \dfrac{\sqrt{3}}{2}i$$

The only real solution is $x = 1$. Therefore, the only point of intersection for the graphs of $y = \dfrac{1}{x^2}$ and $y = x$ occurs when $x = 1$.

Solve rational inequalities.

Solve $\dfrac{x}{1+x} \le 2$.

$$\dfrac{x}{1+x} \le 2, \; 1+x > 0 \quad or \quad \dfrac{x}{1+x} \le 2, \; 1+x < 0$$

$\dfrac{x}{1+x} \le 2$	$\dfrac{x}{1+x} \le 2$
$x \le 2(1+x)$	$x \ge 2(1+x)$
$x \le 2 + 2x$	$x \ge 2 + 2x$
$-x \le 2$	$-x \ge 2$
$x \ge -2$	$x \le -2$

If $1+x > 0$, then $x > -1$. | If $1+x < 0$, then $x < -1$.
Thus, $x > -1$ *and* $x \ge -2$, | Thus, $x < -1$ *and* $x \le -2$,
or simply $x > -1$. | or simply $x \le -2$.

The solution is
$x > -1$ *or* $x \le -2$.

The graphs of
$y = \dfrac{x}{1+x}$ and $y = 2$
verify this solution.

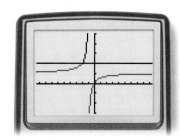

Exercises

Solve each equation.

27. $\dfrac{1}{x^2+1} = \dfrac{1}{2}$

28. $\dfrac{4}{x^2+1} = 1$

29. $\dfrac{3x-1}{x^2+2x} = -1$

30. $\dfrac{2}{1-x^2} = \dfrac{x^2}{x^2+1}$

31. $\dfrac{1}{1-x^2} = -1$

32. $\dfrac{1}{x} = \dfrac{x+2}{x+1}$

Solve each inequality by using algebra.

33. $\dfrac{1}{x} < 1$

34. $\dfrac{1}{x} \ge 2$

35. $\dfrac{1}{x^2+1} < \dfrac{1}{2}$

36. $\dfrac{1}{x^2+1} \ge \dfrac{1}{3}$

37. $\dfrac{1+x}{2x+3} < 1$

38. $\dfrac{1+2x}{2x-1} < 2$

Solve each inequality by graphing.

39. $\dfrac{1}{x} \ge x$

40. $\dfrac{1}{x} < 2x$

41. $\dfrac{x^2+x+1}{x^2+3x+2} \ge x$

42. $\dfrac{x^3+2}{x^2+2x+1} \le 3x$

43. $\dfrac{1}{x^2+2x+1} > 2$

44. $\dfrac{1}{x^2-x+2} < x$

Key Skills

Find the inverse of a quadratic function.

Find the inverse of $y = x^2 - 7x + 10$. Interchange x and y, and solve for y by applying the quadratic formula.

$$x = y^2 - 7y + 10$$

$$y = \frac{-(-7) \pm \sqrt{(-7)^2 - 4(1)(10 - x)}}{2(1)}$$

$$y = \frac{7 \pm \sqrt{9 + 4x}}{2}$$

Describe the transformations applied to the square-root parent function, $f(x) = \sqrt{x}$.

Describe the transformations applied to $f(x) = \sqrt{x}$ to obtain $y = 2\sqrt{3x - 3} + 4$.

$$g(x) = 2\sqrt{3x - 3} + 4 = 2\sqrt{3(x - 1)} + 4$$

The parent function is stretched vertically by a factor of 2, compressed horizontally by a factor of $\frac{1}{3}$, translated horizontally 1 unit to the right, and translated vertically 4 units up.

Exercises

Find the inverse of each quadratic function.

45. $y = 3x + x^2$ **46.** $y = 8x + 12 + x^2$

47. $y = 3x^2 - 16x + 5$ **48.** $y = 2x^2 + 7x + 6$

For each function, describe the transformations applied to $f(x) = \sqrt{x}$.

49. $g(x) = \frac{1}{3}\sqrt{x}$ **50.** $h(x) = 3\sqrt{x} - 5$

51. $k(x) = \sqrt{2x - 3}$ **52.** $g(x) = 4\sqrt{2x + 1} + 2$

53. $h(x) = -2\sqrt{3x} - 6$ **54.** $r(x) = 5\sqrt{3(x - 1)} + 1$

Evaluate each expression.

55. $5\left(\sqrt[3]{-27}\right)^2$ **56.** $\frac{1}{2}\sqrt[3]{8} + 1$

Key Skills

Simplify expressions involving radicals.

Simplify $\dfrac{(24a^8b^5)^{\frac{1}{4}} \cdot \sqrt[4]{4a^3b^2}}{\sqrt[4]{3ab^2}}$.

$$\frac{(24a^8b^5)^{\frac{1}{4}} \cdot \sqrt[4]{4a^3b^2}}{\sqrt[4]{3ab^2}} = \frac{\sqrt[4]{24a^8b^5} \cdot \sqrt[4]{4a^3b^2}}{\sqrt[4]{3ab^2}}$$

$$= \frac{\sqrt[4]{96a^{11}b^7}}{\sqrt[4]{3ab^2}}$$

$$= \sqrt[4]{32a^{10}b^5}$$

$$= \sqrt[4]{2^4a^8b^4 \cdot 2a^2b}$$

$$= 2a^2|b|\sqrt[4]{2a^2b}$$

Rationalize the denominators of expressions.

Write $\dfrac{1}{2 + \sqrt{2}}$ with a rational denominator.

$$\frac{1}{2 + \sqrt{2}} = \frac{1}{2 + \sqrt{2}}\left(\frac{2 - \sqrt{2}}{2 - \sqrt{2}}\right) = \frac{2 - \sqrt{2}}{2}$$

Exercises

Simplify each radical expression. Assume that the value of each variable is positive.

57. $\sqrt{6x^2y^4} \cdot (3x^5y)^{\frac{1}{2}}$ **58.** $(5a^3b^5)^{\frac{1}{3}} \cdot \sqrt[4]{4a^4b}$

59. $\dfrac{\sqrt[3]{42c^4d^{17}}}{(6cd^{11})^{\frac{1}{3}}}$ **60.** $\dfrac{(45s^3t^6)^{\frac{1}{2}}}{\sqrt{3t^2}}$

61. $\dfrac{(6x^5y^7)^{\frac{1}{2}} \cdot \sqrt{3x^2y^4}}{\sqrt{2x}}$ **62.** $\dfrac{(24m^9n)^{\frac{1}{3}} \cdot \sqrt[3]{9m^3n^7}}{\sqrt[3]{3mn^2}}$

Write each expression with a rational denominator and in simplest form.

63. $\dfrac{1}{\sqrt{5}}$ **64.** $\dfrac{1}{\sqrt{7}}$

65. $\dfrac{3}{2 - \sqrt{3}}$ **66.** $\dfrac{4}{-2 + \sqrt{5}}$

67. $\dfrac{1 + \sqrt{2}}{3 - \sqrt{3}}$ **68.** $\dfrac{2 - \sqrt{3}}{3 + \sqrt{2}}$

Key Skills

Solve radical equations.

Solve $2x = \sqrt{3-x}$.

$$2x = \sqrt{3-x}$$
$$4x^2 = 3 - x$$
$$4x^2 + x - 3 = 0$$
$$(4x-3)(x+1) = 0$$
$$x = \frac{3}{4} \quad or \quad x = -1$$

Check for extraneous solutions.

$$2x = \sqrt{3-x} \qquad 2x = \sqrt{3-x}$$
$$2\left(\frac{3}{4}\right) \overset{?}{=} \sqrt{3 - \left(\frac{3}{4}\right)} \qquad 2(-1) \overset{?}{=} \sqrt{3-(-1)}$$
$$\frac{3}{2} = \frac{3}{2} \quad \textbf{True} \qquad -2 = 2 \quad \textbf{False}$$

Solve radical inequalities.

To solve $\sqrt{2x-1} \le 1$, first solve $2x - 1 \ge 0$.

$$2x - 1 \ge 0$$
$$x \ge \frac{1}{2}$$

Then solve the original inequality.

$$\sqrt{2x-1} \le 1$$
$$\left(\sqrt{2x-1}\right)^2 \le 1^2$$
$$2x - 1 \le 1$$
$$2x \le 2$$
$$x \le 1$$

Thus, $x \ge \frac{1}{2}$ and $x \le 1$, or $\frac{1}{2} \le x \le 1$. The solution can be verified by graphing.

Exercises

Solve each radical equation by using algebra. If the inequality has no real solution, write *no solution*. Check your solution.

69. $\sqrt{x+2} = -2$
70. $3\sqrt{x+7} + 8 = 6$
71. $\sqrt[3]{x+2} = -2$
72. $3\sqrt[3]{x+7} + 8 = 6$
73. $\sqrt{x} = 2x$
74. $\sqrt{x+2} = 3$
75. $\sqrt{x} = \sqrt{-x+3}$
76. $\sqrt{2x+1} = \sqrt{4x-4}$
77. $\sqrt[3]{4-x} = \sqrt[3]{3x}$
78. $\sqrt[5]{2x} = \sqrt[5]{x+3}$
79. $\sqrt{x} - 2 = \sqrt{x-2}$
80. $\sqrt{3x} - 1 = \sqrt{x+2}$

Solve each radical inequality by using algebra. Check your solution.

81. $\sqrt{x} \le 5$
82. $\sqrt{x-1} < 2$
83. $\sqrt{x} \ge 5$
84. $\sqrt{x-1} > 2$
85. $\sqrt[4]{x-2} \ge 1$
86. $\sqrt[3]{x-1} < 1$
87. $\sqrt{2x+2} > 4$
88. $-2\sqrt{x-2} < -1$
89. $\sqrt{6x} < 0$
90. $4\sqrt{5x-1} < 0$

Solve each radical inequality by graphing.

91. $\sqrt[3]{x-2} \le \sqrt{x}$
92. $\sqrt[5]{2x+1} \ge 2$

Applications

PHYSICS The weight of an object varies inversely as the square of the distance from the object to the center of Earth, whose radius is approximately 4000 miles.

93. If an astronaut weighs 175 pounds on Earth, what will the astronaut weigh at a point 60 miles above Earth's surface?

94. If an astronaut weighs 145 pounds at a point 80 miles above the Earth's surface, how much does the astronaut weigh on Earth?

8 Alternative Assessment

Performance Assessment

1. WORKER-DAYS A construction foreman estimates that 12 workers will take 180 days to complete a job. Assume that the workers share the job equally and that each works at the same rate.

   a. Make a table for the number of workers, *w*, and the time in days, *t*, that it takes to complete the job.

   b. Graph the values in the table and describe the relationship between them.

   c. Add a column or row to your table for *worker-days* to include the product of the number of workers and the time in days.

   d. Write a function that models the relationship between the number of workers and the time in days.

2. MIXTURES Three hundred milliliters of a 75% citric-acid solution is added to *x* milliliters of water.

   a. Write a rational function for the concentration of citric acid in the mixture.

   b. For each mixture concentration below, find the amount of water in milliliters that is required.
   - a 50% citric-acid mixture
   - a 25% citric-acid mixture
   - a 10% citric-acid mixture
   - a 2.5% citric-acid mixture

   c. Use your results from part **b** to make a table for the mixture concentrations and the amounts of water required. How are they related? Explain.

Portfolio Projects

1. AREA MODELS Using graph paper, sketch several different rectangles that have an area of 24 square units.

   a. What happens to the width of the rectangle as the length increases?

   b. What is the largest possible length for the rectangle? What width corresponds to this length?

   c. Describe the horizontal and vertical asymptotes for the graph of $y = \frac{24}{x}$.

2. RECIPROCAL POLYNOMIAL FUNCTIONS

   a. Graph the reciprocal functions $f(x) = x^3 - x^2 - 6x$ and $g(x) = \frac{1}{x^3 - x^2 - 6x}$.

   b. Compare the functions by examining the zeros, asymptotes, domains, local maxima and minima, and points where the functions are positive, negative, increasing, and decreasing.

   c. Without graphing, compare the functions $f(x) = x(x - 1)(x + 2)$ and $g(x) = \frac{1}{x(x - 1)(x + 2)}$. Then graph *f* and *g* to verify.

3. PERFECT SQUARES AND CUBES The number 64 is the square of 8 and the cube of 4.

   a. Find two other numbers that are both a perfect square and a perfect cube.

   b. Find a formula for generating numbers that are perfect squares and perfect cubes.

QUANTITATIVE COMPARISON. For Items 1–6, write

A if the quantity in Column A is greater than the quantity in Column B;
B if the quantity in Column B is greater than the quantity in Column A;
C if the two quantities are equal; or
D if the relationship cannot be determined from the given information.

	Column A	Column B	Answers
1.	Let $f(x) = 3x - 5$ and $g(x) = x^2 + 1$. $f \circ g$	$g \circ f$	Ⓐ Ⓑ Ⓒ Ⓓ [Lesson 2.6]
2.	$\frac{1}{x}$	x	Ⓐ Ⓑ Ⓒ Ⓓ [Lesson 2.1]
3.	4	$\log_3 50$	Ⓐ Ⓑ Ⓒ Ⓓ [Lesson 6.3]
4.	$-5x < 10$ x	0	Ⓐ Ⓑ Ⓒ Ⓓ [Lesson 1.7]
5.	$x \neq 0$ $\frac{1}{x^2}$	$\frac{1}{x^2 + 1}$	Ⓐ Ⓑ Ⓒ Ⓓ [Lesson 8.2]
6.	$\sqrt[3]{-\frac{1}{3}}$	$\sqrt[4]{\frac{1}{3}}$	Ⓐ Ⓑ Ⓒ Ⓓ [Lesson 5.3]

7. If $\frac{a}{b} = \frac{c}{d}$, which of the following is *not* always true? **(LESSON 1.4)**
a. $ad = bc$
b. $ad = cb$
c. $\frac{a}{d} = \frac{c}{b}$
d. $\frac{a-b}{b} = \frac{c-d}{d}$

8. Solve $2^x = \frac{1}{64}$ for x. **(LESSON 6.3)**
a. 32
b. 6
c. −32
d. −6

9. Simplify $(6\sqrt{8} - 6\sqrt{2})(2\sqrt{2} + 1)$. **(LESSON 8.7)**
a. $6\sqrt{2} - 24$
b. $6\sqrt{2} + 24$
c. $12\sqrt{2} - 23$
d. $6\sqrt{2} - 23$

10. How many solutions does the system $\begin{cases} y = 3x + 2 \\ y = 3x - 2 \end{cases}$ have? **(LESSON 3.1)**
a. 0
b. 1
c. 2
d. infinite

11. Find the remainder when $2x^2 - 5x + 8$ is divided by $x + 4$. **(LESSON 7.3)**
a. 60
b. −44
c. 0
d. 20

12. Simplify $(a^3b^{-2})^{-2}$. Assume that no variable equals zero. **(LESSON 2.2)**
a. $\frac{b^4}{a^6}$
b. $\frac{1}{a^2b}$
c. $\frac{a^6}{b^4}$
d. a^2b

13. Which of the following is *not* a root of $x^3 + x^2 - 9x - 9 = 0$? *(LESSON 7.4)*

    a. -3 **b.** 3 **c.** -1 **d.** 1

14. Which would you add to $x^2 - 10x$ to complete the square? *(LESSON 5.4)*

    a. 5 **b.** -5 **c.** 25 **d.** -25

15. Find the product $\begin{bmatrix} 3 & 6 & 1 \end{bmatrix} \begin{bmatrix} 0 & 5 \\ 1 & -2 \\ -3 & 4 \end{bmatrix}$. *(LESSON 4.2)*

16. Write an equation of the line that contains the points $(-3, 8)$ and $(9, -4)$. *(LESSON 1.3)*

17. Write the function for the graph of $f(x) = |x|$ translated 2 units to the left and 1 unit down. *(LESSON 2.7)*

18. Factor $25x^2 - 60x + 36$ completely. *(LESSON 5.3)*

19. Find the inverse of $f(x) = \frac{2}{3}x + 6$. *(LESSON 2.5)*

20. Simplify $\frac{1 + x}{x^2 + 3x - 4} \div \frac{x^3}{x^2 + 4x}$. *(LESSON 8.3)*

21. Find x if $\log_{10} x + \log_{10} 8 = \log_{10} 16$. *(LESSON 6.4)*

22. Write a polynomial function in standard form by using the information given below. *(LESSON 7.5)*

$P(0) = -12$; zeros: $-4, 3, -1$ (multiplicity 2)

23. Write the parametric equations $\begin{cases} x(t) = 3 - t^2 \\ y(t) = \frac{5}{2}t \end{cases}$ as a single equation in x and y. *(LESSON 3.6)*

24 Find the inverse, if one exists, of the matrix $\begin{bmatrix} 2 & 4 \\ 3 & 5 \end{bmatrix}$. If the inverse does not exist, write *no inverse*. *(LESSON 4.3)*

25. Write with a rational denominator $\frac{8}{5 - 3\sqrt{2}}$. *(LESSON 8.6)*

26. TRAVEL An airplane travels from Hawaii to Los Angeles at 580 miles per hour with a tailwind and returns to Hawaii at 460 miles per hour against a headwind. What is the average speed of the airplane over the entire trip? *(LESSON 8.4)*

27. MAXIMUM/MINIMUM At the Springfield City Fourth of July celebration, a fireworks shell is shot upward with an initial velocity of 250 feet per second. Find its maximum height and the time required to reach it. Use the formula $h = v_0 t - 16t^2$, where v_0 is the initial velocity, t is time in seconds, and h is the height in feet. *(LESSON 5.2)*

FREE-RESPONSE GRID

The following questions may be answered by using a free-response grid such as that commonly used by standardized-test services.

28. Find x if $\log_2 x = 4$. *(LESSON 6.3)*

29. What is the greatest integer x for which $-6x - 1 > 10$? *(LESSON 1.7)*

30. Solve the system for z. *(LESSON 4.4)*

$\begin{cases} x - 2y - z = 2 \\ x - y + 2z = 9 \\ 2x + y + z = 3 \end{cases}$

31. Find $|7 - 24i|$. *(LESSON 5.6)*

32. Solve $2\sqrt{x - 4} = \sqrt{x + 2}$ for x. *(LESSON 8.8)*

Solve each equation. *(LESSONS 1.6 AND 1.8)*

33. $1 - 2x = 5$

34. $-5x + 3 = \frac{1}{2}x - 1$

35. Solve $\log_x 27 = -3$ for x. Give an approximate solution to the nearest hundredth. *(LESSON 6.7)*

36. Approximate to the nearest tenth the real zero of $f(x) = x^3 - 2x^2 + 3x - 1$. *(LESSON 7.5)*

37. Simplify $\sqrt[3]{64^{\frac{1}{2}}}$. *(LESSON 8.7)*

38. ENTERTAINMENT A rectangular stage is 20 meters wide and 38 meters long. To make room for additional seating, two adjacent sides of the stage are shortened by the same amount. If this reduces the stage by 265 square meters, by how many meters are each of the two adjacent sides of the stage shortened? *(LESSON 5.2)*

Keystroke Guide for Chapter 8

Essential keystroke sequences (using the model TI-82 or TI-83 graphics calculator) are presented below for all Activities and Examples found in this chapter that require or recommend the use of a graphics calculator.

 Keystrokes for other models of graphics calculators are found on the HRW Web site.

LESSON 8.1

E X A M P L E S **1** and **3** For Example 1, enter $y = \frac{60.75}{x}$, and use a table to find the
Pages 482 and 483 y-values for the given x-values.

Enter the function:

Y= 60.75 ÷ X,T,Θ,n

Make a table of values:

TBLSET
2nd WINDOW (TblStart=) 0 ENTER (△ Tbl=) 0.5

⇑ TI-82: (TblMin=)

ENTER (Indpt:) **AUTO** ENTER ▼ (Depend:)

TABLE
AUTO ENTER ▼ 2nd GRAPH

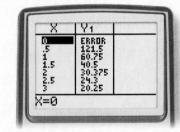

For Example 3, use a similar keystroke sequence. Use (TblStart=) 1.5 and (△ Tbl=) 1.

LESSON 8.2

E X A M P L E **2** Enter $y = \frac{x^2 - 7x + 12}{x^2 + 9x + 20}$, and use a table of values to verify that -4 and -5 are
Page 490 not in the domain.

Enter the function:

Y= (X,T,Θ,n x^2 − 7 X,T,Θ,n
+ 12) ÷ (X,T,Θ,n x^2
+ 9 X,T,Θ,n + 20)

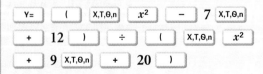

Make a table of values:

Use a keystroke sequence similar to that used
in Example 1 of Lesson 8.1. Use (TblStart=) -8 and (△ Tbl=)1.

Activity

Page 490

For Step 1, enter $y = \dfrac{1}{x-2}$, and use a table to find the y-values for the given x-values.

Use a keystroke sequence similar to that used in Example 1 of Lesson 8.1. For part **a**, use (TblStart=) 1 and ($\triangle$ Tbl=) 0.1. For part **b**, use (TblStart=) 3 and ($\triangle$ Tbl=) −0.1.
For Step 3, use a similar keystroke sequence.

EXAMPLES ③ and ④ Graph the function, and look for asymptotes.

Pages 491–493

Use friendly viewing window [−4.7, 4.7] by [−3.1, 3.1].

Enter the function by using a keystroke sequence similar to that in Example 2 of Lesson 8.2. Then graph.

EXAMPLE ⑥ Enter $y = \dfrac{3x}{0.8x + 25}$, and make a table of values.

Page 501

Enter the function:

| Y= | 3 | X,T,θ,n | ÷ | (| 0.8 | X,T,θ,n | + |
25 |) |

Make a table of values:

Use a keystroke sequence similar to that used in Example 1 of Lesson 8.1. Use (TblStart=) 18 and ($\triangle$ Tbl=) 1.

Activity

Page 501

For Steps 1 and 2, graph $y = \dfrac{\dfrac{x-3}{x+2}}{\dfrac{x-2}{x+2}}$ and $y = \dfrac{x-3}{x-2}$ on the same screen. Then make a table of values with the given x-values.

Use friendly viewing window [−4.7, 4.7] by [−3.1, 3.1].

Graph the functions:

Y=	(	(	X,T,θ,n	−	3	)	÷	(	X,T,θ,n	+	2
)	)	÷	(	(	X,T,θ,n	−	2	)	÷	(	X,T,θ,n
+	2	)	)	(Y2=)	(	X,T,θ,n	−	3	)	÷	(	X,T,θ,n
−	2	)	GRAPH

Make a table of values:

Use a keystroke sequence similar to that used in Example 1 of Lesson 8.1. Use (TblStart=) −3 and ($\triangle$ Tbl=) 1.

E X A M P L E **3** Graph $y = \dfrac{6x}{3x-1} - \dfrac{4x}{2x+5}$ and $y = \dfrac{34x}{6x^2 + 13x - 5}$ on the same screen.

Page 507

Use friendly viewing window $[-6, 4]$ by $[-4, 4]$.

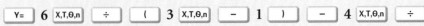

| Y= | 6 | X,T,θ,n | ÷ | (| 3 | X,T,θ,n | − | 1 |) | − | 4 | X,T,θ,n | ÷ |

(2 X,T,θ,n + 5) ENTER (Y2=) 34 X,T,θ,n ÷ (6 X,T,θ,n

x^2 + 13 X,T,θ,n − 5) GRAPH

E X A M P L E **1** Graph $y = \dfrac{64x + 140}{6x(x+5)}$ and $y = 2.5$ on the same screen, and find any points

Pages 512 and 513 of intersection.

Use viewing window $[0, 5]$ by $[0, 7]$.

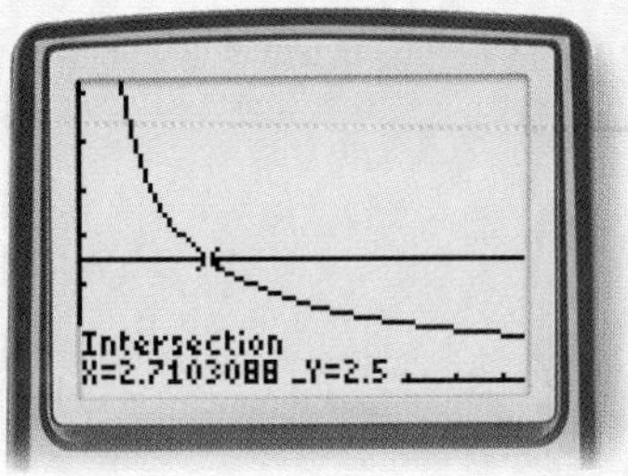

Graph the functions:

Y= (64 X,T,θ,n + 140) ÷ (6 X,T,θ,n (X,T,θ,n

+ 5)) ENTER (Y2=) 2.5 GRAPH

Find any points of intersection:

2nd TRACE **CALC** **5:intersect** (First Curve?) ENTER (Second Curve?) ENTER

(Guess?) ENTER

E X A M P L E S **2** and **3** For Example 2, graph $y = \dfrac{x}{x-6} - \dfrac{1}{x-4}$ and find any zeros.

Pages 513 and 514 Use viewing window $[-2, 4]$ by $[-0.5, 0.5]$.

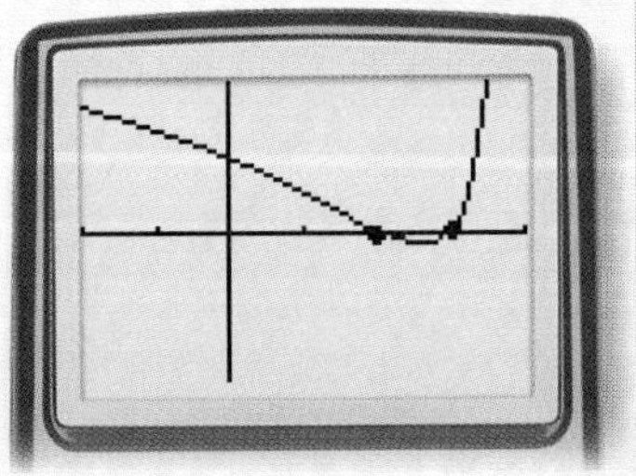

Graph the function:

Use a keystroke sequence similar to that in Example 3 of Lesson 8.4.

CALC
Find any zeros: 2nd TRACE **2:intersect** (Left Bound?) ENTER (Right Bound?)

⇑ TI-82: **2:root**

ENTER (Guess?) ENTER

For Example 3, use a similar keystroke sequence. Use friendly viewing window $[-12.4, 6.4]$ by $[-8, 8]$.

Page 515 For Step 1, graph $y = \dfrac{x+2}{x-4}$, and make a table of values.

Use friendly viewing window $[-6.8, 12]$ by $[-10, 10]$.

Graph the function:

Y= (X,T,θ,n + 2) ÷ (X,T,θ,n − 4) GRAPH

Make a table of values: Use a keystroke sequence similar to that used in Example 1 of Lesson 8.1. Use (TblStart=) −5 and (△ Tbl=) 1.

E X A M P L E ④ Graph $y = \dfrac{x}{2x-1}$ and $y = 1$, and find any points of intersection.

Page 515

Use friendly viewing window $[-4.7, 4.7]$ by $[-3, 3]$.

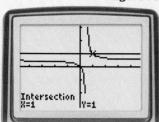

Intersection
X=1   Y=1

Graph the functions:

[Y=] [X,T,θ,n] [÷] [( ] 2 [X,T,θ,n] [–] 1 [ )] [ENTER] (Y2=) 1 [GRAPH]

Find any points of intersection:

Use a keystroke sequence similar to that used in Example 1 of Lesson 8.5.

E X A M P L E ⑤ Graph $y = \dfrac{x-2}{2(x-3)} - \dfrac{x}{x+3}$, and find any zeros of the function. Then make a table of values.

Page 516

Use friendly viewing window $[-9.4, 9.4]$ by $[-3.1, 3.1]$.

Graph the function:

[Y=] [( ] [X,T,θ,n] [–] 2 [ )] [÷] [( ] 2 [( ] [X,T,θ,n] [–] 3 [ )]

⇑ TI-82: [( ]

[ )] [–] [X,T,θ,n] [÷] [( ] [X,T,θ,n] [+] 3 [ )] [GRAPH]

⇑ TI-82: [( ]

Find any zeros:

Use a keystroke sequence similar to that in Example 2 of Lesson 8.5.

Make a table of values:

Use a keystroke sequence similar to that in Example 1 of Lesson 8.1. Use (TblStart=) −4 and (△ Tbl=) 1.

LESSON 8.6

E X A M P L E ① Graph $y = \sqrt{2x-5}$.

Page 521

Use viewing window $[-1, 8]$ by $[-1, 5]$.

$\sqrt{}$ ⇓ TI-82: [( ]

[Y=] [2nd] [x^2] 2 [X,T,θ,n] [–] 5 [ )] [GRAPH]

E X A M P L E S ② and ③ For Example 2, part a, graph $y = \sqrt{x}$ and $y = -2\sqrt{x+1} + 4$ on the same screen, and compare the graphs.

Pages 522 and 523

Use friendly viewing window $[-2.7, 6.7]$ by $[-3, 6]$.

Graph the functions:

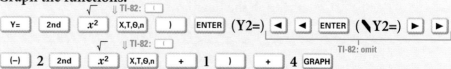

$\sqrt{}$ ⇓ TI-82: [( ]

[Y=] [2nd] [x^2] [X,T,θ,n] [ )] [ENTER] (Y2=) [◄] [◄] [ENTER] (◥Y2=) [►] [►]

$\sqrt{}$ ⇓ TI-82: [( ]   TI-82: omit

[(-)] 2 [2nd] [x^2] [X,T,θ,n] [+] 1 [ )] [+] 4 [GRAPH]

For part **b** of Example 2, use a similar keystroke sequence and the same friendly viewing window.

For Example 3, use friendly viewing window $[-2.7, 6.7]$ by $[-1.6, 4.6]$.

EXAMPLE 4

Page 523

Enter the function $y = 2\pi\sqrt{\dfrac{x}{9.8}}$, and make a table of values.

Enter the function:

`Y=` 2 `2nd` `^`(π) `2nd` `x²`(√) `X,T,θ,n` `÷` 9.8 `)`

Make a table of values:

Use a keystroke sequence similar to that used in Example 1 of Lesson 8.1. Use (TblStart=) 0 and (△ Tbl=) 0.1.

Activity

Page 524

For Step 1, graph each radical function.

Use viewing window $[-5, 5]$ by $[-5, 5]$. Use the fact that $\sqrt[n]{x} = x^{\frac{1}{n}}$ to graph a radical function for $n > 2$. For example, graph $y = \sqrt[3]{x}$:

`Y=` `X,T,θ,n` `^` `(` 1 `÷` 3 `)` `GRAPH`

LESSON 8.7

Activity

Page 528

For Step 1, graph $y = \sqrt{x^2}$.

Use viewing window $[-10, 10]$ by $[-10, 10]$.

`Y=` `2nd` `x²`(√) `X,T,θ,n` `x²` `)` `GRAPH`

⇑ TI-82: omit

For Step 2, graph $y = \sqrt[4]{x^4}$.

`Y=` `(` `X,T,θ,n` `^` 4 `)` `^` `(` 1 `÷` 4 `)` `GRAPH`

For Steps 3–6, use a keystroke sequence similar to that used in Step 2.

LESSON 8.8

EXAMPLES 1 and 3

Pages 537 and 538

For Example 1, graph $y = 2\sqrt{x + 5}$ and $y = 8$ on the same screen, and find any points of intersection.

Use viewing window $[-5, 20]$ by $[-2, 15]$.

Graph the functions:

`Y=` 2 `2nd` `x²`(√) `X,T,θ,n` `+` 5 `)` `ENTER` (Y2=) 8 `GRAPH`

Find any points of intersection:

Use a keystroke sequence similar to that used in Example 1 of Lesson 8.5.

For Example 3, use a similar keystroke sequence and viewing window $[-2, 10]$ by $[-1, 10]$.

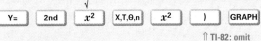

E X A M P L E ❷ Graph $y = \sqrt[3]{x-5}$ and $y = \sqrt[3]{7-x}$ on the same screen, and find any points

Page 537 of intersection.

Use viewing window $[-2, 10]$ by $[-4, 4]$.

Enter the functions:

| Y= | (| X,T,θ,n | − | 5 |) | ^ | (| 1 | ÷ | 3 |) | ENTER | (Y2=)

| (| 7 | − | X,T,θ,n |) | ^ | (| 1 | ÷ | 3 |) | GRAPH

Find any points of intersection:

Use a keystroke sequence similar to that used in Example 1 of Lesson 8.5.

E X A M P L E ❹ Graph $y = \dfrac{286}{2\sqrt{x^2 - 15^2}} + 1$ and $y = 6$ on the same screen, and find any points

Page 538 of intersection. Then make a table of values for $y = \dfrac{286}{2\sqrt{x^2 - 15^2}} + 1$.

Use viewing window $[-2, 50]$ by $[-1, 20]$.

Graph the functions:

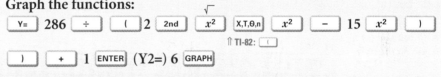

| Y= | 286 | ÷ | (| 2 | 2nd | x^2 | X,T,θ,n | x^2 | − | 15 | x^2 |)

⇑ TI-82: ( )

|) | + | 1 | ENTER | (Y2=) 6 | GRAPH

Find any points of intersection:

Use a keystroke sequence similar to that used in Example 1 of Lesson 8.5.

Make a table of values:

Use a keystroke sequence similar to that used in Example 1 of Lesson 8.1.
Use (TblStart=) 32.25 and (△ Tbl=) 0.01.

Activity

Page 540 Graph $y = \sqrt{x}$ and $y = 1$ on the same screen, and find any points of intersection.

Use viewing window $[-5, 5]$ by $[-5, 5]$.

Use a keystroke sequence similar to that used in Example 1 of Lesson 8.8.

E X A M P L E S ❻ and ❼ For Example 6, graph $y = \sqrt{x+1}$ and $y = 2$ on the same screen,

Pages 540 and 541 and find any points of intersection.

Use viewing window $[-3, 7]$ by $[-5, 5]$.

Use a keystroke sequence similar to that used in Example 1 of Lesson 8.8.

For Example 7, use a keystroke sequence similar to that in Example 2 of this lesson. Use viewing window $[-9.4, 9.4]$ by $[-6.2, 6.2]$.

Conic Sections

CONIC SECTIONS ARE CURVES THAT INCLUDE circles, parabolas, ellipses, and hyperbolas. Parabolas are used to describe the shape of satellite dishes. Ellipses describe the paths of planets around the Sun and of comets that return to the solar system on a regular basis, such as Halley's comet. The lens of a telescope can be either parabolic or hyperbolic. The primary mirror in the Hubble Space Telescope is parabolic.

Lessons

Chapter Project
Focus on This!

About the Chapter Project

In this chapter, you will study the conic sections, their equations, and some of their special properties. In the Chapter Project, *Focus on This!*, you will use an alternative method of graphing to create parabolas, ellipses, and hyperbolas based on their definitions.

After completing the Chapter Project, you will be able to do the following:

- Describe the properties of ellipses, parabolas, and hyperbolas.

- Create ellipses, parabolas, and hyperbolas by using an alternative method of graphing.

About the Portfolio Activities

Throughout the chapter, you will be given opportunities to complete Portfolio Activities that are designed to support your work on the Chapter Project.

- Using wax paper to create a parabolic conic section is included in the Portfolio Activity on page 578.

- Using wax paper to create an elliptical conic section is included in the Portfolio Activity on page 594.

- Using wax paper to create a hyperbolic conic section is included in the Portfolio Activity on page 603.

Introduction to Conic Sections

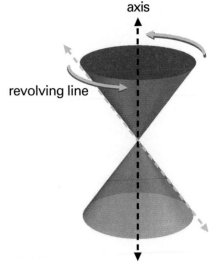

axis

revolving line

Objectives

- Classify a conic section as the intersection of a plane and a double cone.

- Use the distance and midpoint formulas.

Why *The lines or curves that can be created by the intersection of a plane and a double cone, called conic sections, are shapes that can be found in the world around us.*

In the diagram shown at right, a slanted line is revolved all the way around a vertical line, the axis, in three-dimensional space. Because the two lines intersect, the result is a pair of cones that have one point in common. Although the diagram cannot show it, the two cones extend indefinitely both upward and downward, forming a double-napped cone.

The intersection of a double cone and a plane is called a **conic section**. Three conic sections are illustrated below.

parabola

ellipse

hyperbola

A circle, a point, a line, and a pair of intersecting lines are special cases of the three conic sections shown above.

circle
(ellipse)

point
(ellipse)

line
(hyperbola)

pair of intersecting lines (hyperbola)

Since all conic sections are plane figures, you can represent them in a coordinate plane.

EXAMPLE ❶ **Graph each equation and identify the conic section.**

a. $x^2 + y^2 = 25$ **b.** $x^2 - y^2 = 4$

TECHNOLOGY

GRAPHICS CALCULATOR

Keystroke Guide, page 622

SOLUTION

a. Solve for y.

$$x^2 + y^2 = 25$$
$$y^2 = 25 - x^2$$
$$y = \pm\sqrt{25 - x^2}$$

Graph $y = \sqrt{25 - x^2}$ and $y = -\sqrt{25 - x^2}$ together on the same screen.

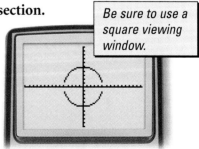

Be sure to use a square viewing window.

The equation $x^2 + y^2 = 25$ represents a circle.

b. Solve for y.

$$x^2 - y^2 = 4$$
$$-y^2 = 4 - x^2$$
$$y^2 = x^2 - 4$$
$$y = \pm\sqrt{x^2 - 4}$$

Graph $y = \sqrt{x^2 - 4}$ and $y = -\sqrt{x^2 - 4}$ together on the same screen.

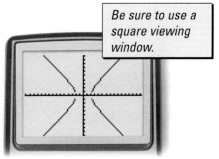

Be sure to use a square viewing window.

The equation $x^2 - y^2 = 4$ represents a hyperbola.

TRY THIS　Graph each equation and identify the conic section.
　　a. $4x^2 + 9y^2 = 36$　　　　　　**b.** $6x - y^2 = 0$

Using the Distance Formula

When conic sections are studied as figures in a coordinate plane, they can be described in terms of distances between points or between points and a line. The *distance formula* will play a role in the definition of each conic section studied in this chapter.

CONNECTION

COORDINATE GEOMETRY

Given points $P(-1, 4)$ and $Q(3, -2)$ in the coordinate plane, you can use the Pythagorean Theorem to find the distance, d, between them.

$$(PQ)^2 = (PR)^2 + (RQ)^2$$
$$d^2 = 6^2 + 4^2$$
$$d = \sqrt{52}$$
$$\approx 7.2$$

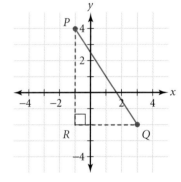

In general, given points $P(x_1, y_1)$ and $Q(x_2, y_2)$ in the coordinate plane, you can use the Pythagorean Theorem to find a formula for the distance, d, between them.

$$(PQ)^2 = (PR)^2 + (RQ)^2$$
$$d^2 = (x_2 - x_1)^2 + (y_2 - y_1)^2$$
$$d = \sqrt{(x_2 - x_1)^2 + (y_2 - y_1)^2}$$

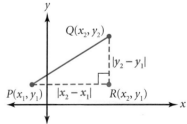

Distance Formula

The distance, d, between $P(x_1, y_1)$ and $Q(x_2, y_2)$ is

$$d = \sqrt{(x_2 - x_1)^2 + (y_2 - y_1)^2}.$$

Activity
Exploring the Distance Formula

You will need: no special materials

1. Let $P(x_1, y_1)$ be the point $(-2, 1)$ and $Q(x_2, y_2)$ be the point $(4, 3)$ in the graph at right. What is x_1? x_2? $(x_2 - x_1)$? $(x_2 - x_1)^2$? Use the distance formula to find PQ.

2. Let $P(x_1, y_1)$ be the point $(4, 3)$ and $Q(x_2, y_2)$ be the point $(-2, 1)$. What is x_1? x_2? $(x_2 - x_1)$? $(x_2 - x_1)^2$? Use the distance formula to find PQ.

3. Is $(x_2 - x_1)$ the same in Steps 1 and 2? Is $(x_2 - x_1)^2$ the same in Steps 1 and 2? Is PQ the same in Steps 1 and 2?

CHECKPOINT ✔ **4.** What seems to happen to the distance between P and Q when you switch the positions of the coordinates in the distance formula? Explain why this happens.

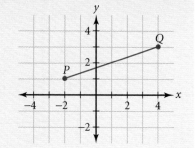

E X A M P L E ❷ Find the distance between $P(-1, 2)$ and $Q(6, 4)$. Give an exact answer and an approximate answer rounded to the nearest hundredth.

● **SOLUTION**

Let (x_1, y_1) be $(-1, 2)$ and let (x_2, y_2) be $(6, 4)$. Use the distance formula.

$d = \sqrt{(x_2 - x_1)^2 + (y_2 - y_1)^2}$

$d = \sqrt{[(6 - (-1)]^2 + (4 - 2)^2}$

$d = \sqrt{53}$ *Exact answer*

$d \approx 7.28$ *Approximate answer*

Thus, the distance between P and Q is $\sqrt{53}$, or about 7.28.

TRY THIS Find the distance between $P(2, 5)$ and $Q(-3, -8)$. Give an exact answer and an approximate answer rounded to the nearest hundredth.

E X A M P L E ❸ An EMS helicopter is stationed at Hospital 1, which is 4 miles west and 2 miles north of an automobile accident. Another EMS helicopter is stationed at Hospital 2, which is 3 miles east and 3 miles north of the accident.

Which helicopter is closer to the accident?

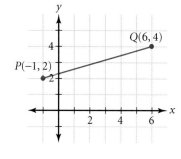

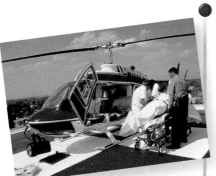

● **SOLUTION**

1. Represent the locations as points in the coordinate plane.

Since the locations of the hospitals are given with reference to the accident, place the accident at the origin. Then $A(-4, 2)$ represents the location of Hospital 1 and $B(3, 3)$ represents the location of Hospital 2.

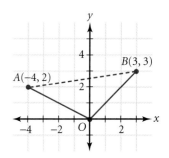

2. Find the distances OA and OB.

$$d = \sqrt{(x_2 - x_1)^2 + (y_2 - y_1)^2}$$
$$OA = \sqrt{[(-4) - 0]^2 + (2 - 0)^2}$$
$$OA = \sqrt{20} \text{ miles, or} \approx 4.47 \text{ miles}$$

$$d = \sqrt{(x_2 - x_1)^2 + (y_2 - y_1)^2}$$
$$OB = \sqrt{(3 - 0)^2 + (3 - 0)^2}$$
$$OB = \sqrt{18} \text{ miles, or} \approx 4.24 \text{ miles}$$

Since $OB < OA$, the helicopter at Hospital 2 is closer to the accident.

Using the Midpoint Formula

The coordinates of the midpoint between two points can be found by using the coordinates of the points.

Midpoint Formula

The coordinates of the midpoint, M, between two points, $P(x_1, y_1)$ and $Q(x_2, y_2)$, are $M\left(\dfrac{x_1 + x_2}{2}, \dfrac{y_1 + y_2}{2}\right)$.

Notice that the x-coordinate of M is the average of the x-coordinates of P and Q and that the y-coordinate of M is the average of the y-coordinates of P and Q. The midpoint formula is used in Example 4.

E X A M P L E **④** **Find the coordinates of the midpoint, M, of the line segment whose endpoints are $P(-4, 6)$ and $Q(5, 10)$.**

● **SOLUTION**

Let (x_1, y_1) be $(-4, 6)$ and (x_2, y_2) be $(5, 10)$.

$$\frac{x_1 + x_2}{2} = \frac{(-4) + 5}{2} = \frac{1}{2} \qquad \frac{y_1 + y_2}{2} = \frac{6 + 10}{2} = 8$$

Thus, $M\left(\dfrac{1}{2}, 8\right)$ is the midpoint.

The graph of points P, M, and Q indicates that the answer is reasonable.

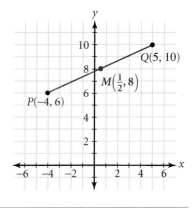

TRY THIS Find the coordinates of the midpoint, M, of the line segment whose endpoints are $A(2.5, 5.5)$ and $B(8.5, -4.5)$.

CRITICAL THINKING A line segment has the endpoints $A(-5, -6)$ and $B(7, 4)$. Find the coordinates of points R, S, and T on segment AB such that $AR = RS = ST = TB$.

CONNECTION
GEOMETRY

Recall from geometry that a chord of a circle is a segment with endpoints on the circle. A **diameter** of a circle is a chord that contains the center. A **radius** of a circle is a segment with one endpoint at the center of the circle and the other endpoint on the circle. The length of the radius is one-half the length of the diameter.

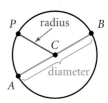

E X A M P L E **5** The endpoints of a diameter of the circle at right are $A(-2, 3)$ and $B(6, 9)$.

Find the center, circumference, and area of the circle.

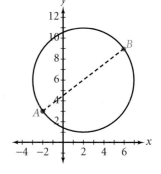

● **SOLUTION**

1. Use the midpoint formula to find the coordinates of the center, C.
$$C\left(\frac{x_1 + x_2}{2}, \frac{y_1 + y_2}{2}\right) \rightarrow C\left(\frac{-2 + 6}{2}, \frac{3 + 9}{2}\right) \rightarrow C(2, 6)$$

2. Use the distance formula to find the radius.
$$CA = \sqrt{(-2 - 2)^2 + (3 - 6)^2} = \sqrt{25} = 5$$

> You can find CA or CB to find the radius.

3. Find the circumference and area.
Circumference $= 2\pi r = 2r(5) = 10\pi$
Area $= \pi r^2 = \pi(5)^2 = 25\pi$

Thus, the center is $(2, 6)$, the circumference is 10π units, and the area is 25π square units.

TRY THIS The endpoints of a diameter of a circle are $A(-3, 2)$ and $B(5, 4)$. Find the center, circumference, and area of the circle.

Exercises

● *Communicate*

1. Illustrate and explain how a plane can intersect a double cone to produce a circle, a parabola, an ellipse, and a hyperbola.

2. Explain why it does not matter which set of coordinates you subtract from the other set when using the distance formula.

3. Explain how to find the circumference and the area of a circle if you are given the coordinates of the center and of a point on the circle.

Guided Skills Practice

Graph each equation and identify the conic section. *(EXAMPLE 1)*

4 $9x^2 - 4y^2 = 100$ **5** $x^2 + y^2 = 100$

6. Find the distance between $P(-7, 12)$ and $Q(6, 5)$. Give an exact answer and an approximate answer rounded to the nearest hundredth. *(EXAMPLE 2)*

APPLICATION

7. EMERGENCY SERVICES If a fire station is 3 miles east and 2 miles south of a fire and the trucks can travel along a straight route to the fire from the station, how long is their route?
(EXAMPLE 3)

8. Find the coordinates of the midpoint, *M,* of the line segment whose endpoints are $P(-3, 10)$ and $Q(6, -12)$.
(EXAMPLE 4)

9. The endpoints of a diameter of a circle are $A(-5, 2)$ and $B(3, 4)$. Find the center, circumference, and area of the circle. *(EXAMPLE 5)*

Practice and Apply

Graph each equation and identify the conic section.

10 $x^2 + y^2 = 36$ **11** $x^2 + y^2 = 121$

12 $x^2 - y^2 = 36$ **13** $4x^2 - 9y^2 = 36$

14 $5x^2 + 9y^2 = 45$ **15** $36x^2 + 5y^2 = 180$

16 $x^2 - 4y = 0$ **17** $y^2 + 4x = 0$

18 $y^2 - 4x = 0$ **19** $x^2 + y^2 = 1$

20 $x^2 + 9y^2 = 9$ **21** $25x^2 - 9y^2 = 225$

Find the distance between *P* and *Q* and the coordinates of *M*, the midpoint of $\overline{PQ}$. Give exact answers and approximate answers to the nearest hundredth when appropriate.

22. $P(-3, -2)$ and $Q(5, -2)$ **23.** $P(-5, -2)$ and $Q(-5, 5)$

24. $P(7, 0)$ and $Q(8, 0)$ **25.** $P(-3, -4)$ and $Q(5, -5)$

26. $P(7, -2)$ and $Q(-5, -1)$ **27.** $P(2.5, 3)$ and $Q(-1.5, 2)$

28. $P(10, 7)$ and $Q(1, 8)$ **29.** $P(10, 2)$ and $Q(8, 0)$

30. $P(7.6, 10.1)$ and $Q(4.6, 3.1)$ **31.** $P\left(2\sqrt{2}, 5\right)$ and $Q\left(\sqrt{2}, 0\right)$

32. $P\left(\frac{1}{2}, \frac{7}{8}\right)$ and $Q\left(3, -\frac{3}{8}\right)$ **33.** $P\left(\frac{3}{2}, \frac{1}{4}\right)$ and $Q\left(-6, \frac{3}{4}\right)$

34. $P\left(5, 5\sqrt{2}\right)$ and $Q\left(6, \sqrt{2}\right)$ **35.** $P\left(2\sqrt{2}, \sqrt{7}\right)$ and $Q\left(\sqrt{2}, 5\sqrt{7}\right)$

36. $P(0, 0)$ and $Q(a, 2a + 1)$ **37.** $P(2a, a)$ and $Q(a, -3a)$

Find the center, circumference, and area of each circle described below.

38. diameter with endpoints $P(-4, -3)$ and $Q(-10, 5)$

39. diameter with endpoints $P(2, 4)$ and $Q(-3, 16)$

40. diameter with endpoints $P(0, 0)$ and $Q(50, 50)$

41. diameter with endpoints $P(-12, -8)$ and $Q(0, 0)$

42. diameter with endpoints $P(-2, 2)$ and $Q(4, 6)$

43. diameter with endpoints $P(8, -3)$ and $Q(-2, 1)$

For $\overline{PQ}$, the coordinates of P and M, the midpoint of $\overline{PQ}$, are given. Find the coordinates of Q.

44. $P(-2, 3)$ and $M(5, 1)$ **45.** $P(2, -3)$ and $M(-5, 1)$

46. $P(3, 11)$ and $M(0, 0)$ **47.** $P(0, 0)$ and $M(-7, 7)$

Three points, A, B, and C, are collinear if they lie on the same line. If A, B, and C are collinear and B is between A and C, then $AB + BC = AC$. For each set of points A, B, and C given below, find AB, BC, and AC, and determine whether the three points are collinear.

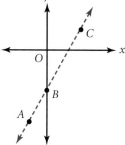

48. $A(0, 0)$, $B(2, 4)$, and $C(3, 6)$

49. $A(0, 0)$, $B(2, 4)$, and $C(3, 7)$

50. $A(-4, 5)$, $B(-2, 2)$, and $C(0, -1)$

51. $A(-3, 1)$, $B(2, 9)$, and $C(7, 17)$

CHALLENGE

52. You are given $P(-3, 2)$, $Q(3, 1)$, and $R(0, 6)$. Find the coordinates of point A such that $PA = QA = RA$, that is, $(PA)^2 = (QA)^2 = (RA)^2$.

CONNECTIONS

COORDINATE GEOMETRY For Exercises 53–55, refer to the coordinate plane at right.

53. a. Find AB, BC, CD, and DA.
     b. Based on your answers to part **a**, are the opposite sides of quadrilateral $ABCD$ equal in length?

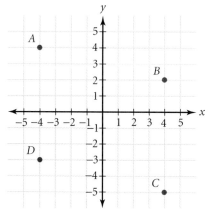

54. a. Find the coordinates of the midpoints of $\overline{AC}$ and of $\overline{BD}$.
     b. Based on your answers to part **a**, what conclusion can you draw about the diagonals of quadrilateral $ABCD$?

55. a. Find the slopes of $\overline{AB}$ and $\overline{CD}$ and of $\overline{AD}$ and $\overline{BC}$.
     b. Based on your answers to part **a**, are the opposite sides of quadrilateral $ABCD$ parallel? Explain.

56. COORDINATE GEOMETRY Determine whether the triangle with vertices at $C(-2, 3)$, $D(1, -1)$, and $E(3, 3)$ is isosceles, equilateral, or both.

57. COORDINATE GEOMETRY Determine whether the triangle with vertices at $F(7, 3)$, $H(6, 9)$, and $L(2, 3)$ is isosceles or scalene. (Hint: No two sides of a scalene triangle are equal in length.)

CONNECTION

58. GEOMETRY A *midsegment* of a triangle is the line segment whose endpoints are the midpoints of two sides of the triangle. A triangle has vertices whose coordinates are $A(0, 0)$, $B(6, 10)$, and $C(10, 3)$. Find an equation for the line containing the midsegment formed by the midpoints of $\overline{AB}$ and $\overline{BC}$.

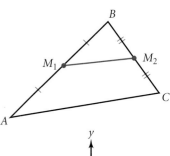

CHALLENGE

59. COORDINATE GEOMETRY The perpendicular bisector of $\overline{PQ}$ in a plane is the line, ℓ, that contains the midpoint of $\overline{PQ}$ and is perpendicular to $\overline{PQ}$. If B is on ℓ, then $BP = BQ$ and $(BP)^2 = (BQ)^2$. Write the equation in standard form for the perpendicular bisector of $\overline{PQ}$ for $P(-5, 7)$ and $Q(9, -3)$.

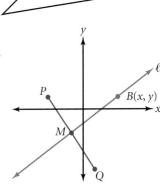

 Look Back

Evaluate. *(LESSON 2.6)*

60. $\lceil -5.1 \rceil - \lceil -3.5 \rceil$ **61.** $\lfloor -0.33 \rfloor + \lceil 2.99 \rceil$ **62.** $\lceil 4.4 \rceil + \lfloor -0.5 \rfloor$

Solve by completing the square. Give exact solutions. *(LESSON 5.4)*

63. $x^2 = 8x - 15$ **64.** $x^2 - 8x = 48$ **65.** $x^2 - 6x - 20 = 0$

Solve by using the quadratic formula. *(LESSON 5.5)*

66. $x^2 - 5x = 50$ **67.** $6x^2 - 7x = -1$ **68.** $2a^2 - 7a + 6 = 0$

Divide by using synthetic division. *(LESSON 7.3)*

69. $(4x^4 - 11x^3 + 8x^2 - 3x - 2) \div (x - 2)$
70. $(5x^4 + 5x^3 + x^2 + 2x + 1) \div (x + 1)$

Let z vary jointly as x and y. Use the given information to find the value of z for the given values of x and y. *(LESSON 8.1)*

71. $z = 3$ when $x = 2$ and $y = 3$; given $x = 5$ and $y = 10$
72. $z = 8$ when $x = 1$ and $y = 4$; given $x = 6$ and $y = 8$

Look Beyond

73. Let $f(x) = x^2$. The point $(1, 1)$ is on the graph of f.
    a. Find the distance between the point $(1, 1)$ and the point $\left(0, \frac{1}{4}\right)$.

    b. Find the shortest distance between the point $(1, 1)$ and the line $y = -\frac{1}{4}$.
    c. Compare the two distances found in parts **a** and **b**.
    d. Pick another point on the graph of f. Repeat parts **a**, **b**, and **c** for your point.
    e. Make a conjecture about the relationship between points on the graph of f, the point $\left(0, \frac{1}{4}\right)$, and the line $y = -\frac{1}{4}$.

Parabolas

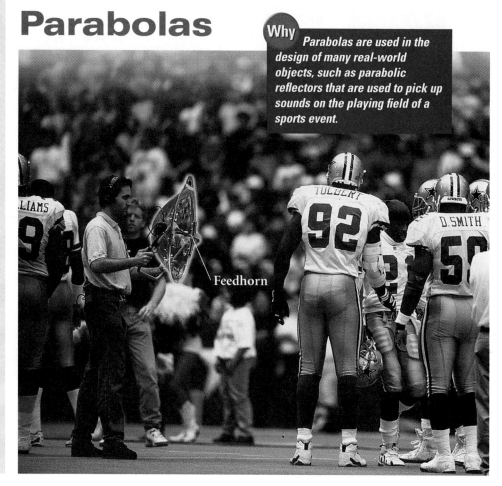

Why *Parabolas are used in the design of many real-world objects, such as parabolic reflectors that are used to pick up sounds on the playing field of a sports event.*

Feedhorn

Objectives

● Write and graph the standard equation of a parabola given sufficient information.

● Given an equation of a parabola, graph it and label the vertex, focus, and directrix.

APPLICATION

COMMUNICATIONS

Sports broadcast technicians often use a parabolic reflector to pick up sounds on the playing field during a sports event. The picture above shows a parabolic reflector whose feedhorn is 10 inches long. The reflector focuses the incoming sounds at the end of the feedhorn. Write the standard equation of the parabola that is a cross section of the reflector. *You will solve this problem in Example 3.*

A parabola is defined in terms of a fixed point, called the **focus**, and a fixed line, called the **directrix**.

In a parabola, the distance from any point, P, on the parabola to the focus, F, is equal to the shortest distance from P to the directrix. That is, $PF = PD$ for any point, P, on the parabola.

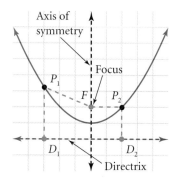

$P_1F = P_1D_1$ and $P_2F = P_2D_2$

Definition of Parabola

A **parabola** is the set of all points $P(x, y)$ in the plane whose distance to a fixed point, called the focus, equals its distance to a fixed line, called the directrix.

If the point $F(0, 3)$ is the focus of a parabola with its vertex at the origin, then the equation for the directrix is $y = -3$. This is shown in the figure at right.

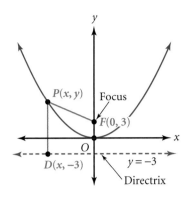

You can find an equation for this parabola by using the definition of a parabola and the distance formula, as shown below.

$$PF = PD$$
$$\sqrt{(x - 0)^2 + (y - 3)^2} = \sqrt{(x - x)^2 + (y + 3)^2}$$
$$x^2 + (y - 3)^2 = (y + 3)^2 \qquad \textit{Square each side.}$$
$$x^2 = (y + 3)^2 - (y - 3)^2$$
$$x^2 = y^2 + 6y + 9 - (y^2 - 6y + 9) \qquad \textit{Expand each binomial.}$$
$$x^2 = 12y$$
$$y = \frac{1}{12}x^2$$

In general, if F is the point $(0, p)$ and the directrix is $y = -p$, then the equation of the parabola is $y = \frac{1}{4p}x^2$.

Recall from Lesson 5.1 that the **axis of symmetry** of a parabola goes through the vertex and divides the parabola into two equal parts. The axis of symmetry also contains the focus and is perpendicular to the directrix. The **vertex** of a parabola is the midpoint between the focus and the directrix.

Standard Equation of a Parabola

The standard equation of a parabola with its vertex at the origin is given below.

Horizontal directrix	**Vertical directrix**
$$y = \frac{1}{4p}x^2$$	$$x = \frac{1}{4p}y^2$$
$p > 0$: opens upward	$p > 0$: opens right
$p < 0$: opens downward	$p < 0$: opens left
focus: $(0, p)$	focus: $(p, 0)$
directrix: $y = -p$	directrix: $x = -p$
axis of symmetry: y-axis	axis of symmetry: x-axis

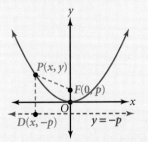

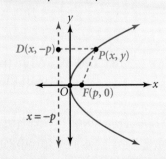

Example 1 shows how to graph a parabola from its equation.

E X A M P L E ❶ **Graph $x = -\frac{1}{8}y^2$. Label the vertex, focus, and directrix.**

● **SOLUTION**

1. Identify p. Rewrite $x = -\frac{1}{8}y^2$ as $x = \frac{1}{4(-2)}y^2$. Thus, $p = -2$.

2. Identify the vertex, focus, and directrix.

Since $p < 0$, the parabola opens to the left.

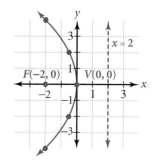

Vertex: $(0, 0)$
Focus: $(p, 0)$, or $(-2, 0)$
Directrix: $x = -p = -(-2)$, or $x = 2$

PROBLEM SOLVING

3. Use a table of values to sketch the graph.

y	-4	-2	0	2	4
x	-2	$\frac{1}{2}$	0	$\frac{1}{2}$	-2

The graph is shown at right.

TRY THIS   Graph $y = \frac{1}{12}x^2$. Label the vertex, focus, and directrix.

When you know the locations of any two of the three main characteristics of a parabola (focus, vertex, and directrix), you can write an equation for the parabola. This is shown in Example 2.

E X A M P L E ❷ **Write the standard equation of the parabola with its vertex at the origin and with the directrix $y = 4$.**

● **SOLUTION**

PROBLEM SOLVING   **Draw a diagram.**

Because the vertex is below the directrix, the parabola opens downward. Since $y = -p$ and $y = 4$, $p = -4$.

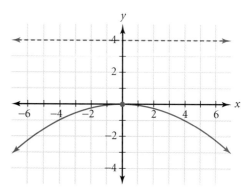

Thus, $y = \frac{1}{4(-4)}x^2$, or $y = -\frac{1}{16}x^2$, is the equation of the parabola.

TRY THIS   Write the standard equation of the parabola with its vertex at the origin and with the directrix $x = 4$.

CRITICAL THINKING   Explain how applying a vertical compression by a factor of $\frac{1}{2}$ to $x = y^2$ produces the same graph as applying a horizontal stretch by a factor of 4 to the graph of $x = y^2$.

3 Refer to the parabolic reflector described at the beginning of the lesson.

Write the standard equation of the parabola that is a cross section of the reflector.

● **SOLUTION**

For convenience, place the vertex of the parabola at the origin. You can let the parabola open upward, downward, to the right, or to the left. If it opens to the right, then the equation is of the form $x = \frac{1}{4p}y^2$.

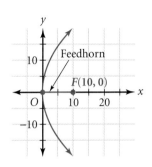

The feedhorn is 10 inches long, so the focus at the end of the feedhorn has coordinates $(10, 0)$ and $p = 10$.

$$x = \frac{1}{4p}y^2$$

$$x = \frac{1}{4(10)}y^2 \quad \textit{Substitute 10 for p.}$$

$$x = \frac{1}{40}y^2$$

Thus, the equation that represents a cross section of the parabolic reflector is $x = \frac{1}{40}y^2$.

The vertex of a parabola can be anywhere in the coordinate plane. In the Activity below, you can explore some of these translations.

Activity

Exploring Translations of Parabolas

You will need: a graphics calculator

1. Graph the parabola described by the equation $y = \frac{1}{4}x^2$.

2. Solve $y - 3 = \frac{1}{4}(x - 2)^2$ for y, and graph the parabola. Find the coordinates of the vertex.

CHECKPOINT ✔ 3. Describe the translation from the graph of $y = \frac{1}{4}x^2$ in Step 1 to the graph of $y - 3 = \frac{1}{4}(x - 2)^2$ in Step 2.

4. Compare the equation $y - 5 = \frac{1}{4}(x - 4)^2$ and the coordinates of the vertex of this parabola. Describe the relationship that you observe.

CHECKPOINT ✔ 5. Predict the coordinates of the vertex of the parabola given by the equation $y + 2 = \frac{1}{4}(x - 1)^2$. Graph the parabola to verify your prediction.

Standard Equation of a Translated Parabola

The standard equation of a parabola with its vertex at (h, k) is given below.

Horizontal Directrix	**Vertical Directrix**
$y - k = \dfrac{1}{4p}(x - h)^2$	$x - h = \dfrac{1}{4p}(y - k)^2$

Horizontal Directrix

$p > 0$: opens upward
$p < 0$: opens downward

focus: $(h, k + p)$
directrix: $y = k - p$
axis of symmetry: $x = h$

Vertical Directrix

$p > 0$: opens right
$p < 0$: opens left

focus: $(h + p, k)$
directrix: $x = h - p$
axis of symmetry: $y = k$

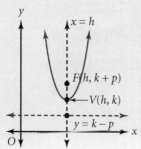
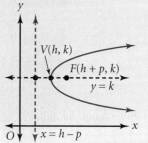

E X A M P L E **4** **Write the standard equation of the parabola graphed at right.**

● **SOLUTION**

The parabola opens upward, so the equation is of the form $y - k = \dfrac{1}{4p}(x - h)^2$ and $p > 0$.

The vertex is halfway between the focus and the directrix. Use the midpoint formula.

Vertex: $\left(2, \dfrac{\frac{10}{3} + \frac{8}{3}}{2}\right)$, or $(2, 3)$ $h = 2$ and $k = 3$

The focus is $(h, k + p)$, or $\left(2, \dfrac{10}{3}\right)$. Solve for p.

$$k + p = \frac{10}{3}$$
$$3 + p = \frac{10}{3}$$
$$p = \frac{1}{3}$$

Write the standard equation. $y - k = \dfrac{1}{4p}(x - h)^2$

$$y - 3 = \frac{1}{4\left(\frac{1}{3}\right)}(x - 2)^2$$

$$y - 3 = \frac{3}{4}(x - 2)^2$$

Thus, the standard equation of the parabola is $y - 3 = \dfrac{3}{4}(x - 2)^2$.

TRY THIS Write the standard equation of the parabola with its focus is at $(-6, 4)$ and with the directrix $x = 2$.

E X A M P L E ⑤ Graph the parabola $y^2 - 8y + 8x + 8 = 0$. Label the vertex, focus, and directrix.

● **SOLUTION**

1. Complete the square to find the standard equation.

$$y^2 - 8y + 8x + 8 = 0$$
$$y^2 - 8y = -8x - 8 \qquad \textit{Isolate the y-terms.}$$
$$y^2 - 8y + (-4)^2 = -8x - 8 + (-4)^2 \quad \textit{Complete the square.}$$
$$(y - 4)^2 = -8x + 8$$
$$(y - 4)^2 = -8(x - 1)$$
$$-\tfrac{1}{8}(y - 4)^2 = x - 1 \qquad \textit{Divide each side by 8.}$$
$$x - 1 = -\tfrac{1}{8}(y - 4)^2 \qquad \textit{Write the standard equation.}$$

2. From the standard equation, the vertex is $(1, 4)$. Find p.

$$\frac{1}{4p} = -\frac{1}{8}$$
$$-4p = 8$$
$$p = -2$$

Focus: $(h + p, k)$ | Directrix: $x = h - p$
$= (1 + (-2), 4)$ | $x = 1 - (-2)$
$= (-1, 4)$ | $x = 3$

PROBLEM SOLVING

3. Use a table of values. Choose y-values from 0 to 8.

$$x = -\tfrac{1}{8}(y - 4)^2 + 1$$

y	0	2	4	6	8
x	-1	$\tfrac{1}{2}$	1	$\tfrac{1}{2}$	-1

The graph is shown at right.

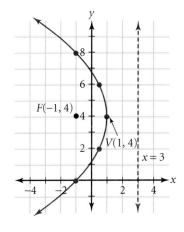

TRY THIS Graph the parabola $x^2 - 6x + 6y + 18 = 0$. Label the vertex, focus, and directrix.

To graph the equation $x - 1 = -\tfrac{1}{8}(y - 4)^2$ from Example 5 on a graphics calculator, first solve for y.

$$x - 1 = -\tfrac{1}{8}(y - 4)^2$$
$$-8(x - 1) = (y - 4)^2$$
$$\pm\sqrt{-8(x - 1)} = y - 4$$
$$4 \pm \sqrt{-8\,(x - 1)} = y$$

Graph $y = 4 + \sqrt{-8(x - 1)}$ and
$y = 4 - \sqrt{-8(x - 1)}$ together on the same screen.

TECHNOLOGY
GRAPHICS CALCULATOR

Keystroke Guide, page 623

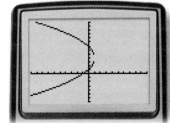

Communicate

1. Explain how to tell from the standard equation of a parabola whether the graph opens upward, downward, to the left, or to the right.

2. How can you determine from the standard equation of a parabola the locations of the focus, vertex, and directrix?

3. Explain how to graph $x = \frac{3}{4}y^2$ on a graphics calculator.

Guided Skills Practice

4. Graph $x = y^2$. Label the vertex, focus, and directrix. *(EXAMPLE 1)*

5. Write the standard equation of the parabola with its vertex at the origin and with the directrix $x = 3$. *(EXAMPLE 2)*

APPLICATION

6. **SPORTS** Refer to the parabolic reflector described at the beginning of the lesson. Write the standard equation of the parabola that is a cross section of a reflector whose feedhorn is 12 inches long. *(EXAMPLE 3)*

7. Write the standard equation for the parabola with its focus at $(-2, 3)$ and with the directrix $x = 3$. *(EXAMPLE 4)*

8. Graph the parabola $x^2 + 10x + 16y - 7 = 0$. Label the vertex, focus, and directrix. *(EXAMPLE 5)*

Practice and Apply

Write the standard equation for each parabola graphed below.

9.
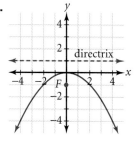

10.
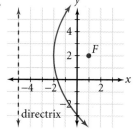

11.
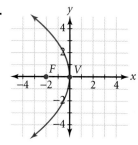

12.
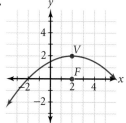

13.
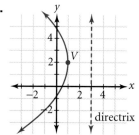

14.
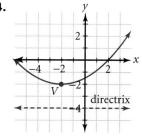

Graph each equation. Label the vertex, focus, and directrix.

15. $y = \frac{1}{4}x^2$ **16.** $y = \frac{1}{8}x^2$ **17.** $x = \frac{1}{20}y^2$

18. $x = \frac{1}{40}y^2$ **19.** $y = x^2$ **20.** $y = 2x^2$

21. $y + 3 = \frac{1}{8}(x + 2)^2$ **22.** $x - 1 = \frac{1}{12}(y + 2)^2$ **23.** $y - 4 = -(x - 1)^2$

24. $y - 1 = \frac{1}{4}(x - 1)^2$ **25.** $y = \frac{1}{8}(x - 1)^2$ **26.** $x - 3 = -\frac{1}{8}(y + 1)^2$

27. $y + 3 = \frac{1}{12}x^2$ **28.** $-12y = (x + 2)^2$ **29.** $x - 1 = \frac{1}{2}(y + 2)^2$

30. $x^2 + 4x - 6y = -10$ **31.** $x^2 - 6x + 10y = 1$ **32.** $x^2 - 8x - y + 20 = 0$

33. $4x + y^2 + 3y = -5$ **34.** $4x + y^2 - 6y = 9$ **35.** $-14x + 2y^2 - 8y = 20$

Write the standard equation for the parabola with the given characteristics.

36. vertex: $(0, 0)$
focus: $(-4, 0)$

37. vertex: $(0, 0)$
focus: $(0, -5)$

38. vertex: $(0, 0)$
directrix: $y = -1$

39. vertex: $(0, 0)$
directrix: $x = 4$

40. vertex: $(0, 0)$
focus: $(0, 3)$

41. vertex: $(0, 0)$
focus: $(2, 0)$

42. vertex: $(0, 0)$
directrix: $x = -3$

43. vertex: $(0, 0)$
directrix: $y = 12$

44. directrix: $y = -4$
focus: $(0, 4)$

45. focus: $(3, 0)$
directrix: $x = -3$

46. focus: $(0, -5)$
directrix: $y = 5$

47. directrix: $x = 8$
focus: $(-8, 0)$

CONNECTIONS

48. TRANSFORMATIONS A parabola defined by the equation $x + 3 = \frac{1}{8}(y + 2)^2$ is translated 4 units down and 3 units to the right. Write the standard equation of the resulting parabola.

49. TRANSFORMATIONS A parabola defined by the equation $4x + y^2 - 6y = 9$ is translated 2 units up and 4 units to the left. Write the standard equation of the resulting parabola.

CHALLENGE

50. COORDINATE GEOMETRY In the diagram at right, points P, F, and Q are collinear, P and Q are on the parabola, and F is the focus of the parabola. Also, $\overline{PQ}$ is perpendicular to the axis of symmetry of the parabola. Let $y - k = \frac{1}{4p}(x - h)^2$ be an equation for the parabola. Write an equation to find PQ in terms of $h, k, p,$ and x.

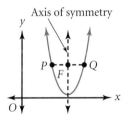

51. COMMUNICATIONS Write an equation for the cross section of a parabolic satellite dish whose focus is 1 foot from its vertex.

52. SPORTS Suppose that a golf ball travels a distance of 600 feet as measured along the ground and reaches an altitude of 200 feet. If the origin represents the tee and the ball travels along a parabolic path that opens downward, find an equation for the path of the golf ball.

53. LIGHTING The lightsource of a flashlight is $\frac{1}{2}$ inch from the vertex of the parabolic reflector and is located at the focus. Assuming that the parabolic reflector is directed upward and the vertex is at the origin, write an equation for a cross section of the reflector.

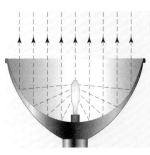

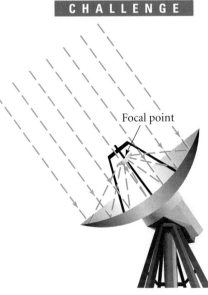

Focal point

Cross section of a parabolic satellite dish

Look Back

Factor each expression. *(LESSON 5.3)*

54. $16x^2 - 1$

55. $3a^2 + 3a$

56. $6x^2y - 18xy^2$

57. $m^2n + 7m^2n^2 - 3mn$

Factor each quadratic expression. *(LESSON 5.3)*

58. $x^2 - 8x + 16$

59. $y^2 - 12y + 20$

60. $7x^2 - 16x + 4$

61. $5x^2 - 15x + 10$

62. $12w^2 - w - 6$

63. $6y^2 - 5y - 25$

Simplify each rational expression. *(LESSON 8.3)*

64. $\dfrac{x^2 - x - 2}{x^2 - 2x - 8} \cdot \dfrac{x + 2}{x^2 + 5x + 4}$

65. $\dfrac{x^2 - x - 6}{x - 1} \cdot \dfrac{x^3 - 1}{x^2 - 2x - 3}$

66. $\dfrac{x^2 - 4}{x^2 + x - 6} \div \dfrac{x + 2}{x^2 + 4x + 3}$

67. $\dfrac{x^2 + 7x + 10}{x^2 + 8x + 15} \div \dfrac{x^2 + 4x + 4}{x + 2}$

Look Beyond

68 Graph $y = 2(x - 3)^2 + 4$ and $x = \frac{1}{4}(y - 3)^2 + 1$ together on the same screen, and find any points of intersection.

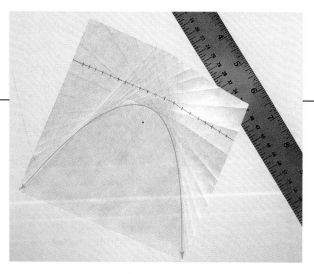

PORTFOLIO ACTIVITY

1. Draw a straight line from one side of the patty paper, or wax paper, to the other. This will be the directrix.

2. Place the focus anywhere except on the directrix.

3. Fold the paper so that the focus lies on one end of the directrix, and crease the paper. Then unfold it.

4. Move the focus along the directrix, making folds as you go, until you come to the other end of the directrix. You should make between 15 and 25 folds.

5. Compare the parabola formed by your creases with your classmates' parabolas. Make a conjecture about how to make a narrower or wider parabola. Verify your conjecture by folding a second parabola.

6. Fold your parabola in half along its axis of symmetry.

7. Explain how the definition of a parabola is related to your folded parabola.

WORKING ON THE CHAPTER PROJECT

You should now be able to complete Activity 1 of the Chapter Project.

578 CHAPTER 9

Circles

Objectives

- Write an equation for a circle given sufficient information.

- Given an equation of a circle, graph it and label the radius and the center.

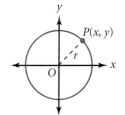

Why **Circles are used to describe the receiving area of radio signals.**

APPLICATION

COMMUNICATIONS

A radio tower is located 25 miles east and 30 miles south of Lorne's home. The radio signal is strong enough to reach homes within a 50 mile radius. Write an equation that represents all ground locations 50 miles from the radio tower. Can someone living 10 miles east and 5 miles north of Lorne receive the radio signal? This is an example of a *locus problem*. *You will solve this problem in Example 3.*

A **locus problem** involves an equation that represents a set of points that satisfy certain conditions. For example, an equation for the set of all points $P(x, y)$ in a plane that are a fixed distance, r, from $O(0, 0)$ can be obtained by using the distance formula.

$$OP = r$$
$$\sqrt{(x - 0)^2 + (y - 0)^2} = r$$
$$\sqrt{x^2 + y^2} = r$$
$$x^2 + y^2 = r^2$$

A **circle** is the set of all points in a plane that are a constant distance, called the radius, from a fixed point, called the **center.**

Standard Equation of a Circle

An equation for the circle with its center at $(0, 0)$ and a radius of r is
$$x^2 + y^2 = r^2.$$

E X A M P L E **1** Write the standard equation of the circle whose center is at the origin and whose radius is 3. Sketch the graph.

SOLUTION

$$x^2 + y^2 = r^2$$
$$x^2 + y^2 = 3^2$$

Thus, an equation for the circle is $x^2 + y^2 = 9$.

Plot the points $(3, 0)$, $(0, 3)$, $(-3, 0)$, and $(0, -3)$, and sketch a circle through these points.

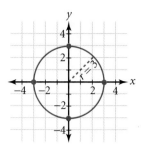

TRY THIS Write the standard equation of the circle whose center is at the origin and whose radius is 2. Sketch the graph.

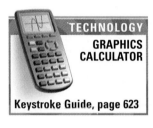

TECHNOLOGY
GRAPHICS CALCULATOR

Keystroke Guide, page 623

Recall from Lesson 9.1 that you can use a graphics calculator to graph a circle. To graph $x^2 + y^2 = 4$, solve for y and graph the two resulting equations together.

$$x^2 + y^2 = 4 \rightarrow \begin{cases} y = \sqrt{4 - x^2} \\ y = -\sqrt{4 - x^2} \end{cases}$$

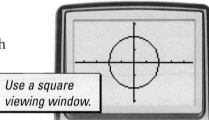

Use a square viewing window.

Activity
Exploring Translations of Circles

You will need: a graphics calculator

1. Graph the circle defined by $x^2 + y^2 = 16$. Find its radius.

2. Graph the circle defined by $(x + 3)^2 + (y - 2)^2 = 16$. Find its radius, and approximate the coordinates of the center.

CHECKPOINT ✔ 3. Describe the transformation of the graph of $x^2 + y^2 = 16$ in Step 1 to the graph of $(x + 3)^2 + (y - 2)^2 = 16$ in Step 2.

4. Compare the equation of the circle $(x + 3)^2 + (y - 2)^2 = 16$ with the coordinates of its center. Describe the relationship you observe.

CHECKPOINT ✔ 5. Predict the radius and center of the circle defined by the equation $(x - 2)^2 + (y + 1)^2 = 9$. Graph the circle to support your prediction.

The standard equation for a translated circle is given below.

Standard Equation of a Translated Circle

The standard equation for a circle with its center at (h, k) and a radius of r is

$$(x - h)^2 + (y - k)^2 = r^2.$$

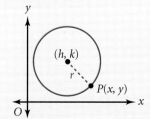

E X A M P L E **2** Write the standard equation for the translated circle graphed at right.

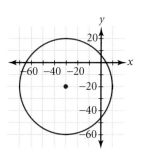

● **SOLUTION**

The center of the circle is $(-30, -20)$.
Substitute -30 for h and -20 for k.
Since the radius is 40, substitute 40 for r.

$$(x - h)^2 + (y - k)^2 = r^2$$
$$[x - (-30)]^2 + [y - (-20)]^2 = 40^2$$
$$(x + 30)^2 + (y + 20)^2 = 1600 \quad \textit{Write the standard equation.}$$

E X A M P L E **3** Refer to the radio-signal problem described at the beginning of the lesson.

a. Write an equation that represents all ground locations 50 miles from the radio tower, given that Lorne's home is located at $(0, 0)$.
b. Can someone who lives 10 miles east and 5 miles north of Lorne's home receive the radio signal?

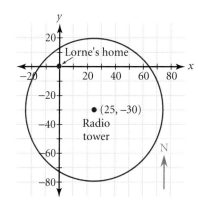

● **SOLUTION**

PROBLEM SOLVING

a. **Select appropriate notation.** Since the origin represents Lorne's home, the radio tower is represented by the point $(25, -30)$. If the radio signal is strong enough to reach homes within a 50-mile radius, then $r = 50$.

Write the standard equation of a circle with its center at $(25, -30)$ and a radius of 50.

$$(x - h)^2 + (y - k)^2 = r^2$$
$$(x - 25)^2 + [y - (-30)]^2 = 50^2$$
$$(x - 25)^2 + (y + 30)^2 = 2500$$

b. The coordinates of a point that lie within the circle will satisfy the inequality $(x - 25)^2 + (y + 30)^2 < 2500$. The point $(10, 5)$ represents a location 10 miles east and 5 miles north of Lorne's home. Test $(10, 5)$ to see if it satisfies the inequality $(x - 25)^2 + (y + 30)^2 < 2500$.

$$(x - 25)^2 + (y + 30)^2 < 2500$$
$$(10 - 25)^2 + (5 + 30)^2 \stackrel{?}{<} 2500$$
$$1450 < 2500 \quad \textbf{True}$$

Thus, someone who lives 10 miles east and 5 miles north of Lorne's home can receive the radio signal.

In order to listen to a radio station, you must be able to receive the radio signal.

TRY THIS Tell whether $A(2, 1)$ is inside, outside, or on the circle whose center is at $(-2, 3)$ and whose radius is 4.

CRITICAL THINKING Explain how to tell whether $A(s, t)$ is inside, outside, or on the circle centered at (h, k) with a radius of r.

To write the standard equation of a translated circle, you may need to complete the square. This is shown in Example 4.

EXAMPLE

Write the standard equation for the circle $x^2 + y^2 + 4x - 6y - 3 = 0$. State the coordinates of its center and give its radius. Then sketch the graph.

● **SOLUTION**

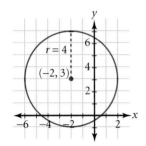

$$x^2 + y^2 + 4x - 6y - 3 = 0$$
$$x^2 + 4x + y^2 - 6y = 3$$
$$(x^2 + 4x + 4) + (y^2 - 6y + 9) = 3 + 4 + 9 \quad \textit{Complete the squares.}$$
$$(x + 2)^2 + (y - 3)^2 = 16 \quad \textit{Write the standard equation.}$$

Thus, the standard equation is $(x + 2)^2 + (y - 3)^2 = 16$. The center is at $(-2, 3)$ and the radius is 4.

TRY THIS   Write the standard equation for the circle $x^2 + y^2 - 2x + 2y - 7 = 0$. State the coordinates of its center and give its radius. Then sketch the graph.

Exercises

● *Communicate*

1. Explain how to read the coordinates of the center of a circle and its radius from the equation $(x - 4)^2 + (y + 1)^2 = 1$.

2. How could you determine whether a given point, such as $(-1, -3)$, lies inside, outside, or on a circle whose equation is given, such as $(x - 2)^2 + (y + 1)^2 = 16$?

3. How would you determine whether the equation $x^2 + 8x + y^2 + 16 = 0$ represents a circle?

● *Guided Skills Practice*

4. Write an equation for the circle whose center is at the origin and whose radius is 6. Sketch the graph. **(EXAMPLE 1)**

5. Write the standard equation for the translated circle graphed at left. **(EXAMPLE 2)**

6. **COMMUNICATIONS** Refer to the radio-signal problem posed at the beginning of the lesson. Can someone who lives 9 miles west and 5 miles south of Lorne's home receive the radio signal? **(EXAMPLE 3)**

7. Write the standard equation for the circle $x^2 + 6x + y^2 - 4y - 3 = 0$. State the coordinates of its center and give its radius. Then sketch the graph. *(EXAMPLE 4)* $(x + 3)^2 + (y - 2)^2 = 16$; $C(-3, 2)$; $r = 4$

Practice and Apply

Write the standard equation for each circle graphed below.

8.
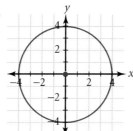

9.
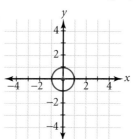

10.
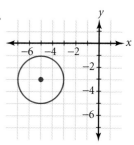

11.
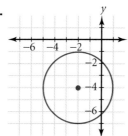

12.
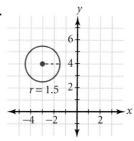

13.
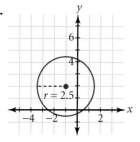

Write the standard equation of a circle with each given radius and center.

14. $r = 4$; $C(0, 0)$ **15.** $r = 5$; $C(0, 0)$

16. $r = 11$; $C(0, 0)$ **17.** $r = 7$; $C(0, 0)$

18. $r = 1$; $C(2, 3)$ **19.** $r = 12$; $C(3, 5)$

20. $r = 10$; $C(-2, -7)$ **21.** $r = 5$; $C(-5, -1)$

22. $r = 4$; $C(-2, 8)$ **23.** $r = 15$; $C(-6, 9)$

24. $r = 2$; $C(0, 12)$ **25.** $r = 3$; $C(0, 4)$

26. $r = \frac{1}{3}$; $C(-2, -2)$ **27.** $r = 2$; $C(3, 3)$

28. $r = \frac{1}{2}$; $C(2, 0)$ **29.** $r = \frac{1}{4}$; $C(1, 0)$

30. $r = 1$; $C(a, a)$, where $a > 0$ **31.** $r = 2$; $C(a, -2a)$, where $a > 0$

Graph each equation. Label the center and the radius.

32. $x^2 + y^2 = 9$ **33.** $x^2 + y^2 = 49$

34. $(x - 2)^2 + y^2 = 4$ **35.** $(x + 5)^2 + y^2 = 36$

36. $x^2 + (y + 3)^2 = 16$ **37.** $x^2 + (y - 2)^2 = 81$

38. $(x + 1)^2 + (y + 5)^2 = 100$ **39.** $(x + 6)^2 + (y + 1)^2 = 4$

40. $(x - 2)^2 + (y + 2)^2 = 64$ **41.** $(x - 3)^2 + (y + 3)^2 = 25$

42. $(x + 4)^2 + (y - 3)^2 = 49$ **43.** $(x + 2)^2 + (y - 4)^2 = 16$

Write the standard equation for each circle. Then state the coordinates of its center and give its radius.

44. $x^2 + y^2 + 4y = 12$ **45.** $x^2 - 2x + y^2 = 8$

46. $x^2 + 2x + y^2 + 2y = 2$ **47.** $x^2 + 2x + y^2 + 6y = 6$

48. $x^2 + y^2 - 10x - 2y = 23$ **49.** $x^2 + y^2 - 12x + 6y = 19$

50. $x^2 + y^2 + 6x - 17 = 0$ **51.** $x^2 + y^2 - 20y + 19 = 0$

52. $x^2 + y^2 + x + y = 0$ **53.** $x^2 + y^2 - x + y = 0$

54. $x^2 + y^2 - x + 3y = 7.5$ **55.** $x^2 + y^2 - x + 7y = 12.5$

56. $x^2 + y^2 - 12x - 2y - 8 = 0$ **57.** $x^2 + y^2 - 6x - 10y - 2 = 0$

58. $x^2 + y^2 + 6x - 14y - 42 = 0$ **59.** $x^2 + y^2 - 10x + 6y = 0$

State whether the graph of each equation is a parabola or a circle. Justify your response.

60. $y = x^2$ **61.** $x^2 = 12 - y^2$

62. $y^2 = 12 - x^2$ **63.** $x = y^2$

64. $x^2 = 4 - (y - 2)^2$ **65.** $10y^2 = 5(x - 2)$

66. $4x = 8(y + 3)^2$ **67.** $(y + 2)^2 = 15 - (x - 2)^2$

State whether the given point is inside, outside, or on the circle whose equation is given. Justify your response.

68. $P(2, 2)$; $x^2 + y^2 = 9$ **69.** $P(1, 6)$; $x^2 + y^2 = 49$

70. $P(5, 1)$; $x^2 - 6x + y^2 + 8y = 24$ **71.** $P(2, -3)$; $x^2 - 4x + y^2 + 6y = 12$

72. $P(0, 0)$; $x^2 + 10x + y^2 + 2y = 10$ **73.** $P(12, 3)$; $x^2 - 12x + y^2 + 2y = 12$

74. $P(0.5, 0.5)$; $x^2 + y^2 = 1$ **75.** $P(1.5, 3.5)$; $x^2 + y^2 = 6$

CHALLENGE

76. Tell whether $P(a, a)$ is inside, outside, or on the circle defined by the equation $x^2 - 2ax + y^2 + 4ay = 4a^2$. Justify your response.

CONNECTIONS

77. COORDINATE GEOMETRY The figure at right shows two circles with centers at C_1 and C_2. An equation for the circle with its center at C_1 is $(x - 3)^2 + (y - 3)^2 = (r_1)^2$, and an equation with the circle for its center at C_2 is $(x - 3)^2 + (y - 1)^2 = (r_2)^2$.

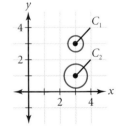

   a. Find one value of r_1 and one value of r_2 such that the circle with its center at C_1 is completely enclosed by the circle with its center at C_2. Justify your response.

   b. Find one value of r_1 and one value of r_2 such that the circles intersect at two points. Justify your response.

   c. Find one value of r_1 and one value of r_2 such that the circles intersect at exactly one point. Justify your response.

78. TRANSFORMATIONS The circle defined by $(x - 1)^2 + (y + 4)^2 = 16$ is translated 3 units to the left and 2 units down. Write the standard equation for the resulting circle.

79. TRANSFORMATIONS The circle defined by $x^2 + y^2 - 8x - 4y + 9 = 0$ is translated 4 units to the right and 6 units up. Write the standard equation for the resulting circle.

80. SPACE SCIENCE A satellite in a stationary orbit rotates once each day about the Earth. Assume that the satellite is 22,300 miles above the surface of Earth and that Earth's radius is 3960 miles. Write an equation that represents the orbit of this satellite on a coordinate plane with the origin representing the center of the Earth.

81. GEOLOGY Vibrations from a certain earthquake were noticeable up to 120 miles away from the earthquake's epicenter. The center of the closest city to the earthquake's epicenter is 85 miles east and 90 miles south of the epicenter. If Alexandra was 15 miles west of this city, could she have noticed the vibrations at the time of the earthquake?

82. COMMUNICATIONS A radio program is broadcast from a van that is located 40 miles east and 30 miles north of a radio tower. The van sends the radio signal to the tower, which then transmits the signal a maximum distance of 70 miles. If Jessica is 30 miles east of the van, is she able to receive the radio program?

Many radio stations have the equipment needed to broadcast from a van.

Look Back

For each quadratic function, find the equation for the axis of symmetry and give the coordinates of the vertex. *(LESSON 5.5)*

83. $y = -11x + 28 + x^2$ **84.** $y = 2x^2 + 3x$ **85.** $y = -3x + 10 - x^2$

Solve each equation. Write the exact solution and the approximate solution to the nearest hundredth, when appropriate. *(LESSON 6.7)*

86. $7^{3x-2} + 2 = 750$ **87.** $e^{-3x} = 12$ **88.** $\log_2 7 = x$

89. $\log_a 8 = \frac{3}{2}$ **90.** $\log_3 x = 4$ **91.** $\ln(x + 1) = 2 \ln 5$

For each function, describe the transformations applied to $f(x) = \sqrt{x}$. *(LESSON 8.6)*

92. $g(x) = 4\sqrt{x - 2}$ **93.** $a(x) = \sqrt{0.5x + 4} - 3$ **94.** $b(x) = 0.5\sqrt{2x - 1} + 6$

Look Beyond

95 In this lesson you learned that the graph of $x^2 + y^2 = r^2$, where r is a positive constant, is a circle centered at the origin. Using a square viewing window, graph $4x^2 + 2y^2 = 12$, and describe the shape of the graph. Graph $8x^2 + y^2 = 24$, and describe the shape of the graph.

Ellipses

Why *Ellipses are used to describe the paths of planets around the Sun.*

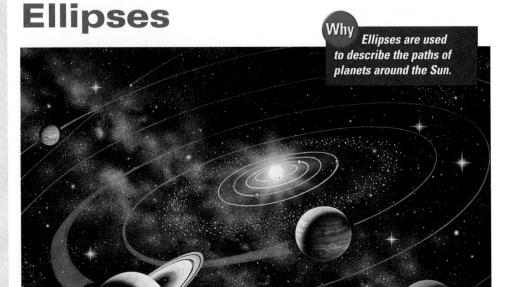

Objectives

- Write the standard equation for an ellipse given sufficient information.

- Given an equation of an ellipse, graph it and label the center, vertices, co-vertices, and foci.

In the Activity below, you will explore the definition of an ellipse by modeling ellipses.

Activity
Modeling Ellipses

You will need: 3 pieces of corrugated cardboard at least 8 inches by 8 inches, 2 tacks, 36 inches of string, and a pencil

Draw each ellipse on a separate piece of cardboard, and write on the cardboard the length of string that was used to create the ellipse.

1. Place two tacks 4 inches apart into a piece of corrugated cardboard. Tie the ends of a 10-inch piece of string together and loop the string around the tacks. Hold the tacks down with one hand, and with the other hand, use the pencil to pull the string taut as shown above. Move your pencil along the path that keeps the string taut at all times. When you return to your starting point, the path of the pencil will have formed an ellipse.

2. Repeat Step 1 with the same locations for the tacks but a 12-inch string.

3. Repeat Step 1 with the same locations for the tacks but a 14-inch string.

CHECKPOINT ✔ 4. How does the length of the string affect the shape of the ellipse that is drawn?

Definition of Ellipse

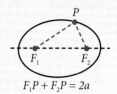

An **ellipse** is the set of all points P in a plane such that the sum of the distances from P to two fixed points, F_1 and F_2, called the **foci**, is a constant.

$F_1P + F_2P = 2a$

You can use the definition of an ellipse and the distance formula to write an equation for an ellipse whose foci are $F_1(-4, 0)$ and $F_2(4, 0)$ and whose constant sum is 10. Let $P(x, y)$ be any point on the ellipse.

$$F_1P + F_2P = 10$$

$$\sqrt{[x - (-4)]^2 + (y - 0)^2} + \sqrt{(x - 4)^2 + (y - 0)^2} = 10$$

$$\sqrt{(x + 4)^2 + y^2} = 10 - \sqrt{(x - 4)^2 + y^2}$$

Square each side. $\quad (x + 4)^2 + y^2 = 100 - 20\sqrt{(x - 4)^2 + y^2} + [(x - 4)^2 + y^2]$

Simplify. $\quad 16x - 100 = -20\sqrt{(x - 4)^2 + y^2}$

Divide each side by 4. $\quad 4x - 25 = -5\sqrt{(x - 4)^2 + y^2}$

Square each side again. $\quad 16x^2 - 200x + 625 = 25[(x - 4)^2 + y^2]$

$$16x^2 - 200x + 625 = 25x^2 - 200x + 400 + 25y^2$$

$$225 = 9x^2 + 25y^2$$

Divide each side by 225. $\quad 1 = \dfrac{x^2}{25} + \dfrac{y^2}{9}$

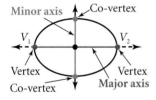

Minor axis · Co-vertex · V_1 · V_2 · Vertex · Vertex · Co-vertex · Major axis

An ellipse has two axes of symmetry. The **major axis** is the longer axis of the ellipse and the **minor axis** is the shorter axis of the ellipse. The endpoints of the major axis are called the **vertices** of the ellipse. The endpoints of the minor axis are called the **co-vertices** of the ellipse. The foci are always on the major axis. The point of intersection of the major and minor axes is called the **center**.

Standard Equation of an Ellipse

The standard equation of an ellipse centered at the origin is given below.

Horizontal major axis

$$\frac{x^2}{a^2} + \frac{y^2}{b^2} = 1$$

$(0, b)$ · $V_1(-a, 0)$ · O · $V_2(a, 0)$ · $F_1(-c, 0)$ · $F_2(c, 0)$ · $(0, -b)$

Vertical major axis

$$\frac{x^2}{b^2} + \frac{y^2}{a^2} = 1$$

$V_2(0, a)$ · $F_2(0, c)$ · $(-b, 0)$ · $(b, 0)$ · O · $F_1(0, -c)$ · $V_1(0, -a)$

In each case: • $a^2 > b^2$, and $a^2 - b^2 = c^2$,
   • the length of the major axis is $2a$, and
   • the length of the minor axis is $2b$.

EXAMPLE **1** Write the standard equation for an ellipse with foci at $(0, -4)$ and $(0, 4)$ and with a minor axis of 6. Sketch the graph.

SOLUTION

The coordinates of the foci are $(0, -4)$ and $(0, 4)$, so $c = 4$. The length of the minor axis is $2b$ and $2b = 6$, so $b = 3$.

Substitute 4 for c and 3 for b to find a.

$$a^2 - b^2 = c^2$$
$$a^2 - 3^2 = 4^2$$
$$a = 5$$

Substitute 5 for a and 3 for b.

$$\frac{x^2}{b^2} + \frac{y^2}{a^2} = 1 \rightarrow \frac{x^2}{9} + \frac{y^2}{25} = 1$$

To sketch the graph, plot the vertices, $(0, -5)$ and $(0, 5)$, and the co-vertices, $(-3, 0)$ and $(3, 0)$. Connect them to form an ellipse.

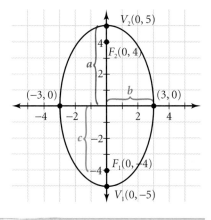

TRY THIS   Write the standard equation for an ellipse with foci at $(-12, 0)$ and $(12, 0)$ and with a major axis of 26. Sketch the graph.

EXAMPLE **2** Mars orbits the Sun in an elliptical path whose minimum distance from the Sun is 129.5 million miles and whose maximum distance from the Sun is 154.4 million miles. The Sun represents one focus of the ellipse.

ASTRONOMY

Write the standard equation for the elliptical orbit of Mars around the Sun, where the center of the ellipse is at the origin.

SOLUTION

PROBLEM SOLVING   Draw a diagram.

1. Find a^2. $V_1V_2 = 154.4 + 129.5$
$$2a = 283.9$$
$$a = 141.95$$
$$a^2 \approx 20{,}149.8$$

2. Find c. $OF_1 = OV_1 - F_1V_1$
$$c = a - 129.5$$
$$c = 141.95 - 129.5$$
$$c = 12.45$$

3. Find b^2. $a^2 - b^2 = c^2$
$$141.95^2 - b^2 = 12.45^2$$
$$19{,}994.8 = b^2$$

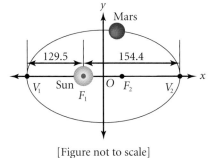

[Figure not to scale]

The standard equation for the orbit of Mars around the Sun in millions of miles is approximately $\dfrac{x^2}{20{,}149.8} + \dfrac{y^2}{19{,}994.8} = 1$.

An image of Mars, composed from 102 Viking Orbiter *images*

TRY THIS Venus orbits the Sun in an elliptical path whose minimum distance from the Sun is 66.7 million miles and whose maximum distance from the Sun is 67.6 million miles. The Sun represents one focus of the ellipse. Write the standard equation for the elliptical orbit of Venus around the Sun, where the center of the ellipse is at the origin.

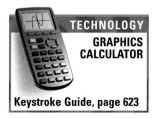

TECHNOLOGY
GRAPHICS CALCULATOR

Keystroke Guide, page 623

You can graph ellipses with a graphics calculator. To graph $\frac{x^2}{25} + \frac{y^2}{9} = 1$, solve for y, and graph the two resulting equations together.

You may wish to simplify the equations before entering them into the graphics calculator, but this is not necessary.

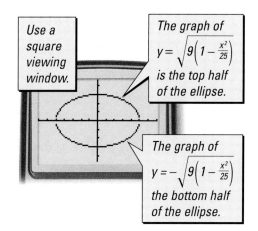

Use a square viewing window.

The graph of $y = \sqrt{9\left(1 - \frac{x^2}{25}\right)}$ is the top half of the ellipse.

The graph of $y = -\sqrt{9\left(1 - \frac{x^2}{25}\right)}$ the bottom half of the ellipse.

The center of an ellipse can be anywhere in a coordinate plane.

Standard Equation of a Translated Ellipse

The standard equation of an ellipse centered at (h, k) is given below.

Horizontal major axis

$$\frac{(x-h)^2}{a^2} + \frac{(y-k)^2}{b^2} = 1$$

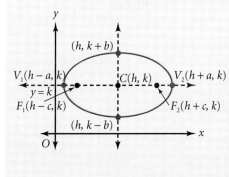

Vertical major axis

$$\frac{(x-h)^2}{b^2} + \frac{(y-k)^2}{a^2} = 1$$

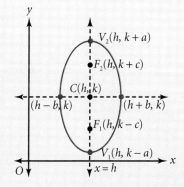

In each case: • $a^2 > b^2$, and $a^2 - b^2 = c^2$,
 • the length of the major axis is $2a$, and
 • the length of the minor axis is $2b$.

The **eccentricity** of an ellipse is a measure of how round or flat it is. The eccentricity, E, is the ratio of the distance, c, between the center and a focus to the distance, a, between the center and a vertex.

$$E = \frac{c}{a}, \text{ where } c = \sqrt{a^2 - b^2}$$

If $c = 0$, then $E = 0$ and the ellipse is a circle. As the value of c approaches the value of a, the value of E approaches 1, and the ellipse becomes flatter.

LESSON 9.4 ELLIPSES **589**

EXAMPLE ❸ Write the standard equation for an ellipse with its center at $(2, -4)$ and with a horizontal major axis of 10 and minor axis of 6. Sketch the graph.

● **SOLUTION**

The center, (h, k), is at $(2, -4)$.
The length of the major axis is $2a = 10$, so $a = 5$.
The length of the minor axis is $2b = 6$, so $b = 3$.

The major axis is horizontal.

$$\frac{(x - h)^2}{a^2} + \frac{(y - k)^2}{b^2} = 1$$

$$\frac{(x - 2)^2}{25} + \frac{(y + 4)^2}{9} = 1$$

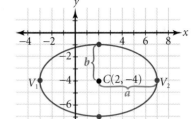

Use the value of a to find the vertices, $(-3, -4)$ and $(7, -4)$.

Use the value of b to find the co-vertices, $(2, -7)$ and $(2, -1)$.

TRY THIS   Write the standard equation for an ellipse with its center at $(-1, -2)$ and with a vertical major axis of 8 and minor axis of 4. Sketch the graph.

EXAMPLE ❹ An ellipse is defined by $4x^2 + y^2 + 24x - 4y + 36 = 0$. Write the standard equation, and identify the coordinates of its center, vertices, co-vertices, and foci. Sketch the graph.

● **SOLUTION**

$$4x^2 + y^2 + 24x - 4y + 36 = 0$$
$$4x^2 + 24x + y^2 - 4y = -36$$
$$4(x^2 + 6x) + (y^2 - 4y) = -36$$
$$4(x^2 + 6x + \mathbf{9}) + (y^2 - 4y + \mathbf{4}) = -36 + 4(\mathbf{9}) + \mathbf{4} \quad \textit{Complete the squares.}$$
$$4(x + 3)^2 + (y - 2)^2 = 4$$
$$\frac{(x + 3)^2}{1} + \frac{(y - 2)^2}{4} = 1 \quad \textit{Divide each side by 4.}$$

From the equation, the center is at $(-3, 2)$, $a^2 = 4$, and $b^2 = 1$. Find c.

$$a^2 - b^2 = c^2$$
$$4 - 1 = c^2$$
$$\sqrt{3} = c$$

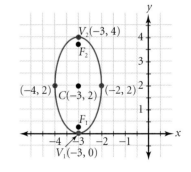

Use the value of c to find the foci.

$$(-3, 2 - \sqrt{3}) \text{ and } (-3, 2 + \sqrt{3})$$

Use the value of a to find the vertices.

$$(-3, 0) \text{ and } (-3, 4)$$

Use the value of b to find the co-vertices.

$$(-4, 2) \text{ and } (-2, 2)$$

CRITICAL THINKING   Identify the graph of $Ax^2 + Cy^2 + E = 0$ given that A and C are positive numbers.

Exercises

Communicate

1. Describe the information you can obtain from the standard equation of a translated ellipse, such as $\frac{x^2}{16} + \frac{(y-2)^2}{25} = 1$.

2. Describe the procedure used to write the standard equation of the ellipse defined by $9x^2 + 4y^2 + 18x - 40y + 73 = 0$.

3. Explain how to graph $\frac{(x-4)^2}{3^2} + \frac{(y-5)^2}{2^2} = 1$.

4. Describe the graph of $\frac{x^2}{25} + \frac{y^2}{25} = 1$.

Guided Skills Practice

5. Write the standard equation for an ellipse centered at the origin with foci at $(5, 0)$ and $(-5, 0)$ and with a minor axis of 8. Sketch the graph. **(EXAMPLE 1)**

APPLICATION

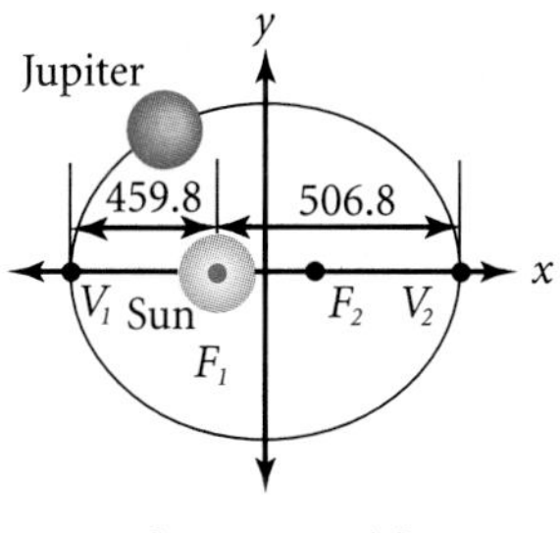

Jupiter

459.8   506.8

V_1 Sun F_2 V_2

F_1

[*Not to scale*]

6. **ASTRONOMY** The diagram at left gives the minimum and maximum distances (in millions of miles) from Jupiter to the Sun. Write the standard equation for Jupiter's elliptical orbit around the Sun. **(EXAMPLE 2)**

7. Write the standard equation for an ellipse centered at $(1, -2)$ with a vertical major axis of 6 and a minor axis of 4. Sketch the graph. **(EXAMPLE 3)**

8. An ellipse is defined by the equation $25x^2 + 4y^2 + 50x - 8y - 71 = 0$. Write the standard equation, and identify the coordinates of the center, vertices, co-vertices, and foci. Sketch the graph. **(EXAMPLE 4)**

Jupiter as seen by Voyager 1

Practice and Apply

Find the vertices and co-vertices of each ellipse.

9. $\frac{x^2}{25} + \frac{y^2}{9} = 1$

10. $\frac{x^2}{16} + \frac{y^2}{49} = 1$

11. $\frac{x^2}{81} + \frac{y^2}{4} = 1$

12. $\frac{x^2}{9} + \frac{y^2}{36} = 1$

13. $\frac{x^2}{1} + \frac{y^2}{64} = 1$

14. $\frac{x^2}{1} + \frac{y^2}{4} = 1$

Write the standard equation of each ellipse. Find the coordinates of the center, vertices, co-vertices, and foci.

15. $3x^2 + 12y^2 = 12$

16. $50x^2 + 2y^2 = 50$

17. $3x^2 + 7y^2 = 28$

18. $5x^2 + 20y^2 = 80$

19. $\frac{x^2}{8} + \frac{y^2}{18} = 2$

20. $\frac{x^2}{3} + \frac{y^2}{12} = 3$

Write the standard equation for each ellipse.

21.

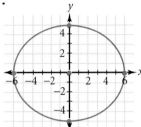

22.

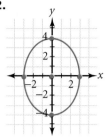

23.

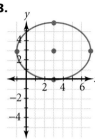

24.

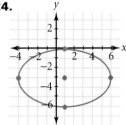

25.

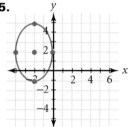

26.

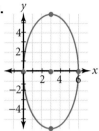

Sketch the graph of each ellipse. Label the center, foci, vertices, and co-vertices.

27. $\dfrac{x^2}{25} + \dfrac{y^2}{4} = 1$

28. $\dfrac{x^2}{1} + \dfrac{y^2}{9} = 1$

29. $\dfrac{x^2}{4} + \dfrac{y^2}{9} = 1$

30. $\dfrac{x^2}{16} + \dfrac{y^2}{1} = 1$

31. $\dfrac{(x+2)^2}{4} + \dfrac{(y+1)^2}{9} = 1$

32. $\dfrac{(x-2)^2}{9} + \dfrac{(y-2)^2}{4} = 1$

33. $\dfrac{x^2}{1} + \dfrac{(y+2)^2}{9} = 1$

34. $\dfrac{(x+1)^2}{4} + \dfrac{y^2}{1} = 1$

35. $\dfrac{(x-1)^2}{4} + \dfrac{(y-1)^2}{4} = 1$

36. $16(x+1)^2 + 9(y-1)^2 = 144$

37. $9(x-1)^2 + 25(y+2)^2 = 225$

38. $4x^2 + 25y^2 = 100$

39. $25x^2 + 9y^2 = 225$

Write the standard equation for the ellipse with the given characteristics.

40. foci: $(5, 0)$, $(-5, 0)$
vertices: $(9, 0)$, $(-9, 0)$

41. foci: $(0, 4)$, $(0, -4)$
vertices: $(0, 8)$, $(0, -8)$

42. foci: $(7, 0)$, $(-7, 0)$
co-vertices: $(0, 3)$, $(0, -3)$

43. foci: $(0, 3)$, $(0, -3)$
co-vertices: $(1, 0)$, $(-1, 0)$

44. co-vertices: $(0, 2)$, $(0, -2)$
vertices: $(3, 0)$, $(-3, 0)$

45. vertices: $(5, 0)$, $(-5, 0)$
co-vertices: $(0, 4)$, $(0, -4)$

State whether each equation represents a parabola, a circle, or an ellipse.

46. $\dfrac{x}{2} = \dfrac{(y-3)^2}{4}$

47. $\dfrac{y}{4} = \dfrac{(x+2)^2}{2}$

48. $\dfrac{(x-1)^2}{12} = 6 - \dfrac{(y+5)^2}{9}$

49. $\dfrac{(y+4)^2}{6} = 8 - \dfrac{(x-1)^2}{4}$

Write the standard equation for each ellipse. Identify the coordinates of the center, vertices, co-vertices, and foci.

50. $x^2 + 4y^2 + 6x - 8y = 3$

51. $16x^2 + 4y^2 + 32x - 8y = 44$

52. $x^2 + 16y^2 - 64y = 0$

53. $25x^2 + y^2 - 50x = 0$

54. $4x^2 + 9y^2 - 16x + 18y = 11$

55. $25x^2 + 9y^2 + 100x + 18y = 116$

56. $9x^2 + 16y^2 - 36x - 64y - 44 = 0$

57. $36x^2 + 25y^2 - 72x + 100y = 764$

58. TRANSFORMATIONS If the ellipse defined by the equation $\frac{(x+5)^2}{36} + \frac{(y-1)^2}{64} = 1$ is translated 1 unit up and 5 units to the right, write the standard equation of the resulting ellipse.

59. TRANSFORMATIONS If the ellipse defined by the equation $16x^2 + 4y^2 + 96x + 8y + 84 = 0$ is translated 4 units down and 7 units to the left, write the standard equation of the resulting ellipse.

60. Use equations to explain why the eccentricity of an ellipse cannot equal 1.

61. Describe the graph of the equation $\frac{(x+2)^2}{3} + \frac{(y-1)^2}{6} = 0$.

62. ASTRONOMY The Moon orbits Earth in an elliptical path with the center of the Earth at one focus. The major axis of the orbit is 774,000 kilometers, and the minor axis is 773,000 kilometers.

a. Using $(0, 0)$ as the center of the ellipse, write the standard equation for the orbit of the Moon around Earth.

b. How far from the center of Earth is the Moon at its closest point?

c. How far from the center of Earth is the Moon at its farthest point?

d. Find the eccentricity of the Moon's orbit around Earth.

James Irwin salutes the flag during the Apollo 15 *mission to the Moon.*

63. ARCHITECTURE The ceiling of the "whispering gallery" of the Statuary Hall in the United States Capitol Building can be approximated by a *semi-ellipse*. Because of the properties of reflection, the whispering of someone standing at one focus can be clearly heard by a person standing at the other focus. It is said that John Quincy Adams used this attribute of the Statuary Hall to eavesdrop on his adversaries. Suppose that the distance between the foci is 38.5 feet and the maximum height of the ceiling above ear level is 37 feet. Find the equation of an elliptical cross section of this gallery, assuming that the center is placed at the origin.

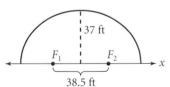

64. LIGHTING A light atop the pole represented by $\overline{PQ}$ illuminates an elliptical region at the base of the pole as shown in the illustration at left, where $PQ = 18$ feet, $CQ = 2$ feet, $AQ = 26$ feet, and $BD = 18$ feet.

a. Using the x- and y-axes shown, write an equation for the boundary of the elliptical region illuminated by the light.

b. Write an inequality in terms of x and y that represents the points in the illuminated area.

c. Describe the region that would be illuminated if the pole stood straight up at point O and the light were directed straight down.

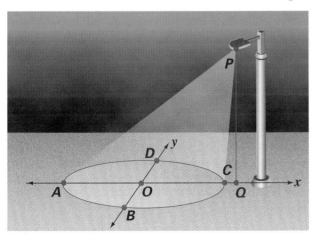

Simplify each expression, assuming that no variable equals zero. Write your answers with positive exponents only. *(LESSON 2.2)*

65. $(4x^3y^4)^2(2x^4y)^{-1}$ **66.** $\left(\dfrac{a^5b^{-3}}{ab^4}\right)^{-2}$ **67.** $\left(\dfrac{6xy^2z^{-5}}{5x^2y^{-2}z}\right)^2$

Solve each equation for *x* by using natural logarithms. Round answers to the nearest hundredth. *(LESSON 6.6)*

68. $10^x = 56$ **69.** $25^x = 123$ **70.** $0.3^{-x} = 0.81$

Write each sum or difference as a polynomial expression in standard form. *(LESSON 7.1)*

71. $(18a^3 - 5a^2 - 6a + 2) + (7a^3 - 8a + 9)$

72. $2x^4 - 3x^2 + 2 - 5x) + (4x^2 + 2x - 7x^4 + 6)$

73. $(9x^2y^2 - 5xy + 25y^2) - (5x^2y^2 + 10xy - 9y^2)$

74. $(-x^2 - y^2) - (-2x^2 + 3xy - 2y^2)$

 Look Beyond

75 Graph $\dfrac{x^2}{9} - \dfrac{y^2}{16} = 1$, and describe its shape. Explain why there are no real-number values of *y* for $-3 < x < 3$.

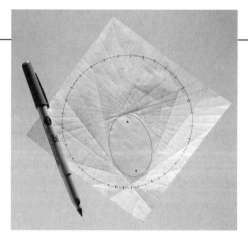

1. Draw a circle with a diameter of at least 4.5 inches in the middle of a piece of patty paper or wax paper.

2. Place at least 20 tick marks on the circle, approximately evenly spaced.

3. Place a point inside the circle anywhere except at the center. Fold the paper so that this inside point lies on one of the tick marks on the circle. Crease the paper, and then unfold it.

4. Repeat this procedure for each tick mark on the circle.

5. Compare the figure formed by the creases with the figures formed by your classmates. How do the figures vary? Could they all be classified as one type of conic section? If so, which one?

6. Make a conjecture about how to make a flatter or rounder figure. Verify your conjecture by repeating the process with the appropriate modification(s).

7. How does the point that you chose in Step 3 appear to be mathematically significant? Explain your reasoning.

WORKING ON THE CHAPTER PROJECT

You should now be able to complete Activity 2 of the Chapter Project.

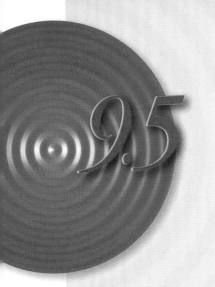

Hyperbolas

Why The principle of the *LORAN* navigation system used by ships at sea is based on the definition of a hyperbola.

Objectives

- Write the standard equation for a hyperbola given sufficient information.

- Graph the equation of a hyperbola, and identify the center, foci, vertices, and co-vertices.

APPLICATION

RADIO NAVIGATION

Ships can navigate by using the LORAN radio navigation system, which is based on the time differences between receiving radio signals from pairs of transmitting stations that send signals at the same time.

For example, the ship at point P in the diagram at right can use the time difference $t_2 - t_1$ and the distance F_1F_2 to locate itself somewhere on the branches of the blue hyperbola. Then, using the time difference $t_3 - t_1$ and the distance F_1F_3, the ship can locate itself somewhere on the branches of the red hyperbola.

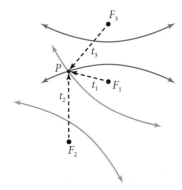

By finding the reasonable intersection of these two hyperbolas, the ship can determine its exact location.

The radio navigation system described utilizes the *definition of a hyperbola* to locate objects.

Definition of a Hyperbola

A **hyperbola** is the set of points $P(x, y)$ in a plane such that the absolute value of the difference between the distances from P to two fixed points in the plane, F_1 and F_2, called the **foci**, is a constant.

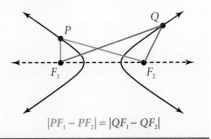

$$|PF_1 - PF_2| = |QF_1 - QF_2|$$

You can use the definition of a hyperbola and the distance formula to find an equation for the hyperbola that contains $P(x, y)$, has foci at $F_1(-5, 0)$ and $F_2(5, 0)$, and has a constant difference of 6.

$$|F_1P - F_2P| = 6$$
$$F_1P - F_2P = \pm 6$$
$$\sqrt{[x - (-5)]^2 + (y - 0)^2} - \sqrt{(x - 5)^2 + (y - 0)^2} = \pm 6$$
$$\sqrt{(x - 5)^2 + y^2} = \pm 6 + \sqrt{(x - 5)^2 + y^2}$$

Square each side.
$$(x + 5)^2 + y^2 = 36 \pm 12\sqrt{(x - 5)^2 + y^2} + (x - 5)^2 + y^2$$
$$x^2 + 10x + 25 + y^2 = 36 \pm 12\sqrt{(x - 5)^2 + y^2} + x^2 - 10x + 25 + y^2$$

Simplify.
$$20x - 36 = \pm 12\sqrt{(x - 5)^2 + y^2}$$

Divide each side by 4.
$$5x - 9 = \pm 3\sqrt{(x - 5)^2 + y^2}$$

Square each side again.
$$25x^2 - 90x + 81 = 9x^2 - 90x + 225 + 9y^2$$
$$16x^2 - 9y^2 = 144$$

Divide each side by 144.
$$\frac{x^2}{9} - \frac{y^2}{16} = 1$$

> Notice that the transverse axis can be shorter than the conjugate axis.

A hyperbola has two axes of symmetry. One axis contains the **transverse axis**, $\overline{V_1V_2}$, of the hyperbola, and the other axis contains the **conjugate axis**, from $(0, -b)$ to $(0, b)$, of the hyperbola. The endpoints of the transverse axis are called the **vertices** of the hyperbola. The endpoints of the conjugate axis are called the **co-vertices** of the hyperbola. The point of intersection of the transverse axis and the conjugate axis is called the **center** of the hyperbola.

Standard Equation of a Hyperbola

The standard equation of a hyperbola centered at the origin is given below.

Horizontal transverse axis

$$\frac{x^2}{a^2} - \frac{y^2}{b^2} = 1$$

Vertical transverse axis

$$\frac{y^2}{a^2} - \frac{x^2}{b^2} = 1$$

In each case:
- $a^2 + b^2 = c^2$,
- the length of the transverse axis is $2a$, and
- the length of the conjugate axis is $2b$.

1 **Write the standard equation for the hyperbola with vertices at $(0, -4)$ and $(0, 4)$ and co-vertices at $(-3, 0)$ and $(3, 0)$. Then sketch the graph.**

● **SOLUTION**

Because the vertices lie along the y-axis and the center is at the origin, the equation is of the form $\dfrac{y^2}{a^2} - \dfrac{x^2}{b^2} = 1$.

From the coordinates of the vertices, $a = 4$. From the coordinates of the co-vertices, $b = 3$. The equation is $\dfrac{y^2}{4^2} - \dfrac{x^2}{3^2} = 1$, or $\dfrac{y^2}{16} - \dfrac{x^2}{9} = 1$.

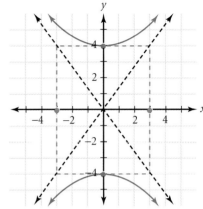

Plot the vertices and co-vertices, and draw the rectangle determined by these points. Sketch the lines containing the diagonals of this rectangle. Then sketch the branches of the hyperbola between the lines that contain the diagonals, as shown at right above.

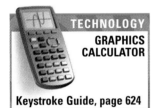

TECHNOLOGY
GRAPHICS CALCULATOR

Keystroke Guide, page 624

CHECK

To graph the hyperbola defined by $\dfrac{y^2}{16} - \dfrac{x^2}{9} = 1$, solve for y and graph the two resulting equations together.

$\dfrac{y^2}{16} - \dfrac{x^2}{9} = 1 \quad \rightarrow \quad y = \pm \sqrt{16\left(1 + \dfrac{x^2}{9}\right)}$

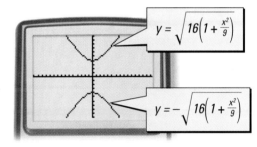

$y = \sqrt{16\left(1 + \dfrac{x^2}{9}\right)}$

$y = -\sqrt{16\left(1 + \dfrac{x^2}{9}\right)}$

TRY THIS   Write the standard equation for the hyperbola with vertices at $(-7, 0)$ and $(7, 0)$ and co-vertices at $(0, -4)$ and $(0, 4)$. Then sketch the graph.

CRITICAL THINKING   Write the standard equation for the hyperbola that has a horizontal transverse axis, is centered at the origin, and passes through the points $(1, 2)$ and $(5, 12)$.

Notice that the hyperbola in Example 1 above is graphed with a pair of dashed lines that contain the diagonals of the rectangle that is determined by the vertices and co-vertices. These lines are **asymptotes of the hyperbola**. In the Activity below, you will explore the equations for the asymptotes of hyperbolas.

Exploring Asymptotes of Hyperbolas

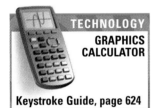

TECHNOLOGY
GRAPHICS CALCULATOR

Keystroke Guide, page 624

You will need: a graphics calculator

1. Solve $\dfrac{x^2}{2^2} - \dfrac{y^2}{3^2} = 1$ for y, and graph the resulting equations with the lines $y = \dfrac{3}{2}x$ and $y = -\dfrac{3}{2}x$ on the same screen. Do the branches of the hyperbola appear to approach these lines?

2. Copy and complete the table of values to the nearest hundredth.

x	$y=\sqrt{9\left(\frac{x^2}{4}-1\right)}$	$y=-\sqrt{9\left(\frac{x^2}{4}-1\right)}$	$y=\frac{3}{2}x$	$y=-\frac{3}{2}x$
10				
20				
30				
40				
50				
60				

3. Do the values in the table above suggest that the branches of this hyperbola approach the lines $y=\frac{3}{2}x$ and $y=-\frac{3}{2}x$? Explain your response.

CHECKPOINT ✔ **4.** Consider $\frac{x^2}{5^2}-\frac{y^2}{4^2}=1$. Predict the equations for the asymptotes of this hyperbola. Use a graph and a table to check your prediction.

Given the standard equation of any hyperbola with a horizontal or vertical transverse axis and with its center at the origin, you can write equations for the asymptotes.

Asymptotes of a Hyperbola

standard equation: $\dfrac{x^2}{a^2}-\dfrac{y^2}{b^2}=1\;\rightarrow\;$ asymptotes: $y=\pm\dfrac{b}{a}x$

standard equation: $\dfrac{y^2}{a^2}-\dfrac{x^2}{b^2}=1\;\rightarrow\;$ asymptotes: $y=\pm\dfrac{a}{b}x$

EXAMPLE ② Find the equations of the asymptotes and the coordinates of the vertices for the graph of $\dfrac{y^2}{16}-\dfrac{x^2}{36}=1$. Then sketch the graph.

SOLUTION

The equation is of the form
$\dfrac{y^2}{a^2}-\dfrac{x^2}{b^2}=1$, where $a=4$ and $b=6$.

The asymptotes, $y=\pm\dfrac{a}{b}x$, are

$y=\pm\dfrac{4}{6}x$, or $y=\dfrac{2}{3}x$ and $y=-\dfrac{2}{3}x$.

The vertices are $(0,-4)$ and $(0,4)$.

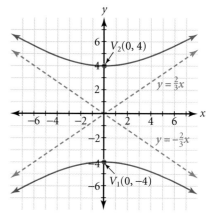

TRY THIS Find the equations of the asymptotes and the coordinates of the vertices for the graph of $\dfrac{x^2}{16}-\dfrac{y^2}{25}=1$. Then sketch the graph.

The center of a hyperbola can be anywhere in a coordinate plane.

Standard Equation of a Translated Hyperbola

The standard equation of a hyperbola centered at (h, k) is given below.

Horizontal transverse axis

$$\frac{(x-h)^2}{a^2} - \frac{(y-k)^2}{b^2} = 1$$

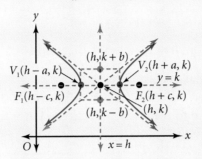

Vertical transverse axis

$$\frac{(y-k)^2}{a^2} - \frac{(x-h)^2}{b^2} = 1$$

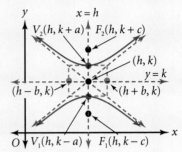

In each case: • $a^2 + b^2 = c^2$,
• the length of the transverse axis is $2a$, and
• the length of the conjugate axis is $2b$.

Given sufficient information, you can write the standard equation of a translated hyperbola.

EXAMPLE 3 Write the standard equation of the hyperbola with foci at $(-1, 1)$ and $(5, 1)$ and vertices at $(0, 1)$ and $(4, 1)$.

SOLUTION

1. To find the center, (h, k), find the midpoint of the transverse axis.

$$\frac{x_1 + x_2}{2} = \frac{0 + 4}{2} = 2 \qquad \frac{y_1 + y_2}{2} = \frac{1 + 1}{2} = 1$$

The center is at $(2, 1)$, so $h = 2$ and $k = 1$.

2. Find a, b, and c. The transverse axis is horizontal and the standard equation is of the form $\dfrac{(x-h)^2}{a^2} - \dfrac{(y-k)^2}{b^2} = 1$.

The vertex $(0, 1)$ is $(h - a, k)$, so $h - a = 0$.

$$h - a = 0$$
$$2 - a = 0$$
$$a = 2$$

The focus $(-1, 1)$ is $(h - c, k)$, so $h - c = -1$.

$$h - c = -1$$
$$2 - c = -1$$
$$c = 3$$

$$a^2 + b^2 = c^2 \quad \rightarrow \quad 2^2 + b^2 = 3^2 \quad \rightarrow \quad b^2 = 5$$

Thus, the standard equation of this hyperbola is $\dfrac{(x-2)^2}{4} - \dfrac{(y-1)^2}{5} = 1$.

TRY THIS Write the standard equation of the hyperbola with foci at $(3, -3)$ and $(3, 7)$ and vertices at $(3, -1)$ and $(3, 5)$.

4 The equation $-2x^2 + y^2 + 4x + 6y + 3 = 0$ represents a hyperbola. Write the standard equation of this hyperbola. Give the coordinates of the center, vertices, co-vertices, and foci. Then sketch the graph.

SOLUTION

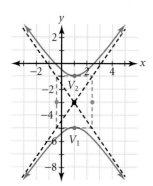

$$-2x^2 + y^2 + 4x + 6y + 3 = 0$$
$$y^2 + 6y - 2x^2 + 4x = -3$$
$$(y^2 + 6y + 9) - 2(x^2 - 2x + 1) = -3 + 9 - 2 \quad \text{Complete the squares.}$$
$$(y + 3)^2 - 2(x - 1)^2 = 4$$
$$\frac{(y + 3)^2}{4} - \frac{(x - 1)^2}{2} = 1$$

From the equation, $h = 1$, $k = -3$, $a = 2$, and $b = \sqrt{2}$. Then $c = \sqrt{4 + 2} = \sqrt{6}$.

The center, (h, k), is at $(1, -3)$.
Use the value of a to find the vertices, $(1, -5)$ and $(1, -1)$.
Use the value of b to find the co-vertices, $\left(1 - \sqrt{2}, -3\right)$ and $\left(1 + \sqrt{2}, -3\right)$.
Use the value of c to find the foci, $\left(1, -3 - \sqrt{6}\right)$ and $\left(1, -3 + \sqrt{6}\right)$.

TRY THIS The equation $4x^2 - 25y^2 - 8x + 100y - 196 = 0$ represents a hyperbola. Write the standard equation of this hyperbola. Give the coordinates of the center, vertices, co-vertices, and foci. Then sketch the graph.

Exercises

Communicate

1. Explain how to find the coordinates of the center, vertices, co-vertices, and foci when given the standard equation of a translated hyperbola.

2. Explain how to use the asymptotes and the coordinates of the vertices of a hyperbola to sketch it.

Guided Skills Practice

3. Write the standard equation for the hyperbola with vertices at $(-4, 0)$ and $(4, 0)$ and co-vertices at $(0, -2)$ and $(0, 2)$. Then sketch the graph. *(EXAMPLE 1)*

4. Find the equations of the asymptotes and the coordinates of the vertices of the graph of $\frac{x^2}{9} - \frac{y^2}{25} = 1$. Then sketch the graph. *(EXAMPLE 2)*

5. Write the standard equation of the hyperbola with foci at $(0, 4)$ and $(6, 4)$ and vertices at $(1, 4)$ and $(5, 4)$. *(EXAMPLE 3)*

6. The equation $x^2 - y^2 + 2x + 4y - 2 = 12$ represents a hyperbola. Write the standard equation of this hyperbola. Give the coordinates of the center, vertices, co-vertices, and foci. Then sketch the graph. *(EXAMPLE 4)*

Write the standard equation for each hyperbola.

7.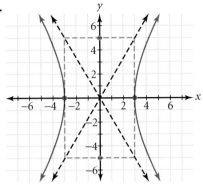

8.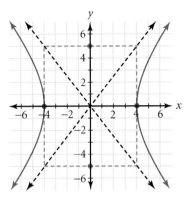

9.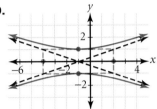

10.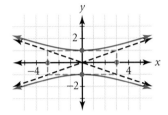

11.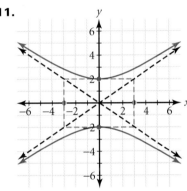

12.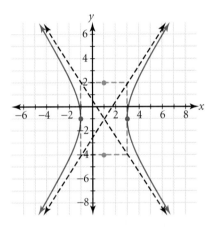

Graph each hyperbola. Label the center, vertices, co-vertices, foci, and asymptotes.

13. $x^2 - y^2 = 1$

14. $y^2 - x^2 = 1$

15. $\dfrac{y^2}{3^2} - \dfrac{x^2}{5^2} = 1$

16. $\dfrac{x^2}{2^2} - \dfrac{y^2}{3^2} = 1$

17. $x^2 - \dfrac{y^2}{2^2} = 1$

18. $y^2 - \dfrac{x^2}{3^2} = 1$

19. $\dfrac{y^2}{100} - \dfrac{x^2}{64} = 1$

20. $\dfrac{x^2}{25} - \dfrac{y^2}{36} = 1$

21. $4x^2 - 25y^2 = 100$

22. $36y^2 - 4x^2 = 144$

23. $\dfrac{(x-1)^2}{2^2} - \dfrac{(y+2)^2}{3^2} = 1$

24. $\dfrac{(x+2)^2}{3^2} - \dfrac{(y-2)^2}{4^2} = 1$

For Exercises 25–32, write the standard equation for the hyperbola with the given characteristics.

25. vertices: $(-3, 0)$ and $(3, 0)$; co-vertices: $(0, -5)$ and $(0, 5)$

26. vertices: $(0, -2)$ and $(0, 2)$; co-vertices: $(-4, 0)$ and $(4, 0)$

27. vertices: $(0, -4)$ and $(0, 4)$; foci: $(0, -5)$ and $(0, 5)$

28. vertices: $(-5, 0)$ and $(5, 0)$; foci: $(-7, 0)$ and $(7, 0)$

29. co-vertices: $(0, -2)$ and $(0, 2)$; foci: $(-3, 0)$ and $(3, 0)$

30. co-vertices: $(-1, 0)$ and $(1, 0)$; foci: $(0, -2)$ and $(0, 2)$

31. center: $(2, 3)$; vertices: $(-1, 3)$ and $(5, 3)$; co-vertices: $(2, -2)$ and $(2, 8)$

32. center: $(-1, -3)$; vertices: $(-6, -3)$ and $(4, -3)$; co-vertices: $(-1, -6)$ and $(-1, 0)$

Write the standard equation for each hyperbola. Give the coordinates of the center, vertices, co-vertices, and foci.

33. $4x^2 - 9y^2 - 8x + 54y = 113$

34. $16x^2 - 25y^2 - 32x + 100y = 484$

35. $4y^2 - 36x^2 - 72x + 8y = 176$

36. $25y^2 - 16x^2 + 64x - 50y = 439$

37. $y^2 - 9x^2 - 6y = 36 + 36x$

38. $16x^2 - 9y^2 + 64x = 89 - 18y$

39. $16x^2 + 64y - 256 = 16y^2 - 64x$

40. $25y^2 + 100x - 100y - 625 = 25x^2$

41. $3y^2 + 20x = 23 + 5x^2 + 12y$

42. $7x^2 - 5y^2 = 48 - 20y - 14x$

Write the standard equations for both hyperbolas whose asymptotes contain the diagonals of rectangle *ABCD* and whose vertices lie on the sides of the given rectangle.

43. $A(-5, 4)$, $B(5, 4)$, $C(5, -4)$, and $D(-5, -4)$

44. $A(-2, 6)$, $B(2, 6)$, $C(2, -6)$, and $D(-2, -6)$

45. $A(1, 12)$, $B(11, 12)$, $C(11, 1)$, and $D(1, 1)$

46. $A(0, 7)$, $B(6, 7)$, $C(6, 4)$, and $D(0, 4)$

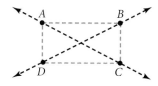

CHALLENGE

47. Let $\dfrac{x^2}{a^2} - \dfrac{y^2}{a^2} = 1$.

  a. Find the coordinates of the vertices and co-vertices.

  b. If the four points in part **a** are joined to form a quadrilateral, classify the quadrilateral.

  c. Justify your conclusion from part **b**.

CONNECTIONS

48. TRANSFORMATIONS If the hyperbola defined by the equation $\dfrac{(x-5)^2}{1} - \dfrac{(y-2)^2}{25} = 1$ is translated 6 units down and 3 units to the right, write the standard equation of the resulting hyperbola.

49. TRANSFORMATIONS Translate the hyperbola defined by the equation $9x^2 - 4y^2 + 54x + 8y + 41 = 0$ up 2 units and to the left 6 units. Write the standard equation of the resulting hyperbola.

APPLICATION

50. LAW ENFORCEMENT An explosion is heard by two law enforcement officers who are 1000 meters apart. One officer heard the explosion 1.5 seconds after the other officer. The speed of sound in air (at 20°C) is approximately 340 meters per second. Write an equation for the possible locations of the explosion, relative to the two law enforcement officers.

Use substitution to solve each system of equations. (LESSON 3.1)

51. $\begin{cases} x = y + 1 \\ x + 4y = 11 \end{cases}$

52. $\begin{cases} 9m + 8n = 21 \\ 2m = 7 - n \end{cases}$

53. $\begin{cases} 15x + 4y = 23 \\ 10x - y = -3 \end{cases}$

Use elimination to solve each system of equations. (LESSON 3.2)

54. $\begin{cases} 5x - 2y = 30 \\ x + 2y = 6 \end{cases}$

55. $\begin{cases} 3x + 2y = 5 \\ 4x = 22 + 5y \end{cases}$

56. $\begin{cases} 5x - 2y = 3 \\ 2x + 7y = 9 \end{cases}$

Let $A = \begin{bmatrix} -2 \\ 1 \\ 5 \end{bmatrix}$, $B = [4 \quad 0 \quad -5]$, and $C = \begin{bmatrix} 2 & 4 & 1 \\ -6 & 0 & -1 \\ 3 & 2 & 9 \end{bmatrix}$. **Find each product, if it exists.** (LESSON 4.2)

57. AB **58.** BA **59.** BC **60.** CA

61. CB **62.** $(AB)C$ **63.** $C(AB)$ **64.** $A(BC)$

 Look Beyond

65 Consider $2x^2 + 5y^2 = 22$ and $3x^2 - y^2 = -1$.
  a. What two figures are represented by these equations?
  b. Solve both equations for y.
  c. Graph the equations from part **b** on your graphics calculator. Use a viewing window that allows you to see all points of intersection for the four graphs. Find all points of intersection.

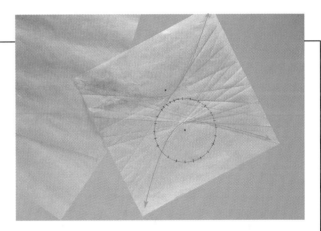

1. Draw a circle with a diameter between 2 and 4 inches on the left side of a piece of wax paper.

2. Place at least 20 tick marks on the circle, approximately evenly spaced.

3. Place a point outside and to the right of the circle. Fold the paper so that this outside point lies on one of the tick marks on the circle. Crease the paper, and then unfold it.

4. Repeat Step 3 for each tick mark on the circle.

5. Compare the figure formed by the creases with those of your classmates. How do the figures vary? Could they all be classified as one type of conic section? If so, which one?

6. Make a conjecture about how to make a flatter or more open figure. Verify your conjecture by repeating the process with the appropriate modification(s).

7. How does the point that you placed in Step 3 appear to be mathematically significant? Explain your reasoning.

WORKING ON THE CHAPTER PROJECT

You should now be able to complete Activity 3 of the Chapter Project.

WHAT'S SO FUZZY?

Time for Some Fuzzy Thinking

By Philip Elmer-Dewitt

In the pages of *Books in Print*, listed among works like *Fuzzy Bear* and *Fuzzy Wuzzy Puppy*, are some strange sounding titles: *Fuzzy Systems, Fuzzy Set Theory* and *Fuzzy Reasoning & Its Applications*. The bedtime reading of scientists gone soft in the head? No, these academic tomes are the collected output of 25 years of mostly American research in fuzzy logic, a branch of mathematics designed to help computers simulate the various kinds of vagueness and uncertainty found in everyday life. Despite a distinguished corps of devoted followers, however, fuzzy logic has been largely relegated to the back shelves of computer science—at least in the U.S.

But not, it turns out, in Japan. Suddenly the term fuzzy and products based on principles of fuzzy logic seem to be everywhere in Japan: in television documentaries, in corporate magazine ads and in novel electronic gadgets ranging from computer-controlled air conditioners to golf-swing analyzers.

What is fuzzy logic? The original concept, developed in the mid-'60s by Lofti Zadeh, a Russian-born professor of computer science at the University of California, Berkeley, is that things in the real world do not fall into neat, crisp categories defined by traditional set theory, like the set of even numbers or the set of left-handed baseball players.

[*Source: Time, September 25, 1989*]

But this on-or-off, black-or-white, 0-or-1 approach falls apart when applied to many everyday classifications, like the set of beautiful women, the set of tall men or the set of very cold days.

This mathematics turns out to be surprisingly useful for controlling robots, machine tools and various electronic systems. A conventional air conditioner, for example, recognizes only two basic states: too hot or too cold. When geared for thermostat control, the cooling system either operates at full blast or shuts off completely. A fuzzy air conditioner, by contrast, would recognize that some room temperatures are closer to the human comfort zone than others. Its cooling system would begin to slow down gradually as the room temperature approached the desired setting. Result: a more comfortable room and a smaller electric bill.

Fuzzy logic began to find applications in industry in the early '70s, when it was teamed with another form of advanced computer science called the expert system. Expert systems solve complex problems somewhat like humans experts do—by applying rules of thumb. (Example: when the oven gets very hot, turn the gas down a bit.)

Fuzzy-logic controllers create a smoother ride for passengers and use less energy than human conductors or automated systems that are based on traditional logic.

What is fuzzy logic? How can it make things work more efficiently? Does fuzzy logic resemble the way we think more than traditional logic does?

To answer questions like these, you need to explore the basis of fuzzy logic—something called *fuzzy sets.*

According to traditional logic, if someone belongs to the set of *people who are tall*, then they cannot belong to the set of *people who are not tall*. With fuzzy sets, the distinction is not so sharp, as you will see.

Traditional Logic

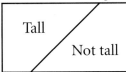

Tall

Not tall

Cooperative Learning

For Steps 1 and 2, use the data in the table at right or use the heights of 12 students from your class.

Student	Height
A	5' 11"
B	5' 3"
C	6' 1"
D	4' 11"
E	5' 4"
F	5' 10"
G	5' 1"
H	5' 8"
I	5' 5"
J	5' 7"
K	5' 6"
L	5' 9"

1. Before looking at fuzzy sets, examine how you might use sets in traditional logic to categorize a group of students by height.
   a. Create a 2-column table. In the left column, list the heights of the students you think are tall. List the rest in the right column.
   b. Which heights were hardest to place? Why?
   c. At what height did you draw the line between *tall* and *not tall*? Compare your response with other groups. Describe the disagreements.
   d. Why would you expect there to be disagreements?

2. Now, try using fuzzy sets.
   a. For each student letter in the table, assign a value from 0 to 1 to indicate the extent to which that person belongs to the set *tall*. For example:
      0 for someone who definitely does not belong
      0.5 for someone who *may be* tall
      0.8 for someone who is *fairly* tall
      1 for someone who definitely belongs on the *tall* list
   b. On a graph, plot the 12 values you assigned in part **a**. Draw a smooth curve through the points.
   c. How does the graph show what you think the word *tall* means?
   d. Compare your graph with the graphs of other groups. How are they a like and how are they different?

3. What sort of difficulties can you run into when you apply traditional logic to real-world situations? How can fuzzy sets help resolve those difficulties?

Solving Nonlinear Systems

Why *Solving nonlinear systems of equations is required to solve many real-world problems, such as finding the dimensions of a beam that is to be cut from a log.*

A mill operator wants to cut a rectangular beam from a cylindrical log whose circular cross section has a diameter of 10 inches. The rectangular cross section of the beam is to have a length that is twice its width.

To find the dimensions of the beam, you need to solve a *system of nonlinear equations*. *You will solve this problem in Example 2.*

Objectives

• Solve a system of equations containing first- or second-degree equations in two variables.

• Identify a conic section from its equation.

A **system of nonlinear equations** is a collection of equations in which at least one equation is not linear.

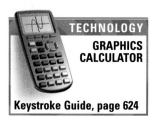

TECHNOLOGY
GRAPHICS CALCULATOR

Keystroke Guide, page 624

Activity
Exploring Nonlinear Systems

You will need: a graphics calculator

1. Graph the system of equations in part **a.** Record the number of points of intersection. Repeat this for the systems of equations in parts **b, c,** and **d.**

   a. $\begin{cases} x^2 + y^2 = 25 \\ y = 2x \end{cases}$ **b.** $\begin{cases} x^2 + y^2 = 25 \\ x^2 - y^2 = 9 \end{cases}$ **c.** $\begin{cases} y = x^2 \\ y = 2x + 1 \end{cases}$ **d.** $\begin{cases} x^2 + y^2 = 1 \\ y = x^2 \end{cases}$

CHECKPOINT ✔   2. The equations in part **a** of Step 1 represent a circle and a line. Consider all of the ways in which a circle and a line can intersect. Make a conjecture about the number of possible intersection points for a circle and a line, and sketch an example of each.

CHECKPOINT ✔   3. The equations in part **b** of Step 1 represent a circle and a hyperbola. Consider all of the ways in which a circle and a hyperbola can intersect. Make a conjecture about the number of possible intersection points for a circle and a hyperbola, and sketch an example of each.

CHECKPOINT ✔   4. The equations in part **c** of Step 1 represent a parabola and a line. Consider all of the ways in which a parabola and a line can intersect. Make a conjecture about the number of possible intersection points for a parabola and a line, and sketch an example of each.

CHECKPOINT ✔   5. The equations in part **d** of Step 1 represent a circle and a parabola. Consider all of the ways in which a circle and a parabola can intersect. Make a conjecture about the number of possible intersection points for a circle and a parabola, and sketch an example of each.

A system of two second-degree equations in x and y can have no more than four real solutions, unless the system is dependent. This is demonstrated below for an ellipse and hyperbola.

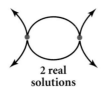
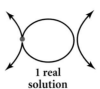
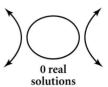

| 4 real solutions | 3 real solutions | 2 real solutions | 1 real solution | 0 real solutions |

CRITICAL THINKING   Give an example of a dependent system of nonlinear equations. How many solutions does it have?

Solving Systems of Nonlinear Equations

Just as you can use substitution to solve some systems of linear equations, you can use substitution to solve some systems of nonlinear equations, as shown in Example 1 below.

E X A M P L E ❶ Solve $\begin{cases} y^2 = 3x - 1 \\ x^2 + y^2 = 9 \end{cases}$ by substitution.

● **SOLUTION**

Substitute $3x - 1$ for y^2 in $x^2 + y^2 = 9$.

$$x^2 + y^2 = 9$$
$$x^2 + (3x - 1) = 9$$
$$x^2 + 3x = 10$$
$$x^2 + 3x - 10 = 0$$
$$(x - 2)(x + 5) = 0$$
$$x = 2 \quad or \quad x = -5$$

Then find the corresponding y-values.

Substitute 2 for x.
$$y^2 = 3x - 1$$
$$y^2 = 3(2) - 1$$
$$y = \pm\sqrt{5}$$

Substitute -5 for x.
$$y^2 = 3x - 1$$
$$y^2 = 3(-5) - 1$$
$$y = \pm\sqrt{-16}$$
$$y = \pm 4i$$

The real solutions are $(2, \sqrt{5})$ and $(2, -\sqrt{5})$. The nonreal solutions, $(-5, 4i)$ and $(-5, -4i)$, are meaningless in this coordinate plane.

TECHNOLOGY
GRAPHICS CALCULATOR

Keystroke Guide, page 625

CHECK
Solve $y^2 = 3x - 1$ and $x^2 + y^2 = 9$ for y. Enter each of the four resulting functions separately, and graph them together in a square viewing window. From the graph, the only real solutions are $(2, \sqrt{5})$ and $(2, -\sqrt{5})$.

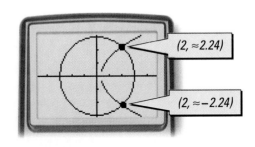

(2, ≈2.24)

(2, ≈−2.24)

TRY THIS   Solve $\begin{cases} x^2 + y^2 = 25 \\ y^2 = 2x + 1 \end{cases}$ by substitution.

EXAMPLE ② Refer to the mill problem described at the beginning of the lesson.

APPLICATION

BUSINESS

Find the dimensions of the rectangular cross section of the beam to the nearest hundredth of an inch.

● **SOLUTION**

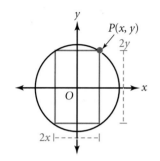

The diagram at left shows the beam inscribed in the circular cross section of the log, with the center of the circle at the origin of the coordinate plane. Since the diameter is 10, $P(x, y)$ is on a circle with a radius of 5. The equation of the circle is $x^2 + y^2 = 25$. The length of the beam is twice the width, so $y = 2x$. Solve $\begin{cases} x^2 + y^2 = 25 \\ y = 2x \end{cases}$.

$$x^2 + y^2 = 25$$
$$x^2 + (2x)^2 = 25 \quad \textit{Substitute 2x for y.}$$
$$5x^2 = 25$$
$$x^2 = 5$$
$$x = \pm\sqrt{5} \approx \pm 2.24$$

Since x represents a measurement, $\sqrt{5}$ is the only reasonable solution. The width is $2x$, or about 4.48 inches; the length is $2(2x)$, about 8.94 inches.

You can also use the elimination method to solve nonlinear systems, as shown in Example 3.

EXAMPLE ③ **Use the elimination method to solve** $\begin{cases} 4x^2 + 25y^2 = 100 \\ x^2 + y^2 = 9 \end{cases}$**. Give your answers to the nearest hundredth.**

● **SOLUTION**

1. Multiply each side of the equation $x^2 + y^2 = 9$ by -4. Solve the resulting system by using elimination.

$$\begin{cases} 4x^2 + 25y^2 = 100 \\ x^2 + y^2 = 9 \end{cases} \rightarrow \begin{cases} 4x^2 + 25y^2 = 100 \\ -4x^2 - 4y^2 = -36 \end{cases}$$

$$\begin{array}{r} 4x^2 + 25y^2 = 100 \\ \underline{-4x^2 - 4y^2 = -36} \\ 21y^2 = 64 \end{array}$$

$$y = \pm\sqrt{\frac{64}{21}} \approx \pm 1.75$$

2. Substitute $\frac{64}{21}$ for y^2 in $x^2 + y^2 = 9$.

$$x^2 + y^2 = 9$$
$$x^2 + \frac{64}{21} = 9$$
$$x = \pm\sqrt{9 - \frac{64}{21}} \approx \pm 2.44$$

The approximate solutions are $(2.44, 1.75)$, $(-2.44, 1.75)$, $(-2.44, -1.75)$, and $(2.44, -1.75)$.

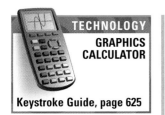

TECHNOLOGY
GRAPHICS
CALCULATOR

Keystroke Guide, page 625

CHECK
Solve each equation in the
system for y, and enter each
of the resulting functions separately,
and graph them together.

$$\begin{cases} y = \pm\sqrt{\dfrac{100 - 4x^2}{25}} \\ y = \pm\sqrt{9 - x^2} \end{cases}$$

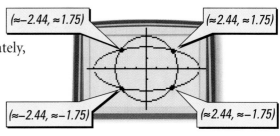

$(\approx -2.44, \approx 1.75)$ $(\approx 2.44, \approx 1.75)$
$(\approx -2.44, \approx -1.75)$ $(\approx 2.44, \approx -1.75)$

TRY THIS   Use the elimination method to solve $\begin{cases} 4x^2 + 9y^2 = 36 \\ 9x^2 - y^2 = 9 \end{cases}$. Give your answers to the
nearest hundredth.

Classifying a Conic Section

The equation $Ax^2 + Bxy + Cy^2 + Dx + Ey + F = 0$, where A, B, and C are not all
equal to zero, represents a conic section. When $B = 0$, the axes of symmetry of
the conic section are parallel to the x-axis or y-axis. When $B \neq 0$, the conic
sections are rotated. This book discusses only the first case, in which $B = 0$.
When $B = 0$, the equation reduces to $Ax^2 + Cy^2 + Dx + Ey + F = 0$.

CLASSIFYING A CONIC SECTION $Ax^2 + Cy^2 + Dx + Ey + F = 0$	
Type of conic	**Coefficients**
ellipse (or circle)	$AC > 0$
circle	$A = C, A \neq 0, C \neq 0$
parabola	$AC = 0$
hyperbola	$AC < 0$

Using the information in the table above, you can classify an equation of the
form $Ax^2 + Cy^2 + Dx + Ey + F = 0$ without completing the square.

EXAMPLE   **4**   Let $4x^2 + 8x = y^2 + 6y + 13$ be the equation of a conic section.
   a. Classify the conic section defined by this equation.
   b. Write the standard equation for this conic section.
   c. Sketch the graph.

SOLUTION

   a. Rewrite $4x^2 + 8x = y^2 + 6y + 13$ in the form $Ax^2 + Cy^2 + Dx + Ey + F = 0$.
   $4x^2 - y^2 + 8x - 6y - 13 = 0$, where $A = 4$ and $C = -1$
   Because $4(-1) < 0$, the equation represents a hyperbola.

   b.
   $$4x^2 + 8x = y^2 + 6y + 13$$
   $$4x^2 + 8x - y^2 - 6y = 13$$
   $$4(x^2 + 2x + 4) - (y^2 + 6y + 9) = 13 + 4(4) - 9 \quad \textit{Complete the squares.}$$
   $$4(x + 2)^2 - (y + 3)^2 = 20$$
   $$\frac{(x + 2)^2}{5} - \frac{(y + 3)^2}{20} = 1$$

c. center: $(-2, -3)$

vertices: $(-2 - \sqrt{5}, -3)$ and $(-2 + \sqrt{5}, -3)$

co-vertices: $(-2, -3 + \sqrt{20})$ and $(-2, -3 - \sqrt{20})$

The graph of $4x^2 + 8x = y^2 + 6y + 13$, or $\dfrac{(x+2)^2}{5} - \dfrac{(y+3)^2}{20} = 1$, is shown at right.

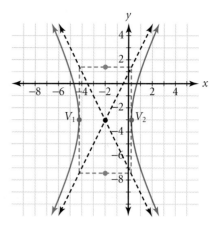

TRY THIS   Let $9x^2 + 18x + 4y^2 + 8y = 23$ be the equation of a conic section. Classify the conic section defined by this equation, write the standard equation for this conic section, and sketch the graph.

Exercises

Communicate

1. Explain how to apply the substitution method to solve $\begin{cases} y = 2x \\ x^2 + y^2 = 10 \end{cases}$.

2. Explain how to apply the elimination method to solve $\begin{cases} 2x^2 - y^2 = 1 \\ x^2 + y^2 = 5 \end{cases}$.

3. Use an illustration to help describe all of the ways in which two ellipses can intersect.

4. Given the equation $Ax^2 + Cy^2 + Dx + Ey + F = 0$, what can be said about A and C if $AC > 0$? if $AC < 0$? if $AC = 0$?

Guided Skills Practice

5. Solve $\begin{cases} y^2 = 2x + 1 \\ x^2 + y^2 = 16 \end{cases}$ by substitution. *(EXAMPLE 1)*

6. FORESTRY Refer to the mill problem described at the beginning of the lesson. Find the dimensions of the rectangular cross section of the beam that can be cut from a log whose circular cross section has a diameter of 12 inches. *(EXAMPLE 2)*

7. Use the elimination method to solve $\begin{cases} x^2 + y^2 = 16 \\ 4x^2 - 9y^2 = 36 \end{cases}$. Give answers to the nearest hundredth. *(EXAMPLE 3)*

8. Let $4x^2 + 9y^2 + 8x + 18y - 23 = 0$ be the equation of a conic section. Classify the conic section defined by this equation, write the standard equation of this conic section, and sketch the graph. *(EXAMPLE 4)*

Practice and Apply

Use the substitution method to solve each system. If there are no real-number solutions, write *none*.

9. $\begin{cases} y = 5 \\ y = x^2 \end{cases}$
10. $\begin{cases} y = 2 \\ y = x^2 \end{cases}$
11. $\begin{cases} y = 2x \\ y = x^2 \end{cases}$
12. $\begin{cases} y = x \\ x = y^2 \end{cases}$

13. $\begin{cases} y = x \\ x^2 + y^2 = 4 \end{cases}$
14. $\begin{cases} y = 3x \\ x^2 + y^2 = 9 \end{cases}$
15. $\begin{cases} y = x \\ x^2 - y^2 = 4 \end{cases}$
16. $\begin{cases} y = x^2 \\ x^2 - y^2 = 4 \end{cases}$

17. $\begin{cases} y = x^2 \\ x^2 + y^2 = 1 \end{cases}$
18. $\begin{cases} x^2 = 4 - y^2 \\ y = x^2 \end{cases}$
19. $\begin{cases} x^2 = y \\ x^2 = 4 + y^2 \end{cases}$
20. $\begin{cases} x = y \\ 9x^2 - 4y^2 = 36 \end{cases}$

Use the elimination method to solve each system. If there are no real-number solutions, write *none*.

21. $\begin{cases} x^2 + y^2 = 1 \\ 4x^2 + y^2 = 1 \end{cases}$
22. $\begin{cases} x^2 + y^2 = 9 \\ 9x^2 + y^2 = 9 \end{cases}$
23. $\begin{cases} x^2 + y^2 = 1 \\ x^2 + y^2 = 4 \end{cases}$

24. $\begin{cases} x^2 - y^2 = 1 \\ x^2 - y^2 = 4 \end{cases}$
25. $\begin{cases} x^2 + y^2 = 25 \\ 4x^2 + 25y^2 = 100 \end{cases}$
26. $\begin{cases} x^2 + y^2 = 25 \\ 25x^2 + 4y^2 = 100 \end{cases}$

27. $\begin{cases} x^2 - y^2 = 36 \\ 4y^2 - 9x^2 = 36 \end{cases}$
28. $\begin{cases} 9x^2 + 4y^2 = 36 \\ 4x^2 + 9y^2 = 36 \end{cases}$
29. $\begin{cases} x^2 + y^2 = 36 \\ 4x^2 - 9y^2 = 36 \end{cases}$

30. $\begin{cases} 9x^2 + 4y^2 = 36 \\ 4x^2 - 9y^2 = 36 \end{cases}$
31. $\begin{cases} x^2 + y^2 = 9 \\ 4x^2 + 9y^2 = 36 \end{cases}$
32. $\begin{cases} x^2 + y^2 = 4 \\ 4x^2 - 9y^2 = 36 \end{cases}$

Use any method to solve each system. If there are no real-number solutions, write *none*.

33. $\begin{cases} y = x^2 \\ x = y^2 \end{cases}$
34. $\begin{cases} x^2 + y^2 = 16 \\ x + y = 1 \end{cases}$
35. $\begin{cases} y^2 - x^2 = 1 \\ 9x^2 - y^2 = 9 \end{cases}$

36. $\begin{cases} y = x^2 + 4 \\ x = y^2 + 4 \end{cases}$
37. $\begin{cases} x^2 - 4y^2 = 20 \\ y^2 = 4 \end{cases}$
38. $\begin{cases} y - x^2 = 0 \\ x^2 = 20 - y^2 \end{cases}$

39. $\begin{cases} 4x^2 - 25y^2 = 100 \\ 4x^2 - 9y^2 = 36 \end{cases}$
40. $\begin{cases} x^2 = y \\ x^2 = 4 - y^2 \end{cases}$
41. $\begin{cases} x = y^2 + 4 \\ y = x \end{cases}$

Solve each system by graphing. If there are no real-number solutions, write *none*.

42 $\begin{cases} x^2 + y^2 = 9 \\ 4x^2 - 4y^2 = 16 \end{cases}$
43 $\begin{cases} 4y^2 + 25x^2 = 100 \\ 5x^2 - 2y^2 = 10 \end{cases}$

44 $\begin{cases} 4x^2 + 9y^2 = 36 \\ 16x^2 + 36y^2 = 144 \end{cases}$
45 $\begin{cases} 25x^2 - 4y^2 = 9 \\ 100x^2 - 16y^2 = 36 \end{cases}$

Classify the conic section defined by each equation. Write the standard equation of the conic section, and sketch the graph.

46. $x^2 + 2x + y^2 + 6y = 15$
47. $x^2 - 2x + y^2 - 2y - 6 = 0$

48. $4x^2 + 9y^2 - 8x - 18y - 23 = 0$
49. $4x^2 + 9y^2 + 16x - 36y = -16$

50. $4y^2 - 8y - x^2 - 4x - 4 = 0$
51. $4x^2 + 8x - 9y^2 + 36y - 68 = 0$

52. $4x^2 - 75 = 50y - 25y^2$
53. $9y^2 + 18y + 9 = 24x - 4x^2$

54. $9x^2 - 3 = 18x + 4y$
55. $y^2 - 2x = 6y - 5$

56. $x^2 - 8y - 16 = 4y^2 + 4x$
57. $-18x - 4y - 109 = y^2 - x^2$

Solve each system of equations. If there are no real-number solutions, write *none*.

58. $\begin{cases} (x-1)^2 + (y-1)^2 = 4 \\ (x-1)^2 + (y+1)^2 = 9 \end{cases}$

59. $\begin{cases} (x+2)^2 + (y-2)^2 = 9 \\ (x-1)^2 + (y-2)^2 = 16 \end{cases}$

60. $\begin{cases} (x-1)^2 + y^2 = 4 \\ (x-1)^2 + y^2 = 1 \end{cases}$

61. $\begin{cases} (x+2)^2 + y^2 = 9 \\ (x+2)^2 + y^2 = 25 \end{cases}$

62. $\begin{cases} \dfrac{(x-1)^2}{9} + \dfrac{y^2}{4} = 1 \\ \dfrac{(x-1)^2}{9} + y^2 = 1 \end{cases}$

63. $\begin{cases} \dfrac{(y-1)^2}{9} - x^2 = 1 \\ \dfrac{(y-1)^2}{9} - \dfrac{x^2}{9} = 1 \end{cases}$

64. $\begin{cases} x^2 + y^2 + 2x + 6y = 15 \\ x^2 + y^2 - 2x - 6y = -1 \end{cases}$

65. $\begin{cases} x^2 + y^2 - 4x + 4y = 8 \\ x^2 + y^2 - 6x - 6y = -2 \end{cases}$

66. The graphs of two nonlinear equations in x and y are shown at right.
  a. What conic sections are graphed?
  b. Describe any solutions to the system of equations represented.
  c. Write the system of equations represented by the graphs.

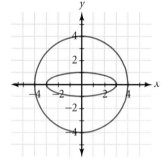

67. A positive two-digit number is represented by $10t + u$. The sum of the squares of the digits is 26. If the number is decreased by the number with its digits reversed, the result is 36. Find the two-digit number.

68. Find two negative numbers such that the sum of their squares is 170 and twice the square of the first minus 3 times the square of the second is 95.

CHALLENGES

69 You can write $\begin{cases} 4x^2 + 9y^2 = 36 \\ x^2 + y^2 = 9 \end{cases}$ as $AX = B$, where $A = \begin{bmatrix} 4 & 9 \\ 1 & 1 \end{bmatrix}$, $X = \begin{bmatrix} x^2 \\ y^2 \end{bmatrix}$, and $B = \begin{bmatrix} 36 \\ 9 \end{bmatrix}$. Use a matrix equation to find x^2 and y^2. Then find x and y.

70. Solve $\begin{cases} x^2 + y^2 < 16 \\ x^2 - 6y \le 3 \end{cases}$ by graphing.

CONNECTIONS

71. GEOMETRY Find the dimensions of a rectangle with an area of 12 square feet and a diagonal of 5 feet.

72. GEOMETRY The area of a rectangle is 48 square meters. The length of a diagonal is 10 meters. Find the perimeter of the rectangle.

73. GEOMETRY The area of a rectangle is 12 square inches. The perimeter is 24 inches. Find the dimensions of the rectangle.

APPLICATION

74. BUSINESS A company determines that its total monthly production cost, P, in thousands of dollars is defined by the equation $P = 8x + 4$. The company's monthly revenue, R, in thousands of dollars is defined by $8R - 3x^2 = 0$. In both equations, x is the number of units, in thousands, of its product manufactured and sold per month. When the cost of manufacturing the product equals the revenue obtained by selling it, the company breaks even. How many units must the company produce in order to break even?

BUSINESS The cross section of a log is circular. A mill operator wants to cut a beam from the log as shown below. Find the dimensions of each rectangular cross section described below to the nearest tenth of an inch.

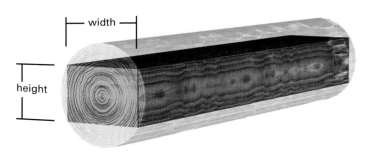

75. Find the dimensions of the cross section if the circular cross section has a 16-inch diameter and the beam's height is $\frac{1}{2}$ its width.

76. Find the dimensions of the cross section if the circular cross section has an 18-inch diameter and the beam's height is $\frac{1}{2}$ its width.

77. Find the dimensions of the cross section if the circular cross section has an 18-inch diameter and the beam's width is 3 times its height.

 Look Back

Find all rational zeros of each polynomial function. *(LESSON 7.5)*

78 $P(x) = x^3 - 8x^2 + 5x + 14$ **79** $P(x) = x^3 + 2x^2 - x - 2$

80 $P(x) = x^4 + x^2 - 2$ **81** $P(x) = x^4 + 7x^2 + 12$

Find all zeros of each polynomial function. *(LESSON 7.5)*

82 $P(x) = x^3 + 4x^2 - 17x - 60$ **83** $P(x) = 2x^3 - 5x^2 + 1$

84 $P(a) = 3a^4 - 5a^3 - 5a^2 - 19a - 6$ **85** $P(a) = 3a^4 - 2a^3 + 8a^2 - 6a - 3$

Simplify. *(LESSON 8.4)*

86. $\dfrac{x}{x+1} + \dfrac{1}{x^2-1}$ **87.** $\dfrac{2}{x(x-2)} - \dfrac{x+1}{x^2-4}$

Solve each radical equation. *(LESSON 8.8)*

88. $\sqrt{x+4} = 2$ **89.** $\sqrt{x-1} = 3\sqrt{x-2}$ **90.** $\sqrt{-x} = 4\sqrt{-x-1}$

Solve each radical inequality. *(LESSON 8.8)*

91. $\sqrt{3x+2} > 5$ **92.** $0 \geq 3\sqrt{x-2} - 2$ **93.** $-6 > 2\sqrt{x-2} - 4$

 Look Beyond

Classify the conic section defined by each equation. Then graph the conic section and describe its graph.

94 $4x^2 + y^2 = 0$ **95** $y^2 = 4$ **96** $x^2 = 4$

97 $y^2 - x^2 = 0$ **98** $(x-1)^2 = (y+1)^2$ **99** $(x-2)^2 + (y+2)^2 = 0$

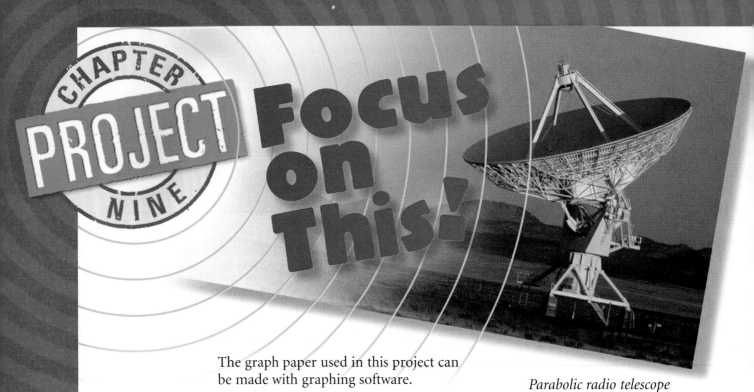

The graph paper used in this project can be made with graphing software.

Parabolic radio telescope in New Mexico

Activity 1 **Parabolas**

The figure at right shows a parabola with its focus at $(0, 1)$ and a directrix of $y = -1$. Equally spaced concentric circles with their center at the parabola's focus enable you to measure distances from the focus. Equally spaced horizontal lines parallel to the parabola's directrix enable you to measure vertical distances from the directrix. This type of graph paper is called focus-directrix graph paper.

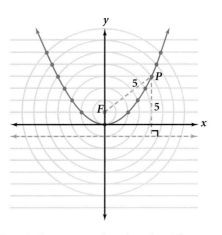

Notice that P is the point of intersection of the circle centered at $(0, 1)$ with a radius of 5 and the horizontal line 5 units above the directrix. Thus, P is equidistant from the focus and directrix. Examine the figure above and note that all points on the parabola are equidistant from the focus and the directrix.

1. Create focus-directrix graph paper with the focus at $(0, 3)$ and a directrix of $y = 3$. Label the focus, directrix, x-axis, and y-axis.
   a. Plot points that are equidistant from the focus and directrix.
   b. Identify the vertex of the resulting parabola.
   c. Identify p as defined for the standard equation of a parabola.
   d. Write the equation of the parabola.

2. Repeat Step 1 with the focus at $(0, -3)$ and a directrix of $y = 3$.

3. Repeat Step 1 with the focus at $(3, 0)$ and a directrix of $x = -3$. This time the focus-directrix graph paper should have concentric circles centered at $(3, 0)$ and vertical lines parallel to the directrix, $x = -3$.

4. Repeat Step 1 with the focus at $(-3, 0)$ and a directrix of $x = 3$.

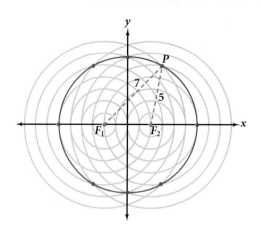

 Ellipses

The figure at right shows an ellipse with foci at $F_1(-2, 0)$ and $F_2(2, 0)$. Equally spaced concentric circles centered at the two foci enable you to measure distances from the foci. This is called focus-focus graph paper.

Notice that P is the point of intersection of the two circles: one circle is centered at F_1 with a radius of 7, and the other circle is centered at F_2 with a radius of 5. Thus, $F_1P + F_2P = 7 + 5 = 12$. Notice that all points on the ellipse satisfy the equation $F_1P + F_2P = 12$.

1. Create focus-focus graph paper with foci at $F_1(-4, 0)$ and $F_2(4, 0)$. Label the foci, x-axis, and y-axis.
  a. Plot points that satisfy the equation $F_1P + F_2P = 10$.
  b. Identify the vertices and co-vertices of the resulting ellipse.
  c. Identify a, b, and c as defined for the standard equation of an ellipse, and find the lengths of the major and minor axes.
  d. Write the standard equation of the ellipse.

2. Repeat Step 1 with the foci at $F_1(0, -4)$ and $F_2(0, 4)$.

 Hyperbolas

The figure below shows a hyperbola with foci at $F_1(-6, 0)$ and $F_2(6, 0)$. Equally spaced concentric circles are centered at the foci. This is also called focus-focus graph paper.

Notice that P is the point of intersection of two circles: one circle is centered at $F_1(-6, 0)$ with a radius of 9, and the other circle is centered at $F_2(6, 0)$ with a radius of 5. Thus, $|F_1P - F_2P| = |9 - 5| = 4$. Notice that all points on the hyperbola satisfy the equation $|F_1P - F_2P| = 4$.

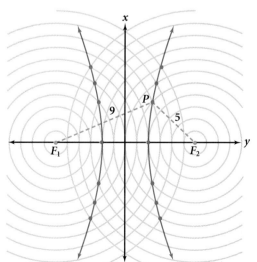

1. Create focus-focus graph paper with foci at $F_1(-5, 0)$ and $F_2(5, 0)$. Label the foci, x-axis, and y-axis.
  a. Plot points that satisfy the equation $|F_1P - F_2P| = 6$.
  b. Identify the vertices and co-vertices of the resulting hyperbola.
  c. Identify a, b, and c as defined for the standard equation of a hyperbola, and find the lengths of the transverse and conjugate axes.
  d. Write equations for the asymptotes of the hyperbola, and sketch them on your graph.
  e. Write the standard equation of the hyperbola.

Chapter Review and Assessment

Key Skills & Exercises

LESSON 9.1

Key Skills

Use the distance and midpoint formulas.

Find the distance between points $P(1, 2)$ and $Q(-3, 5)$.

$$d = \sqrt{(x_2 - x_1)^2 + (y_2 - y_1)^2}$$
$$d = \sqrt{(-3 - 1)^2 + (5 - 2)^2} = \sqrt{25} = 5$$

Find the coordinates of M, the midpoint of $P(1, 2)$ and $Q(-3, 5)$.

$$M\left(\frac{x_1 + x_2}{2}, \frac{y_1 + y_2}{2}\right) = \left(\frac{1 + (-3)}{2}, \frac{2 + 5}{2}\right) = \left(-1, \frac{7}{2}\right)$$

Exercises

Find PQ and the coordinates of M, the midpoint of PQ.

1. $P(0, 4)$ and $Q(3, 0)$
2. $P(2, 7)$ and $Q(10, 13)$
3. $P(-3, 5)$ and $Q(3, 1)$
4. $P(-1, 2)$ and $Q(-6, -8)$
5. $P(11, -9)$ and $Q(-2, -5)$

LESSON 9.2

Key Skills

Find the vertex, focus, and directrix of a parabola. Graph the parabola.

Given $y^2 - 6y - 12x + 57 = 0$, complete the square and write the standard equation of the parabola.

$$x - 4 = \frac{1}{12}(y - 3)^2$$

From the equation, $h = 4$, $k = 3$, and $p = 3$.

The vertex is at $(4, 3)$, the focus is at $(7, 3)$, and the directrix is $x = 1$.

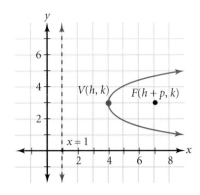

Exercises

Write the standard equation for each parabola. Find the vertex, focus, and directrix. Then sketch the graph.

6. $y = x^2 - 4x$
7. $x - 2 = y^2 - 10y$
8. $y = -2x^2 - 4x + 6$
9. $x^2 + 8x - y + 20 = 0$
10. $4y^2 - 8y - x + 1 = 0$

LESSON 9.3

Key Skills

Find the radius and center of a circle. Sketch the graph.

Given $x^2 + y^2 - 10x + 8y + 5 = 0$, complete the square and write the standard equation of the circle.

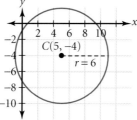

$(x - 5)^2 + (y + 4)^2 = 6^2$

The center is at $(5, -4)$, and the radius is 6.

Exercises

Write the standard equation for each circle. Find the center and radius. Then sketch the graph.

11. $x^2 + y^2 = 100$

12. $3x^2 + 3y^2 = 36$

13. $(x - 1)^2 + (y - 49)^2 = 81$

14. $x^2 + y^2 - 10x + 8y + 5 = 0$

15. $x^2 + y^2 + 8y + 4x - 5 = 0$

LESSON 9.4

Key Skills

Find the coordinates of the center, vertices, co-vertices, and foci of an ellipse. Sketch the graph.

Given $16x^2 + 4y^2 - 96x + 8y + 84 = 0$, complete the square and write the standard equation.

$$\frac{(x - 3)^2}{4} + \frac{(y + 1)^2}{16} = 1$$

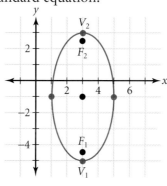

From the equation, $h = 3$, $k = -1$, $a = 4$, $b = 2$, and $c = 2\sqrt{3}$.

center: $(3, -1)$

vertices: $(3, -5)$, $(3, 3)$

co-vertices: $(1, -1)$, $(5, -1)$

foci: $(3, -1 + \sqrt{12})$, $(3, -1 - \sqrt{12})$

Exercises

Write the standard equation for each ellipse. Find the center, vertices, co-vertices, and foci. Then sketch the graph.

16. $\dfrac{(x + 1)^2}{16} + \dfrac{(y - 3)^2}{4} = 1$

17. $\dfrac{(x - 4)^2}{9} + \dfrac{(y + 1)^2}{25} = 1$

18. $25x^2 + 4y^2 = 100$

19. $x^2 + 4y^2 + 10x + 24y + 45 = 0$

20. $16x^2 + 4y^2 - 96x + 8y + 84 = 0$

LESSON 9.5

Key Skills

Find the center, vertices, co-vertices, and foci of a hyperbola. Sketch the graph.

Given $4x^2 - y^2 + 24x + 4y + 28 = 0$, complete the square and write the standard equation.

$$\frac{(x + 3)^2}{1} - \frac{(y - 2)^2}{4} = 1$$

center: $(-3, 2)$

vertices: $(-4, 2)$, $(-2, 2)$

co-vertices: $(-3, 4)$, $(-3, 0)$

foci: $(-3 + \sqrt{5}, 2)$, $(-3 - \sqrt{5}, 2)$

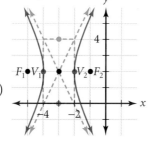

Exercises

Write the standard equation for each hyperbola. Find the center, vertices, co-vertices, and foci. Then sketch the graph.

21. $\dfrac{(x + 5)^2}{36} - \dfrac{(y - 1)^2}{64} = 1$

22. $\dfrac{(y + 5)^2}{4} - \dfrac{(x - 4)^2}{9} = 1$

23. $4y^2 - 25x^2 = 100$

24. $9x^2 - 16y^2 - 90x + 32y + 65 = 0$

25. $36y^2 - 4x^2 + 216y - 40x + 80 = 0$

Key Skills

Solve a system of nonlinear equations.

Use elimination or substitution to solve a
nonlinear system algebraically. Independent
systems of two conic sections can have 0, 1, 2, 3,
or 4 solutions.

Identify a conic section from its equation.

$Ax^2 + Cy^2 + Dx + Ey + F = 0$ represents the
following:

- a parabola if $AC = 0$
- a circle if $A = C$ ($A \neq 0$ and $C \neq 0$)
- an ellipse if $AC > 0$
- a hyperbola if $AC < 0$

Exercises

Solve each system. If there are no real-number
solutions, write *none*.

26. $\begin{cases} 2x^2 + y^2 = 22 \\ x^2 + 3y^2 = 21 \end{cases}$
27. $\begin{cases} 4x^2 + 2y^2 = 20 \\ 3x^2 - 4y^2 = 4 \end{cases}$

28. $\begin{cases} x + y = 5 \\ x^2 + y^2 = 1 \end{cases}$
29. $\begin{cases} y - x = 5 \\ 9x^2 + 16y^2 = 144 \end{cases}$

Classify the conic section defined by each
equation. Write the standard equation of the
conic section, and sketch the graph.

30. $x^2 + y^2 - 2x + 8y - 8 = 0$

31. $4x^2 - 9y^2 - 24x - 18y - 9 = 0$

32. $y^2 - 8y + 4x - 8 = 0$

Applications

33. **PHYSICS** In a 220-volt electric circuit, the available power in watts, W, is
given by the formula $W = 220I - 15I^2$, where I is the amount of current
in amperes. Find the maximum amount of power available in the circuit.

34. **ASTRONOMY** Earth orbits the Sun in an elliptical path with the Sun
at one focus of the ellipse. The closest that Earth gets to the Sun is 91.4
million miles and the farthest it gets is 94.6 million miles. Write an
equation for Earth's orbit around the Sun with the center of the ellipse
at the origin.

35. **BIOLOGY** To locate a whale, two microphones are placed 6000 feet apart
in the ocean. One microphone picks up a whale's sound 0.5 second
after the other microphone picks up the same sound. The speed of
sound in water is about 5000 feet per second.
   a. Find the equation of the hyperbola that describes the possible
   locations of the whale.
   b. What is the shortest distance that the whale could be to either
   microphone?

36. **GEOLOGY** An earthquake transmits its energy in seismic waves that
radiate from its underground focus in all directions. A seismograph
station determines that the earthquake's epicenter (the point on the
Earth's surface directly above the focus) is 100 miles from the
station.
   a. Write the standard equation for the possible locations of the
   epicenter, using (0, 0) as the location of the seismograph station.
   b. A second station is 120 miles east and 160 miles south of the first
   station and 100 miles from the earthquake's epicenter. Write a second
   standard equation for the possible locations of the epicenter.
   c. Find the coordinates of the epicenter by solving the system formed by
   the equations you wrote in parts **a** and **b**.

*Tail of a humpback whale
near Alaska*

Alternative Assessment

Performance Assessment

1. MODELING CONIC SECTIONS Obtain two plastic cones and a large container of water, such as a fish tank. Make a double cone and place the cones in the water in such a way that the surface of the water forms each of the following conic sections on the surface of the cone:

- circle
- ellipse
- hyperbola
- parabola
- point
- line

Then describe how each conic section is formed.

2. CONIC TRANSLATIONS Graph each equation, and describe the translations.

a. $(x - 2)^2 = 8(y + 3)$

b. $\dfrac{(x - 6)^2}{25} + \dfrac{(y + 10)^2}{9} = 1$

c. $\dfrac{(x + 1)^2}{8} - \dfrac{(y - 2)^2}{1} = 1$

d. $(x + 2)^2 + y^2 = 12$

3. NONLINEAR SOLUTIONS

a. Illustrate all of the possible solutions for a system of equations that represents a parabola and a hyperbola. Then write a system of equations for each possibility.

b. Write a nonlinear system that represents a hyperbola and a circle and that has three real-number solutions. Solve your system.

Portfolio Projects

1. SUMMARY CHART Make a summary chart for the parabola, circle, ellipse, and hyperbola. Draw each conic section and label the points discussed in this chapter. Give the standard equation for each conic section, and indicate how the equations differ from one another. Describe the properties of each conic section, and give a real-world application in which each could be used.

2. KEPLER'S LAWS Johannes Kepler (1571–1630) devoted 16 years to finding a mathematical model for the orbits of the planets around the Sun.

a. Research Kepler's three laws of planetary motion and summarize each of them.

b. Describe how the speed of a planet changes as it moves around the Sun.

c. Explain how the change in seasons is related to the orbit of Earth around the Sun.

3. ORBITS OF COMETS The orbits of comets in our solar system can be described by conic sections.

a. Draw the Sun at one focus and a point V as a vertex directly opposite the Sun.

b. Draw two different elliptical orbits around the Sun that pass through V.

c. Draw a parabolic orbit around the Sun that passes through V.

d. Draw a hyperbolic orbit around the Sun that passes through V.

e. Which type of orbit means that a comet will be seen from Earth only once?

---

internetconnect

The HRW Web site contains many resources to reinforce and expand your knowledge of conic sections. This Web site also provides Internet links to other sites where you can find information and real-world data for use in research projects, reports, and activities that involve conic sections. Visit the HRW Web site at **go.hrw.com,** and enter the keyword **MB1 CH9** to access the resources for this chapter.

College Entrance Exam Practice

QUANTITATIVE COMPARISON For Items 1–6, write:
A if the quantity in Column A is greater than the quantity in Column B;
B if the quantity in Column B is greater than the quantity in Column A;
C if the quantities are equal; or
D if the relationship cannot be determined from the given information.

	Column A	Column B	Answers
1.	The value of x		
	$\dfrac{1}{5} = \dfrac{7}{x}$	$\dfrac{-4x}{3} = x - 1$	Ⓐ Ⓑ Ⓒ Ⓓ [Lesson 1.4]
2.	$(-2)^3$	$\left(\dfrac{1}{2}\right)^{-3}$	Ⓐ Ⓑ Ⓒ Ⓓ [Lesson 2.2]
3.	$\log 200$	2	Ⓐ Ⓑ Ⓒ Ⓓ [Lesson 6.5]
4.	$x > 0$		
	$\dfrac{x^2 - 25}{x + 5}$	$x - 1$	Ⓐ Ⓑ Ⓒ Ⓓ [Lesson 8.2]
5.	The distance between the points		
	$(-2, 5)$ and $(-3, 2)$	$(6, -2)$ and $(-1, -4)$	Ⓐ Ⓑ Ⓒ Ⓓ [Lesson 9.1]
6.	The degree of the polynomial function		
	$f(x) = 5x^2 - x^3 + 6x - 1$	$f(x) = 8x(x + 1)^2$	Ⓐ Ⓑ Ⓒ Ⓓ [Lesson 7.1]

7. How many solutions does an independent system of linear equations have?
(LESSON 3.1)
  a. 0   **b.** 1
  c. at least 1   **d.** infinitely many

8. Which statement is true for $f(x) = 3x - 6$ and $g(x) = 12 - 6x$? **(LESSONS 2.4 AND 2.7)**
  a. $f \circ g = g \circ f$ **b.** $2(f \circ g) = g \circ f$
  c. $-2(f \circ g) = g \circ f$ **d.** none of these

9. Evaluate $f(x) = 2x^2 - 9x - 12$ for $x = -2$.
(LESSON 2.3)
  a. 8   **b.** 14   **c.** 2   **d.** −22

10. Which describes the slope of a vertical line?
(LESSON 1.2)
  a. 0   **b.** undefined
  c. negative   **d.** positive

11. For matrices A and B, each with dimensions $m \times n$, which statement is always true?
(LESSONS 4.1 AND 4.2)
  a. $A = B$ **b.** $A + B = B + A$
  c. $AB = BA$ **d.** $A - B = B - A$

12. Solve $7 - \sqrt{4a - 3} = 4$. *(LESSON 8.8)*

   a. 0   **b.** −3   **c.** 3   **d.** $\sqrt{3}$

13. Which equation represents $5^x = 625$ in logarithmic form? *(LESSON 6.3)*

   a. $\log_x 5 = 625$ **b.** $\log_5 625 = x$
   c. $\log_x 625 = 5$ **d.** $\log_{625} x = 5$

14. Which binomial is a factor of $x^3 - 2x^2 - 6x - 3$? *(LESSON 7.3)*

   a. $x - 3$ **b.** $x + 3$
   c. $x + 1$ **d.** $x - 1$

15. Simplify $\dfrac{3 + i}{1 - 3i}$. *(LESSON 5.6)*

   a. $\dfrac{9}{10} + i$ **b.** i

   c. $\dfrac{3}{10} + \dfrac{7}{10}i$ **d.** $\dfrac{3}{5} + i$

16. Which equation defines a circle with its center at $(0, -2)$ and a radius of 5? *(LESSON 9.3)*

   a. $x^2 + (y - 2)^2 = 25$
   b. $x^2 + (y - 2)^2 = 5$
   c. $x^2 + (y + 2)^2 = 25$
   d. $x^2 + (y + 2)^2 = 5$

17. Write an equation in slope-intercept form for the line that contains $(-3, 4)$ and is parallel to $y = -\dfrac{1}{5}x + 2$. *(LESSON 1.3)*

18. Solve the literal equation $A = p + prt$ for p. *(LESSON 1.6)*

19. Use the quadratic formula to solve $x^2 + 4x - 1 = 0$. *(LESSON 5.5)*

20. Solve $\begin{cases} 3x - y = -4 \\ 2x - 3y = 2 \end{cases}$ by graphing.

   (LESSON 3.1)

21. Graph $2y > -1$. *(LESSON 3.3)*

22. Find the determinant of $\begin{bmatrix} 4 & -2 \\ 3 & -1 \end{bmatrix}$.

   (LESSON 4.3)

23. Factor $9x^2 - 18x + 8$, if possible.

   (LESSON 5.3)

24. Write the function for the graph of $f(x) = x^2$ stretched vertically by a factor of 5 and translated 2 units up. *(LESSON 2.7)*

25. Factor $6x^3 - 15x^2 - 4x + 10$, if possible.

   (LESSON 7.3)

26. Write $(x + 2)(x^2 - 3x - 5)$ as a polynomial expression in standard form. *(LESSON 7.3)*

27. Write the standard equation for a circle with its center at $(-5, 4)$ and a radius of 6.

   (LESSON 9.3)

28. Find the domain of $h(x) = \dfrac{3x^2}{-5 + 2x}$.

   (LESSON 8.2)

29. Simplify $\dfrac{3x - 10}{x^2 - 8x + 12} - \dfrac{2}{x - 6}$. *(LESSON 8.4)*

30. Find the domain of $h(x) = \sqrt{5x - 7}$.

   (LESSON 8.6)

FREE RESPONSE GRID The following questions may be answered by using a free-response grid such as that commonly used by standardized-test services.

31. A truck travels 245 kilometers on 35 liters of gasoline. How many kilometers should the truck be able to travel on 100 liters? *(LESSON 1.4)*

32. Evaluate $2^{\log_2 9}$. *(LESSON 6.4)*

33. Solve $10^x = 222$ for x. Round your answer to the nearest hundredth. *(LESSON 6.3)*

34. Find the maximum value of the function $y = -2x^2 + 8x + 4$. *(LESSON 5.1)*

SPORTS A swimmer jumps from a platform that is 10 feet above the water. The vertical height of the swimmer at three different times is given in the table. *(LESSON 5.7)*

Time (s)	Vertical height (ft)
0.0	10
0.5	8
0.75	4

35. Use a quadratic function to predict the time in seconds when the swimmer enters the water.

36. Find the maximum height of the swimmer.

Keystroke Guide for Chapter 9

Essential keystroke sequences (using the model TI-82 or TI-83 graphics calculator) are presented below for all Activities and Examples found in this chapter that require or recommend the use of a graphics calculator.

internetconnect

Keystrokes for other graphics calculator models are found on the HRW Web site.

LESSON 9.1

E X A M P L E ① For part a, graph $y = \sqrt{25 - x^2}$ and $y = -\sqrt{25 - x^2}$ together.

Page 562

Begin with viewing window $[-10, 10]$ by $[-10, 10]$.

Entering {−1, 1} implements the ± sign.

For part b, graph $y = \sqrt{x^2 - 4}$ and $y = -\sqrt{x^2 - 4}$ together.

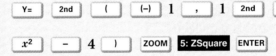

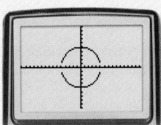

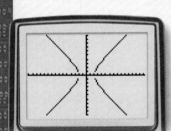

LESSON 9.2

Activity

Page 573

For Steps 1 and 2, graph $y = \frac{1}{4}x^2$ and $y = \frac{1}{4}(x - 2)^2 + 3$ on the same screen, and find the coordinates of the vertices.

Use viewing window $[-10, 10]$ by $[-10, 10]$.

Graph the functions:

Find the vertex:

| 2nd | TRACE (CALC) | 3:minimum | ENTER | (LeftBound?) | ENTER |

(RightBound?) ENTER (Guess?) ENTER

Repeat this keystroke sequence to find the other vertex.

Graph $y = 4 + \sqrt{-8(x-1)}$ and $y = 4 - \sqrt{-8(x-1)}$ together.

Begin with viewing window $[-10, 10]$ by $[-7, 13]$.

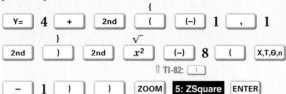

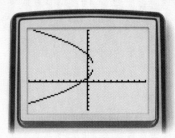

LESSON 9.3

Graph $y = \sqrt{4 - x^2}$ and $y = -\sqrt{4 - x^2}$ together.

Begin with viewing window $[-5, 5]$ by $[-5, 5]$.

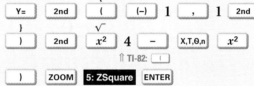

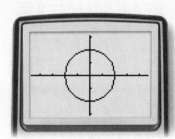

Activity

Graph $x^2 + y^2 = 16$ and $(x + 3)^2 + (y - 2)^2 = 16$ on the same screen, and find the center of each.

Use friendly viewing window $[-9.4, 9.4]$ by $[-6.2, 6.2]$.

Graph the functions:

Solve for y, and use a keystroke sequence similar to that given in Example 1 of Lesson 9.1.

Find the centers:

Use the cursor keys ▲ ▼ ◄ ► to find the approximate coordinates of the center.

LESSON 9.4

Graph $y = \sqrt{9\left(1 - \dfrac{x^2}{25}\right)}$ and $y = -\sqrt{9\left(1 - \dfrac{x^2}{25}\right)}$ together.

Begin with viewing window $[-7, 7]$ by $[-5, 5]$.

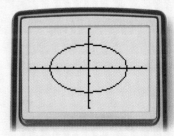

E X A M P L E **1** Graph $y = \sqrt{16\left(1 + \frac{x^2}{9}\right)}$ and $y = -\sqrt{16\left(1 + \frac{x^2}{9}\right)}$ together.

Page 597

Begin with viewing window $[-15, 15]$ by $[-10, 10]$.

Activity

Page 597

Graph $\frac{x^2}{2^2} - \frac{y^2}{3^2} = 1$, $y = \frac{3}{2}x$, and $y = -\frac{3}{2}x$ on the same screen.

Use viewing window $[-10, 10]$ by $[-10, 10]$.

Graph the functions:

Solve for y, and use a keystroke sequence similar to that given in Example 1 of this lesson.

Activity

Page 606

For part a of Step 1, graph $x^2 + y^2 = 25$ and $y = 2x$ on the same screen.

Begin with viewing window $[-10, 10]$ by $[-10, 10]$.

Solve for y, and use a keystroke sequence similar to that given in the Technology example of Lesson 9.3.

For part b of Step 1, graph $x^2 + y^2 = 25$ and $x^2 - y^2 = 9$ on the same screen.

Use viewing window $[-10, 10]$ by $[-10, 10]$.

Solve for y, and use keystroke sequences similar to those given in the Technology example of Lesson 9.3 and in Example 1 of Lesson 9.5.

For parts **c** and **d** of Step 1, use the same viewing window and similar keystroke sequences.

E X A M P L E **1**
Page 607

Graph $y = \sqrt{3x - 1}$, $y = -\sqrt{3x - 1}$, $y = \sqrt{9 - x^2}$, and $y = -\sqrt{9 - x^2}$ on the same screen. Find any points of intersection.

Begin with viewing window $[-5, 5]$ by $[-5, 5]$.

> If equations are not entered separately, it may be difficult to find the intersection points.

Graph the functions:

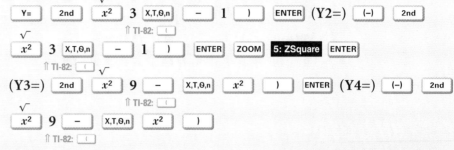

Find any points of intersection:

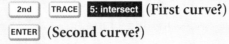

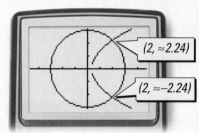

E X A M P L E **3**
Page 609

Graph $y = \sqrt{\dfrac{100 - 4x^2}{25}}$, $y = -\sqrt{\dfrac{100 - 4x^2}{25}}$, $y = \sqrt{9 - x^2}$, and $y = -\sqrt{9 - x^2}$ on the same screen. Find any points of intersection.

Use viewing window $[-6, 6]$ by $[-4, 4]$.

Graph the functions:

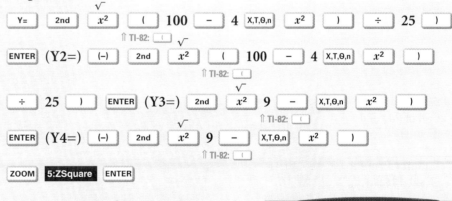

Find any points of intersection:

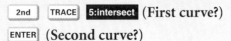

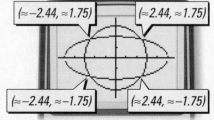

DISCRETE MATHEMATICS
Counting Principles and Probability

PROBABILITY IS THE RELATIVE LIKELIHOOD, or chance, that an event will occur. Some events, such as those shown here, are unlikely, or have a low probability of occurence. In this chapter, you will use the Fundamental Counting Principle to find the number of ways in which an event can occur.

Probability is used in many real-world fields, such as insurance, medical research, law enforcement, and political science.

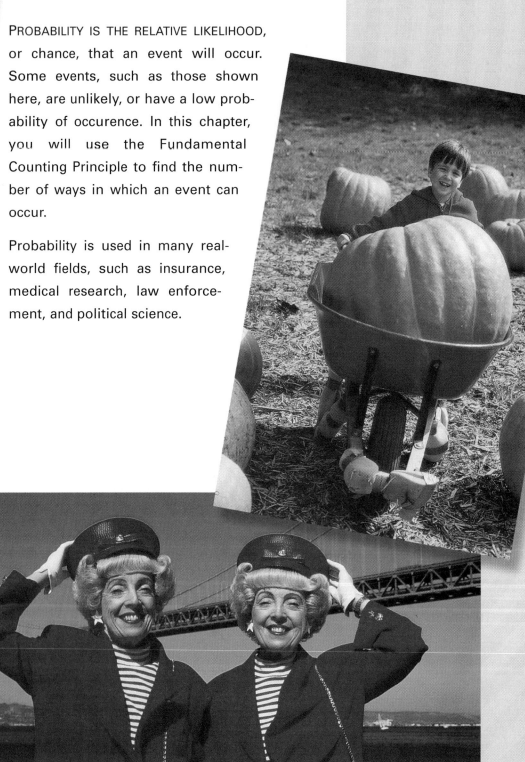

Rubber ducks float down the Singapore River in the Great Duck Race fund-raiser.

About the Chapter Project

Making reasonable predictions about random events plays an important role in decision-making strategies from the simplest problems to the most complex problems. In many situations, the probability of a random event occurring can be determined empirically by observing the number of times the event occurs. When the random event is complex, the actual observation of the event may be impossible. In these cases, simulations are used. In the Chapter Project, *Next, Please . . .*, you will simulate random events and estimate probabilities.

After completing the Chapter Project, you will be able to do the following:

- Set up models that simulate random events.

- Use data from simulations to estimate probabilities.

About the Portfolio Activities

Throughout the chapter, you will be given opportunities to complete Portfolio Activities that are designed to support your work on the Chapter Project.

- You will use a spinner to model the possible outcomes of a geometric probability problem in the Portfolio Activity on page 635.

- You will use a random-number generator to model the possible outcomes of an event in the Portfolio Activity on page 649.

- You will use a random-number generator to model two-event probabilities in the Portfolio Activity on page 658.

Introduction to Probability

Why *Probability is often studied using everyday objects, such as number cubes, coins, and darts.*

Objectives

- Find the theoretical probability of an event.

- Apply the Fundamental Counting Principle.

How do some businesses, such as life insurance companies and gambling establishments, make dependable profits on events that seem unpredictable? The answer is that the overall likelihood, or **probability**, of an event can be discovered by observing the results of a large number of repetitions of the situation in which the event may occur.

The terminology used to discuss probabilities is given below. An example related to rolling a number cube is given for each term.

DEFINITION	EXAMPLE
Trial: a systematic opportunity for an event to occur	rolling a number cube
Experiment: one or more trials	rolling a number cube 10 times
Sample space: the set of all possible outcomes of an event	1, 2, 3, 4, 5, 6
Event: an individual outcome or any specified combination of outcomes	rolling a 3 rolling a 3 *or* rolling a 5

Outcomes are **random** if all possible outcomes are equally likely. Although it is impossible to prove that the result of a real-world event is completely random, some outcomes are often assumed to be random. For example, the results of tossing a coin, the roll of a number cube, the outcome of a spinner, the selection of lottery numbers, and the gender of a baby are often assumed to be random.

Probability is expressed as a number from 0 to 1, inclusive. It is often written as a fraction, decimal, or percent.
- An impossible event has a probability of 0.
- An event that must occur has a probability of 1.
- The sum of the probabilities of all outcomes in a sample space is 1.

In mathematics, the probability of an event can be assigned in two ways: *experimentally* (inductively) or *theoretically* (deductively).

Experimental probability is approximated by performing trials and recording the ratio of the number of occurrences of the event to the number of trials. As the number of trials in an experiment increases, the approximation of the experimental probability improves.

Theoretical probability is based on the assumption that all outcomes in the sample space occur randomly.

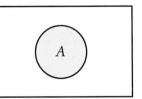

Sample space

Theoretical Probability

If all outcomes in a sample space are equally likely, then the theoretical probability of event A, denoted $P(A)$, is defined by

$$P(A) = \frac{\text{number of outcomes in event } A}{\text{number of outcomes in the sample space}}.$$

E X A M P L E **1** **Find the probability of randomly selecting a red disk in one draw from a container that contains 2 red disks, 4 blue disks, and 3 yellow disks.**

● **SOLUTION**

The event is selecting *1 red disk.*

Because there are 2 red disks, the number of outcomes in the event is 2.

The sample space is the set of all disks, so the total number of outcomes in the sample space is 2 + 4 + 3, or 9.

$$P(1 \text{ red disk}) = \frac{\text{number of outcomes in the event}}{\text{number of outcomes in the sample space}}$$

$$= \frac{2}{9}, \text{ or about } 22\%$$

Thus, the probability of randomly selecting a red disk in one draw is about 22%.

TRY THIS   Find the probability of randomly selecting a blue disk in one draw from a container that contains 2 red disks, 4 blue disks, and 3 yellow disks.

In the next two examples, area models are used to find probabilities for situations in which the number of outcomes in the sample space is infinite, such as with area or time.

E X A M P L E ②

CONNECTION
GEOMETRY

Assume that a dart will land on the dartboard and that each point on the dartboard is equally likely to be hit.

Find the probability of a dart landing in region *A*, the outer ring.

● **SOLUTION**

The event is landing in region *A*.

The sample space consists of all points on the dartboard.

$$P(A) = \frac{\text{area of region } A}{\text{total area}} = \frac{\pi(3)^2 - \pi(2)^2}{\pi(3)^2} = \frac{5\pi}{9\pi} = \frac{5}{9} \approx 0.556$$

The probability of a dart landing in region *A* is about 55.6%.

TRY THIS   Find the probability of a dart landing in region *B* of the dartboard.

E X A M P L E ③

APPLICATION
COMPUTERS

Eduardo logs onto his electronic mail once during the time interval from 1:00 P.M. to 2:00 P.M.

Assuming that all times are equally likely, find the probability that he will log on during each time interval.

a. from 1:30 P.M. to 1:40 P.M.   **b.** from 1:30 P.M. to 1:35 P.M.

● **SOLUTION**

a. The event is the interval from 1:30 P.M. to 1:40 P.M.

The sample space is the interval from 1:00 P.M. to 2:00 P.M.

Divide the sample space into 10-minute intervals to represent the equally likely events.

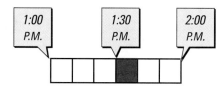

The event is $\frac{1}{6}$ of the sample space. Thus, the probability is $\frac{1}{6}$, or about 16.7%.

b. The event is the interval from 1:30 P.M. to 1:35 P.M.

The sample space is the interval from 1:00 P.M. to 2:00 P.M.

Divide the sample space into 5-minute intervals to represent the equally likely events.

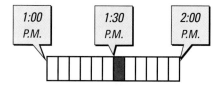

The event is $\frac{1}{12}$ of the sample space. Thus, the probability is $\frac{1}{12}$, or about 8.3%.

TRY THIS   Janice leaves home for work sometime between 7:30 A.M. and 8:00 A.M. Assuming that all times are equally likely, find the probability that she will leave home during each time interval.

a. from 7:30 A.M. to 7:40 A.M.   **b.** from 7:30 A.M. to 7:32 A.M.

In the Activity below, a tree diagram is used to count all possible choices of pizza toppings.

Activity

Investigating Tree Diagrams

You will need: no special tools

A pizza shop offers a special price on a 2-topping pizza. You can choose 1 topping from each of the following groups:
- provolone cheese or extra mozzarella cheese
- pepperoni, sausage, or hamburger

1. Begin a tree diagram with the two cheese choices, as shown at right.

        < provolone
          mozzarella

2. From each cheese choice, extend a line for each meat choice.

3. How many possible different combinations of two toppings are possible?

CHECKPOINT ✔ 4. If the special included a third topping of either onions or green peppers, how would you extend your diagram to show the additional possibilities? How many total 3-topping combinations are there?

There are several ways to determine the size of a sample space for an event that is a combination of two or more outcomes. One way is a tree diagram.

For example, a cafe's lunch special is a hamburger meal. It comes with a choice of beverage (soda or tea) and a choice of salad (garden, potato, or bean). The tree diagram below shows that there are 2 × 3, or 6, choices.

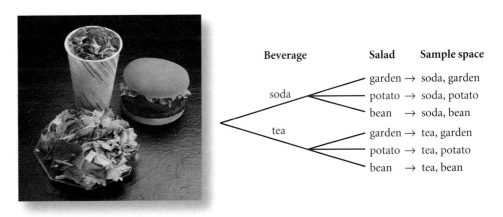

CHECKPOINT ✔ Make a tree diagram with the salad as the first choice and the beverage as the second choice. Does the order in which the choices are made affect the number of possible choices for the lunch special?

Tree diagrams illustrate the *Fundamental Counting Principle*.

Fundamental Counting Principle

If there are *m* ways that one event can occur and *n* ways that another event can occur, then there are *m* × *n* ways that both events can occur.

EXAMPLE 4

APPLICATION
COMPUTERS

Ann is choosing a password for her access to the Internet. She decides not to use the digit 0 or the letter *O*. Each letter or number may be used more than once.

How many passwords of 2 letters followed by 4 digits are possible?

SOLUTION

Use the Fundamental Counting Principle. There are **25** possible letters and **9** possible digits.

1st letter		2nd letter		1st digit		2nd digit		3rd digit		4th digit
25	×	25	×	9	×	9	×	9	×	9

The number of possible passwords for Ann is $25^2 \times 9^4$, or 4,100,625.

EXAMPLE 5

APPLICATION
TRANSPORTATION

A license plate consists of 2 letters followed by 3 digits. The letters, *A–Z*, and the numbers, 0–9, can be repeated.

Find the probability that your new license plate contains the initials of your first and last names in their proper order.

SOLUTION

1. Find the number of outcomes in the event.

	1st letter	2nd letter	1st number	2nd number	3rd number
Number of ways possible →	1 ×	1 ×	10 ×	10 ×	10

2. Find the number of outcomes in the sample space.

	1st letter	2nd letter	1st number	2nd number	3rd number
Number of ways possible →	26 ×	26 ×	10 ×	10 ×	10

3. Find the probability of this event.

$$P(A) = \frac{1 \times 1 \times 10 \times 10 \times 10}{26 \times 26 \times 10 \times 10 \times 10} = \frac{1000}{676,000} = \frac{1}{676} \approx 0.0015$$

Thus, the probability that your new license plate contains the initials of your first and last names is about 0.15%, which is more than 1 in 1000.

Exercises

Communicate

1. Give three examples of an event with more than one outcome.

2. How are theoretical and experimental probabilities similar? different?

3. Explain how an area model can be used to find probabilities.

4. Find the probability of randomly selecting a red marble in one draw from a bag of 5 blue marbles, 3 red marbles, and 1 white marble. *(EXAMPLE 1)*

5. Assume that a dart will land on the dartboard and that each point on the dartboard is equally likely to be hit. Find the probability of a dart landing in region *C*, the inner ring. *(EXAMPLE 2)*

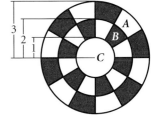

6. Sue logs onto her electronic mail once during the time interval from 7:00 A.M. to 8:00 A.M. Assuming that all times are equally likely, find the probability that she will log on during the interval from 7:30 P.M. to 7:45 P.M. *(EXAMPLE 3)*

7. John is deciding on a password for his access to the Internet. He decides not to use the digit 0 or the letter *Q*. How many possible passwords are there if he uses 2 letters followed by 3 digits? *(EXAMPLE 4)*

8. In a lottery, a 4-digit number from 0000 to 9999 is randomly selected. Find the probability that the number selected begins with 3 and ends in 2 or 0. *(EXAMPLE 5)*

● *Practice and Apply*

A bag contains 3 white cards, 2 black cards, and 5 red cards. Find the probability of each event for one draw.

9. a white card   **10.** a black card   **11.** a red card

Calculate the probability of each event for one roll of a number cube.

12. 1   **13.** 4

14. an even number   **15.** an odd number

16. a number less than 3   **17.** a number greater than 3

18. a number greater than 6   **19.** a number less than 6

A bus arrives at Jason's house anytime from 8:00 A.M. to 8:05 A.M. If all times are equally likely, find the probability that Jason will catch the bus if he begins waiting at the given times.

20. 8:04 A.M.   **21.** 8:02 A.M.   **22.** 8:01 A.M.   **23.** 8:03 A.M.

For Exercises 24 and 25, create a tree diagram that shows the sample space for each event.

24. Involvement in one of each type of extracurricular activity

> Sports: football, soccer, tennis
> Arts: music, painting
> Clubs: science, French

25. Involvement in one of each type of leisure activity

> Outdoor: biking, gardening, rappeling
> Indoor: reading, watching television, playing board games

Find the number of possible passwords (with no letters or digits excluded) for each of the following conditions:

26. 2 digits followed by 3 letters followed by 1 digit

27. 3 digits followed by 2 letters followed by 1 digit

28. 3 letters followed by 3 digits

29. 2 letters followed by 4 digits

The odds in favor of an event are defined as the number of ways the event can happen divided by the number of ways it can fail to happen. If the odds in favor of an event are $\frac{a}{b}$, or a to b, then the probability of the event is $\frac{a}{a+b}$. Find the probability of each event, given the odds in favor of the event.

30. 3 to 8   **31.** 4 to 5   **32.** 3 to 7   **33.** 1 to 20

CONNECTION

GEOMETRY To the nearest tenth of a percent, find or approximate the probability that a dart thrown at the square dartboard at right will land in the regions indicated below.

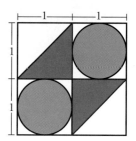

34. one of the circular regions

35. one of the red triangular regions

36. one of the white triangular regions

CHALLENGE

37. one of the white regions

APPLICATIONS

38. PUBLISHING When a book is published, it is assigned a number called an International Standard Book Number (ISBN). The number consists of 10 digits that provide information about the language in which the book is printed, the publisher of the book, the book itself, and a check digit. How many ISBN numbers are possible?

39. ACADEMICS A multiple-choice exam consists of 14 questions, each of which has 4 possible answers. How many different ways can all 14 questions on the exam be answered?

DEMOGRAPHICS The table at right shows the 1993 college enrollment statistics, in thousands, for the United States. Based on this data, find the probability that a randomly selected person enrolled in college in the United States in 1993 is in the given age group. [*Source: Statistical Abstract of the United States, 1996*]

40. 18–24   **41.** 25–29

42. 30–34   **43.** 30 or over

Age	Male	Female
14–17	83	93
18–19	1224	1416
20–21	1294	1414
22–24	1260	1263
25–29	950	1058
30–34	661	811
35 and over	955	1824

44. TRANSPORTATION How many different license plates can be made if each plate consists of 2 letters followed by 2 digits (1 through 9) followed by 3 letters?

 **CHALLENGE**

45. SECURITY A security specialist is designing a code for a security system. The code will use only the letters A, B, and C. If the specialist wants the probability of guessing the code at random to be less than 0.001, how long must the code be?

 *Look Back*

For each function, find an equation of the inverse. Then use composition to verify that the equation you wrote is the inverse. *(LESSON 2.5)*

46. $f(x) = 3x + 10$ **47.** $g(x) = \dfrac{3x - 2}{6}$ **48.** $h(x) = \dfrac{1}{2} - 5x$

For each function, describe the transformations from $f(x) = \sqrt{x}$ to g. Graph each transformation. *(LESSON 8.6)*

49. $g(x) = \dfrac{1}{2}\sqrt{x} - 5$ **50.** $g(x) = 3\sqrt{x - 2}$ **51.** $g(x) = \sqrt{2x} + 1$

 *Look Beyond*

52. When Scott accesses his electronic mail, he enters a 6-symbol code that is a string of letters, numbers, or the 10 symbols which appear at the top of his keyboard (such as !, @, #).
  a. How many codes are possible if uppercase and lowercase letters (such as B and b) are considered the same?
  b. How many codes are possible if uppercase and lowercase letters are considered different?
  c. How long would it take to try all of the codes in part **b** if you could enter one code per second? Give your answer in years.

Refer to Example 3 on page 630. Assuming that all the times are equally likely, you can perform an experiment with a spinner to model the probability that Eduardo logs onto his mail during the time interval from 1:30 P.M. to 1:40 P.M.

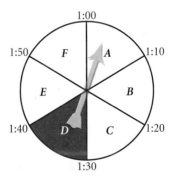

1. Divide a spinner into 6 equal sections, each representing a 10-minute interval. Let region D represent the 10-minute interval from 1:30 P.M. to 1:40 P.M.

2. Spin the spinner 40 times, and record the number of times that the spinner lands in region D.

3. Use your results to estimate the probability that Eduardo logs onto his mail in the interval from 1:30 P.M. to 1:40 P.M.

4. Compare your estimated probability with the theoretical probability obtained in the lesson. How well do you think the spinner models this problem? Explain.

WORKING ON THE CHAPTER PROJECT

You should now be able to complete Activity 1 of the Chapter Project.

Permutations

10.2

Why *There are many situations that involve an ordered arrangement, or permutation, of objects. For example, 12-tone music, developed by Arnold Schoenberg, consists of permutations of all 12 tones in an octave.*

Arnold Schoenberg, 1874–1951

Objectives

- Solve problems involving linear permutations of distinct or indistinguishable objects.

- Solve problems involving circular permutations.

In 12-tone music, pioneered by Arnold Schoenberg, each note of the chromatic scale must be used exactly once before any are repeated. A set of 12 tones is called a *tone row*. How many different tone rows are possible? *You will answer this question in Example 1.*

A **permutation** is an arrangement of objects in a specific order. When objects are arranged in a row, the permutation is called a **linear permutation**. Unless otherwise noted, the term *permutation* will be used to mean *linear permutations*.

PROBLEM SOLVING

ABCD	BACD	CABD	DABC
ABDC	BADC	CADB	DACB
ACBD	BCAD	CBAD	DBAC
ACDB	BCDA	CBDA	DBCA
ADBC	BDAC	CDAB	DCAB
ADCB	BDCA	CDBA	DCBA

Make an organized list. Each of the possible permutations of the letters *A*, *B*, *C*, and *D* are listed in the table at left.

The number of different permutations, 24, can be obtained by using the Fundamental Counting Principle, as shown below.

Number of possible → choices	1st choice		2nd choice		3rd choice		4th choice		
	4	×	3	×	2	×	1	=	24

Thus, there are $4 \times 3 \times 2 \times 1$, or 24, possible arrangements. You can use *factorial notation* to abbreviate this product: $4! = 4 \times 3 \times 2 \times 1 = 24$.

If *n* is a positive integer, then ***n* factorial**, written *n*!, is defined as follows:

$$n! = n \times (n-1) \times (n-2) \times \cdots \times 2 \times 1$$

Note that the value of 0! is defined to be 1.

You can find the number of permutations of any number of objects by using the Fundamental Counting Principle and factorials as follows:

Permutations of *n* Objects

The number of permutations of *n* objects is given by *n*!.

E X A M P L E ❶ In 12-tone music, each of the 12 notes in an octave must be used exactly once before any are repeated. A set of 12 tones is called a tone row.

APPLICATION
MUSIC

How many different tone rows are possible?

SOLUTION

Find the number of permutations of 12 notes.

$$12! = 12 \times 11 \times 10 \times 9 \times 8 \times 7 \times 6 \times 5 \times 4 \times 3 \times 2 \times 1$$
$$= 479{,}001{,}600$$

There are 479,001,600 different tone rows for 12 tones.

TRY THIS How many different ways can the letters in the word *objects* be arranged?

The number of ways that you can listen to 3 different CDs from a selection of 10 CDs is a *permutation of 10 objects taken 3 at a time*.

	1st CD		2nd CD		3rd CD
Number of CDs available →	10	×	9	×	8

By the Fundamental Counting Principle, there are $10 \times 9 \times 8$, or 720, ways that you can listen to 3 different CDs from a selection of 10 CDs.

Permutations of *n* Objects Taken *r* at a Time

The number of permutations of n objects taken r at a time, denoted by $P(n, r)$ or $_nP_r$, is given by $P(n, r) = {}_nP_r = \dfrac{n!}{(n-r)!}$, where $r \leq n$.

Note the use of 0! in calculating the number of permutations of n objects taken n at a time.

$$P(n, n) = {}_nP_n = \frac{n!}{(n-n)!} = \frac{n!}{0!} = n!$$

E X A M P L E ❷ **Find the number of ways to listen to 5 different CDs from a selection of 15 CDs.**

APPLICATION
MUSIC

SOLUTION

Find the number of permutations of 15 objects taken 5 at a time.

$$_{15}P_5 = \frac{15!}{(15-5)!}$$
$$= \frac{15 \times 14 \times 13 \times 12 \times 11 \times \cancel{10!}}{\cancel{10!}}$$
$$= 15 \times 14 \times 13 \times 12 \times 11$$
$$= 360{,}360$$

TRY THIS Find the number of ways to listen to 4 CDs from a selection of 8 CDs.

Exploring Formulas for Permutations

You will need: a calculator

1. **a.** Evaluate $_7P_3$ and $7 \times 6 \times 5$.   **b.** Evaluate $_7P_4$ and $7 \times 6 \times 5 \times 4$.
   c. Evaluate $_7P_5$ and $7 \times 6 \times 5 \times 4 \times 3$.

2. **a.** Write $_7P_r$ as a product.   **b.** Write $_nP_r$ as a product.

CHECKPOINT ✓ 3. Using your answer from part **b** of Step 2, write products to represent $_8P_4$, $_8P_5$, and $_{10}P_8$. Verify your results.

As you have seen, there are 4! permutations of the 4 letters A, B, C, and D. However, if 2 of the 4 letters are identical, as in **OHIO**, there will be less than 4! permutations because arrangements such as O_1HIO_2 and O_2HIO_1 are indistinguishable. To account for the 2 identical letters, divide by 2! because there are 2! ways of arranging the 2 **O**s.

$$\frac{4!}{2!} \quad \begin{matrix} \leftarrow \textit{permutation of 4 objects} \\ \leftarrow \textit{2 identical objects} \end{matrix}$$

Permutations With Identical Objects

The number of distinct permutations of n objects with r identical objects is given by $\frac{n!}{r!}$, where $1 \le r \le n$.

The number of distinct permutations of n objects with r_1 identical objects, r_2 identical objects of another kind, r_3 identical objects of another kind, . . . , and r_k identical objects of another kind is given by $\dfrac{n!}{r_1!r_2!r_3! \cdots r_k!}$

EXAMPLE ③ T'anna is planting 11 colored flowers in a line.

In how many ways can she plant 4 red flowers, 5 yellow flowers, and 2 purple flowers?

● **SOLUTION**

PROBLEM SOLVING

Use the formula for permutations with repeated objects.

$$\frac{11!}{4! \times 5! \times 2!} = \frac{11 \times 10 \times 9 \times 8 \times 7 \times 6 \times 5!}{4! \times 5! \times 2!}$$

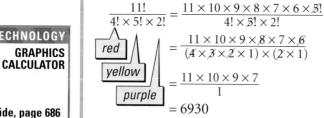

$$= \frac{11 \times 10 \times 9 \times 8 \times 7 \times 6}{(4 \times 3 \times 2 \times 1) \times (2 \times 1)}$$

$$= \frac{11 \times 10 \times 9 \times 7}{1}$$

$$= 6930$$

There are 6930 ways that T'anna can plant the flowers in a line.

TECHNOLOGY
GRAPHICS
CALCULATOR

Keystroke Guide, page 686

TRY THIS In how many ways can T'anna plant 11 colored flowers if 5 are white and the remaining ones are red?

CHECKPOINT ✔ How does the formula for the number of permutations with repeated objects give the number of permutations of n objects when all of the objects are distinct?

CRITICAL THINKING A row of daisies consists of r yellow and s white flowers. In terms of r and s, write a formula for the number of permutations of all of the flowers.

In how many ways can you arrange 4 objects around the edge of a circular tray? The letters A, B, C, and D are arranged in a circle, as shown below. This type of a permutation is called a **circular permutation**.

A	B	C	D
B	C	D	A
C	D	A	B
D	A	B	C

Circular permutations   Linear permutations

Notice that all 4 distinct linear permutations of the letters A, B, C, and D, give a single distinct circular permutation. Therefore, to find the number of *circular permutations* of 4 objects, divide the total number of linear permutations by 4. The result, 3!, is also $(4 - 1)!$, as shown below.

$$\frac{4!}{4} = \frac{4 \times 3 \times 2 \times 1}{4} = 3!$$

Circular Permutations

If n distinct objects are arranged around a circle, then there are $(n - 1)!$ circular permutations of the n objects.

E X A M P L E ❹ In how many ways can 7 different appetizers be arranged on a circular tray as shown at right?

APPLICATION
CATERING

● **SOLUTION**

PROBLEM SOLVING

Use the formula for circular permutations with $n = 7$.

$(n - 1)! = (7 - 1)! = 6! = 720$

There are 720 distinct ways to arrange the appetizers on the tray.

TRY THIS In how many ways can seats be chosen for 12 couples on a Ferris wheel that has 12 double seats?

● Communicate

1. Explain how the Fundamental Counting Principle is used to find the number of permutation of 4 objects.

2. Which number of permutations of 4 letters is greater, 2 at a time or 3 at a time? Explain.

3. Explain why $_4P_4 = {_4P_3}$ is true. Is $_nP_n = {_nP_{n-1}}$ always true? Explain.

4. Does a circular permutation of 5 distinct objects always have fewer arrangements than a linear permutation of 5 distinct objects? Explain.

● Guided Skills Practice

5. How many different ways can the letters in the word *orange* be arranged? **(EXAMPLE 1)**

6. Find the number of ways to watch 3 videos from a selection of 7 videos. **(EXAMPLE 2)**

7. In how many ways can 5 pennies, 2 quarters, and 3 dimes be arranged in a straight line? **(EXAMPLE 3)**

8. In how many ways can 12 different spices be arranged around a circular spice rack? **(EXAMPLE 4)**

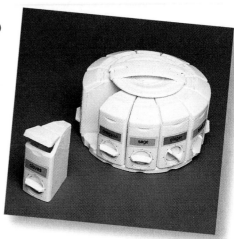

● Practice and Apply

Evaluate each expression.

9. $7! - 5!$ **10.** $6! - 4!$ **11.** $(7 - 5)!$ **12.** $(6 - 4)!$

13. $\dfrac{8!}{3! \times 5!}$ **14.** $\dfrac{10!}{4! \times 6!}$ **15.** $\dfrac{5! \times 0!}{(4-1)!}$ **16.** $\dfrac{(7-2)! \times 3!}{0!}$

17. $_{10}P_7$ **18.** $_7P_3$ **19.** $_{50}P_1$ **20.** $_{1000}P_1$

21. $\dfrac{_{12}P_5}{_6P_5}$ **22.** $\dfrac{_4P_3}{_8P_3}$ **23.** $_4P_2 \times {_7P_7}$ **24.** $_{15}P_5 \times {_5P_5}$

Find the number of permutations of the first 8 letters of the alphabet for each situation.

25. taking 5 letters at a time **26.** taking 3 letters at a time
27. taking 4 letters at a time **28.** taking 6 letters at a time
29. taking 1 letter at a time **30.** taking all 8 letters at a time

In how many ways can 8 new employees be assigned to the following number of vacant offices?

31. 8 **32.** 9 **33.** 10 **34.** 15

In how many ways can a teacher arrange 6 students in the front row of a classroom with the following number of students?

35. 18   **36.** 24   **37.** 28   **38.** 30

Find the number of permutations of the letters in each word.

39. *barley*   **40.** *pencil*   **41.** *trout*

42. *circus*   **43.** *football*   **44.** *vignette*

45. *bookkeeper*   **46.** *Mississippi*   **47.** *correspondence*

48. Five different stuffed animals are to be placed on a circular display rack in a department store. In how many ways can this be done?

49. Seven different types of sunglasses are to be displayed on one level of a circular rack. In how many ways can they be arranged?

50. Franklin High School has 4 valedictorians. In how many different ways can they give their graduation speeches?

51. Suppose that a personal identification number (PIN) consists of 4 digits from 0 through 9.
   a. How many PIN numbers are possible?
   b. How many PIN numbers are possible if no digit can be repeated?

52. In how many different ways can the expression $a^4b^2c^5d$ be written without exponents?

53. A spinner is divided into 8 equal regions to represent the digits 1–8. In how many ways can the digits be arranged?

CHALLENGES

54. In how many different ways can 4 blue counters and 4 red counters be placed in a circle if red and blue counters are alternated?

55. In how many ways can 3 males (Joe, Jerry, and John) and 3 females (Jamie, Jenny, and Jasmine) be seated in a row if the genders alternate down the row?

56. In how many ways can 5 seniors, 3 juniors, 4 sophomores, and 3 freshmen be seated in a row if a senior must be seated at each end? Assume that the members of each class are distinct.

CONNECTION

GEOMETRY Geometric figures are often represented by the letters that identify each vertex. Determine the number of ways that each figure below can be named with the letters *A*, *B*, *C*, *D*, *E*, and *F*. Assume that each figure is irregular.

57. triangle   **58.** quadrilateral

59. hexagon   **60.** pentagon

APPLICATIONS

61. SPORTS In a track meet, 7 runners compete for first, second, and third place. How many different ways can the runners place if there are no ties?

62. SMALL BUSINESS A caterer is arranging a row of desserts. The row will contain 8 platters of cookies, 5 trays of fruit, and 3 pies. In how many distinct ways can the 3 types of desserts, cookies, fruit, and pies, be arranged in a row?

63. SPORTS A basketball team of 5 players is huddled in a circle along with their coach. In how many ways can the players and their coach be arranged in the huddle?

 Look Back

64. NUTRITION You are given the diet information below. *(LESSON 3.5)*

	Food X	Food Y	Total
Carbohydrates	2 units/ounce	3 units/ounce	at least 12 units
Fat	1 unit/ounce	2 units/ounce	at most 16 units
Protein	1 unit/ounce	3 units/ounce	at least 18 units
Cost	$0.20/ounce	$0.25/ounce	

Let x represent the required number of ounces of food X and let y represent the required number of ounces of food Y.
   a. Write the set of constraints and the objective function.
   b. Sketch the feasible region.
   c. Find the minimum cost of a meal with foods X and Y.

Simplify each expression. *(LESSON 5.6)*

65. $(3i - 2) + (5 - 7i)$ **66.** $(-1 + 4i)(2 - i)$ **67.** $\dfrac{-1 - 8i}{2 + 5i}$

68. SMALL BUSINESS The revenue earned from selling x items is given by the revenue function $R(x) = 6x$. The cost of producing x items is given by the cost function $C(x) = -0.1x^2 + 5x + 40$. Find the number of items that must be produced and sold to generate a profit (when revenue exceeds cost). *(LESSON 5.8)*

Write each expression as a single logarithm. Then simplify, if possible. *(LESSON 6.4)*

69. $\log_b 6 + \log_b 2 - \log_b 3$ **70.** $3 \log 5^2 - 2 \log 5^3$

71. $\dfrac{1}{2} \log_2 36 - \log_2 12$ **72.** $8 \log_5 x + \log_5 4$

73. MAXIMUM/MINIMUM A rectangular piece of cardboard measures 12 inches by 16 inches. Find the maximum volume of an open-top box created by cutting squares of the same size from each corner and folding up the sides. *(LESSON 7.3)*

74. Solve the nonlinear system at right. If there is no solution, write *none*. $\begin{cases} y = x^2 + 1 \\ 3x - y = -11 \end{cases}$ *(LESSON 9.6)*

Look Beyond

75. List all of the ways in which 2 of the letters A, B, C, D, and E can be chosen if the order in which letters are chosen is not important, that is, if AB is considered to be the same choice as BA.

76. Find the number of ways in which 2 of 26 letters can be chosen if the order in which letters are chosen is not important.

Combinations

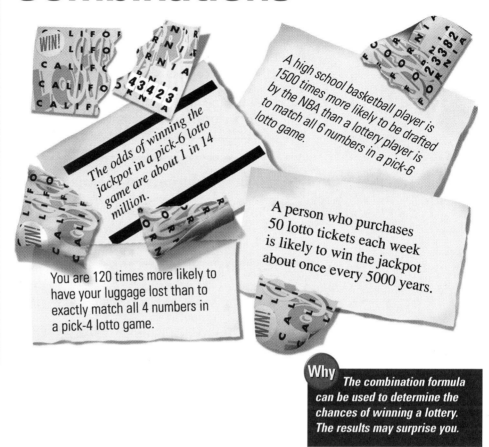

The odds of winning the jackpot in a pick-6 lotto game are about 1 in 14 million.

A high school basketball player is 1500 times more likely to be drafted by the NBA than a lottery player is to match all 6 numbers in a pick-6 lotto game.

A person who purchases 50 lotto tickets each week is likely to win the jackpot about once every 5000 years.

You are 120 times more likely to have your luggage lost than to exactly match all 4 numbers in a pick-4 lotto game.

Objectives

- Solve problems involving combinations.

- Solve problems by distinguishing between permutations and combinations.

Recall from Lesson 10.2 that a permutation is an arrangement of objects in a specific order. An arrangement of objects in which order is *not* important is called a **combination**.

In the Activity below, you can see the distinction between a permutation and a combination and learn how to count combinations.

Activity
Comparing Combinations and Permutations

APPLICATION
LOTTERY

You will need: no special tools

Consider a state lottery in which 3 numbers from 0 to 9 are selected. The numbers are not repeated. A lottery player can choose whether to play *exact match* or *any-order match*.

1. A person selects the numbers 8-4-1 and plays *exact match*. Write all of the ways that winning numbers can be drawn.

2. A person selects the numbers 8-4-1 and plays *any-order match*. Write all of the ways that winning numbers can be drawn.

3. Which has more ways to win: exact match or any-order match?

CHECKPOINT ✔ 4. Explain why the prize is greater for winning with an exact match.

The number of ways to listen to 2 of 5 CDs is $_5P_2 = 5 \times 4 = 20$. If you want to find the number of ways to purchase 2 of 5 CDs, their order does not matter. For example, choosing to purchase CD #1 and then CD #2 is no different than choosing CD #2 and then CD #1 because they are *combined* in the total purchase. To find the number of *combinations* of 2 CDs taken from 5 CDs, divide $_5P_2$ by 2 to compensate for duplicate combinations.

Notice that the formula for $_nC_r$ below is like the formula for $_nP_r$, except that it contains the factor $r!$ to compensate for duplicate combinations.

Combinations of *n* Objects Taken *r* at a Time

The number of combinations of n objects taken r at a time, is given by
$$C(n, r) = {}_nC_r = \binom{n}{r} = \frac{n!}{r!(n-r)!}, \text{ where } 0 \le r \le n.$$

The notations $C(n, r)$, $_nC_r$, and $\binom{n}{r}$ have the same meaning. All are read as "n choose r." In this chapter, we will use the notation $_nC_r$.

EXAMPLE ❶ **Find the number of ways to purchase 3 different kinds of juice from a selection of 10 different juices.**

SOLUTION

The order in which the 3 juices are chosen is not important. Find the number of combinations of 10 objects taken 3 at a time.

$$_{10}C_3 = \frac{10!}{3!(10-3)!}$$
$$= \frac{10 \times 9 \times 8 \times 7!}{3! \times 7!}$$
$$= \frac{10 \times 9^3 \times 8^4}{3 \times 2 \times 1}$$
$$= 10 \times 3 \times 4$$
$$= 120$$

There are 120 ways to purchase 3 different kinds of juice from a selection of 10 different kinds.

TRY THIS Find the number of combinations of 9 objects taken 7 at a time.

CHECKPOINT ✔ Which is larger, $_{10}C_7$ or $_{10}P_7$? Does a given number of objects have more combinations or permutations? Explain.

When reading a problem, you need to determine whether the problem involves permutations or combinations.

EXAMPLE 2 **Use a permutation or combination to answer each question.**

APPLICATION
VOTING

a. How many ways are there to choose a committee of 3 people from a group of 5 people?

b. How many ways are there to choose 3 separate officeholders (chairperson, secretary, and treasurer) from a group of 5 people?

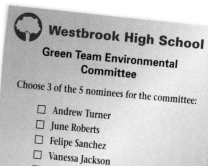

Westbrook High School
Green Team Environmental Committee
Choose 3 of the 5 nominees for the committee:

☐ Andrew Turner
☐ June Roberts
☐ Felipe Sanchez
☐ Vanessa Jackson
☐ Brandon Plummer

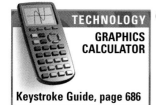

TECHNOLOGY
GRAPHICS CALCULATOR

Keystroke Guide, page 686

● **SOLUTION**

a. The members chosen for the committee will be members regardless of the order in which they are chosen. Find $_5C_3$.

$$_5C_3 = \frac{5!}{3!2!} = \frac{5 \times 4}{2} = 10$$

There are 10 ways to choose a committee of 3 people from a group of 5 people.

b. The officeholders are chosen to fulfill particular positions. Therefore, order is important. Find $_5P_3$.

$$_5P_3 = \frac{5!}{2!} = 5 \times 4 \times 3 = 60$$

There are 60 ways to choose a chairperson, a secretary, and a treasurer from a group of 5 people.

TRY THIS How many ways are there to choose a committee of 2 people from a group of 7 people? How many ways are there to choose a chairperson and a co-chairperson from a group of 7 people?

EXAMPLE 3 **How many different ways are there to purchase 2 CDs, 3 cassettes, and 1 videotape if there are 7 CD titles, 5 cassette titles, and 3 videotape titles from which to choose?**

APPLICATION
SHOPPING

● **SOLUTION**

Consider the CDs, cassettes, and videotapes separately, and apply the Fundamental Counting Principle.

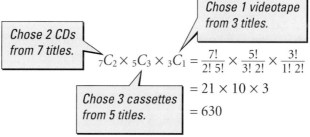

Chose 2 CDs from 7 titles.

Chose 1 videotape from 3 titles.

Chose 3 cassettes from 5 titles.

$$_7C_2 \times _5C_3 \times _3C_1 = \frac{7!}{2!\,5!} \times \frac{5!}{3!\,2!} \times \frac{3!}{1!\,2!}$$
$$= 21 \times 10 \times 3$$
$$= 630$$

There are 630 different ways to make the purchase.

TRY THIS How many different ways are there to purchase 3 CDs, 4 cassettes, and 2 videotapes if there are 3 CD titles, 6 cassette titles, and 4 videotape titles from which to choose?

Using Combinations and Probability

Recall from Lesson 10.1 that you can find the probability of event A by using the following ratio:

$$P(A) = \frac{\text{number of outcomes in event } A}{\text{number of outcomes in the sample space}}$$

In many situations, you can find and evaluate the numerator and the denominator by applying the formula for combinations.

EXAMPLE ④ In a recent survey of 25 voters, 17 favor a new city regulation and 8 oppose it.

APPLICATION
SURVEYS

Find the probability that in a random sample of 6 respondents from this survey, exactly 2 favor the proposed regulation and 4 oppose it.

Survey of 25 people

17 favor	8 oppose
2 of 17	4 of 8

● **SOLUTION**

1. Find the number of outcomes in the event. Use the Fundamental Counting Principle.

$$_{17}C_2 \times {}_8C_4$$

Choose 2 respondents of 17 respondents who favor.

Choose 4 respondents of 8 respondents who oppose.

2. Find the number of outcomes in the sample space.

$$_{25}C_6$$ ◁ *Choose 6 people from the 25 respondents.*

3. Find the probability.

$$\frac{\text{number of outcomes in event } A}{\text{number of outcomes in the sample space}} = \frac{_{17}C_2 \times {}_8C_4}{_{25}C_6} \approx 0.05$$

TECHNOLOGY
GRAPHICS CALCULATOR

Keystroke Guide, page 686

Thus, the probability of selecting exactly 2 respondents who favor the proposed regulation and 4 who oppose it in a randomly selected group of 6 respondents is about 0.05, or 5%.

```
(17 nCr 2)*(8 nCr 4)/(25 nCr 6)
    .0537549407
```

TRY THIS Find the probability that in a random sample of 10 respondents from the above survey, all 10 favor the proposed regulation.

CRITICAL THINKING Sets A and B are two nonoverlapping sets. Set A contains a distinct objects and set B contains b distinct objects. You wish to choose x objects randomly from both set A and set B. Find the probability of choosing r objects from set A and s objects from set B. Are there any restrictions on r and s?

Set A	Set B
a objects	b objects
r	s

Exercises

Communicate

1. Describe the difference between a combination and a permutation. Give examples to illustrate your descriptions.

2. Describe the relationship between $_5P_3$ and $_5C_3$. Then explain how the formula for combinations is related to the formula for permutations.

3. Using the definition of a combination and the values for $_8C_8$ and $_8C_1$, find and describe $_nC_n$ and $_nC_1$ for any whole number n.

Guided Skills Practice

4. Find the number of ways to rent 4 comedy videos from a collection of 9 comedy videos. *(EXAMPLE 1)*

5. Use a permutation or combination to answer each question. *(EXAMPLE 2)*

 a. How many ways are there to choose a committee of 3 from a group of 12 people?

 b. How many ways are there to choose 3 separate officeholders (chairperson, secretary, and treasurer) from a group of 12 people?

6. How many different ways are there to purchase 3 CDs, 4 cassettes, and 2 videotapes if there are 8 CD titles, 5 cassette titles, and 5 videotape titles from which to choose? *(EXAMPLE 3)*

7. A survey of 30 people showed that 19 people favor a new city regulation and that 11 people oppose it. Find the probability that in a random sample of 8 respondents from the survey, exactly 3 favor the proposed regulation and 5 oppose it. *(EXAMPLE 4)*

Practice and Apply

Find the value of each expression.

8. $_7C_4$

9. $_8C_4$

10. $_{10}C_7$

11. $_9C_5$

12. $_9C_1$

13. $_{11}C_1$

14. $_{15}C_{15}$

15. $_{12}C_{12}$

16. $\dfrac{6!}{2!4!} \times \dfrac{5!}{4!1!}$

17. $\dfrac{4!}{3!1!} \times \dfrac{9!}{5!4!}$

18. $\dfrac{_6C_5 \times {}_{15}C_2}{_{21}C_7}$

19. $\dfrac{_{14}C_5 \times {}_9C_7}{_{23}C_{12}}$

Find the number of ways in which each committee can be selected.

20. 3 people from a group of 5

21. 7 people from a group of 8

22. 8 people from a group of 12

23. 6 people from a group of 10

24. How many different 12-member juries can be chosen from a pool of 32 people?

25. A test consists of 20 questions, and students are told to answer 15 of them. In how many different ways can they choose the 15 questions?

A pizza parlor offers a selection of 3 different cheeses and 9 different toppings. In how many ways can a pizza be made with the following ingredients?

26. 1 cheese and 3 toppings   **27.** 1 cheese and 4 toppings
28. 2 cheeses and 4 toppings   **29.** 2 cheeses and 3 toppings

A bag contains 5 white marbles and 3 green marbles. Find the probability of selecting each combination.

30. 1 green and 1 white   **31.** 2 green and 1 white
32. 2 green and 2 white   **33.** 3 green and 2 white

For Exercises 34–38, determine whether each situation involves a permutation or a combination.

34. Four recipes were selected for publication and 302 recipes were submitted.
35. Nine players are selected from a team of 15 to start the softball game.
36. Four out of 200 contestants were awarded prizes of $100, $75, $50, and $25.
37. A president and vice-president are elected for a class of 210 students.
38. The batting order for the 9 starting players is announced.

39. **a.** Find the number of different 5-card hands that can be dealt from a standard deck of 52 playing cards.
     b. Find the probability that 4 kings and a queen are randomly drawn from a standard deck of 52 playing cards.

CHALLENGE

40. Use the formula for $_nC_r$ to verify each statement below.
     a. $_nC_n = 1$ for all positive integer values of n
     b. $_nC_1 = n$ for all positive integer values of n
     c. $_nC_0 = 1$ for all positive integer values of n
     d. $_nC_r = {_nC_{n-r}}$ for all positive integer values of n and r, where $0 \leq r \leq n$
     e. Give an intuitive explanation for your answers to parts **a–d**.

41. **CULTURAL CONNECTION: ASIA** Around 600 B.C.E. in the Vedic period of Indian history, a writer named Sushruta found all combinations of the 6 different tastes: bitter, sour, salty, astringent, sweet, and hot. How many total combinations of the tastes are possible when taken 1 at a time, 2 at a time, etc?

APPLICATION

42. **HEALTH** From a group of 10 joggers and 15 nonjoggers, a university researcher will choose 5 people to participate in a study of heart disease.
     a. In how many ways can this be done if it does not matter how many of those chosen are joggers and how many are nonjoggers?
     b. In how many ways can this be done if exactly 3 joggers must be chosen?
     c. Find the probability that exactly 3 of the 5 people randomly selected from the group are joggers.

43. LOTTERY In many lotteries, contestants choose 6 out of 50 numbers (without replacement).

Event (applies to U.S. population)	Experimental probability
Undergo an audit by the IRS this year	$\frac{1}{100}$
Being hit by lightning	$\frac{1}{9100}$
Being hit by a baseball in a major league game	$\frac{1}{300,000}$

[*Source: Les Krantz,* What the Odds Are, *Harper Perennial, 1992*]

a. Find the probability of winning this kind of lottery with one set of numbers.

b. Determine how many times more likely than winning the lottery it is for each of the events in the table at left to occur.

 *Look Back*

BUSINESS A movie theater charges $5 for adults and $3 for children. The theater needs to sell at least $2500 worth of tickets to cover expenses. Graph the solution for each situation below. *(LESSON 3.3)*

44. The theater fails to sell at least $2500 worth of tickets.
45. The theater breaks even, selling exactly $2500 worth of tickets.
46. The theater makes a profit, selling more that $2500 worth of tickets.

Graph the solution to each inequality. *(LESSON 5.8)*

47. $y \leq x^2 - 5$ **48.** $y \geq (x + 1)^2$ **49.** $y < (x - 1)^2 + 3$

 Look Beyond

50. A governor appointed 5 department heads from a group of people that consisted of 8 acquaintances and 22 others. Assuming that all choices are equally likely, find the probability of each event below.
  a. All 5 were acquaintances.
  b. Exactly 4 of the 5 were acquaintances.
  c. At least 3 of the 5 were acquaintances.

Refer to Example 4 on page 646. Assign numbers from 1 to 25 to the survey respondents. Let the numbers from 1 to 17 represent the people who favor the new city regulation, and let the numbers from 18 to 25 represent the people who oppose it.

1. Generate 6 random integers from 1 to 25 inclusive. (Refer to page 687 of the Keystroke Guide.) This represents a random sample of 6 respondents. Repeat this generation of 6 random integers for a total of 30 trials. Record the outcomes.

2. For the 30 trials, count the total number of times that exactly 2 of the 6 random integers were between 1 and 17 inclusive. Use your outcomes to approximate the probability

that exactly 2 of the 6 respondents chosen favor the proposed regulation.

3. Compare your approximate probability with the theoretical probability obtained in the lesson. How well do you think the random-number generator models this problem? Explain.

WORKING ON THE CHAPTER PROJECT

You should now be able to complete Activity 2 of the Chapter Project.

Let's Make a Deal

You have reached the final round of a TV game show called *Let's Make a Deal*. Behind one of the three numbered doors is a new car. Behind each of the other two doors is a goat. You have chosen door number 1. The host, Monty Hall, knows what's behind each door. He opens door number 3 to show you a goat.

Behind one of these doors is a new car.

Should you stick with number 1 or switch to number 2?

Then he pops the question: "Do you want to change your mind?"

What would you do? Would you stick with door number 1 or switch to door number 2?

Many contestants faced such a dilemma on the show, which ran for over 25 years. In 1990, a question based on this situation was submitted to a columnist, Marilyn vos Savant, who is reported to have the highest IQ in the world.

BY MARILYN VOS SAVANT

Ask Marilyn®

Suppose you're on a game show, and you're given the choice of three doors: Behind one door is a car; behind the others, goats. You pick a door, say No. 1, and the host, who knows what's behind the doors, opens another door, say No. 3, which has a goat. He then says to you, "Do you want to pick door No. 2?" Is it to your advantage to switch your choice?

—Craig F. Whitaker, Columbus, Md.

Yes; you should switch. The first door has a one-third chance of winning, but the second door has a two-thirds chance. Here's a good way to visualize what happened. Suppose there are a million doors, and you pick door No. 1. Then the host, who knows what's behind the doors and will always avoid the one with the prize, opens them all except door #777,777. You'd switch to that door pretty fast, wouldn't you?

By permission of Parade, copyright ©1990

Nearly a year later, an article in the *New York Times* reported that Marilyn vos Savant had received about 10,000 letters in response to her answer. Most of the letters disagreed with her. Many came from mathematicians and scientists with arguments like this:

...You blew it! Let me explain: If one door is shown to be a loser, that information changes the probability of either remaining choice—neither of which has any reason to be more likely—to ½. As a professional mathematician, I'm very concerned with the general public's lack of mathematical skills. Please help by confessing your error and, in the future, being more careful...

Cooperative Learning

1. Before you analyze the problem in detail, explain which strategy you think is best and why.

2. Make three cards (two goats, one car) to model the situation. Try 10 games in which you stick with your choice. Then try 10 games in which you switch. Compare the results.

3. Make a table with the column headings shown, and complete it using all possible options. According to your table, should you switch? Explain.

4. Suppose that you wrote the response for Marilyn vos Savant's column. How would you answer the question about the game show?

Door with car	Door you choose	Door you are shown	Result if you switch	Result if you stick
1	1	2 or 3	Lose	Win
1	2	3	Win	Lose
1				
2				
⋮				

Using Addition With Probability

DRAMA CLUB

Objectives

- Find the probabilities of mutually exclusive events.

- Find the probabilities of inclusive events.

Why *You can often use addition to determine the probability of two or more events occurring.*

The drama, mathematics, and jazz clubs at Gloverdale High School have 32 members, 33 members, and 39 members, respectively. Some club members belong to more than one club, as indicated in the diagram at right. What is the probability that a randomly selected club member belongs to at least two clubs? *You will answer this question in Example 3.*

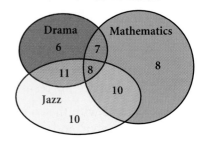

Events that can occur at the same time are called **inclusive events.** For example, a student can belong to more than one club at the same time.

Events that cannot occur at the same time are called **mutually exclusive events.** For example, if you flip a coin, you cannot get *both* heads and tails.

Activity
Exploring Two-Event Probabilities

You will need: a pair of number cubes, preferably of two different colors

1. Copy and complete the following table by rolling two number cubes 10 times:

Toss	1st cube	2nd cube	Sum	Product
1				
2				
3				
⋮				

2. Using your 10 trials, copy and complete the table of experimental probabilities for each pair of events listed below.

	a.	b.	c.
$P(A)$			
$P(B)$			
$P(A \text{ or } B)$			
$P(A) + P(B)$			

  a. Let A be the event that the first cube is a 6 and let B be the event the first cube is a 3.

  b. Let A be the event that the first cube is a 6 and let B be the event that the sum is 7.

  c. Let A be the event that the sum is less than 5 and let B be the event that the product is greater than 5.

CHECKPOINT ✔ **3.** Based on your results, does $P(A \text{ or } B) = P(A) + P(B)$? When can you be sure that this statement is true?

Mutually exclusive events and inclusive events are illustrated below with a number cube.

Mutually exclusive events	**Inclusive events**
Let A represent an even number.	Let A represent an even number.
 $P(A) = \frac{3}{6}$	 $P(A) = \frac{3}{6}$
Let B represent 3.	Let C represent 4.
$P(B) = \frac{1}{6}$	 $P(C) = \frac{1}{6}$
$P($an even number *or* 3$)$	$P($an even number *or* 4$)$
$P(A \text{ or } B)$	$P(A \text{ or } C)$

Because A and B are mutually exclusive events, you can add $P(A)$ and $P(B)$ to find $P(A \text{ or } B)$.

$$P(A \text{ or } B) = \frac{3}{6} + \frac{1}{6} = \frac{4}{6}, \text{ or } \frac{2}{3}$$

Because A and C are inclusive events, you must *subtract* $P(A \text{ and } C)$ from the sum of $P(A)$ and $P(C)$ to find $P(A \text{ or } C)$.

$$P(A \text{ or } C) = \frac{3}{6} + \frac{1}{6} - \frac{1}{6} = \frac{3}{6}, \text{ or } \frac{1}{2}$$

A or B, exclusive

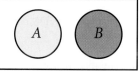

Sample space

A or B, inclusive

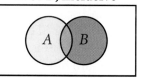

Sample space

Probability of *A or B*

Let A and B represent events in the same sample space.

If A and B are mutually exclusive events, then
$$P(A \text{ or } B) = P(A) + P(B).$$

If A and B are inclusive events, then
$$P(A \text{ or } B) = P(A) + P(B) - P(A \text{ and } B).$$

CHECKPOINT ✔ Which formula for $P(A \text{ or } B)$ can be used with any events A and B in the same sample space? Why?

	Men	Women	Total
Favor	18	9	27
Oppose	12	25	37
No opinion	20	16	36
Total	50	50	100

E X A M P L E ❶ In a survey about a change in public policy, 100 people were asked if they favor the change, oppose the change, or have no opinion about the change. The responses are indicated at right.

A P P L I C A T I O N
SURVEYS

Find the probability that a randomly selected respondent to the survey opposes *or* has no opinion about the change in policy.

SOLUTION

The events "oppose" and "no opinion" are mutually exclusive events.

$P(\text{oppose or no opinion}) = P(\text{oppose}) + P(\text{no opinion})$

$$= \frac{37}{100} + \frac{36}{100}$$

$$= \frac{73}{100}, \text{ or } 73\%$$

The probability that a respondent opposes the change *or* has no opinion is 73%.

TRY THIS Find the probability that a randomly selected respondent to this survey favors *or* has no opinion about the change in policy.

E X A M P L E ❷ Refer to the survey results given in Example 1.

A P P L I C A T I O N
SURVEYS

Find the probability that a randomly selected respondent to the survey is a man *or* opposes the change in policy.

SOLUTION

The events "man" and "opposes" are inclusive events.

$P(\text{man or opposes}) = P(\text{man}) + (\text{opposes}) - P(\text{man and opposes})$

$$= \frac{50}{100} + \frac{37}{100} - \frac{12}{100}$$

$$= \frac{75}{100}, \text{ or } 75\%$$

The probability that a respondent is a man *or* opposes the change is 75%.

TRY THIS Find the probability that a randomly selected respondent to this survey is a woman *or* has no opinion about the change in policy.

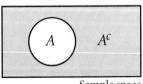

Sample space

The **complement** of event A consists of all outcomes in the sample space that are not in A and is denoted by A^c. For example, let A be the event "favor." Then the complement A^c is the event "oppose" *or* "no opinion." Conversely, if A is the event "oppose" *or* "no opinion," then A^c is the event "favor." The sum of the probabilities of all of the outcomes in a sample space is 1. Thus, $P(A) + P(A^c) = 1$.

CHECKPOINT ✔ Refer to the survey results given in Example 1. Let A be the event "favor." Verify that $P(A) + P(A^c) = 1$ is true.

654 CHAPTER 10

Probability of the Complement of *A*

Let *A* represent an event in the sample space.

$$P(A) + P(A^c) = 1 \qquad P(A) = 1 - P(A^c) \qquad P(A^c) = 1 - P(A)$$

CRITICAL THINKING

Let *A* be any event in a sample space. Why is $P(A \text{ or } A^c) = P(A) + P(A^c)$ true? Explain how this equation leads to the equations in the box above.

E X A M P L E ❸

APPLICATION
EXTRACURRICULAR ACTIVITIES

The drama, mathematics, and jazz clubs have 32 members, 33 members, and 39 members, respectively.

Find the probability that a randomly selected club member belongs to at least two clubs.

● **SOLUTION**

Let *A* represent membership in exactly one club. Then A^c represents membership in two or three clubs.

$$P(A^c) = 1 - P(A)$$
$$P(A^c) = 1 - \frac{6 + 8 + 10}{60}$$
$$= \frac{36}{60}$$
$$= 0.6$$

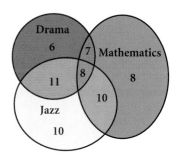

The probability that a randomly selected club member belongs to at least two clubs is 60%.

TRY THIS

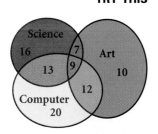

The science, art, and computer clubs have 45 members, 38 members, and 54 members, respectively. Some club members belong to more than one club, as indicated in the diagram at left. Find the probability that one of these club members selected at random will belong to more than one club.

Exercises

● *Communicate*

1. Explain the meaning of mutually exclusive events and of inclusive events. Give examples of each.

2. Describe how to find the complement of the event "rolling 1" *or* "rolling 2" on a number cube.

3. Explain how to find the probability of "rolling an odd number" *or* "rolling 3" on a number cube.

Guided Skills Practice

For Exercises 4 and 5, refer to the results of the survey about a change in public policy given on page 654.

4. Find the probability that a randomly selected respondent to the survey favors *or* opposes the change in policy. *(EXAMPLE 1)*

5. Find the probability that a randomly selected respondent to the survey is a man *or* favors the change in policy. *(EXAMPLE 2)*

APPLICATION

6. EDUCATION The economics, computer, and anatomy classes have 28 students, 29 students, and 24 students, respectively. Some students are taking more than one of these classes, as indicated in the diagram at right. Find the probability that a randomly selected student from these classes is taking at least two of the classes. *(EXAMPLE 3)*

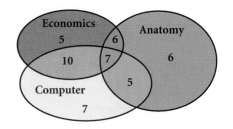

Practice and Apply

A number cube is rolled once, and the number on the top face is recorded. Find the probability of each event.

7. 5 *or* 6

8. 1 *or* 4

9. even *or* 3

10. odd *or* 2

11. less than 4 *or* 1

12. greater than 2 *or* 6

13. not 1

14. not even

15. even *or* odd

The table at right shows all of the possible outcomes of rolling two number cubes. Using the table, state whether the events in each pair below are inclusive or mutually exclusive. Then find the probability of each pair of events.

(1, 1)	(1, 2)	(1, 3)	(1, 4)	(1, 5)	(1, 6)
(2, 1)	(2, 2)	(2, 3)	(2, 4)	(2, 5)	(2, 6)
(3, 1)	(3, 2)	(3, 3)	(3, 4)	(3, 5)	(3, 6)
(4, 1)	(4, 2)	(4, 3)	(4, 4)	(4, 5)	(4, 6)
(5, 1)	(5, 2)	(5, 3)	(5, 4)	(5, 5)	(5, 6)
(6, 1)	(6, 2)	(6, 3)	(6, 4)	(6, 5)	(6, 6)

16. a sum of 2 *or* a sum of 4

17. a sum of 8 *or* a sum of 12

18. a sum of less than 3 *or* a sum of greater than 5

19. a sum of less than 7 *or* a sum of greater than 8

20. a sum of greater than 2 *or* a sum of greater than 6

21. a sum of less than 3 *or* a sum of less than 10

22. a sum of greater than 4 *or* a sum of less than 7

23. a sum of greater than 5 *or* a sum of less than 8

24. a product of greater than 8 *or* a product of less than 6

25. a product of greater than 16 *or* a product of less than 9

26. a product of greater than 6 *or* a product of less than 8

27. a product of greater than 9 *or* a product of less than 16

28. **a.** How many integers from 1 to 600 are divisible by 2 or by 3?
   b. Find the probability that a random integer from 1 to 600 is divisible by neither 2 nor 3.

29. **a.** How many integers from 1 to 3500 are divisible by 5 or by 7?
   b. Find the probability that a random integer from 1 to 3500 is divisible by neither 5 nor 7.

For Exercises 30–35, use the given probability to find $P(E^c)$.

30. $P(E) = \frac{1}{3}$ **31.** $P(E) = \frac{4}{11}$ **32.** $P(E) = 0.782$

33. $P(E) = 0.324$ **34.** $P(E) = 0$ **35.** $P(E) = 1$

Find the probability of each event.

36. 2 heads *or* 2 tails appearing in 2 tosses of a coin

37. 3 heads *or* 2 tails appearing in 3 tosses of a coin

38. at least 2 heads appearing in 3 tosses of a coin

39. at least 3 heads appearing in 4 tosses of a coin

CHALLENGE **40.** A number cube is rolled 3 times. Find the probability of getting at least one 4.

41. In a group of 300 people surveyed, 46 like only cola A, 23 like only cola B, 18 like only cola C, 80 like both colas A and B, 66 like both colas A and C, 45 like both colas B and C, and 12 like all three colas. Find the probability that a randomly selected person from this survey likes none of these colas.

CONNECTION **42.** **GEOMETRY** A circle with a radius of 3 and a 6×6 square are positioned inside a 10×10 square so that the top edge of the 6×6 square forms a diameter of the circle, as shown at right. A point inside the 10×10 square is selected at random. Find the probability of each event below.
   a. The point is within the circle.
   b. The point is within the 6×6 square.
   c. The point is within the 6×6 square *and* within the circle.
   d. The point is within the 6×6 square *or* within the circle.

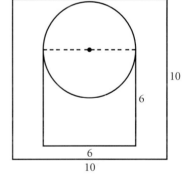

APPLICATION **POLITICS** The table shows the composition of the 106th Congress of the United States (1999–2001) according to political party.

Find the probability that a randomly selected member of Congress is the following:

43. a House Democrat *or* a Senate Republican

44. a House Republican *or* a Senate Democrat

45. a Democrat *or* a Senator

46. a Republican *or* a Senator

	Democrat	Republican	TOTAL
House	211	222	433
Senate	45	55	100
Total	266	267	533

Independent Events

Objective

● Find the probability of two or more independent events.

Why *You can use the probability of independent events to find many interesting probabilities, such as the probability that two people at a party have the same birthday.*

In a group of 35 individuals, what is the probability that 2 or more individuals have the same birth month and day? *You will answer this question in Example 3.*

To answer this question, you need to know how to identify *independent* and *dependent events* and how to find probabilities of independent events. In the Activity below, you will investigate independent events.

Investigating Independent Events

You will need: no special tools

1. Let event *A* be the outcome of tossing heads on a coin. Find *P*(*A*).

2. Let event *B* be the outcome of rolling a 3 on a number cube. Find *P*(*B*).

3. Does event *A* have an effect on event *B*? Does event *B* have an effect on event *A*? Explain.

4. List all of the possible combinations for tossing a coin and rolling a number cube. Find the probability that both event *A* *and* event *B* occur, or *P*(*A and B*).

5. Find *P*(*A*) × *P*(*B*). Does *P*(*A and B*) equal *P*(*A*) × *P*(*B*)?

6. Let even *C* be the outcome of rolling an odd number on a number cube. Find *P*(*C*).

7. Find *P*(*A and C*) by using your list from Step 4. Does *P*(*A and C*) equal *P*(*A*) × *P*(*C*)?

CHECKPOINT ✔
8. What can you say about the probability that two events will both occur if they have no effect on one another?

Two events are **independent** if the occurrence or non-occurrence of one event has no effect on the likelihood of the occurrence of the other event. For example, tossing two coins is an example of a pair of independent events. If one event does affect the occurrence of the other event, the events are **dependent**.

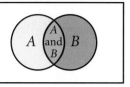
Sample space

Probability of Independent Events

Events A and B are independent events if and only if
$P(A \text{ and } B) = P(A) \times P(B)$. Otherwise, A and B are dependent events.

E X A M P L E ① Bag A contains 9 red marbles and 3 green marbles. Bag B contains 9 black marbles and 6 orange marbles.

Find the probability of selecting one green marble from bag A and one black marble from bag B in one draw from each bag.

SOLUTION

Bag A

$P(\text{green marble}) = \dfrac{3}{9+3} = \dfrac{3}{12} = \dfrac{1}{4}$

Bag B

$P(\text{black marble}) = \dfrac{9}{9+6} = \dfrac{9}{15} = \dfrac{3}{5}$

The events are independent.

$$P(\text{green marble } and \text{ black marble}) = \dfrac{1}{4} \times \dfrac{3}{5} = \dfrac{3}{20}$$

The probability of selecting a green marble from bag A and a black marble from bag B in one draw from each bag is 0.15, or 15%.

E X A M P L E ② Two seniors, one from each government class, are to be randomly selected to travel to Washington, D.C. John is in a class of 18 students, and Peter is in another class of 20 students.

Find the probability that both John and Peter will be selected.

SOLUTION

Event A
The probability that John will be chosen is $\dfrac{1}{18}$.
Event B
The probability that Peter will be chosen is $\dfrac{1}{20}$.
Events A and B are independent events.

$$P(A \text{ and } B) = P(A) \times P(B)$$
$$= \dfrac{1}{18} \times \dfrac{1}{20} = \dfrac{1}{360},$$
$$\text{or about } 0.003$$

The probability that both John and Peter will be selected is about 0.3%.

WASHINGTON, D.C.

The formula for the probability of independent events can be extended to 3 or more events. For example, the probability of obtaining 3 heads in 3 tosses of a coin is $\frac{1}{2} \times \frac{1}{2} \times \frac{1}{2} = \frac{1}{8} = 0.125$, or 12.5%.

CRITICAL THINKING

Find the probability of obtaining 4 heads in 4 tosses of a coin. Write a formula for the probability of obtaining n heads in n tosses of a coin.

EXAMPLE ③

Refer to the birthday problem described at the beginning of the lesson.

What is the probability that in a group of 35 people, 2 or more people have the same birth month and day?

APPLICATION
ENTERTAINMENT

● **SOLUTION**

PROBLEM SOLVING

Change your point of view. Use the complementary event, which is that all birthdays are different. Use 365 days for a year (ignoring leap years).

The first person's birthday can be any day.	$\frac{365}{365}$
The second person's birthday cannot be the same day.	$\frac{364}{365}$
The third person's birthday cannot be the same day as either the first or the second person's.	$\frac{363}{365}$

Continue this pattern for all 35 individuals. The probability that all individuals have different birthdays is as follows:

$$P(\text{different birthday}) = \frac{365}{365} \times \frac{364}{365} \times \frac{363}{365} \times \cdots \times \frac{331}{365} \approx 0.19$$

Find the probability that 2 or more individuals have the same birthday.

$$P(\text{same birthday}) = 1 - P(\text{different birthday})$$
$$\approx 1 - 0.19 \approx 0.81$$

The probability that 2 or more individuals have the same birth month and day is about 81%.

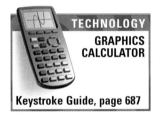

TECHNOLOGY
GRAPHICS CALCULATOR

Keystroke Guide, page 687

TRY THIS

What is the probability that in a group of 45 people, 2 or more people have the same birth month and day?

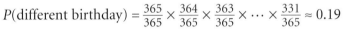

Exercises

● *Communicate* ━━━━━━━━━━━━━━━━━━━━

1. Give an example of independent events and of dependent events.

2. Explain how to find the probability of two independent events occurring.

3. Explain the difference between mutually exclusive events and independent events. Give an example.

4. Bag A contains 5 black marbles and 5 white marbles. Bag B contains 1 green marble and 2 red marbles. Find the probability of selecting a black marble from bag A and a green marble from bag B in two draws. *(EXAMPLE 1)*

5. Two students, one from each science class, are to be randomly selected to attend a national science conference. Melinda is in a class of 22 students, and Seth is in another class of 19 students. Find the probability that both Melinda and Seth will be selected. *(EXAMPLE 2)*

6. What is the probability that in a group of 40 people, 2 or more people have the same birth month and day? *(EXAMPLE 3)*

● *Practice and Apply* ▬▬▬▬▬▬▬

Events *A*, *B*, *C* and *D* are independent, and *P*(*A*) = 0.5, *P*(*B*) = 0.25, *P*(*C*) = 0.75, and *P*(*D*) = 0.1. Find each probability.

7. $P(A \text{ and } B)$ 8. $P(A \text{ and } C)$ 9. $P(C \text{ and } B)$

10. $P(C \text{ and } D)$ 11. $P(A \text{ and } D)$ 12. $P(B \text{ and } D)$

Use the definition of independent events to determine whether the events below are independent or dependent.

13. the event *even* and the event *2 or 4* on one roll of a number cube

14. the event *even* and the event *1 or 4* on one roll of a number cube

15. the event *less than 5* and the event *6* on one roll of a number cube

16. the event *greater than 3* and the event *4* on one roll of a number cube

Refer to the spinner shown below in which each numbered section is exactly $\frac{1}{8}$ of the circle. Find the probability of each event in three spins of the spinner.

17. All three numbers are 3 *or* greater than 5.

18. All three numbers are 4 *or* less than 6.

19. Exactly one number is 5 *or* less than 7.

20. Exactly one number is 8 *or* greater than 3.

21. Suppose that the probability of Kevin coming to a party is 80% and the probability of Judy coming to a party is 95%. Assuming that these events are independent, what is the probability that they both will come to a party?

22. The integers 1 through 15 are written on slips of paper and placed into a box. One slip is selected at random and put back into the box, and then another slip is chosen at random.
   a. What is the probability that the number 8 is selected both times?
   b. What is the probability that the number 8 is selected exactly once? (Hint: Find the probability that an 8 is selected on the first or second draw, but not on *both* draws.)

CHALLENGE

APPLICATIONS

23. TRAVEL An airline's records show
that its flights from Los Angeles to
Dallas arrive on schedule 92% of
the time. They also show that its
flights from Dallas to Miami leave
on schedule 97% of the time. If
you fly from Los Angeles to Miami
with a connection through Dallas,
what is the probability that you
will arrive at Dallas and leave from
Dallas at your scheduled times?

A passenger checking flight information

SECURITY Suppose that a security system consists of four components: a
motion detector, a glass-break detector, magnetic door and window contacts,
and a video camera. The probabilities of escaping detection by each of the
four devices are 0.2, 0.3, 0.4, and 0.6, respectively. Assume that all of the
components act independently.

24. What is the probability that a thief can get past the magnetic contacts and
the video camera?

25. What is the probability that a thief can get past the glass-break detector
and the motion detector?

26. What is the probability that a thief can get past all four components?

Look Back

Simplify each expression. Assume that no variable equals zero.
(LESSON 2.2)

27. $(x^{-2}y^3)^2(3xy^0)^3$ **28.** $(2x^2y^{-2})^{-3}(-x^2y)^3$ **29.** $\left(\dfrac{3x^2y^{-2}}{5x^2y}\right)^2$

30. Find the maximum and minimum values of the objective function
$C = 2x + 3y$ given the constraints $\begin{cases} y \geq x \\ y \leq 5 \\ x \geq 0 \end{cases}$. *(LESSON 3.5)*

**Solve each equation for x. Round your answers to the nearest
hundredth.** *(LESSONS 6.5 AND 6.6)*

31. $e^x = 3$ **32.** $5^x = 11$ **33.** $e^{x+1} = 9$

**Write the standard equation of the parabola with the given
characteristics.** *(LESSON 9.2)*

34. vertex: $(3, 2)$ **35.** vertex: $(1, 0)$ **36.** directrix: $x = -4$
      focus: $(4, 2)$ directrix: $y = 4$ focus: $(3, 0)$

Look Beyond

37. Three coins are tossed. What is the probability of 3 heads appearing given
the conditions below?
    a. All three coins are regular, fair coins.
    b. One of the three coins is a two-headed coin.
    c. Two of the three coins are two-headed coins.

Dependent Events and Conditional Probability

Why *Conditional probability applies to many real-world situations in which the probability of one event is affected by the occurrence of another event.*

Objective

- Find conditional probabilities.

APPLICATION
HEALTH

The ELISA test is used to screen donated blood for the presence of HIV antibodies. When HIV antibodies are present in the blood tested, ELISA gives a positive result 98% of the time. When HIV antibodies are not present in the blood tested, ELISA gives a positive result 7% of the time, which is called a *false positive*.

Suppose that 1 out of every 1000 units of donated blood actually contains HIV antibodies. What is the probability that a positive ELISA result is accurate? *You will answer this question in Example 4.*

To solve the problem above, you need to calculate a *conditional probability*. The Activity below will help you understand conditional probabilities.

Activity
Exploring Conditional Probability

You will need: no special materials

Suppose that you select a card at random from a standard deck of playing cards. (Note: In a standard deck of 52 playing cards, 12 cards are face cards, and 4 of the face cards are kings.)

1. Find the probability that the card drawn is a king.

2. Find the probability that the card drawn is a king if you know that the card is a face card.

3. Find the probability that the card drawn is a king if you know that 2 queens were previously removed from the deck.

4. Find the probability that the card drawn is a king if you know that 2 kings were previously removed from the deck.

CHECKPOINT ✔ 5. How does what you know in Steps 2 and 3 affect the resulting probabilities? How does what you know in Step 4 affect the resulting probability? Describe how probabilities can be affected by knowledge of a previous event.

Knowing the outcome of one event can affect the probability of another event.

EXAMPLE ❶ The band at Villesdale High School has 50 members, and the student council has 20 members. Five student council members are also in the band. Suppose that a student is randomly selected from these two groups.

APPLICATION
EXTRACURRICULAR
ACTIVITIES

Find the probability that the student is a member of the band if you know that he or she is on the student council.

SOLUTION

Because the student is on the student council, the sample space is 20 members.

$$P(\text{band, given council}) = \frac{5}{20} = \frac{1}{4}$$

Thus, the probability that the student is also a member of the band is 25%.

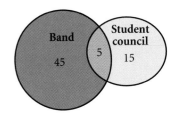

If a marble is selected from a bag of marbles and replaced and then a second marble is selected, the two selections are independent events. On the other hand, if a marble is selected from a bag of marbles and a second marble is selected *without* replacing the first marble, the second selection is a dependent event. That is, the probability of the second event changes, depending on the outcome of the first event.

EXAMPLE ❷ **A bag contains 9 red marbles and 3 green marbles. For each case below, find the probability of randomly selecting a red marble on the first draw and a green marble on the second draw.**

    a. The first marble is replaced.   **b.** The first marble is not replaced.

SOLUTION

a. If the first marble is replaced before the second marble is selected, then the events are independent.

$$P(\text{red}) = \frac{9}{9 + 3} = \frac{9}{12} = \frac{3}{4}$$

$$P(\text{green}) = \frac{3}{9 + 3} = \frac{3}{12} = \frac{1}{4}$$

$$P(\text{red } and \text{ green}) = \frac{3}{4} \times \frac{1}{4} = \frac{3}{16}$$

The probability is $\frac{3}{16}$, or 18.75%.

b. If the first marble is *not* replaced before the second marble is selected, then the size of the sample space for the second event changes from 12 to 11.

$$P(\text{red}) = \frac{9}{9 + 3} = \frac{9}{12} = \frac{3}{4}$$

$$P(\text{green}) = \frac{3}{8 + 3} = \frac{3}{11}$$

$$P(\text{red } and \text{ green}) = \frac{3}{4} \times \frac{3}{11} = \frac{9}{44}$$

The probability is $\frac{9}{44}$, or about 20.5%.

The probability of event *B*, given that event *A* has happened (or will happen), is called *conditional probability*.

Conditional Probability

The **conditional probability** of event *B*, given event *A*, denoted by $P(B|A)$, is given by $P(B|A) = \frac{P(A \text{ } and \text{ } B)}{P(A)}$, where $P(A) \neq 0$.

✔ Use the conditional probability formula to verify the solution in Example 1.

Using the Multiplication Property of Equality, the conditional probability formula $P(B|A) = \frac{P(A \text{ and } B)}{P(A)}$ can be rewritten as $P(A) \times P(B|A) = P(A \text{ and } B)$. You can use this form to verify the solutions in Example 2, as shown below.

Independent Events	Dependent Events
The first marble is replaced.	The first marble is not replaced.
Event A: red first	Event A: red first
Event B: green second	Event B: green second
$P(A) \times P(B|A) = P(A \text{ and } B)$	$P(A) \times P(B|A) = P(A \text{ and } B)$
$\frac{3}{4} \times \frac{1}{4} = \frac{3}{16}$	$\frac{3}{4} \times \frac{3}{11} = \frac{9}{44}$

CHECKPOINT ✔ Explain why $P(B|A) = P(B)$ if A and B are independent events.

E X A M P L E ③

APPLICATION
CONTEST

In a school contest, a class (sophomore, junior, or senior) will be selected according to the probabilities listed at right. Then a student from that class will be randomly selected. The distribution of the possible contest winners is shown in the table.

$P(\text{sophomore}) = \frac{1}{4}$

$P(\text{junior}) = \frac{1}{4}$

$P(\text{senior}) = \frac{1}{2}$

Find the probability that a girl is selected.

	Girls	Boys	Total
Sophomores	10	13	23
Juniors	7	4	11
Seniors	9	5	14

● **SOLUTION**

To find the probability that a girl from any of these classes is selected, find the sum of probabilities of selecting a sophomore girl, a junior girl, and a senior girl.

Use the formula $P(A \text{ and } B) = P(A) \times P(B|A)$.

$P(\text{sophomore and girl}) = P(\text{sophomore}) \times P(\text{girl}|\text{sophomore})$
$$= \frac{1}{4} \times \frac{10}{23} = \frac{5}{46}$$

$P(\text{junior and girl}) = P(\text{junior}) \times P(\text{girl}|\text{junior})$
$$= \frac{1}{4} \times \frac{7}{11} = \frac{7}{44}$$

$P(\text{senior and girl}) = P(\text{senior}) \times P(\text{girl}|\text{senior})$
$$= \frac{1}{2} \times \frac{9}{14} = \frac{9}{28}$$

Then add.

$$P(\text{girl}) = \frac{5}{46} + \frac{7}{44} + \frac{9}{28} = 0.589$$

The probability that a girl will be selected is about 58.9%.

TRY THIS Let $P(\text{sophomore}) = \frac{1}{6}$, $P(\text{junior}) = \frac{1}{3}$, and $P(\text{senior}) = \frac{1}{2}$ and let the distribution of the possible winners remain as shown in Example 3. Find the probability that a boy is selected.

EXAMPLE ④

APPLICATION
HEALTH

Refer to the donated blood problem from the beginning of the lesson.

What is the probability that a positive ELISA result for a unit of donated blood is accurate?

● SOLUTION

PROBLEM SOLVING

Draw a tree diagram to show each possibility.

$$P(A) \quad \times \quad P(B|A) \quad = \quad P(B \text{ and } A)$$

Unit of blood
- 0.001 antibodies
  - 0.98 → ELISA + → 0.00098
  - 0.02 → ELISA − → 0.00002
- 0.999 no antibodies
  - 0.07 → ELISA + → 0.06993
  - 0.93 → ELISA − → 0.92907

(Total: 1.0)

Use the formula for conditional probability.

$$P(\text{antibodies present}|\text{ELISA +}) = \frac{P(\text{antibodies present } and \text{ ELISA +})}{P(\text{ELISA +})}$$

$$= \frac{0.00098}{0.00098 + 0.06993}$$

$$= 0.014$$

Thus, the probability that a positive ELISA result is accurate is only about 1.4%. This surprising result is because most positive ELISA results are *false positives*.

TRY THIS

Refer to Example 4. Suppose that 75 out of every 1000 units of donated blood are contaminated, instead of 1 out of every 1000 units. What is the probability that a positive ELISA result is accurate?

CRITICAL THINKING

If 1 out of every 1000 units of donated blood is contaminated, what is the probability that a negative ELISA result is accurate? Which do you feel is more important, an accurate negative result or an accurate positive result? Why?

Exercises

● *Communicate*

1. Explain what the notation $P(B|A)$ represents.

2. Describe the difference between $P(A \text{ and } B)$ and $P(B|A)$.

3. Explain why $P(B|A) = 0$ if A and B are mutually exclusive events.

LESSON 10.6   DEPENDENT EVENTS AND CONDITIONAL PROBABILITY   **667**

4. The band at Washington High School has 25 members, and the pep club has 18 members. Five students belong to both groups. Find the probability that a student randomly selected from these two groups is a member of the band if you know that he or she is in the pep club. *(EXAMPLE 1)*

A bag contains 12 blue disks and 5 green disks. For each case below, find the probability of selecting a green disk on the first draw *and* a green disk on the second draw. (EXAMPLE 2)

5. The first disk is replaced.   **6.** The first disk is *not* replaced.

7. Refer to the table on page 666 about the student body and the respective probabilities for each class. Use the method shown in Example 3 to find the probability that a boy is selected. *(EXAMPLE 3)*

8. HEALTH Refer to Example 4. Suppose that 5 out of every 1000 units of donated blood are contaminated with HIV antibodies. Find the probability that a positive ELISA result for a unit of donated blood is *not* accurate. *(EXAMPLE 4)*

● *Practice and Apply*

A bag contains 8 red disks, 9 yellow disks, and 5 blue disks. Two consecutive draws are made from the bag *without* replacement of the first draw. Find the probability of each event.

9. red first, red second   **10.** yellow first, yellow second

11. red first, blue second   **12.** blue first, red second

13. red first, yellow second   **14.** yellow first, red second

15. yellow first, blue second   **16.** red first, blue second

Two number cubes are rolled, and the first cube shows a 5. Find the probability of each event below for the two cubes.

17. a sum of 9   **18.** two odd numbers   **19.** a sum of 7 or 9

For one roll of a number cube, let *A* be the event "even" and let *B* be the event "2." Find each probability.

20. a. $P(A)$ **b.** $P(A \ and \ B)$ **c.** $P(B|A)$

21. a. $P(B)$ **b.** $P(B \ and \ A)$ **c.** $P(A|B)$

For one roll of a number cube, let *A* be the event "odd" and let *B* be the event "1 *or* 3." Find each probability.

22. a. $P(A)$ **b.** $P(A \ and \ B)$ **c.** $(B|A)$

23. a. $P(B)$ **b.** $P(B \ and \ A)$ **c.** $P(A|B)$

24. Given $P(A \ and \ B) = \frac{1}{4}$ and $P(A) = \frac{1}{2}$, find $P(B|A)$.

25. Given $P(A \ and \ B) = 0.38$ and $P(A) = 0.57$, find $P(B|A)$.

26. Given $P(B|A) = \frac{1}{3}$ and $P(A) = \frac{1}{2}$, find $P(A \ and \ B)$.

27. Given $P(B|A) = 0.27$ and $P(A) = 0.76$, find $P(A \ and \ B)$.

28. Given $P(B|A) = 0.87$ and $P(A \ and \ B) = 0.75$, find $P(A)$.

29. Given $P(B|A) = \frac{3}{5}$ and $P(A \ and \ B) = \frac{1}{2}$, find $P(A)$.

GEOMETRY A point is randomly selected in the 10×10 square at right. Find the probability of each event.

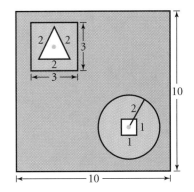

30. **a.** The point is inside the triangle.
  b. The point is inside the triangle, given that it is within the 3×3 square.

31. **a.** The point is inside the 1×1 square.
  b. The point is inside the 1×1 square, given that it is inside the circle.

DEMOGRAPHICS The table below gives data from a survey on marital status in the United States for 1995.

Age	Number of persons (in thousands)				
	Total in age group	Never married	Married	Widowed	Divorced
18 to 19	7016	6643	357	2	13
20 to 24	18,142	13,372	4407	17	347
25 to 29	19,401	8373	9913	23	1090
30 to 34	21,988	5186	14,645	80	2077
35 to 39	22,241	3649	15,664	155	2773
40 to 44	20,094	2271	14,779	205	2838
45 to 54	30,694	2173	23,465	808	4248
55 to 64	20,756	961	15,640	1680	2474
65 to 74	18,214	750	12,120	4045	1299
75 and older	13,053	561	5670	6346	473
Total	191,599	43,939	116,660	13,361	17,632

[*Source: Statistical Abstract of the United States, 1996*]

Suppose that a person were chosen at random from the population in 1995. Find the probability of each event.

32. The person is married, given that the person is 20 to 24 years old.

33. The person is married, given that the person is 20 to 29 years old.

34. The person is divorced, given that the person is 20 to 29 years old.

35. The person is divorced, given that the person is 30 to 39 years years old.

36. The person has never been married, given that the person is 20 to 29 years old.

37. The person has never been married, given that the person is 30 to 44 years old.

APPLICATIONS

38. ADVERTISING Suppose that 20% of a newspaper's readers see an ad for a new product. If 9% of the readers who see the ad purchase the product, what is the probability that a newspaper reader sees the ad and purchases the product?

39. Market research indicates that 77% of all computer owners buy their computers in an electronics store as opposed to a department or general merchandise store. Furthermore, 41% of all computer owners buy their computers and software from electronics stores. If Frances purchased a computer in an electronics store and is interested in buying software, what is the probability that he will buy it in an electronics store?

40. HEALTH Suppose that for a particular test, 97% of people who have the illness test positive and 98% of people who do not have the illness test negative. If the probability of having the illness is 0.004, find each probability.
    a. that a positive test result is inaccurate
    b. that a positive test result is accurate

CHALLENGE

41. On 3 tosses of a coin, 2 were heads. What is the probability that the first toss was heads?

 *Look Back*

Solve each equation. *(LESSON 1.8)*

42. $|x - 4| = 9$ **43.** $|3x| - 6 = -2$ **44.** $|3 - 4x| = 21$

45. Factor $72x - 24x^2 + 2x^3$, if possible. *(LESSON 5.3)*

46. Factor $x^4 - 81$ completely. *(LESSON 5.3)*

47. Use the quadratic formula to solve $a^2 - 5a - 2 = 0$. *(LESSON 5.5)*

48. Find the zeros of the polynomial function $f(x) = x^3 - 7x^2 + 7x + 15$. *(LESSON 7.5)*

Find the domain of each radical function. *(LESSON 8.6)*

49. $f(x) = \sqrt{3x - 3}$ **50.** $f(x) = \sqrt{3(x - 3)}$ **51.** $f(x) = \sqrt{4 - 3(x + 1)}$

Find PQ and the coordinates of M, the midpoint of $\overline{PQ}$. Give exact answers and approximate answers to the nearest hundredth when appropriate. *(LESSON 9.1)*

52. $P(3, -4)$ and $Q(-2, -5)$ **53.** $P(-2, 7)$ and $Q(-8, 2)$

54. Classify the conic section defined by $16x^2 + 4y^2 - 96x + 8y + 84 = 0$. Write the standard equation for this conic section and sketch the graph. *(LESSON 9.6)*

APPLICATION

55. VOTING A 3-person committee is to be elected from a group of 6 boys and 4 girls. If each person has an equal chance of being elected, find the probability that the elected committee consists of 2 boys and 1 girl. *(LESSON 10.3)*

 *Look Beyond*

56. Show that $_5C_0 + {}_5C_1 + {}_5C_2 + {}_5C_3 + {}_5C_4 + {}_5C_5 = 2^5$.

57. Show that $_6C_6 + {}_6C_5 + {}_6C_4 + {}_6C_3 + {}_6C_2 + {}_6C_1 = 2^6 - 1$.

CHALLENGE

58. Prove that $_nC_r + {}_nC_{r+1} = {}_{n+1}C_{r+1}$ is true for all integers r and n, where $0 \leq r \leq n$.

Experimental Probability and Simulation

Objective

- Use simulation methods to estimate or approximate the experimental probability of an event.

Why *Simulations can be used to estimate probabilities. For example, you can use a simulation to estimate the probability that a family with 3 children has all boys or all girls.*

Recall from Lesson 10.1 that the experimental probability of an event is approximated by performing trials and recording the ratio of the number of occurrences of the event to the number of trials.

Exploring Experimental Probability

You will need: a coin

You can model, or *simulate*, two random events with coin tosses. Let H, heads, represent a female and let T, tails, represent a male. Each trial will represent a family with three children. Assume that genders are random.

Follow the steps below to investigate *P*(all males *or* all females).

1. Toss a coin three times, and record the outcomes, such as HTH or HHH, as a single trial. Perform 10 trials for the experiment. Find the number of occurrences of the event "TTT *or* HHH." What is the ratio of this number to the total number of trials?

2. Repeat Step 1 four more times.

3. Find the total number of occurrences of the event "TTT *or* HHH" in all five experiments. What is the ratio of this number to the total number of trials in all five experiments? (Let this be called the *average ratio*.)

4. Find the theoretical probability of the event "TTT *or* HHH."

5. Compare the experimental probability ratios that you obtained in each experiment with the theoretical probability. Compare your *average ratio* from Step 3 with the theoretical probability.

CHECKPOINT ✔ 6. Which of your ratios is closest to the theoretical probability? Compare your results with those of your classmates. Make a generalization about the value of experimental probability ratios as the number of trials in an experiment increases.

Recall from Lesson 10.1 that as the number of trials in an experiment increases, the results will more closely approximate the actual probability.

One way to perform large numbers of trials is to use *simulation*. A **simulation** is a reproduction or representation of events that are likely to occur in the real world. Simulations are especially useful when actual trials would be difficult or impossible.

This lesson will concentrate on the use of *random-number generators* to perform simulations.

E X A M P L E ❶

APPLICATION

TRANSPORTATION

Traffic analysts counted the number of motorists out of 200 that went in each direction at an intersection. The results are shown in the table below.

Straight	63
Left	89
Right	48

Use a simulation to estimate the probability that 3 or more out of 5 consecutive motorists will turn right.

● **SOLUTION**

1. Copy the table, and add a third column. In the third column, write numbers from 1 to 200 according to the number of motorists recorded for each direction.

Straight	63	1–63	← *The first 63 numbers*
Left	89	64–152	← *The next 89 numbers*
Right	48	153–200	← *The last 48 numbers*

2. Each trial will represent 5 consecutive motorists.

Generate 5 random integers from 1 to 200 inclusive. Categorize each resulting number as a motorist who goes straight, turns left, or turns right.

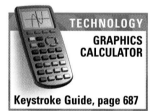

TECHNOLOGY

GRAPHICS CALCULATOR

Keystroke Guide, page 687

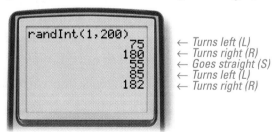

randInt(1,200)
          75   ← *Turns left (L)*
         180   ← *Turns right (R)*
          55   ← *Goes straight (S)*
          85   ← *Turns left (L)*
         182   ← *Turns right (R)*

Trial	Result
1	LRSLR
2	LSLLS
3	LLSRR
4	SRRLR
5	LSLRL
6	RSRRR
7	LSLLS
8	RLSLL
9	LRRRS
10	SLSSR

3. Perform 10 trials, and record your results in a table such as the one shown at right.

4. Estimate the probability.

In this experiment, there are 3 trials in which 3 or more motorists turned right.

The estimated probability is $\frac{3}{10}$.

EXAMPLE **2**

An airline statistician made the table at right for customer arrivals per minute at a ticket counter during the time period from 11:00 A.M. to 11:10 A.M. In the table, X represents the number of customers that may arrive at the counter during a one-minute interval, and $P(X)$ represents the probability of X customers arriving during that one-minute interval. For example, the probability that 5 customers arrive during a given minute is 0.189, or 18.9%.

X	$P(X)$
0	0.006
1	0.034
2	0.101
3	0.152
4	0.193
5	0.189
6	0.153
7	0.137
8	0.035

Find a reasonable estimate of the probability that 50 or more customers arrive at the counter between 11:00 A.M. and 11:10 A.M. inclusive.

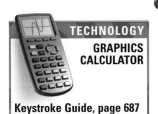

TECHNOLOGY
GRAPHICS
CALCULATOR

Keystroke Guide, page 687

SOLUTION

1. Copy the probability table and add a new column labeled *Random numbers*. In this column, write numbers from 1 to 1000 according to the given values of $P(X)$.

   For example:
   $P(X) = 0.006$: first 6 numbers, 1–6
   $P(X) = 0.034$: next 34 numbers, 7–40
   $P(X) = 0.101$: next 101 numbers, 41–141

X	$P(X)$	Random numbers
0	0.006	1–6
1	0.034	7–40
2	0.101	41–141
3	0.152	142–293
4	0.193	294–486
5	0.189	487–675
6	0.153	676–828
7	0.137	829–965
8	0.035	966–1000

2. Generate 10 random integers from 1 to 1000 inclusive. The results of the first trial are 684, 461, 145, 947, 832, 521, 302, 250, 947, and 926.

Trial	Total number of customers
1	53
2	40
3	55
4	42
5	62
6	32
7	45
8	58
9	64
10	29

Use the table to find the corresponding number of customers that arrived for this trial.

$$6, 4, 3, 7, 7, 5, 4, 3, 7, 7$$

Add these numbers together to find the total number of customers for this 10-minute interval.

$$6 + 4 + 3 + 7 + 7 + 5 + 4 + 3 + 7 + 7 = 53$$

3. Perform 10 trials, and record your results as shown at left.

4. For this simulation, there were 50 or more customers in 5 out of 10 trials, so an estimate of the probability is $\frac{5}{10}$, or $\frac{1}{2}$.

Using a Geometric Simulation

You can also use simulations to analyze geometric probability problems.

EXAMPLE

CONNECTION

GEOMETRY

3 Suppose that 3 darts are thrown at the dartboard at right and that any point on the board is equally likely to be hit.

Use a simulation to estimate the probability that exactly 2 of the 3 darts land in ring B.

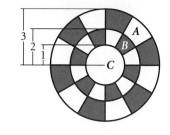

SOLUTION

1. Find the probability of a dart landing in region A (the outer ring), B (the inner ring), and C (the circle).

$$P(A) = \frac{\text{area of region } A}{\text{area of dartboard}} = \frac{9\pi - 4\pi}{9\pi} = \frac{5}{9}$$

> The area of a circle is πr^2.

$$P(B) = \frac{\text{area of region } B}{\text{area of dartboard}} = \frac{4\pi - \pi}{9\pi} = \frac{3}{9} = \frac{1}{3}$$

$$P(C) = \frac{\text{area of region } C}{\text{area of dartboard}} = \frac{\pi}{9\pi} = \frac{1}{9}$$

2. Make a table of the probabilities and their respective random integers from 1 to 9 inclusive.

Probability	Random numbers
$P(A) = \frac{5}{9}$	1, 2, 3, 4, 5
$P(B) = \frac{3}{9}$	6, 7, 8
$P(C) = \frac{1}{9}$	9

TECHNOLOGY

GRAPHICS CALCULATOR

Keystroke Guide, page 687

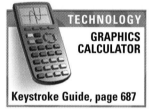

3. Generate a trial of 3 random integers. The results of the first trial are 1, 8, and 3. Therefore, there were 2 hits in region A (1 and 3), 1 hit in region B (8), and 0 hits in region C.

4. Perform 10 trials, and record your results as shown in the table at right.

5. In 4 of the 10 trials, exactly 2 darts landed in region B, so an estimate of the probability is $\frac{4}{10}$, or $\frac{2}{5}$.

Trial	Result
1	1 in B
2	2 in B
3	0 in B
4	3 in B
5	2 in B
6	1 in B
7	2 in B
8	1 in B
9	0 in B
10	2 in B

TRY THIS Refer to the dartboard in Example 3. Use a simulation to estimate the probability that exactly 2 of 3 darts land in ring A.

CRITICAL THINKING Calculate $_3C_2\left(\frac{1}{3}\right)^2\left(\frac{2}{3}\right)$, the theoretical probability of the event described in Example 3 above. Compare the experimental probability from Example 3 with the theoretical probability. How can you account for the discrepancy?

You can also use a geometric simulation to approximate π. Refer to the figure at right.

Let event R be a point in the square that is also in the circle.

$$P(R) = \frac{\text{area of circle}}{\text{area of square}} = \frac{\pi(1)^2}{2^2} = \frac{\pi}{4}$$

Make a spreadsheet that contains 20 random decimals between -1 and 1 inclusive in both columns A and B. For column C, use the following rule:

If $x^2 + y^2 \leq 1$, (where x and y are the values in columns A and B), print 1, otherwise print 0.

Then compute the experimental probability:

$$P(R) = \frac{\text{number of 1s}}{20}$$

The data from one simulation gives $P(R) = 0.8$. Thus, $\frac{\pi}{4} \approx 0.8$, or $\pi \approx 3.2$. The actual value of π is $3.14159\ldots$

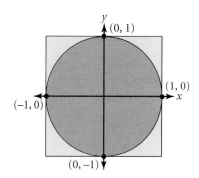

	A	B	C
1	X	Y	
2	-0.79355678	0.34678998	1
3	0.82410872	-0.92525235	0
4	0.68198496	0.38564413	1
5			
17			
18			
19	0.31884303	0.45645644	0
20	0.56456678	-0.52534556	1
21	0.25647562	0.2947445	1
22			3.2

Exercises

Communicate

1. How can you use random numbers to simulate rolling a number cube?

2. For what type of event is flipping a coin an appropriate model? Explain.

3. Which experiment would generally produce better results, an experiment with 1 trial or an experiment with 100 trials? Explain.

Guided Skills Practice

APPLICATIONS

4. TRANSPORTATION Refer to the traffic data from page 672. Use a simulation with 10 trials to estimate the probability that 2 or more out of 6 consecutive motorists will go straight. **(EXAMPLE 1)**

5. MANAGEMENT Refer to the probability table for customer arrival on page 673. Use a simulation with 10 trials to estimate the probability that 30 or more customers will arrive during the given 10-minute period. **(EXAMPLE 2)**

CONNECTION

6. GEOMETRY Refer to the dartboard on page 674. Use a simulation with 10 trials to estimate the probability that exactly 1 of 4 darts land in region C. **(EXAMPLE 3)**

7. Use a simulation with 20 trials to estimate the number of coin tosses needed to obtain 2 consecutive heads. (Hint: Outcomes such as **HH**, **THH**, and **THTHTHH** meet the condition.)

8. Use a simulation with 20 trials to estimate the number of coin tosses needed to obtain heads followed by tails. (Hint: Outcomes such as **THT**, **HHT**, **TTHT**, and **THHHT** meet the condition.)

9. Use a simulation with 10 trials to estimate the number of times a 6-sided number cube must be rolled to obtain 2 consecutive numbers less than 5.

10. Use a simulation with 10 trials to estimate the number of times a 6-sided number cube must be rolled to obtain a number less than 5 followed by a 5 or 6.

Use the table of traffic data below and a simulation with 10 trials to estimate the probability of each event.

11. Exactly 2 out of 3 consecutive motorists turn right.

12. Exactly 3 out of 4 consecutive motorists turn left.

Straight	73
Left	53
Right	69

13. No more than 2 out of 5 consecutive motorists go straight.

14. At least 3 out of 5 consecutive motorists go straight.

A restaurant chain is giving away 1 of 4 different prizes with each purchase of a dinner. Assume that each prize is equally likely to be awarded.

15. Use a simulation with 10 trials to estimate the probability that you will have all 4 prizes after 5 dinner purchases.

16. Use a simulation with 10 trials to estimate the probability that you will have all 4 prizes after 8 dinner purchases.

17. Use a simulation with 10 trials to estimate how many dinners you must purchase to collect all 4 prizes.

A multiple-choice test consists of 10 questions. Use the number of possible answers given below, and assume that each answer is a guess.

18. Suppose that each question has 4 possible answers. Use a simulation to find the probability of answering at least 6 questions correctly.

19. Suppose that each question has 3 possible answers. Use a simulation to find the probability of answering at least 6 questions correctly.

20. Suppose that each question has only 2 possible answers, true or false. Use a simulation to find the probability of answering at least 6 questions correctly.

CHALLENGES

Use a simulation to estimate the indicated area.

21. the area of the ellipse $\frac{x^2}{4} + \frac{y^2}{9} = 1$

22. the area under the curve $y = e^x$ from $x = 0$ to $x = 5$

23. the area under the curve $y = x^2 - 2x + 3$ from $x = 0$ to $x = 5$

24. GEOMETRY A toothpick has a length of ℓ units. Parallel lines are drawn at a distance of d units apart, where $\ell < d$. When the toothpick is dropped above the parallel lines, it either intersects one of the lines or rests between them. What is the probability that the toothpick will intersect one of the lines?

a. Obtain a toothpick and paper. Perform a simulation with 20 trials to estimate the probability.

b. Compare your answer with French naturalist Compte de Buffon's theoretical value of $\frac{2\ell}{\pi d}$.

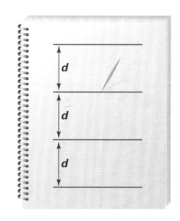

SPORTS A baseball player's batting statistics are given in the table at right. Use a simulation with 10 trials to find an approximate answer for each question below.

25. How many times will the player bat before he gets a hit (a single, double, triple, or home run)?

26. How many times will the player bat before he makes a ground out, fly out, or strike out?

27. How many times will the player bat before he makes a ground out or fly out?

Batting Statistics

Outcome	Probability
Single	0.198
Double	0.061
Triple	0.020
Home run	0.032
Walk	0.118
Ground out	0.264
Fly out	0.187
Strike out	0.120
Total	**1.000**

Look Back

Solve each system of linear equations. *(LESSONS 3.1 AND 3.2)*

28. $\begin{cases} 21x + 2y = 3 \\ 3x + 4y = 5 \end{cases}$

29. $\begin{cases} -3x + y = -2 \\ 2x - y = 3 \end{cases}$

30. $\begin{cases} 7x - 3y = 1 \\ 2x + 5y = 2 \end{cases}$

Solve each nonlinear system of equations. *(LESSON 9.6)*

31. $\begin{cases} x^2 + y^2 = 4 \\ 3x - y = 0 \end{cases}$

32. $\begin{cases} 2x + y = 0 \\ x^2 + y^2 = 9 \end{cases}$

33. $\begin{cases} 2x^2 + \dfrac{y^2}{8} = 1 \\ x^2 + y^2 = 4 \end{cases}$

34. How many 5-digit zip codes are possible? Assume that 00000 is not a valid zip code. *(LESSON 10.1)*

A bag contains 4 red marbles, 7 white marbles, and 14 black marbles. Find the probability of each event for one random selection. *(LESSON 10.4)*

35. red *or* white

36. red *or* black

37. black *or* white

Look Beyond

38. Find the next two terms in each sequence of numbers.

    a. 1, 5, 9, 13, 17, . . .

    b. 20, 10, 5, 2.5, . . .

Next, Please . . .

A customer arrives at the ticket counter of an airline. A delay at the counter caused by a long line might result in the customer missing a flight or might cause the airline to delay the departure time so that the customer does not miss the flight. Both events are undesireable for the airline. Therefore, the airline is greatly concerned about its customer's arrival time and processing time in order to minimize delays.

Suppose that an airline is going to start operations in a new terminal. The airline must develop a strategy for providing the optimum number of check-in counters and service staff. Trial-and-error methods in this situation could be very expensive. Instead the airline decides to use a probability experiment.

Activity 1

Airline statisticians want to analyze the time that it takes to process customers who arrive at the ticket counter between 1:00 P.M. and 1:10 P.M. To do this, they begin by researching the time it takes to process each of 50 customers. As a result of this research, the following table of probabilities is generated:

Process Times (in seconds)

Processing time, t	10	20	30	40	50	60
Probability, $P(t)$	0.052	0.132	0.158	0.135	0.123	0.104

Processing time, t	70	80	90	100	110	120
Probability, $P(t)$	0.058	0.034	0.116	0.050	0.026	0.012

Another term for a waiting line is a queue. In real-world situations, queues can vary considerably. They grow for a while, then disappear, and then occur again.

In the table, t represents the processing time to the nearest 10 seconds, and $P(t)$ represents the probability that processing a customer will take t seconds. The probabilities in the table are given to the nearest thousandth.

In order to set up a random-number simulation, first group numbers, N, from 1 to 1000 according to the given probabilities. For example, the first 52 numbers (1–52) correspond to $t = 10$. The next 132 numbers (53–184) correspond to $t = 20$, the next 158 numbers (185–342) correspond to $t = 30$, and so on. Complete the table in this manner.

Table for Processing Time Simulations

t	$P(t)$	N
0	0	000
10	0.052	001–052
20	0.132	053–184
30	0.158	185–342
⋮	⋮	⋮

Perform a simulation for 50 customers who arrive at the counter between 1:00 P.M. and 1:10 P.M.

1. Using a random-number generator, generate 50 random numbers between 1 and 1000 inclusive.

2. Create a table like the one shown at right, and record your random numbers in the *Number* column. Each random number represents a customer.

3. Refer to the table you created in Activity 1. For each random number that you generated, write the corresponding value of t in the *Time* column. The corresponding value of t represents the time it takes to process that customer. For example, if the first random number generated is 179, then the corresponding value of t is 20. This simulates a processing time of 20 seconds for the first customer.

Simulated Processing Time for 50 Consecutive Customers

Customer	Number, N	Time, t
1		
2		
3		
⋮		
49		
50		

1. Perform 10 trials of the simulation for 50 customers who arrive at the counter between 1:00 P.M. and 1:10 P.M. Estimate the probability that processing 50 customers takes longer than 50 minutes.

2. From the activities that you have completed in this project, you can see that efficient handling of customers, particularly in high-volume situations, is complicated and is not an exact science. From your own experiences, what are some situations in which these simulation techniques might be used to estimate probabilities? Describe how simulations might be designed for these situations.

Chapter Review and Assessment

Chapter Review and Assessment

10

10 Chapter Review and Assessment

10 Chapter Review and Assessment

VOCABULARY

Key Skills & Exercises

LESSON 10.1

Key Skills

Find the theoretical probability of an event.

A bag contains 2 green marbles and 11 red marbles. The theoretical probability of drawing a green marble is $P(\text{green}) = \frac{2}{13}$, or about 15%.

A rehearsal is to begin at some time between 3:00 P.M. and 3:15 P.M. Assuming that all times are equally likely, find the probability that the rehearsal begins in the interval from 3:00 P.M. to 3:03 P.M.

Divide the 15-minute interval into 5 equal parts. The 3-minute interval from 3:00 P.M. to 3:03 P.M. is $\frac{1}{5}$ of the total interval. Thus, the probability is $\frac{1}{5}$.

Apply the Fundamental Counting Principle.

At a cafe, there are 5 choices of entrees and 4 choices of side dishes. By the Fundamental Counting Principle, there are 5×4, or 20, ways to choose an entree and a side dish.

Exercises

Find the probability of each event.

1. drawing a red marble from a bag that contains 3 red marbles and 5 purple marbles

2. drawing a red marble from a bag that contains 4 red marbles and 10 black marbles

A party is to begin at some time between 8:00 P.M. and 8:30 P.M. Assuming that all times are equally likely, find the probability that the first guest arrives during each given time interval.

3. from 8:00 P.M. to 8:05 P.M.

4. from 8:12 P.M. to 8:18 P.M.

5. from 8:21 P.M. to 8:24 P.M.

6. If repetition is *not* allowed, how many 4-letter codes can be formed from only 5 letters of the alphabet?

7. If repetition is allowed, how many 4-letter codes can be formed from 5 letters of the alphabet?

LESSON 10.2

Key Skills

Find the number of linear permutations.

Five books on a shelf can be arranged $_5P_5 = 5! = 5 \times 4 \times 3 \times 2 \times 1 = 120$ different ways.

Two of the five books can be chosen and arranged in $_5P_2 = \frac{5!}{(5-2)!} = 20$ different ways.

Exercises

8. In how many ways can the letters in the word *pencil* be arranged?

Find the number of ways that a coach can assign each number of basketball players to 5 distinct positions.

9. 8   10. 10   11. 12

The letters in the word *hollow* can be arranged in $\frac{6!}{2!2!} = \frac{6!}{4} = 180$ different ways.

Find the number of circular permutations.

Five objects can be arranged around a circle in $(5 - 1)! = 4!$, or 24, different ways.

12. How many arrangements of the letters in the word *tomorrow* are possible?

13. In how many ways can 5 children be positioned around a merry-go-round?

14. In how many ways can 8 employees be seated at a circular conference table?

Key Skills

Find the number of combinations.

Find the number of ways to purchase 2 games from a display of 7 games.

$$_7C_2 = \frac{7!}{2!(7-2)!} = \frac{7 \times 6 \times 5!}{2!5!} = 21$$

Exercises

15. Find the number of ways to choose 2 books from a set of 10 books.

16. In how many ways can 2 of 27 ice cream flavors be chosen?

17. In how many ways can 3 student representatives be chosen from 100 students?

Key Skills

Find the probability of event *A or B*.

For one roll of a number cube:

Mutually exclusive events: Find $P(2 \text{ or } 3)$.

$$P(A \text{ or } B) = P(A) + P(B)$$

$$P(2 \text{ or } 3) = \frac{1}{6} + \frac{1}{6} = \frac{2}{6} = \frac{1}{3}$$

Inclusive events: Find $P(\text{even or multiple of } 3)$.

$$P(A \text{ or } B) = P(A) + P(B) - P(A \text{ and } B)$$

$$P(\text{even or multiple of } 3) = \frac{1}{2} + \frac{1}{3} - \frac{1}{6} = \frac{4}{6} = \frac{2}{3}$$

Use the complement of an event to find a probability.

$$P(A) = 1 - P(A^c)$$

$$P(\text{less than } 6) = 1 - P(6)$$

$$= 1 - \frac{1}{6} = \frac{5}{6}$$

Exercises

Find the probability of each event for one roll of a number cube.

18. 4 *or* 7

19. 1 *or* 6

20. an odd number *or* a number greater than 4

21. an even number *or* a number less than 4

22. greater than 1

23. greater than 2

Key Skills

Find the probability of independent events.

For 2 rolls of a number cube:

$$P(A \text{ and } B) = P(A) \times P(B)$$

$$P(6 \text{ first and even second}) = \frac{1}{6} \times \frac{3}{6} = \frac{3}{36} = \frac{1}{12}$$

Exercises

Find the probability of each event.

24. 3 heads on 3 tosses of a fair coin

25. 2 even numbers on 2 rolls of a number cube

Key Skills

Find conditional probabilities.

For 1 roll of a number cube, find the probability that the number 2 is rolled if you know that the number is even.

$$P(2|even) = \frac{P(even\ and\ 2)}{P(even)} = \frac{\frac{1}{6}}{\frac{1}{2}} = \frac{1}{3}$$

Exercises

Find the probability of each event for one roll of a number cube.

26. 5, given that it is an odd number

27. 1, given that it is *not* an odd number

28. 2, given that it is less than or equal to 5

Key Skills

Use simulations to estimate probabilities.

The probability table gives the probabilities of the number of traffic tickets written by one officer between 3:00 A.M. and 4:00 A.M.

X	P(X)
0	0.20
1	0.30
2	0.35
3	0.15

Use a simulation with 10 trials to estimate the probability that the officer writes less than 2 tickets during this time.

Add a column, N, as shown below. Generate 10 random integers.

X	P(X)	N	Random integers
0	0.20	1–20	14
1	0.30	21–50	38, 34, 23, 28
2	0.35	51–85	72, 57, 73
3	0.15	86–100	95, 97

In this experiment, less than 2 traffic tickets occurred 5 out of 10 times, so the probability is estimated to be $\frac{1}{2}$, or 50%.

Exercises

29. The table at right gives the probabilities, $P(X)$, of the number, X, of drinks ordered at a fast-food restaurant during a 1-minute interval between 3:00 P.M. and 3:20 P.M.

X	P(X)
0	0.18
1	0.37
2	0.22
3	0.10
4	0.07
5	0.06

    Use a simulation with 10 trials to estimate the probability that more than 6 drinks are ordered between 3:00 P.M. and 3:20 P.M. inclusive.

30. The table below gives the number of customers out of 100 that went up, down, or stayed on the same level after entering a mall.

    Use a simulation with 10 trials to estimate the probability that 3 or more out of 5 consecutive customers go up.

Up	36
Down	20
Same	44

Applications

31. **HEALTH** A test of 100 adults showed that 40 of them consumed on average more than the recommended maximum of 2400 milligrams of sodium per day. Of those with the high sodium consumption, 50% had higher-than-normal blood pressure. Of the 60 adults whose sodium intake was at or below 2400 milligrams per day, only 15% had higher-than-normal blood pressure. Using this data as a sample of the general population, find the probability that a person with higher-than-normal blood pressure has a daily intake of more than 2400 milligrams of sodium.

Alternative Assessment

Performance Assessment

1. **GAMES** A popular game is played with 5 number cubes. One desirable outcome in the game is to roll the same number on all 5 number cubes.
   a. Find the number of combinations of rolls for 5 number cubes.
   b. Find the probability of rolling 5 ones.
   c. Find the probability of rolling 5 of any kind.
   d. Perform a simulation to estimate the probability for Step 3. How does your estimate compare with the theoretical probability?

2. **BIRTHDAY PROBLEM** In Lesson 10.5 you studied the probability that 2 or more people in a group will have the same birth month and day.
   a. Make a table of the probabilities that 2 or more people have the same birth month and day for groups of 5, 10, 15, . . . , 55 people.
   b. Graph the data from Step 5, connecting the points with a smooth curve. What does the graph indicate?
   c. Use the graph to determine the number of students that need to be in the group in order for the probability to be 50%.
   d. How many students must be in the group in order for the probability to be 100%? Explain.

Portfolio Projects

1. **CUSTOMER SERVICE** The probabilities that a large retail store receives from 0 to 10 complaints in a given week are given in the table at right.
   a. Why do you think a probability for 11 complaints is not shown?
   b. Describe two ways you could perform a simulation to estimate the probability of receiving 20 or more complaints in a 4-week period.

Complaints Received	
Number	**Probability**
0	0.06
1	0.08
2	0.14
3	0.19
4	0.15
5	0.11
6	0.08
7	0.07
8	0.06
9	0.04
10	0.02
Total	**1.00**

2. **BAR CODES** The UPC bar code found on products is a 12-digit computer code.
   a. If the first and last digit are fixed, how many UPC numbers are possible?
   b. If 5 of the remaining 10 digits identify the manufacturer, how many numbers are available to identify manufacturers?

---

internetconnect

The HRW Web site contains many resources to reinforce and expand your knowledge of probability. This Web site also provides Internet links to other sites where you can find information and real-world data for use in research projects, reports, and activities that involve probability. Visit the HRW Web site at **go.hrw.com**, and enter the keyword **MB1 CH10** to access the resources for this chapter.

QUANTITATIVE COMPARISON For Items 1–5, write
A if the quantity in Column A is greater than the quantity in Column B;
B if the quantity in Column B is greater than the quantity in Column A;
C if the two quantities are equal; or
D if the relationship cannot be determined from the given information.

	Column A	Column B	Answers
1.	— The value of x		
	$-\dfrac{1}{3}x = 2x + 1$	$5 + \dfrac{1}{2}x = 6(x + 1)$	Ⓐ Ⓑ Ⓒ Ⓓ [Lesson 1.6]
2.	$\log 12$	10^{12}	Ⓐ Ⓑ Ⓒ Ⓓ [Lesson 6.3]
3.	$\begin{cases} y = -3x + 4 \\ y + 3x = -3 \end{cases}$		
	x	y	Ⓐ Ⓑ Ⓒ Ⓓ [Lesson 3.1]
4.	The number of real solutions		
	$3x^2 - 2x + 1 = 0$	$2x^2 - 5x - 2 = 0$	Ⓐ Ⓑ Ⓒ Ⓓ [Lesson 5.6]
5.	$f(x) = 2x - 1$		
	$f(2)$	$f^{-1}(2)$	Ⓐ Ⓑ Ⓒ Ⓓ [Lesson 2.5]

6. Which of the following is a solution of the system $\begin{cases} 2y + x \le 6 \\ y - 3x \ge 4 \end{cases}$? **(LESSON 3.4)**

　　a. $(0, 5)$　　　　**b.** $(-1, 2)$
　　c. $(1, -1)$　　　**d.** $(0, 0)$

7. Solve $2(x + 2) - 7 < 8x + 15$. **(LESSON 1.7)**

　　a. $x > -3$　　　**b.** $x < -3$
　　c. $x > 2$　　　 **d.** $x < 2$

8. Which value would you add to $x^2 - 10x$ to complete the square? **(LESSON 5.4)**

　　a. 5　　**b.** -5　　**c.** 25　　**d.** -25

9. Simplify $\left(-\dfrac{1}{125}\right)^{-\frac{2}{3}}$. **(LESSON 2.2)**

　　a. $\dfrac{1}{25}$　　**b.** $-\dfrac{1}{25}$　　**c.** 25　　**d.** -25

10. If $f(x) = 2x - 6$ and $g(x) = 12 - 6x$, which statement is true? **(LESSON 2.4)**

　　a. $f \circ g = g \circ f$　　　**b.** $2(f \circ g) = g \circ f$
　　c. $-2(f \circ g) = g \circ f$　　**d.** none of these

11. Which of the following describes the relationship between the lines $y = \dfrac{1}{2}x$ and $y = -2x - 3$? **(LESSON 1.3)**

　　a. horizontal　　　**b.** vertical
　　c. perpendicular　**d.** parallel

12. Solve $4y^2 + 7 = 0$. **(LESSON 5.6)**

　　a. $y = \dfrac{7i}{2}$　　　　**b.** $y = \dfrac{-\sqrt{7}}{4}$
　　c. $y = \dfrac{\sqrt{7}}{4}$　　　**d.** $y = \pm\dfrac{i\sqrt{7}}{2}$

13. Find the coordinates of the midpoint of the segment with endpoints at $(-4, -1)$ and $(2, -7)$. **(LESSON 9.1)**

   a. $(-1, -3)$ **b.** $(-3, 3)$

   c. $(-1, -4)$ **d.** $(-3, -3)$

14. Which expression is not equivalent to the others? **(LESSON 6.4)**

   a. $2 \log_b \frac{5}{3}$ **b.** $\log_b \sqrt[3]{5^2}$

   c. $\frac{1}{3} \log_b 25$ **d.** $\frac{2}{3} \log_b 5$

15. Write $(5x^3 - 2x^2 + x - 10) + (2x^3 - 3x - 1)$ in standard form. **(LESSON 7.1)**

   a. $3x^3 - 2x^2 - 4x - 9$

   b. $3x^3 + 2x^2 + 4x - 9$

   c. $7x^3 - 2x^2 - 2x - 9$

   d. $7x^3 - 2x^2 - 2x - 11$

16. Simplify $\frac{a^2 + 3a - 4}{a^2} \cdot \frac{a^2 - 2a}{2a + 8}$. **(LESSON 8.3)**

   a. $-(a - 4)$ **b.** $\frac{(a - 1)(a - 2)}{2a}$

   c. $\frac{(a + 4)(a - 2)}{2a}$ **d.** $\frac{(a + 4)(a - 1)}{a}$

17. Find the coordinates of the center of the circle defined by $x^2 + y^2 - 2x - 8y = 8$. **(LESSON 9.6)**

   a. $(-1, -4)$ **b.** $(1, 2)$

   c. $(1, 4)$ **d.** $(-1, -8)$

18. Write an equation in slope-intercept form for the line containing the points $(3, -4)$ and $(2, 7)$. **(LESSON 1.3)**

19. Find the zeros of $f(x) = x^2 - 8x + 12$. **(LESSON 5.3)**

20. Find the product $-2 \begin{bmatrix} 7 & -6 & 0 \\ -3 & 5 & 1 \end{bmatrix}$, if it exists. **(LESSON 4.1)**

21. Factor $5x^2 + 10x - 40$, if possible. **(LESSON 5.3)**

22. Find the inverse of $\{(2, -1), (4, 3), (6, 0), (3, 1)\}$. **(LESSON 2.5)**

23. Simplify $(1 - 2i) - (3 - 4i)$. **(LESSON 5.6)**

24. Factor $8x^3 + 64$. **(LESSON 7.3)**

25. Describe the end behavior of $P(x) = -2x^3 + x^2 - 11x + 4$. **(LESSON 7.2)**

26. Simplify $\left(\sqrt{-36x^4}\right)^2$. **(LESSON 8.7)**

27. Write equations for all vertical and horizontal asymptotes in the graph of $f(x) = \frac{(x + 2)^2}{3x}$. **(LESSON 8.2)**

28. Write the standard equation for $x^2 + y^2 + 6x - 4y = 12$. **(LESSON 9.6)**

29. Factor $6x^2 + 8x - 15x - 20$, if possible. **(LESSON 7.3)**

30. Simplify $\dfrac{\frac{x + 4}{9x^3}}{\frac{x - 6}{3x^4}}$. **(LESSON 8.3)**

FREE-RESPONSE GRID

The following questions may be answered by using a free-response grid such as that commonly used by standardized-test services.

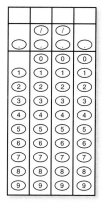

31. Find the slope, m, of the line $y = 8$. **(LESSON 1.2)**

32. Find the determinant of $\begin{bmatrix} -3 & 5 \\ -1 & 6 \end{bmatrix}$. **(LESSON 4.3)**

33. Solve $\frac{6x + 2}{3x} = 6$. **(LESSON 8.5)**

34. Solve $3^x = 9^5$. **(LESSON 6.7)**

35. What value would you add to $x^2 + 8x$ to complete the square? **(LESSON 5.4)**

36. Find the value of v in $v = \log_{10} \frac{1}{1000}$. **(LESSON 6.3)**

EXTRACURRICULAR ACTIVITIES The Outdoors Club has 12 students—5 girls and 7 boys. **(LESSON 10.5)**

37. How many different committees of 6 students can be formed if at least 3 are girls?

38. How many different committees of 6 students can be formed if at least 3 are boys?

39. How many different committees of 6 students can be formed if no more than 3 are boys?

Keystroke Guide for Chapter 10

Essential keystroke sequences (using the model TI-82 or TI-83 graphics calculator) are presented below for all Activities and Examples found in this chapter that require or recommend the use of a graphics calculator.

 internet**connect**

HRW Keystrokes for other models of graphics calculators are found on the HRW Web site.

LESSON 10.2

EXAMPLE ❸ Evaluate $\dfrac{11!}{4!5!2!}$.

Page 638

11 [MATH] [PRB] [4:!] [ENTER] [÷]

[(] 4 [MATH] [PRB] [4:!] [ENTER]

[×] 5 [MATH] [PRB] [4:!] [ENTER]

[×] 2 [MATH] [PRB] [4:!] [ENTER] [)] [ENTER]

```
11!/(4!*5!*2!)
            6930
```

LESSON 10.3

EXAMPLE ❷ Evaluate $_5C_3$ and $_5P_3$.

Page 645

5 [MATH] [PRB] [3:nCr] [ENTER] 3 [ENTER]

5 [MATH] [PRB] [2:nPr] [ENTER] 3 [ENTER]

```
5 nCr 3
            10
5 nPr 3
            60
```

EXAMPLE ❹ Evaluate $\dfrac{_{17}C_2 \times \,_8C_4}{_{25}C_6}$.

Page 646

[(] 17 [MATH] [PRB] [3:nCr] [ENTER] 2 [)]

[×] [(] 8 [MATH] [PRB] [3:nCr] [ENTER] 4

[)] [÷] [(] 25 [MATH] [PRB] [3:nCr]

[ENTER] 6 [)] [ENTER]

```
(17 nCr 2)*(8 nC
r 4)/(25 nCr 6)
        .0537549407
```